Communications in Computer and Information Science 704

Commenced Publication in 2007
Founding and Former Series Editors:
Alfredo Cuzzocrea, Xiaoyong Du, Orhun Kara, Ting Liu, Dominik Ślęzak, and Xiaokang Yang

Editorial Board

More information about this series at http://www.springer.com/series/7899

Ming Xu · Zheng Qin
Fei Yan · Shaojing Fu (Eds.)

Trusted Computing and Information Security

11th Chinese Conference, CTCIS 2017
Changsha, China, September 14–17, 2017
Proceedings

Springer

Editors
Ming Xu
National University of Defense Technology
Changsha
China

Zheng Qin
Hunan University
Changsha, Hunan
China

Fei Yan
Wuhan University
Wuhan
China

Shaojing Fu
National University of Defense Technology
Changsha, Hunan
China

ISSN 1865-0929   ISSN 1865-0937 (electronic)
Communications in Computer and Information Science
ISBN 978-981-10-7079-2   ISBN 978-981-10-7080-8 (eBook)
https://doi.org/10.1007/978-981-10-7080-8

Library of Congress Control Number: 2017957551

Printed on acid-free paper

This Springer imprint is published by Springer Nature
The registered company is Springer Nature Singapore Pte Ltd.
The registered company address is: 152 Beach Road, #21-01/04 Gateway East, Singapore 189721, Singapore

Preface

The 11th Chinese Conference on Trusted Computing and Information Security (CTCIS 2017) continued in a series of events dedicated to trusted computing and information security, focusing on new theories, mechanisms, infrastructures, services, tools, and benchmarks. CTCIS provides a forum for researchers and developers in academia, industry, and government to share their excellent ideas and experiences in the areas of trusted computing and information security in the broad context of cloud computing, big data, Internet of Things, etc.

This year, CTCIS received 390 submissions. After a thorough reviewing process, 28 English papers and 87 Chinese papers were selected for presentation as full papers, with an acceptance rate of 29.2%. Furthermore, this year's CTCIS also included 11 English papers and 14 Chinese papers as posters, with an acceptance rate of 12.32%. Additionally, five industrial/demo papers were selected. This volume contains the 28 English full papers presented at CTCIS 2017

The high-quality program would not have been possible without the authors who chose CTCIS 2017 as a venue for their publications. We are also very grateful to the Program Committee members and Organizing Committee members, who put a tremendous amount of effort into soliciting and selecting research papers with a balance of high quality and new ideas and new applications.

We hope that you enjoy reading and benefit from the proceedings of CTCIS 2017.

September 2017

Ming Xu
Zheng Qin
Fei Yan
Shaojing Fu

Organization

CTCIS 2017 was organized by the China Computer Federation, National University of Defense Technology, and Hunan University.

Organizing Committee

Conference Honorary Chair

Changxiang Shen   Chinese Academy of Sciences, China

Conference Co-chairs

Huanguo Zhang   Wuhan University, China
Huaiming Wang   National University of Defense Technology, China

Conference Assistant Chair

Bo Zhao   Wuhan University, China

Program Co-chairs

Ming Xu   National University of Defense Technology, China
Qin Zheng   Hunan University, China

Program Associate Chair

Fei Yan   Wuhan University, China

Organizing Chair

Yongjun Wang   National University of Defense Technology, China

Organizing Associate Chair

Shaojing Fu   National University of Defense Technology, China

Steering Committee

Changxiang Shen	Chinese Academy of Sciences
Huanguo Zhang	Wuhan University
Zhong Chen	Peking University
Kefei Chen	Hangzhou Normal University
Dengguo Feng	Beijing Science Technology Academy
Zhen Han	Beijing Jiaotong University
Yeping He	Chinese Academy of Sciences
Jianhua Li	Shanghai Jiao Tong University

Zhoujun Li	Beihang University
Jianfeng Ma	Xidian University
Dan Meng	Institute of Information Engineering
Zhiguang Qin	University of Electronic Science and Technology of China
Shuming Song	Collaborative Innovation Center of Cryptography
Jinshu Su	National University of Defense Technology
Xiaoyun Wang	Tsinghua University
Zhiying Wang	National University of Defense Technology
Xiaoyao Xie	Guizhou Normal University
Xiaoyuan Yang	Engineering University of CAPF
Yixian Yang	Beijing University of Posts and Telecommunications
Zhiqiang Zhu	Information Engineering University

Program Committee

Zuling Chang	Zhengzhou University
Fei Chen	Shenzhen University
Jiagen Chen	Central China Normal University
Jing Chen	Wuhan University
Kai Chen	Chinese Academy of Sciences
Rongmao Chen	National University of Defense Technology
Qingfeng Cheng	Information Engineering University
Yong Ding	Guilin University of Electronic Technology
Zhongrui Du	Hebei University
Xiutao Ma	Chinese Academy of Sciences
Wei Fu	Naval University of Engineering
Zhangjie Fu	Nanjing University of Information Science and Technology
Jianming Fu	Wuhan University
Shanqing Guo	Shandong University
Yuanbo Guo	Information Engineering University
Weili Hanhang	Fudan University
Debiao He	Wuhan University
Yupeng Hu	Hunan University
Qiang Huang	National Laboratory of Information Security
Qiong Huang	South China Agricultural University
Xinyi Huang	Fujian Normal University
Chunfu Jia	Nankai University
Wenjun Jiang	Hunan University
Weijin Jiang	Hunan University of Commerce
Fagen Li	University of Electronic Science and Technology of China
Hongwei Li	University of Electronic Science and Technology of China
Qi Li	Tsinghua University
Yunchang Li	Hunan University of Technology
JingQiang Lin	Chinese Academy of Sciences
Bo Liu	National University of Defense Technology, China
Ting Liu	Xi'an Jiaotong University

Organizers

Organized by

China Computer Federation, China

Hosted by

National University of Defense Technology   Hunan University

In Cooperation with:

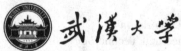

Wuhan University

Sponsoring Institutions

Bluedon Inc.   Trusted Computing Group   Hetian Inc.

Tsinghua University Press

Contents

Homology Analysis Method of Worms Based on Attack and Propagation Features

Liyan Wang, Jingfeng Xue, Yan Cui, Yong Wang, and Chun Shan[✉]

School of Software, Beijing Institute of Technology, Beijing, China
cuiyan_72@163.com, sherrychan@bit.edu.cn

Abstract. Internet worms pose a serious threat to the Internet security. In order to avoid the security detection and adapt to diverse target environment, the attackers often modify the existing worm code, then get the variants of original worm. Therefore, it is of practical significance to determine the cognate relationship between worms quickly and accurately. By extracting the semantic structure, attack behavior and propagation behavior of the worm, the worm feature set is generated, and the worm sensitive behavior library is built with the idea of association analysis. On this basis, combined with random forest and sensitive behavior matching algorithm, the homology relationship between worms was determined. The experimental results show that the method proposed can fully guarantee the time performance of the algorithm, what's more further improve the accuracy of the results of the homology analysis of worms.

Keywords: Feature engineering · Frequent pattern mining · Sensitive behavior match · Homology analysis · Worm

1 Introduction

With the rapid popularization of the Internet, the development of network information technology and the rapid expansion of Internet users, the spread of worms is more convenient, and the negative impact of the attacks is further expanding. The distinctive feature of worms is the ability to self replicate and quickly spread, it can use network connectivity in the absence of human intervention, through a large number of copying own code or code fragments to achieve rapid propagation. In this paper, based on the attack propagation features, the worm feature set is filtered, and the sensitive behavior database of worms is constructed with the idea of association analysis. Finally, homology analysis of worms is carried out by combining the random forest classification model and the sensitive behavior matching algorithm. The rest of this paper is organized as follows: In Sect. 2, we introduce the related work. Section 3 focuses on feature engineering. Section 4 discusses the method and process of homology analysis of worms in detail. Section 5 proves the feasibility of the proposed method. Finally, we summarize and conclude our work in Sect. 6.

© Springer Nature Singapore Pte Ltd. 2017
M. Xu et al. (Eds.): CTCIS 2017, CCIS 704, pp. 1–15, 2017.
https://doi.org/10.1007/978-981-10-7080-8_1

2   Related Work

Domestic and foreign research institutions and scholars on the research of worms cover the work mechanism of worms, scanning strategy, transmission mode, automatic feature generation technology and worm detection and other areas. Feature extraction is the precondition of homology analysis, how to extract effective worm features has become an important research direction. In 2012, a feature classification framework based on graph is proposed, which uses the subordinate relation between the common substring and the substring of the worm copy to analyze [1]. In 2014, Liang et al. proposed a method of using positional relationship between worms to detect worms [2]. This method has good effect on worm detection by combining the relation between byte character and byte of worm code itself. And in the same year, Wang et al. proposed a method of automatic worm feature extraction based on seed expansion [3]. This method has good noise identification ability, and it can extract effective worms features in the presence of noise interference features. In addition, in the field of homology analysis of malicious code such as worms, it can be analyzed from the aspects of malicious code module structure, compiler architecture, core function realization, important data structure, and also combine with coding psychology to analyze attacker's coding psychology [4]. In 2015, Qian and others proposed a method of malware homology analysis based on clustering model [5], which is based on the worms features, using clustering algorithm based on density to determine and analyze the homology of malicious code. In 2016, Ge et al. proposed a method of malicious code homology analysis based on dynamic BP neural network [6], which introduces BP neural network algorithm for homologous analysis of malicious code.

3   Feature Engineering

3.1   Feature Extraction

In this paper, worms are described by the combination of dynamic and static features, that is relevant to the semantic structure, and pay more attention to the attack propagation features. The static features of worm are the semantic structures of worm codes. The dynamic features of worm include the characteristics of worm attack behavior and the propagation behavior [7].

(1) Extraction of semantic structure features

Portable executable files contain important information about program code information, application types, required library functions and space requirements. Therefore, by acquiring the disassembly file of PE file format, extracting the important features that can fully reflect the semantic structure of worm, it will be beneficial to the homologous analysis of worm.

In the worm disassembly files, different PE sections can map different program functions, extracting the names of PE sections from the worm disassembly file is helpful to predict the possible behavior of the worm. Dynamic link library is a unique way to share code among multiple applications in windows operating system, so the useful information of worm code loading function can be obtained from the DLL dependency relation of worm. The opcode is the basis of the machine language, it can be used to specify the action to be performed. For different source worms, the opcode distribution has obvious differences, so the opcode sequence with no parameter can be used to represent the worm [8]. At the same time, the n-gram model partly contains some semantic features. By extracting the n-gram features of worms opcodes, it can better recognize the difference of semantic structure between different worm [9].

Therefore, in this paper, we extract names of PE sections, DLL and opcode n-gram features from worm disassembly files. And count the frequency of these features in the disassembled files of each worm. Finally, the merged statistics are used as the representation of the semantic structure of worms.

(2) Extraction of attack behavior features

In addition, in order to avoid the influence of original features in different dimension, and to ensure the convergence speed of the algorithm, we need dimensionless the original features to eliminate the dimensional differences between the features. In this paper, the mean-variance method is used for standardizing the processing of features, so that all worm features can meet the standard normal distribution, that is, all values are clustered near 0, and the variance is equal to 1.

The worm is a highly autonomous attack program, usually launched against a specific vulnerability. The worm attack behavior causes a large number of network requests in a short time, and these network requests are sent to the service port of the specific vulnerability in the target host. This behavior makes the communication protocol, destination port number and packet length in the worm attack basically remain unchanged [10].

So we use triples <PROTOCOL, DPORT, LENGTH> to describe the attack behavior of worms. The triples sequence is extracted from the network behavior report of each worm. But the extracted sequence is a text type, it needs to be converted to the vector of word bag mapping. So we use TF-IDF algorithm to deal with the text sequence of worm attack behavior. Based on this idea, each text sequences of the worm attack behaviors is mapped to the vector of word bag, and the words in the word bag model as the transformed feature names, and the weight of each word as the numerical representation of the features. Through this method, we can get the worms attack behavior features.

(3) Extraction of propagation behavior features

When worms complete the attack, they will spread by copying itself and sending it to the infected host. Due to worms are not parasitic, propagation do not depend on other programs in the infected host, but by modifying the registry, and using existing system vulnerabilities to send copies to the infected host. Therefore, we focus on worm modification of registry behavior and self replication behavior, which can be described by worms API call sequence [11]. The API call sequences which can reflect worm modification of registry and self replication behavior are shown in Fig. 1.

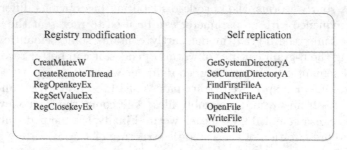

Fig. 1. API call sequences of worms propagation behavior

3.2 Feature Preprocessing

For the original features, there may be missing values and original features in different dimensions. This problem will cause that these features cannot be used directly as an input to a feature selection algorithm. Therefore, the original features of worms need to be preprocessed.

The value of the semantic structure of worms is the statistical value of the frequency of each feature, and the value of attack behavior is TF-IDF weight, hence we use number zero to fill the missing value of the original features.

In addition, in order to avoid the influence of original features in different dimension, and to ensure the convergence speed of the algorithm, we need dimensionless the original features to eliminate the dimensional differences between the features. In this paper, the mean-variance method is used for standardizing the processing of features, so that all worm features can meet the standard normal distribution, that is, all values are clustered near 0, and the variance is equal to 1.

3.3 Feature Selection and Dimensionality Reduction

Due to the high dimensionality of the worm features after preprocessing, the time performance of homology analysis method of worms will be affected. To improve the learning efficiency of homology analysis method of worms, it is necessary to select and reduce the feature set. That is, to eliminate the redundant features while ensuring the validity of worm features, the feature sets with lower dimensionality and higher abstraction degree are obtained.

In this paper, we use recursive feature elimination algorithm to select features and use principal component analysis to reduce the feature set. The process is shown in Fig. 2.

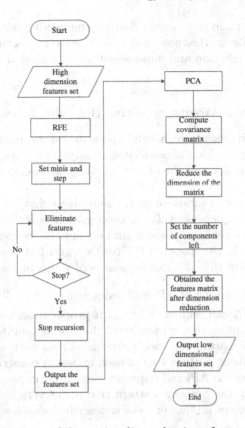

Fig. 2. Selection and dimensionality reduction of worms features.

The process is described as follows:

(1) Select features by using recursive feature elimination algorithms. We use ExtraTreesClassifier as the base model of the algorithm to conduct several rounds of training. After each round of training, 10 features are eliminated and the next round of training is performed based on the removed feature set. When the algorithm satisfies the stopping criterion, the recursive process is ended and the filtered feature set is output. By using the recursive elimination algorithm to select features, it can remove the features without distinction, which can not only keep the divergence of features but also reduce the dimensionality of worms feature set.

(2) Reduce features by using principal component analysis. Firstly, the covariance matrix of the feature is calculated. Secondly the singular value decomposition algorithm is used to compute the eigenvalues and eigenvectors of the covariance matrix to obtain the matrix with low dimension. By calculating the empirical mean of each feature in the reduced dimension matrix, the importance of features is sorted. Set the target dimension and generate the target matrix according to the importance of the features. Finally, convert the matrix into the worm feature set.

According to the main processes of feature engineering, we carry out extraction of semantic structure features and attack behavior features, features preprocessing, features selection and dimensional reduction, and finally obtain features set.

3.4 Construction of Worms Sensitive Behavior Library

For the API call sequences which can represent the propagation behavior of worms, we introduce the idea of association analysis to construct the sensitive behavior library of worms, and then carry out the homologous analysis of worms on this basis.

The core of the construction of worm sensitive behavior feature library is to dig the API call sequences of worm propagation behavior deeply, find out the correlation between API sequences, and obtain the frequent pattern sets of these sequences [12]. In this paper, FP-Growth algorithm is used for obtaining frequent pattern sets of the API call sequences of worm propagation behavior.

(1) Frequent pattern mining of API call sequences

Firstly, the set of API call sequences of worm propagation behavior is cut into multiple subsets according to the identity of the worms family, and each subset represents a class of worms behavior patterns. Then, each subset is scanned in turn, and the frequent pattern tree of each subset is constructed. Lastly, the frequent pattern set of the API call sequence of each worm propagation behavior is obtained by mining the frequent pattern tree recursively.

The frequent patterns mining process is described as follows:

① Mark the complete set of API call sequences for worm propagation behavior as S and the set S is composed of API call sequences of n worms' propagation behavior. According to the labels, the set S is divided into n subsets and denoted as $\{S_1, S_2 \cdots, S_i, S_i + 1, \cdots, S_n\}$, where $1 \leq i \leq n$. Put all the S_i into a queue q_1.

② Sets the minimum number of support thresholds for the algorithm and records it as minimum support. The threshold needs to satisfy the size of the frequent pattern set that enables the API call sequences of each class of worm families to be as homogeneous as possible.

③ Construct FP-Tree. The specific construction process is described as follows:

a. Take a S_i from the q_1 as input to this iteration. Scan set S_i, count the occurrences of all items in the S_i as the support of the item, and create the header table. All items with less than minimum support in the head pointer table will be filtered, and the frequent 1-itemset of S_i is obtained. According to the support number, the frequent 1-itemset is arranged in descending order, and the frequent 1-itemset after sorting is denoted as L.

b. Put S_i into the queue q_2 to indicate that S_i has been accessed. Initialize an empty FP-Tree, filter and reorder the items in each API call sequence in S_i, and mark the processed S_i as S_i'.

c. Create the FP-Tree root node, mark it as R, and mark the value of R as null. Call the insert function to insert the set of items from S_i' into FP-Tree in turn. If a set of S_i' has the same prefix path as the child node C, the prefix path is reused and the number of support for each item on the prefix path is increased by 1, otherwise a new node is created in the FP-Tree. Executes the header insert while updating the header pointer table. The ③-c is then recursively executed for the remaining element entries of the current itemset and the corresponding child nodes of the current element entry.

④ Frequent pattern mining. The recursive mining process is described as follows:

a. Call the FP-Growth ($Tree, \alpha$) function, where α represents the root node of the current tree. To determine whether there is a single path P in FP-Tree, if it exists, jump to step ④-b, if not, jump to step ④-c.

b. The set of items corresponding to all nodes in P is denoted as β, and the schema $\alpha \cup \beta$ is generated. The support number of the schema is equal to the minimum of the number of support items contained in β. If the support of the pattern is not less than the minimum support number min-sup, then the pattern is a frequent pattern.

- c. Access each α_i in the header table in reverse order and generate the schema $\beta = \alpha_i \cup \alpha$, whose support number is equal to the support number of α_i. Then, we construct the conditional pattern base (CPB) of β and the conditional FP-Tree (Tree β) to find frequent pattern sets. If Tree is not empty, jump to step ④-a, call FP-growth ($Tree\beta, \beta$) function, otherwise perform step ⑤ operation.

⑤Output the frequent pattern set of the API call sequence of the current worm propagation behavior. If the queue q_1 is not empty, jump to step ③, otherwise the process ends.

(2) Construction of sensitive behavior feature library

After mining the frequent pattern sets of the API call sequences of worm propagation behavior, we can construct the sensitive behavior feature library of worms.

Firstly, we create a new database as the sensitive behavior feature library. Then n tables are created in this database, which are used to store frequent pattern sets of API call sequences of n kinds of worm propagation behavior. Each frequent pattern in a frequent pattern set corresponds to a record in the table, where n is the total number of existing worm families.

4   Homology Analysis of Worm

In this paper, we analyze the worms by the way of cell division. For the worm feature set, the random forest classification model is used for measuring the similarity. For the API call sequence of worm propagation behavior, it combines the sensitive behavior feature library and calculates the hit rate to measure the similarity of worms. Then combining the results of the two methods, we analyze and judge the homologous relationship among worms.

This paper defines the similarity criterion of worms is that one of the worm samples are mapped into the corresponding probability distribution matrix, then the worm family corresponding to each probability value in the row and column to the similarity analysis between the worm sample values measured by probability. The higher the probability value, the higher the similarity.

4.1 Worms Similarity Measure Based on Random Forest Classification Model

Worm feature set is input. The output calculates for all decision trees in random forest for worms, comprehensive consideration and the prediction results are converted to probability distribution matrix. The probability distribution matrix represents the similarity of the measurement results of worms [13].

The random forest algorithm is based on the following assumptions. The worms feature set contains W kinds of worms, and each worm sample has F feature attributes. The feature set is divided into training set and test set, in which the training set is denoted as X, and the test set is denoted as Y.

The process of constructing a random forest classification model using the training set X is described as follows:

(1) Set the number t of decision trees in a random forest.
(2) Some samples are extracted from X in random and back way as the training set of the current decision tree.
(3) Randomly select f attributes from the feature attribute set F as the feature attributes of the current decision tree, and then use the f feature attributes to train the current decision tree.
(4) Recursive execution step 2 and step 3 until all decision trees are trained in a random forest, that is, the recursive process is executed t times. A random forest classification model is used for subsequent similarity measurement of worms.

The random forest classification model is used for measuring the similarity of the test set Y to generate the worm probability distribution matrix. The flow chart is shown in Fig. 3.

A detailed description of the process is as follows:

(1) The feature set Y is divided into m parts and each part represents a worm sample, denoted as $\{Y_1, Y_2, Y_3, \cdots, Y_m\}$.
(2) For each $Y_i(i \in (i, m))$ and input it to a random forest classification model, the Y_i will be classified and predicted by each decision tree in the random forest, and t prediction results can be obtained.
(3) According to the t prediction results, the voting result is used to generate the probability distribution matrix of worms.

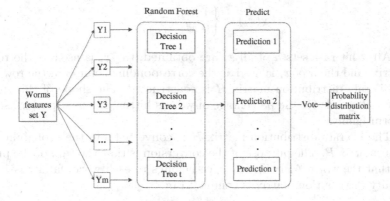

Fig. 3. Worms similarity measure based on random forest classification model.

4.2 Worms Similarity Measure Based on Sensitive Behavior Matching Algorithm

Input in this part is API call sequence of worm propagation behavior. By calculating the hit rate of the API sequence of worm propagation behavior in the sensitive behavior feature library, then convert the hit rate to the probability distribution matrix. The probability distribution matrix represents the similarity measurement results of worms.

The sensitive behavior matching algorithm is based on the assumption that the number of worms is T, and the API call sequence of each worm propagation behavior is denoted as x_i, where $i \in [1, T]$. There are M tables in sensitive behavior library and the length of each table is N. Each table represents a frequent pattern set of the API call sequence of a kind of worm, and the length of the table represents the number of frequent items with the frequent pattern set. M_j represents the first j table in the sensitive behavior feature library, that is, the frequent pattern set of the API call sequence of the first j worm family. M_{j_i} represents the first n frequent item of the frequent pattern in the API call sequence of the first j worm, where $j \in [1, M]$ and $n \in [1, N]$.

A detailed description of the process is as follows:

(1) For the API calling sequence x_i of the worm propagation behavior to be matched, mark the hit rate as h_j. The hit rate of x_i in the frequent pattern set M_j of the first j worm is calculated by

$$h_j = \frac{\sum\limits_{n=1}^{N} \chi(x_i)}{N} \tag{1}$$

where $\chi(x_i)$ indicates whether the API call sequence x_i hits the frequent item of the current frequent pattern set. When x_i contains the current frequent item M_{j_n}, it means hit, and when x_i doesn't contain the current frequent item M_{j_n}, it means no hit. $\chi(x_i)$ is computed by

$$\chi(x_i) = \begin{cases} 1 & M_{j_n} \subseteq x_i \\ 0 & M_{j_n} \not\subseteq x_i \end{cases} \tag{2}$$

(2) After hit rate sets h of all x_i are obtained, the x_i is used as the row of the matrix, and the h of x_i is used as the corresponding column of the row. The worms hit rate distribution matrix H is constructed. The shape of this matrix is $T \times M$. H stands for the percentage of worms hitting frequent pattern sets in each worm family.

(3) The hit rate distribution matrix H is converted into the probability distribution matrix P. The purpose of the conversion is that the sum of the probabilities that the worm API call sequence belongs to each worm family is 1. The probability distribution matrix is computed by

$$P_{i,j} = \frac{H_{i,j}}{\sum\limits_{j=1}^{M} H_{i,j}} \tag{3}$$

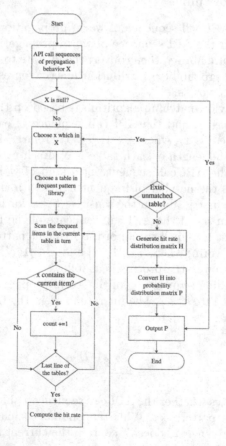

Fig. 4. Worms similarity measure based on sensitive behavior matching algorithm.

where $P_{i,j}$ represents the probability that the first i worm belongs to the first j worm family. $H_{i,j}$ represents the hit rate that the first j worm family contains the first i worm. $\sum_{j=1}^{M} H_{i,j}$ represents the sum of the line i of the hit rate distribution matrix, that is, the sum of hit rates of the first i worms in each worm family. In the probability distribution matrix P, each row corresponds to

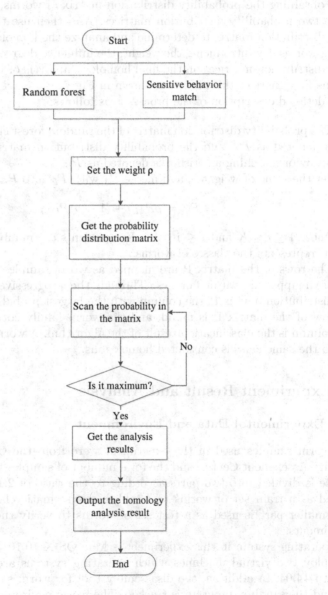

Fig. 5. Homology analysis based on worm similarity measurement matrix.

a worm sample, and each column represents a known worm family. The flow chart of this process is shown in Fig. 4.

4.3 Homology Analysis Based on Worm Similarity Measurement Matrix

After obtaining the probability distribution matrix of worms, it is necessary to merge two probability distribution matrices. And then use the merged probability distribution matrix to determine and analyze the homologous relationship among worms. By introducing the weight, the influence degree of the two probability distribution matrices on the final homology analysis of worms is adjusted.

The flow chart of this process is shown in Fig. 5.

A detailed description of the process is as follows:

(1) The probability distribution matrix of the random forest classification model is denoted as P_A, and the probability distribution matrix of the sensitive behavior matching algorithm is denoted as P_B.

(2) Set the value of weight ρ, and merge P_A with P_B into P. P is computed by

$$P_{i,j} = \rho P_{Ai,j} + (1 - \rho) P_{Bi,j} \qquad (4)$$

where $1 \leq i \leq K$ and $1 \leq j \leq W$. K represents the numbers of worms, and W represents the classes of worms.

(3) The rows of the matrix P are mapped as worm samples, and the columns are mapped as worm families. Through the progressive scan probability distribution matrix P, the column with the largest probability value in each row of the matrix P is found, and the worm family corresponding to the column is the classification result of the algorithm. A worm sample assigned to the same class is considered homologous.

5 Experiment Result and Analysis

5.1 Experimental Data and Environment

The worm samples used in the experiment were from the China Information Security Assessment Center, and the total number of samples was 910. The total sample is divided into two parts according to the ratio of 2:1. The larger part is used as a train set of worms to establish a systematic classification model. The smaller part is used as a test set of worms to verify the effect of system experiments.

Operating system in this experiment is Mac OS X 10.10. And use VMware to deploy two virtual machines which operating systems are Windows 7 and Ubuntu 14.04. In addition, the disassembly tool for worm samples is IDA Pro 5.5, and the sandbox program is Cuckoo. The worm environments simulated in sandbox include Window XP and Window 7.

5.2   Experimental Evaluation Method

The proposed homology analysis method of worms is compared with the existing methods, and the experimental results are evaluated from two aspects which are the accuracy of results and the time performance of the method.

The accuracy, precision, recall rate and F value are used as the evaluation indexes of the accuracy of the results of the homology analysis. It can be used for evaluating whether the worm similarity method proposed in this paper can improve the accuracy of the results of worm homology analysis. The running time of the algorithm is used as an evaluation index of the time performance of the algorithm, which is used to evaluate whether the time performance of the worm similarity analysis method is guaranteed and whether it has been improved or not.

5.3   Experimental Results and Comparative Analysis

In order to prove the method proposed in this paper, three sets of comparative experiments were conducted. And three experiments use the same experimental group. That is, to extract features based on attack propagation characteristics, and to analyze worm homology combined with the random forest classification model and the sensitive behavior matching algorithm. The experimental group was marked by symbolic A.

Three groups of experimental control groups are shown in Table 1.

Table 1. Experimental control groups

No.	Label
Use the full worms feature set, combine with random forest classification model and sensitive behavior matching algorithm for homology analysis of worms	B
Use the filtered worms feature set, just use random forest classification model for homology analysis of worms	C
Use the full worms feature set, just use random forest classification model for homology analysis of worms	D

Experiments were carried out according to the experimental set, and experimental evaluation index were used to statistically analyze the experimental results. The statistical results are shown in Table 2.

Table 2. Experimental results statistics

Number	Accuracy	Precision	Recall	F value	Time (s)
A	93.7%	93.7%	93.1%	93.2%	17.26
B	92.4%	93.2%	92.4%	92.6%	20.01
C	91.1%	91.4%	91.1%	91.1%	13.33
D	90.8%	91.2%	90.8%	90.8%	18.71

(a) Data from China Information Security Assessment Center.

The experimental results are analyzed as follows:

(1) When worm features are extracted based on attack propagation behavior, the accuracy, precision, recall rate and F value of homology analysis of worms are improved slightly, and the running time of the algorithm is obviously reduced. Through this experiment, it can be proved that worms feature extraction based on attack propagation behavior can improve the time performance of the algorithm without reducing the accuracy of the results of the same analysis.
(2) When combined with the random forest classification model and sensitive behavior matching algorithm, the results of homology analysis of worms in accuracy, precision, recall and F value have obviously improved, but the performance of the algorithm's running time decreased slightly.
(3) The third set of experiments integrated the two set of experiments were designed to verify feature extraction based on worm attack propagation behavior and method combined random forest classification model and sensitive behavior matching algorithm for results of homology analysis of worms. The experimental results show that the optimization effect of this method is more obvious, and the accuracy of homology analysis is improved under the premise of ensuring the time performance of the algorithm.

Through simulation experiments, the proposed homology analysis method of worms in this paper can not only guarantee the time performance of the algorithm but improve the accuracy of analysis results. Hence the feasibility of this method is proved.

6   Conclusions

With the increasingly close connection between the Internet and people's daily work and life, the economic losses and security threats caused by worm attacks are becoming more and more serious. Therefore, this paper studies the attack propagation mode of worms, and proposes a method based on the worm attack propagation features, combined with the random forest classification model and sensitive behavior matching algorithm for the homology analysis of worms.

Experimental results show that the method can guarantee the time performance of algorithm, and improve the accuracy of homology analysis of worms. The method has a certain value in the field of homology analysis of worms.

Acknowledgments. This work was supported by the National Key R & D Program of China (Grant No. 2016YFB0801304).

References

1. Bayoğlu, B., Soğukpınar, İ.: Graph based signature classes for detecting polymorphic worms via content analysis. Comput. Netw. **56**(2), 832–844 (2012)
2. Liang, H., Chai, J., Tang, Y.: Polymorphic worm detection using position-relation signature. In: Wong, W.E., Zhu, T. (eds.) Computer Engineering and Networking. LNEE, vol. 277, pp. 1365–1372. Springer, Cham (2014). https://doi.org/10.1007/978-3-319-01766-2_155
3. Wang, J., He, X.: Automatic extraction method of feature based on seed extended polymorphic worm. J. Commun. **35**(9), 12–19 (2014)
4. Li, W., Song, K.: Exploring the mystery of Duqu Trojan horse. Duqu and Stuxnet homology analysis. Programmer **5**, 117–121 (2012)
5. Qian, Y., Peng, G., Wang, Y., et al.: Homology analysis of malicious code and family clustering. Comput. Eng. Appl. **51**(18), 76–81 (2015)
6. Ge, Y., Kang, F., Peng, X.: Homology analysis of malicious code based on dynamic BP neural network. Small Microcomput. Syst. **37**(11), 2527–2531 (2016)
7. Alazab, M., Layton, R., Venkataraman, S., et al.: Malware detection based on structural and behavioural features of API call (2010)
8. Moskovitch, R., Feher, C., Tzachar, N., Berger, E., Gitelman, M., Dolev, S., Elovici, Y.: Unknown malcode detection using OPCODE representation. In: Ortiz-Arroyo, D., Larsen, H.L., Zeng, D.D., Hicks, D., Wagner, G. (eds.) EuroIsI 2008. LNCS, vol. 5376, pp. 204–215. Springer, Heidelberg (2008). https://doi.org/10.1007/978-3-540-89900-6_21
9. Shabtai, A., Moskovitch, R., Feher, C., et al.: Detecting unknown malicious code by applying classification techniques on Op-Code patterns. Secur. Inform. **1**(1), 1 (2012)
10. Xin, Y., Fang, B., He, L., et al.: Research of worm detection and feature extraction based on communication feature analysis. J. Commun. **28**(12), 1–7 (2007)
11. Fang, W., Zhou, B., An, J.: Windows API Development Detailed: Function, Interface, Programming Examples. Posts and Telecommunications Press (2011)
12. Ravi, C., Manoharan, R.: Malware detection using windows API sequence and machine learning. Int. J. Comput. Appl. **43**(17), 12–16 (2012)
13. Katz, J., Linde, Y.: Introduction to modern cryptography, vol. 207 (2014)
14. Alam, M.S., Vuong, S.T.: Random forest classification for detecting android malware. In: IEEE International Conference on Green Computing and Communications and IEEE Internet of Things and IEEE Cyber, Physical and Social Computing, pp. 663–669. IEEE Computer Society (2013)

Modeling and Analysis of Information Propagation Model of Online/Offline Network Based on Coupled Network

Wanting Qin and Tongrang Fan[✉]

School of Information Science and Technology, Shijiazhuang Tiedao University,
Shijiazhuang 050043, China
fantr@stdu.edu.cn, fantr2009@126.com

Abstract. Currently, more and more scholars believe that most networks are not isolated, but interact with each other. Internet-based social network (online network), and physical contact networks (offline network) are a coupled network that interact with each other. Person have online virtual identity and offline social identity. In this paper, the double SIR information spreading model with unilateral effect is constructed according to the characteristics of online and offline information dissemination. And two typical types of coupled networks, BA_BA network and WS_WS network, are used to simulate. The experimental results show that the online information propagation can inhibit the scope of offline. This inhibition is slightly weaker for the BA_BA network that the inter degree-degree correlation (IDDC) is positive. At the same time, it is found that the increase of the interlayer influence rate can enhance the synchronization of information transmission on online and offline so that effectively promote the information propagation of online/offline.

Keywords: Online/offline · The coupled network · SIR · The inter degree-degree correlation · Interlayer influence rate

1 Introduction

The evolution of the Internet is from a single network to the "Super Network" [1]. Once a network fails, cascading failures may result in other networks. Most of real networks are a more complex system formed by the interaction of various types of networks. Such as in power system, power network and computer control system composed of coupled network [2]; in the social network, the interpersonal network formed in real life and the interpersonal network formed in the virtual world can produce coupled network [3]; in the traffic network, the road network and railway network presents a kind of coupled cooperation system [4]. Research on information propagation dynamics only from single network tends to ignore some important factors that affect the spread, for example the interaction of the inter-layer communication in multiplex network. In the real world, the channels

© Springer Nature Singapore Pte Ltd. 2017
M. Xu et al. (Eds.): CTCIS 2017, CCIS 704, pp. 16–25, 2017.
https://doi.org/10.1007/978-981-10-7080-8_2

of receiving and spreading messages have physical contact networks (offline), such as face to face or telephone, and Internet-based social network (online), such as MSN or twitter. These two channels, online and offline, not only have the relationship of mutual collaboration but also have competition relationship. Study on this information dissemination process which is different from single network has a great significance to more really response the regulars and features of information propagation and to maintain network security and stability. This paper researches online/offline information propagation model based on coupled network.

2   Related Work

At present, Network of networks, Multiplex network and Multiplex network and interdependent networks [1,5] are presented at international. These concepts have become one of the most important areas of complex network. In 2010, Buldyrev et al. [6] proposed a cascading failure model of interdependent networks and found that robustness was lower in interdepend networks. Since then more and more scholars pay attention to multiplex networks, and study various dynamic process based on multiplex networks. Dickison et al. [7] who investigated SIR epidemics on the coupled network found that the diseases spread over a large area in the strong interconnection coupled network and the virus more likely spread one side of the weak interconnection coupled network. Min et al. [8] extended the SIS, SIR model to the coupled or multiplex network and found that the critical values of disease broken out was significantly different from single network. Zhao et al. [9] researched immunization strategy on the multiplex network. They presented two immunization strategies, Multiplex node-based random (targeted) immunization and Layer node-based random (targeted) immunization. They found that these both types of random immunization strategy can effectively control the disease for multiplex consisting of ER and ER network but targeted immunization strategy effect was better than random for multiplex consisting of BA and BA. Granell et al. [10] researched asymmetric transmission dynamic characteristics on coupled network composed of information diffusion network and disease spreading network. Yu [11] constructed on the online/offline BCN information dissemination model based on symmetric transmission mechanisms and asymmetric transmission mechanism. Dong et al. [12] studied the robustness of partial dependence on the N interdependent network. It was found that the N layer ER network will undergo a process which was from the two-order phase transition to the first-order phase transition. Wang et al. [13] studied asymmetrically spreading dynamic on information epidemic network and found that the increase in the rate of information transmission can increase the threshold of disease outbreaks. Therefore, not only the network but also the related network should be considered to maintain the stability of the network.

3 Information Propagation and Coupled Network

3.1 Analysis of the Characteristics of Online/Offline Information Propagation

The Information propagation often both occur simultaneously on these two communication networks, online/offline, but there are obvious differences. Online communications network can span geographical limitations [14]. Such as, one in China and the other person in United States can completely real-time communicate through online network. This phenomenon is impossible on offline network. Cooperation and competition mechanism embodied in coupled network [15]. Online communication network and offline communication network not only exist cooperative relations that promote the information spreading, but also exit competitive relations because of different media. Both cooperation and competition existing in online/offline network, make the information spreading on the coupled network different from on single network. The event happened will trigger online network and offline network at the same time and then transmit the message. But because of the development of internet technology, online has wider range and efficiency on information spreading than offline. Information dissemination process generally radiate message from the online to the offline [16]. Because online radiate message to offline, the double SIR information dissemination constructed in this paper is unilateral effect.

3.2 The Classic Model of Information Propagation

Most of researches on information propagation model make use of epidemic spreading model. Social network has a close relationship with disease transmission network. In fact, disease spreads through the contact between people. Therefore, it's suitable to make use of epidemic model to study information dissemination in social networks. There are three classical epidemic spreading models, susceptible-infected model (SI), susceptible-infected-susceptible model (SIS) and susceptible-infected-recovered model (SIR). S (susceptible) means that some people is illness and easy to be infected by sick person, which represent the group who do not receive message in this paper; I (infected) means that some people can infect susceptible person, which represent those who get the message and reproduce or transport the message in this paper; R(recovered) means that some people are isolated or immunized, and in this paper, it represents some people who lost interest and will not spread it after getting the message. The classic SIR virus propagation model is shown in Fig. 1:

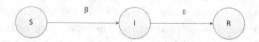

Fig. 1. The classic SIR virus propagation model

3.3   The Topology of Coupled Network

The type of coupled network built in this paper is inter-dependent networks, as shown in Fig. 2. There have two types of edges in this coupled network: (1) Interdependent edge: represents a connection between nodes at different network layers; (2) Intralayer edge: represents a connection between nodes in the same network layer. The general topology of interdependent networks is given by Ref. [17]. This topology introduces the concept of interdependent matrix based on the adjacency matrix of single network. And this topology represents the topology of interdependent edge. The topology of interdependent networks is shown in Eq. 1. In this matrix, A1, A2 represent the adjacency matrix of Layer A and Layer B, and B_{12} is interdependent matrix representing connections between Layer A's node and Layer B's node.

$$\tilde{A} = \begin{bmatrix} A_1 & B_{12} \\ B_{12}^T & A_2 \end{bmatrix} \tag{1}$$

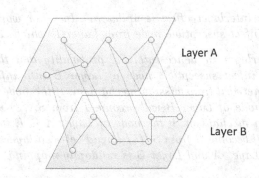

Fig. 2. Interdependent network

3.4   The Inter Degree-Degree Correlation (IDDC)

In the single network, degree correlation describes different degree of nodes in the network preferentially connect. The inter degree-degree correlation describes degree of relevance between different layers in the coupled network. Parshani [18] mentioned the IDDC that based on degree correlation in single network, as shown Eq. 2. The IDDC exits the following three types: (1) The value of IDDC is positive ($r^{AB} \to 1$). Represent a larger degree node of Layer A tends to connect with a larger degree node of Layer B. The greater value of IDDC is, the more obvious the tendency is. (2) The value of IDDC is negative ($r^{AB} \to -1$). Represent a larger degree node of Layer A tends to connect with a smaller degree node of Layer B. (3) The value of IDDC is approximately equal to 0 ($r^{AB} \approx 0$). The nodes between two layers randomly connect with equal probability.

$$r^{AB} = \frac{1}{\sigma^2} \sum_{jk} jk \left(e_{jk} - p_j^A p_k^B \right) \tag{2}$$

Which, e_{jk}, the probability of choosing an interdependent edge that degree of Layer A vertex is j and degree of Layer B vertex is k. p_j^A, p_k^B represent that the probability that degree of Layer A node is and the degree of Layer B node is k. $\sigma^2 = \sqrt{\sigma_A} * \sqrt{\sigma_B}$, which $\sigma_A = \sum_k k^2 p_k^A - [\sum_k k p_k^A]^2$, $\sigma_B = \sum_k k^2 p_k^B - [\sum_k k p_k^B]^2$.

4   The Information Propagation Model of Online/Offline

Virus propagation model in single network does not apply to information spreading on multiplex network. A double SIR information propagation model with unilateral effect is given.

4.1   Model Definition

Definition 1. *SIR virus transmission dynamic process in single network simultaneously exist in Layer A and Layer B.*

Definition 2. *The interlayer effect is unilateral. In other word, infected node from Layer A can infect susceptible node from Layer B which can't reverse.*

Definition 3. *Interlayer influence rate, the probability that the infected node from Layer A can infect susceptible node of Layer B into infected state, and (1) interlayer symmetrical transmission mechanism, if the node of Layer A is I, the corresponding node of Layer B will become I from S. (2) interlayer asymmetric transmission mechanism, if the node of Layer A is I, the corresponding node of Layer B will become R from S. (3) spread between layers for the random state. The node of Layer A and Layer B is randomly mapping.*

Definition 4. *What the node of Layer A lose interest for information will lead to the corresponding nodes of Layer B losing interest. If Layer A node is recovered, the corresponding node of Layer B will be recovered. The double SIR information propagation model with unilateral effect is shown in Fig. 3.*

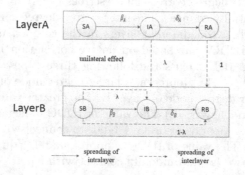

Fig. 3. The double SIR information propagation model

4.2 Algorithm Description Based on Double SIR Information Propagation Model

Node status information is asynchronous update on spreading of intralayer and synchronous update on spreading of interlayer. When the initial $t = 0$, it means that a node was selected as infected node from Layer A randomly, and the corresponding node of Layer B is also infected node. When $t = t_i$, it means that the status of node B_i is determined by its own state and its neighboring node status at $t = t_i - 1$ and corresponding layer node at $t = t_i$.

1. The spreading of intralayer in Layer A (principle of asynchronous update) (1) At $t_i - 1$, if node A_i is S, then judge whether the neighbor of A_i exist I status node. If don't have, node A_i will keep S status at $t = t_i$ and if the number of node I is m, node A_i will become I with probability $1 - (1 - \beta)^m$ at $t = t_i$. (2) If node A_i is I at node A_i will become R with probability δ at $t = t_i$. (3) If node A_i is R at $t_i - 1$, node will keep R status at $t = t_i$.
2. The spreading of intralayer in Layer B is similar with Layer A.
3. The spreading of interlayer between Layer A and Layer B (principle of synchronous update): (1) If node A_i is S at $t = t_i$, corresponding node B_i of Layer B will keep status at $t = t_i$. (2) If node A_i is I and corresponding node B_i is S at $t = t_i$, node B_i will change to I with probability λ. (3) If node A_i is R at $t = t_i$, the node B_i will change to R at $t = t_i$.
4. When there is no node I on the coupled network, the process of propagation will be end.

5 The Simulation of Information Propagation Process on Online/Offline

5.1 The Construction of Coupled Network

Based on Matlab, the double SIR information propagation process is run. First, construct two classic types of online/offline network, BA_BA network and WS_WS network, which the subnetworks attributes is shown in the following Table 1. For convenience, the interlayer connection is one-to-one in this paper. Sort the nodes of Layer A and Layer B according to the size of degree: $k_1^A \geq k_2^A \geq k_3^A \geq \cdots \geq k_N^A, k_1^B \geq k_2^B \geq k_3^B \geq \cdots \geq k_N^B$. If the way of interlayer connection is $k_1^A \leftrightarrow k_1^B, \cdots, k_N^A \leftrightarrow k_N^B$, the value of IDDC is maximum; if the way of interlayer connection is $k_1^A \leftrightarrow k_N^B, \cdots, k_N^A \leftrightarrow k_1^B$, the value of IDDC is minimum.

5.2 The Settings of Experiment and Results

The value of IDDC is approximately set to 1, −0.2, 0 for BA_BA network; the value of IDDC is approximately set to 1, −0.9, 0 for WS_WS network. The interlayer influence rate λ is 0.1, 0.5, 0.9; the infection rate of Layer B is set to $\beta_B = 0.3$. In order to accelerate the process of experiment; the recovery rates

Table 1. The two types of subnetworks attributes

Types	Number	Average path length	Average degree	Clustering coefficient	Connectivity
WS	1000	3.3846	10	0.094672	Yes
BA	1000	2.975	10	0.042318	Yes

of Layer A and Layer B are both set to $\delta_A = \delta_B = 0.8$. Select one node of Layer A as infected node and corresponding node of Layer B is also infected node and then run the double SIR information propagation process on the constructed coupled network, BA_BA network and WS_WS network. After end of each process, statistic the proportion of infected nodes to the total nodes (I/N), and average value of 20 groups of experimental data.

When λ the is 0.1, 0.5, 0.9, the simulation results of I/N change with infected rate β_A of Layer A for BA_BA network and WS_WS network is shown in Figs. 4, 5 and 6. In the following simulation results graph, the solid red line represents I/N of Layer A; black dotted line represents I/N of Layer B. And the star-shape, triangular-shape and square-shape separately represent the value of IDDC is positive, negative or 0.

From Figs. 4, 5 and 6, both for BA_BA network and WS_WS network, when the β_A of Layer A increases, the I/N of Layer A is gradually increasing, however, the I/N of Layer B is gradually decreasing. This phenomenon shows there is a competing relation between Layer A and Layer B. The spreading of Layer A can inhibit Layer B. With the β_A of Layer A increases, the difference of I/N between Layer A and Layer B is becoming larger and larger. In other word, online information spreading has an impulsion on the scope of offline. The bigger the propagation rate of online is, the stronger the effect of inhibition is. From Figs. 5a and 6a, when the value of IDDC is 1, the I/N of Layer B is higher than that the value of IDDC is −0.2 or 0. The value of IDDC more tend to maximum, and the I/N of Layer B will be higher which means that IDDC has slightly effect on BA_BA network. From Figs. 3b, 4b and 5b, different IDDC don't have obvious influence on WS_WS network. This inhibition is also consistent with the spreading characteristics of information disease network. The information spread more quickly on information layer so that people will early receive the disease messages. The infected number of person will be reduced because people have received the message and take appropriate measures to protect themselves.

Both the infected rate of Layer A and Layer B are set to $\beta_A = \beta_B = 0.3$, both the recovery rate of Layer A and layer B are set to $\delta_A = \delta_B = 0.3$. The simulation results of I/N of Layer A and Layer B change with the influence rate is shown in Fig. 7.

From Fig. 7, both for BA_BA network and WS_WS network, the I/N of Layer B increases with λ the increasing, and finally tends to Layer A's. That means Layer A and Layer B will become more synchronously when λ increases. When λ tends to 1, this is symmetrical transmission mechanism. Layer B is more

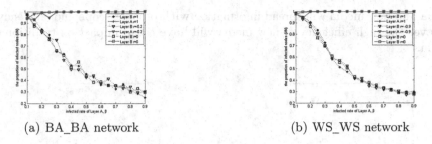

(a) BA_BA network   (b) WS_WS network

Fig. 4. $\lambda = 0.1$, the proportion of infected nodes (I/N) change with infected rate β_A of Layer A

(a) BA_BA network   (b) WS_WS network

Fig. 5. $\lambda = 0.5$, the proportion of infected nodes (I/N) change with infected rate β_A of Layer A

(a) BA_BA network   (b) WS_WS network

Fig. 6. $\lambda = 0.9$, the proportion of infected nodes (I/N) change with infected rate β_A of Layer A

synchronous with Layer A, so the proportion of infected nodes is bigger in this situation. Conversely, when λ tends to 0, this is asymmetrical transmission mechanism, and the synchronization of Layer A and Layer B is weaker. Symmetric dissemination mechanisms contribute to dissemination of information. The partnerships between layer and layer are highlighted at this time and synchronicity is more noticeable. However, asymmetric transmission mechanisms would highlight competition. The above analysis show that the transmission of online/offline has broader range than single way transmission. However, because online/offline are substitute so that they have a competitive relationship. For example, Traditional media and new media will spread information with broader scope and efficiency, however the high efficiency of new media will have a bad impact on traditional media.

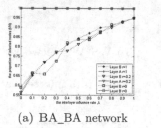

(a) BA_BA network

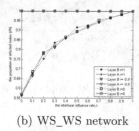

(b) WS_WS network

Fig. 7. The proportion of infected nodes (I/N) change with interlayer influence rate λ

6   Conclusion

At present, the research of information dissemination model is based on single layer network. In this paper, the research object is to take the online/offline as an interdependent coupled network. This is more conform to the process of information propagation of online/offline. The information dissemination and public opinion can be better controlled and guided through study information propagation on online/offline. Especially, when face unexpected events, be able to guide public opinion and stop the spread of rumors. Therefore, the study of information transmission from the coupled network can better maintain the flow of information security in the network.

A double SIR information propagation model based on the spreading characteristics of online/offline is put up in this paper. Simulation results show that as the inflected rate of Layer A increases, it has an inhibitory effect on Layer B. The inhibitory effect will slightly weaken for BA_BA network with larger value of IDDC. However, this effect has no clear distinction with different IDDC of WS_WS network as the inflected rate of Layer A increases, and will conduct a follow-up study. Layer A and Layer B tend to sync with the interlayer influence rate increase. It needs to increase cooperation between the different transmission routes and lessen competition, if want to expand dissemination of information. The increase of interlayer influence rate can make online and offline partnerships highlight and the competitive relationship weakened so that online/offline can be in sync. Epidemic spreading model is used to study information spreading in this paper. Due to the information dissemination process is different from the spread of the virus, the process of information propagation can reflect the characteristics of the information itself. In the subsequent work, the above imperfections should be taken into account. And the double SIR information propagation model should be refined further and will be more prefect.

Acknowledgements. This work was supported by the National Natural Science Foundation of China (61373160,61402300) and the Founded Projects for Introduction of Overseas Scholars of Hebei Province, and the Funds for Excellent Young Scholar of Shijiazhuang Tiedao University.

References

1. Nagurney, A., Dong, J.: Supernetworks: Decision-Making for the Information Age. Edward Elgar Publishers, Cheltenham (2002)
2. Shi-Ming, C., Xiao-qun, Z., Hui, L., Qing-Gang, X.: Research on robustness of interdependent network for suppressing cascading failure. Acta Phys. Sin. **63**(2), 432–441 (2014)
3. Yiran, G., Huang, Z.: Analying and modeling of student communication behavior based on bilayer network. J. Nanjing Univ. Posts Telecommun. (Nat. Sci. Ed.), **36**(2), 41–48 (2016)
4. Wen-ju, D., Li, Y.-Z., An, X., Ma, C.-X.: A new class of two layers public traffic coupled network model. J. Transp. Syst. Eng. Inf. Technol. **16**(4), 131–138 (2016)
5. Yang, L.S., Junde, W., Liang, B.: Review of interdependent networks. J. Nat. Univ. Defense Technol. **1**, 122–128 (2016)
6. Buldyrev, S.V., Parshani, R., Paul, G., Stanley, H.E., Havlin, S.: Catastrophic cascade of failures in interdependent networks. Nature **464**(7291), 1025–1028 (2010)
7. Dickison, M., Havlin, S., Stanley, H.E.: Epidemics on interconnected networks. Phys. Rev. E Stat. Phys. Plasmas Fluids Relat. Interdisc. Topics **85**(2), 1380–1404 (2012)
8. Min, B., Goh, K.I.: Layer-crossing overhead and information spreading in multiplex social networks. In: APS March Meeting 2014. American Physical Society (2013)
9. Zhao, D., Wang, L., Li, S., et al.: Immunization of epidemics in multiplex networks. Plos One **9**(11), e112018 (2014)
10. Granell, C., Gmez, S., Arenas, A.: Dynamical interplay between awareness and epidemic spreading in multiplex networks. Phys. Rev. Lett. **111**(12), 1–7 (2013)
11. Yu, K.: Research on information spreading model on bilayer coupled network. Dalian University of Technology (2015)
12. Dong, G., Tian, L., Zhou, D., et al.: Robustness of n interdependent networks with partial support dependence relationship. EPL **102**(102), 68804 (2013)
13. Wang, W., Tang, M., Yang, H., et al.: Asymmetrically interacting spreading dynamics on complex layered networks. Sci. Rep. **4**(7502), 5097 (2014)
14. Ming, D.: Research on model online/offline network and information spreading. University of Electronic Science and technology of China (2016)
15. Kai-Jun, L.I., Chang-Gui, G.U., Yan-Qing, Q.U., et al.: Onset of co-operation in some real world layered networks. Complex Syst. Complex. Sci. **9**(2), 79–83 (2012)
16. Hengmin, Z., Liu, Y., Jing, M., Jing, W.: Study on public opinion propagation model based on coupled network under online to offline interaction. J. Intell. (0.2), 139–144+450 (2016)
17. Wang, H., Li, Q., D'Agostino, G., Havlin, S., Stlanely, H.E., Van, M.P.: Effect of the interconnected network structure on the epidemic threshold. Phys. Rev. E Stat. Nonlinear Soft Matter Phys. **88**(2), 279–311 (2013)
18. Parshani, R., Rozenblat, C., Ietri, D., Ducruet, C., Havlin, S.: Inter-similarity between coupled networks. EPL **96**(6), 2470–2484 (2011)

A Signature-Sharing Based Auditing Scheme with Data Deduplication in Cloud Storage

Liang Wang[1], Baocang Wang[1,2(✉)], and Shuquan Ma[1]

[1] State Key Laboratory of Integrated Service Networks, Xidian University, Xi'an 710071, People's Republic of China
bcwang79@aliyun.com
[2] Key Laboratory of Cognitive Radio and Information Processing, Ministry of Education, Guilin University of Electronic Technology, Guilin 541004, People's Republic of China

Abstract. With the rapid development of cloud computing, more and more individuals and enterprises trend to store their massive data in the cloud to reduce the expenses of data maintenance and achieve more convenient access. As the cloud service provider is not fully trusted, the accidents involving software or hardware in cloud servers may cause damage of the users' data, which might be covered by the cloud servers deliberately for its reputation. What's worse, the cloud servers may also maliciously discard the rarely accessed data for saving storage space. Data auditing can timely detect and restrict the malicious behaviors of the cloud servers, therefore it can improve the quality of cloud service. Meanwhile there are a large amount of data storing in the cloud repeatedly, the data deduplication technique can make the cloud keep the only physical duplicate for the same data, therefore eliminate redundant data and achieve the efficient storage. To achieve auditing with data deduplication, the existing schemes need different users to sign the same data, which consume a large amount of computing resources of the users, especially it is difficult to be accomplished in the case of poor computation in client side's portable devices. Based on the public verifiability and batch auditing of the POR, we propose a signature-sharing based scheme, for the same data, it only needs the first user to sign and share its signature with the after users for data auditing, this can effectively reduce the burden of the signature computation of the users, consequently achieves both data integrity and storage efficiency.

Keywords: Cloud computing · Signature-share · Public auditing · Data deduplication

1 Introduction

Cloud computing technology has developed rapidly in recent years, one of the most important service in cloud computing is data storage, which allows enterprises and individuals to store their data in the cloud. Cloud storage can provide

© Springer Nature Singapore Pte Ltd. 2017
M. Xu et al. (Eds.): CTCIS 2017, CCIS 704, pp. 26–40, 2017.
https://doi.org/10.1007/978-981-10-7080-8_3

low-cost and on-demand use of vast storage and processing resources, which can relieve users from the heavy burden of storage management and maintenance. It makes the outsourced data can be accessed from anywhere via the internet and the data owners can easily share their data to others, consequently those advantages lead to the cloud storage of exponential growth. Cloud storage not only stands for the massive computing infrastructure but also brings great economic benefits. Commercial cloud storage services such as Microsoft Azure, Amazon AWS and Google Cloud Storage have attracted millions of users. Under such a trend, it becomes urgent to assure the quality of data storage services which involves two frequent concerns from both cloud users and cloud service providers: data integrity and storage efficiency.

As for the users, the cloud service provider is not fully trusted, this inevitably raises users concerns on the integrity of their data as the data is no longer stored locally and not under control of the users at all. The software or hardware fault may occur in cloud storage, which may lead to the loss or damage of the user's data, the cloud may deliberately hide some incidents involving data damage for its good reputation, what is worse is that the cloud servers may deliberately delete the rarely accessed data for saving space. Considering the users' concerns, the data auditing scheme is proposed that the client can efficiently perform integrity verification periodically without the local copy of the data.

As for the cloud servers, a large amount of data is stored in the cloud, storage efficiency has been a main concern for cloud service providers. According to a recent survey by EMC [1], more than 75% of today's digital data are duplicated copies, repeated storage of massive data means a huge waste of storage resources. The secure deduplication technique is proposed to reduce the unnecessarily redundant copies, the cloud storage servers would deduplicate by keeping only one copy for each file and just making a link to the file for every owner who stored the file.

In order to achieve both data integrity and storage efficiency, simple combination of the two techniques results in a storage overhead for each file, because lack of mutual trust, the data owners need to separately store their own authentication tags in cloud for integrity auditing, since these tags are created for auditing the same file, storing such copies represents a type of duplication itself. For efficient proof of storage with deduplication, many related works have been done.

Related Work. To verify the availability and integrity of the storage outsourced data, Juels and Kaliski [2] first presented a proof of retrievability (POR) scheme, in which clients apply erasure codes and generate authentications for each block for data auditing. Similar to POR, Ateniese et al. [3] were the first to consider public auditing in the provable data possession (PDP) model, the scheme utilizes the RSA-based homomorphic linear authenticator for ensuring possession of outsourced data. In their subsequent work, Ateniese et al. [4] proposed a dynamic version of the prior PDP scheme, but it doesn't support fully dynamic data operations. Based on the works of Juels et al. [2] and Ateniese et al. [3], some other POR schemes and models give a study on different variants of POR with private auditing. In contrast, public auditing schemes [5–7] allow anyone who has the public key to perform the auditing task, which makes it possible to delegate the auditing task to an external third party auditor (TPA). A TPA can perform the integrity verification on behalf of the data owner and honestly report the auditing result to the user. Other schemes in [8,9] provide support for data dynamic operations. Tan et al. [10] reduces the computations of the sign phase by transferring some exponentiation operations into normal operations, which also supports data dynamics and public verifiability. Jin et al. [11] designs an index switcher to achieve efficient handling of data dynamics with fairness arbitration of potential disputes.

Several deduplication schemes [12–14] have been proposed showing that deduplication allows very appealing reductions in the usage of storage resources, but most of their works didn't consider security issues. Convergent encryption is a cryptographic primitive proposed by Douceur et al. [15] and by Storer et al. [16], attempting to achieve data confidentiality with deduplication. Later, Bellare et al. [17] formalized convergent encryption under message locked encryption (MLE) and proved that it offers confidentiality for unpredictable messages only. As a follow-up work, Bellare et al. [18] presented an enhanced version called interactive MLE providing privacy even for correlated messages depending on the public parameters. Li et al. [19] attempt to solve the problem of management of many convergent keys that arises when deduplicating many files or their parts. Meye et al. [20] presented a two-phase data deduplication scheme trying to solve some of the known convergent encryption issues. Stanek et al. [21] presented a threshold data deduplication scheme in which the files are encrypted with two layers, deduplication only happens when a file reaches the popular status.

To achieve both data integrity auditing and storage deduplication, Li et al. [22] proposed a SecCloud system in which the TPA replace the users to generate tags, it needs the TPA with enormous computing power and be fully trusted. Alkhojandi et al. [23] presented the mediator who aggregates the signatures of the duplicate blocks and performs a block-level deduplication. Yuan and Yu [24] proposed a scheme based on the polynomial-based authentication tags and homomorphic linear authenticators. He et al. [25] proposed the scheme by using the method of proxy re-encryption and aggregating the tags from different owners. All above schemes need the owners sign their data even if for the same duplicate data, which costs a lot of computing resources.

Our Contribution. The research in [10] shows that the cost of generating the metadata is expensive, the signature phase for 1 GB data need dozens of hours, especially for various kinds of accessed devices, e.g., mobile devices, the client cannot spend too much computation resources on both the generating metadata and executing auditing phase. All the existing schemes need the different users generate metadata for the same duplicated data, which cost a lot of computation resources of the clients. Based on the properties of public auditing and batch auditing in current auditing schemes, we propose the signature-sharing auditing scheme with data deduplication.

Our scheme presents the signature-sharing method, for the duplicated data, only the first client needs to generate the metadata and shares the metadata with others who have the same data. So anyone who has the same data can use the first one's metadata to execute the data integrity auditing. In this way, only the first client uploading data needs to execute the signature phase while the other later users possessing the same data do not, thus it effectively reduces the computation resource in the client's side.

2 Preliminary

Before introducing our scheme, we should first briefly introduce some related concepts as follows:

Definition 1. Bilinear Maps. Let G, G_T be two multiplicative cyclic groups of prime order p, A bilinear map is the map $e : G \times G \to G_T$ with the following properties:

- Bilinear: $\forall g_1, g_2 \in G$ and $\forall a, b \in Z_p$, it has $e(g_1^a, g_2^b) = e(g_1, g_2)^{ab}$.
- Non-degenerate: for some $g_1, g_2 \in G$, it has $e(g_1, g_2) \neq 1$.
- Computable: $\forall g_1, g_2 \in G$, there exists efficient algorithm to compute $e(g_1, g_2)$.

Such groups can be found in hyperelliptic curves or supersingular elliptic curves over finite fields, and the bilinear pairings can be derived from the Weil or Tate pairings.

Definition 2. CDH Problem. The Computational Diffie-Hellman Problem (CDH Problem) is that, unknown $x, y \in Z_p^*$, for given $g, g^x, g^y \in G$, to compute g^{xy}.

If no polynomial time algorithm has advantage at least ε in solving the CDH problem in G, we declare the CDH assumption holds in G, which means it is computational infeasible to solve the CDH problem in G. The security of our proposed scheme is based on the hardness of CDH problem.

Definition 3. Convergent Encryption. Convergent encryption would encrypt or decrypt the data copy with a convergent key that would be derived by computing the cryptographic hash value of the data content itself. Since convergent encryption makes use of a deterministic symmetric encryption scheme and its key depends only on the data content, the same data copy could generate the same ciphertext, it has been extensively adopted for secure deduplication.

3 Problem Statement

3.1 System Model

Aiming at allowing for auditable and deduplicated storage, our signature-sharing scheme is illustrated in Fig. 1, which contains three entities:

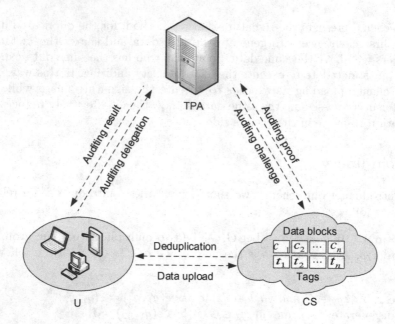

Fig. 1. System model

(1) Cloud Users (U): U has large number of data need to store in the cloud and depends on the cloud for data maintenance and computation. They can be either individual consumers or commercial organizations.

(2) Cloud Server (CS): CS provides storage and computing service for users, and has a strong computing power and storage space. Typically, the cloud users may buy or lease storage capacity from cloud servers, and store their individual data in these bought or rented spaces for future utilization.

(3) Third Party Auditor (TPA): TPA has a rich of experience knowledge in auditing, it performs audit task with fair arbitration, and the TPA can greatly alleviate the auditing burden of users.

3.2   Threat Model

The users encrypt their data, then sign and upload those ciphertext, but their dishonest behaviors on the encryption may do harm to other users, they may forge the signature to cheat the CS. The TPA is allowed to check the integrity of the data fairly, but it is prohibited from seeing the content of the data. The CS is semi-trusted and allowed to see the content of the data and its signatures, but it is required to follow the steps of the auditing process.

3.3 Design Goals

In order to design an efficient auditing scheme with data deduplication for cloud data storage under the above model, our protocol should achieve the following security and performance guarantees.

(1) Signature-sharing: For the duplicate data, the later owners of the same data needn't to compute the signature repeatedly.
(2) Justice and equity: Either the user's or the cloud server's cheat behaviors could be found timely.
(3) Public audibility: Allow TPA to verify the correctness of the stored data in the cloud.
(4) Storage correctness: Ensure that the cloud cannot cheat and pass the auditing process without having stored the data intactly.
(5) Client-side deduplication: Deduplication happens before the client upload the data to the cloud.
(6) Batch auditing: Allow the TPA to perform multiple auditing tasks at the same time.
(7) Lightweight: Consider constrained computation capability of users' accessed device, our scheme mainly allows the user to perform signature phase with minimum computation overhead.

4 Scheme Details

Our signature-sharing auditing scheme with data deduplication contains four steps, the details are described as follows:

4.1 Setup

In this step, we initiate the parameters of the system:

$\textbf{KeyGen}$:$(1^\lambda) \to (pk, sk)$, This is a probabilistic key generation algorithm that is run by the client, λ is the security parameter. It random choose $x \leftarrow Z_p$ and $u \leftarrow G$, compute $y \leftarrow g^x$. The user's secret key is $sk = x$, public key is $pk = \{g, u, y\}$. The user's main key is K, which is used for encrypting the user's convergent keys.

$\textbf{HashFunction}$: there are three collision-resistant cryptographic hash functions in our scheme, they are all public security hash functions:

- $H(\bullet) : \{0,1\}^* \to G$ is a collision-resistant map-to-point hash function which maps a string with arbitrary length into a point in G.
- $h(\bullet) : \{0,1\}^* \to \{0,1\}^l$ is a collision-resistant hash function which maps a string with arbitrary length into l bit, it is used for generating the characteristic value of the data.
- $h_{ck}(\bullet) : \{0,1\}^* \to \{0,1\}^{ck}$ is a collision-resistant hash function which maps a string with arbitrary length to generate the convergent key.

Identification: In our scheme, every user has a unique serial number, denoted as Uid. The user numbers its files, the file is split into blocks, every block has its serial number. The identifications are set as follows:

- $Uid = UserNumber.$
- $Fid = UserNumber \parallel FileNumber.$
- $Bid = UserNumber \parallel FileNumber \parallel BlockNumber.$

By doing this, we can easily learn the file owner from the Fid, and learn the Uid and Fid from the Bid.

4.2 Deduplicate and Upload

When a user has a file ready to be stored in the cloud, the deduplicate and upload step is described in Fig. 2.

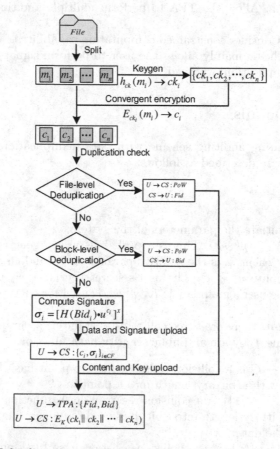

Fig. 2. Uploading file with the file-level and block-level deduplication

File Split: Based on the length of one block the system set, The user split F into n blocks, the data file F can be presented as $F \rightarrow (m_1, m_2, \cdots, m_n) \in Z_p$.

Convergent Encryption: The user runs the convergent key hash function $h_{ck}(\bullet) : \{0,1\}^* \rightarrow \{0,1\}^{ck}$, generates the key for each block $\{ck_i \leftarrow h_{ck}(m_i)\}_{i=1,2,\cdots,n}$, which is used to encrypt each corresponding block, then use the public symmetric cryptographic algorithm to encrypt each block respectively and obtains the ciphertext blocks $\{c_i \leftarrow E_{ck_i}(m_i)\}_{i=1,2,\cdots,n}$.

Data Deduplication: In the case of using plaintext for deduplication, a dishonest user may not follow the rules to encrypt the file, the same data owners could not get the valid plaintext from the ciphertext. So in order to avoid this risk, we adopt the ciphertext at the stage of deduplication.

First, it executes the check in the file-level deduplication, the user utilizes the ciphertext blocks $(c_1, c_2, \cdots, c_n)$ to construct the Merkle Hash Tree (MHT) and send h_{root} to the cloud for deduplication check, if it failed, next executes the duplication check in the block level, otherwise the user need to perform the proof of ownership (PoW) then the CS sends the Fid to the user. To execute the block-level deduplication check, the user sends the characteristic values of the ciphertext blocks $\{h(c_i)\}_{i=1,2,\cdots,n}$ to the cloud to perform the duplication check. As for the failed blocks $CF \in (c_1, c_2, \cdots, c_n)$, it executes the operations of signature and upload. As to the duplicated blocks, it goes to the PoW phase, after CS confirms its validity, the cloud sends the initial Bid to the user.

SignGen: For the blocks $c_i \in CF$, it means the cloud hadn't store the data yet, we call them fresh data. The user is the first one who upload the data and need to sign those blocks $\{\sigma_i = [H(Bid_i) \cdot u^{c_i}]^x\}_{c_i \in CF}$.

Upload: For the fresh data, the user uploads the blocks and its tags $\{c_i, \sigma_i\}_{c_i \in CF}$ to the cloud. Considering dishonest users may utilize a fake signature to cheat the cloud, in order to prevent such case, the cloud verifies the correctness of the data. It compute $\sigma = \prod_{(c_i \in CF)} \sigma_i$ and $\mu = \sum_{(c_i \in CF)} c_i$, then verify

$$e(\sigma, g)? = e(\prod_{(c_i \in CF)} H(Bid_i) \cdot u^\mu, y)$$

Whenever the above equation holds true, the cloud accept those data. For the duplicated file, the identification Fid would be uploaded to the TPA so as for auditing. As for the data that fails to be deduplicated, all of Bid would be uploaded to the TPA so as to it could execute auditing. Finally, the users encrypt all of the convergent keys and upload to the cloud. Concretely, the users utilize the main key to encrypt them, which adopts the public standard symmetric encryption algorithm, and obtain the key ciphertext $FK \leftarrow E_K(ck_1 \parallel ck_2 \parallel \cdots \parallel ck_n)$, then uploads FK to the cloud.

4.3 Proof of Ownership

In a deduplication system, a client claims it has the file F to upload when F has been stored in the cloud, the client needn't really upload the data. A malicious client may use a fictitious claim to visit the data it doesn't really own, in order to prevent this cheating behaviors, the user needs to pass the challenge-response to prove he really possesses the data.

Challenge: Cloud server generates a set of challenge and sends it to the user. If the number of the duplicated blocks is s, CS randomly chooses a set of blocks $I_c \subseteq \{1, 2, \cdots, s\}$ as challenge and sends is to the user. As shown in Fig. 3, eight blocks construct the MHT and CS chooses $I_c = (2, 5)$ as the challenge.

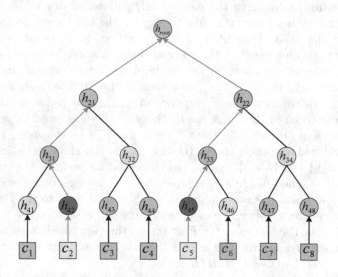

Fig. 3. Auxiliary information in Merkle hash tree

Response: The user responds with the proof for data ownership. The user constructs the MHT on the s blocks, we denote $Path(B_i)$ as the set of nodes from the leaf node indentified by B_i to the root node of the MHT, and $Sibl(B_i)$ is the set of sibling nodes of each node in $Path(B_i)$, for each $i \in I_c$, the user sends $\{h_i, Sibl(B_i)\}$ to the cloud server as the response. As the example described in Fig. 3, $h_i = (h_{42}, h_{45})$, $Sibl(B_i) = (h_{41}, h_{32}, h_{46}, h_{34})$.

Verification: The CS verifies the validity of the proof. If CS could recover the h_{root} from the received nodes, then accepts the proof, otherwise it rejects.

4.4   Auditing

The TPA is delegated by the users to audit the integrity of the data in the cloud and feedbacks the result to the users. Due to the existence of the sharing signature, a user's data may correspond different users' signature. Suppose a user's data blocks refer to k different users' signature, their secret keys and public keys are $\{x_i, y_i\}_{i=1,2,\cdots,k}$. The TPA uses the challenge-response to execute the auditing task as described in Fig. 4.

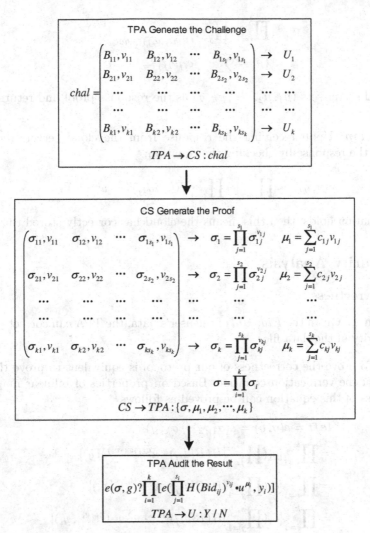

Fig. 4. Integrity auditing with signature-sharing

Challenge: The TPA randomly chooses a set of user's blocks, and obtains the Bid, then it puts the blocks which are signed by the same user together and generates the challenge $chal = \{Bid_{ij}, v_{ij}\}_{i=(1,2,\cdots,k), j=(1,2,\cdots,s_i)}$, s_i denotes the number of blocks that the user U_i signed, B_{ij} denotes the jth signed block of the user U_i, $v_{ij} \in Z_p$ is a set of random numbers. Next, TPA sends $chal$ to the cloud.

Response: Upon receiving the request $chal$ from the TPA, the cloud server generates the proof of data storage correctness. The proof consists of two parts: the aggregated signature value and the linear combination of the specified blocks:

$$\sigma = \prod_{i=1}^{k} \left(\prod_{j=1 \, (Bid_{ij}, \nu_{ij}) \in chal}^{s_j} \sigma_{ij}^{\nu_{ij}} \right)$$

$$\{\mu_i = \sum_{j=1}^{s_j} c_{ij} \nu_{ij}\}_{i=1,2,\cdots,k}$$

The cloud server sets $(\mu_1, \mu_2, \cdots, \mu_k, \sigma)$ as the response proof and returns it to the TPA.

Verification: Upon receiving the response from the cloud server, the TPA validates the response by checking the equation:

$$e(\sigma, g)? = \prod_{i=1}^{k} [e(\prod_{j=1}^{s_i} H(Bid_{ij})^{\nu_{ij}} \cdot u^{\mu_i}, y_i)].$$

If the equation holds, then this means the cloud has correctly stored the data.

5   Security Analysis

5.1   Correctness

Theorem 1. Given the Fid, Bid of the user's data, the TPA can correctly check the integrity of the data file.

Proof. To prove the correctness of our protocol is equivalent to prove the correctness of the verification equation. Based on properties of bilinear maps, the correctness of this equation can be proved as follows

$$left = e(\sigma, g) = e(\sigma_1 \sigma_2 \cdots \sigma_k, g)$$
$$= \prod_{i=1}^{k} [e((\prod_{j=1}^{s_i} [H(Bid_{ij}) \cdot u^{c_{ij}}]^{x_i \cdot \nu_{ij}}), g)]$$
$$= \prod_{i=1}^{k} [e((\prod_{j=1}^{s_i} [H(Bid_{ij}) \cdot u^{c_{ij}}]^{\nu_{ij}}), y_i)]$$
$$= \prod_{i=1}^{k} [e((\prod_{j=1}^{s_i} [H(Bid_{ij})]^{\nu_{ij}} \cdot u^{\sum_{j=1}^{s_i} c_{ij} \nu_{ij}}, y_i)]$$
$$= \prod_{i=1}^{k} [e((\prod_{j=1}^{s_i} [H(Bid_{ij})]^{\nu_{ij}} \cdot u_i^{\mu}, y_i)]$$
$$= right$$

5.2   Unforgeability

Theorem 2. For a probabilistic polynomial time adversary A, it is computationally infeasible to generate a forgery of an auditing proof under our protocol.

Proof. Following the security model, we can prove that, if A could pass our verification by forging an auditing proof, then we can find a solution to CDH problem, which contradicts to the CDH assumption.

Given the same challenge C from the TPA, the proof on correct data F should be $proof = \{\sigma, \mu_1, \mu_2, \cdots, \mu_k\}$, which should pass the verification equation.

$$e(\sigma, g) = \prod_{i=1}^{k}[e(\prod_{j=1}^{s_i} H(Bid_{ij})^{v_{ij}} \cdot u^{\mu_i}, y_i)]$$

However, the forged $proof' = \{\sigma', \mu_1', \mu_2', \cdots, \mu_k'\}$, where $proof' \neq proof$. If this forged proof can still pass the verification performed by the TPA, according to the verification equation.

$$e(\sigma', g) = \prod_{i=1}^{k}[e(\prod_{j=1}^{s_i} H(Bid_{ij})^{v_{ij}} \cdot u^{\mu_i'}, y_i)]$$

Based on the properties of bilinear maps, we can learn that $e(\sigma/\sigma', g) = \prod_{i=1}^{k} e(u^{\Delta\mu_i}, y_i)$, where $\Delta\mu_i = \mu_i - \mu_i'$, then gets

$$e(\sigma/\sigma', g) = \prod_{i=1}^{k} e(u^{x_i\Delta\mu_i}, g) = e(u^{\sum_{i=1}^{k} x_i\Delta\mu_i}, g)$$

That is for given $g, g^{x_1}, g^{x_2}, \cdots, g^{x_k}, u \in G$, we can get $u^{\sum_{i=1}^{k} x_i\Delta\mu_i}$, which contradicts to the assumption that CDH problem is computationally infeasible in G.

5.3 Confidentiality

Theorem 3. Our scheme achieves confidentiality of file with the assumption of secure hash functions.

Proof. The convergent key and characteristic value for duplication check are hash values of the file content, an adversary cannot obtain any information of the file from the hash values. Without actually own the whole file, an adversary cannot generate a valid convergent key for any file with non-negligible probability. All the data has been encrypted with the traditional symmetric encryption scheme before they are outsourced, the convergent key is encrypted by another master key and stored in the cloud server. Furthermore, based on the assumption of secure PoW scheme, any adversary without the file cannot convince the cloud storage server to allow him to get the corresponding access privilege. Thus, our deduplication system is secure in terms of the security model.

5.4 Performance Evaluation

In this section, we will analyze the storage overhead, communication cost and computation cost in our scheme. Let n is the number of blocks in the data file, s is the number of elements in a data block, W is the number of owners of the file, k is the number of users related to the auditing phase, c is the number of challenged blocks, and $|p|$ is the element size of the G, G_T, Z_p.

The storage overhead is one of the most significant issues of deduplication in cloud storage systems. In our scheme, the storage overhead on the cloud server consists of data file, tags and identifications of files and blocks. Comparing to the data file and tags, the size of identifications could be negligible. The storage overhead of data file is $n|p|$, while the storage overhead of tags is $(n/s)|p|$. The total storage overhead of our scheme is $n|p| + (n/s)|p|$.

To compute the communication cost during integrity auditing. In our scheme, the communication cost of auditing process is the challenging message $chal = \{Bid_{ij}, v_{ij}\}$ and the proof $proof = \{\sigma, \mu_1, \mu_2, \cdots, \mu_k\}$, where Bid_{ij} is negligible compared to others. Thus the total communication cost of auditing is $n|p| + (k+1)|p|$.

The computation costs of deduplication and auditing phase are the same compare with other deduplication and auditing system. We proposed the signature-sharing mechanism, in this proposal users needn't to compute the signature of the blocks that had stored in the cloud. Since computing the signature is an expensive operation, our scheme could save plenty of computing resources for the users.

6   Conclusion

In this paper, we proposed an auditing scheme for encrypted data which can achieve data integrity auditing and storage deduplication simultaneously. By using deduplication, the cloud server only needs to store one copy of encrypted data. By utilizing the idea of signature-sharing, only the first client uploading data needs to perform the signature phase while the other later users possessing the same data do not, thus it effectively reduces the computation resource in the client's side. The integrity of deduplicated data can be correctly checked by the auditor fairly. The analyses show that our scheme is secure and efficient.

Acknowledgments. This work was supported by the National Natural Science Foundation of China under Grants No. 61572390, the National Key Research and Development Program of China under Grants No. 2017YFB0802002, the National Natural Science Foundation of Ningbo City under Grants No. 201601HJ-B01382, and the Open Foundation of Key Laboratory of Cognitive Radio and Information Processing, Ministry of Education (Guilin University of Electronic Technology) under Grants No. CRKL160202.

References

1. Yuan, J., Yu, S.: Secure and constant cost public cloud storage auditing with deduplication. In: Communications and Networking Symposium, pp. 145–153 (2013)
2. Juels, A., Kaliski, B.S.: Proofs of retrievability for large files. In: Computer and Communications Security, pp. 584–597 (2007)
3. Ateniese, G., Burns, R., Curtmola, R., et al.: Provable data possession at untrusted stores. In: Computer and Communications Security, pp. 598–609 (2007)
4. Ateniese, G., Pietro, R.D., Mancini, L.V., et al.: Proceedings of the 4th International Conference on Security and Privacy in Communication Network (Secure-Comn 2008), Istanbul, Turkey, 22–25 September 2008, vol. 9, pp. 1–10. ACM, New York (2008)

5. Shacham, H., Waters, B.: Compact proofs of retrievability. In: International Conference on the Theory and Application of Cryptology and Information Security, pp. 90–107 (2008)
6. Wang, Q., Wang, C., Li, J., et al.: Enabling public verifiability and data dynamics for storage security in cloud computing. In: European Symposium on Research in Computer Security, pp. 355–370 (2009)
7. Wang, C., Ren, K., Lou, W., et al.: Toward publicly auditable secure cloud data storage services. IEEE Netw. **24**(4), 19–24 (2010)
8. Erway, C.C., Kupcu, A., Papamanthou, C., et al.: Dynamic provable data possession. In: Computer and Communications Security, pp. 213–222 (2009)
9. Zhu, Y., Wang, H., Hu, Z., et al.: Dynamic audit services for integrity verification of outsourced storages in clouds. In: ACM Symposium on Applied Computing, pp. 1550–1557 (2011)
10. Shuang, T., Lin, T., Xiaoling, L., et al.: An efficient method for checking the integrity of data in the cloud. China Commun. **11**(9), 68–81 (2014)
11. Jin, H., Jiang, H., Zhou, K., et al.: Dynamic and public auditing with fair arbitration for cloud data. IEEE Trans. Cloud Comput. **1** (2016)
12. Meister, D., Brinkmann, A.: Multilevel comparison of data deduplication in a backup scenario. In: Proceedings of SYSTOR 2009: The Israeli Experimental Systems Conference 2009, Haifa, Israel, p. 8, 4–6 May 2009
13. Aronovich, L., Asher, R., Bachmat, E., Bitner, H., Hirsch, M., Klein, S.T.: The design of a similarity based deduplication system. In: Proceedings of SYSTOR 2009: The Israeli Experimental Systems Conference, Haifa, Israel, 4–6 May 2009, p. 6 (2009)
14. Mandagere, N., Zhou, P., Smith, M.A., Uttamchandani, S.: Demystifying data deduplication. In: ACM/IFIP/USENIX 9th International Middleware Conference, Middleware 2008, Companion Proceedings, Leuven, Belgium, 1–5 December 2008, pp. 12–17 (2008)
15. Douceur, J.R., Adya, A., Bolosky, W.J., et al.: Reclaiming space from duplicate files in a serverless distributed file system. In: International Conference on Distributed Computing Systems, pp. 617–624 (2002)
16. Storer, M.W., Greenan, K.M., Long, D.D.E., Miller, E.L.: Secure data deduplication. In: Proceedings of the 2008 ACM Workshop on Storage Security and Survivability, StorageSS 2008, Alexandria, VA, USA, 31 October 2008, pp. 1–10 (2008)
17. Bellare, M., Keelveedhi, S., Ristenpart, T., et al.: Message-locked encryption and secure deduplication. In: Theory and Application of Cryptographic Techniques, pp. 296–312 (2013)
18. Bellare, M., Keelveedhi, S.: Interactive message-locked encryption and secure deduplication. In: Public Key Cryptography, pp. 516–538 (2015)
19. Li, J., Chen, X., Li, M., et al.: Secure deduplication with efficient and reliable convergent key management. IEEE Trans. Parallel Distrib. Syst. **25**(6), 1615–1625 (2014)
20. Meye, P., Raipin, P., Tronel, F., et al.: A secure two-phase data deduplication scheme. In: High Performance Computing and Communications, pp. 802–809 (2014)
21. Stanek, J., Kencl, L.: Enhanced secure thresholded data deduplication scheme for cloud storage. IEEE Trans. Dependable Secure Comput. **1** (2016)
22. Li, J., Li, J., Xie, D., et al.: Secure auditing and deduplicating data in cloud. IEEE Trans. Comput. **65**(8), 2386–2396 (2016)

23. Alkhojandi, N., Miri, A.: Privacy-preserving public auditing in cloud computing with data deduplication. In: Cuppens, F., Garcia-Alfaro, J., Zincir Heywood, N., Fong, P.W.L. (eds.) FPS 2014. LNCS, vol. 8930, pp. 35–48. Springer, Cham (2015). https://doi.org/10.1007/978-3-319-17040-4_3
24. Yuan, J., Yu, S.: Secure and constant cost public cloud storage auditing with deduplication. In: Communications and Network Security, pp. 145–153. IEEE (2013)
25. Kai, H.E., Huang, C., Zhou, H., et al.: Public auditing for encrypted data with client-side deduplication in cloud storage. Wuhan Univ. J. Nat. Sci. 20(4), 291–298 (2015)

A Trusted VM Live Migration Protocol in IaaS

Xinfeng He[1,2](✉) and Junfeng Tian[1,2]

[1] School of Management, Hebei University, Baoding 071002, China
hxf@hbu.edu.cn
[2] School of Computer Science and Technology, Hebei University,
Baoding 071002, China

Abstract. Trusted computing is an important means for the security of the IaaS platform. One of the key problem is how to migrate a virtual machine (VM) from one host to another trustily. To solving it, the lifecycle of VM, trusted proof of VM and other notions are presented in this paper. Moreover, the paper proposes a Trusted Virtual Machine Migration Protocol (TVMMP) which can guarantee the coherence and continuity of trusted status during the VM migration and provide secure aids for trusted migration of VM in the IaaS platform. Through the security analysis and comparison, it can be proved that the protocol is suitable for trusted computing cloud platform.

Keywords: Trusted migration protocol · Trusted proof · Virtual machine (VM) migration · IaaS · Trusted computing

1 Introduction

Cloud computing is the research focus in academia and industry. In particular, the convenient and economical services provided by IaaS (Infrastructure as a Service) are concerted and applied broadly. IaaS becomes the preferred solution for private clouds and public clouds. As it developed, the problems of security and privacy are obviously affected and become the constraints for the further progress of IaaS. The uses suspect that IaaS will harm the security and privacy of their data. Therefore, IaaS is not adopted in many sensitive field, such as, government, military, finance, securities, transportation, medicine and etc.

Recently, the technology of secure IaaS is arising. Especially based on trusted computing (TC), the trusted cloud computing platform is introduced to solve the problem of security and privacy in cloud computing. TC's aim is to promote the trustworthiness of computer system and guarantee the behaviors of computer in expected ways. TC can provide trusted boot, security isolations, remote attestation, keys protection etc., which can help to enforce the security of IaaS. TC can boost the uses' confidence to the security of IaaS and trustworthiness to cloud computing platform.

This work was supported by the Natural Science Foundation of Hebei province (Grant No. F2016201064, F2016201244) and the Natural Science Foundation of Hebei institution (Grant No. ZD2015088).

However, the fact that IaaS is very different from ordinary computer system makes it difficult for TC to cover all the security needs of IaaS. Managements of virtual machine (VM), e.g. producing, allocating, retrieving, migrating of VM, are the core services of IaaS. The security of VM's lifecycle is the foundation of IaaS. In the lifecycle, one of key problems is how to guarantee the trusted status of a VM after it migrating to another node? For different aims, TC cannot provide comprehensive supports to VM security management for IaaS platform.

To address the problems above, a Trusted Virtual Machine Migration Protocol (TVMMP) based on TC is proposed in this paper. Trusted proofs is presented in the protocol to ensure the coherence and continuity of trusted status during the VM migration. The protocol can provide secure aids for trusted migration of VM in the IaaS platform.

The contributions of this paper are:

1. Presenting a new concept of Trusted Proof of VM (TPV) to measure the trustworthiness of VM;
2. Proposing a VM migration protocol C TVMMP for trust-ed cloud computing platform, which can maintain the coherence and continuity of trusted status during the VM live migration.

2   Related Works

Virtualization of secure cryptoprocessor is the most popular fashion for TC working with cloud computing. Virtualizing the Trusted Platform Module (vTPM) [1] is the first TC technology used for virtualization. There are some trusted cloud platform based on vTPM.

Liu [2] proposes TCEE (trusted cloud execution environment), which extends the current trusted chain into virtual machine's architecture stack. By using vTPM, TCG software stack and OpenPTS, it can provide a dynamic trustworthiness verification mechanism for the tenants' virtual execution environment. A method to build trusted virtual execution environment based on trust extension was proposed to ensure the integrity and security of virtual machine and service software in [3]. It establishes mapping of virtual PCR (vPCR) to hardware TPM's PCR. A multi-tenancy trusted computing environment model (MTCEM) is designed for IaaS delivery model in [4]. Its purpose is to assure a trusted cloud infrastructure to customers. MTCEM presents a dual level transitive trust mechanism and supports a security duty separation function simultaneously. With MTCEM, Cloud service providers and customers can cooperate to build and maintain a trusted cloud computing environment. In [5], a framework of end to end (E2E) trusted cloud infrastructure based on vTPM is proposed to protect the security of communication.

Some advanced trusted cloud model have emerged to improve performance of cryptoprocessor, such as TPM (Trusted Platform Module) or TCM (Trusted Cryptography Module).

Santos et al. in [6] propose the design of a trusted cloud computing platform (TCCP) to provide a closed box execution environment that guarantees confidential execution of guest virtual machines. TCCP use Trusted Coordinator (TC) to manage all the trusted nodes in the cloud. However, the overhead of the management is intolerable for massive scale cloud. For this reason, Excalibur is presented in [7]. Excalibur uses attribute-based encryption, which reduces the overhead of key management and improves the performance of the distributed protocols employed.

Additional, Chen et al. in [8] presents cTPM, an extension of the TPM's design that adds an additional root key to the TPM and shares that root key with the cloud. As a result, the cloud can create and share TPM-protected keys and data across multiple devices owned by one user. It is helpful to reduce dependence on the resource of TPM. Sayler et al. [9] present Jobber: a highly autonomous multi-tenant network security framework designed to handle both the dynamic nature of cloud data centers and the desire for optimized inter-tenant communication.

Trusted cloud platform can enhance the trustworthiness of cloud by attesting the computing nodes. But the trustworthiness of VM in cloud is not ensure for the lack of attesting for the VM during its lifecycle.

The importance of VM migration solution for the IaaS clouds have been identified. [10] used the X.805 security standard to investigate attacks on live virtual machine migration. It also surveyed and compared different proposals in the literature to secure the live migration. [11] conducted a systematic literature review (SLR) of 23 selected studies, published from 2010 to 2013. It classified and compared the selected studies based on a characterization framework.

To a certain extent, the research work above can solve the VM migration in cloud. But, most of their aims are the effective use and allocation for the cloud resources, not for the trustworthiness of VM.

[12] presented a protocol enabling secure migration of vTPM-based virtual machines in private clouds. In the public clouds, [13] proposed a secure VM migration mechanism for VM migration from one CSP (cloud service provider) to the others. [14] dealt with the opportunity to leverage the Trusted Computing technology for encouraging the federation in trustiness among heterogeneous clouds, in particular when VM migration taken place between federated providers.

Previous works on migration based on vTPM proposed in [12,15] can prove the trustworthiness of VM after migration. However, the protocols based on vTPM is not suitable for massive VM in cloud because of the limitation of the computing capacity of TPM/TCM.

The protocol proposed in this paper can guarantee the coherence and continuity of trusted status during the whole VM lifecycle. Additional, the protocol requires considerable computing capacity to the cryptoprocessor. So, it is scalable and suitable for the massive cloud environment due to its low computing demands.

3   Notions

Some definitions and notions are given to illustrate the migration protocol firstly.

Definition 1. *Lifecycle of VM*. *The lifecycle of VM in this paper is the procedure for a VM from its loading from VM image to its shutting down. That is, a lifecycle represent a process of a VM image.*

To achieve the goal of trusted working in the lifecycle, a VM is bound with a Trusted Proof of VM (TPV) when it is born in IaaS platform. TPV will be the companion for the VM during the lifecycle illustrated by Fig. 1.

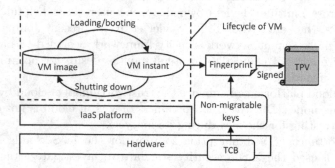

Fig. 1. Lifecycle of VM

Definition 2. *Trusted Proof of VM (TPV)*. *TPV is the confidential data to guarantee the coherence and continuity of trusted status during the VM lifecycle. It be produced with non-migratable keys in Trusted Computing Base (TCB) (See Sect. 4.1) and fingerprint data.*

TPV The structure of TPV is shown by Fig. 2.

- UUID: the unique identification of a VM, produced by IaaS platform.
- VMIK: Virtual Machine Identity Key. It is the credential binding with a VM for authenticating itself to a verifier as AIK [17]. VMIK is produced companioning with a new VM instant as a part of TPV. The private key of VMEK is protect by TCB.
- Residence (Res): the location information of a VM. It can be represented by a host's ID.
- Static & Dynamic fingerprint (FPData): the unique data of a VM. They can delegate the static and dynamic trusted status of a VM. These data can be obtained by many means, such as vPCR in vTPM, VMI and etc.
- Signature: the digital signature made by VMEK of the corresponding VM. It can be express by

$$Sign_{VMEK}(UUID||VMIK||Res||FPData)$$

in which VMEK is a non-migratable key in TCB.

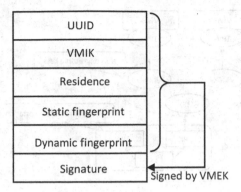

Fig. 2. The structure of TPV

TPV is the trusted measure of a VM. How to guarantee the coherence and continuity of TPV becomes the key issue for VM trusted migration.

4 Trusted Virtual Machine Migration Protocol (TVMMP)

TVMMP can protect the trusted certification data of VM from loss in the procedure of VM migration. Thus, the security status of VM in the source node can be reproduced in the destination node. This is called the coherence and continuity of VM trusted status. With TPV and TPH, TVMMP can be used to support the trusted VM migration in IaaS.

4.1 The Key Hierarchy

Traditional TC technology is intended for single terminal rather than for the collaboration of TCB in many terminals. Furthermore, the computing capacity of TCB is very low due to the implementation technique. It takes one second or even more times consuming [8] for a trusted attestation. All of these cannot meet the needs of massive cloud environment. Base on traditional TC, a novel key hierarchy is proposal in Fig. 3. The keys are illustrate as follow:

- EK: Endorsement Key of TPM/TCM. It is the public and private key pair that is created randomly on the chip at manufacture time and cannot be changed. The private key never leaves the chip, while the public key is used for attestation and for encryption of sensitive data sent to TCB.
- AIK: Attestation Identity Key. It is an asymmetric non-migratable signing key generated inside the TCB. It is used as a one-time key to establish authenticity of the TCB during attestation. The AIK certificate proves the AIK was created by a genuine TCB. More information about EK and AIK can refer to DAA protocol [17].

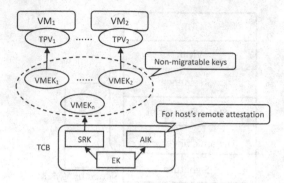

Fig. 3. The key hierarchy

- SRK: Storage Root Key. It is a non-migratable encryption key that is used to protect the storage of other keys outside the TCB.
- VMEK: Virtual Machine Endorsement Key. It is a public and private key pair produced with a new VM instant and the signature key used in TPV. There is one-to-one relationship between VMEK and VM instant. The private key of VMEK is protect by EK and never leaves the TCB.

4.2 Attacker Model

In cloud computing, side-channels attacks are conducted through gaining access to the physical node hosting the target VM. The attackers can co-locate their VMs with target VMs on the same server, and obtain sensitive information from the victims using side channels. These attacks are often called co-resident attacks. TVMMP proposed in this paper can resist co-resident attacks.

Firstly, some assumptions are given as follow:

- The attacker can invade a physical computing node, obtain the privilege of administrator;
- The attacker can access the VM arbitrarily in the intruded node;
- The attacker can trick a VM to migrate to an invaded node;
- The keys protected by TCB cannot be revealed to the attacker.

The assumptions above fit the current situation of cloud computing and TC.

The co-resident attacks with VM migration can be performed as Fig. 4.

 (1) The attacker A intrudes and take control of D;
(2.1) The VM owner O lost it availability by DDoS attacks;
(2.2) A fake O's identity and initiate the migration procedure to D;
 (3) The data of VM_O is migrated to D;
 (4) A launches a VM_A in D;
 (5) A uses VM_A as the side-channel to access VM_O illegally. The co-resident attacks in VM migration achieves its ends.

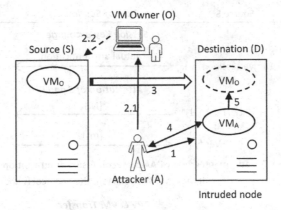

Fig. 4. The attacker model

4.3 Description of TVMMP

TVMMP can be expressed by 4 phases: (1) Session key exchange; (2) Attestation of nodes; (3) TPV and VM Transfer; (4) Refactor of TPV. The description of TVMMP are illustrated in Fig. 5.

Session Key Exchange. The purpose of the phase is to derive the encrypted channel between S and D by using the session key K. The session key K can be derived by any method of securely exchanging cryptographic keys, such as Diffie-Hellman key exchange.

Attestation of Nodes. The trustworthiness of nodes is the basis of trusted VM migration. In this phase, S can verifies D platform integrity by a random number N_s and the AIK in DAA protocol. A similar attestation of S can also be performed by D. If these verifications fail, the protocol is aborted.

TPV and VM Transfer. After the attestation of nodes, the protocol will perform the transfer process of TPV and VM. During the process, the integrity of TPV will be verify by the signature in TPV, and the integrity of VM will be verify by the fingerprint data in TPV. So, TPV is the key to the trusted VM migration.

Refactor of TPV. The phase is to solve the problem that TPV is not cohere with bound VM after migration. According to the definition of TPV, some fields and the signature must be update. D will produce a new VMEK K_v, update the Res field of TPV, and resign the TPV with K_v.

The integration and trustworthiness of VM can be guarantee by new TPV. TPV also preserves all the trusted attestation for VM, that is, the whole trusted status in source can be duplicated into destination.

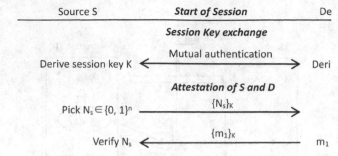

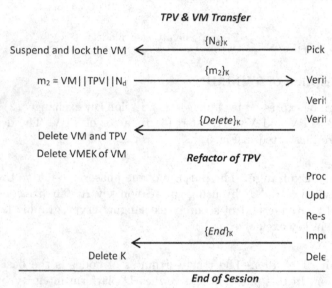

Fig. 5. Description of TVMMP

4.4 Security Proof and Analysis

The key trustworthiness points of TVMMP are: (1) the destination node is trusted; (2) the integration of VM is not wrecked during the migration.

Lemma 1. *S can attest the trustworthiness of D in TVMMP.*

D's identification can be verified by DAA protocol in phase (2) of TVMMP (See Sect. 4.3). The security of DAA protocol is based on group signature and proved safety. Meanwhile, m_1 in phase (2) of TVMMP can also attest the he trustworthiness of D's configuration and status. So, S can attest the trustworthiness of D, and Lemma 1 is proved.   □

Lemma 2. *TPV can be migrated to destination safely.*

TPV is protected by the session key K in TVMMP. K is established by using Diffie-Hellman key exchange and the parties' AIK, which can provide the identity authentication for the key exchange between interactive parties. Therefore, K can resist the middle-man attack and keep the confidentiality of TPV during the migration. Thus, Lemma 2 is reasonable.   □

Theorem 1. *TVMMP can guarantee the trustworthiness of VM in migration.*

Trusted migration is decided by two aspects: the trust of destination node and the trusted status of VM. The trustworthiness of destination node is ensured by Lemma 1. The security of TPV can be keep by Lemma 2. Furthermore, TPV can confirm the VM's trust status. In summary, TVMMP is safe for trusted VM migration.   □

To demonstrate the correctness of TVMMP further, applied Pi calculus [18,19] and ProVerif [20] are introduced to describe and prove the protocol. Applied Pi calculus is based Dolev-Yao model which assumes the attacker having the ability of intercepting, accessing, modifying and sending messages in the channel. ProVerif is an automatic cryptographic protocol verifier, which use the applied Pi calculus as its input. It can handle many different cryptographic primitives, including encryption, signatures, hash functions, Diffie-Hellman key agreements and so on. TVMMP can be abstracted by applied Pi calculus as Fig. 6.

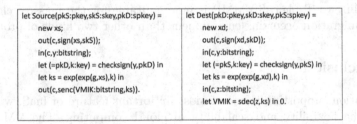

Fig. 6. Abstract of TVMMP

By using the query statement "query attacker (VMIK)", the result of ProVerif showed as Fig. 7. It is clear that the attacker cannot access the VMIK, which is the key point for security of TPV and the process of VM migration.

Fig. 7. Result of ProVerif

Table 1. Comparisons of VM Migration Protocol

	vTPM based [12,15]	Key-shared based [13]	TVMMP
Migration overhead	vTPM + VM	Some keys + VM	TPV + VM
Attestation for destination	Yes	No	Yes
Trusted Third Party (TTP)	Needless	Need	Needless
Coherence of trusted status	Yes	No	Yes
Continuity of trusted status	No	Yes	Yes
Scalability	Poor	Good	Good
Interaction frequency	Few	More	More

The characteristic comparisons between TVMMP and other secure or trusted migration protocols show as Table 1.

The vTPM based protocols depends on the migration of TCB, which will bring higher overhead than the key-shared based protocols. In addition, the scalability is also the shortage of vTPM based protocols because of the hard binding relationship between VM and TCB. On the other hand, key migration is convenient in the key-shared based protocols, but the protection of shared keys is insufficient. The coherent trusted status of VM is difficult to be ensured. And these protocols need a TTP normally. TVMMP only uses TPV to seal the keys (e.g. VMEK, VMIK), which will take few resources. Unlike vTPM based protocols, VM is bound to VMIK that can be migrate instead of a certain TCB in TVMMP. Both coherence and continuity of trusted status can be achieved.

According to Table 1, TVMMP is more suitable for the massive cloud and the more migration occurring environment than other two kinds of protocols.

5   Conclusion

VM migration supporting is one of most important feature of IaaS, which can embody the flexibility and scalability of cloud computing. The VM trusted migration is key issue for trusted cloud platform. Several conceptions such as lifecycle of VM, TPV are presented to solve the problem above. Moreover, the paper proposes a Trusted Virtual Machine Migration Protocol (TVMMP) which can guarantee the coherence and continuity of trusted status during the VM migration. TVMMP can provide secure aids for trusted migration of VM in the IaaS platform. Additional, the protocol gives considerable performance and safety, which is suitable for massive cloud platform.

However, VM's behaves in the cloud are very complex because the platforms are open to public. It is difficult to cover all the trust property of VM by using TPV defined in this paper. The future work will extend the scopes of TPV for more accurate trusted measurement.

References

1. Berger, S., Cáceres, R., Goldman, K.A., et al.: vTPM: virtualizing the trusted platform module. Usenix Secur. **15**, 305–320 (2006)
2. Liu, C.Y., Lin, J., Tang, B.: A dynamic trustworthiness verification mechanism for trusted cloud execution environment. J. Softw. **24**(1), 1240–1252 (2013). (in Chinese)
3. Wang, L.N., Gao, H.J., Yu, R.W., et al.: Research of constructing trusted virtual execution environment based on trust extension. J. Commun. **32**(9), 1–8 (2011). (in Chinese)
4. Li, X.Y., Zhou, L.T., Shi, Y., et al.: A trusted computing environment model in cloud architecture. In: International Conference on Machine Learning and Cybernetics, pp. 2843–2848. IEEE (2010)
5. Wang, J., Zhao, B., Zhang, H., et al.: POSTER: an E2E trusted cloud infrastructure. In: Proceedings of the 2014 ACM SIGSAC Conference on Computer and Communications Security, pp. 1517–1519 (2014)
6. Santos, N., Gummadi, K., Rodrigues, R.: Towards trusted cloud computing. In: Conference on Hot Topics in Cloud Computing. USENIX Association (2009)
7. Santos, N., Rodrigues, R., Gummadi, K.P., et al.: Policy-sealed data: a new abstraction for building trusted cloud services. In: Usenix Conference on Security Symposium, p. 10 (2012)
8. Chen, C., Raj, H., Saroiu, S., et al.: cTPM: a cloud TPM for cross-device trusted applications. In: Proceedings of the 11th USENIX Conference on Networked Systems Design and Implementation, pp. 187–201. USENIX Association (2014)
9. Sayler, A., Keller, E., Grunwald, D.: Jobber: automating inter-tenant trust in the cloud. In: Proceedings of Workshop on Hot Topics in Cloud Computing (HotCloud) (2013)
10. Aiash, M., Mapp, G., Gemikonakli, O.: Secure live virtual machines migration: issues and solutions. In: International Conference on Advanced Information NETWORKING and Applications Workshops, pp. 160–165. IEEE (2014)
11. Jamshidi, P., Ahmad, A., Pahl, C.: Cloud migration research: a systematic review. Cloud Comput. IEEE Trans. **1**(2), 142–157 (2013)
12. Danev, B., Masti, R.J., Karame, G.O., et al.: Enabling secure VM-vTPM migration in private clouds. In: Twenty-Seventh Computer Security Applications Conference, pp. 187–196 (2011)
13. Aslam, M., Gehrmann, C., Bjorkman, M.: Security and trust preserving VM migrations in public clouds. In: Proceedings of the 2012 IEEE 11th International Conference on Trust, Security and Privacy in Computing and Communications, pp. 869–876. IEEE Computer Society (2012)
14. Celesti, A., Salici, A., Villari, M., et al.: A remote attestation approach for a secure virtual machine migration in federated cloud environments. In: First International Symposium on Network Cloud Computing and Applications, pp. 99–106. IEEE (2012)
15. Hong, Z., Wang, J., Zhang, H.G., et al.: A trusted VM-vTPM live migration protocol in clouds. In: Proceedings of International Workshop on Cloud Computing & Information Security, vol. 52, no. 1391, pp. 299–302 (2013)
16. Garfinkel, T., Rosenblum, M.: A virtual machine introspection based architecture for intrusion detection. In: Proceedings of the Network & Distributed Systems Security Symposium, pp. 191–206 (2003)

17. Brickell, E., Camenisch, J., Chen, L.: Direct anonymous attestation. In: ACM Conference on Computer and Communications Security, pp. 132–145. ACM (2004)
18. Abadi, M., Blanchet, B.: Analyzing security protocols with secrecy types and logic programs. J. ACM **52**(01), 102–146 (2005)
19. Abadi, M., Blanchet, B.: Computer-assisted verification of a protocol for certified email. Sci. Comput. Program. **58**(1/2), 3–27 (2005)
20. Blancher, B.: ProVerif user manual (2016). http://www.proverif.ens.fr/manual.pdf

Double-Layered Predictor for High-Fidelity Reversible Data Hiding

Fuqiang Di, Junyi Duan, Jia Liu$^{(\boxtimes)}$, Guangwei Su, and Yingnan Zhang

Department of Electronic Technology,
Engineering University of Chinese Peoples Armed Police, Xi'an, China
18710752607@163.com, 1054165690@qq.com

Abstract. The high-fidelity reversible data hiding aims to reduce the embedding distortion as far as possible, especially when the embedding capacity is low. To improve the embedding performance, a novel high-fidelity reversible data hiding method based on double-layered predictor is proposed. At first, the cover image is divided into two sets. The one set is used to predict the pixels in the other set according to the rhombus prediction method. Then, the prediction errors are used to embed data using pixel value ordering method. At last, the marked pixels in the first set are used to implement the process of embedding in the other set. To the best of our knowledge, the proposed predictor is the first double-layered predictor in the field of reversible data hiding. Extensive experiments demonstrate that the proposed method can significantly improve the embedding performance of the existing high-fidelity reversible data hiding method methods, especially for the relatively smooth images.

Keywords: Reversible data hiding · Double-layered predictor · Rhombus prediction · Pixel value ordering

1 Introduction

Reversible data hiding (RDH) embeds data into a cover image which can be recovered exactly after the embedded data is extracted from the marked image. Highly desired in copyright protection field and data hiding of sensitive images, the RDH has become a very active research area in the past two decades [1–6]. The embedding capacity (EC) and the embedding distortion are two important criteria to evaluate the RDH method.

The early RDH schemes are based on lossless compression [7,8]. In these schemes, the cover image is firstly losslessly compressed, and the released space is utilized to embed data. However, the EC of this kind of scheme is very low. A large number of approaches have been proposed later to obtain a tradeoff between the EC and the embedding distortion. One popular method is called difference expansion (DE) which is firstly proposed by Tian [9]. In this algorithm, the pixel difference generated by the integer Haar wavelet transform is expanded to embed data. To reduce the embedding distortion of Tians algorithm,

© Springer Nature Singapore Pte Ltd. 2017
M. Xu et al. (Eds.): CTCIS 2017, CCIS 704, pp. 53–65, 2017.
https://doi.org/10.1007/978-981-10-7080-8_5

Thodi and Rodriguez proposed an extension method called prediction error expansion (PEE) [10], which uses the prediction error instead of pixel difference to embed data. The PEE algorithm and the improved PEE-based algorithms [11–15] provide a much high EC while the embedding distortion caused by expansion is difficult to control. Besides, Ni et al. proposes another kind of popular method called histogram shifting (HS) [16]. In his method, the peak point of image histogram modified to embed data. Later on, many improved methods called HS-PEE use the prediction error to generate histogram and better balance the EC and the embedding distortion [17–21]. However, all the above methods use the traditional single-layered predictor which predicts the pixel value using some neighboring pixel values.

Recently, to achieve the high-fidelity performance, the pixel value ordering (PVO) predictor is proposed by Li et al. [22] and has attracted much attention from researchers. In Lis method, the data hider firstly divides the cover image into non-overlapped equal-sized blocks, and orders the pixels within a given block according to the pixel value. Then, the maximum pixel is predicted by the second largest pixel and the minimum pixel is predicted by the second smallest pixel. At last, the obtained prediction error is used to embed data using the HS-PEE method. But in the PVO method, the bin 0 (i.e., the bin with the prediction error equals to 0) is not used to embed data, and thus the embedding capacity is relatively low.

Many RDH methods have been proposed to further improve the PVO embedding performance. One type of improved PVO methods pays attention to improve the process of selecting bin of histogram. To achieve a higher EC, Peng et al. has proposed the improved pixel value ordering (IPVO) method [23]. In this method, the relative location relationship between the maximum and second largest value is considered and the bin 0 can be used to embed data. In order to utilize the bin 0, another similar method named PVO-K [24] treats many pixels with same pixel value as a unit to embed data and thus produces higher EC compared with PVO method. Another type of improved PVO methods focuses on optimizing the image partition process. Qu et al. proposed a pixel-based PVO (PPVO) [25] method which adopted a pixel-by-pixel embedding manner instead of the traditional block-by-block embedding manner. In the PPVO method, each pixel is predicted by its sorted content pixels, and a sliding window is used to improve the embedding performance. In addition, another PVO-based adaptive method (PVO-A) is proposed by Weng et al. [26]. Unlike the prior works, Wengs method partitions the smooth blocks into sub-blocks of arbitrary size by the local complexity and utilizes different pixel modification method for blocks of different levels. Wang et al. divides the cover image adaptively into various-sized blocks and partitions the flat image areas into smaller blocks [27]. The dynamic blocking strategy can improve the embedding capacity significantly while keep the embedding distortion low. In summary, the key idea of all the above PVO-based methods is to design the single-layered predictor which can be more suitable for high-fidelity reversible data hiding. However, the estimation method of the prediction value is not sufficiently precise.

In this paper, a novel high-fidelity RDH method based on double-layered predictor is proposed. To better exploit the correlation between the adjacent pixels and improve the accuracy of prediction method, the cover image is double-layered predicted by the earlier prediction errors obtained using the rhombus prediction method. Instead of the traditional single-layered predictor, the proposed double-layered predictor combines the rhombus prediction method with the pixel value ordering method. The experimental results show that the proposed method can effectively improve the embedding performance of the existing high-fidelity RDH methods, especially for the relatively smooth images.

The rest of this paper is organized as follows. In Sect. 2, the related work of IPVO embedding method is described. The detailed procedures of the proposed algorithm are described in Sect. 3. Section 4 elaborates the experimental results and the performance comparisons. Conclusions of our work are given in Sect. 5.

2   IPVO Embedding

In this subsection, we give a brief introduction to the improved pixel value ordering (IPVO) method. The main embedding steps of IPVO can be summarized as follows:

Step 1: Partition the cover image into non-overlapped equal-sized blocks. Here, we take 22 sized blocks as an example. For a block (x_1, x_2, x_3, x_4), sort the pixel values in ascending order to obtain $(x_{\sigma(1)}, x_{\sigma(2)}, x_{\sigma(3)}, x_{\sigma(4)})$, where $x_{\sigma(1)} \leq x_{\sigma(2)} \leq x_{\sigma(3)} \leq x_{\sigma(4)}$. If $x_{\sigma(i)} = x_{\sigma(j)}$, and $i < j$, then $\sigma(i) < \sigma(j)$.

Step 2: For each block, calculate the difference

$$PE_{\max} = x_u - x_v \tag{1}$$

where $u = \min(\sigma(3), \sigma(4))$, $v = \max(\sigma(3), \sigma(4))$. The maximum $x_{\sigma(4)}$ is modified to embed data by

$$\bar{x}_{\sigma(4)} = \begin{cases} x_{\sigma(4)} + b & PE_{\max} = 1 \\ x_{\sigma(4)} + 1 & PE_{\max} > 1 \\ x_{\sigma(4)} + b & PE_{\max} = 0 \\ x_{\sigma(4)} + 1 & PE_{\max} < 0 \end{cases} \tag{2}$$

where $\bar{x}_{\sigma(4)}$ is the marked pixel value, and $b \in \{0, 1\}$ is a data bit to be embedded.

Step 3: For each block, calculate the difference

$$PE_{\min} = x_s - x_t \tag{3}$$

where $s = \min(\sigma(1), \sigma(2))$, $t = \max(\sigma(1), \sigma(2))$. The minimum $x_{\sigma(1)}$ is modified to embed data by

$$\bar{x}_{\sigma(1)} = \begin{cases} x_{\sigma(1)} - b & PE_{\min} = 1 \\ x_{\sigma(1)} - 1 & PE_{\min} > 1 \\ x_{\sigma(1)} - b & PE_{\min} = 0 \\ x_{\sigma(1)} - 1 & PE_{\min} < 0 \end{cases} \tag{4}$$

Note that, since the maximum $x_{\sigma(4)}$ is never decreased and minimum $x_{\sigma(1)}$ is never increased, the decoder can extract the embedded data directly and recover the cover image losslessly (refer to [23] for the details).

3 Proposed Method

In this section, we will describe the embedding steps and the extracting steps in this proposed method.

3.1 Date Embedding

As is shown in Fig. 1, the detailed embedding steps are as follows:

Step 1: Divide the cover image I into two non-overlapped sets: Set A and Set B. As is shown in Fig. 2, the Set A is made up of the blankpixels, and the Set B is made up of the shadowpixels.

Step 2: Layer 1 prediction for the blankpixels using the shadowpixels. The prediction method utilizes the rhombus prediction method. As is shown in Fig. 2,

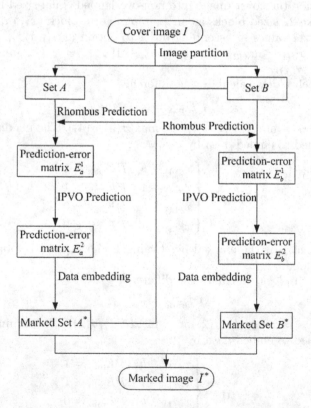

Fig. 1. The flowchart of the embedding procedure

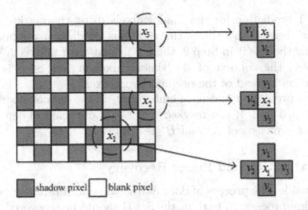

Fig. 2. The sketch of the image partition and rhombus prediction

the blankpixels have three types: the inner pixel such as x_1, the edge pixels such as x_2, and the corner pixels such as x_3. The predicted values of different types of pixels are calculated as follows.

$$e_1 = \left\lfloor \frac{v_1 + v_2 + v_3 + v_4}{4} \right\rfloor - x_1 \tag{5}$$

$$e_2 = \left\lfloor \frac{v_1 + v_2 + v_3}{3} \right\rfloor - x_2 \tag{6}$$

$$e_3 = \left\lfloor \frac{v_1 + v_2}{2} \right\rfloor - x_3 \tag{7}$$

where $\lfloor \bullet \rfloor$ means the floor function and e_i represents the corresponding prediction-errors. Note that the neighboring pixel v_i belongs to the shadowpixels. All the prediction-errors of the blankpixels make up a prediction-error matrix E_a^1.

Step 3: Layer 2 prediction for the blankpixels. The prediction method utilizes IPVO method. In the Layer 2 prediction, the prediction-error matrix E_a^1 is used as the new cover image of the IPVO method described in Sec. 2, and the Layer 2 prediction-error matrix E_a^2 is then obtained. Specifically, E_a^1 is firstly divided as blocks and the prediction-errors in the given block are sorted. The matrix E_a^2 is calculated by using the second largest value to predict the maximum value and the second smallest value to predict the minimum value.

Step 4: Data embedding in the blankpixels. Firstly, divide the secret message to be embedded into two parts, and the matrix E_a^2 is used to embed the half of the secret message. After embedding, the marked Layer 2 prediction-errors is obtained and then used to calculate the marked Layer 1 prediction-errors. According to the marked Layer 1 prediction-errors, the marked Set A^* is obtained.

Step 5: Layer 1 prediction for the shadowpixels using the marked Set A^*. The prediction method utilizes the rhombus prediction method. Using the same method as it in Step 2, the prediction-error matrix E_b^1 is obtained. However, the context of the shadowpixel in this Step is the marked blankpixel instead of the original blankpixel.

Step 6: Layer 2 prediction and data embedding in the shadowpixels. Similar to the Step 3 and 4, the marked Set B^* is obtained. Then, the marked image I^* consists of A^* and B^* is achieved.

3.2 Data Extraction and Image Recovery

At the decoder side, the process of data extraction and image recovery is similar to the embedding process. Note that, the Set B should be recovered at first. As is shown in Fig. 3, the following steps are used to extract data and recover image:

Step 1: Divide the marked image I^* into two non-overlapped sets: Set A^* and Set B^*.

Step 2: Layer 1 prediction for the shadowpixels using the blankpixels. The prediction method utilizes the rhombus prediction method. The prediction-error matrix E_b^1 is obtained by the same method as it in the embedding process.

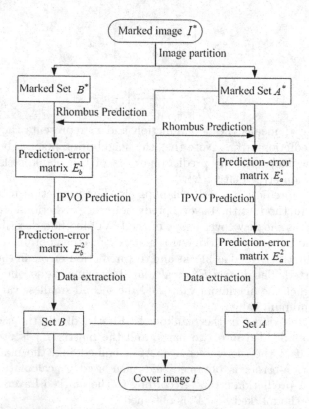

Fig. 3. The flowchart of the extraction procedure

Step 3: Layer 2 prediction for the shadowpixels. The prediction method utilizes IPVO method. Then, the matrix E_b^2 is calculated.

Step 4: Data extraction in the shadowpixels. The matrix E_b^2 is used to embed the rest half of the secret message. After embedding, the original Set B is obtained, and the half of embedded data can be extracted.

Step 5: Layer 1 prediction for the blankpixels using the recovered Set B. The prediction method utilizes the rhombus prediction method, and the prediction-error matrix E_a^1 is obtained.

Step 6: Layer 2 prediction and data embedding in the blankpixels. Similar to the Step 3 and 4, the original Set A is recovered, and the rest half of embedded data can be extracted. Then, the original cover image I is achieved.

4 Experimental Results

In this section, the proposed method is evaluated by comparing it with some contemporary high-fidelity RDH methods. Some standard test images used in our experiment are all eight-bit gray-scale images with the size of 512×512. All the payloads used in this section are random bit stream.

The embedding performance of the proposed method is significantly related to the prediction-error of the predictor. To verify the performance improvement of the proposed double-layered prediction process, we compare the prediction-error histograms generated by the single-layered IPVO predictor and the proposed double-layered predictor. Figure 4 shows the prediction-error histogram comparisons between the two kinds of predictors for test image "Lena". From the Fig. 4, it can be seen that the prediction-error histogram of the proposed double-layered predictor is sharper than the one of the single-layered IPVO predictor, which means that the double-layered predictor can improve the rate-distortion performance of the existing high-fidelity predictor. Furthermore, the histogram of double-layered predictor has a much higher 0 bin (i.e., the bin that represents the frequency of prediction-error 0) and 1 bin than the histogram of single -layered predictor, which means that the double-layered predictor can increase the embedding capacity. The main reason for the above results is that the traditional PVO-based single-layered predictor processes the pixels value directly, while the proposed double-layered predictor processes the prediction-errors which have the better correlation between the neighboring values. Thus, the prediction-error of the double-layered predictor is better for high-fidelity reversible data hiding than the existing single-layered predictor.

In addition, we validate the embedding performance of the proposed method compared with the following three existing high-fidelity reversible data hiding methods: Li et al. PVO method [22], Peng et al. IPVO method [23] and Qu et al. PPVO method [25]. Figure 5 shows the performance comparisons between the proposed method and three typical RDH methods on nine test images. The figures clearly illustrate that the proposed method can achieve the better

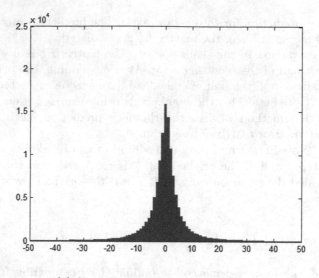

(a) Single-layered predictor on Lena

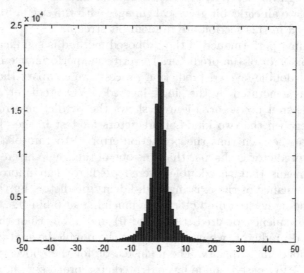

(b) Double-layered predictor on Lena

Fig. 4. Histogram comparisons between one-layered and double-layered predictor

rate-distortion performance (i.e., the PSNR is higher with the same payload). In addition, the superiority of the proposed method is more obvious on smooth images (e.g., image House and image F16). However, this level of EC (e.g. 10000 bits) is sufficient for many practical applications. For instance, an EC of 3500 bits is enough for the RDH application in the medical image sharing field [28].

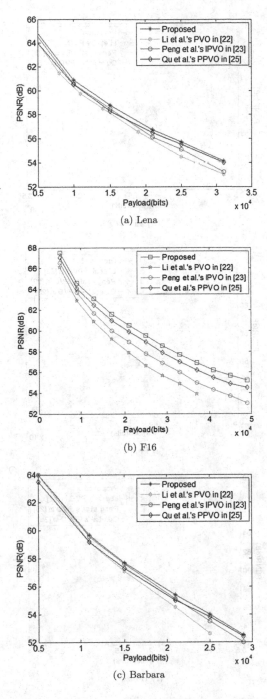

(a) Lena

(b) F16

(c) Barbara

Fig. 5. Performance comparisons between the proposed method and three typical methods

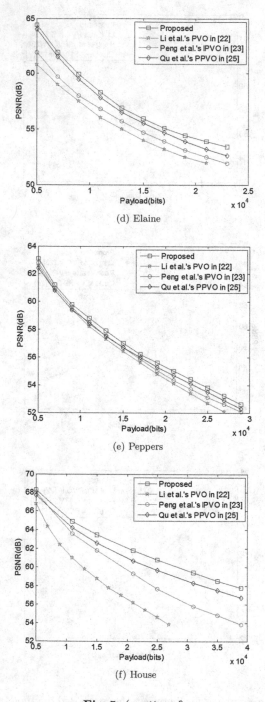

(d) Elaine

(e) Peppers

(f) House

Fig. 5. (*continued*)

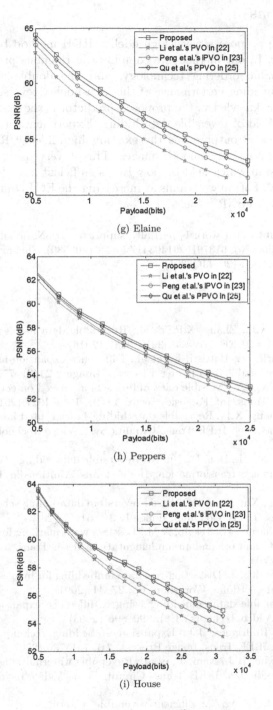

(g) Elaine

(h) Peppers

(i) House

Fig. 5. (*continued*)

5 Conclusions

In this paper, we propose a novel high-fidelity RDH method based on double-layered predictor. In our method, we combine the rhombus prediction method and the pixel value ordering technology, and the double-layered predictor improves the embedding performance of the high-fidelity reversible data hiding. To the best of our knowledge, the proposed predictor is the first double-layered predictor in the field of reversible data hiding. Experimental results show that the proposed method outperforms the existing high-fidelity RDH algorithms, especially for the relatively smooth images. This is very useful for some practical applications, in which field the low EC is sufficient and the image quality demand is desired. Future work aims at increasing the EC in our method as well as keeping the high PSNR value.

Acknowledgments. This work is partially supported by National Natural Science Foundation of China (No. 6137915261403417 and 61402530), Shaanxi Provincial Natural Science Foundation (2014JQ8301).

References

1. Shi, Y.Q., Li, X.L., Zhang, X.P., et al.: Reversible data hiding: advances in the past two decades. IEEE Access **4**, 3210–3237 (2016)
2. Boato, G., Carli, M., Battisti, F., et al.: Difference expansion and prediction for high bit-rate reversible data hiding. Electron. Imaging **21**(3), 777–793 (2012)
3. Ma, B., Shi, Y.Q.: A reversible data hiding scheme based on code division multiplexing. IEEE Trans. Inf. Forensics Secur. **11**(9), 1914–1927 (2016)
4. Qian, Z.X., Zhang, X.P.: Reversible data hiding in encrypted images with distributed source encoding. IEEE Trans. Circuits Syst. Video Technol. **26**(4), 636–646 (2016)
5. Zhang, W., Wang, H., Hou, D., Yu, N.: Reversible data hiding in encrypted images by reversible image transformation. IEEE Trans. Multimedia **18**(8), 1469–1479 (2016)
6. Liu, Y., Qu, X., Xin, G.: A ROI-based reversible data hiding scheme in encrypted medical images. J. Vis. Commun. Image R **39**, 51–57 (2016)
7. Celik, M.U., Sharma, G., Tekalp, A.M.: Lossless watermarking for image authentication: a new framework and an implementation. IEEE Trans. Image Process. **15**, 1042–1049 (2006)
8. Goljan, M., Fridrich, J.: Distortion-free data embedding for images. In: Proceedings of 4th Information Hiding Workshop, pp. 27–41 (2001)
9. Tian, J.: Reversible data embedding using a difference expansion. IEEE Trans. Circuits Syst. Video Technol. **13**(8), 890–896 (2003)
10. Thodi, D.M., Rodriguez, J.J.: Expansion embedding techniques for reversible watermarking. IEEE Trans. Image Process. **16**, 721–730 (2007)
11. Sachnev, V., Kim, H.J., Nam, J., et al.: Reversible watermarking algorithm using sorting and prediction. IEEE Trans. Circuits Syst. Video Technol. **19**, 989–999 (2009)
12. Li, X., Yang, B., Zeng, T.: Efficient reversible watermarking based on adaptive prediction-error expansion and pixel selection. IEEE Trans. Image Process. **20**, 3524–3533 (2011)

13. Gui, X., Li, X., Yang, B.: A high capacity reversible data hiding scheme based on generalized prediction-error expansion and adaptive embedding. Signal Process. **98**, 370–380 (2014)
14. Coltuc, D.: Low distortion transform for reversible watermarking. IEEE Trans. Image Process. **21**, 412–417 (2012)
15. Coltuc, D.: Improved embedding for prediction-based reversible watermarking. IEEE Trans. Inf. Forensics Secur. **6**, 873–882 (2011)
16. Ni, Z., Shi, Y.Q., Ansari, N., et al.: Reversible data hiding. IEEE Trans. Circ. Syst. Video Technol. **16**, 354–362 (2006)
17. Luo, L., Chen, Z., Chen, M., et al.: Reversible image watermarking using interpolation technique. IEEE Trans. Inf. Forensics Secur **5**, 187–103 (2010)
18. Chen, X., Sun, X., Sun, H., et al.: Histogram shifting based reversible data hiding method using directed-prediction scheme. Multimedia Tools Appl. 1–19 (2014)
19. Li, X., Li, B., Yang, B., et al.: General framework to histogram-shifting-based reversible data hiding. IEEE Trans. Image Process. **22**, 2181–2191 (2013)
20. Li, X., Zhang, W., Gui, X., et al.: A novel reversible data hiding scheme based on two-dimensional difference-histogram modification. IEEE Trans. Inf. Forensics Secur. **8**, 1091–1100 (2013)
21. Ou, B., Li, J., Zhao, Y., et al.: Pairwise prediction-error expansion for efficient reversible data hiding. IEEE Trans. Image Process. **22**, 5010–5021 (2013)
22. Li, X.L., Li, J., Li, B., et al.: High-fidelity reversible data hiding scheme based on pixel-value-ordering and prediction-error expansion. Signal Process. **93**(1), 198–205 (2013)
23. Peng, F., Li, X.L., Yang, B.: Improved PVO-based reversible data hiding. Digit. Signal Process. **25**, 255–265 (2014)
24. Ou, B., Li, X.L., Zhao, Y., et al.: Reversible data hiding using invariant pixel-value-ordering and prediction-error expansion. Signal Process. Image Commun. **29**(7), 760–772 (2014)
25. Qu, X.C., Kim, H.J.: Pixel-based pixel value ordering predictor for high-fidelity reversible data hiding. Signal Process. **111**, 249–260 (2015)
26. Weng, S.W., Liu, Y.J., Pan, J.S., et al.: Reversible data hiding based on flexible block-partition and adaptive block-modification strategy. J. Vis. Commun. Image R. **41**, 185–199 (2016)
27. Wang, X., Ding, J., Pei, Q.Q.: A novel reversible image data hiding scheme based on pixel value ordering and dynamic pixel block partition. Inf. Sci. **310**, 16–35 (2015)
28. Goatrieux, G., Guillou, C.L., Cauvin, J.M., et al.: Reversible watermarking for knowledge digest embedding and reliability control in medical images. IEEE Trans. Inf. Technol. Biomed. **13**(2), 158–165 (2009)

A New FPGA PUF Based on Transition Probability Delay Measurement

Zhenyu Guan, Yuyao Qin[✉], and Junming Liu

School of Electronic and Information Engineering,
Beihang University, XueYuan Road 37, Beijing, China
qinyuyao@buaa.edu.cn

Abstract. By extracting the physical random differences produced in the manufacturing process on chip itself, a unique identification of any FPGA could be obtained with certain excitation, which has brought new opportunities to research and development of key generation and storage. Based on the transition probability method to measure the delay of LUT, this paper proposes a new PUF (Physical Unclonable Function) scheme. By choosing the LUT under measurement intentionally, such as 2D barcode, it realizes the multi-dimensional information utilization. An overlapping route comparison method is adopted in this scheme to measure the delay of a single LUT with high accuracy and low resource consumption, which has been significantly optimized compared to previous work in accuracy, granularity and resource consumption.

Keywords: LUT · PUF (Physical Unclonable Function) · Transition probability · Multi-dimensional information utilization

1 Introduction

With the rapid development of electronic communications, electronic devices have become ubiquitous and interoperable. Integrated circuits (ICs) or programmable chips, providing a trusted communications environment, are widely used to perform encryption process or to carry, transmit and process sensitive information where information security issues attract more attention. In the traditional cryptography information technology, authentication and encryption are two kinds of useful and effective means to protect information. For the authentication technology, people often use a unique identity ID to verify the authenticity, to ensure that the identity of the entity in the communication system. The encryption and decryption work with the secret key and the security of the classic encryption depends on the security of the key, which are often stored in nonvolatile on-chip memory. Although a certain amount of secure hardware can be used to store key, it is vulnerable to physical attacks such as invasive attacks, side channel attacks, cloning attacks and software attacks such as virus attacks.

The development of PUF brings new research space to key generation and storage and authentication. PUF refers a nominal function that by inputting

© Springer Nature Singapore Pte Ltd. 2017
M. Xu et al. (Eds.): CTCIS 2017, CCIS 704, pp. 66–75, 2017.
https://doi.org/10.1007/978-981-10-7080-8_6

an excitation to a designed circuit on the specific chip, an unpredictable but consistent response is output. This function reflect the randomness difference introduced in the manufacturing process in the chip. By adapting the response of PUF, it can be used as a unique identification of a specific IC. Theoretically, PUF can avoid intrusion and semi-intrusion attack tamper. It can also provide the Intellectual Property (IP) core protection by assigning an ID for each chip. In addition, chip authentication, key generation and other security scheme can be achieved based on PUF.

In this paper, a new DTP-PUF based on TP delay measurement on basic units (such as LUT) is proposed. Compared with previous work, this scheme can reduce the complexity of PUF circuit and improve efficiency. The space of challenge and response pair sets of DTP-PUF is magnified because of small granularity measurement. Furthermore, by choosing the location of LUT under test ac-cording to two-dimension code, variously chip ID can be produced to serve multipurpose security scheme.

The rest of this paper is structured as follows: the Sect. 2 briefly introduce the previous work about PUF, TP measurement technology and existing PUF scheme based on LUT delay. This is followed by the research motivation in Sect. 3. The specific DTP-PUF is described in Sect. 4. Then, the simulation results is presented in Sect. 5. Section 6 shows the conclusion of the whole paper. Finally, the future work is discussed briefly in Sect. 7.

2   Background

2.1   Previous Work

In 2002, Physical One-Way Functions proposed by Pappu et al. was published, pioneering the study of PUF [1]. Then, the concept of CDs PUF and paper PUF subsequently presented respectively by Hammouri et al. [2] and Bulens et al. [3]. In 2006, Tuyls et al. proposed a representative coatings PUF for analog circuits [4]. In addition, PUF based on threshold voltage was proposed by Lofstrom et al. [5] and PUF based on the resistance was proposed by Helinski et al. using the resistance of the resistor to identify the IC power distribution system [6]. Besides, the development of digital circuit PUF has also made great progress, which is often divided into storage-based PUF and delay-based PUF. The former uses unpredictable steady state of uninitialized digital memory, such as PUF based on SRAMs, flip-flops or latches. The latter, the delay-based PUF derives the response directly using the delay variation of the wires and logic element [7,8].

Habib et al. put forward an FPGA PUF scheme based on the delay of LUT in 2013 [9]. The design uses the internal differences of LUTs to generate PUF responses. It makes an improvement on the scheme based on programmable delay line published by Majzoobi et al. [12]. By keeping the path outside the LUT constant to minimize the effect of path delay on the frequency of the ring oscillator, it ensure that the randomness is only determined by the inherent randomness of the LUT. Bilal's scheme is to use a LUT as an AND gate to reflect input changes. Three LUTs playing as inverters are connected forming a ring oscillator structure inside one CLB. And 130 CLBs in the scheme are configured in the center of the chip as a 13 * 10 matrix. In essence, Bilal Habib's PUF scheme can be considered as classical RO (Ring Oscillator) PUF. In this scheme, it is necessary to count the eight frequency results of each oscillator from 000 to 111, and the results can act as a response to the PUF after comparing. The results shown in this work are pretty good with inter-device Hamming distance of 48.3%, uniformity 50.13%, bit-aliasing 51.8%, reliability 97.88%, and steadiness 99.5%.

2.2 Transition Probability Delay Measurement

Transition probability is the probability that the node will change state when the next input stimuli is applied to the circuit [9,10]. Suppose that k represents the output of one combinatorial circuit, the input of the circuit is a sequence of vectors $C(n), n = 1, 2$, and results in a sequence of output values $R(n)$. The probability of a transition $D(k)(D(k)$ represents the transition probability of the primary output node$k$) can be defined as:

$$
P\left\{k(n+1) = \overline{k(n)}\right\} = P\left\{k(n) = 0\right\} P\left\{k(n+1) = 1\right\} \\
+ P\left\{k(n) = 1\right\} P\left\{k(n+1) = 0\right\}
$$
(1)

By detecting the changes of TP, the highest frequency CUT (Circuit under test) can achieve is observed and its propagation delay can be calculated. The use of TP measurement technology has many advantages: First, this method requires less prior knowledge of the internal structure; Second, it can measure the delay of arbitrary circuits; Third, TP method needs no external test equipment, and its less resource consumption, high efficiency.

During measurement, the CUT output captured by a register at clock frequency that has been tracked. The CUT is fault-free when clock frequency is low enough. Because of the propagation delay, the output changes over a period of time after the input is applied to the CUT, then at a point in the CUT began to fail to find the TP that maximum deviates from its fixed operating frequency, so that the prop-agation delay can be known. The structure of TP measurement is shown in the Fig. 1. In this example, the CUT is a simple 4-bit carry-chain adder including four LUTs and dedicated interconnections. The Test Vector Generator (TVG) is used to generate test vector. Launch Register are used to feed the test vector into CUT with different clock signal. The generated signal is switched at each clock cycle under a stable transition probability. The Transition Activity Counter (TAC) is implemented as an asynchronous counter to calculate the number of transitions for a given test cycle at different clock frequencies. With the gradual failure of the CUT, the circuit corresponds to the maximum operating frequency and the delay can be determined by the average statistical center of the random jitter of the test clock.

PUF is a challenge-response function that when an external input (challenge) is excited, it outputs an unclonable, unpredictable but unique response, the

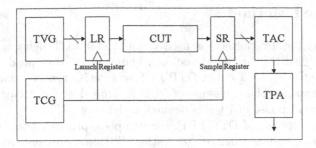

Fig. 1. The general test circuit.

excitation and response, called Challenge-Response pair (CPR). All sets of CPRs constitute the mapping space of the PUF. With reference to the general test circuit scheme and the single critical path test scheme from Justin, we can achieve the measurement of the FPGA base unit LUT delay [9]. This greatly extends the CPRs sets space and is significantly optimized in granularity.

3 Motivation

By analyzing the PUF design based on the delay of LUT in FPGA proposed by Bilal et al., it shows that further improvement can be made from three aspects. Firstly, although [9] ring oscillator is simple and easy to be constructed, this PUF scheme needs to track the outputs on each circuit under the eight inputs motivated. Besides that, it takes a certain amount of time to achieve the desired vibration state of the ring oscillator. Because of the structure of negative feedback, ring oscillator is easy to cause local overheating, leading to that the result of output is not stable. It is meaningful to find another low timing cost and workload test circuit in PUF design. Secondly, the location of CUT in traditional PUF is chosen randomly. It is possible to design the location of CUT purposely loading complex multidimensional data. By combining the two-dimensional code into PUF scheme, it can realize the multi-dimensional information storage and utilization. For example, in the scheme of intellectual property protection, the CUT of PUF can be chosen as a 2D code including the information of IP core provider. It associates the fingerprint of hardware and the information of manufacturer directly without any more cost. Furthermore, TP measurement technique and the route comparison method are combined to obtain the delay of a single specific unit such as a wire segment, which achieves more accurate and smaller granularity [9,13]. The DTP-PUF will not rely on the external complex circuit but only depends on the delay characteristic of the LUT of the FPGA chip itself. Considering the characteristics of such as uniqueness, robustness, unpredictability and unclonability, it can be used flexibly in authentication, key generation, random oracle and so on.

4   Proposed Method

In the scheme, the TP method is used to carry out LUT delay measurement for our PUF called DTP-PUF. Based on schemes [9,12] that produce the PUF response output using LUT delay, DTP-PUF scheme is proposed that makes use of TP measurement. The challenge of PUF is defined as the location of CUT, e.g. LUTs. The response of PUF is defined as delay of CUTs.

To get the response of DTP-PUF, the complete process should include the following steps: Challenge matrix generation, TP measurement, and Response matrix generation. The response result of PUF can be corrected to keep consistency in key generation if necessary. C_M represents the challenge matrix whose c_{ij} is 0 or 1, R_M is the response matrix and each element r_{ij} is the frequency of the corresponding position, and DTP-PUF can be expressed as follows:

$$f_{DTP-PUF} : C_M \xrightarrow{TP} R_M \tag{2}$$

(a) Challenge matrix generation

DTP-PUF is a challenge response function, since we have to carry out the TP measurement of LUT distributed in the FPGA CLB, the primary problem is to determine the location of the measurement point. Inspired by the two-dimensional code technology, challenge matrix is de-signed as a two-dimensional code, which means that the input is no longer limited to numbers, but can be expanded to text and even images and videos. It not only increase the diversity of challenges, but also improve the security. When a "two-dimensional code" of a binary distribution is obtained by input, that is, the challenge matrix, each ele-ment of the matrix is mapped to the corresponding LUT measurement circuit block location in the area on the FPGA, and the position of the value "1" (c_{ij} =1) is measured.

(b) TP measurement

The challenge matrix can be generated in binary form. When the measurement area is determined on the FPGA, we carry out the TP measurement of LUT in the CLB cor-responding to "1" in the selected matrix.

Figure 1 depicts the TP measurement test circuit. We simplify the circuit in the scheme [9] to get the delay of the specific unit. The TVG and the Launch register are single toggle flip-flops, and they are used to generate test vector. The TAC is an asynchronous counter that calculates the number of measured cycle transitions at different clock frequencies. The CUT is gradually deactivated when the test clock frequency is increased. And the output delay of the LUT is obtained by observing the maximum operating frequency of the circuit. In addition, the tiny delay of one switch means that the test frequency required for the measurement is extremely high which may heat up of the chips and decrease the accuracy of measurement. The idea of GROK-LAB measurement is to measure a set of overlapping paths with TP measurement [13] to form a system of linear equations. The individual delay of components in those paths can be given if the equations can be solved [14].

To obtain the delay of each LUT, the measured path has multiple units at the beginning. We test several paths and establish a linear set to obtain the delay of a single LUT. In the Ref. [13], for example, the three paths are measured, the path 1 consists of A and B, and the path 2 consists of B and C. The path 3 consists of C and A. And the delay is 5 ps, 4 ps and 3 ps respectively, which can lead to the following equations:

$$\begin{cases} A + B = 5\,\text{ps}, path1 \\ B + C = 4\,\text{ps}, path2 \\ C + A = 3\,\text{ps}, path3 \end{cases} \tag{3}$$

And A, B, C specific value can be obtained by solving the equation. That is, from linear combination of single LUT and the total delay, the delay of a single LUT can be gotten by computing.

(c) Response matrix generation

By measuring the position of the challenge matrix with the value of "1", the values of delay of corresponding LUTs can be obtained, and the response matrix can be formed by these values. However, the value in the matrix is a specific value, and cant be applied directly.

Enlightened by the two methods of processing the re-sults from Bilal Habib's scheme, we can compare adjacent rows or adjacent columns to get the response "1" or "0". Likewise, we can rely on some sort of rule to compare the values in the matrix to get the response result of 0 or 1.

(d) Key generation processing

Applying DTP-PUF response to key generation includes error correcting processing. The process of generation of DTP-PUF response may be affected by the fluctuation of internal control voltage and ambient temperature. To ensure that the same challenge can eventually produce the same key, the response result from the same challenge excitation needs to be corrected. If necessary, we introduce the syndrome in the error correcting coding process to ensure we could get same result every time. Hashed response can be as a seed key. After further processed, the seed key can be available for the specific algorithm.

5   Simulation Results

Table 1 lists the comparison of parameters of Bilal Habib's scheme (reference scheme) and DTP-PUF scheme [11], and both of them are based on 520 LUTs.

Table 1. Comparison of parameters of Bilal Habib's scheme and DTP-PUF scheme

	Bilal Habib's scheme	DTP-PUF scheme
CUT composition	One LUT as an AND gate to and three LUTs as inverters, connected in a ring oscillator structure	4-bit adder using four LUTs and dedicated carry-chain interconnec-tions.
Input data	8 different LUT_input from "000" to "111"	20 × 26 matrix, whose element is 1 or 0, there are possible inputs
Output data	1032 bit response	Depending on the way of comparison, there may be up to 1.34×10^5 different response results.
Frequency comparison	129	CUT (including 4 LUTs) comparison within groups and between groups

Frequency comparison 129 CUT (including 4 LUTs) comparison within groups and between groups After simulation, Fig. 2 shows the number of response bits that may be generated under the same LUT resource, the x-axis represents the number of LUTs, and the y-axis represents the number of possible response bits. Because of the introduction of multidimensional form, the DTP-PUF scheme has a greater response space. At the same time, Fig. 3 represents the LUT resource comparison required to produce the same response bit. For Bilal Habib's scheme, the input is eight combinations from 000 to 111, however, DTP-PUF has a greater challenge space (from Fig. 4), which is imparted to the input data of more practical significance.

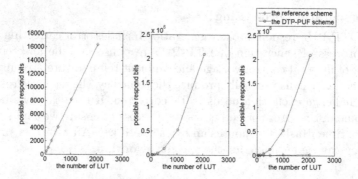

Fig. 2. Comparison of response bits generated under the same LUT resource

From the results of the simulation, the results shown in these figures are in line with the expectations. The proposed scheme greatly extends the input space a by adopting 2D barcode challenge and response matrix. And it has been significantly optimized in granularity and resource consumption.

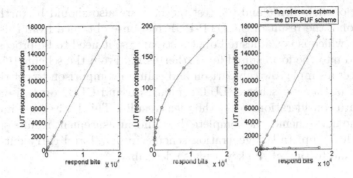

Fig. 3. Comparison of LUT resource required to produce the same response bit

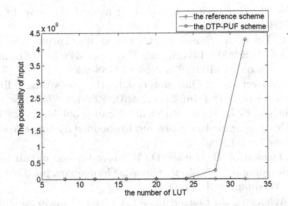

Fig. 4. Comparison of challenge space

6   Conclusion

This paper presents a DTP-PUF construction scheme based on FPGA LUT delay, combined with TP measurement technology and route comparison method. The input and output are in form of challenge matrix and response matrix, which achieve the multi-dimensional information utilization. Compared to previous work, the strength of DTP-PUF is its ability that it can provide better PUF scheme in terms of accuracy and granularity because it choose to measure simple CUT to calculate the delay of single LUT to pro-duce challenge and response pair. In addition, the new scheme has advantage of simple circuit, great input space, less resource consumption.

7   Future Work

The future work will focus on the following aspects: First, the data processing methods in the DTP-PUF scheme needs complete and theoretical proof. And the test circuit of the scheme and the test method are also should be further optimized. Second, the result of the DTP-PUF response obtained from this scheme is a matrix, which is not a desired digital stream, so it need to be processed and transformed into the form suited for further using. From the scheme [11] we can see that after a simple row comparison and column comparison to get the result of 0/1, but in the new scheme, LUT comparison and CLB comparison should be taken into consideration to get the ideal results. Third, after the implementation of the new scheme, the complete data and measurement results should be analyzed, the complete key generation scheme in detail and carry out security evaluation and testing of the key are also described.

References

1. Pappu, R., Recht, B., Taylor, J., et al.: Physical one-way functions. Science **297**(5589), 2026–2030 (2002)
2. Hammouri, G., Dana, A., Sunar, B.: CDs have fingerprints too. In: Clavier, C., Gaj, K. (eds.) CHES 2009. LNCS, vol. 5747, pp. 348–362. Springer, Heidelberg (2009). https://doi.org/10.1007/978-3-642-04138-9_25
3. Bulens, P., Standaert, F.X., Quisquater, J.J.: How to strongly link data and its medium: the paper case. IET Inf. Secur. **4**(3), 125–136 (2010)
4. Tuyls, P., Schrijen, G.J., Koric, B., et al.: Read-proof hardware from protective coatings. In: Cryptographic Hardware and Embedded Systems Workshop, pp. 369–383. ACM , New York (2006)
5. Lofstrom, K., Daasch, W.R., Taylor, D.: IC identification circuit using device mismatch. In: Proceedings of Solid-State Circuits Conference. pp. 372–373. IEEE Computer Society, Washington, DC (2000)
6. Helinski, R., Acharyya, D., Plusquellic, J.: A physical unclonable function defined using power distribution system equivalent resistance variationC. In: Proceedings of the 46th Annual Design Automation Conference, pp. 676–681. ACM, New York (2009)
7. Holcomb, D.E., Burleson, W.P., Fu, K.: Initial SRAM state as a finger-print and source of true random numbers for RFID tags. In: Proceedings of the Conference on RFID Security, pp. 11–13. RFID Publications, Malaga, Spain (2007)
8. Maes, R., Tuyls, P., Verbauwhede, T.: Intrinsic PUFs from flipflops on reconfigurable device [EB/OL], 18 March 2012. http://www.Cosic.Esat.Kuleuven.be/publications/article-1173.pdf
9. Wong, J.S.J., Sedcole, P., Cheung, P.Y.K.: A transition probability based delay measurement method for arbitrary circuits on FPGAs. In: International Conference on ICECE Technology, pp. 105–112. IEEE Xplore (2008)
10. Wong J.S.J., Cheung P.Y.K.: Improved delay measurement method in FPGA based on transition probability. In: ACM/SIGDA, International Symposium on Field Programmable Gate Arrays, FPGA 2011, Monterey, California, USA, 27 February, March 2011, pp. 163–172. DBLP (2011)
11. Habib, B., Gaj, K., Kaps, J.P.: FPGA PUF based on programmable LUT delays. In: Digital System Design, pp. 697–704 (2013)
12. Majzoobi, M., Koushanfar, F., Devadas, S.: FPGA PUF using programmable delay lines. In: IEEE International Workshop on Information Forensics and Security, pp. 1–6. IEEE Xplore (2011)

13. Gojman, B., Nalmela, S., Mehta, N., et al.: GROK-LAB: Generating real on-chip knowledge for intracluster delays using timing extractio. ACM Trans. Reconfigurable Technol. Syst. **7**(4), 81–90 (2014)
14. Gojman, B., Mehta, N., Rubin, R., DeHon, A.: Component-specific mapping for low-power operation in the presence of variation and aging. In: Bhunia, S., Mukhopadhyay, S. (eds.) Low-Power Variation-Tolerant Design in Nanometer Silicon, pp. 381–432. Springer, Boston (2011). https://doi.org/10.1007/978-1-4419-7418-1_12

A New Service Selection Method Based on Service Depository Relevance

WeiJin Jiang[1,2,3] and YuHui Xu[1(✉)]

[1] School of Computer and Information Engineering,
Hunan University of Commerce, Changsha 410205, China
nudtjwj@163.com
[2] Electronic Information Engineering Department, Changsha Normal University,
Changsha 410100, China
[3] School of Computer Science and Technology,
Wuhan University of Technology, Wuhan, China

Abstract. In view of the current service selection method, the service attribute of the service requester itself and the service selection method based on collaborative filtering are not considered. The paper will combine the filtering technology with the trust measurement method. According to the service requestor's personality attribute characteristics of the service selection process, the introduction of the user (service requestor) relevance, and calculate the recommended credibility, the use of analytic hierarchy process to determine the weight of the service reputation value. A Trusted Service Selection Model Based on Collaborative Filtering. The simulation results show that the proposed method can effectively avoid the malicious attacks of service providers and improve the efficiency of service selection.

Keywords: Trust computing · User relevance · Service selection · Collaborative filtering

1 Introduction

Service selection is an important part of achieving service sharing and reusing. The traditional service selection scheme is based on Service (Quality of, QoS), that is, to select the QoS global or local optimal service under the premise of meeting the functional attributes [1, 2]. However, the expansion of the application scale, the malicious spoof of the service provider, the lag of the QoS data update or the external environment and other factors, resulting in the authenticity of QoS data cannot be guaranteed [3]. The main task of the current service selection is to use the trust metric theory to correct the QoS data, and to realize the service selection by maximizing the credibility of the data. However, the QoS value of the service provider in most of these methods [4, 5] is often a simple weighted average of all the feedback QoS data, ignoring the inherent correlation between users, without considering the impact of the user's personality and categories of services. Collaborative Filtering (CF) was first proposed by Goldberg et al. [6] in 1992. The recommended system Tapestry is primarily intended to solve the problem of Xerox's information overload in the Palo Alto

© Springer Nature Singapore Pte Ltd. 2017
M. Xu et al. (Eds.): CTCIS 2017, CCIS 704, pp. 76–86, 2017.
https://doi.org/10.1007/978-981-10-7080-8_7

Research Center, whose basic idea can be refined as to predict the services which some requests who share the same interests and common experiences are interested in among a large number of users [7]. Therefore, with the increase of the size of candidate services, collaborative filtering technology is more and more applied to the reliable prediction of QoS data. At present, the service selection method based on collaborative filtering [8, 9] mostly assumes that the QoS data given by the service provider and the service referrer are true and credible, and that the service provider may not provide false information or service recommendation due to personal benefits. There may be malicious spoofing behavior, resulting in QoS data is not credible, and these untrusted QoS data will directly affect the effectiveness of Web services selection.

In view of the shortcomings existing in the above service selection scheme, this paper proposes a trusted Trustworthy Services Selection Model Based on Collaborative Filtering (UPFSRTM), which is based on the combination of collaborative filtering technology and trust measurement method. There are two major innovations as following:

Firstly, to make a introduction of user relevance to reflect the degree of close between two users (service requester) under the network environment; to apply the user's personality attribute characteristics to the service provider reputation value during the prediction, to improve the accuracy of service selection by reducing the size of service providers.

Secondly, combining user relevance and recommendation credibility organically, using AHP to determine the weight of relevant factors in the service selection index system so that we can make the reputation of the predicted service provider more reliable and effectively resist the malicious user feedback.

2 Trusted Service Selection Method Based on User's Personality Feature and Service Recommendation (UPFSRTM)

2.1 Related Conceptions

In the environment of the network, entity can be divided into 3 categories: Firstly, Service Requester (SR), an service request entity, sometimes called "user", is also described as service recommender when sharing service experience. Secondly, Service Registration Center (SRC), which contains the description information of the service provider and the service requester. Thirdly, the Service Provider (SP), which provides the software service distributed in the network.

Definition 1. User Evaluation Values

This paper does not set up a central node that is responsible for collecting, updating, and broadcasting service reputation. Each service requester records only the evaluations of the service providers that interacted with. This evaluation is called the service requester or user evaluation value. It is also called the recommended value of service recommender in the case of recommendation information. The evaluation value r (sr_i, sp_j) of the service provider sp_j given by the service requester sr_i is defined $r(sr_i)$ as

$$r(sr_i) = \begin{cases} 1, \text{Completely satisfied} \\ 0, \text{Completely dissatisfied}, \\ e, \text{other} \end{cases} \quad (1)$$

"1" indicates that the service requester sr_i is completely satisfied with the service provided by the service provider sp_j and "0" is completely dissatisfied. In the remaining cases, the greater the value of e $(0 < e < 1)$ indicates the higher satisfaction.

Definition 2. The concept of user relevance

Correlation is established in the process of systematical research and development, and has become a basic concept of modern system theory. In the service selection process, there is a certain link between the user's own personality attribute information and the user's ranking of the service. The user evaluation values are more or less reflecting the user's personality characteristics. To this end, this paper introduces user relevance to reflect the close relationship between two users. Taking into account the relevance of the impact on the choice of the content, user relevance is defined as the evaluation of similarity and domain correlation of two aspects, the specific meaning and calculation methods are as follows.

Definition 3. Evaluating Similarity

Considering the effects of different types of services on the evaluation of service requesters are not equivalent, the weight of the service provider sp_m is added to the Pearson correlation measure, which is based on the idea of literature [10]. The evaluation similarity $sim(sr_i, sr_j)$ of the requester sr_i and sr_j is calculated as

$$sim(sr_i, sr_j) = \frac{\sum_{m \in I} \frac{|I| d_m^\gamma}{d_m^\gamma}(r_{i,m} - \bar{r}_i)(r_{j,m} - \bar{r}_j)}{\sqrt{\sum_{m \in I}(r_{i,m} - \bar{r}_i)^2 \sum_{m \in I}(r_{j,m} - \bar{r}_j)^2}} \quad (2)$$

"$r_{i,m}$" and "$r_{j,m}$" respectively represent the user evaluation value of the service requester sr_i, sr_j to the service provider sp_m. "$I = Isr_i \cap Isr_j$", which represents the set of service providers that were used by the two service requesters. $\bar{r}_i$ and $\bar{r}_j$ represent the average of the user evaluations of the service requesters sr_i and sr_j is for all service providers in I, and "d_m" represents the weight of the service m according to its personality attribute or category. The parameter γ determines the influence factor of the service weight when calculating the similarity degree. If $\gamma = 0$, it means that the weight of the service has no effect on the service requestor's similarity.

Definition 4. Domain correlation

The attribute information for sr_i and sr_j is defined as: $att_i = \{att_{i1}, att_{i2}, att_{in}\}$ and $att_j = \{att_{j1}, att_{j2}, att_{jn}\}$. atti represents the set of attributes of the service requester sri, including the age, sex, occupation and other information. If $att_i \cap att_j \neq \Phi$ and $| att_i \cap att_j | \geq M$, that the service requestor sr_i and sr_j have some of the same attributes and the same number of attributes greater than a certain threshold M, then service requester sri is domain-related to the service requester srj, and the domain affinity dom (sr_i, sr_j) is defined as

$$\mathrm{dom}(\mathrm{sr}_i, \mathrm{sr}_j) = N'/N \tag{3}$$

The N' is the total number of registered service requesters and N the number of service requesters whose similarity satisfies a certain threshold M.

Definition 5. Neighbor users

If we consider only the recommendation information of the neighbor user [11], we can effectively reduce the calculation scale and improve the service selection efficiency. There are two algorithms for selecting neighbors: one is the number of neighbors fixed, and only take the user with the nearest K users; the second is to select the current point as the center, the distance from the K area of all users as a neighbor user basing on the similarity threshold. The number of neighbors calculated through this method is uncertain, but the similarity will not be a large deviation. As this paper mainly considers the recommendation information of the neighbor users to participate in the service selection, and focuses on improving the accuracy of the recommendation. Therefore, the second method is used to determine the neighbor user, the second method is adopted. The calculation formula of the neighbor user of sr_i is

$$nb(\mathrm{sr}_i) = \{\mathrm{sr}_j | \mathrm{sim}(\mathrm{sr}_i, \mathrm{sr}_j) \geq \delta\} \tag{4}$$

The δ refers to the similarity threshold between the selected service requesters sr_i and sr_j. Neighbor users are the elements of the neighborhood called Sri Neighbors. The larger the δ is, the more harsh the condition that the neighbor of the service requester is determined. The smaller the δ, the more relaxed the determining condition.

Definition 6. The credibility of recommendation

This model is used to measure the credibility of the neighbor user as the recommender using the method of calculating the credibility in the literature [4]. The service requester sr_i recommends the recommended user sr_j from time t to time $t + 1$. The update formula for the credibility $\mathrm{cre}(\mathrm{sr}_i, \mathrm{sr}_j)$ is

$$\mathrm{cre}_{t+1}(\mathrm{sr}_i, \mathrm{sr}_j) =$$
$$\mathrm{cre}_t(\mathrm{sr}_i, \mathrm{sr}_j) \left((1 \pm (1 - |v_{\mathrm{sr}_j} - M|)) \frac{\left|2 - \left(\sqrt{\sum_{k=1}^{n}(M - V_{\mathrm{sr}_k})^2} + \sqrt{\sum_{k=1}^{n}(A - V_{\mathrm{sr}_k})^2}\right)/\sigma\right|}{\rho} \frac{\sum_{k=1}^{m} U_{\mathrm{sr}_k}}{\sum_{k=1}^{n} V_{\mathrm{sr}_k}} \right) \tag{5}$$

M denotes the maximum central evaluation value, V_{sr_k} denotes the credibility evaluation value of the recommended user sr_k to the service provider sp, and U_{sr_k} denotes the "useful" recommendation in the literature [4]. σ represents the average of all recommended user trust ratings, and ρ determines the degree of urgency of the recommended reliability update as a penalty factor. A indicates the average value of the service provider's reputation value for the most recent period.

Definition 7. User Recommendation

The user recommendation level indicates the size of the recommended value of the service requester to the service requester [12]. As the user recommendation degree and evaluation similarity, domain relevance, recommended credibility are time-related, so the user recommendation degree of sr_j to sr_i at time t is

$$rec(sr_i, sr_j, t) = (\omega_1 sim(sr_i, sr_j) + \omega_2 dom(sr_i, sr_j) + \omega_3 cre(sr_i, sr_j))(1 - \ell^{t-t_0}) \quad (6)$$

"t" is the time recommended by the service, t_0 is the initial time, and the weight vector $W = [w_1, w_2, w_3]$ is calculated according to the specific network environment. It should be noted that the recommendation here refers only to the recommendation of the neighbor user.

Definition 8. Service Reputation Value

It is assumed that the service information can be shared between the service requester and the neighbor user [13]. From the perspective of the service requester sr_i, the reputation value of the service provider sp_k can be defined as

$$rep(sr_i, sp_k, t) = \frac{\sum_{j=1}^{L} rec(sr_i, sr_j, t) r(sr_i, sp_k)}{L} \quad (7)$$

L represents the number of neighbors of the sr_i, and $rec(sr_i, sr_j, t)$ represents the user recommendation of the service requester sr_j at the time t.

2.2 UPFSRTM Architecture

On the basis of inheriting the traditional Web service architecture, UPFSRTM has added the functions of evaluation similarity, domain correlation and recommendation credibility calculation. The model includes service registration center, service requester, service provider, collaborative filtering module, trust management module and recommendation weighting algorithm engine module. The structure is shown in Fig. 1 [8, 11].

2.2.1 Collaborative Filtering Module

The Collaborative Filtering module is responsible for calculating the correlation between users. This model divides user relevance into evaluation similarity and domain relevance. Among them, the evaluation similarity degree is based on the different degree of service impact on the service selection, and the service weighting factor is introduced to make the evaluation similarity more accurate. The domain relevance distinguishes the recommended users in the same domain from the ordinary users in the service requesters. To avoid the different areas of the user evaluation of the same service differences arising from the impact.

2.2.2 Trust Management Module

The trust management module is responsible for calculating the trustworthiness of the recommender [14, 15]. From (5) we can see that this model determines the

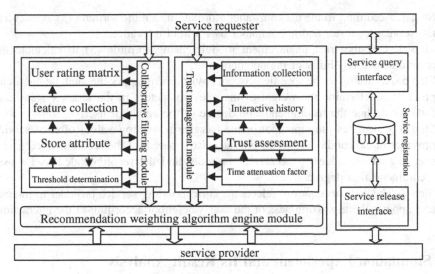

Fig. 1. UPFSRTM model

recommended credibility based on the user's credibility evaluation value of the service provider. When it is recommended that the user's trustworthiness assessment value of the service provider be closer to the majority of the user's evaluation value of the service provider's trustworthiness and the change in the reliability rating value is maintained within a certain period of time, the user's recommendation credibility is high. The recommended credibility obtained by this method is not only effective in avoiding the adverse effects of malicious group feedback, but also the recommendation that the recommended value is not continuous. In addition, the trust management module updates the trustworthiness of the recommender based on the result of the interaction of the service requester with the service provider.

2.2.3   Recommendation Degree Weight Algorithm Engine Module

As the user recommendation degree is a multi-level, multi-factor complex problem, the model of the recommendation weight algorithm engine module using AHP (Analytic Hierarchy Process, AHP) thinking on the user recommendation to construct a hierarchical analysis of the structural model to achieve the user to determine the degree of recommendation.

2.3   UPFSRTM-Based Service Selection Process

Step 1. The service requester sr issues a service request to the service registry. The service registry returns the list of providers that have this service L $\{sp_1, sp_2, sp_n\}$.

Step 2. The service requester uses Eq. (2) to calculate the similarity of the service requester and the service recommender, and then obtain the service requestor neighbor according to the corresponding algorithm.

Step 3. According to the user attribute information, use the formula (3) to calculate the service requester and the neighbor user's field relevance.

Step 4. Call the trust management module, using formula (5) to calculate the recommended reliability of the neighbor user.

Step 5. According to the specific network environment, apply the analytic hierarchy process to determine the weight of the relevant factors in the index system, and finally calculate the recommendation degree of the neighbor user.

Step 6. Calculates the reputation value (service reputation value) of each service provider in the candidate service provider list L based on the recommended user's user evaluation value of the service provider and the recommended user's user recommendation degree.

Step 7. The service requester selects the corresponding service provider to interact and updates the trustworthiness of the user's neighbor according to the interaction.

3 Simulation Experiment and Its Result Analysis

In order to explain in detail the role and significance of combining user relevance and recommendation credibility in service selection, this paper validates the effectiveness of the proposed UPFSRTM service selection model to the service provider's reputation value by simulation experiments to prove the effectiveness of the method.

3.1 Experimental Environment

The experimental hardware environment is Intel (R) Core (TM) i3 CPU M350 @ 2.27 GHz 2.27 GHz, 4 GB RAM. Software environment for win7 ultimate, eclipse-SDK-3.5.2-Win32, simulation program written in java language.

3.2 Experimental Scene Settings

In this paper, the UPFSRTM system, which includes the data preprocessing module, the collaborative filtering module, the trust management module and the weight assignment module, are formed according to the cooperative filtering algorithm in the machine learning field of Mahout's open source project. Among them, the test data from the Grouplens research group [12], including 6040 MovieLens users of 3952 films for the 1000209 evaluation. The attributes of the user include ID, gender, age, occupation and zip code. This experiment uses the user attribute as the registration information to calculate the domain relevance of the user.

Intuitive, different gender, age and occupation of the user's understanding of the film will be very different. Usually, people who are less than 20 years old tend to science fiction, children and other themes of the film, while those who aged 20 and 50 years old of the lawyers, scientists, doctors crowd tend to documentary, economic other themes of the film. For those 20 to 50 years old workers, individual and private groups tend to war, adventure and other themes of the film, and the age of 50 years people tend to drama, life and other themes of the film. The model is divided into four categories according to the user's attributes:

> Class A: {age, occupation | age $\leq$ 25, occupation = student/college/grad student}
> Class B: {age, occupation | 25 <age <50, occupation = lawyer/scientist/writer/ doctor/artist}
> Class C: {age, occupation | 25 <age <50, occupation = homemaker/self-employed}
> Class D: {age, occupation | age $\geq$ 50, occupation = retired/academician/educator}

User evaluation of the film is divided into 1 to 5 levels, respectively, said: very poor, poor, general, good, very good. At the initial stage, each service requester evaluates at least 20 movies.

3.3 Average Absolute Error

The experiment uses the mean absolute error (Mean Absolute Error, MAE) as one of the evaluation indicators. MAE indicates the absolute difference between the predicted credit value and the actual reputation value, the formula is

$$MAE = \frac{\sum_{i}^{N} |rep_i - rep_i'|}{N} \tag{8}$$

$\{rep_1', rep_2', \text{ and } rep_N'\}$ indicate that the service requester has a true reputation evaluation value for n service providers, $\{rep_1, rep_2, rep_N\}$ represents the service provider calculated by the model predict the reputation value, and N the number of service providers. The smaller the MAE is, the more accurate the predicted value, and the better the algorithm.

3.4 Experiments and Results Analysis

By comparing the UPFSRTM model proposed in this paper with the service selection method based on trust and collaborative filtering, the RATEWeb model proposed in [4] is selected based on the trust service selection method. The service selection method based on collaborative filtering is used to select the literature [9]. The WSQPA model is proposed to evaluate the WSQPA model. In order to verify whether the model can achieve the expected function, the performance of the user is the adaptability to the user, the resistance of the malicious user and the user neighbor threshold.

Experiment 1 Fig. 2 reflects the changes in MAE as the number of service requesters and service providers grows [12]. It can be seen from the figure that the RATEWeb model is based on the similarity calculation method. With the increase of the number of users, the recommendation information provided to the service requesters is also increased, the service provider credit value calculation is more accurate, However, to a certain threshold, due to the problem of sparse data, the similarity of the neighbor is reduced, the viscosity is decreased and the predicted value is no longer accurate. The MAE is in the ascending trend. When the WSQPA model calculates the service reputation value, the number of users and services The impact of the service provider's reputation value is not very obvious, MAE fluctuations are relatively flat, but because there is no consideration between the intrinsic relationship between users, provided to the service requester's service is credible, but can not meet the service requester's personality attributes. The MAE is higher than the other two methods. When the number of users increases to a certain threshold, the model avoids the problem of data sparseness due to the recommended credibility, and filters a large number of user sets into a small amount by user correlation Neighbor users, to meet the characteristics of user attributes, so this model MAE value is better than the first two models.

Experiment 2 Fig. 3 reflects the effect of different thresholds on MAE results when selecting neighbors. When δ = 0.9, it means that only a very similar user can serve as a neighbor of the service requester. When the user and the service are relatively few, the recommendation information is not accurate enough due to the harsh conditions [13]. As the user and the service increase, the situation will be improved, but will still cause errors. When δ = 0.5, it means that the condition is relatively loose, and it is not very similar to the service requester. It can be a neighbor. Although some dissimilar users are filtered out, because the neighbor threshold is too loose, the model tends to be based on trust service selection model; when δ = 0.7, this time can better reflect the advantages of this model, that is, to select the valuable recommendation information to provide users, you can filter out a small part of the value of the user.

Experiment 3 Fig. 4 reflects the three models for the proportion of malicious users caused by the difference in the success rate of service situation. With the increase in malicious nodes, as there is no resistance mechanism, the success rate of interactive decline quickly in RATEWeb model [11]. Because of the use of the service request between the trust, the malicious node in WSQPA model is less, the success rate is higher, however, with the increase in malicious nodes, even if you can identify malicious recommendations, as the recommendations are less and less available, success rate will inevitable decline. This paper takes two aspects of user relevance and recommendation credibility, and the success rate decreases with the increase of

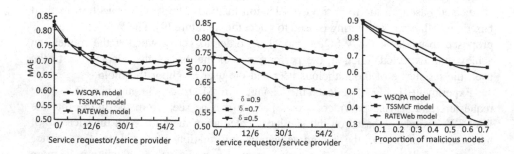

Fig. 2. Comparison of three models with user size changes MAE

Fig. 3. The effect of different thresholds on MAE when calculating user neighbors

Fig. 4. Comparison of the three models' resistance to malicious users

malicious nodes. Since the proportion of malicious nodes in real life is generally impossible to reach 70%, so in general, this model can better resist malicious attacks.

4 Conclusion

Based on the characteristics of the personality of the service requester, this paper describes the user correlation by defining the similarity and domain relevance of the user, and the calculation method of the recommended credibility is given by using the credible measurement theory. Using the analytic hierarchy process (AHP) to determine the weight of each correlation factor, this paper proposes a credible service selection model based on collaborative filtering UPFSRTM. The simulation results show that the model can effectively improve the efficiency of service selection and resist the attack of malicious feedback.

Acknowledgments. This work was supported by the National Natural Science Foundation of China (61472136; 61772196), the Hunan Provincial Focus Social Science Fund (2016ZBB006) and Hunan Provincial Social Science Achievement Review Committee results appraisal identification project (Xiang social assessment 2016JD05).

References

1. Li, M., Zhao, J., Wang, L.: CoWs: an internet-enriched and quality-aware web services search engine. In: 2011 IEEE International Conference on Web Services, Washington, DC, pp. 419–427 (2011)
2. Hu, J., Li, J., Liao, G.: A multi-QoS based local optimal model of service selection. Chin. J. Comput. **33**(3), 526–534 (2010)
3. Jiang, W., Zhang, L., Wang, P.: Research on grid resource scheduling algorithm based on MAS cooperative bidding game. Sci. China F **52**(8), 1302–1320 (2009)
4. Wang, H.M., Yin, G., Xie, B., et al.: Research on network-based large-scale collaborative development and evolution of trustworthy software. Sci. Sin. Inf. **44**, 1–19 (2014)
5. Tao, Q., Chang, H.Y., Gu, C.Q., et al.: A novel prediction approach for trustworthy QoS of web services. Expert Syst. Appl. **39**(3), 3676–3681 (2012)
6. Ding, Y., Wang, H., Shi, P., et al.: Trusted cloud service. Chin. J. Comput. **38**(1), 133–149 (2015)
7. Jiang, W., Xu, Y., Guo, H., Zhang, L.: Dynamic trust calculation model and credit management mechanism of online transaction. Sci. China F Inf. Sci. **44**(9), 1084–1101 (2014). https://doi.org/10.1360/N112013-00202
8. Zhang, S.B., Xu, C.X.: Study on the trust evaluation approach based on cloud model. Chin. J. Comput. **36**(2), 422–431 (2013)
9. Jiang, W.J., Zhong, L., Zhang, L.M., Shi, D.J.: Dynamic cooperative multi-agent model of complex system based-on sequential action' logic. Chin. J. Comput. **36**(5), 115–1124 (2013)
10. Lim, S.L., Finkelstein, A.: StakeRare: using social networks and collaborative filtering for large-scale requirements elicitation. IEEE Trans. Softw. Eng. **38**(3), 707–735 (2012)
11. Xu, J., Si, G.N., Yang, J.F., et al.: An internetware dependable entity model and trust measurement based on evaluation. Sci. Sin. Inf. **43**, 108–125 (2013)

12. Li, L.H., Zhang, J.P., Yang, J.: Based time-series aware of social network nodes set context aggregation method. Sci. Sin. Inf. **43**, 1079–1095 (2013)
13. Jiang, W.: Dynamic Modeling and Quantification Trust More Research Methods Agent, p. 6. Science Press, Beijing (2014)
14. Wang, J., Li, S.-J., Yang, S., Jin, H., Yu, W.: A new transfer learning model for cross-domain recommendation. Chin. J. Comput. **40**(33), 1–15 (2017). Online publication number
15. Zhang, W.-L., Guo, B., Shen, Y., et al.: Computation offloading on intelligent mobile terminal. Chin. J. Comput. **39**(5), 1021–1038 (2016)

Real-Time Trusted Computing Technology for Xenomai

Mingdi Xu[1], Xueyuan Gao[1], Yang Gao[1], and Fan Zhang[2]([⊠])

[1] Wuhan Digital Engineering Institute, Wuhan, China
mingdixu@163.com
[2] School of Mathematics and Computer Science,
Wuhan Polytechnic University, Wuhan, China
whpuzf@whpu.edu.cn

Abstract. With the development of science and technology, embedded system plays an indispensable part in our daily life. Real time operating system (RTOS) is the critical part of it. To meet the stringent response time requirements, Xenomai is developed as a software framework adding real-time capabilities to the mainline linux kernel. And on the hand, the security of RTOS is a rising issue for computer industrial development, as RTOS used to be considered safer than other system. Therefore, trusted platform module (TPM) is proposed to ensure security form a hardware perspective. In this work, we built a trusted real-time platform based on dual kernel architecture. It comprises host OS and guest OS, which are implemented by trusted virtualization platform (TVP) and Xenomai respectively. In the platform, TVP was based on SW-TPM. Then some tests were carried out to verify performance of system that we built. The result shows that compared with original linux kernel, the average rate of time saving by our platform is 49.52%. The TPM commands executed in the present system is faster than that runs as binary file in the SW-TPM alone.

Keywords: Xenomai · SW-TPM · RTOS

1 Introduction

In the past few years, we have seen the rise in demand and rapid development of embedded system. From airplane to smartphones, it gradually permeates our information society. Most of these systems need RTOS to meet a strict task [1,2]. The purpose of RTOS is to serve real-time applications without buffering latency. This means task completion is time limited. Both premature and late completion of the task could cause problems. Xenomai was born to meet stricter time needs for applications for linux platforms. And it has already been widely used in industrial control systems. With the widespread use of RTOS, security issue has become plain. For example, the problem of cyber-security in automotive electronic systems, security of intra-RTOS communication and supervisory control and data acquisition (SCADA)[3,4].

© Springer Nature Singapore Pte Ltd. 2017
M. Xu et al. (Eds.): CTCIS 2017, CCIS 704, pp. 87–96, 2017.
https://doi.org/10.1007/978-981-10-7080-8_8

As trusted computing group (TCG) addressed, the trust in trusted computing stands for an entity can be trusted if it always behaves in the expected manner for the intended purpose [5]. Trusted platform module (TPM) was presented as a hardware component, enhancing the trustworthiness of the platform. However, TPM has platform dependencies, and simulation often does not work [6]. Due to those reasons, software TPM (SW-TPM) has been developed. Unlike hardware TPM, SW-TPM solves the limitations and generally runs faster.

Although TPM can solve some security problems, but most of them are achieved by sacrificing real-time performance. Khalid [7] implemented trusted boot for embedded systems. In their work, trusted computing hardware not only includes TPM, but also CPU, memory controller hub and I/O controller hub. Besides they implemented two processors, the main processor acted as application processor, another worked as secure coprocessor. And as a result, the startup time was prolonged to 25%.

Different from the previous work, we built a trusted real-time platform based on dual kernel architecture. It runs RTOS in a trustworthy virtualization environment. In the platform, TVP implemented by SW-TPM working as host OS, Xenomai working as guest OS.

The remainder of this paper is organized as follows: In Sect. 2, we summarize the main features and capabilities of Xenomai. We outline the structure and implementation of host OS and guest OS in Sect. 3. Performance and commands testing are arranged in Sect. 4. Section 5 summed up conclusions.

2   Xenomai

Xenomai is a real-time extension of the linux kernel that based on dual kernel technology. Different from PREEMPT-RT, Xenomai modifies the entire system architecture. As a result, linux does not bring extra influence on the real-time tasks. Xenomai implements dual kernel mechanism based on adaptive domain environment for operating system (ADEOS) technology.

ADEOS is a virtual layer of resources between operating system and hardware resources. Its purpose lies in providing a compatible environment, which allows hardware resources to be shared between different operating systems or applications. Those operating systems or applications are called as domain [8]. From Fig. 1, we can see that the domains do not necessarily to see each other, but can communicate with ADEOS. In order to meet stringent real-time requirements, ADEOS is preferentially allowed to handle the incoming interrupts before linux kernel. Figure 2 is the dual kernel (aka cobalt) architecture of Xenomai3. It provides interface with the cobalt core of RTOS APIs, including the subset and extensions of POSIX (aka libcobalt) in user mode. Copperplate interface mediates between two parts, one is the real-time emulator used by user applications, another is real-time core. In this way, applications are able to easily migrate to other environment without visible code changes. Hardware abstract layer (HAL) is used to wrap i-pipe and underlying information.

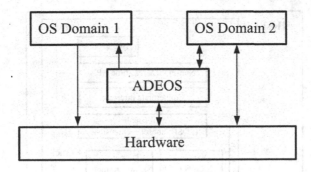

Fig. 1. Architecture of ADEOS

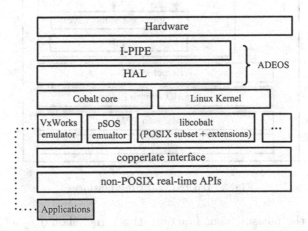

Fig. 2. Xenomai3 architecture

3 Design and Implementation

In Fig. 3, host OS is TVP, working as trusted kernel in the dual kernel architecture. Guest OS is Xenomai, acting as user kernel by dealing with the real-time tasks efficiently. In the paper, SW-TPM was used to replace hardware TPM due to the factors of efficiency and convenience.

3.1 Host OS and SW-TPM

The startup process of our platform can be described as follows. First, kernel-IMA measures the binary value of the application and dynamic link libraries loaded with modules. The metric expands and measurement records are written to PCR (Platform Configuration Registers) and SML (Stored Measurement Log) respectively. After the loading of TPM driver, TCSD (Trusted Core Service daemon) provides trusted services and encryption algorithms to the application layer as TSS (TCG Software Stack).

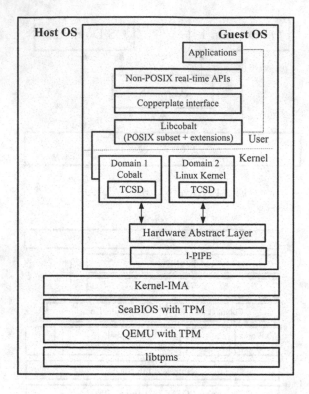

Fig. 3. Trusted real-time platform

To achieve the measurement function, the kernel should be fitted with the IBM IMA patches. However, the patches have been integrated into the main kernel stream since 2.6.30. The version of Ubuntu and kernel in our environment is 14.0.4 and 4.2.0, thus there is no need to for installation work.

In order to install trusted computing in guest OS, here are two indispensable parts, they are SeaBIOS and TPM driver. The former is an open source implementation of a 16bit X86 BIOS, for most cases it is default in QEMU and KVM [9]. TPM driver are compiled by default as kernel modules.

Before introducing SW-TPM, the paper gives a general description of TPM architecture. In Fig. 4, C1 implements cryptographic operations into TPM, which contains RSA, SHA1 and random number generation (RNG) for the generation of random data and asymmetric keys, etc. In addition, TPM may also achieve different singing and wrapping due to the realization of the above algorithms. C6 manages TPM power state as TCG requires TPM to master the power state changes of platform. C7 provides flags to realize the control of TPM hardware, and this requires the permission of TPM owner or the assertion of physical presence, the result is that a remote entity cannot easily change the status of TPM without two conditions above. SW-TPM was created by IBM and is open-source. It is mainly oriented to application development, education, and virtualization. It consists of three parts: libtpm, tpm and tpm_proxy. The contents of libtpm are TPM commands. The last part is proxies that connect TPM interface with hardware TPM device driver. In our platform, TPM driver module does exist on our current guest OS.

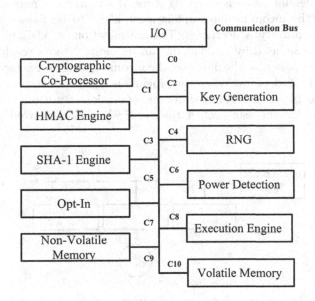

Fig. 4. TPM component architecture

3.2   Guest OS and ADEOS

After identifying the above components in host OS, we create a QEMU virtual machine to run the guest OS. To meet strict real-time requirements in Guest OS, a patch, called Xenomai, was built into the Linux kernel.

To reduce system overhead and improve the performance of guest OS, some options need to be disabled when we configure the kernel, such as CONFIG_CPU_FREQ and CONFIG_CPU_IDLE. Because CONFIG_CPU_FREQ creates issues with Xenomai timing code, as well as unpredictable run-time for the real-time threads, and high latencies when CPU frequency is changed dynamically. And the impact of CONFIG_CPU_IDLE is similar to CONFIG_CPU_FREQ.

The missions of fundamental ADEOS technology are summarized as follow. ADEOS handles all the incoming interrupts before linux kernel. With this strategy, ADEOS deals with interrupts immediately, regardless of any current attempt from the linux kernel. Besides, it also needs to ensure that each thread has the proper priority managements. These can be achieved by pipeline, Fig. 5 gives a general view of its architecture. In Fig. 5, all active domains form the pipeline, domain priority decreases from left to right. As each domain is assigned by a static priority except linux kernel, the incoming events are dispatched in an orderly manner to various domains, and the delivery time of events can also be predictable. Because linux kernel stands for root domain, and the other domains need linux kernel to install them, thus the position of linux kernel of Fig. 5 might be can be anywhere. Typically, a domain can receive, discard or terminate an interrupt, the default mode is receiving state. If an interrupt enters a receiving state domain, the incoming interrupt is most likely to be passed to the next domain and its priority is decreased. The optimization of ADEOS is that any segment of pipeline used by the domain can be blocked. As a result, instead of being handled or passed to the next one, the incoming interrupt is recorded in the interrupt log of the domain. When the pipeline is non-block state, the interrupt will be handled by an internal synchronous operation. By using this optimization technique, domains can protect their critical areas and avoid unnecessary preemption.

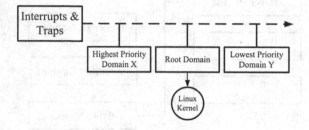

Fig. 5. Per-CPU ADEOS pipeline

4   Performance Evaluation

In order to estimate the real-time performance of our platform, we used cyclictest to examine it. After that, a number of TPM commands were tested. They were measurements commands, ownership commands, cryptographic commands, capability commands, storage and key management commands. These tests were conducted on a Samsung (core i5@2.4 GHz and 3 G Byte RAM) using linux kernel-4.2.0 as trusted kernel and linux kernel-4.1.18 with xenomai-3.0.3 as user kernel.

To confirm the real-time performance of our platform, we choose another new platform as a comparison. The new platform also uses SW-TPM to meet the demand of trustworthy, without being patched with Xenomai-3.0.3. And it is based on the same Ubuntu 14.0.4 and linux kernel 4.2.0 as our platform.

Cyclictest is a highly resolution test program. It is mainly used to test latency, which determines the real-time performance of the kernel. The principle of Cyclictest is to compute delays by constantly making a thread sleep and waking the threads.

Test parameters PRIO represents the priority of the highest thread, we assign it to the maximum to exclude priority preemption. The study selects parameters INTERVAL and LOOPS as test variables. INTERVAL is the basic interval of thread (μs), representing the specified sleep time of thread. LOOPS is the number of times that we repeatedly make the thread sleep (or the number of times that we wake up the thread). In the testing, we selected INTERVAL value as $200\mu s$ and $1000\mu s$ (default), LOOPS as 10000, 100000 and 1000000. The test values were divided into 6 groups, and each group was executed 100 times. Figure 6 shows the experiment results. Different from PREEMPT-RT, Xenomai changes the architecture of entire system, a new scheduler and IRQ management mechanism is added into the system. With this mechanism, Xenomai simplifies the processing of the real-time task to the point where only ipipe-scheduler is left to execute. In this way, the complex architecture of linux will have no influence on the process of real-time tasks. Therefore, it can be easy to understand that the average rate of time saving by Xenomai is 49.52%.

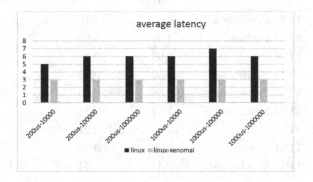

Fig. 6. Real-time performance comparison between original host OS and host OS patched Xenomai

On the other hand, to evaluate the performance of Xenomai in trusted virtualization platform, we used some TPM commands by calling TSPI [10], as shown in Table 1. They were PCR read and write, TPM authorization protocols, TPM key management. The experiments were conducted on a Samsung (core i5 @ 2.4 GHz and 3 G Byte RAM) using linux kernel-4.2.0 as trusted kernel and linux kernel-4.1.18 with Xenomai-3.0.3 as user kernel. Table 1 shows the average execution time for a set of TPM commands. The performance of our trusted virtualization platform built in this paper is 60% higher than reference data. Cryptographic commands (TPM_GetRandom and TPM_Sign) take longer to execute. The timing issue happens because that digital signatures and random number generation may cause other consumption (such as the random number generator). In the case of command TPM_GetCapacity. We analyze the execution time of Fig. 7. The distribution of ordinate is relatively even, but the variance is quite large, we attribute the result to machine performance problems. In the host OS, ADEOS makes sure that events are dispatched in the sequence of the two domains according to their respective priority in the pipeline. By defining each domain with a static priority, it is possible to provide timely and predictable delivery for those events. According to the mechanism of Xenomai, those TPM commands such as TPM_LoadKey is pushed to the higher priority domain, which is Xenomai domain. Regardless of the complexity of linux, CPU deals with the real-time events in the current Xenomai domain without being interrupted by the lower priority system calls from another domain. Apparently, the average execution time of the TPM commands have a rapidly improvement compared to the previous works. However, as ADEOS and virtual machine take up more resources, some of the TPM commands' execution time such as TPM_TakeOwnership increases as we expected.

Table 1. The TPM command execution time

	Xenomai in TVP (ms)	SW-TPM (ms)
TPM_PcrExtend	4.01	12.46
TPM_PcrRead	3.07	6.69
TPM_Quote	0.01	0.31
TPM_ReadPubek	0.02	0.09
TPM_TakeOwnership	0.66	0.83
TPM_GetRandom	1.77	0.19
TPM_Sign	10.59	0.21
TPM_LoadKey	0.05	0.06
TPM_GetCapacity	1.44	0.04

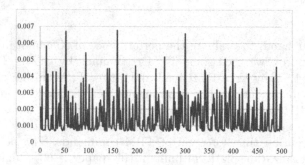

Fig. 7. Real-time performance of vTPM command TPM_TakeOwnership

5   Conclusions

As real-time and security are the two critical parts of industrial control system, looking for a way to balance performance between the two parts is becoming more and more important. To provide Xenomai with TPM support from lower level, we implement SW-TPM in host OS. The implementation creates a TVP, which can provide TPM support for the QEMU virtual machine. This platform can meet our real-time and security needs to a certain extent.

We still have a lot to do in the near future. Due to the effects of time and efficiency, the study chooses SW-TPM to replace hardware TPM. Although SW-TPM can implement most of the TPM functions, its limitation still exists. Besides hardware TPM is usually shipped with endorsement key (EK), but not SW-TPM. Users can create their own EKs and certificates, which is also one disadvantage of using SW-TPM.

In addition, public keys and signatures are six-times larger for RSA than that of ECC in the 128-bit security level. Private keys are 12 times larger for RSA compared to ECC [11]. The size matters when it comes to the cost of secure storage of the keys. We will replace RSA with ECC to improve the system. Besides, Loongson CPU and NeoKylin will be implemented in the current system. In order to save resources, the trusted kernel should be reduced by kernel tailoring.

Acknowledgments. This work is supported by National Nature Science Foundation of China under grant 61502438, 61272452 and 61403350.

References

1. Koeberl, P., Schulz, S., Sadeghi, A.R., et al.: TrustLite: a security architecture for tiny embedded devices. In: EuroSys 2014 Proceedings of the Ninth European Conference on Computer Systems. ACM Press, Amsterdam, pp. 1–14, 14–16 April 2014
2. Hambarde, P., Varma, R., Jha, S.: The survery of real time operating system RTOS. In: Proceeding of International Conference on Electronic Systems, Signal Processing and Computing Technologies (ICESC). IEEE Press, Nagpur, pp. 34–39, 9–11 Jan 2014
3. Rautmare, S.: SCADA system security: challenges and recommendations. In: Annual of IEEE India Conference. IEEE Press, Hyderabad, pp. 1–4, 16–18 Dec 2011
4. Chung, W.L., Zhu, Q., Phung, C., et al.: Security-aware mapping for CAN-based real-time distributed automotive system. In: International Conference on Computer-Aided Design. IEEE Press, San Jose, pp. 115–121, 18–21 Nov 2013
5. Mohd, A.M.I., Jamalul, A.M., Haibah, H., et al.: Trusted real time operating System: identifying its characteristics. In: IEEE Symposium on Computer Applications and Industrial Electronics (ISCAIE). IEEE Press, Kota Kinabalu, pp. 83–88, 3–4 Dec 2012
6. Strasser, M., Stamer, H.: A software-based trusted platform module emulator. In: Lipp, P., Sadeghi, A.-R., Koch, K.-M. (eds.) Trust 2008. LNCS, vol. 4968, pp. 33–47. Springer, Heidelberg (2008). https://doi.org/10.1007/978-3-540-68979-9_3
7. Khalid, O., Rolfes, C., Ibing, A.: On implementing trusted boot for embedded systems. In: IEEE International Symposium on Hardware-oriented Security and Trust (HOST). IEEE Press, Austin, pp. 75–80, 2–3 June 2013
8. Xenomai.: Xenomai White paper[EB/OL] (2014). http://xenomai.org/2014/06/xenomai-white-paper/

9. TVP Trusted Virtualization Platform Deployment[EB/OL] (2015). https://www.oerc.ox.ac.uk/sites/default/files/uploads/ProjectFiles/MyTrustedCloud/TrustedVirtualizationPlatformDeployment.pdf
10. Aaraj, N., Raghunathan, A., Ravi, S., et al.: Energy and execution time analysis of a software-based trusted platform module. In: Proceedings of Design, Automation and Test in Europe Conference and Exhibition (DATE). IEEE Press, Nice, pp. 1–6, 16–20 April 2007
11. Kerry, M.: RSA vs. ECC comparison for embedded systems white paper[EB/OL] (2016).   http://www.atmel.com/Images/Atmel-8951-CryptoAuth-RSA-ECC-Comparison-Embedded-Systems-WhitePaper.pdf

Cryptanalysis of Rijndael-192/224 in Single Key Setting

Jingyi Cui, Jiansheng Guo$^{(\boxtimes)}$, and Yipeng Liu

Information Science and Technology Institute, Zhengzhou, China
tsg_31@126.com

Abstract. Rijndael was the finalist of Advanced Encryption Standard (AES) competition and Rijndael-128 with the 128-bit block size was selected as the standard. In this paper, we concentrate on the security of large-block Rijndael under impossible differential attack. First, the differential properties of S-box and MixColumn in Rijndael were analyzed to construct a 6-round impossible differential distinguisher of Rijndael-192. Based on the new distinguisher, the first impossible differential attack on 9-round Rijndael-192 was proposed. Then the flaws in the impossible differential attack on 10-round Rijndael-224 introduced by Minier in 2016 were presented. And a new impossible differential attack on 10-round Rijndael-224 was introduced in this paper. Finally, the optimal techniques such as: early abort technique, quick sort algorithm and time-memory tradeoff strategy could be used to improve the security of Rijndael-160 and Rijndael-256 under the impossible differential attack.

Keywords: Block cipher · Cryptanalysis · Rijndael · Impossible differential attack · Early abort technique

1 Introduction

Rijndael [1] is an SPN-based block cipher family designed by Belgian cryptographers, Daemen and Rijmen, which was submitted to AES competition organized by NIST (National Institute of Standards and Technology). The finalist is Rijndael-128 and is published as a block cipher standard, FIPS-197 [2] in 2001. In the initial Rijndael, there were 25 block ciphers with five different block sizes and five key sizes, from 128-bit to 256-bit with a step of 32-bit. The block size of AES is 128-bit and the key sizes are 128-bit, 192-bit and 256-bit. The rest Rijndaels with the block sizes of 160/192/224/256-bit are called large-block Rijndael.

Impossible differential attack is a powerful and widely used cryptanalytic method. Impossible differential attack was first proposed by Knudsen [3] and Biham [4] respectively. Knudsen pointed that there was a 5-round impossible characteristic of Feistel when the F-function is bijection while he analyzed the AES candidate, DEAL. Biham introduced miss-in-the-middle technique to construct impossible differential characteristic in FSE 1999. Impossible differential attack is introduced to analyze the security of various block ciphers, such as

© Springer Nature Singapore Pte Ltd. 2017
M. Xu et al. (Eds.): CTCIS 2017, CCIS 704, pp. 97–111, 2017.
https://doi.org/10.1007/978-981-10-7080-8_9

Table 1. Comparison of impossible differential attacks on Rijndael-192/224

Cipher	Key	Round	Data	Time	Memory	Reference
Rijndael-192	192	8	2^{179}	$2^{81.4}$	–	[15]
Rijndael-192	192	8	2^{158}	$2^{177.4}$	–	[15]
Rijndael-192	192	9	$2^{183.4}$	$2^{188.4}$	$2^{164.1}$	Sect. 3
Rijndael-224	224	9	$2^{198.1}$	$2^{195.2}$	$2^{140.4}$	[16]
Rijndael-224	256	10	$2^{185.38}$	$2^{246.93}$	$2^{201.38}$	[17]
Rijndael-224	256	10	$2^{214.2}$	$2^{236.02}$	$2^{194.2}$	Sect. 4

AES [5–7], CLEFIA [8], Camellia [9], ARIA [10], LBlock [11]. In recent years, there are many attacks deduced from impossible differential attack, such as related-key impossible differential attack [12] and zero-correlation liner cryptanalysis [13].

The first impossible differential attacks on Rijndael were proposed by J. Nakabara Jr. [14] in ISC 2007. He analyzed the security of 6-round Rijndael-160, 6-round Rijndael-192, 7-round Rijndael-224 and 7-round Rijndael-256. In ISC 2008, Zhang et al. [15] improved the attacks on Rijndael and they gave the impossible differential attacks on 7-round Rijndael-160, 8-round Rijndael-192, 9-round Rijndael-224 and 9-round Rijndael-256. In ISC 2012, Wang et al. [16] introduced the impossible differential attacks on 9-round Rijndael-224 and 10-round Rijndael-256. In 2016, Minier [17] analyzed the security of 8-round Rijndael-160 and 10-round Rijndael-224 under impossible differential attack.

Contribution. In this paper, the security of Rijndael-192 and Rijndael-224 under impossible differential attack is analyzed. First, a new 6-round impossible differential distinguisher of Rijndael-192 is introduced. Based on this distinguisher, the impossible differential attack on 9-round Rijndael-192 is proposed with the usage of early abort technique, quick sort algorithm and time-memory tradeoff technique. Then, the flaws of the attack in [17] are corrected. And by using a 6-round distinguisher, the impossible differential attack on 10-round Rijndael-224 is given. The results in this paper are shown in Table 1.

The paper is organized as follows. In Sect. 2, the notations and the description of Rijndael are given. Section 3 introduces the security analysis of Rijndael-192 and Sect. 4 improves the impossible differential attack on Rijndael-224. Section 5 concludes the paper.

2   Preliminaries

2.1   Notations

Here are some notations used in the following paper.

x_i: The i-th round state after AK;

y_i: The i-th round state after SB;

z_i: The i-th round state after SC;

w_i: The i-th round state after MC;

$x_{i,col(j)}$: The j-th column of x_i;

$x_{i,row(j)}$: The j-th row of x_i;

k_i: The i-th round key;

k_i^*: The i-th round key after $SC^{-1} \circ MC^{-1}$, $k_i = MC \circ SC(k_i^*)$;

$x_i[j]$: The j-th byte of x_i;

Nb: The number of columns in a state;

Nk: The number of columns in a key;

2.2 Description of Rijndael

Rijndael is an SPN block cipher family. There are five block sizes: 128/160/192/224/256 bits. The corresponding ciphers are called Rijndael-b, b=128/160/192/224/256. Each cipher has five key sizes: 128/160/192/224/256 bits. The state of Rijndael can be represented as a byte matrix shown in Fig. 1.

The ciphers have different iterated rounds with different block sizes and key sizes shown in Table 2.

The round function of Rijndael consists of four transformations: SubBytes, ShiftRows, MixColumns and AddRoundKey. The details are shown below.

SubBytes (SB): In Rijndael, there is a nonlinear byte-oriented S-box applied to transform each byte in the state.

ShiftRows (SR): Each row of the state needs to rotate left for specific bytes shown in Table 3.

0	4	8	12	16	20	24	28
1	5	9	13	17	21	25	29
2	6	10	14	18	22	26	30
3	7	11	15	19	23	27	31

Fig. 1. The state of Rijndael.

Table 2. The iterated rounds of Rijndael

	$Nk=4$	$Nk=5$	$Nk=6$	$Nk=7$	$Nk=8$
$Nk=4$	10	11	12	13	14
$Nk=5$	11	11	12	13	14
$Nk=6$	12	12	12	13	14
$Nk=7$	13	13	13	13	14
$Nk=8$	14	14	14	14	14

Table 3. The offsets of ShiftRows

	$Nk = 4$	$Nk = 5$	$Nk = 6$	$Nk = 7$	$Nk = 8$
$Row = 0$	0	0	0	0	0
$Row = 1$	1	1	1	1	1
$Row = 2$	2	2	2	2	3
$Row = 3$	3	3	3	4	4

MixColumns (MC): With the usage of a binary matrix over $GF(2^8)$, each column of the state is updated as follows.

$$\begin{pmatrix} a_0 \\ a_1 \\ a_2 \\ a_3 \end{pmatrix} = \begin{pmatrix} 0x2\ 0x3\ 0x1\ 0x1 \\ 0x3\ 0x1\ 0x1\ 0x2 \\ 0x1\ 0x1\ 0x2\ 0x3 \\ 0x1\ 0x2\ 0x3\ 0x1 \end{pmatrix} \cdot \begin{pmatrix} b_0 \\ b_1 \\ b_2 \\ b_3 \end{pmatrix}$$

AddRoundKey (AK): The key is XORed to the corresponding state.

The full encryption of Rijndael needs to XOR a prewhitening key WK in the forward direction and omit ShiftRows and MixColumns in the last round.

2.3   Properties of Rijndael

Here are some properties of Rijndael used in the following attacks.

Proposition 1 [17]. The MixColumns operation uses an MDS matrix over $GF(2^8)$, with the knowledge five bytes of the input and output, the other three bytes can be determined uniquely.

When it comes to XOR operation, the MixColumns is linear. The Property 2 can be deduced from Property 1 directly.

Proposition 2. With the knowledge of the differences in five bytes of the input and output, the differences in the other three bytes can be determined uniquely.

Like the property of AES used in the attacks [18], the similar property of Rijndael is introduced as follows.

Proposition 3. The S-box in Rijndael is bijective. Given the input difference and output difference, there is one input and output in average.

3   Impossible Differential Attack on 9-Round Rijndael-192

A new 6-round impossible differential distinguisher is proposed. Based on this distinguisher, encrypt for two rounds and decrypt for one round to introduce the impossible differential attack on 9-round Rijndael-192 with the usage of early abort technique, quick sort algorithm and time-memory tradeoff strategy.

The whole attack is divided into two phases: Pre-computation phase and online attack phase.

In the Pre-computation phase, we need to precompute and store the partial encryption and decryption in six tables: $T_0, T_1, T_2, T_3, T_4, T_5$.

Table T_0: When the difference $\Delta w'_{8,col(0)}$ is only active in the 0th byte, $\Delta x_{9,col(0)}$ can take 2^8 values. With the knowledge of Proposition 3, given the difference $\Delta C[0, 15, 18, 21]$, we can deduce 2^8 pairs $(x_{9,col(0)}, y_{9,col(0)})$. Take $\Delta C[0, 15, 18, 21]$ as indexes, store the pairs $(x_{9,col(0)}, y_{9,col(0)})$ in the table T_0.

Table T_1: When the difference $\Delta w'_{8,col(3)}$ is only active in the 15th byte, $\Delta x_{9,col(3)}$ can take 2^8 values. Similar with the table T_0, take $\Delta C[3, 6, 9, 12]$ as indexes, store the pairs $(x_{9,col(3)}, y_{9,col(3)})$ in the table T_0.

Table T_2: When the difference $\Delta w'_{8,col(4)}$ is only active in the 18th byte, $\Delta x_{9,col(4)}$ can take 2^8 values. Take $\Delta C[7, 10, 13, 16]$ as indexes, store the pairs $(x_{9,col(4)}, y_{9,col(4)})$ in the table T_2.

Table T_3: When the difference $\Delta w'_{8,col(5)}$ is only active in the 21st byte, $\Delta x_{9,col(5)}$ can take 2^8 values. Take $\Delta C[11, 14, 17, 20]$ as indexes, store the pairs $(x_{9,col(5)}, y_{9,col(5)})$ in the table T_3.

Table T_4: If there is only one active byte in the first column of $\Delta w'_{7,col(0)}$, $\Delta x_8[0, 1, 2, 3]$ can take 2^{10} possible values. Take $\Delta y_{8,col(0)}$ as indexes, store the 2^{10} pairs $(x_{8,col(0)}, y_{8,col(0)})$ in the table T_4.

Table T_5: If there is only one active byte in the first column of $\Delta w_{1,col(0)}$, $\Delta y_1[0, 5, 10, 15]$ can take 2^{10} possible values. Take ΔP as indexes, store the 2^{10} pairs $(x_1[0, 5, 10, 15], y_1[0, 5, 10, 15])$ in the table T_5.

In the online attack phase, there are nine steps to recover the full master key.

Step 1. Select 2^n structures: a set of plaintexts take all possible values in 0, 5, 10, 15-th bytes and take the fixed values in other bytes. A structure contains 2^{32} plaintexts and $C_{2^{32}}^2 \approx 2^{63}$ plaintext pairs. So we choose 2^{n+32} plaintexts and 2^{n+63} pairs in this attack.

Step 2. Filter the pairs with the usage of quick sort algorithm. Select the plaintext pairs that satisfy the ciphertext difference $\Delta C[1, 2, 4, 5, 8, 19, 22, 23]$ is 0 and the other bytes are active. Store the remaining $2^{n+63} \times 2^{-64} = 2^{n-1}$ pairs in the table Ω with the index of the pair number. We need to store 0, 5, 10, 15-th bytes of plaintext and 0, 3, 6, 7, 9, 10, 11, 12, 13, 14, 15, 16, 17, 18, 20, 21-th bytes of ciphertext.

Step 3. Guess $k_{10}[0, 15, 18, 21]$. For the rest 2^{n-1} pairs in the table Ω, look up the table T_0 to deduce 2^8 values $y_{9,col(0)}$ and $y'_{9,col(0)} = y_{9,col(0)} \oplus \Delta C[0, 15, 18, 21]$. With the usage of the pairs $C[0, 15, 18, 21]$ and $C'[0, 15, 18, 21]$ in the table Ω, deduce 2^8 keys $k_{10}[0, 15, 18, 21] = y_{9,col(0)} \oplus C[0, 15, 18, 21]$ and $(x_{9,col(0)}, x'_{9,col(0)})$. Take 2^{32} possible values of $k_{10}[0, 15, 18, 21]$ as indexes, store the pairs $(x_{9,col(0)}, x'_{9,col(0)})$ and the pair number in the table Ω_1. For each index, there are $2^{n-1} \times 2^8/2^{32} = 2^{n-25}$ plaintext pairs.

Step 4. Guess $k_{10}[3, 6, 9, 12]$. Known $k_{10}[0, 15, 18, 21]$, for 2^{n-25} pairs in the table Ω_1, look up the table T_1 to deduce 2^8 pairs $(y_{9,col(3)}, y'_{9,col(3)})$. Known the pairs $(C[3, 6, 9, 12], C'[3, 6, 9, 12])$ in the table Ω, deduce 2^8 keys $k_{10}[3, 6, 9, 12]$ and the corresponding pairs $(x_{9,col(3)}, x'_{9,col(3)})$. Take 2^{32} possible values of $k_{10}[3, 6, 9, 12]$ as indexes to store the pair number and the pairs $(x_{9,col(0,3)}, x'_{9,col(0,3)})$ in the table Ω_2. For each index, there are $2^{n-25} \times 2^8/2^{32} = 2^{n-49}$ plaintext pairs.

Step 5. Guess $k_{10}[7, 10, 13, 16]$. For the rest 2^{n-49} pairs in the table Ω_2, look up the table T_2 to deduce 2^8 pairs $(y_{9,col(4)}, y'_{9,col(4)})$. Known the pairs $(C[7, 10, 13, 16], C'[7, 10, 13, 16])$ in the table Ω, deduce 2^8 keys $k_{10}[7, 10, 13, 16]$ and the corresponding pairs $(x_{9,col(4)}, x'_{9,col(4)})$. Take 2^{32} possible values of $k_{10}[7, 10, 13, 16]$ as indexes to store the pair number and the pairs $(x_{9,col(0,3,4)}, x'_{9,col(0,3,4)})$ in the table Ω_3. For each index, there are $2^{n-49} \times 2^8/2^{32} = 2^{n-73}$ plaintext pairs.

Step 6. Guess $k_{10}[11, 14, 17, 20]$. For the rest 2^{n-73} pairs in the table Ω_3, look up the table T_3 to deduce 2^8 pairs $(y_{9,col(5)}, y'_{9,col(5)})$. Known the pairs $(C[11, 14, 17, 20], C'[11, 14, 17, 20])$ in the table Ω, deduce 2^8 keys $k_{10}[11, 14, 17, 20]$ and the corresponding pairs $(x_{9,col(5)}, x'_{9,col(5)})$. Take 2^{32} possible values of $k_{10}[11, 14, 17, 20]$ as indexes to store the pair number and the pairs $(x_{8,col(0,3,4,5)}, x'_{9,col(0,3,4,5)})$ in the table Ω_4. For each index, there are $2^{n-73} \times 2^8/2^{32} = 2^{n-97}$ plaintext pairs.

Step 7. Guess $k^*_{9,col(0)}$. For the remaining 2^{n-97} pairs in the table Ω_4, look up the table T_4 to deduce 2^{10} values $(y_{8,col(0)}, y'_{8,col(0)})$. Known the pairs $(z'_{8,col(0)}, z''_{8,col(0)})$ from the table Ω_4, deduce 2^{10} keys $k^*_{9,col(0)} = y_{8,col(0)} \oplus z'_{8,col(0)}$. Take 2^{32} possible values of $k^*_{9,col(0)}$ as indexes to store the pair number in the table Ω_5. There are $2^{n-97} \times 2^{10}/2^{32} = 2^{n-119}$ pairs for each index.

Step 8. For each possible $(k^*_{9,col(0)}, k_{10}[0, 3, 6, 7, 9, 10, 11, 12, 13, 14, 15, 16, 17, 18, 20, 21])$, establish a table T. The table T takes 2^{32} possible $k_1[0, 5, 10, 15]$ as indexes and stores 1 bit for each index. Initialize each address to store 0 and a counter satisfies $flag = 0$. For 2^{n-119} pairs in the table Ω_5, look up the table T_5 to deduce $k_1[0, 5, 10, 15]$. Then look up the table T to find the corresponding address. If the address stores 0, set it 1 and add 1 to the counter $flag$. Otherwise, do nothing. If the counter satisfies $flag = 2^{32}$, the key $(k^*_{9,col(0)}, k_{10}[0, 3, 6, 7, 9, 10, 11, 12, 13, 14, 15, 16, 17, 18, 20, 21])$ should be discarded and try another. If the counter satisfies $flag < 2^{32}$ when the plaintext pairs in the table Ω_5 are exhaustively tested, store the key $(k^*_{9,col(0)}, k_{10}[0, 3, 6, 7, 9, 10, 11, 12, 13, 14, 15, 16, 17, 18, 20, 21])$ and find the index $k_1[0, 5, 10, 15]$ stores 0.

Step 9. Known the key $(k^*_{9,col(0)}, k_{10}[0, 3, 6, 7, 9, 10, 11, 12, 13, 14, 15, 16, 17, 18, 20, 21])$ from Step 8, exhaustively test the remaining key bytes to search the master key.

The differential path is shown in Fig. 2. Black and red bytes mean active and white bytes are inactive. Mesh bytes are the key bytes needed to be guessed. The complexity of this attack is give in the Theorem 1.

Theorem 1. With the usage of a 6-round distinguisher, the impossible differential attack on 9-round Rijndael-192 could recover the master key with a time complexity of $2^{188.4}$, a data complexity of $2^{183.4}$ and a memory complexity of $2^{163.1}$.

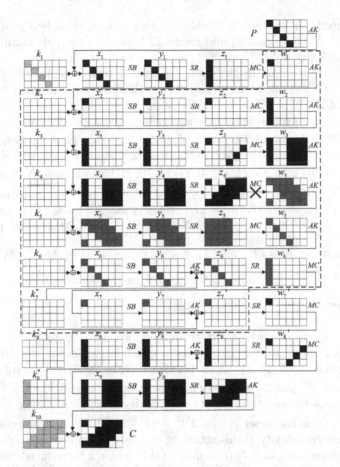

Fig. 2. Impossible differential attack on 9-round Rijndael-192. (Color figure online)

Proof. Compared with the complexity of the online attack phase, the complexity of pre-computation phase could be ignored. In Step 2, filtering 2^{n+63} plaintext pairs by using the quick sort algorithm needs $2^{n+32}\mathrm{lb}2^{32} = 2^{n+37}$ comparisons. The table Ω stores 2^{n-1} plaintext pairs with a memory complexity of $2^{n-1} \times 2 \times (4 + 12) = 2^{n+4}$ bytes.

Step 3 looks up the table T_0 for 2^{n-1} plaintext pairs with a time complexity of $2^{n-1} \times 2^8 = 2^{n+7}$ table-lookups. The table Ω_1 need to store 8 bytes and the pair number with a memory complexity of $2^{n-25} \times 2^{32} \times (8 + (n-1)/8)$ bytes.

Step 4 needs to look up the table T_1 with a time complexity of $2^{n-25} \times 2^8 \times 2^{32} = 2^{n+15}$ table-lookups and stores 16 bytes and the pair number with a memory complexity of $2^{n-49} \times 2^{32} \times (16 + (n-1)/8)$ bytes.

Step 5 needs to look up the table T_2 with a time complexity of $2^{n-49} \times 2^8 \times 2^{64} = 2^{n+23}$ table-lookups and stores 24 bytes and the pair number with a memory complexity of $2^{n-73} \times 2^{32} \times (24 + (n-1)/8)$ bytes.

Step 6 needs to look up the table T_3 with a time complexity of $2^{n-73} \times 2^8 \times 2^{96} = 2^{n+31}$ table-lookups and stores 32 bytes and the pair number with a memory complexity of $2^{n-97} \times 2^{32} \times (32+(n-1)/8)$ bytes.

Step 7 needs to look up the table T_4 with a time complexity of $2^{n-97} \times 2^8 \times 2^{128} = 2^{n+39}$ table-lookups and stores the pair number with a memory complexity of $2^{n-119} \times 2^{32} \times (n-1)/8$ bytes.

In Step 8, the probability for a wrong key guess $(k_1[0,5,10,15], k_{9,col(0)}^*, k_{10}[0,3,6,7,9,10,11,12,13,14,15,16,17,18,20,21])$ to pass a test is $1 - 2^{10}/2^{32} = 1 - 1/2^{22}$. So the probability that 2^{32} keys $(k_1[0,5,10,15], k_{9,col(0)}^*, k_{10}[0,3,6,7,9,10,11,12,13,14,15,16,17,18,20,21])$ can't pass N tests is $[1-(1-2^{-22})^N]^{2^{32}}$ which is the probability that one key $(k_{9,col(0)}^*, k_{10}[0,3,6,7,9,10,11,12,13,14,15,16,17,18,20,21])$ can't pass N tests. The probability for $(k_{9,col(0)}^*, k_{10}[0,3,6,7,9,10,11,12,13,14,15,16,17,18,20,21])$ to pass $2^{22}t$ tests, but not to pass $2^{22}(t+1)$ tests is $p_t = [1-(1-2^{-22})^{2^{22}t}]^{2^{32}} - [1-(1-2^{-22})^{2^{22}(t+1)}]^{2^{32}}$. The mathematical expectation is $E(t) = \sum_{t=1}^{\infty} t p_t = \sum_{t=1}^{\infty} t[e^{-2^{32-1.4425(t+1)}} - e^{-2^{32-1.4425t}}] \approx 2^{4.48}$.

With the usage of early abort technique, we need to test $2^{22} \times 2^{4.48} = 2^{26.48}$ plaintext pairs in average to get a candidate. Known the 160-bit key $(k_{9,col(0)}^*, k_{10}[0,3,6,7,9,10,11,12,13,14,15,16,17,18,20,21])$, look up the table T_5 and T for $2^{26.48}$ plaintext pairs. The time complexity is $2^{160} \times 2^{26.48} \times 2^{10} = 2^{196.48}$ table-lookups and the memory complexity is 2^{32} bits.

The size of candidate set is $\varepsilon = 2^{170} \times (1 - 2^{-22})^{2^{n-119}}$. When we set $n = 151.4$, the time complexity of this attack in mainly determined by Step 8. We use the method mentioned in [17] to transfer table-lookups to reduced-round Rijndael encryptions. The time complexity is $2^{196.48}/30 \times 1/9 = 2^{188.4}$ 9-round Rijndael encryptions and the data complexity is $2^{183.4}$ chosen plaintexts. The memory complexity determined by Step 3 is $2^{126.4} \times 2^{32} \times (8+(151.4-1)/8) = 2^{163.1}$ bytes.

4   Impossible Differential Attack on 10-Round Rijndael-224

The flaws in the impossible differential attack on 10-round Rijndael-224 proposed by Minier in [17] are mentioned. A new impossible differential attack on 10-round Rijndael-224 with the usage of early abort technique is introduced.

4.1   Impossible Differential Attack on 10-Round Rijndael-224 in [17]

The first impossible differential attack on 10-round Rijndael-224 was proposed by Minier in 2016. But there are two flaws in this attack:

1. The distinguisher used in this attack is not impossible with a probability of 1. The following differential characteristics I and II are used to construct the

contrast in the first column. When the input of MC is active on one byte, the fact that there are at most three bytes active is impossible. 1 means the active byte, 0 means the inactive bytes, * means unknown.

$$
\text{I.} \quad
\begin{pmatrix}
0\ 0\ 0\ 0\ 0\ 0\ 1 \\
0\ 0\ 0\ 0\ 0\ 0\ 0 \\
0\ 0\ 0\ 0\ 0\ 0\ 0 \\
0\ 0\ 0\ 0\ 0\ 0\ 0
\end{pmatrix}
\xrightarrow{2.5R}
\begin{pmatrix}
0\ 1\ 0\ 0\ 1\ 1\ 1 \\
1\ 0\ 0\ 1\ 1\ 1\ 0 \\
0\ 0\ 1\ 1\ 1\ 0\ 1 \\
0\ 1\ 1\ 1\ 0\ 1\ 0
\end{pmatrix}
$$

$$
\text{II.} \quad
\begin{pmatrix}
0\ *\ *\ *\ *\ *\ * \\
*\ 0\ *\ *\ *\ *\ * \\
*\ *\ 0\ *\ *\ *\ * \\
*\ *\ *\ *\ 0\ *\ *
\end{pmatrix}
\xleftarrow{3.5R}
\begin{pmatrix}
0\ 0\ 0\ 0\ 0\ 0\ 0 \\
1\ 0\ 0\ 0\ 0\ 0\ 0 \\
1\ 0\ 0\ 0\ 0\ 0\ 0 \\
1\ 0\ 0\ 0\ 0\ 0\ 0
\end{pmatrix}.
$$

But when we encrypt the input of distinguisher in [17] for 2.5 rounds, we can get the following state which is different from it in [17]. So we correct it in this paper.

$$
\begin{pmatrix}
0\ 0\ 0\ 0\ 0\ 0\ 1 \\
0\ 0\ 0\ 0\ 0\ 0\ 0 \\
0\ 0\ 0\ 0\ 0\ 0\ 0 \\
0\ 0\ 0\ 0\ 0\ 0\ 0
\end{pmatrix}
\xrightarrow{2.5R}
\begin{pmatrix}
0\ 0\ 1\ 0\ 1\ 1\ 1 \\
0\ 1\ 0\ 1\ 1\ 1\ 0 \\
1\ 0\ 1\ 1\ 1\ 0\ 0 \\
1\ 1\ 1\ 0\ 0\ 1\ 0
\end{pmatrix}
$$

2. The differential path is incorrect when encrypt the output of distinguisher for two rounds. Encrypt the output of MC operation in the 8th round to give the full different path of 9-round Rijndael-192. The following different path used in [17] is wrong.

$$
\begin{pmatrix}
0\ 0\ 0\ 0\ 0\ 0\ 0 \\
0\ 0\ 0\ 0\ 0\ 0\ 0 \\
1\ 0\ 0\ 0\ 0\ 0\ 0 \\
1\ 0\ 0\ 0\ 0\ 0\ 0
\end{pmatrix}
\xrightarrow{2R}
\begin{pmatrix}
0\ 0\ 1\ 0\ 1\ 0\ 0 \\
0\ 0\ 0\ 1\ 0\ 1\ 0 \\
0\ 0\ 0\ 0\ 1\ 0\ 1 \\
0\ 1\ 0\ 0\ 0\ 0\ 1
\end{pmatrix}
$$

The left rotation operation is used in the round function. So we correct it as follows.

$$
\begin{pmatrix}
0\ 0\ 0\ 0\ 0\ 0\ 0 \\
0\ 0\ 0\ 0\ 0\ 0\ 0 \\
1\ 0\ 0\ 0\ 0\ 0\ 0 \\
1\ 0\ 0\ 0\ 0\ 0\ 0
\end{pmatrix}
\xrightarrow{2R}
\begin{pmatrix}
0\ 0\ 0\ 1\ 0\ 1\ 0 \\
0\ 0\ 0\ 0\ 1\ 0\ 1 \\
1\ 0\ 0\ 0\ 0\ 1\ 0 \\
1\ 0\ 1\ 0\ 0\ 0\ 0
\end{pmatrix}
$$

4.2 New Impossible Differential Attack on 10-Round Rijndael-224

Based on a new 6-round impossible differential distinguisher, by encrypting for two rounds in the backward direction and decrypting for two rounds in the forward direction, we can give the impossible differential attack on 10-round Rijndael-224. The whole attack can be divided into two phases: pre-computation phase and online attack phase.

Pre-computation phase: Store the partial encryption and decryption in 8 tables.

Table T_0: When $\Delta w'_{9,col(3)}$ is only active on the 15th byte, $\Delta x_{10,col(3)}$ can take 2^8 values. Given a possible value of $\Delta C[6, 9, 12, 27]$, we can deduce 2^8 possible pairs $(x_{10,col(3)}, y_{10,col(3)})$. Take $\Delta C[6, 9, 12, 27]$ as indexes to store 2^8 pairs $(x_{10,col(3)}, y_{10,col(3)})$.

Table T_1: Similar with the table T_0. When $\Delta w'_{9,col(5)}$ is only active on the 22nd byte, take $\Delta C[7, 14, 17, 20]$ as indexes to store 2^8 pairs $(x_{10,col(5)}, y_{10,col(5)})$.

Table T_2: When $\Delta w'_{8,col(0)}[1, 2, 3]$ are active and $\Delta x_{9,col(0)}[2, 3]$ are active, there are 2^8 possible values according to Proposition 2. Take $\Delta y_9[2, 3]$ as indexes to store 2^8 pairs $(x_9[2, 3], y_9[2, 3])$.

Table T_3: When $\Delta x_{2,col(0)}$ is only active on the 0th byte, take $\Delta P[0, 5, 10, 19]$ as indexes to store 2^8 pairs $(x_1[0, 5, 10, 19], y_1[0, 5, 10, 19])$.

Table T_4: When $\Delta x_{2,col(1)}$ is only active on 5th byte, take $\Delta P[4, 9, 14, 23]$ as indexes to store 2^8 pairs $(x_1[4, 9, 14, 23], y_1[4, 9, 14, 23])$.

Table T_5: When $\Delta x_{2,col(2)}$ is only active on 10th byte, take $\Delta P[8, 13, 18, 27]$ as indexes to store 2^8 pairs $(x_1[8, 13, 18, 27], y_1[8, 13, 18, 27])$.

Table T_6: When $\Delta x_{2,col(3)}$ is only active on 19th byte, take $\Delta P[7, 16, 21, 26]$ as indexes to store 2^8 pairs $(x_1[7, 16, 21, 26], y_1[7, 16, 21, 26])$.

Table T_7: When there is only one byte active in $\Delta w_{2,col(0)}$ and $\Delta y_2[0, 5, 10, 19]$ are active, there are 2^{10} possible values. Take $\Delta x_2[0, 5, 10, 19]$ as indexes to store 2^{10} pairs $(x_2[0, 5, 10, 19], y_2[0, 5, 10, 19])$.

Online attack phase contains 10 steps.

Step 1. Select 2^n structures: a set of plaintexts take all possible values in 0, 4, 5, 7, 8, 9, 10, 13, 14, 16, 18, 19, 21, 23, 26, 27-th bytes and take the fixed values in other bytes. A structure contains 2^{128} plaintexts and $C_{2^{128}}^2 \approx 2^{255}$ plaintext pairs. So we choose 2^{n+128} plaintexts and 2^{n+255} pairs.

Step 2. Filter the pairs with the usage of quick sort algorithm. Select the plaintext pairs that satisfy the ciphertext difference $\Delta C[6, 7, 9, 12, 14, 17, 20, 27]$ is active and the other bytes are inactive. Store the remaining $2^{n+255} \times 2^{-160} = 2^{n+95}$ pairs in the table Ω with the index of the pair number. We need to store 0, 4, 5, 7, 8, 9, 10, 13, 14, 16, 18, 19, 21, 23, 26, 27-th bytes of plaintext and 6, 7, 9, 12, 14, 17, 20, 27-th bytes of ciphertext.

Step 3. Guess $k_{11}[6, 9, 12, 27]$. For the 2^{n+95} pairs in the table Ω, look up the table T_0 to deduce 2^8 values $y_{10,col(3)} = z_{10}[6, 9, 12, 27]$. Then deduce 2^8 keys

$$k_{11}[6, 9, 12, 27] = z_{10}[6, 9, 12, 27] \oplus \Delta C[6, 9, 12, 27]$$

and $(x_{10,col(3)}, x'_{10,col(3)})$. Take 2^{32} possible values of $k_{11}[6, 9, 12, 27]$ as indexes, store the pairs $(x_{10,col(3)}, x'_{10,col(3)})$ and the pair number in the table Ω_1. For each index, there are $2^{n+95} \times 2^8/2^{32} = 2^{n+71}$ plaintext pairs.

Step 4. Guess $k_{11}[7, 14, 17, 20]$. For the rest 2^{n+71} pairs in the table Ω_1, look up the table T_1 to deduce $y_{10,col(5)} = z_{10}[7, 14, 17, 20]$. Then deduce 2^8 keys $k_{11}[7, 14, 17, 20] = z_{10}[7, 14, 17, 20] \oplus \Delta C[7, 14, 17, 20]$. Take 2^{32} possible values of $k_{11}[7, 14, 17, 20]$ as indexes to store the pair number and the pairs $(x_{10,col(3,5)}, x'_{10,col(3,5)})$ in the table Ω_2. For each index, there are $2^{n+71} \times 2^8/2^{32} = 2^{n+47}$ plaintext pairs.

Step 5. Guess $k_{10}^*[2, 3]$. Known $k_{11}[6, 7, 9, 12, 14, 17, 20, 27]$, for the rest 2^{n+47} pairs in the table Ω_2, look up the table T_2 to deduce 2^8 pairs $y_9[2, 3]$. Take 2^{16}

possible values of $k_{10}^*[2,3]$ as indexes to store the pair number in the table Ω_3. For each index, there are $2^{n+47} \times 2^8/2^{16} = 2^{n+39}$ plaintext pairs.

Step 6. Guess $k_1[0,5,10,19]$. Known $(k_{10}^*[2,3], k_{11}[6,7,9,12,14,17,20,27])$, For the rest 2^{n+39} pairs in the table Ω_3, look up the table T_3 to deduce 2^8 keys $k_1[0,5,10,19]$ and the corresponding pairs $(y_1[0,5,10,19], y_1'[0,5,10,19])$. Take 2^{32} possible values of $k_1[0,5,10,19]$ as indexes to store the pair number and the pairs $(y_1[0,5,10,19], y_1'[0,5,10,19])$ in the table Ω_4. For each index, there are $2^{n+39} \times 2^8/2^{32} = 2^{n+15}$ plaintext pairs.

Step 7. Guess $k_1[4,9,14,23]$. For the remaining 2^{n+15} pairs in the table Ω_4, look up the table T_4 to deduce 2^8 keys $k_1[4,9,14,23]$. Take 2^{32} possible values of $k_1[4,9,14,23]$ as indexes to store the pair number and $(y_1[0,4,5,9,10,14,19,23], y_1'[0,4,5,9,10,14,19,23])$ in the table Ω_5. There are $2^{n+15} \times 2^8/2^{32} = 2^{n-9}$ pairs for each index.

Step 8. Guess $k_1[8,13,18,27]$. For the remaining 2^{n-9} pairs in the table Ω_5, look up the table T_5 to deduce 2^8 keys $k_1[8,13,18,27]$. Take 2^{32} possible values of $k_1[8,13,18,27]$ as indexes to store the pair number and $(y_1[0,4,5,8,9,10,13,14,18,19,23,27], y_1'[0,4,5,8,9,10,13,14,18,19,23,27])$ in the table Ω_6. There are $2^{n-9} \times 2^8/2^{32} = 2^{n-33}$ pairs for each index.

Step 9. Guess $k_1[7,16,21,26]$. For the remaining 2^{n-33} pairs in the table Ω_6, look up the table T_6 to deduce 2^8 keys $k_1[7,16,21,26]$. Take 2^{32} possible values of $k_1[7,16,21,26]$ as indexes to store the pair number in the table Ω_7. There are $2^{n-33} \times 2^8/2^{32} = 2^{n-57}$ pairs for each index.

Step 10. For each 208-bit key $(k_1[0,4,5,7,8,9,10,13,14,16,18,19,21,23, 26,27], k_{10}^*[2,3], k_{11}[6,7,9,12,14,17,20,27])$, establish a table T. The table T takes 2^{32} possible $k_2[0,5,10,19]$ as indexes and stores 1 bit for each index. Initialize each address to store 0 and a counter satisfies $flag = 0$. For 2^{n-57} pairs in the table Ω_7, look up the table T_7 to deduce $k_2[0,5,10,19]$. Then look up the table T to find the corresponding address. If the address stores 0, set it 1 and add 1 to the counter $flag$. Otherwise, do nothing. If the counter satisfies $flag=2^{32}$, the key

$$(k_1[0,4,5,7,8,9,10,13,14,16,18,19,21,23,26,27], k_{10}^*[2,3],$$
$$k_{11}[6,7,9,12,14,17,20,27])$$

should be discarded and try another. If the counter satisfies $flag < 2^{32}$ when the plaintext pairs in the table Ω_5 are exhaustively tested, store the key $(k_1[0,4,5,7,8,9,10,13,14,16,18,19,21,23,26,27], k_{10}^*[2,3], k_{11}[6,7,9,12,14,17, 20,27])$ and find the index $k_2[0,5,10,19]$ stores 0.

The differential path is shown in Fig. 3. Black and red bytes mean active and white bytes are inactive. Mesh bytes are the key bytes needed to be guessed. The complexity of this attack is give in the Theorem 2.

Theorem 2. With the usage of a 6-round distinguisher, the impossible differential attack on 10-round Rijndael-224 is proposed with a time complexity of $2^{236.03}$, a data complexity of $2^{214.2}$ and a memory complexity of $2^{194.1}$.

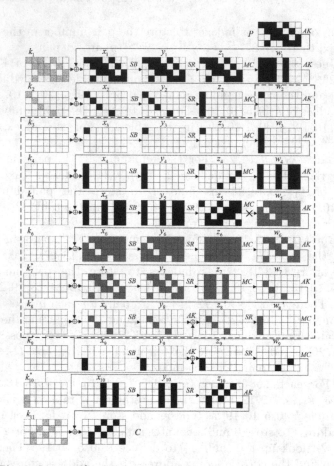

Fig. 3. Impossible differential attack on 10-round Rijndael-224.

Proof. In Step 2, filtering 2^{n+255} plaintext pairs by using the quick sort algorithm needs $2^{n+128}\text{lb}2^{128} = 2^{n+135}$ comparisons. The table Ω stores 2^{n+95} plaintext pairs with a memory complexity of $2^{n+95} \times 2 \times (16+8) \approx 2^{n+100.58}$ bytes.

Step 3 looks up the table T_0 for 2^{n+95} plaintext pairs with a time complexity of $2^{n+95} \times 2^8 = 2^{n+103}$ table-lookups. The table Ω_1 needs to store 8 bytes and the pair number with a memory complexity of $2^{n+71} \times 2^{32} \times (8 + (n + 95)/8)$ bytes.

Step 4 needs to look up the table T_1 with a time complexity of $2^{n+71} \times 2^{32} \times 2^8 = 2^{n+111}$ table-lookups and stores 16 bytes and the pair number with a memory complexity of $2^{n+47} \times 2^{32} \times (16 + (n + 95)/8)$ bytes.

Step 5 needs to look up the table T_2 with a time complexity of $2^{n+47} \times 2^{64} \times 2^8 = 2^{n+119}$ table-lookups and stores the pair number with a memory complexity of $2^{n+39} \times 2^{16} \times (n + 95)/8$ bytes.

Step 6 needs to look up the table T_3 with a time complexity of $2^{n+39} \times 2^{80} \times 2^8 = 2^{n+127}$ table-lookups and stores 8 bytes and the pair number with a memory complexity of $2^{n+15} \times 2^{32} \times (8+(n+95)/8)$ bytes.

Step 7 needs to look up the table T_4 with a time complexity of $2^{n+15} \times 2^8 \times 2^{112} = 2^{n+135}$ table-lookups and stores 16 bytes and the pair number with a memory complexity of $2^{n-9} \times 2^{32} \times (16+(n+95)/8)$ bytes.

Step 8 needs to look up the table T_5 with a time complexity of $2^{n-9} \times 2^8 \times 2^{144} = 2^{n+143}$ table-lookups and stores 24 bytes and the pair number with a memory complexity of $2^{n-33} \times 2^{32} \times (24+(n+95)/8)$ bytes.

Step 9 needs to look up the table T_6 with a time complexity of $2^{n-33} \times 2^8 \times 2^{176} = 2^{n+151}$ table-lookups and stores the pair number with a memory complexity of $2^{n-57} \times 2^{32} \times (n+95)/8$ bytes.

In Step 10, the probability for a wrong key guess ($k_1[0,4,5,7,8,9,10,13,14,$ $16,18,19,21,23,26,27], k_2[0,5,10,19], k_{10}^*[2,3], k_{11}[6,7,9,12,14,17,20,27]$)   to pass a test is $1 - 2^{10}/2^{32} = 1 - 1/2^{22}$. So the probability that 2^{32} keys ($k_1[0,4,$ $5,7,8,9,10,13,14,16,18,19,21,23,26,27], k_2[0,5,10,19], k_{10}^*[2,3], k_{11}[6,7,9,12,$ $14,17,20,27]$) can't pass N tests is $\left[1 - (1 - 2^{-22})^N\right]^{2^{32}}$ which is the probability that one key

$$(k_1[0,4,5,7,8,9,10,13,14,16,18,19,21,23,26,27], k_{10}^*[2,3],$$
$$k_{11}[6,7,9,12,14,17,20,27])$$

can't pass N tests. The probability for ($k_1[0,4,5,7,8,9,10,13,14,16,18,19,21,$ $23,26,27], k_{10}^*[2,3], k_{11}[6,7,9,12,14,17,20,27]$) to pass $2^{22}t$ tests, but not to pass $2^{22}(t+1)$ tests is $p_t = \left[1 - (1 - 2^{-22})^{2^{22}t}\right]^{2^{32}} - \left[1 - (1 - 2^{-22})^{2^{22}(t+1)}\right]^{2^{32}}$. The mathematical expectation is $E(t) = \sum_{t=1}^{\infty} tp_t = \sum_{t=1}^{\infty} t[e^{-2^{32-1.4425(t+1)}} - e^{-2^{32-1.4425t}}] \approx 2^{4.48}$.

With the usage of early abort technique, we need to test $2^{22} \times 2^{4.48} = 2^{26.48}$ plaintext pairs in average to get a candidate. Known the 208-bit key

$$(k_1[0,4,5,7,8,9,10,13,14,16,18,19,21,23,26,27], k_{10}^*[2,3],$$
$$k_{11}[6,7,9,12,14,17,20,27]),$$

look up the table T_7 and T for $2^{26.48}$ plaintext pairs. The time complexity is $2^{208} \times 2^{26.48} \times 2^{10} = 2^{244.48}$ table-lookups and the memory complexity is 2^{32} bits.

The size of candidate set is $\varepsilon = 2^{218} \times (1 - 2^{-22})^{2^{n-57}}$. When we set $n = 86.2$, the time complexity of this attack in mainly determined by Step 8. The time complexity is $2^{244.48}/35 \times 1/10 = 2^{236.03}$ 10-round Rijndael-224 encryptions and the data complexity is $2^{214.2}$ chosen plaintexts. The memory complexity determined by Step 3 is $2^{157.2} \times 2^{32} \times (8 + (86.2+95)/8) = 2^{194.1}$ bytes.

5   Conclusion

In this paper, the security of Rijndael-192 and Rijndael-224 under the impossible differential attack is analyzed. With the usage of time-memory tradeoff technique, the attack is divided into two phases: pre-computation phase and online attack phase. The time complexity of filtering plaintext pairs is reduced by using quick sort algorithm and we can reduce the time complexity of matching the wrong key guesses by using early abort technique. With the usage of these technique, the new impossible differential attacks on Rijndael-192 and Rijndael-224 are proposed. These techniques can also be used to improve the security analysis of Rijndael-160 and Rijndael-256.

References

1. Daemen, J., Rijmen V.: AES proposal: Rijndael [EB/OL] (2011). (2017-05-10). http://csrc.nist.gov/archive/aes/rijndael/Rijndael-ammended.pdf
2. National Institute of Standards and Technology: FIPS-197: Advanced Encryption Standard (AES) [EB/OL], November 2001. (2017-05-10). http://www.nist.org/nist_plugins/content/content.php?content.39
3. Knudsen, L.R.: DEAL - a 128-bit block cipher [EB/OL] (1998). (2017-05-10). http://repo.hackerzvoice.net/depot_madchat/crypto/hash-lib-algo/deal/deal.pdf
4. Biham, E., Bivyukov, A., Shamir, A.: Cryptanalysis of Skipjack reduced 31 rounds using impossible differentials. J. Cryptol. **18**(4), 291–311 (2005)
5. Liu, Y., Gu, D.W., Liu, Z.Q., et al.: New improved impossible differential attack on reduced-round AES-128. In: (Jong Hyuk) Park, J.J., Chao, H.C., Obaidat M.S., Kim, J. (eds.): Computer Science and Convergence, pp. 453–461. Springer, Dordrecht (2016). https://doi.org/10.1007/978-94-007-2792-2_43
6. Mala, H., Dakhilalian, M., Rijmen, V., et al.: Improved impossible differential cryptanalysis of 7-round AES-128. In: INDOCRYPT 2010, Hyderabad, India, pp. 282–291, December 2010
7. Hu, H.J., Jin, C.H., Li, X.R.: Improved impossible differential attack on 7-round AES-128. J. Cryptol. Res. **2**(1), 92–100 (2015)
8. Boura, C., Naya-Plasencia, M., Suder, V.: Scrutinizing and improving impossible differential attacks: applications to CLEFIA, Camellia, LBlock and Simon. In: ASIACRYPT 2014, Kaoshiung, Taiwan, pp. 179–199, December 2014
9. Blondeau, C.: Impossible differential attack on 13-round Camellia-192. Inf. Process. Lett. **115**(9), 660–666 (2015)
10. Akshima, Chang, D., Ghosh, M., et al.: Improved meet-in-the-middle attacks on 7 and 8-round ARIA-192 and ARIA-256. In: INDOCRYPT 2015, Bangalore, India, pp. 198–217, December 2015
11. Wang, N., Wang, X., Jia, K.: Improved impossible differential attack on reduced-round LBlock. In: ICISC 2015, Seoul, Korea, pp. 136–152, November 2015
12. Wen, L., Wang, M., Zhao, J.: Related-key impossible differential attack on reduced-round LBlock. J. Comput. Sci. Technol. **29**(1), 165–176 (2014)
13. Sun, B., Liu, Z., Rijmen, V., et al.: Links among impossible differential, integral and zero correlation linear cryptanalysis. In: CRYPTO 2015, Santo Barbara, CA, USA, pp. 95–115, August 2015
14. Nakahara Jr., J., Pavao, I.C.: Impossible-differential attacks on large-block Rijndael. In: ISC 2007, Valparaso, Chile, pp. 104–117, October 2007

15. Zhang, L., Wu, W.L., Park, J., et al.: Improved impossible differential attacks on large-block Rijndael. In: ISC 2008, Taipei, Taiwan, pp. 298–315, September 2008
16. Wang, Q.J., Gu, D.W., Rijmen, V., et al.: Improved impossible differential attacks on large-block Rijndael. In: ICISC 2012, Seoul, Korea, pp. 126–140, November 2012
17. Minier, M.: Improving impossible-differential attacks against Rijndael-160 and Rijndael-224. Des. Codes Cryptogr. **82**(1), 117–129 (2016)
18. Li, R.J., Jin, C.H.: Meet-in-the-middle attacks on 10-round AES-256. Des. Codes Cryptogr. **80**(3), 459–471 (2016)

Exception Detection of Data Stream Based on Improved Maximal Frequent Itemsets Mining

Saihua Cai[1], Ruizhi Sun[1]([✉]), Chunming Cheng[1], and Gang Wu[2]

[1] College of Information and Electrical Engineering,
China Agricultural University, Beijing, China
{caisaih,sunruizhi}@cau.edu.com, ccm@cau.edu.cn
[2] Secretary of Computer Science Department, Tarim University, Alar, China

Abstract. The security of data stream attracts more attention in daily life, the huge number of data stream makes it impossible to detect its exceptions, and the maximal frequent itemsets (MFIs) can perfectly imply data stream and the number is smaller, therefore, the time cost and memory usage are much more efficient. This paper proposes DMFI to detect the exceptions of data stream, an improved method called MRMFI and a pattern matching method called IM-Sunday and included in DMFI. MRMFI mines the MFIs from data stream and it uses two matrices to store the information, the frequent multiple-itemsets are generated by the extension of frequent 2-itemsets. Then, the exceptions are detected by using IM-Sunday algorithm to match the patterns in MFIs. Some experimental studies are conducted based on proposed method, the results show that the MRFIM method can mine MFIs in less time and DMFI can efficiently detect the exceptions of data stream.

Keywords: Exception detection · Data stream · Maximal frequent itemsets mining · Pattern matching

1 Introduction

With the rapid development of information and network technology, the amount of information is increasing faster than ever in various domains [1], and the speed of data generation has grown in several times. The exceptions are contained in almost all measurement data and they may produce deviation or mislead data processing. In order to detect the exceptions of data better, the abnormal data need to be mined effectively.

Data stream is a form of data that generated in continuous stream [2] and constituted of massive unbounded sequences with a large amount of data elements at a rapid rate, it is generated in many aspects of applications and its amount is huge. Due to the number of maximal frequent itemsets (MFIs) is relatively smaller and they can imply all the frequent itemsets perfectly, in this case, the time cost for mining the MFIs is lower and the memory usage is also

© Springer Nature Singapore Pte Ltd. 2017
M. Xu et al. (Eds.): CTCIS 2017, CCIS 704, pp. 112–125, 2017.
https://doi.org/10.1007/978-981-10-7080-8_10

much smaller, therefore, the problems of frequent itemsets mining can be transformed into the operation of MFIs mining. The frequent itemsets [3,4] mean that their support is not smaller than predefined minimum support (denoted as min_sup), and the support means the ratio of the number of containing itemsets over the total number. Based on this concept, Li et al. [5] presented an algorithm called DSM-MFI to mine the MFIs and used prefix tree structure to store the information of data stream, Fan and Yin proposed the TMFI algorithm [6] that transferred the information of data stream into one matrix first and then stored the frequent itemsets into another matrix for mining MFIs.

The effect of exception detection is to detect the abnormal information, it aims to examine the data with a significant difference between other data in data stream. The traditional exception detection methods can be included in distance-based [7], density-based [8], clustering-based [9] and frequent pattern-based [10] exception detection. Augiulli and Fassetti [11] presented a method for detecting distance-based outliers existing in data stream, they first used stream manager to receive incoming data stream objects and efficiently update a suitable data structure, and then stored all the window objects and returned an approximate answer based on accurate estimations with a statistical guarantee. Wang et al. [12] proposed a novel framework of autonomic intrusion testing over unlabeled traffic streams in computer networks, the framework employed the affinity propagation algorithm to learn a subject's behaviors through dynamical clustering of the data stream, and it automatically labeled the data and adapted to normal behavior changes while identifying anomalies.

The huge number of data stream makes it impossible to store all the data into main memory, and previous algorithms applied to static datasets are not feasible for data stream, in this case, new structures and mining algorithms need to be used to support one-time and continuous mining. Besides that, the drawback of traditional exception detection method is that the amount of training data is very large, which causes the computational cost and the influence on the real-time detection much higher. In this paper, we propose an improved method called MRMFI to mine MFIs over data stream and present a method called DMFI to detect the exceptions of data stream. The main contributions of this paper are summarized as follows:

(1) Mine the maximal frequent itemsets using two matrices to store the information of each item based on redundancy mechanism.
(2) Match the maximal frequent itemsets with the patterns existing in abnormal pattern library and in correct pattern library to detect the exceptions.

The remainder of this paper is organized as follows. The problems description and preliminaries are introduced in Sect. 2. The exception detection framework, maximal frequent itemsets mining and pattern matching methods are presented in Sect. 3. The performance evaluation is discussed in Sect. 4, and the conclusions are stated in Sect. 5.

2   Problems Description and Preliminaries

2.1   Problems Description

The huge nature of data stream makes it impossible to store all the frequent itemsets into main memory or secondary storage because they can easily consume all resources of systems and bring difficulties to the underlying detecting tasks, besides that, the existing exception detection methods are mainly face to intrusion detection and malicious attacks of network.

The DSM-MFI algorithm [5] used the summary frequent itemset forest to store the projection of every sub-projection of affairs, a large memory storage was wasted due to some of these sub-projections were not frequent at all, besides that, more time was wasted because these sub-projections need to be deleted from the forest. In TMFI algorithm [6], the infrequent itemsets existing in the matrix were also conducted in extension operation, of course, more time and memory usage were wasted. In general, the memory storage, time cost and accuracy are the most important problems in the process of mining maximal frequent itemsets.

2.2   Preliminaries

2.2.1   Definitions

Definition 1. *Itemset: let $I = \{i_1, i_2, i_3, \cdots, i_m\}$ be a set of literals called items, and an arbitrary subset of I is an itemset.*

If the connection of itemsets α and β is $\alpha \subseteq \beta$, then α is a sub-itemset of β and β is a super-itemset of α.

Definition 2. *Support: The number of contained itemset x_i in data stream (DS, denoted count(x_i, DS)) is the support number, the frequency of x_i in DS is defined as support, that is to say support = count(x_i, DS)/ $|W|$, $|W|$ is the size of basic window.*

Definition 3. *Frequent itemsets (FIs): The FIs mean the support of each itemset is not less than the predefined min_sup.*

Definition 4. *Maximal frequent itemsets (MFIs): The MFIs mean that each itemset in MFIs is not a subset of any frequent itemsets.*

2.2.2   Redundancy Mechanism

Theorem 1. All nonempty subsets of frequent itemsets are frequent.

Proof. Assume that s is a frequent itemset, of course, support(s) $\geq min\_sup$. s_1 is a nonempty subset of s, it is known from the definition of support that s_1 is contained in the transactions which contain s, therefore, support(s_1) $\geq$ support(s) $\geq min\_sup$ and s_1 is also a frequent itemset.

Theorem 2. The super-itemsets of infrequent itemsets are infrequent.

Proof. Assume that s is an infrequent itemset, s_s is a super-itemset of s and s_s is also a frequent itemset, in this case, s is a subset of s_s and s is a frequent itemset according to Theorem 1, it is contradicted with the assumption.

3   Exception Detection of Data Stream

In this section, we propose a new exception detection method to detect the abnormal data over data stream using the improved maximal frequent itemsets mining method called MRMFI and the pattern matching method called IM-Sunday.

3.1   Exception Detection Framework

To detect exceptions in data stream, a new framework of exception detection method of data stream called DMFI is outlined in Fig. 1.

The DMFI mines the MFIs using improved maximal frequent itemsets mining method firstly, and then the MFIs are matched with the patterns existing in abnormal pattern library and correct pattern library using pattern matching method. The generated MFIs are matched with abnormal pattern library and regard as exceptions if they are fully consistent with the known abnormal patterns in abnormal pattern library, otherwise the current MFIs are matched with correct pattern library. Then the MFIs are trained if they are not matched with the patterns in pattern library or the matching degree is lower than predefined support. The detection result of data stream is generated in the end.

3.2   Mining Recent Maximal Frequent Itemsets

In this section, we propose an improved method called MRMFI to mine MFIs from data stream referring to TMFI [6], which uses two matrices to store the current information of data stream, and the MFIs mining is depending on the extension of frequent itemsets.

MRMFI method adopts matrix A to store the detail information of current data stream, the size of A is $(n+1) * m$, n is the size of sliding window and m is the maximal size of items. Row i stands for transaction T_i and row $(n+1)$ stands

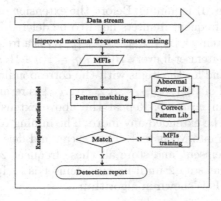

Fig. 1. Exception detection framework

for the total appearing times of items, column j stands for item i_j. Transactions are scanned and added into matrix A in turn if the data is in the sliding window, $A_{d,k}$ is set to 1 if item i_k is appearing in T_d, otherwise $A_{d,k}$ is set to 0. The old items are covered by new ones directly to improve the mining efficiency, the position of the new transaction T_d is determined with the formula $pos = d\%n$, and the information of transaction is recorded in row n if pos is 0. The construction of matrix A is shown in Algorithm 1.

Algorithm 1. Construct Matrix A

Input: Data Stream, n(the size of sliding window $|W|$)
Output: Matrix A
1.if $|W| < n$ **then**
2. **for** $k=1$ to m **do**
3.   **if** i_k in T_d **then**
4. $A_{d,k}=1$
5.   **else**
6. $A_{d,k}=0$
7.   **end if**
8. **end for**
9.**else**
10. $pos=d\%n$ //pos is the position of T_d
11. go to 2
12.**end if**   //Matrix A is constructed

Matrix B records the information of frequent 1-items, the original element of matrix B is 0. The maximal size of matrix B is $(m-1)*(m-1)$, but the real size of matrix B is depending on the number of frequent itemsets. Doing logic and operation for every element of columns p and q in matrix A, and then $B_{p,q}$ is set to 1 if the support of the logic and result is not less than min_sup, otherwise $B_{p,q}$ is 0. The construction of frequent matrix B is listed in algorithm 2.

The main idea of MRMFI method includes two parts, one is the extension of FIs and the other is the MFIs mining. Before the extension of FIs, every itemset is checked and these infrequent itemsets need to be deleted immediately.

In matrix B, if the itemset $\{i_{k,1}, i_{k,2}, \cdots, i_{k,(p-1)}\}$ is a frequent (p-1)-itemset, it can be extended to p-itemset if every $B[ky, kq] = 1(y \in [1, p-1])$. Then, doing the operation of logic and for the items with the corresponding items of row k in matrix A, and the p-FI of $\{i_{k,1}, i_{k,2}, \cdots, i_{k,(p-1)}, i_{k,p}\}$ is retained if the obtained values are not less than min_sup. Repeat the above extension operation until the last item $i_{p,q}$ can't be extended any more. The mining operation of MFIs is that store all the 1-FIs into MFIs first. Then, scan and delete each sub-itemset of all the frequent 2-itemsets, and store all these frequent 2-itemset into MFIs in order. Thirdly, repeat step 2 until no sub-itemset is included in MFIs. The function of mining MFIs is shown in algorithm 3.

Algorithm 2. Construct Matrix B

Input: Matrix A, min_sup

Output: Frequent Matrix B

1.for k=1 to A.column do
2. if $sup(i_k) \geq min\_sup$ then
3.   matrix $B \leftarrow i_k$ //i_k is added to matrix B
4. end if
5.end for
6.for k=1 to m do
7. for s=k+1 to m do
8.   if $sup(i_k, i_s) > m\_sup$ then
9. $B_{k,s}$=1
10. $MFIs \leftarrow \{i_{k+1}, i_{s+1}\}$ //add i_{k+1}, i_{s+1} to MFIs
11.   else
12. $B_{k,s}$=0
13.   end if
14. end for
15.end for   //frequent matrix B is constructed

Algorithm 3. Mine Recent Maximal Frequent Itemsets

Input: Frequent Matrix B

Output: MFIs

1.for k=1 to B.column do
2. find (p-1)-FI of $\{i_{k1}, i_{k2}, \cdots, i_{k(p-1)}\}$
3. if B[ky,kq]= 1 $(y \in [1, p-1])$ then
4.   p-itemset $\leftarrow$ (p-1)-FIs   //extend the (p-1) FIs to p-itemset of $\{i_{k1}, i_{k2}, \cdots, i_{k(p-1)}, i_{kq}\}$
5. end if
6. if $sup(i_{k1}, i_{k2}, \cdots, i_{k(p-1)}, i_{kq}) \geq min\_sup$ then
7.   delete each sub-itemset of p-itemset
8.   MFIs $\leftarrow$ MFI   //add the MFI of $\{i_{k1}, i_{k2}, \cdots, i_{k(p-1)}, i_{kq}\}$ to MFIs
9. end if
10.end for

3.3   Pattern Matching Method

Pattern matching is an important step in exception detection of data stream, and is executed using string-searching algorithms. It takes the patterns in abnormal pattern library and correct pattern library as the main string and takes current MFIs as the pattern string, the main string and pattern string are matched to identify whether or not the exceptions are existing in data stream. Some classic string-searching algorithms were proposed in the past years, the most widely used of these algorithms are KMP algorithm [13,14], BM algorithm [15] and Sunday algorithm [16,17]. The efficiency of Sunday algorithm is much higher than KMP and BM, fortunately, it also can be further improved in some aspects. In this section, we propose an improved string-searching algorithm (called IM-Sunday) based on Sunday algorithm to achieve effective performance.

The core idea of IM-Sunday algorithm is using "least appearance" rule and "good suffix" rule to reduce the matching times, the matching sequence is from right to left. The "least appearance" rule is sorting the character of pattern string based on the frequency of occurrence, and finding the character (denoted as la) which appearing least and in the rightest compared with the same character of pattern string. The "good suffix" rule is that finding the characters (denoted as gs) which are equal to the ones matching successfully in pattern string (T) from right to left, it means that $T[x, x+1, x+2, \cdots, i-1] = T[m-i+x, m-i+x+1, m-i+x+2, \cdots, m-1]$ and $T[x-1] \neq T[m-i+x]$ $(0 < x \leq i < m)$.

The basic ideas of IM-Sunday algorithm are generalized as follows:

(1) Find la according to "least appearance" rule.
(2) Match the character of la with the corresponding character in main string (S), and then match the characters in T if la matched successfully, otherwise move the distance of Sunday algorithm and denoted it as $dis1$.
(3) Find the gs and calculate the distance of gs that is away from $T[m-1]$, and the distance is recorded as $dis2$.
(4) Take the larger distance (record as dis) between $dis1$ and $dis2$ as the moving distance and move T in dis, the dis is set to $dis1$ directly without comparison if la is not matched.
(5) Repeat (2) to (4) until matching successful or failed.

4 Performance Evaluation

In this section, we evaluate the performance of the proposed method through the data sets of $T10.I5.1000K$ and $T30.I10.D1000K$ generated from IBM data generator, $T10.I5.1000K(T10)$ is the sparse data and $T30.I10.D1000K(T30)$ is the dense data. The experiments are implemented on the same machine running Windows 7 with an Intel dual core i3-2020 2.93 GHz processor, and the development environment is Microsoft Visual Studio 2010. The experiments are conducted to test the time cost and memory usage of MRMFI method compared with DSM-MFI and TMFI, and the time cost of IM-Sunday algorithm. Then, some faults are injected into data stream and the effect of DMFI is evaluated.

4.1 Time Cost and Memory Usage of MFIs Mining

Each group of experiments is conducted for 50 times, the average time cost and average memory usage are calculated.

4.1.1 Time Cost and Memory Usage with Different min_sup

The time cost and memory usage for mining MFIs over data stream with different min_sup are shown in Figs. 2 and 3, the size of sliding window is 20 and the number of transaction is $600K$ (K represents thousand), the min_sup ranges from 0.05 to 0.4 in turn.

As can be seen from Fig. 2, the time cost of the three methods shows a decreasing trend with the increasing of min_sup. The time cost of MRMFI method is the lowest due to in the process of mining MFIs, the work of MRMFI is just the logic and operation for the information existed in matrices, which

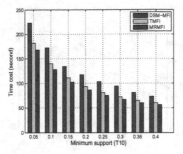
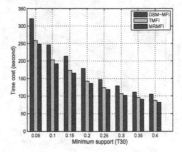

Fig. 2. Time cost with different min_sup

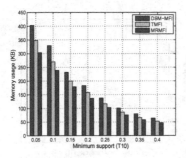
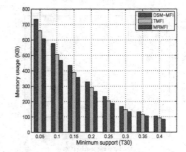

Fig. 3. Memory usage with different min_sup

reduces iteration, sorting and pruning, and these infrequent itemsets are not included in the operation of extension. Time cost of $T30$ is much more than that of $T10$ due to the former is a dense data and the latter is a sparse one.

From Fig. 3, we can see that the memory usage of three methods have reduced with the increasing of min_sup. The memory usage of MRMFI method is less than TMFI and DSM-MFI methods, the reason is that the infrequent itemsets have been deleted in MRMFI method in the beginning, so these infrequent itemsets have not been extended or storage in memory at all.

4.1.2 Time Cost and Memory Usage with Different Number of Transactions

The time cost and memory usage with different number of transactions are shown in Figs. 4 and 5, the size of sliding window is 20 and the min_sup is 0.1, the number of transactions ranges from 200K to 900K.

Figure 4 shows that the time cost of three methods are increasing with the number of transactions increased, the reason is that the frequent itemsets have increased gradually with the rising number of transactions. The time cost of MRMFI method is less than DSM-MFI and TMFI methods, and time cost of $T30$ is much more than that of $T10$.

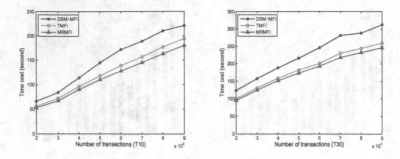

Fig. 4. Time cost with different number of transactions

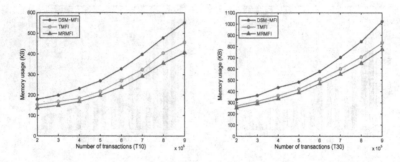

Fig. 5. Memory usage with different number of transactions

It can be seen from Fig. 5 that the memory usage of MRMFI, TMFI and DSM-MFI methods have increased smoothly, and the memory usage of MRMFI method is lower than that of DSM-MFI method in a certain extent.

4.1.3   Time Cost and Memory Usage with Different Size of Sliding Window

The time cost and memory usage for different size of sliding window are shown in Figs. 6 and 7, the min_sup is 0.1 and the number of transactions is 600K, the size of sliding window ranges from 20 to 70.

It can be seen from Fig. 6 that with the increasing size of sliding window, the time cost of $T30$ and $T10$ are also increasing due to the number of frequent itemsets is rising, and the increasing speed of $T30$ is faster than that of $T10$.

Figure 7 shows that the memory usage of $T10$ and $T30$ grows up gradually when the increasing number of sliding window, the reason is that the number of MFIs becomes much larger with the extending size of sliding window. The memory usage of $T10$ is much smaller than $T30$ because it is a sparse data.

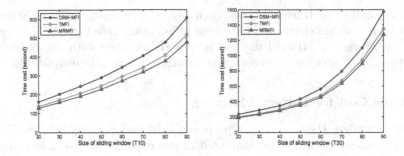

Fig. 6. Time cost with different size of sliding window

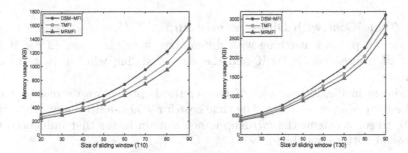

Fig. 7. Memory usage with different size of sliding window

4.2 Accuracy of MRMFI Method

The accuracy rate of MRMFI method is shown in Fig. 8. In the left figure, the number of transactions is 600K and the size of sliding window is 20. In the middle figure, the *min_sup* is 0.1 and the size of sliding window is 20. The *min_sup* is 0.1 and the number of transactions is 600K in the right figure.

We can see from Fig. 8 that the accuracy rate of the mining results is slowly improving with the arising of *min_sup*, it is owing to the number of FIs shows a decreasing trend and the influence of infrequent itemsets disappears gradually.

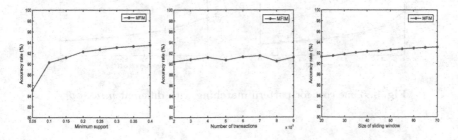

Fig. 8. Accuracy rate of MRMFI method

With the number of transactions is changing, the accuracy rate of MRMFI method is in a stable status and the range of accuracy rate is 90.4% to 91.8%. The accuracy rate of MRMFI method is in a rising trend with the increasing size of the sliding window, in general the accuracy rate is relatively stable.

4.3   Time Cost for Pattern Matching

In order to analyze the time cost of proposed IM-Sunday algorithm, the KMP, BM and Sunday algorithms are compared in the experiment. We take a recent MFI as the pattern string and the MFIs as the main string in the experiment, each group of experiments is repeated for 50 times and the average time cost is calculated.

4.3.1   Time Cost with Different min_sup

Time cost for pattern matching with different min_sup is shown in Fig. 9, the number of transactions is 600K and the size of sliding window is 20 in this experiment.

As shown in Fig. 9, time cost of four methods presents a decreasing trend with the increasing of min_sup. The time cost for $T30$ is a little more than that for $T10$, to some extent, the min_sup is not a main factor that influenced the time cost of pattern matching.

4.3.2   Time Cost with Different Number of Transactions

Time cost for pattern matching with different number of transactions is shown in Fig. 10, the min_sup is 0.1 and the size of sliding window is 20 in this experiment.

From Fig. 10, we can see that time cost of four methods presents an increasing trend with the increasing number of transactions, and the IM-Sunday algorithm is efficiency king of these four methods.

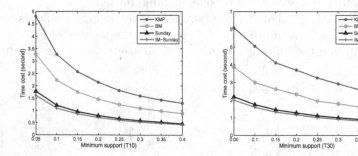

Fig. 9. Time cost for pattern matching with different min_sup

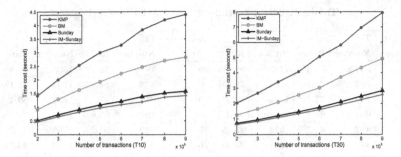

Fig. 10. Time cost for pattern matching with different number of transactions

4.3.3 Time Cost with Different Size of Sliding Window

Time cost for pattern matching with different size of sliding window is shown in Fig. 11, the min_sup is 0.1 and the number of transactions is 600K in this experiment.

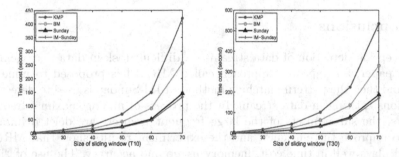

Fig. 11. Time cost for pattern matching with different size of sliding window

We can see from Fig. 11 that the time cost of pattern matching shows the exponential growth with the increasing size of sliding window, the change of sliding window plays core role in time cost. Under the conditions of accuracy allowed, we should choose the small size of sliding window to save the time cost.

4.4 Detection Rate of DMFI Method

We inject 1000 faults into $T10$ and 2000 faults into $T30$ to detect the efficiency of DMFI method, the number of transactions in this test is 600K. Table 1 shows the detection rate of DMFI method with different min_sup and the detection rate with different size of sliding window, and the size of sliding window is set to 20 and the min_sup is set to 0.1 respectively. The number means the detected number of injected faults, the rate means the ratio of the detected faults to the total injected faults.

Table 1. The detection rate of DMFI method

Data sets	T_{10}		T_{30}		Data sets	T_{10}		T_{30}	
min_sup	Number	Rate	Number	Rate	Size	Number	Rate	Number	Rate
0.05	854	85.4%	1772	88.6%	20	797	79.7%	1595	79.8%
0.1	797	79.7%	1595	79.8%	30	844	84.4%	1702	85.1%
0.15	713	71.3%	1406	70.3%	40	871	87.1%	1787	89.4%
0.2	601	60.1%	1187	59.4%	50	898	89.8%	1823	91.2%
0.25	487	48.7%	913	45.7%	60	912	91.2%	1850	92.5%
0.3	372	37.2%	648	32.4%	70	925	92.5%	1862	93.1%
0.35	261	26.1%	430	21.5%	80	934	93.4%	1870	93.5%
0.4	174	17.4%	205	10.3%	90	939	93.9%	1878	93.9%

It can be seen from Table 1 that the number of detected faults shows a decreasing trend with the increasing of min_sup, and the detecting rate is gradually larger with the increasing size of sliding window, the reason is that the number of frequent itemsets is becoming much larger when the size of window is turning bigger.

5   Conclusions

The exception detection of data stream is a difficult task in data management. In this paper, an improved approach called MRMFI is proposed to mine the MFIs and then the pattern matching method of IM-Sunday is used to detect the exceptions existing in data stream. In the process of mining maximal frequent itemsets, the sub-itemsets of the large frequent itemsets are deleted immediately to improve the efficiency, and the experiment results show that MRMFI method plays well in time cost, memory usage and accuracy. The use of "least appearance" rule and "good suffix" rule makes IM-Sunday algorithm much more outstanding in time cost of detecting, which has improved about 9%–10% compared with Sunday algorithm. In general, in small size of sliding window, the detection rate of DMFI method is in a high degree. In the future, the training of data need to be further improved to enhance the accuracy of exception detection.

Acknowledgments. This work was supported by Scientific and technological key projects of Xinjiang Production & Construction Corps (Grant No. 2015AC023).

References

1. Calders, T., Dexters, N., Gillis, J.J.M., et al.: Mining frequent itemsets in a stream. Inf. Syst. **39**, 233–255 (2014)
2. Nori, F., Deypir, M., Sadreddini, M.H.: A sliding window based algorithm for frequent closed itemset mining over data streams. J. Syst. Softw. **86**(3), 615–623 (2013)
3. Deng, Z.H.: DiffNodesets: an efficient structure for fast mining frequent itemsets. Appl. Soft Comput. **41**, 214–223 (2016)

4. Shin, S.J., Lee, D.S., Lee, W.S.: CP-tree: an adaptive synopsis structure for compressing frequent itemsets over online data streams. Inf. Sci. **278**, 559–576 (2014)
5. Li, H.F., Lee, S.Y., Shan, M.K.: Online mining (recently) maximal frequent itemsets over data streams. In: 15th International Workshop on Research Issues in Data Engineering: Stream Data Mining and Applications (RIDE-SDMA 2005), pp. 11–18. IEEE (2005)
6. Fan, G.D., Yin, S.H.: A frequent itemsets mining algorithm based on matrix in sliding window over data streams. In: 3rd International Conference Intelligent System Design and Engineering Applications, pp. 66–69 (2013)
7. Yan, Q.Y., Xia, S.X., Feng, K.W.: Probabilistic distance based abnormal pattern detection in uncertain series data. Knowl.-Based Syst. **36**, 182–190 (2012)
8. Liu, J., Deng, H.F.: Outlier detection on uncertain data based on local information. Knowl.-Based Syst. **51**, 60–71 (2013)
9. Böhm, C., Plant, C., Shao, J., et al.: Clustering by synchronization. In: Proceedings of 16th ACM SIGKDD International Conference on Knowledge Discovery and Data Mining, pp. 583–592. ACM (2010)
10. Kao, L.J., Huang, Y.P.: Association rules based algorithm for identifying outlier transactions in data stream. In: International Conference on Systems, Man, and Cybernetics (SMC), pp. 3209–3214. IEEE (2012)
11. Angiulli, F., Fassetti, F.: Detecting distance-based outliers in streams of data. In: Proceedings of the 16th Conference on Information and Knowledge Management, pp. 811–820. ACM (2007)
12. Wang, W., Guyet, T., Quiniou, R., et al.: Autonomic intrusion detection: adaptively detecting anomalies over unlabeled audit data streams in computer networks. Knowl.-Based Syst. **70**, 103–117 (2014)
13. Knuth, D.E., Morris, J.H., Pratt, V.R.: Fast pattern matching in strings. SIAM J. Comput. **6**(2), 323–350 (1977)
14. Cho, S., Na, J.C., Park, K., et al.: A fast algorithm for order-preserving pattern matching. Inf. Process. Lett. **115**(2), 397–402 (2015)
15. Boyer, R.S., Moore, J.S.: A fast string searching algorithm. Commun. ACM **20**(10), 762–772 (1977)
16. Sunday, D.M.: A very fast substring search algorithm. Commun. ACM **33**(8), 132–142 (1990)
17. Chen, J.F., Cai, S.H., Zhu, L.L., et al.: An improved string-searching algorithm and its application in component security testing. Tsinghua Sci. Technol. **21**(3), 281–294 (2016)

A Dictionary Sequence Model to Analyze the Security of Protocol Implementations at the Source Code Level

Fu-Sheng Wu[1,2] and Huan-Guo Zhang[1,2(✉)]

[1] Computer School, Wuhan University, Wuhan 430072, China
liss@whu.edu.cn
[2] Key Laboratory of Aerospace Information Security and Trusted Computing
of Ministry of Education, Wuhan University, Wuhan 430072, China

Abstract. It is one of most important parts in the field of information security to set up models for the security analysis of cryptographic protocols, especially for the security analysis of cryptographic protocol implementations at the source code level. On the base of the dictionary sequence, a model is set up in this paper, aimed at the security analysis of cryptographic protocol implementations at the source code level. It is a new way to evaluate whether protocols are secure or not through the change of the sequences of function returning values in the process of the implementation at the source code level. Based on the new model, an experiment is carried out. It is shown in the experiment that our new model has advantage over previous models. Our new model will be helpful for designing and evaluating cryptographic protocol implementations at the source code level.

Keywords: Cryptographic protocol · Code · Model · Security analysis

1 Introduction

The cryptographic protocol security analysis model is a significant part of information security researches [1] as well as the important evaluating reference when analyzing the security of a cryptographic protocol. For example, Dolev-Yao model is always used to evaluate whether a cryptographic protocol is secure or not. Based on Dolev-Yao model, many methods have been proposed and used [2, 3], such as formal approach, computing method, computational soundness formal and so on. At the same time, two representative tools automatically analyzing cryptographic protocols have been developed: ProVerif [4] and CryptoVerif [5]. There have been fruitful achievements [6, 7] in the field of cryptographic protocol security analysis by using these methods or these tools. However, there are many problems in them and they can't guarantee the security analysis of cryptographic protocol implementations at the source code level. There are several reasons for that: (1) any well-designed cryptographic protocol has to be transferred into codes

This work is supported by the State Key Program of National Natural Science of China (No. 61332019), and the National Basic Research Program (973 Program) of China (No. 2014CB340601).

© Springer Nature Singapore Pte Ltd. 2017
M. Xu et al. (Eds.): CTCIS 2017, CCIS 704, pp. 126–142, 2017.
https://doi.org/10.1007/978-981-10-7080-8_11

to be implemented so as to reach its aim. (2) some cryptographic protocols can't be securely implemented at the source code level due to imperfect designing language structures (such as the pointer operation of C language, incomplete semantic structure, etc.). (3) although some cryptographic protocols are theoretically proved to be secure, some insecure factors will still arise during the process of implementation at the source code level (such as memory leak, malicious codes, etc.), which will inevitably lead to a gap between the security analysis on theory level and that at the source code level [8, 9]. Therefore, it is worth focusing on the model of cryptographic protocol implementations security analysis. And there are rich achievements in this field [10, 11].

Now two representative models are used to analyze the security of cryptographic protocol implementations: model extraction and code generation. In literature [12], the security analysis of Needham-Schroeder protocol (NS protocol for short) written in C has been proposed. On the base of Horn clause logic, it uses assertion method and sets up a model, on which an adversary has Dolev-Yao capacity, to analyze the security of cryptographic protocol implementations. But this method does not provide authentication function. Basing on this, searchers have proposed some methods. Literature [13] has proposed a general method to verify protocols written in C. In literature [14], based on computational semantic security a method has been proposed to verify the logic security of a protocol. In literature [15], a method has been proposed to automatically analyzing the security of cryptographic protocols on the base of logic event authentication. Compared with traditional ways, the methods mentioned above take the security of protocol implementations into account, but they still analyze the security of cryptographic protocols on the theory level, so they can't guarantee the security of cryptographic protocol implementations at the source code level. In order to solve this problem, some improved approaches have been proposed in [16–18].

Function returning values are both the key to implement program languages at the source code level and the direct display of the behaviors when implementing programs. In order to solve the problem that the previous methods can't guarantee the security analysis of cryptographic protocol implementations at the source code level, the traditional way of dictionary matching query and function returning value sequences are exploited to set up a model to analyze the security of cryptographic protocol implementations at the source code level. That is, the dictionary sequence of function returning values is used as the security evaluating reference when analyzing the security of a cryptographic protocol. This method is called the dictionary sequence model. Here are the specific steps: execute *XOR* operation on function returning value sequences and dictionary sequences and find the insecure factors in the process of the cryptographic protocol implementation at the source code level, such as the incapability of generating shared key, the failure of encryption and decryption, memory overflow attacks and so on.

Our original contributions:

(1) Proposing a simple model for the security analysis of cryptographic protocol implementations at the source code level.
(2) On the base of the dictionary matching query way, analyzing the security of cryptographic protocol implementations at the source code level.

On the base of the methods mentioned in the literatures, the dictionary sequence model is proposed in this paper to analyze the security of cryptographic protocol implementations at the source code level. Our scheme will provide valuable help for designing and evaluating cryptographic protocols.

2   Related Work

It is a new research direction to analyze the security of cryptographic protocol implementations at the source code level. At first, mature model checking techniques were exploited to analyze the security of cryptographic protocols. Literature [12] first proposed to analyze the security of cryptographic protocol (written in C) implementations. After that, researchers focused on the security analysis of cryptographic protocol implementations at the source code level [11], such as the analysis security of cryptographic protocols written in C [17], Java [20] and F# [21], etc.

Among the researches on the security analysis of cryptographic protocol (written in C) implementations at the source code level, literature [17] first proposed a evaluating method to automatically analyze the security of cryptographic protocols by exploiting the framework ASPIER with the model checking technique and SSMs mechanism, and gave an example for analyzing the security of cryptographic protocols on the base of OpenSSL. In order to avoid pointer operation of C, memory leaks and so on. Literature [8, 17] applied Intermediate model language like C to the security analysis of cryptographic protocols with tools Proverif and CryptoVerif. Recently, researchers have had new achievements. In literature [14], computational semantics has been used to analyze the security of a cryptographic protocol's logic, and authentication checking has been applied into the program abstract model in the logic analysis, and items have been used to prove the security of a protocol. On the base of logic event analysis, literature [15] has proposed a method to automatically analyze the security of cryptographic protocols, but this method can be only applied to symbolic logic reasoning. In literature [22], a new model has been proposed to analyze the security of protocols by using information flow (that is reading and writing flowing model, RWFM for short). Till now, many methods and models have been proposed and used to analyze the security of cryptographic protocols, but there is still a great gap between the security analysis of the cryptographic protocols on the theory level and the security analysis of cryptographic protocol implementations at the source code level. Therefore, more should be done on this field.

3   Preliminaries

For better understanding the model proposed in this paper to analyze the security of cryptographic protocol implementations at the source code level, it is required to have a basic knowledge of the operational semantics of labelled transition system and the formal of cryptographic protocol implementations.

3.1 Labelled Transition System

In line with the automata theory, a labelled transition system is a transferring model composed of start point, input label and terminal point. Different from automata, a labelled transition system has no fixed start states and accepting states so that any state can act as a start state in a labelled transition system. Therefore, running a program is a labelled transition system, for cryptographic protocols are implemented on the base of automata theory.

Definition 1 (Labelled transition system [19] (LTS for short)). A labelled transition system over Act is a pair (Q, T) consisting of

(1) a set of states Q
(2) a ternary relation T, known as a transition relation, $T \subseteq (Q \times Act \times Q)$.

If $(q, \alpha, q') \in T$, we write $q \xrightarrow{\alpha} q'$, and we call q the source and q' the target of the transition. If $q \xrightarrow{\alpha_1} q_1 \xrightarrow{\alpha_2} \ldots \xrightarrow{\alpha_n} q_n$, we call q_n a derivate of q under $\alpha_1 \alpha_2 \ldots \alpha_n$. According to definition 1 (LTS), we write the definition of the labelled transition system of a protocol implementation at the source code level as follow (Definition 2).

Definition 2 (The LTS of a cryptographic protocol implementation). Let p be a cryptographic protocol, and when implementing p, its labelled transition system is a 4-tuple $(S, F, \rightarrow, P)$:

(1) S is the state set of running
(2) F is concrete functions related to protocol in the process of the cryptographic protocol P implementation at the source code level, such as sending massage functions $send()$, receiving massage functions $recv()$ and encrypting and decrypting functions of openSSL.

3.2 The Operational Semantics of Cryptographic Protocol Implementations

According to the LTS of cryptographic protocol implementations, we define the operational semantics of cryptographic protocol implementations as follow:

Definition 3 (The state of a cryptographic protocol implementation). $S = P(RunTerm) \times P(Run).P(RunTerm)$ represents the items of the cryptographic protocol, and $P(Run)$ represents running the codes of the cryptographic protocol.

Definition 4 (The functions of the cryptographic protocol implementation at source code level). $F = P(RunFunc) \times P(Run) \times ReturnValue.P(RunFunc)$ represents the functions related to the cryptographic protocol implementation; $ReturnValue$ represents the function returning values.

To analyze the security of cryptographic protocol implementations at the source code level, it is necessary to define the rules of operational semantics. The model proposed

in this paper to analyze the security of cryptographic protocols is based on function returning value sequences, so the rules of operational semantics are defined as follow:
(R_1):

$$send: \frac{P(Run), v_s \in ReturnValue, v_s = true| - v_{s1} \prec_R v_{s2} \prec_R, \ldots, \prec_R v_{sn}}{send_{success}}$$

(R_2):

$$recv: \frac{P(Run), v_r \in ReturnValue, v_r = true| - v_{r1} \prec_R v_{r2} \prec_R, \ldots, \prec_R v_{rn}}{recv_{success}}$$

(R_3):

$$P_{excute}: \frac{P(Run), send_{success}, recv_{success}}{P_{secure}}$$

There, the symbol $\prec_R$ represents a strict partial order relation of the functions ($send()$) and the functions ($recv()$) during the process of cryptographic protocol implementations at the source code level. Because $\prec_R$ satisfies the conditions for irreflexivity, asymmetry and transitivity, it is a strict partial order relation over $RetruValue \times RetruValue.| -$ denotes the capacity of deducing. For example, $M| - N$ means that N can be deduced from M.

3.3 Cryptographic Protocol Specification

For clearly presenting the concrete process of the cryptographic protocol implementation at the source code level, the specification of the cryptographic protocol implementation at the source code level is defined in the form of BNF. Let P be a cryptographic protocol. A complete cryptographic protocol consists of many components, such as the participants of the protocol, calling function of the implementation at the source code level, etc. Here is the BNF form of the cryptographic protocol:

$P:: = Role|RunEevent|ReturnValue$

$Role:: = send|recv$

$RunEevent: = function|other\_sentence$

$Function: = encryption\_func|$

$dencryption\_func|rand\_func| \ldots$

$ReturnValue: = true|false$

According to the BNF form, the specification of a cryptographic protocol implementation consists of two parts: the behavior process and the function returning values of the cryptographic protocol implementation at the source code level. Function returning values directly display the execution of the program codes. Hence, the sequences composed of function returning values directly display the cryptographic protocol implementation at the source code level.

4   Establishment of the New Model

The new model is established to analyze the security of cryptographic protocol implementations based on the inherent function returning values of program languages as well as the function returning values and the operational semantics of cryptographic protocol implementations at the source code level. It is different from the traditional ways of analyzing the security of cryptographic protocols and other analysis models mentioned in the literatures.

4.1   The Function Returning Value Dictionary

Most program languages have calling functions in the process of implementations at the source code level, like C language, Java language and Python language etc., and each calling function has a function returning value. Hence, if a cryptographic protocol is written in different program languages, it will get different function returning values correspondingly.

Definition 5 (The function returning value dictionary(FRVD)). When implementing a cryptographic protocol at source code level, the inherent function returning values(Inherent function returning value: function returning value conventionalized by a program language structure. For example, function strcmp() of C language returns 0, a positive integer and a negative integer so that 0, the positive integer and the negative integer are its inherent function returning values) of the calling functions form a set, called the function returning value dictionary, denoted by D. Then there exists: $D = \{v^* | v \in ReturnValue\}$.

Definition 6 (The dictionary sequence of function returning values). If the inherent function returning value set $\{v_1, v_2, \ldots, v_i\}, i \in N$ satisfies:

(1) $\{v_1, v_2, \ldots, v_i\} \in D, i \in N$,
(2) $v_1 \prec_R v_2 \prec_R, \ldots, \prec_R v_i, i \in N$, and satisfies strict partial order relation, then $\{v_1, v_2, \ldots, v_i\}, i \in N$ is called the dictionary sequence of function returning values.

4.2   The Function Returning Value Sequence

When program languages are executed at the source code level, functions will be called to execute an event. Every called function will produce a function returning value. Similarly, in the process of a cryptographic protocol implementation at the source code level, functions are called, and their returning values consist of a sequence, called function returning value sequence.

Definition 7 (The item of cryptographic protocol implementations). A single function returning value of a cryptographic protocol implementation at the source code level is called an item, such as the returning value of the function RSA_new() and the returning value of the function BN_new() in the OpenSSL cryptographic library.

Definition 8 (The event node of cryptographic protocol implementations). When sending and receiving massages interactively in the process of cryptographic protocol implementations at the source code level, the function *send*() and the function *recv*() are called running event nodes. Here v_s denotes sending event nodes and v_r denotes receiving event nodes. Generally, there exist two or more sending nodes and receiving nodes in the process of a cryptographic protocol implementation, denoted by v_{si} and v_{ri} respectively. Here $i \in N$.

Definition 9 (The sequence of related to event nodes). Before finishing an event node, the events related to it have to be finished. These related to events consist of a sequence, called the sequence of related to event nodes.

According to Definitions 7, 8, and 9, there exists the sequence of a cryptographic protocol implementation at the source code level when sending or receiving massages, represented as:

(1) The sequence of sending nodes is $\{< v_1, v_2, \ldots, v_i >, v_{si}\}$, and $i \in N$ $v_i \in ReturnValue$.

(2) The sequence of receiving nodes is $\{< v_1, v_2, \ldots, v_j >, v_{rj}\}$, and $j \in N$ $v_j \in ReturnValue$.

(3) The sequence of the cryptographic protocol implementation is $tr = \{v_1, v_2, \ldots, v_j v_{si}, v_1, v_2, \ldots, v_j v_{ri}, \ldots \ | v \in ReturnValue\}$, and $i, j \in N$. Here v_{si} denotes the function returning values of sending function nodes, and v_{ri} denotes the function returning values of receiving function nodes.

4.3   The Security Analysis of Cryptographic Protocol Implementations at the Source Code Level

Grammars and semantic structures of program languages are different. When executing calling functions, different program languages have different returning values. When calling functions, there are two cases: successfully executing calling functions or failing to execute calling functions. For clearly presenting the sequences of function returning values of cryptographic protocol implementations at the source code level, two kinds of functions returning values are discussed respectively.

(1) The inherent returning value of a function is 1 or 0, and it won't be changed in the process of execution.

(2) When the inherent returning value of a function is not 1 or 0 but success or failure, it will be transferred into 1 or 0 respectively through mathematical method. Here is the definition:

$$\sigma(v) = \begin{cases} 1 & v\text{: } \textit{The function is called successfully} \\ & \textit{and the returning value is not } 1 \\ 0 & v\text{: } \textit{The function is called unsuccessfully} \\ & \textit{and the returning value is not } 0 \end{cases} \tag{1}$$

According to the definition of $\sigma(v)$, we can transfer $D = \{v^* | v \in ReturnValue\}$ into the dictionary of function returning values with the binary form: $D = \{0, 1\}^*$. When analyzing the security of cryptographic protocol implementations at the source code level, there are 5 steps:

(1) Acquire the sequence of function returning values in the process of cryptographic protocol implementations at the source code level. According to Definition 9, the sequence of the cryptographic protocol implementations at the source code level is
$\{v_1, v_2, \ldots, v_j v_{si}, v_1, v_2, \ldots, v_j v_{ri}, \ldots | v \in ReturnValue, i, j \in N\}$.

(2) The binary sequence of the cryptographic protocol implementations will be obtained by transferring the function $\sigma(v)$ and let it be $\{v_{b1}, v_{b2}, \ldots, v_{bj} v_{bsi}, v_{b1}, v_{b2}, \ldots, v_{bj} v_{bri}, \ldots | v_b \in \{0, 1\}, i, j \in N\}$.

(3) Similarly a binary sequence of the dictionary D can be obtained by transferring the function $\sigma(v)$, and let it be $\{v_{db1}, v_{db2}, \ldots, v_{dbj} v_{dbsi}, v_{db1}, v_{db2}, \ldots, v_{dbj} v_{dbri}, \ldots | v_{db} \in \{0, 1\}, i, j \in N\}$ and satisfy a strict partial order relation.

(4) Judge whether the binary sequence of (2) satisfies a strict partial order relation or not (that is, it is satisfies:
$\{v_{b1} \prec_R v_{b2} \prec_R \cdots \prec_R v_{bj} \prec_R v_{bsi} \prec_R v_{b1} \prec_R v_{b2} \prec_R \cdots \prec_R v_{bj} \prec_R v_{bri} \prec_R \cdots\}$). If the binary sequence satisfies that, execute 5. If the binary sequence does not satisfy that, it indicates that the cryptographic protocol implementation at the source code level does not abide by the specifications, so the cryptographic protocol is not secure. That is, the sent message mismatches the received massage.

(5) Execute the *XOR* operation on the binary sequences of (2) and (3) respectively, or $\overline{V}_b \oplus \overline{V}_{db}$. If $\overline{V}_b \oplus \overline{V}_{db} \neq \overline{0}$, it indicates that there are insecure factors in the process of the cryptographic protocol implementation at the source code level, like memory leaks, abnormal interruptions and so on. Here $\overline{V}$ denotes vectors; $\overline{0}$ denotes null vectors.

In the process of executing the codes of a program language, function returning values directly display the execution of the program at the source code level. Cryptographic protocols are written in program languages. The sequence of function returning values of cryptographic protocol implementations at the source code level directly displays the specifications of cryptographic protocols' interactive communication. Therefore, the result of the *XOR* operation on the function returning value sequence reflects the flaws of cryptographic protocol implementations at the source code level, such as the incapability to generate the share key, the failure of encryption and decryption, memory overflow attacks and so on.

5   Implementation and Experiment

It is a requirement of cryptographic protocol communications that at least two participants take part in an interactive communication in accordance with certain specifications. A symbolic flow graph is used to represent the process of the cryptographic
protocol implementation at the source code level. Generally, an ITU-standardized
protocol specification language (ITU: International Telecommunication Union [23]) is
used to express Massage Sequence Charts (MSC) of protocol interactive communications (in this paper, the specifications of cryptographic protocols are expressed by the
ways from ITU and the literature [24]). Classical NS protocol has been theoretically
proved to be insecure. So we take Needham-Schroeder-Lowe protocol (NSL for short)
for example, which is the improvement of NS protocol and has been theoretically proved
to be secure (It can resist man-in-the-middle attacks), and analyze the security of the
NSL protocol implementation at the source code level through our new model. The
symbolic description of NSL protocol is shown in Fig. 1.

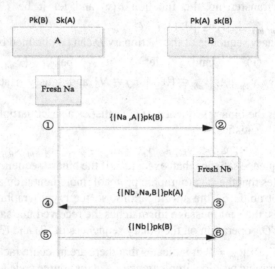

Fig. 1.   The symbolic description of the NSL protocol

Here A and B denote two participants of the protocol; pk(A) and pk(B) denote the
public keys of the protocol participants; sk(A) and sk(B) denote the private keys of the
protocol participants; Na and Nb respectively denote the temporary values of A and B;
$\{|Na, Al\}_{pk(B)}$ denotes encrypting massage {Na, A} with the public key B. The numbers
(①, ②, ③, ④, ⑤ and ⑥) in Fig. 2 respectively denote the event nodes of the protocol
implementation at the source code level.

A

① send1(A,B,+{Na,A}pk(B))

④ recv2(B,A,-{Na,Nb,B}pk(A))

⑤ send3(A,B,+{Nb}pk(B))

B

② recv1(A,B,-{Na,A}pk(B))

③ send2(B,A,+{Na,Nb,B}pk(A))

⑥ recv3(A,B,-{Nb}pk(B))

Fig. 2. The specification of the NSL protocol implementation

5.1 Symbolic Specifications of the NSL Protocol Implementation

The conception of strand spaces is exploited to denote the concrete specifications of the NSL protocol implementation at the source code level. According to strand spaces, + denotes sending events, and − denotes receiving events. According to Fig. 2 and the conception of strand spaces, the symbolic specification of the NSL protocol implementation at the source code level is obtained, shown in Fig. 2.

The illustration of the specification: ① send1(A, B, + {Na, A}$_{pk(B)}$) denotes that the event nodes of A send massage {Na, A}$_{pk(B)}$ to B. ② recv1 (A, B, −{Na, A}$_{pk(B)}$) denotes that the event nodes of B receive massage {Na, A}$_{pk(B)}$ from A. Other expressions are used in the same way.

5.2 Part of the Source Codes (Written in C) of the NSL Protocol

As is shown in Fig. 2, a series of events must be finished before triggering every event node. That is to say, calling functions must be executed. For example, before event node send1, these must be finished: ① generating the random numbers of A; ② encrypting data {Na, A} with public key of B; ③ sending data {N$_a$, A}$_{pk(B)}$ to event node send1. Main function source codes of NSL protocol implemented at the source code level are displayed in Fig. 3.

```
A
//Generated a random number:Na
1BN_new();
2BN_pseudo_rand();
3BN_bn2dec();
4strcpy();
//The public key pk(B) encrypts the data:{Na,A}pk(B)
5BN_new();
6BN_new();
7BN_dec2bn();
8BN_dec2bn();
9RSA_new();
10RSA_size();
11RSA_public_encrypt();
//The private key sk(A) decrypts the data:{Na,Nb,B}pk(A)
25RSA_size();
26RSA_private_decrypt();
//The public key pk(B)encrypts the data:{Nb}pk(B)
27BN_new();
28BN_new();
29BN_dec2bn();
30BN_dec2bn();
31RSA_new();
32RSA_size();
33RSA_public_encrypt();
//Data process
34memcpy();
35strcpy();
//①The event node(send1()) sends a message:+{Na,A}pk(B)
36send();
//④The event node(recv2())receives a message:-{Na,Nb,B}pk(A)
37recv();
//Data process
38memcpy();
39memcpy();
//⑤The event node(send3())sends a message:+{Nb}pk(B)
40send();
```

```
B
//The private key sk(B) decrypt the data:{Na,A}pk(B)
12RSA_size();
13RSA_private_decrypt();
//Generated a random number:Nb
14BN_new();
15BN_pseudo_rand();
16BN_bn2dec();
17strcpy();
//The public key pk(A) encrypts the data:{Na,Nb,B}pk(A)
18BN_new();
19BN_new();
20BN_dec2bn();
21BN_dec2bn();
22RSA_new();
23RSA_size();
24RSA_public_encrypt();
//The private key sk(B)decrypt the data:{Nb}pk(B)
41RSA_size();
42RSA_private_decrypt();
//②The event node(recv1())receives a message:-{Na,A}pk(B)
43recv();
//Data process
44memcpy();
45memcpy();
46strcpy();
//③The event node(send2())sends a message:+{Na,Nb,B}pk(A)
47send();
//⑥The event node(recv3())receives a message:-{Nb}pk(B)
48recv();
//Data process
49memcpy();
```

Fig. 3. Main function source codes of the NSL protocol implementation

As is shown in Fig. 3, the functions related to the NSL protocol implementation are displayed and their function returning values are exploited to analyze the security of the cryptographic protocol implementation at the source code level.

5.3   The Security Analysis of the NSL Protocol Implementation

Classic NSL protocol, written in C, is taken as an example in this paper. The running environment of the protocol is: Win7, Visual studio 2010, Intel(R) CPU G3240, memory 4 GB, openssl-1.0.1s. The functions and the big number in the OpenSSL cryptographic library are used to the cryptographic protocol implementations at the source code level. The mechanism of the RSA public key is exploited to encrypt and decrypt the data of the protocol. By linking TCP based on Socket API, participants take part in the inter-active communication. A simulate experiment is carried out in the pattern of Client/Server.

(1) Acquiring the function returning value dictionary

According to Definitions 5 and 6, the function returning values of the NSL protocol implementation are acquired from the function returning value dictionary, shown in Table 1. The binary returning values of the NSL protocol implementation are acquired by transferring function $\sigma(v)$, shown in Table 2.

Table 1. The function returning values of the NSL protocol implementation

Called function	Successfully calling	Unsuccessfully calling
BN_new()	Returning new structure pointer values	Returning NULL or error codes
BN_pseudo_rand()	1	0
BN_bn2dec()	Returning a character string ending with null	NULL
BN_dec2bn();	Returning number length	0
RSA_new();	Returning new structure pointer values	Returning NULL or error codes
RSA_size();	Returning byte number	0
send()	Returning sending data length	Returning SOCKET_ERROR
recv()	Returning receiving data length	SOCKET_ERROR Link ends and returns 0, or SOCKET_ERROR
strcpy()	Returning destination address	NULL
memcpy()	Returning destination address	NULL
RSA_public_encrypt()	Returning signature size	−1
RSA_private_decrypt()	Returning abstract size	−1

Table 2. The binary returning values of each function of the NSL protocol implementation

Called function	Successfully calling	Unsuccessfully calling
BN_new()	1	0
BN_pseudo_rand()	1	0
BN_bn2dec()	1	0
BN_dec2bn();	1	0
RSA_new();	1	0
RSA_size();	1	0
send()	1	0
recv()	1	0
strcpy()	1	0
memcpy()	1	0
RSA_public_encrypt()	1	0
RSA_private_decrypt()	1	0

As is shown in Table 2 and by the process of the NSL protocol implementation at the source code level in Sect. 5.2, the dictionary sequence of function returning values of the NSL protocol implementation at the source code level is:

$$D = \{\underbrace{1, \ldots, 1}_{49}\} \tag{2}$$

(2) Acquiring the function returning values sequences of the NSL protocol implementation at the source code level. In the given experiment environment, NSL protocol is implemented at the source code level. Function returning values are obtained and consist of sequences, written as $SG_i (i \in N)$, shown in Table 3.

Table 3. The function returning value sequences of the NSL protocol implementation

Types of implementations	Function returning value sequences of the NSL implementation
SG_1	1111111111111111111111111111111111111111111111111
SG_2	1111111111111111111111111111011100100000000000000000
SG_3	1111111111011111111111111101111110101111111111111100
SG_4	1111111111111111111111001111111111111111111011100100

(3) The *XOR* operation of function returning value sequences

Let function returning value sequences of the NSL protocol implementation at the source code level at each situation be $\overline{V}_1, \overline{V}_2, \overline{V}_3$ and $\overline{V}_4$. It is known that the dictionary sequence of function returning values is $D = \{1, \ldots, 1\}$. According to Sect. 3.3, each result

$$\underbrace{\{1, \ldots, 1\}}_{49}$$

sequence is obtained after calculating $\overline{V}_b \oplus \overline{V}_{db}$, called the calculated sequence, written as $CSG_i (i \in N)$. shown in Table 4.

Table 4. The $\overline{V}_b \oplus \overline{V}_{db}$ values

Types of implementations	$\overline{V}_b \oplus \overline{V}_{db}$	$\overline{V}_b \oplus \overline{V}_{db} = \overline{0}$
CSG_1	0000000000000000000000000000000000000000000000000	Yes
CSG_2	0000000000000000000000000000100011011111111111111111	No
CSG_3	0000000000100000000000000001000000010000000000000011	No
CSG_4	0000000000000000000000000110000000000000000100011011	No

After analyzing the *XOR* operation sequences in Table 4, it can be found that these 4 types of sequences correspond to 4 cases (including attacking cases) of the NSL protocol implementation at the source code level: ① the participants of the protocol generating the share key; ② interrupting buffer overflow (buffer overflow attacks) and failing to run the protocol; ③ failing to encrypt and decrypt; ④ mismatching between the sending messages and the receiving messages (failing to satisfy the operational semantic rules). Therefore, it can be concluded after the security analysis:

(1) If the result vector is zero, NSL protocol is successfully implemented at the source code level. Otherwise, there are flaws or attacks when implementing NSL protocol at the source code level.

(2) It can be found by analyzing the result of *XOR* operation that the cryptographic protocol implementation at the source code level is interrupted due to memory overflow. That is, the execution of the protocol fails.

(3) The error nodes of the NSL protocol implementation at the source code level can be quickly found from the result of the operation. For example, from the result of the operation of ③ in Table 4, it can be quickly found in Fig. 3 that failing to generate share keys is due to 11.RSA_public_encrypt(), 26. RSA_private_decrypt() going wrong. The reason is that functions are wrongly padded. Other errors can be quickly found like this.

(4) From the result of the *XOR* operation of ① in Table 4 and the rules of the operational semantics R1, R2 and R3 of the cryptographic protocol implementation, it can be concluded that when implementing the cryptographic protocol, the strict order relation $\prec_R$ of send() and recv() when sending and receiving messages can not satisfy partial order relation. Hence, the cryptographic protocol fails to encrypt and decrypt. When implemented at the source code level.

It is shown by the analysis of the experiment that the new model proposed in this paper can quickly check out the error nodes and find the flaws or the attacks in the process of the cryptographic protocol implementations at the source code level. At the same time, taking NSL protocol as an example, our experiment has proved that though a protocol has theoretically proved to be secure, its implementation may be insecure. Of course, there are many factors that may influence the security of protocol implementations due to the complex running environments, which can't be discussed here owing to the limited length of the paper.

5.4 Comparing the New Model and the Previous Models

Different from other analysis models mentioned in the literatures, our model is aimed to analyze the security of cryptographic protocol implementations at the source code level. Table 5 shows the comparison between our model and the previous models from Table 5 aspects (authentication, attacks, model language and so on). ✓ denotes that the security analysis of this item can be achieved in the process of cryptographic protocol implementation at the source code level. ✗ denotes that the security analysis of this item can't be achieved.

Table 5. The comparison between common models

Type method	Authentication	Model kind	Model language	Dynamic analysis	Buffer overflow	Protocol evaluation
Model extraction	✓	Symbolic/Computation	✓	✗	✗	✗
Code generation	✓	Symbolic/Computation	✓	✗	✗	✗
Our scheme	✓	Source code level	✗	✓	✓	✓

As is shown in Table 5, the analysis methods based on model extraction and code generation only provide theoretical security analysis of cryptographic protocols. Although sometimes they are involved in codes, the security analysis of cryptographic protocols relies on symbolic models or computing models, and they are not aimed at the security analysis of cryptographic protocol implementations at the source code level. In that case, it can't guarantee the security of protocol implementations at the source code. Our model, the sequence dictionary method, is established to analyze the security of cryptographic protocol implementations at the source code level and it doesn't use abstract model language and symbolic models as well as computing models. Based on the implementation at the source code level, our method can discover memory overflow attacks in the process of cryptographic protocol implementations, and can dynamically analyze the security of cryptographic protocol implementations. This can't be achieved by the previous extract models or code generations. Therefore, our model guarantees the security of cryptographic protocol implementations at the source code level.

Our new model is established on the base of the labelled transition system of automata theory so it satisfies the security analysis of cryptographic protocol implementation in different kinds of program language environments. The function returning value dictionary and the conception of the dictionary sequence of function returning values are proposed and can be exploited to analyze the security of cryptographic protocol implementations at the source code level, which are written in the program languages with function returning values (like C, C++, Java and F#, etc.).

6   Conclusion and Future Work

Based on program languages, a new model is established and an experiment is carried out in this paper to analyze the security of cryptographic protocol implementations at the source code level. As is described in Sect. 5, the function returning values of program language library are exploited as the dictionary sequence and the function returning value sequences of cryptographic protocol implementations at the source code are exploited as analysis objects. And their *XOR* operations are executed to analyze the security of cryptographic protocol implementations. It is shown by our experiment that many cryptographic protocols are theoretically proved to be secure, but they are not secure in the process of implementations at the source code level. Our method focuses on the security analysis of cryptographic protocol implementations at the source code level and is not involved in the analysis of formal and computing theory, so it can guarantee the secure application of cryptographic protocols in practice. As the environments of cryptographic protocol implementations at the source code level are becoming more and more complex (such as different language structures and paralleling running environments [25], etc.), the security analysis of cryptographic protocol implementations is more complex than ever. Hence, how to analyze cryptographic protocol implementations in the complex environments [26] is the direction that researchers need to consider in the future.

References

1. Zhang, H.G., Han, W.B., Lai, X.J., et al.: Survey on cyberspace security. Sci. China Inf. Sci. **58**(11), 1–43 (2015)
2. Zheng, H., Qin, J., Jiankun, H., Qianhong, W.: Threshold attribute-based signcryption and its application to authenticated key agreement. Secur. Commun. Netw. **9**, 4914–4923 (2016)
3. Zhao, S., Xi, L., Zhang, Q., Qin, Y., Feng, D.: Security analysis of SM2 key exchange protocol in TPM2.0. Secur. Commun. Netw. **8**, 383–395 (2015)
4. Abadi, M., Blanchet, B.: Computer-assisted verification of a protocol for certified email. Sci. Comput. Progr. **58**(1–2), 3–27 (2005)
5. Blanchet, B.: A computationally sound mechanized prover for security protocols. In IEEE Symposium on Security and Privacy, Oakland, California, pp. 140–154, May 2006
6. Bhargavan, K., Fournet, C., Corin, R.J., Zalinescu, E.: Cryptographically verified implementations for TLS. In: Ning, P., Syverson, P.F., Jha, S. (eds.) 15th ACM Conference on Computer and Communications Security (ACM CCS 2008), Alexandria, USA, pp. 459–468. ACM, New York (2008)
7. Bhargavan, K., Fournet, C., Gordon, A.D.: Modular verification of security protocol code by typing. In: Hermenegildo, M.V., Palsberg, J. (eds.) 37th ACM SIGPLAN-SIGACT Symposium on Principles of Programming Languages (POPL 2010), Madrid, Spain, pp. 445–456. ACM, New York (2010)
8. Aizatulin, M., Gordon, A.D., Jürjens, J.: Extracting and verifying cryptographic models from C protocol code by symbolic execution. In: Chen, Y., Danezis, G., Shmatikov, V. (eds.) 18th ACM Conference on Computer and Communications Security (ACM CCS 2011), Chicago, USA, pp. 331–340. ACM, New York (2011)
9. Sprenger, C., Basin, D.A.: Refining key establishment. In: Chong, S. (ed.) 25th IEEE Computer Security Foundations Symposium (CSF 2012), Cambridge, USA, pp. 230–246 (2012)
10. Backes, M., Maffei, M., Unruh, D.: Computationally sound verification of source code. In: CCS 2010, 4–8 October 2010
11. Avalle, M., Pironti, A., Sisto, R.: Formal verification of security protocol implementations: a survey. Formal Aspects Comput. **26**(1), 99–123 (2014)
12. Goubault-Larrecq, J., Parrennes, F.: Cryptographic protocol analysis on real C code. In: Cousot, R. (ed.) VMCAI 2005. LNCS, vol. 3385, pp. 363–379. Springer, Heidelberg (2005). https://doi.org/10.1007/978-3-540-30579-8_24
13. Dupressoir, F., Gordon, A.D., Jürjens, J., Naumann, D.A.: Guiding a general-purpose C verifier to prove cryptographic protocols. J. Comput. Secur. **22**(5), 823–866 (2014)
14. Tang, C., Lu, Z., Feng, C.: A verification logic for security protocols based on computational semantics. Acta Electronica Sinica, **42**(6) (2014)
15. Xiao, M., Ma, C., Deng, C., Zhu, K.: A novel approach to automatic security protocol analysis based on authentication event logic. Chin. J. Electron. **24**(1), 187–192 (2015)
16. Chaki, S., Datta, A.: ASPIER: an automated framework for verifying security protocol implementations. In: 2009 22nd IEEE Computer Security Foundations Symposium
17. Aizatulin, M., Gordon, A.D., Jürjens, J.: Computational verification of C protocol implementations by symbolic execution. In: CCS 2012, Raleigh, North Carolina, 16–18 October 2012
18. Hasabnis, N., Sekar, R.: Extracting instruction semantics via symbolic execution of code generators. In: FSE 2016, Seattle, WA, USA, 13–18 November 2016
19. Milner, R.: Communication and Mobile Systems: The π - Calculus. Cambridge University Press, Cambridge (1999)

20. Jürjens, J.: Automated security verification for crypto protocol implementations: verifying the JESSIE project. Electron. Notes Theor. Comput. Sci. **250**(1), 123–136 (2009)
21. Backes, M., Busenius, A., Hriţcu, C.: On the development and formalization of an extensible code generator for real life security protocols. In: Goodloe, A.E., Person, S. (eds.) NFM 2012. LNCS, vol. 7226, pp. 371–387. Springer, Heidelberg (2012). https://doi.org/10.1007/978-3-642-28891-3_34
22. Narendra Kumar, N.V., Shyamasundar, R.K.: POSTER: dynamic labelling for analyzing security protocols. In: CCS 2015, Denver, Colorado, USA, 12–16 October 2015
23. ITU-TS: Recommendation Z.120: Message Sequence Chart (MSC) ITU-TS, Geneva (1999)
24. Cremers, C., Mauw, S.: Operational Semantics and Verification of Security Protocols. Spring, Heidelberg (2012)
25. Yao, A.C.-C., Yung, M., Zhao, Y.: Concurrent knowledge extraction in public-key models. J. Cryptol. **2**, 156–219 (2016)
26. Wang, J., Shi, Y., Peng, G., Zhang, H., et al.: Survey on key technology development and application in trusted computing. China Commun. **13**(11), 70–90 (2016)

The Analysis of Malicious Group Based on Suspicious Communication Behavior Aggregation

Guolin Shao[1], Xingshu Chen[2(✉)], Xuemei Zeng[2], Xueyuan Yin[1], Xiaoming Ye[1], and Yonggang Luo[2]

[1] Department of Computer Science, Sichuan University, Chengdu, Sichuan, People's Republic of China
[2] Institute of Cybersecurity Research, Sichuan University, Chengdu, Sichuan, People's Republic of China
chenxsh@scu.edu.cn

Abstract. Evasive and persistent network attack is a kind of serious cyber security threat, which hides communication data in massive legitimate network traffic, to achieve the goal of avoiding detection, and reach the purpose of long-term latent and information theft. The Trojan, spyware, botnet and some APT can be classified as such attacks. To cope with this, this paper proposed an analysis approach of the malicious group based on suspicious communication behavior aggregation. Firstly, the evasive and persistent characteristics of the communication behaviors were studied, several features were extracted from the perspective of evasive and persistent characteristics, and the suspicious communication behavior detection model was built based on this. Furthermore, to determine the nature and purpose of such suspicious behavior, they are further studied by aggregation analysis from the perspective of communication behavior similarity, a behavior group discovery algorithm was presented based on density clustering method, and a framework was proposed for tracking and analyzing the behavior groups. Experimental results demonstrate that this approach can detect and excavate unknown attack and unknown malware, such as botnet, slow scanning, persistent service probe etc. Besides, it also found that some normal services have shown similar communication characteristics, such as NTP service, DHCP service etc.

Keywords: Evasive and persistent threat · Communication behavior · Aggregation analysis · Malicious group · Malware detection

1 Introduction

Motivated by political and economic interests, evasive and persistent network threats turn into the main challenges to national cyber security. An evasive and persistent network attack is a kind of confrontational network attack which hides communication data in massive legitimate network traffic to evade the detection

M. Xu et al. (Eds.): CTCIS 2017, CCIS 704, pp. 143–164, 2017.
https://doi.org/10.1007/978-981-10-7080-8_12

of security devices and achieve the purpose of long-term latent and information theft [1]. The current existing cyber-attacks, such as the Trojan, spyware, botnet and some APT, can be classified as such type attacks [2]. However, the evasive and persistent network attacks are hard to detect because their network activities are subtle and do not cause target network sharp fluctuation or disruption in contrast to DoS attacks. Moreover, these attacks are often organized as groups, and the attacks caused by a single node are not obvious enough to arouse suspicion. Once that happened, they are very destructive in terms of mass and collaborative. Therefore, finding the malicious groups in this type attacks through correlation analysis and group analysis is a current urgent task needed to be realized.

In this paper, an analysis approach towards malicious groups based on suspicious communication behavior aggregation is proposed to detect security threats that have evasive and persistent communication behaviors, such as botnets, hidden Trojans, APT attacks, etc. Firstly, we study the suspicious communication behaviors with the evasive and persistent characteristics, several features are extracted, e.g. communication frequency, frequency stability, the average packet length, receive and send ratio, duration ratio. On this basis, the detection model is built to detect the suspicious communication behaviors. Secondly, the group natures of suspicious communication behaviors are further studied and analyzed from the perspective of behavior similarity. As the traditional rule-based aggregation approaches are inadequacy for the problem scene of this paper, it is imperative to design a new common, adaptive aggregation approach. To cope with it, we put forward a communication behavior group discovery algorithm based on density clustering method. Finally, it is necessary to make a collaborative analysis based on the detailed communication data, threat intelligence information, and expert knowledge to determine the natures of the groups. We present a framework for tracking and analyzing the suspicious group. The Group Sketch Construction phase, Group Pruning phase, Deep Analysis and Tracking phase are included in the framework. In our experiments with real network traffic, some malicious communication behavior groups have been detected, such as botnets, slow scanning, persistent service probe etc. It also found that some normal services show similar communication characteristics.

The rest of this paper is organized as follows. Section 2 gives an overview of the related work. Section 3 gives a brief description of the problem definition and preliminaries, and points out that the purposes of this paper include: firstly, detecting the suspicious communication behaviors with the evasive and persistent characteristics; furthermore, studying and tracking the group nature of suspicious behaviors from the perspective of behavior similarity. Section 4 presents the analysis approach towards malicious groups in detail. Firstly, the suspicious communication behavior detection method was described, then the behavior group discovery method was proposed, finally, the tracking framework was introduced. Section 5 gives the experimental results. Section 6 concludes the paper and discusses the future work.

2   Related Work

Botnet detection. Many researchers have adopted the botnet feature of similar or group behaviors among a set of infected machine, DNS logs or communication traffic are utilized to detect this kind of malicious group. Numerous DNS-based schemes were proposed, Choi et al. [3,4] proposed an approach named BotGAD to reveal the domain names of C&C servers, they distinguished group activities in DNS traffic using the concept of the client set of a domain name. It allegedly can detect botnets from a large-scale network in real-time. Moreover, BotGAD can detect not only individual botnets but also correlated evasive botnets. Thomas et al. [5] illustrated typical malware DNS lookup patterns and clustered groups of domain names that are queried by infected machines, this work can detect and accurately cluster malware domains to a particular variant or malware family without the need for obtaining a malware sample. Sharifnya et al. [6] present DFBotKiller, a negative reputation system that considers the history of both suspicious group activities and suspicious failures in DNS traffic to detect domain-flux botnets. To identify randomly or algorithmically generated domain names, it uses three measures, namely the Jensen-Shannon divergence, Spearman's rank correlation coefficient, and Levenshtein distance. The experimental results show that DFBotKiller can make a good trade-off between the detection and false alarm rates.

On the other hand, numerous communication-based detection schemes were proposed, Felix et al. [7] proposed a set of metrics for efficient botnet detection, the proposed metrics captures the unique group behavior that is inherent in bot communications, it uses three standard network traffic characteristics: topological properties, traffic pattern statistics and protocol sequence and usage. Wang et al. [8] found that there exist great similarity and synchronization among the behaviors and the C&C traffic of the centralized botnets, then proposed a common detection mechanism. Firstly, they determine if the groups of flows are suspectable by performing the evaluation on the payload similarity and sequence correlation. Furthermore, they monitor and keep tracking with the collective and simultaneous behaviors of the suspicious groups of hosts. The experimental results show that the proposed method can detect and hold back the centralized botnets effectively. Aresu et al. [9] performed an analysis of Android botnets that employ HTTP traffic for their communications. Firstly, it effectively groups mobile botnets families by analyzing the HTTP traffic, the results showed that the samples belonging to the same malware family have similar HTTP traffic statistics. Moreover, it is possible to precisely detect new malware that belong to the clustered families.

Malware detection. Apart from botnet, other malwares are also the focus of research. Numerous DNS-based detection schemes were proposed. Lee et al. [10] introduce a malware activity detection mechanism, GMAD: Graph-based Malware Activity Detection that utilizes a sequence of DNS queries in order to achieve robustness against evasion techniques. To detect malicious domain names utilized to malware activities, GMAD applies domain name clustering using the graph structure and determines malicious clusters by referring to public blacklists. The results show that the proposed method is effective for detecting multi-domain malware activities irrespective of evasion techniques. Shalaginov et al. [11] utilize common behavior of malware called beacon, which implies that infected hosts communicate to C&C servers at regular intervals which have relatively small time variations. The DNS log files represented as a graph in this paper, based on the graph structure, it uses four periodicity detection algorithms for each pair of internal-external communications, it infers the existence of other infected hosts and malicious domains enrolled in the attack activities.

Yen et al. [12] proposed a detection system called TAMD (Traffic Aggregation for Malware Detection) to identify infected hosts by finding out aggregated communication involving multiple internal hosts. The aggregated features include flows communicating with the same external network, sharing similar payload, and involving internal hosts with similar software platforms. Johnson et al. [13] proposed a volumetric analysis methodology that aggregates traffic at the Autonomous System (AS) level. The methodology reduces the number of flows, while still detecting traffic anomalies. The results showed the feasibility of detecting various attack types when aggregate metrics are summarized at the AS level. Perdisci et al. [14] proposed a method and system for network-based detecting of malware from behavioral clustering. Firstly, clustering the malware samples based on network behavioral information from the HTTP traffic; after that, extracting network signatures from the HTTP traffic information for each cluster, the network signatures being indicative of malware infection. Ogawa et al. [15] proposed a malware HTTP traffic detection utilizing the cluster appearance ratio, the method clusters HTTP traffic features and calculates the cluster appearance ratio per communication host pairs, then it classify communication host pairs of traffic for evaluation by utilizing the cluster appearance ratio.

3   Problem Definition and Preliminaries

3.1   Background

The communication behaviors are described using the various flow fields (e.g. extracted from IP header, transport header, flow properties), and are depicted based on different fields values. Each communication behavior record includes the source IP, destination IP, destination port, protocol, send packets, receive packets, send bytes, receive bytes, suspicious communication lasting days, session count, daily communication details, etc. The objects studied in this paper are the suspicious communication behaviors which are directed against evasive and persistent communication behaviors. Hence, one of the purpose is detecting and extracting the suspicious behavior records from the real network in the perspective of evasive and persistent characteristics.

Besides, the analysis results turn out that a part of suspicious communication behaviors are normal services, such as the DHCP service, NTP service, etc. the other parts are the real security threats, such as slow port scan, persistent service probe, botnets, etc. Therefore, they need further analysis. However, due to the huge amount of data, it is hard to tracking analysis for every suspicious record; in addition, many suspicious records have the similarity and should be aggregated into a group. At the meanwhile, there are still many suspicious communication behaviors are individual behaviors. Therefore, the another purpose of this paper is that, aggregating the suspicious communication behaviors which share the same characteristic into the same group, then tracking and analyzing the behavior groups to determine their natures and purpose.

3.2   Problem Statement

For the sake of description, we will define the key concepts as follow.

Definition 1. *Suspicious communication behavior. A data record that specifies the source, destination, and communication characteristics c = $(sip, dip, dport, prot, sp, rp, sb, rb)$.*

The properties in c represent source IP, destination IP, destination port, protocol, send packet number, receive packet number, send byte number, receive byte number, etc.

Definition 2. *Suspicious communication behavior group. A set of $g = \{c_i, i = 1, 2, \cdots, l\}$, which has the same property value on certain properties, the suspicious behavior records in the same group exhibit similar behavior.*

Let the communication behavior set is $C = \{c_i, i = 1, 2, \cdots, n\}$, where c_i is one of the suspicious communication behavior record. As a result, the goal of aggregation analysis is shown in the formula (1), it aims at aggregating the similar behavior records to groups.

$$C \to G = \{g_1, g_2, g_3, \cdots, g_m\} \tag{1}$$

where $g_i \subset C$, $g_1 \cup g_1 \cup \cdots \cup g_m = C$, $g_i \cap g_j = \varnothing$.

Traditional aggregation analysis methods are usually based on specific rules that specify some properties based on known attack patterns. The properties indicate that the data records which have the same property values are clustered in one group. For example, you can set rules based on the port scan pattern $R = (sip, dip, sp, sb)$, all the behavior records that have the same source IP, destination IP, number of packets, and number of bytes are gathered together. According to practical experience, this kind of rule-based aggregation method can only be used in situations where the group pattern is simple. On the other hand, the granularity of the rules is difficult to control and generalize in actual situation and different data sets.

The analysis results show that the groups in G contain different patterns: 1-n pattern, n-1 pattern, 1-n-1 pattern, individual pattern. The 1-n pattern indicates a behavior group between a source IP and numerous destination IP, as presented in Fig. 1, in this kind of group, all the fields are the same except destination IP. The n-1 pattern indicates a behavior group between numerous source IP and a destination IP, which means all the fields are the same except source IP in

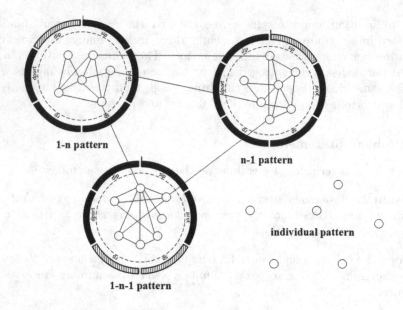

Fig. 1. Communication behavior group pattern

the group. The 1-n-1 pattern indicates a behavior group between a source IP and a destination IP, but some behavior properties vary greatly. The individual pattern indicates the behavior record show few similarities with other records.

Therefore, it is unviable to adopt the rule-based methods, it needs to study a common, adaptive aggregation approach. The aggregation analysis can be used to study the methods of group discovery. However, it is clear that aggregation analysis and cluster analysis are different issues. The aggregation problems aim to identify the records which in the same group share common properties, however, the cluster problems aim to identify the records which close to each other, it is judged by distance which is a value indicating the amount of similarity between two records. For example, there are three communication behavior records c_i, c_j and c_k, they are not equal to each other in every property value. c_i and c_j are close in each property value, but c_i and c_k have big difference. In the cluster analysis, c_i and c_j are closer to each other, and may be classified into the same class, but c_i and c_k are far away. However, in aggregation analysis, c_i, c_j and c_k should belong to three completely different categories, and there is no different between them. Hence, it requires research into a common, adaptive aggregation approach.

4   Communication Behavior Group Aggregation

4.1   Suspicious Communication Behavior Detection

Compared to traditional cyber-attacks, evasive and persistent network threats usually adopt confrontational evasive communication technology, and hide communication data in massive normal traffic, common protocols and legal services, to achieve the purpose of long-term latency and information theft. Based on the evasive and persistent communication characteristics, this paper extracted five communication features to distinguish suspicious communication behavior from normal network communication behavior.

– Communication Frequency

In order not to cause the change of host and network traffic characteristics, malicious softwares usually reduce the frequency of communication, and submerge communication data in massive legitimate network traffic, to achieve the goal of avoiding detection, reaching long-term latent and information theft. Therefore, suspicious communication is characterized by low communication frequency. This paper divided the observation window into different periods of time (by the day). For behavior record c_i, the number of communication in the time window k was regarded as its communication frequency, donated by $cf(c_i, k)$, then the communication frequency of c_i is defined as formula (2).

$$cf(c_i) = \frac{\sum\limits_{k=1}^{n} cf(c_i, k)}{n} \tag{2}$$

– Frequency Stability

According to the long-term traffic observation of the evasive Trojan communication, the communications which designated by programs have the characteristic of frequency stability. It shows that even within a short period (e.g., minutes or hours) communication frequency has no stability, but in the long period of time (such as days or longer), it tends to be stable. In this paper, the stability coefficient is used to describe the stability of frequency. It reflects the stability of communication frequency in different time periods, it donated by formula (3).

$$\alpha = 1 - c_v = 1 - \frac{\sigma}{\mu} \tag{3}$$

where c_v is the coefficient of variation, σ is the standard deviation, and μ is the average. The variation coefficient is the absolute indicator that reflects the change degree of the data, there is no requirement for the size and dimensionality of the multi-group data.

– The Average Packet Length

It needs to establish a connection with the control side to announce the survival and work status at regular intervals after the malware is embedded in the target computer, it is also known as the heartbeat packet. These communication characteristics result in the small packets ratio is higher in the communication process. Based on it, this paper measures this feature through the average packet length.

– Receive and Send Ratio

The purpose of malware is to steal a certain amount of information from the target, and the data upload and download ratio in the communication process must not be consistent with the normal communication (e.g. in web browsing, the user data is mostly downloaded data, the amount of uploaded data is minimal). Through the analysis of theft Trojan communication behavior, it found that the ratio is different from normal communication completely, it shows that the amount of upload data even higher than the download data. Thus, the ratio of upload and download data can be used as another important indicator for the detection of theft Trojan. This paper measures it by the receive and send ratio, which donated by $rsr = RB/SB$, where SB indicates the number of sending bytes, RB indicates the number of receiving bytes.

– Duration Ratio

Evasive and persistent characteristics are the two main types of communication behaviors that are concerned in this article, the above features are mainly evasive characteristics. At the same time, because the purpose of such attacks is to achieve long-term latency and information theft, the persistent characteristics of the communication behavior is an essential attribute. Those behaviors which having long term continuous evasive behavior are more suspicious, e.g. lasting several ten days or months. To analyze the persistence characteristics of behavior, we set one day as an observation unit, the whole observable period is 30 days or more, donated by D. For a communication behavior record, the number of observation units (days) during the observation period was examined, donated by d, then the duration ratio was defined as $dr = \frac{d}{D}$.

As the evasive and persistent cyber threats are usually unknown attack or unknown malware, so it is difficult to come up with a unified detection model. Therefore, this paper uses a threshold-based approach to detect suspicious communication behaviors that are reflected both in evasive and persistent characteristics, namely assign a threshold for each feature as needed.

4.2   Communication Behavior Group Discovery

The group discovery algorithm based on clustering method was adopted in this paper, by improving the distance measurement method in the clustering process, so as to realize aggregation analysis of suspicious communication behaviors. Many clustering algorithms such as k-means, spectral clustering algorithms are required to specify the cluster number k. However, the communication behavior group aggregation analysis problem is much more complicated, cluster number cannot be known in advance. On the other hand, according to the suspicious behavior analysis results, only a part of communication behaviors show group character, the other individual behaviors should not be divided into a certain cluster. However, in the common clustering algorithm, this kind of noise data can easily be gathered in a certain cluster, the more serious consequence is that it is likely to affect the data distribution, which affects the clustering results.

Through the comprehensive consideration, the DBSCAN algorithm was adopted to achieve the clustering process, because DBSCAN algorithm does not need to specify the cluster number k, and has strong anti-noise capability. There are two other parameters need to be specified: epsilon (*eps*) and minimum number of points (*minpts*). *eps* is the distance around an object that defines its eps-neighborhood. The two parameters are related to the analysis process, so this is acceptable for us.

The DBSCAN algorithm has been widely used due to its simplicity and the ability to detect clusters of different sizes and shapes compared to other clustering algorithms [16]. The DBSCAN algorithm is based on the concepts of density-reachability and density-connectivity. According to the given parameters, search space area and find the core objects and density-connected objects [17]. A cluster is defined as the set of objects in a data set that are density-connected to a particular core object. Any object that is not part of a cluster is categorized as noise. This is in contrast to k-means, which assign every object to a cluster.

For convenience of explaining, we defined the related definitions used in the DBSCAN algorithm firstly. Let X be the set of data points to be clustered using DBSCAN.

Definition 3. *eps-neighborhood. The neighborhood of a point $x \in X$ within a given radius eps is called the eps-neighborhood of x, denoted by $N_{eps}(x) = \{x' \in X | dist(x, x') \le eps\}$, where $dist(x, x')$ is the distance between x and x'.*

Definition 4. *core point. A point $x \in X$ is referred to as a core point if its eps-neighborhood contains at least a minimum number of points (minpts), more formally, $|N_{eps}(x)| \ge minpts$.*

Definition 5. *directly density-reachable. A point $x' \in X$ is directly density-reachable from $x \in X$ if x' is within the eps-neighborhood of x and x is a core point.*

Definition 6. *density-reachable. A point $x' \in X$ is density-reachable from $x \in X$ if there is a chain of points $x_1, x_2, \cdots, x_n$, with $x_1 = x$ and $x_n = x'$, and x_{i+1} is directly density-reachable from x_i for all $1 \le i \le n$, $x_i \in X$.*

Definition 7. *density-connected. A point $x' \in X$ is density-connected to $x \in X$ if there is a point $x'' \in X$ such that both x and x' density-reachable from x''.*

Definition 8. *noise. A point $x \in X$ is a noise point if x is not directly density-reachable from any core point.*

These notions of density-reachability and density-connectivity are used to define what the DBSCAN algorithm as a cluster. In order to describe the DBSCAN clustering process and the relevant concepts, we explain by example. Assume the *minpts* is 3 in Fig. 2, as you can see from the Fig. 2, m, p, o, r are all the core objects, because they contain more than *minpts* (3) objects inside. Object q is directly density-reachable from m. Object m is directly density-reachable from p. Object q is density-reachable from p, because q is directly

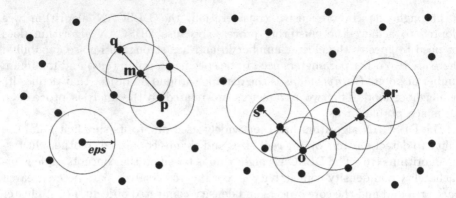

Fig. 2. DBSCAN algorithm schematic diagram

density-reachable m, and m is directly density-reachable p. r and s are density-reachable from o, and o is density-reachable from r, so o, r and s are density-connected.

Based on the definitions above, a density-based clustering algorithm for communication behavior group discovery is proposed as Algorithm 1.

Algorithm 1. Behavior Aggregation Algorithm

Input: suspicious behavior set C, eps, $minpts$;
Output: a set of communication behavior clusters;

1 **for** *each unvisited behavior item $c \in C$* **do**
2   mark c as visited;
3   $N_{eps}(c) \leftarrow NeighborPts(c, eps)$;
4   **if** $|N| < minpts$ **then**
5 | mark c as noise;
6   **end**
7   **else**
8    $g \leftarrow \{c\}$;
9   **for** *each item $c' \in N$* **do**
10   **if** c' *is not visited* **then**
11   mark c' as visited;
12     $N'_{eps}(c') \leftarrow NeighborPts(c', eps)$;
13   **if** $|N|' \geq minpts$ **then**
14 | $N \leftarrow N \cup N'$
15   **end**
16   **end**
17   **if** c' is not member of any cluster $g \leftarrow g \cup \{x'\}$
18   **end**
19 **end**
20 **end**

The DBSCAN algorithm works as follows. Initially, all behavior records in suspicious behavior set C are assumed to be unvisited. DBSCAN then chooses an arbitrary unvisited behavior item c from C. If DBSCAN finds c is a core object, it will fetch all the density-connected objects based on *eps* and *minpts*. It assigns all these objects to a new cluster. If DBSCAN finds c is not a core object, then c is considered as a noise and DBSCAN moves onto the next unvisited behavior record. Once every record is visited, the algorithm stops.

In order generate the *eps*-neighborhood, a distance measurement must be established. The common distance measurements such as Euclidean distance are not applicable for this paper, on account of it aims to cluster the groups share common properties. Due to this characteristic, we proposed a self-defined distance measurement based on the aggregation coefficient. For any behavior record c_i and c_j, the aggregation coefficient $ae(c_i, c_j)$ indicates the similarity between them. The aggregation coefficient defined as formula (4). As defined above, behavior record c is consists of r properties, the k-th property of c_i denoted by c_{ik}, $w(k)$ indicates the weight of the k-th property in c, $\nabla(c_{ik}, c_{jk})$ indicates that, the result is set to 1 if c_{ik} is equal to c_{ik}, otherwise, the result is set to 0.

$$ae(c_i, c_j) = \sum_{k=1}^{r} \nabla(c_{ik}, c_{jk}) w(k) \tag{4}$$

Based on the aggregation coefficient, the distance measurement was proposed.

$$dist(c_i, c_j) = \frac{2^{max-ae} - 2^{ae(c_i, c_j)}}{ae(c_i, c_j) + 1} \tag{5}$$

4.3   Communication Behavior Group Tracking

DBSCAN algorithm is able to aggregate communication behaviors into a group, which share common properties. However the clustering results are not all evasive and persistent security threats, some behaviors might be normal services which just have similar communication behavior characteristics. Therefore, further analysis is needed to determine the groups natures. The evasive and persistent security threats are usually unknown attack or unknown malware, so it is unable to obtain their features in advance. It is necessary to make a collaborative analysis based on the detailed communication data, threat intelligence information, and expert knowledge to determine its nature. Therefore, we present a framework for tracking and analyzing communication behavior group. The framework includes the Group Sketch Construction phase, Group Pruning phase, Deep Analysis and Tracking phase. The Group Sketch Construction phase mainly extracts Group characteristics based on clustering results, which prepares for Group Pruning and Deep Analysis and Tracking phase. However, not all groups need to be tracked, as a result, the Group Pruning phase mainly filters known-groups, and then analyzes the unknown-groups in Deep Analysis and Tracking phase. In the deep tracking phase, the unknown malwares can be excavated, and the infected hosts can be obtained (Fig. 3).

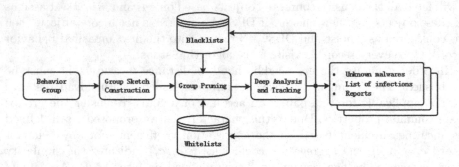

Fig. 3. Communication behavior group tracking architecture

– Group Sketch Construction

In order to facilitate the tracking analysis, this paper presents a group feature automatic extraction algorithm. By constructing the outline of the suspected communication group, the algorithm automatically forms the decision-making tree of the common characteristics of the group, provide the analysis foundation for Group Pruning, Deep Analysis and Tracking phase. For any communication group, it consists of communication behavior records $c = (sip, dip, dport, prot, sp, rp, sb, rb)$, The purpose of this algorithm is to extract the common properties that describe the vast majority of records within a group. Therefore, the principle of the algorithm is to analyze the data distribution of all properties, select the properties that most records have the same property value, then build group sketch based on this, thus the characteristics of the whole group are quantified. Naturally, not all properties show commonality in groups, according to its characteristics, the properties can be divided into three types: uniqueness property, subjectivity property and clutter property. The uniqueness property is that all records in the group have the same value on this property, the subjectivity property indicates that a small number of property values can cover most records on this property, a clutter property is a property that the records in the group do not have a common sense in this property. The algorithm is shown as Algorithm 2. For the group g, the sketch $SK = \{(p_k : vset_k),\ k = 1, 2, \cdots, r\}$ will be obtained, p_k indicates the k-th property in c, $vset_k$ indicates the set of corresponding property values. Several thresholds are needed during the calculation: $maxcumper$, $minper$, $maxdiff$ and $mincumper$.

Algorithm 2. Group Sketch Construction Algorithm

    Input: g,$maxcumper$,$minper$,$maxdiff$,$mincumper$;
    Output: SK- the sketch of group g;
1 **for** *each property p_k in c, $1 \leq k \leq r$* **do**
2     $V = \{c_{ik}, i = 0, 1, \cdots, n\} \leftarrow g$;
3     $KVC = \{(v_i : cnt_i),\ i = 0, 1, \cdots, m\} \leftarrow V$;
4     $KVC' \leftarrow KVC$ sort by cnt in desc-order;
5     $KVP = \{(v_i : per_i), i = 0, 1, \cdots, m\} \leftarrow KVC'$;
6     $vset_k = \{\}$, $sk = (p_k : vset_k)$;
7   **if** $|KVP| = 1$ **then**
8         $vset_k \leftarrow vset_k \cup \{v_1\}$;
9   continue;
10   **end**
11     $cumper = 0$,$lastper = 0$;
12   **for** *each $(v_i : per_i) \in KVP$, $1 \leq i \leq m$* **do**
13   **if** $cumper \geq maxcumper$ **then**
14   break;
15   **end**
16   **if** $i = 1$ **then**
17   **if** $per_i \leq minper$ **then**
18   break;
19   **end**
20   **end**
21   **else**
22   **if** $lastper/per_i \geq times$ **then**
23   break;
24   **end**
25   **end**
26         $vset_k \leftarrow vset_k \cup \{v_1\}$;
27         $cumper \leftarrow cumper + per_i$,$lastper \leftarrow per_i$;
28   **if** $cumper \geq mincumper$ **then**
29             $SK \leftarrow SK \cup \{sk\}$
30   **end**
31   **end**
32 **end**

– Group Pruning

Tracking analysis requires a lot of computing and expertise, and not all groups need to be tracked, e.g. the known or unconsidered group will not be analyzed. Therefore, through the Group Pruning phase, the groups that do not need analysis are filtered. The basis of pruning is mainly divided into the following aspects:

(1) Whitelist
    The analysis found that some groups are not belong to malware, it also

includes some normal services with similar communication characteristics, such as DHCP service, NTP service etc. Thus, these known normal service communication behavior characteristics are added to the whitelist, avoiding repeated analysis.

(2) Blacklist

For malicious communication groups that have been identified in previous work, the group characteristics can be added to the blacklist, avoiding repeated analysis. The blacklist data is mainly derived from the feedback of Deep Analysis and Tracking phase.

(3) Concerned Area

Not all host communication behaviors require attention, this paper focuses on the important assets of the campus network, namely some kernel servers. Therefore, the communication behaviors that do not need to be analyzed are filtered through source IP or destination IP.

(4) Concerned Groups

This paper focuses on the large-scale, specific group communication behavior (e.g. suspicious port). Therefore, small groups or unconsidered groups will be filtered based on the actual situation.

– Deep Analysis and Tracking

The purpose of the Deep Analysis and Tracking phase is to determine the natures of the unknown suspicious communication behaviors, e.g. normal services, botnets, trojans et al. Suspicious behavior tracking analysis is a decision-making problem based on domain knowledge, so must be combined with detailed communication data, threat intelligence information, as well as the expert knowledge. For the identified groups, the characteristics can be added to the whitelist or blacklist. As the feedback mechanism builds up, there will be fewer and fewer suspicious communication groups that need to be tracked. At the meanwhile, it can also analyze, excavate and detect unknown attacks and malwares at the same time. In addition, there is a question that needs to be discussed, the suspicious group tracking analysis may include various unknown attacks, rather than a specific type of attack. Therefore, a uniform model cannot be used to detect it, it is more depends on the analysis of threat intelligence information and expertise. Therefore, the main function of the module is to explore the unknown attack.

5   Experimental Results and Discussion

5.1   Data Set Description

Our network traffic was obtained from the edge routers on the Sichuan University campus network, we researched and analyzed the communication data from 2017.3.1 to 2017.3.31, during the observation, the number of sessions reaches 506,475,339. After the suspicious behavior detection phase, we extracted some suspicious communication behaviors from the perspective of evasive and persistent characteristics, 53,449 kinds of behavior records were extracted. Each communication behavior item includes the source IP, destination IP, destination port, protocol, send packets, receive packets, send bytes, receive bytes, suspicious communication lasting days, session count, daily communication details, etc.

5.2   Parameters Selection and Discussion

DBSCAN algorithm can discover any shape clusters, and effectively identify the outliers. It does not need to specify the clustering categories number k, but other two parameters should be specified: eps and $minpts$, the results of clustering directly depends on the selection of parameters. Therefore, the parameters selection of eps and $minpts$ is discussed here. According to the principle of the DBSCAN algorithm, the influence of parameters selection is described as follows.

Given the eps value, when $minpts$ is too large, the number of core points decreases, causing some natural clusters with fewer objects to be discarded, these objects are treated as noise; when $minpts$ is too small, a large number of objects are marked as core points, so that the noises are clustered into the group. Given the $minpts$ value, when eps is too small, a large number of objects are mistakenly marked as noise, and a natural cluster may be also wrongly split into multiple clusters; when eps is too large, many noises may wrongly clustered into groups, and a number of natural clusters may be wrongly combined into a cluster.

The parameters selection of $minpts$ and eps has a mutually reinforcing relationship, it usually requires set $minpts$ firstly and then select eps based on the statistical properties of the dataset itself. DBSCAN clustering using the concept of the k-distance [18], k-distance means: given a data set $P = \{p(i), i = 0, 1, \cdots, n\}$, for any point $p(i)$, calculate all the distance between $p(i)$ and other points in set P (not include $p(i)$ itself), and then sort them according to the distance in ascending order. Assume the sorted distance set is $D = d(1), d(2), \cdots, d(k), \cdots, d(n-1)$, then $d(k)$ is called k-distance, that is, the k-distance of $p(i)$ is the k-th nearest distance from the point $p(i)$ to the other points. Calculate the k-distance for each point $p(i)$ in the set P, and then the k-distance set E of all points is obtained. After that, sort set E in ascending order to get the set E', fit a distance change curve, the position that changes dramatically in the curve is the recommended value of eps [19].

For the value of $minpts$, the four values of 1, 5, 10, 15 are selected in the experiment, then the corresponding k-distance set E is calculated, after that the k-distance curve is plotted. The results are shown in Fig. 4. From the fitting curve, it shows that the variation of the k-distance curve is basically the same. As shown in Fig. 4, the curve will change drastically when the distance is about 60 in different $minpts$ condition, so the eps is set as 60 in this paper.

5.3   Aggregation Results Analysis

As discussed above, the eps is set to 60, in order to select the appropriate $minpts$ parameters, and study the impact of eps and $minpts$ parameters on the aggregated results, two sets of experiments were conducted. In the first set

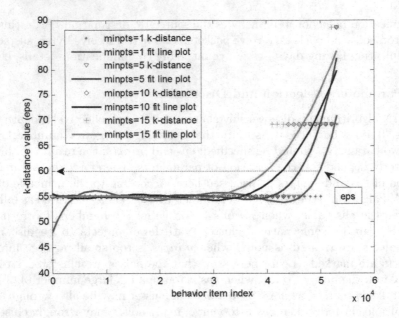

Fig. 4. K-distance curve

of experiments, the *eps* parameter was set to 60, and the *minpts* parameters were chosen as 1, 5, 10, 15, 20, 25, 30, the purpose is to select the appropriate *minpts* parameter. The second set of experiment was a controlled experiment, the purpose is to study the effect of selecting the wrong *eps* and *minpts* parameters on the aggregated results.

A distance-based clustering algorithm, such as k-means, usually evaluates the clustering results using methods such as SSE (Sum of squared errors). However, this kind of method is not suitable to the density-based clustering algorithm. Because the distance-based similarity measure only takes the distance between two data points into account, but in the density-based situation, it needs to calculate the distance of all data points within a certain range, there is a big difference between the number of involved data points and the calculation mode.

This paper puts forward the coverage (*cover*) and the average description length (*adl*) to evaluate the clustering results. For the group $g_i \in G$, g_i' is the behavior records set which satisfies the condition of Group Sketch, and $g_i' \subset g_i$, then *cover* can be defined as below.

$$cover = \frac{\sum\limits_{i=1}^{n} |g'_i|}{\sum\limits_{i=1}^{n} |g_i|} \qquad (6)$$

The larger the *cover*, the better the clustering results will be, at least to a certain degree. Yet this is not absolute, On the one hand, *cover* is determined by the clustering results, but on the other hand, it is determined by the extraction of Group Sketch as well. The coarser granularity the Group Sketch extracted, the higher the *cover* is, namely the fewer properties you can use to describe the Group Sketch, the more records that meet the criteria due to fewer restrictions. In order to solve this problem, the average description length (*adl*) is proposed to measure it. Let $||g_i||$ be the number of properties which used to describe the Group Sketch of g_i, then

$$adl = ||g_i|| * \frac{|g_i|}{|C|} \tag{7}$$

The larger the *adl*, the greater the number of properties describing the Group Sketch, that is the more concentrated the data records in the group, the better the clustering results. This paper studies the different *eps* and *minpts* parameters, and the results are shown in Table 1. In the controlled experiment, when the *eps* was set to 55, the group number was 0, indicating that the *eps* was too small, it is unable to find the core object, and a large number of objects were marked as noisy by mistake. When the *eps* was set to 85, the number of groups and noise are small, indicating that the *eps* value is too great, a number of separate natural groups were wrongly combined into a group, and many noises were also clustered into certain groups. However, the clustering effect is not ideal according to *cover* and *adl*. This also illustrates that the *cover* and *adl* indicators can measure the clustering results effectively.

Table 1. Aggregation results with different parameters

ID	eps	minpts	groups	noisy	ratio	L-groups	cover	adl
#1-1	60	1	5692	0	1	129	0.934	4.56
#1-2	60	2	2433	3259	0.94	129	0.929	4.46
#1-3	60	3	1245	5635	0.89	129	0.925	4.41
#1-4	60	4	1004	6452	0.88	129	0.924	4.4
#1-5	60	5	837	7295	0.86	129	0.924	4.39
#1-6	60	10	362	12382	0.77	125	0.923	4.41
#1-7	60	15	245	14558	0.73	118	0.929	4.43
#1-8	60	20	154	16675	0.69	111	0.932	4.45
#1-9	60	25	125	17807	0.67	106	0.935	4.46
#1-10	60	30	103	18979	0.64	101	0.941	4.56
#2-1	55	4	0	53449	0	0	#	#
#2-2	85	4	102	505	0.99	12	0.886	0.619

In the first set of experiment, the *eps* was set to 60, and the *minpts* was set to 1, 2, 3, 4, 5, 10, 15, 20, 25, 30. According to Fig. 5, with the increase of *minpts*, the values of *cover* and *adl* show the "V" trend, that is when *minpts* takes the

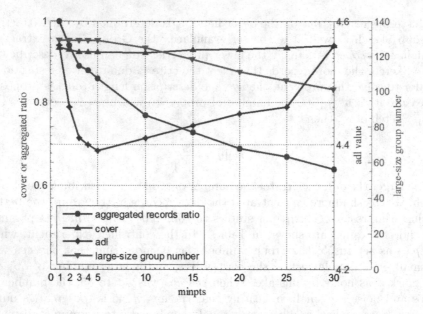

Fig. 5. Clustering results evaluation

minimum or maximum value, the effect is better. However, with the increase of *minpts*, the ratio of aggregated records is getting smaller (change from 100% to 64%). It demonstrates that more and more data records are marked as noises. The number of noise is affected by *minpts*, because when *minpts* was chosen too large, small groups which size are less than *minpts* are marked as noise. To cope with this, we also examined the large-size groups, and these large-size groups are also the focus of this paper. It will be treated as a large-size group if the group size is greater than 30. According to the results, the number of large-size groups is not significantly affected by *minpts*, it ranges from 101 to 129. As a conclusion, when the *minpts* value is set to 1, it can perform well in all respects.

5.4 Suspicious Behavior Group Analysis

Some malicious communication behavior groups have been detected, such as botnet, slow scanning, etc. It also found that some normal services have shown similar communication characteristics.

– Detecting Malware

Based on the group sketch, it is possible to make in-depth analysis of the suspicious groups according to the information such as port and IP, so as to determine their natures. Servral malwares were detected, e.g. the SQL Server probe and RDP probe in Table 2, the group sizes reach 598 and 171 respectively, duration reach 27 days and 24 days, respectively. Through their port information and the

Table 2. Examples of detected malwares

Type	Description	Sketch	Size
Botnet	Communicates frequency about tens to hundreds per day for a request IP, lasts for 22 days, most of the request IP are outside China and associate with malware according to threat intelligence from VirusTotal	dip = 202.*.*.186 dport = 7275 prot = udp sp = 1 rp = 1	1919
SQL Server probe	Communicates frequency is stable every day, about 16 per day for a probed IP, lasts for 27 days, 220.*.*.190 is associate with malware according to threat intelligence from ThreatBook	sip = 220.*.*.190 dport = 1433 prot = tcp sp = 2 rp = 0	598
RDP probe	Communicates frequency is stable every day, 2/day for a probed IP, lasts for 24 days, 111.*.*.12 is associate with malware according to threat intelligence from ThreatBook, the IP resolves to w*.wrjlife.cn, f*.f3322.org, p*.p7yy.com, etc	sip = 111.*.*.12 dport = 3389 prot = tcp sp = 1 rp = 0	171
Slow port scan	Communicates frequency is stable every day, 2/day for a probed IP, lasts for 27 days, 80.*.*.38 is associate with malware according to threat intelligence from ThreatBook	sip = 80.*.*.38 prot = tcp sp = 1 rp = 0	3310

analysis results of communication details, it is easy to determine that they are probe attacks on port 1433 and 3389, which correspond to the SQL Server service and RDP service. In addition, for some large or special-port groups, we will focus on them. With the aid of raw traffic analysis, it found that a group was a botnet, and another is a slow port scan attack. Open source threat intelligence is also one of the main basis of analysis. According to the threat intelligence from VirusTotal [20] and ThreatBook [21], the natures of many suspicious IP are validated, that further confirmed the credibility of the results.

– Normal Service

It found that some groups also show the evasive and persistent communication behavior, such as only few communications every day, and this kind of

Table 3. Examples of detected normal services

Type	Description	Sketch	Size
Windows Teredo	Communicates frequency about 10 per day for a request IP, lasts for 15 days, the IP resolves to win10.ipv6.microsoft.com and teredo.ipv6.microsoft.com	dip = [51.**.**.244, 157.**.**.207] dport = 3544 prot = udp sp = 2rp = 1	132
NTP service	Communicates frequency about tens to hundreds per day for a request IP, lasts for 22 days	dport = 123 prot = udp sp = 1 rp = 1	127
DHCP service	Communicates frequency about tens to hundreds per day for a request IP, lasts for 22 days, 202.**.**. 56 and 202.**.**. 57 are the DHCP servers of campus network	dip = [202.*.*.56, 202.*.*.57] dport = 67 prot = udp sp = 1 rp = 1	2249
SNMP	Communicates frequency is stable every day, about 230 per day for a request IP, lasts for 16 days	sip = 202.*.*.199 dport = 161 prot = udp sp = 51 rp = 51	60

communication pattern lasts for a long term duration etc. Through the analysis results of communication details, it found that they are normal service, such as Windows Teredo service, NTP service, DHCP service, SNMP etc. (Table 3).

6   Conclusion and Future Work

The objective of this paper is to detect the security threats that have evasive and persistent communication behaviors, such as botnets, hidden trojans, APT attacks, etc. Firstly, we studied the behavior features from the perspective of evasive and persistent characteristics, then we proposed a suspicious communication behavior detection approach. Furthermore, to determine the natures and purpose of such evasive and persistent threats, we put forward a communication behavior group discovery algorithm based on density clustering method, and proposed a framework for tracking and analyzing the behavior groups.

However, this paper is inadequate in many respects. Firstly, the current feature set which used to describe the evasive and persistent characteristics is not enough systematic, besides, the suspicious behavior detection mechanism is simple. As future work, we aim to improve the feature set and detection mechanism. Secondly, the threat intelligence is one of the crucial adjective references. The current intelligence information mainly comes from open source information repositories, which has some limitations on automated analysis. In the future work, we expect to be able to set up a threat intelligence repository, which provides support for analysis.

Acknowledgments. The authors would like to thank the editors and anonymous reviewers for their valuable suggestions which considerably helped us to enhance this paper. This work was partially funded by the National Natural Science Foundation of China (Grant No. 61272447).

References

1. Chen, P., Desmet, L., Huygens, C.: A study on advanced persistent threats. In: De Decker, B , Zúquete, A. (eds.) CMS 2014. LNCS, vol. 8735, pp. 63–72. Springer, Heidelberg (2014). https://doi.org/10.1007/978-3-662-44885-4_5
2. Cao, Z.G.: Research on the key issues in evasive network attack detection. Beijing University of Posts and Telecommunications (2015)
3. Choi, H., Lee, H.: Identifying botnets by capturing group activities in DNS traffic. Comput. Netw. **56**(1), 20–33 (2012)
4. Choi, H., Lee, H., Kim, H.: BotGAD: detecting botnets by capturing group activities in network traffic. In: Proceedings of the Fourth International ICST Conference on COMmunication System softWAre and middlewaRE, p. 2. ACM (2009)
5. Thomas, M., Mohaisen, A.: Kindred domains: detecting and clustering botnet domains using DNS traffic. In: Proceedings of the 23rd International Conference on World Wide Web, pp. 707–712. ACM (2014)
6. Sharifnya, R., Abadi, M.: DFBotKiller: domain-flux botnet detection based on the history of group activities and failures in DNS traffic. Digital Invest. **12**, 15–26 (2015)
7. Felix, J., Joseph, C., Ghorbani, A.A.: Group behavior metrics for P2P botnet detection. In: Chim, T.W., Yuen, T.H. (eds.) ICICS 2012. LNCS, vol. 7618, pp. 93–104. Springer, Heidelberg (2012). https://doi.org/10.1007/978-3-642-34129-8_9
8. Wang, T., Yu, S.Z.: Centralized botnet detection by traffic aggregation. In: IEEE International Symposium on Parallel and Distributed Processing with Applications, pp. 86–93. IEEE (2009)
9. Aresu, M., Ariu, D., Ahmadi, M., et al.: Clustering android malware families by http traffic. In: 2015 10th International Conference on Malicious and Unwanted Software (MALWARE), pp. 128–135. IEEE (2015)
10. Lee, J., Lee, H.: GMAD: Graph-based Malware Activity Detection by DNS traffic analysis. Comput. Commun. **49**, 33–47 (2014)
11. Shalaginov, A., Franke, K., Huang, X.: Malware beaconing detection by mining large-scale DNS logs for targeted attack identification. In: 18th International Conference on Computational Intelligence in Security Information Systems. WASET (2016)
12. Yen, T.-F., Reiter, M.K.: Traffic aggregation for malware detection. In: Zamboni, D. (ed.) DIMVA 2008. LNCS, vol. 5137, pp. 207–227. Springer, Heidelberg (2008). https://doi.org/10.1007/978-3-540-70542-0_11
13. Johnson, T., Lazos, L.: Network anomaly detection using autonomous system flow aggregates. In: 2014 IEEE Global Communications Conference (GLOBECOM), pp. 544–550. IEEE (2014)

14. Perdisci, R., Lee, W., Ollmann, G.: Method and system for network-based detecting of malware from behavioral clustering. U.S. Patent 8,826,438, 2 Sept 2014
15. Ogawa, H., Yamaguchi, Y., Shimada, H., et al.: Malware originated HTTP traffic detection utilizing cluster appearance ratio. In: 2017 International Conference on Information Networking (ICOIN), pp. 248–253. IEEE (2017)
16. Karami, A., Johansson, R.: Choosing DBSCAN parameters automatically using differential evolution. Int. J. Comput. Appl. **91**(7), 1–11 (2014)
17. Tran, T.N., Drab, K., Daszykowski, M.: Revised DBSCAN algorithm to cluster data with dense adjacent clusters. Chemom. Intell. Lab. Syst. **120**, 92–96 (2013)
18. Zhou, H.F., Wang, P.: DBSCAN research on adaptive parameters determination in DBSCAN algorithm. J. Xi'an Univ. Technol. **28**(3) (2012)
19. Zhou, Z.P., Wang, J.F., Zhu, S.W., et al.: An improved adaptive and fast AF-DBSCAN clustering algorithm. CAAI Trans. Intell. Syst. **1**, 93–98 (2016)
20. The VirusTotal threat intelligence information platform homepage. https://www.virustotal.com/. Accessed 8 June 2017
21. The ThreatBook threat intelligence information platform homepage. https://x.threatbook.cn/. Accessed 8 June 2017

Analysis of Vulnerability Correlation Based on Data Fitting

Long Wang, Rui Ma$^{(\boxtimes)}$, HaoRan Gao, XiaJing Wang, and ChangZhen Hu

Beijing Key Laboratory of Software Security Engineering Technology,
School of Software, Beijing Institute of Technology, Beijing 100081, China
mary@bit.edu.cn

Abstract. Discovering the correlation between vulnerability is a significant method of vulnerability analysis. The traditional way focuses on single vulnerability rather than considers the relationship between several vulnerabilities. That may spend much time but achieve a poor effect. This paper presents a new method working on the vulnerability distribution data. This method applies logarithmic normal distribution to the distribution data of different categories of vulnerability to calculate their correlation coefficient. Then, the correlativity between different vulnerability classifications could be qualitatively determined. The experiment was performed on two types of vulnerability database, namely CNNVD and SecurityFocus. The correlativity of different vulnerability classification obtained by the proposed method is verified both quantitative and qualitative ways. The results highlight the effectiveness of the proposed method.

Keywords: Vulnerability correlation · Logarithmic normal distribution · Correlation coefficient · Correlativity · CNNVD · SecurityFocus

1 Introduction

Nowadays, a variety of security issues caused by vulnerabilities have been the greatest threat to the Internet [1]. Therefore, the vulnerability detection or vulnerability analysis methods have become a hot issue. Many of these methods focus on single vulnerability rather than consider the correlation between vulnerabilities. As a result, after repairing some vulnerabilities with the current technology, new vulnerabilities often appear again. Fixing vulnerability so frequently not only consumes many resources, but also does not make it sure the security of software.

One of the major causes is not fully considered the correlation between vulnerabilities. That results in the phenomenon that the security objective is not achieved although many vulnerabilities are repaired. In fact, the correlation among different categories of vulnerabilities are various. This correlation may be symbiotic or causal, which is very important for the discovery and repair of vulnerabilities. Currently, there are only a few researches on this aspect. One of

© Springer Nature Singapore Pte Ltd. 2017
M. Xu et al. (Eds.): CTCIS 2017, CCIS 704, pp. 165–180, 2017.
https://doi.org/10.1007/978-981-10-7080-8_13

the major cause is the classifications of vulnerabilities are extremely numerous and fuzzy. Therefore, it is difficult to analyze the association on two categories of vulnerabilities. Thanks to the development of related works, including the data fitting, big data [2], vulnerability database and vulnerability association analysis technology. With the related works, this paper quantifies and qualifies the correlation between vulnerabilities.

This paper starts from the characteristics of vulnerability distribution to analyze the proportion of different categories of vulnerabilities meanwhile. Then the logarithmic normal distribution [3] was used to fit the distributed data in order to quantify the correlation degree. Next, the correlation is analyzed between various vulnerability categories.

In the Sect. 2, we will introduce the related research, including vulnerability database and vulnerability association analysis technology mentioned previously. In the Sect. 3, combining with the technical purpose, the model would be put forward of the correlation between different categories of vulnerability. Later, we make a detailed description of the key points - correlation coefficient matrix and correlativity matrix. The former matrix is quantitative analysis to quantify the correlation strength of different categories of vulnerability, while the latter is qualitative analysis to give a judgment whether there is a correlation, strong or weak. In the Sect. 4, different data sources are considered to obtain more than one matrices. That is helpful for a higher confidence conclusion. Then, the matrices would be analyzed with the common knowledge to judge the credibility and discover the correlation between categories. Finally, a conclusion would be drawn of this paper.

2   Related Works

2.1   Vulnerability Database

The vulnerability database stores known or published vulnerabilities and their information associated for sharing. Various types of vulnerability databases formulate the name, category, time, distribution of information and other data of vulnerabilities, which provide an indispensable data support for research on aspects of vulnerability and information security. For example, Stephan Neuhaus and Thomas Zimmermann found prevalent vulnerability types and new trends according to the data of CVE [4].

There are more than one vulnerabilities database, which can be divided into national vulnerability database and enterprise vulnerability database.

China National Vulnerability Database of Information Security (CNNVD) was a famous and authoritative national database. CNNVD was maintained by China Information Technology Security Evaluation Center. The data of CNNVD [5] would be used in this paper.

In addition to national vulnerability database, there are enterprise vulnerability databases. The typical case is SecurityFocus [6]. There are nearly 100,000 vulnerabilities in SecurityFocus database, even more than CVE. The data of SecurityFocus would also be used in this paper.

2.2   The Technology of Vulnerability Correlation Analysis

At present, the study of vulnerability correlation is more focused on the attack graph. As early as 2000, Ritchey R.W. [7] proposed the concept of vulnerability association between systems and attack graphs. In the typical attack graph, each node represents a vulnerability and a vector connect one node to another. This means that the vulnerability can be used continuously. Multiple vulnerabilities connect with each other to constitute the attack path, by which the relation between vulnerabilities could be discovered.

However, as Big Data was referred, this paper adopted absolute different method. The information was extracted from a dense large data sets incomplete, noisy, fuzzy, and even random. In 2006, Wang Fenghui [8] applied the data mining with the vulnerability database to discover the data rules between vulnerabilities according to the statistical theory. Zhang Xueqin [9] constructed an information security vulnerability ontology based on CWE. They took the ontology as the base of vulnerability domain semantics. Then, the Apriori algorithm was used to analyze the distribute of vulnerabilities in software, and discover hidden vulnerability association rules.

3   Analysis Method to Vulnerability Correlation Based on Data Fitting

3.1   Workflow

This paper establishes the vulnerability correlation model first, then quantifies the correlation between vulnerabilities by analyzing the distribution data of vulnerabilities. After that, the vulnerability correlation matrices could be constructed. Next, according to the matrices, the correlations analyzed between various vulnerability categories. Meanwhile, the credibility of the resulting correlations verified based on existing knowledge list.

Specific ideas are as follows.

(1) Establish the vulnerability correlation model. This model is constructed as a graph. Therefore, the step would define the vertex, edge, weight and threshold. Then, the correlation coefficient matrix and correlativity matrix would be constructed according to model. The former matrix is quantitative analysis to quantify the correlation strength of various categories of vulnerability. The latter is qualitative analysis to give a judgment whether there is a correlation, strong or weak.

(2) Obtain the distribution data of vulnerabilities. Including the category and amount of vulnerabilities in different software. Some processing necessary may be carried out. Then, calculate the weights and thresholds. Consequently, construct the correlation coefficient matrix and correlativity matrix according to the definition of the correlation model.

(3) Analyze the matrices and compare different results with existing knowledge.

Step 1 is the core and theoretical basis of this method, while Step 2 and 3 are dependent on specific vulnerability data. Therefore, this section focuses on Step 1, which refers to the vulnerability correlation model. Steps 2 and 3 will be described in Sect. 4.

3.2   Vulnerability Correlation Model

In this method, the vulnerability correlation model is constructed as a graph to facilitate the subsequent analysis of vulnerabilities correlation. As a result, the meaning should be defined first, including the vertex, edge and weight of edge in the vulnerability correlation graph.

Vertex. As this paper is to study the correlation between different categories of vulnerabilities, the vertexes are used to denote different categories. The number of vertexes is equal to the number of categories. In the practice, we can set the amounts of vertexes according to different methods of vulnerability classification used. In this paper, the vulnerabilities are classified according the security threats.

Edge. The edges of vulnerability correlation graph are the full outer join of the vertexes. Edges represent the correlation between vertexes. There is a weight on each edge. The larger the weight, the stronger the relevance between the vulnerabilities corresponding.

Weight. As the quantification measure of the correlation of vulnerabilities, the weight of edge is one of the focuses of this paper. There is a weight on each edge, but they are usually not equal to each other. The weight represents the strength of correlation between the two categories of vulnerabilities.

As the amount of different vulnerability categories varies enormously on different software. If the correlation was calculated according that amount, there would be huge deviation between different categories.

Therefore, this method considers the ratio between the vulnerabilities. If the correlation between two categories of vulnerabilities is high, their distribution feature should be high or low at the same time. It is easy to explain. If one category of vulnerability causes another to appear (possibly one or more), then their ratio will remain at a fixed value (for example, each vulnerability of category A will cause three vulnerabilities of category B). Assuming that there exists the referred correlation between the two categories of vulnerabilities A and B, then the ratio in each single software will be roughly consistent with that in all software. The most exaggerating situation is that in all software, the ratios of category A to B are all 1:3. On the contrary, the distribution of vulnerabilities should be consistent with some distribution regularity.

The first to describe is the fitting coefficient of the ratio of two categories of vulnerabilities. Specifically, it is to find a suitable probability-distribution function, which denotes the probability that this actual value appears. This function has the following two characteristics.

Gradual change. When the ratio of vulnerabilities in a single software to the total ratio of vulnerabilities in all software approaches, the fitting coefficient approaches 1. On the contrary, it approaches 0. For example, assume that the ratio of category A to B is 1:3, if the ratio in a single software is also 1:3, then the fitting coefficient is 1, which is the highest situation. If the ratio in a single software is 2:7, then the value is close to 1. If the ratio is 20:1, then the coefficient will be very low. If the amount of one or two categories of vulnerabilities is 0, such as 0:0 or 0:3, then the fitting coefficient is 0.

Symmetry. Through analysis of the characteristics of the fitting coefficient, it is easy to find that if the total ratio of two categories of vulnerabilities is 1:1, then for the ratio 1:2 and 2:1 in a single software, their deviations to 1:1 are the same. So the logarithms are symmetrical about the center. Therefore, the distribution of the fitting coefficient of vulnerabilities should meet the logarithmic distribution.

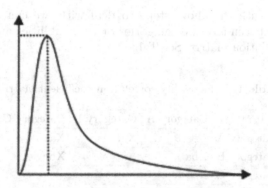

Fig. 1. Distribution of fitting coefficient

Based on the characteristics above, the logarithmic normal distribution [10] is used to define the fitting coefficient of the ratio between the various categories of vulnerabilities. First, for each software, calculate the fitting coefficients according to the Formula (1). The fitting coefficients indicates the deviation between the ratio of single software and the total ratio. In this formula, the σ values 1. The μ is the logarithm of total ratio. The x is the logarithm of the ratio on single software. Then, the front coefficient is remove because it's need to divide the maximum value.

$$w = \sum_i f(i) \tag{1}$$

The distribution law is shown in Fig. 1.

Second, deal with the fitting coefficient in all software, to get the weighted fitting coefficient. Considering that the amounts of the same two categories of vulnerabilities in different software can still be different, so the weights of the fitting coefficients are also different. Therefore, this method carries out weighting processing on the fitting coefficients obtained in the previous step. Assuming that the number of the vulnerabilities of category A in software i is C_{ia} and the number of the vulnerabilities of category B is C_{ib}, then the total numbers of the vulnerabilities of category A and B in all software are $\sum C_{ia}$ and $\sum C_{ib}$. The formula is shown in (2).

$$w = \sum_i f(i) \tag{2}$$

In the third step, we can get the correlation coefficient $\sum f(i)$ between the two categories of vulnerabilities by simply summing up the fitting coefficients. This coefficient is the weight on each edge in the graph. The formula is shown in (3).

$$w = \sum_i f(i) \tag{3}$$

In accordance with the above steps to deal with, we can get the correlation coefficients between any two categories of vulnerabilities and construct the vulnerability correlation matrix. See Table 1.

Table 1. Vulnerability correlation coefficient matrix

	Category A	Category B	Category C
Category A		Xab	Xac
Category B	Xba		Xbc
Category C	Xca	Xcb	

In this table, the rows and columns both denote the categories of vulnerabilities, and the values which are less or equal to 1 denote the correlation coefficients between the two corresponding categories of vulnerabilities. The matrix is symmetric because the correlation is mutual. For example, X_{ab} and X_{ba} both denote the correlation between the vulnerabilities of category A and B. The value on the diagonal position does not exist, because the correlation of the same category of vulnerability does not make sense.

Threshold. After establishing the vulnerability correlation matrix, it's easy to see that the correlations between different vulnerabilities are different. In this step, the threshold is set to judge the correlativity. When the correlation between two categories of vulnerabilities is too low, it needs to be identified as irrelevant. So two thresholds are set here. The correlativity corresponding to the threshold is shown in Table 2. As in the Table 2, if the correlation coefficient is less than the lower threshold, the correlativity is considered "None". If the

Table 2. Vulnerability correlativity corresponding to the coefficient and threshold

Correlation coefficient	Compared to the two threshold		Correlativity
	Lower threshold	Higher threshold	
Φ 1	Higher	Higher	Strong
Φ 2	Higher	Lower	Middle
Φ 3	Lower	Lower	None

coefficient is between the two thresholds, the correlation is considered "Middle". The correlation is 'Strong' if the coefficient is greater than the higher threshold.

It's very helpful for the analysis of the results to set the threshold, but there isn't any prior data about it. In some similar studies, some scholars will take the mean or median as the threshold, or just set past 10% of the data to 0. It lacks logic support to set the threshold directly, so several thresholds will be used to provide a reference.

According to the obtained results in subsequent experiment, we calculate the average and variance, and set $(\mu - \sigma, \mu)$ and $(\mu, \mu + \sigma)$ as the thresholds. With the thresholds, the correlation could be got, then we construct the vulnerability correlativity matrix.

4   The Analysis Based on Data Fitting

4.1   Construction of Correlation Matrices

Section 3 has described the method to construct model. In this Section, the data of CNNVD and SecurityFocus would be used to construct the vulnerability correlation matrix.

First of all, vulnerability distribution data should be gathered sort by software name and vulnerability category through spider program. The name of software and the category of vulnerability can both be obtained from vulnerability database. In practice, because there are only a few vulnerabilities in minority of the software, the minimum requirements of the vulnerability may not be achieved if the vulnerabilities are sorted by version rather than merged together. So, second, the data is processed during the experiment, including ignoring the number of the software name and merging the different versions of the software, such as Ubuntu14.04 and Ubuntu14.10. This step will cut down the accuracy, but its influence is not significant because there are many codes reused in each series of software, which causes that vulnerabilities are hereditary. For example, the vulnerability, CVE-2010-4314, appears in Windows XP/Vista/Win7.

In addition, it's useful to do some processing on the noise data. For example, in CNNVD data, the number of Path Traversal vulnerability is only '1'. So this category of vulnerability is cleared.

The data of one of the files is shown in Table 3.

Table 3. Example of vulnerability distribution data in a single software

No.	Category of vulnerability	Vulnerability number
1	Buffer overflow	4
2	SQL injection	0
3	XSS	1
4	Resource management error	0
5	Permission and access control	0
6	CSRF	0
7	Numeric error	0
8	Authorization issue	0
9	Trust management	0
10	Configuration error	3
11	Design error	2
12	Input validation	0
13	Information leakage	0
14	Code injection	0
15	Encryption issue	0
16	Race condition	0
17	Format string	2
18	Command injection	0
19	Post link	0
20	Environment condition error	0
21	Boundary condition error	2
22	Access validation error	3
23	Path traversal	0
24	Lack of information	2
25	Unknown	8
26	Other	4

The numbers on the left denotes different categories of vulnerabilities corresponding to 26 categories of vulnerabilities in CNNVD, and the numbers on the right denotes the number of vulnerabilities corresponded. Only the top 22 categories are used in this following.

After obtaining the data, it can calculate the correlation coefficient according to 3.2.3, so that the correlation coefficient matrix could be constructed.

Part of the correlation coefficient matrix of CNNVD is given in Table 4. The graph of this table can be seen in Fig. 2.

After getting the correlation coefficient matrix, the threshold value could be calculated according to 3.2.4. For the matrix of CNNVD, the threshold value is μ

and $\mu - \sigma$. For the matrix of SecurityFocus, the threshold value is μ and $\mu + \sigma$. With the threshold, the correlativity matrices could be constructed, seeing in Tables 5 and 7. This matrices would be used in the analysis of the correlation between categories.

Table 4. Correlation coefficient Matrix_CNNVD (Part)

No.	Buffer overflow	Resource management error	Cross-site request forgery	Numeric error	Input validation error
	1	2	3	4	5
1		0.502	0.196	0.545	0.540
2	0.502		0.255	0.556	0.483
3	0.196	0.255		0.134	0.311
4	0.545	0.556	0.134		0.369
5	0.540	0.483	0.311	0.369	

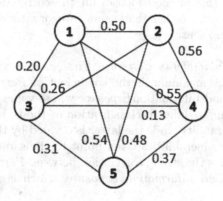

Fig. 2. Graph with correlation coefficient

4.2 The Analysis of Correlation

After getting the correlation coefficient matrices and correlativity matrices, the data contained could be analyzed. On one hand, the correlation coefficient could be compared and verified by the knowledge about vulnerabilities. On the other hand, the correlation coefficient could quantify the correlation between vulnerabilities. The next two parts would respectively analyze the matrices from the CNNVD and SecurityFocus. The third part would compare the conclusion with each other to judge the credibility.

Analysis with the Matrix of CNNVD. First, as CNNVD has been selected as the vulnerability database, the correlation coefficient matrix and correlativity matrix could be got, according to the method proposed in this paper. On this basis, the correlation between various categories of vulnerabilities can be analyzed.

The Method to Analyze the Correlation. First, part of the correlation coefficient matrix of CNNVD has been shown in Table 4. In the Table 4, each nature number surrounded by parenthesis responds to one category of vulnerabilities, and each cell with a decimal denotes the correlation coefficient of two categories of vulnerabilities. From the Table 4, the correlation coefficient of *Buffer Overflow* and *Numeric Error* values 0.545, which means there is a strong correlation between them. The correlation coefficient of *Input Validation Error* and *Cross-site Request Forgery* values 0.311. Compared with the average valuing 0.274, this coefficient of *Input Validation Error* and Cross-site Request For*gery* shows there is a middle correlation between them. For *Numeric Error* and *Cross-site Request Forgery,*whose correlation coefficient values 0.134, there is little correlation between this two categories. The correlation coefficient matrix is consistent with the actual situation.

The Table 4 is a diagonal matrix because the correlation between vulnerabilities is mutual. As this method focuses on the correlation between various categories of vulnerabilities rather than same category, there is no value on the diagonal which make no sense.

Analysis of Typical Vulnerability Category. First, in the correlation coefficient matrix of CNNVD, the maximum is the coefficient of *Permissions, Privileges, and Access Controls* and Information*Exposure* whose value is 0.709. These two categories in fact belong to different classification methods: the former is divided by the reason of vulnerability while the latter is divided by the outcome. In fact, the two categories of vulnerabilities often point to the same vulnerability. The high coefficient indicates the strong correlation between *Permissions, Privileges, and Access Controls* and *Information Exposure*, which is about two to three times the average.

Second, the correlation coefficients of *Design Error* are always high, except the *Environment Error*. Because the error in a design of a system or software will lead to Design *Error* or *Code Error*. So there may be correlation between the *Design Error* and the categories of *Code Error*. But for the *Environment Error*, the coefficients are always lower than the average. According to the classification of CWE, the *Environment Error* is far different from the Design Er*ror* and the *Code Error*. In conclusion, the correlation coefficient conforms to the common cognizance.

The Correlativity Between Different Categories of Vulnerabilities. After analyzing the correlation coefficients, this part is a qualitative study of the correlativity between different categories of vulnerabilities.

According to the method of threshold value in 3. B.d, the correlativity of different vulnerability categories could be constructed with the correlation coefficient matrix. The $\mu - \sigma$ valued 0.120 and μ valued 0.275 are used as the thresholds, by which the correlativity matrix could be constructed as Table 5. The serial numbers surrounded by parenthesis of Table 5 are same to the top 22 categories of Table 3, which means a category of vulnerabilities. The numbers '0', '1', '2' denote there is no/middle/strong correlation. For example, the '1' in the 6th row, 12th column means that there is middle correlation between the No. 6, Cross-site Request Forgery, and the No. 12, *Input Validation Error*. This correlativity of these two categories is authentic as it has been discussed in Part A. In the same way, the '2' in the first row, eighth column means that there is strong correlation between the No. 1, *Buffer Overflow*, and the No. 8, *Improper Authentication*.

Table 5. Correlativity Matrix_CNNVD

	1	2	3	4	5	6	7	8	9	10	11	12	13	14	15	16	17	18	19	20	21	22
1		1	2	2	2	1	2	2	2	2	2	2	2	2	1	2	2	1	2	0	2	2
2	1		2	0	1	1	0	1	1	1	1	2	1	2	0	0	1	1	1	0	1	1
3	2	2		1	2	2	1	2	1	1	2	2	2	2	1	1	1	1	1	0	1	2
4	2	0	1		2	1	2	2	2	2	2	2	2	2	1	2	1	1	1	1	2	2
5	2	1	2	2		2	2	2	2	2	2	2	2	2	2	2	1	2	2	0	2	2
6	1	1	2	1	2		1	2	2	2	1	2	2	1	1	1	1	1	1	0	1	1
7	2	0	1	2	2	1		1	1	2	2	2	2	2	1	2	1	1	2	1	2	2
8	2	1	2	2	2	2	1		2	2	2	2	2	2	1	2	2	2	1	0	2	2
9	2	1	1	2	2	2	1	2		2	2	2	2	1	1	1	1	2	1	0	1	2
10	2	1	1	2	2	2	2	2	2		2	2	2	2	1	2	2	1	2	0	2	2
11	2	1	2	2	2	1	2	2	2	2		2	2	2	1	2	2	1	2	1	2	2
12	2	2	2	2	2	2	2	2	2	2	2		2	2	1	2	1	1	1	0	2	2
13	2	1	2	2	2	2	2	2	2	2	2	2		2	2	2	1	2	2	0	2	2
14	2	2	2	2	2	1	2	2	1	2	2	2	2		1	2	1	1	1	1	2	2
15	1	0	1	1	2	1	1	1	1	1	1	1	1	2		1	1	1	1	0	1	1
16	2	0	1	2	2	1	2	2	1	2	2	2	2	2	1		1	1	1	1	2	2
17	2	1	1	1	1	1	1	1	2	1	2	2	1	1	1	1		1	1	0	2	2
18	1	1	1	1	2	1	1	1	2	2	1	1	1	2	1	1	1		1	0	1	1
19	2	1	1	1	2	1	2	1	1	2	2	1	2	1	1	1	1	1		0	1	1
20	0	0	0	0	1	0	0	1	0	0	0	1	0	0	1	0	1	0	0		1	0
21	2	1	1	2	2	1	2	2	1	2	2	2	2	2	1	2	2	1	1	1		2
22	2	1	2	2	2	1	2	2	2	2	2	2	2	2	1	2	2	1	1	0	2	

(a) The number '0' stands for no correlation, '1' stands for middle correlation, '2' stands for strong correlation

Analysis with the Matrix of SecurityFocus

The Method to analyze the correlation. In the same way, this part would analyze the matrices of SecurityFocus. Part of the correlation coefficient matrix of SecurityFocus has been shown in Table 6.

Just as the Table 4, each cell in Table 6 with a decimal denotes the correlation coefficient of two categories of vulnerabilities. From the Table 6, the correlation coefficient of *Input Validation Error* and *Design Error* is 0.448, which means there is a strong correlation between them. The correlation coefficient of *Boundary Condition Error* and *Input Validation Error* is 0.213. Compared with the average value 0.163, this coefficient of Boundary Condi*tion Error* and *Input Validation Error* shows there is a middle correlation between them. For the Boundary Con*dition Error* and *Environment Error*, whose correlation coefficient is 0.048, there is little correlation between these two categories. The correlation coefficient would be analyzed in the following.

Table 6. Correlation coefficient Matrix_SecurityFocus (Part)

	Environment error	Input validation error	Design error	Race condition error
Configuration error	0.115	0.087	0.134	0.199
Boundary condition error	0.048	0.213	0.419	0.217
Environment error		0.008	0.033	0.156
Input Validation error	0.008		0.448	0.059

Analysis of Typical Vulnerability Category. In the correlation coefficient matrix of SecurityFocus, the maximum is the coefficient of Failure to Handle Excep*tional Conditions* and *Design Error*, whose value is 0.476. The *Failure to Handle Exceptional Conditions* is little mentioned, which denotes improper check or handling of exceptional conditions. For example, the CVE-2016-6170 is a vulnerability of *Failure to Handle Exceptional Conditions*, which allowed attackers to cause a denial of service via a large AXFR/IXFR response or UPDATE message. This type of vulnerability is due to the improper check, which is related with the design. So the coefficient is appropriate to the fact.

The Correlativity Between Different Categories of Vulnerabilities. This part is a qualitative study of the correlativity between different categories of vulnerabilities. The μ valued 0.1633 and $\mu + \sigma$ valued 0.3017 are used as the threshold,

Table 7. The serial numbers and the corresponding categories

No.	Category of vulnerability
0	Configuration error
1	Boundary condition error
2	Environment error
3	Input Validation error
4	Design error
5	Race condition error
6	Origin validation error
7	Access validation error
8	Failure to handle exceptional conditions
9	Atomicity error
10	Configuration error

by which the correlativity matrix could be constructed as Table 8. There is a Table 7 corresponding to the serial numbers of Table 8, which contains the serial numbers and the corresponding categories. The numbers '0', '1', '2' in Table 8 denote there is no/middle/strong correlation. For example, the '1' in the 8th row, 4th column means that there is strong correlation between the No. 8, Failure to Handle Exceptional Conditions, and the No. 4, DesignError. This correlativity of these two categories is authentic as it has been discussed in the Part B. In the same way, the '0' in the first row, third column means that there is little correlation between the No. 1, Configuration Error, and the No. 8, Environment Error. According to the 4.2.1.B, the correlativity is also authentic.

Table 8. Correlativity Matrix_SecurityFocus

	1	2	3	4	5	6	7	8	9	10
1		1	0	0	0	1	1	1	0	0
2	1		0	1	2	1	0	2	2	0
3	0	0		0	0	0	0	0	0	0
4	0	1	0		2	0	0	2	2	0
5	0	2	0	2		1	0	2	2	0
6	1	1	0	0	1		2	1	1	0
7	1	0	0	0	0	2		1	0	0
8	1	2	0	2	2	1	1		2	0
9	0	2	0	2	2	1	0	2		0
10	0	0	0	0	0	0	0	0	0	

Comparing the Two Results of CNNVD and SecurityFocus. The results are difficult to compare with each other because of the different classifications. But they are comparable on some common categories. For this part of data, some correlativities are shown by the two matrices of CNNVD and SecurityFocus, which was shown in Table 9.

Table 9. The comparison between CNNVD and SecurityFocus in correlation coefficient

Vulnerability name	Vulnerability name	Correlation coefficient		Correlativity
		CNNVD	SecurityFocus	
Boundary condition error	Design error	0.528	0.419	Strong
Access validation error	Input validation error	0.445	0.344	Strong
Design error	Access validation error	0.578	0.377	Strong
Race condition error	Boundary condition error	0.391	0.216	Middle
Access validation error	Race condition error	0.392	0.182	Middle
Race condition error	Environment error	0.234	0.156	Middle
Boundary condition error	Environment error	0.113	0.475	None
Input validation error	Environment error	0.072	0.082	None
Configuration error	Environment error	0.082	0.059	None
Configuration error	Boundary condition error	0.416	0.181	Unconformable
Input validation error	Race condition error	0.342	0.0589	Unconformable

In the Tables 5 and 8, the correlation coefficients corresponding are similar, particularly on the high and low value. However for the middle value, there are some different result between matrices of two source. The coefficients of *Design Error* are always higher than the average from CNNVD source, expect the *Environment Error*. This characteristic also takes part in the table of SecurityFocus source, expect the *Atomicity Error*. Meantime, in all the matrices, the coefficients of *Environment Error* are lower than the average.

Apart from that, as the different classifications, many categories in one table could not match a category on the other table, such as the *Cross-site Request Forgery* and *Numeric Error* in CNNVD data and the *Failure to Handle Exceptional Conditions* and, *Atomicity Error* in SecurityFocus data. It is remarkable to combine the two matrices so that we can gain a comprehensive correlativity matrix of different categories of vulnerabilities.

Referring the two matrices, these two paragraphs would make analysis with the typical, *Buffer Overflow*. There are four categories of vulnerabilities whose correlation with *Buffer Overflow* is stronger, including *Numeric Error*, *Input Validation Error*, *Access Validation Error* and *Resource Management Error*. First, the *Numeric Error*, also named Integer overflow, result from the insufficient size of data type, which was similar to *Buffer Overflow*. Second, the *Input Validation Error* is one of the main cause of *Buffer Overflow*. So there should be some correlation between them.

Third, as for the *Access Validation Error*, whose coefficient with *Buffer Overflow* is far higher than the average in both the matrices. These two categories also belong to different classification methods: the former was divided by the outcome of vulnerability while the latter was divided by the reason. Some buffer overflow, such as CVE-2016-3871, may cause the privilege escalation, which would be divided into *Access Validation Error*. In fact, the two categories of vulnerabilities often point to the same vulnerability. The Resource Management Error is in the same way, so there is no more detailed description.

5   Conclusion

It is vulnerability correlation technologies that have added new vitality to the current vulnerability security research, which have attracted the attention of many scholars. In this paper, a new method to the analysis of the correlation between vulnerabilities is proposed. This method establishes a new vulnerability correlation model by exploiting the characteristic that the amounts of two categories of vulnerabilities will be high or low at the same time if there is correlation between them. Then, it obtains the corresponding quantitative data of the correlation between vulnerabilities and constructs the vulnerability correlation matrices combining with the data of multiple vulnerability databases. Finally, it can analyze the correlation between various vulnerability categories according to the quantified data and verify the credibility of the resulting correlation based on existing knowledge list.

At present, there are some shortcomings in this method. For example, the majority of the correlation between vulnerabilities should be directed. Sometimes, vulnerability A may lead to vulnerability B, while vulnerability B will not have an impact on vulnerability A. So it is need to use the directed graph for analysis. This method also lacks experimental validation. The next step is to get more source data and use more experimental material to verify this method.

Acknowledgments. This work was supported by the National Key R&D Program of China (No. 2016YFB0800700).

References

1. China Internet Network Information Center, The 37th China Internet network development state statistic report, January 2016
2. Deng, M., Liu, Q., Wang, J., Shi, Y.: A general method of spatio-temporal clustering analysis. Sci. China (Inf. Sci.) **10**, 158–171 (2013)
3. Long, Y.H.: Probability Theory and Mathematical Statistics. Higher Education Press, Beijing (2004)
4. Neuhaus, S., Zimmermann, T.: Security trend analysis with CVE topic models. In: IEEE, International Symposium on Software Reliability Engineering, pp. 111–120. IEEE (2010)
5. CNNVD/China National Vulnerability Database of Information Security [EB/OL], 14 December 2016. http://www.cnnvd.org.cn
6. SecurityFocus [EB/OL] (2017). http://www.securityfocus.com/
7. Ritchey, R.W., Ammann, P.: Using model checking to analyze network vulnerabilities. In: Proceedings of Security and Privacy 2000, S&P 2000, 2000 IEEE Symposium on IEEE, pp. 156–165 (2000)
8. Wang, F.H.: Research on Vulnerability Related Technologies. Beijing University of Posts and Telecommunications (2006)
9. Zhang, X.Q., Xu, J.Y., Gu, C.H.: Information security vulnerability association analysis based on ontology technology. J. East China Univ. Sci. Technol. (Nat. Sci. Ed.) **40**(1), 125–131 (2014)
10. Herrmann, H., Bucksch, H.: Logarithmic Normal Distribution. Springer, Heidelberg (2014). https://doi.org/10.1007/978-3-642-41714-6_122137

Tracking the Mobile Jammer in Wireless Sensor Network by Using Meanshift Based Method

Liang Pang[✉], Pengze Guo, Zhi Xue, and Xiao Chen

School of Electronic Information and Electrical Engineering, Engineering Research
Center of Network Information Security Management and Service,
Shanghai Jiao Tong University, Shanghai, China
cyclone0000@163.com, {guopengze,zxue,chenxiao}@sjtu.edu.cn

Abstract. Due to the openness of the wireless transmission medium, wireless communications can be vulnerable to malicious jamming attackers. Such Denial-of-Service (DOS) attacks can cause serious influence on the network performance of Wireless Sensor Networks (WSN). To address this issue, the jammer localization methods are widely researched. However, the localization methods focus on the static jammer. The realtime requirements will make these localization methods disabled when the jammer is mobile. Moreover, in WSN, the mobile jammer tracking method must be lightweight enough to bring less additional computation and communication overhead onto the sensor nodes. Therefore, a lightweight Meanshift based jammer tracking method which is independent of the wireless propagation parameters is proposed in this paper. The method uses the positions of nodes as basis and weights the "mass" of each node through the node state. Then, it tracks the jammer by searching the area with highest jamming density. We simulate a series of experiments in Matlab. The experimental results suggest that our proposed method is effective, and it can achieve the acceptable accuracy with less additional overhead when it is used to track the jammer source.

Keywords: Mobile jammer · Jammer tracking · Meanshift · Jamming attack · Wireless sensor network

1 Introduction

As the rapid development of wireless communication, wireless networks can provide the communication infrastructure for sensor nodes. As a result, the wireless sensor networks (WSN) become commonly available in recent years. They have been widely used in industrial, civilian and military applications. A typical wireless sensor network usually contains many sensor nodes which can communicate with each other over multiple wireless hops instead of some preexisting infrastructures.

However, in wireless sensor network, the wireless transmission medium is shared by nature, it makes wireless communications vulnerable to malicious

© Springer Nature Singapore Pte Ltd. 2017
M. Xu et al. (Eds.): CTCIS 2017, CCIS 704, pp. 181–197, 2017.
https://doi.org/10.1007/978-981-10-7080-8_14

jamming attacks. The adversaries can easily observe the communications, then they can launch simple Denial-of-Service attacks against the wireless network by injecting false messages. Such attacks can easily prevent sensor nodes from communicating with each other.

In order to cope with this kind of Denial-of-Service attacks, many strategies and techniques have been developed to detect and defend against jamming, such as detection by jamming measurements [18], jamming evasion by channel surfing [20], DSSS (Direct sequence spread spectrum) and FHSS (Frequency hopping spread spectrum) [13]. Compared to these methods which detect the jammer or try to communicate under jamming, finding the location of jamming source is critical to launch certain security actions against the adversary for restoring network service and ensuring Quality of Service (QoS).

Based on the localization methodology, the localization algorithms can be divided into two categories: range-based and range-free algorithms. Range-based algorithms involve estimating distance to landmarks which are located at known positions by utilizing the measurements of various physical properties. Range-free algorithms use the features of jammer and the positional information of sensor nodes to estimate the jammer location. However, most of existing methods cannot cope with the challenges produced by mobile jammers, which can move around the applied region of WSN.

The mobile jammer can dynamically change its position and spatial distribution of jamming signal which will enable the jammer to adapt to the changes of wireless network configuration. This mobility will make the jammer localization process more challenging:

1. In WSN, the location of mobile jammer must be calculated on every sensor node to further ensure the quality of network service. (Nodes will change their routing table to avoid the jammed nodes or stop working when a jammer is nearby.)
2. In WSN, the sensor nodes are always energy constrained or computing capability constrained, the sophisticated localization algorithm is inapplicable to be implemented on the nodes.
3. For the existing range-based and range-free algorithms, they require the time varying measurements or positions of jammed nodes when they localize jammer with grow of time. This process will generate additional communication traffic which seriously affects the normal communications among sensor nodes.
4. In WSN, jamming attack can severely affect or even disrupt legitimate transmission or information sharing in the jammed region which increases the difficulty of collecting useful information.

To address the challenges of tracking the mobile jammer source, we first studied the impact of jamming on sensor nodes at various locations. Based on the level of interference, we divided the sensor nodes into three main categories: no-jammed nodes, jammed nodes and unaffected jammed nodes. Further, we use the connectivity of WSN to make a more detailed division on the jamming states of sensor nodes. There are six states which can be stayed at: no-jammed state, completely jammed state, boundary state of jammed which is close to unaffected jammed region, boundary state of unaffected jammed which is close to jammed region, middle unaffected jammed state, boundary state of unaffected jammed which is close to no-jammed region.

Secondly, we propose a Meanshift based tracking algorithm which utilizes the states of sensor nodes to estimate the location of jammer source when the jammer is moving around. Instead of localizing a jammer with grow of time, our tracking algorithm starts to work only when the state of any sensor node has been changed. The algorithm uses the jamming states to weight the "mass" of each sensor node. Then, an adaptive window of Meanshift algorithm is generated by the positions of unaffected jammed nodes. We finally use the iterative Meanshift algorithm to converge to the local maxima of density, and the center of window at this time is used as the estimated position of jammer source.

Finally, we conducted our experiments in Matlab and performed extensive simulations under different network configurations, such as various sensor node densities and different distributions of sensor nodes. The experimental results indicate that our method is effective when tracking the mobile jammer, and it can achieve the acceptable localization accuracy with lower additional overhead which is performed on each sensor node. Further, simulation results show that our approach is sensitive to the density and distribution of sensor nodes. It will get the more accurate localization with higher density of sensor nodes.

The rest of the paper is organized as follows: We place our work in the context of related research in Sect. 2. Our network assumption is presented in Sect. 3. We provide our theoretical analysis and describe how to track the mobile jammer source in Sect. 4. We make the comprehensive simulations to evaluate our proposed method in Sect. 5. Finally, we conclude our work in Sect. 6.

2   Related Work

Localizing a wireless device is usually solved by using signal processing based physical layer communication techniques [3]. But these methods always need additional hardware to measure the required signal features. Further, the issue of detecting jammers is studied by Wood et al. [17] and Xu et al. [19]. The authors presented several jamming models and explored the need for more advanced detection algorithms to identify jamming. Our work focuses on tracking jammers after jamming attacks have been detected by using the proposed jamming detection strategies.

In recent years, without specialized devices, many jammer localization techniques have been researched widely by scholars and professions. They can be categorized into range-based and range-free methods. Range-based methods involve distance estimation by using the measurements of various physical properties such as Received Signal Strength (RSS) [1,4,7], Time Of Arrival (TOA) [11], Time Difference Of Arrival (TDOA), and Direction Of Arrival (DOA) [21]. However, all the range-based methods rely on the landmarks at various positions to collect their measurements. Especially in [16], authors have proposed a mobile jammer tracking scheme which uses the common nodes in wireless network to monitor the jammer and collect the measurements. Then, a well-known range-based trilateration algorithm is used to localize a mobile jammer with grow of time. But this method needs a lot of data exchanges among sensor nodes, it will affect the common communications. Range-free methods only use the positions of nodes as basis and combine them with the characteristics of jammers. For example, Liu et al. have developed a jammer localization algorithm called Virtual Force Iterative Localization (VFIL) [10]. In [4], authors have proposed a Centroid Localization (CL) method to estimate the jammer location by averaging the coordinates of several jammed nodes. Further, Blumenthal et al. have proposed Weighted Centroid Localization (WCL) to improve the localization accuracy to some extent [2]. Also, some geometry covering based (GCL) range-free localization methods are developed. Sun et al. [14] use convex hull to locate the jammer. Cheng et al. have proposed an algorithm called Double Circle Localization (DCL) [5], which is based on minimum bounding circle and maximum inscribed circle. In a slightly different context, authors in [12] use gradient descent minimization to get the position where has minimal Packet Delivery Ratio (PDR), and this position is taken as the estimated result. However, when these range-free methods are used in tracking mobile jammer, they seem too simple to get the inaccurate estimated location, or too complex to bring heavy additional overhead to WSN.

Our work differs from the previous studies in that we use a simple Meanshift algorithm to track the jammer source only when any state of sensor node has been changed. The method is easy to be deployed on every node in WSN and can achieve an acceptable accuracy. Moreover, our proposed method produces a lightweight additional communication overhead.

3   Network Model and Jamming Model

3.1   Network Model

We consider a wireless sensor network over a large area. A lot of sensor nodes are numbered and deployed with known positions. Their positions remain unchanged during the tracking process. In another word, we consider static sensor nodes in our work. Each sensor node in the network has a number of neighbors, and it maintains a table to record its neighbors' information, such as their numbers and states. Also, we assume that each node records the locations of all the sensor nodes which are corresponding to their numbers and states. Moreover, each sensor node is equipped with an omnidirectional antenna, and each node has the same radio range in all directions. Other nodes which can successfully receive and decode messages from the transmitting node are called its neighbors. Thus, each node can periodically broadcast a hello message to help their neighbors in determining whether it has been jammed. The state-updated messages also can be broadcasted by each node when its state has been changed.

In this work, we focus on tracking a jammer after it has been detected. We assume that each sensor node in WSN is able to detect a jamming attack. (A lot of researches focus on this detection technique, such as [17,19]).

3.2   Jamming Model

The mobile jammer uses intentional radio interference to harm wireless communications. The effect of such jamming attack is twofold: on the side of the transmitters, it renders the medium busy resulting in large back-off times; while on the side of the receivers, it dramatically decreases the SNR resulting in a large number of packet collisions. The mobile jammer is also equipped with an omnidirectional antenna.

3.3   States of Sensor Nodes Under Jamming Attack

Path loss and fading are unique features of wireless propagation, respectively referring to the rapid decay in the jamming signal envelop with distance and to the random fades present in the jamming signal power. As a result, the sensor nodes which are located near a jammer, their communications are severely disrupted, whereas a node which is far away from a jammer may not be affected by the jammer at all. There also exists some critical nodes which can broadcast and receive messages as usual. Based on the degree of interference to a node, we can divide sensor nodes into three non-overlapping categories under jamming attacks: jammed nodes, no-jammed nodes and unaffected jammed nodes.

However, when using Meanshift based tracking algorithm to search the local area with maximum density, the mass degree of each sensor node is closely related to the accuracy of tracking results. The reason is that the node which is close to the jammer must represent a bigger "mass" to increase the local density. In another word, the tracking results should be located near the nodes which have bigger "mass". The best choice of weighting the "mass" of each node is the measurements of RSS which are closely related to the distance to the jammer. But the quality of communication must be seriously affected when the RSS values are measured frequently (Other nodes must keep quiet when a node is measuring the RSS value). Therefore, we propose to use some own states of sensor nodes to weight the mass of each node. And a more detailed division on the states of sensor nodes is necessary. To address this issue, we assume the number of used sensor nodes is n, and the nodes can be represented as $N = \{n_1, n_2, \ldots, n_n\}$. Then, we use l_{ij} to represent the link state between a pair of neighbor nodes n_i and n_j. We define that l_{ij} equals to 1 when n_j can receive packets from n_i, otherwise l_{ij} equals to 0. We emphasize that the link state l_{ij} equals to l_{ji}, the reason is that jamming takes effect on both sides of a communication. That means any sensor node cannot receive messages from its neighbors, it also cannot use the channel to send any message. Further, we use $Nbr\{n_i\}$ to represent the set which is consisted of the neighbors of node n_i before the mobile jammer becomes active. We also use N_J, N_U and N_N to represent the jammed node set, unaffected jammed node set and no-jammed node set respectively. (These three node set can be determined by using the received SNR [9]). Finally, we define six different states of sensor nodes, and they can be described as follows:

1. **Nodes at no-jammed state:** $N_a = \{n_a | (\forall n_i \in Nbr\{n_a\}, l_{ia} = 1) \wedge (n_a \in N_N)\}$.
   A node is not changed by the jammer at no-jammed state. It can exchange packets with all of its neighbors.

2. **Nodes at boundary state of unaffected jammed which is close to no-jammed region:** $N_b = \{n_b | (\forall n_i \in Nbr\{n_b\}, l_{ib} = 1) \wedge (n_b \in N_U) \wedge (\exists n_j \in Nbr\{n_b\}, n_j \in N_N)\}$.
   A node at this state can be seen as the boundary of no-jammed region and unaffected jammed region. It can receive and send packets as usual.

3. **Nodes at middle unaffected jammed state:** $N_c = \{n_c | (\forall n_i \in Nbr\{n_c\}, l_{ic} = 1, n_i \in N_U) \wedge (n_c \in N_U)\}$.
   A node at this state should be located at the middle area of unaffected jammed region. It also can communicate with its neighbors as before. But all of its neighbors are located in the unaffected jammed region.

4. **Nodes at boundary state of unaffected jammed which is close to jammed region:** $N_d = \{n_d | (\exists n_i \in Nbr\{n_d\}, l_{id} = 1, n_i \in N_U \cup N_N) \wedge (n_d \in N_U) \wedge (\exists n_j \in Nbr\{n_d\}, l_{jd} = 0, n_j \in N_J)\}$.
   A node at this state represents the boundary of jammed region and unaffected jammed region, and it is located in unaffected jammed region where it can find at least one neighbor to exchange packets. Another important function of the nodes at this state is that they can determine any of their neighbors is located in jammed region or not. Then, they can transmit this information to its neighbors which are located in the other two regions. It is important for us to get the states of the nodes which lose their communication abilities. Especially, we involve the special condition in this state, which can be described as the neighbors of a node are located both in jammed and no-jammed regions.

5. **Nodes at boundary state of jammed which is close to unaffected jammed region:** $N_e = \{n_e | (\forall n_i \in Nbr\{n_e\}, l_{ie} = 0) \wedge (n_e \in N_J) \wedge (\exists n_j \in Nbr\{n_e\}, n_j \in N_U \cup N_N)\}$.
   A node at this state represents the boundary of jammed region and unaffected jammed region, and it is located in jammed region where makes it impossible to exchange packets with its neighbors as usual. Especially, we involve another special condition in this state, which can be described as there exists any neighbor of a jammed node is located in no-jammed region.

6. **Nodes at completely jammed state:** $N_f = \{n_f | (\forall n_i \in Nbr\{n_f\}, l_{if} = 0, n_i \in N_J) \wedge (n_f \in N_J)\}$.
   A node at completely jammed state loses its communication ability. Also, it cannot find any usable link to transmit its state to the other nodes. However, we assume every sensor node knows the positions of all the nodes, and the node set N_e can be determined by using the nodes in N_d. Similarly, we can determine the node set N_f by using the nodes in N_e. It can be described as $N_f = \{(x_f, y_f) | (x_f, y_f) \in N, x_f \in [x_{min}, x_{max}], y_f \in [y_{min}, y_{max}]\}$, where (x_f, y_f) represents the coordinates of nodes in N_f, x_{min} and x_{max} represents

the minimum and maximum value of x among the nodes in N_e respectively, y_{min} and y_{max} represents the minimum and maximum value of y among the nodes in N_e respectively.

As mentioned above, we can get that $N_J = N_e \cup N_f$, $N_U = N_b \cup N_c \cup N_d$ and $N_N = N_a$. And we use S_a, S_b, S_c, S_d, S_e and S_f to represent the different states which are corresponding to $N_a \sim N_f$. It is obvious that the state of a node can be transformed as $S_a \to S_b \to S_c \to S_d \to S_e \to S_f$ when the mobile jammer moves toward the node. Also, the state can be transformed as $S_f \to S_e \to S_d \to S_c \to S_b \to S_a$ when the mobile jammer moves away. Additionally, due to the non-uniformly distributed sensor nodes and the radio range, some transformations are allowed in our work like $S_a \to S_d$, $S_b \to S_d$ and $S_c \to S_e$. Figure 1 shows the general view of the different states of sensor nodes when the mobile jammer is active.

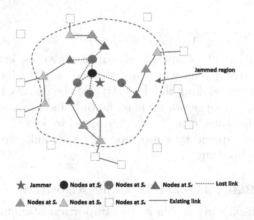

Fig. 1. The different states of sensor note under jamming

4   Tracking Method

In this paper, we propose to use basic form of Meanshift algorithm to track the jammer dynamically. Meanshift algorithm is widely used in dynamic objective tracking [6] and multiclass clustering [15].

4.1   Basic Form of Meanshift Algorithm

The basic form of Meanshift can be described as follows: Given a set $X = \{x_i\}_{i=1...n}$ of n points in the d-dimensional space $\Re^d$, then the basic Meanshift vector can be obtained by (1), where $M_h(x)$ represents the Meanshift vector, k represents k points in X located in the area S_k and x represents the centroid of S_k. S_k is a d-dimensional sphere area which can be described as

(2), where x represents the centroid of $S_h(x)$ and h represents the sphere radius (window-width).

$$M_h(x) = \frac{1}{k} \sum_{x_i \in S_k} (x_i - x) \tag{1}$$

$$S_h(x) = \{y : (y - x)^{\mathrm{T}}(y - x) < h^2\} \tag{2}$$

When using Meanshift algorithm, the window width h and initial centroid $x(0)$ are determined in advance. Then, a iterative process is performed, it computes the Meanshift vector and uses this vector to update the centroid as (3) in each iteration, where $x(i)$ is the centroid in ith iteration and $M_h(x(i))$ is the Meanshift vector in ith iteration. The iteration will stop when $|x(i+1) - x(i)| < \varepsilon$, where $\varepsilon > 0$ is close to zero. It is clear that the centroid x is the "mass" centroid which converges to the area with the highest node density, otherwise there must exist another area with higher node density to lead the centroid to move toward this area.

$$x(i + 1) = x(i) + M_h(x(i)), i = 0, 1, 2, \ldots, +\infty \tag{3}$$

A standard version of Meanshift algorithm involves kernel functions to smooth and weight the points which are located in the window. It computes the Meanshift vector by making the derivative of the density function equals to 0. In our work, the state of sensor node is the only factor we used to weight the points in X. And the states cannot be determined by kernel functions. Instead, they are detected and spread by sensor nodes. As a result, we choose this basic form of Meanshift algorithm.

4.2   Meanshift Based Jammer Tracking Algorithm

The state and position can be seen as two important attributes of each sensor node in WSN. As described in Sect. 3.3, if we use d_a, d_b, d_c, d_d, d_e and d_f to represent the distance between jammer and the node at $S_a \sim S_f$ respectively, we can easily get that $d_a > d_b > d_c > d_d > d_e > d_f$ when the nodes are located at the same direction of jamming signal propagation. It indicates that the nodes in jammed region are located closer to the jammer. In order to lead the "mass" centroid to move toward the location of jammer, the "mass" degree of each node must be inversely proportional to its distance to jammer. In another word, if we use $W_a \sim W_f$ to represent the weight value of the node at $S_a \sim S_f$ respectively, the relationship among these weight values can be described as $W_a < W_b < W_c < W_d < W_e < W_f$. When we use the 2-dimisional point set $P = \{p_i | p_i = (x_i, y_i)\}_{i=1,2,\ldots,n}$ to represent the locations of all the sensor nodes in WSN and use $c = (x_c, y_c)$ to represent the mass centroid, the Meanshift vector should be transformed into (4), where k is the number of nodes which are located in S_k, S_k is a circle area with circle center c and radius h.

$$\begin{cases} M_h(c) = \frac{1}{k}(\sum_a + \sum_b + \sum_c + \sum_d + \sum_e + \sum_f) \\ \sum_j = \sum_{(p_i \in S_k) \wedge (p_i \in N_j)} W_j(p_i - c), j = a, b, c, d, e, f \\ S_k = S_h(c) = \{(x_q, y_q) | \sqrt{(x_q - x_c)^2 + (y_q - y_c)^2} < h\} \end{cases} \tag{4}$$

How to determine the initial value of c and h is also an important factor of using Meanshift to track the jammer. In our work, because of the jammer is near to the nodes at S_f, we easily define the initial centroid c as the center of the rectangle which is built by the maximum and minimum value of x and y in N_f. And the window width h is defined as the maximum distance between the mass centroid and the unaffected jammed nodes. They can be described as shown in (5).

$$\begin{cases} c^{initial} = (x_c^{initial}, y_c^{initial}) \\ x_c^{initial} = \frac{x_{min}^f + x_{max}^f}{2}, y_c^{initial} = \frac{y_{min}^f + y_{max}^f}{2} \\ h = \max_{p_i \in N_U} \{d | d = \sqrt{(p_i - c)^T (p_i - c)}\} \end{cases} \tag{5}$$

Actually, h is a dynamically adaptive window width, because it changes with the centroid c and node set N_U when the iterative process is performed. The consideration of designing this adaptive width is based on the following two points: On one side, the result of Meanshift is more accurate when the window width is smaller. But the non-uniform distribution and lower density of sensor nodes are not allowed to use such small width, the result will be leaded to a local optimum. Thus, we use N_U instead of N_J as the reference of distance, and it is a trade-off choice. On the other side, the jammer can change its jamming power to avoid to be detected by nodes. Such an adaptive window can effectively reduce the errors generated by this changing power. In addition, the used circle area not means that the jammed region can be seen as a circle. The circle area only makes it easy to determine whether a node is located in the density-related area.

Finally, the Meanshift based tracking algorithm is a triggered method. It starts to calculate the position of mobile jammer only when the recorded states of one or some sensor nodes have been changed. It can be performed on every sensor node in WSN and can be described as follows:

- **Step 1:** Calculate the initial centroid c through (5);
- **Step 2:** Calculate the window width h through (5);
- **Step 3:** Calculate the Meanshift vector $M_h(c)$ through (4);
- **Step 4:** If $M_h(c) < \varepsilon$, return the value of c as the estimated position of mobile jammer. Otherwise, update the centroid c through (3) and go back to step 2.

This algorithm also converges to the area with highest density through iterations. We must emphasize that the initial centroid of step 1 is only computed once when the jammer is active. The later tracking triggered by the moving jammer can use the tracking result at last time as the initial centroid. It is a continuous tracking process.

5 Experimental Results and Analysis

In this section, we evaluate the effectiveness of our Meanshift based jammer tracking approach through simulation experiments and analyze the performance of the experimental results.

5.1   Network Configuration

We implemented our simulations in Matlab. We simulated a wireless sensor network environment on a $400 \times 400\,\text{m}^2$ map. The distribution of sensor nodes was considered from two types which are uniform distribution and random distribution. A single jammer equipped with omnidirectional antenna moved at a random speed and produced a jamming signal with variable power. The mobile jammer started to move at $(90, 90)$, and the moving path of the jammer can be described as a piecewise function as shown in (6).

$$\begin{cases} y = 2x - 90 & (90 \leq x \leq 150) \\ y = -\frac{1}{3}x + 260 & (150 \leq x \leq 210) \\ y = \frac{1}{3}x + 120 & (210 \leq x \leq 270) \\ y = \frac{1}{9}x + 180 & (270 \leq x \leq 330) \end{cases} \tag{6}$$

In the simulation, the signal propagation follows the path loss and shadowing model [8] which can be described as (7), where P_r is the received power with the unit dBm, P_t is the transmitted power, $\lambda = c/f_c$ is the signal wavelength ($c = 3 \times 10^8\,\text{m/s}$ is the speed of light, f_c is the center frequency of signal), d is the distance between receiver and transmitter, K is a unitless constant which depends on the antenna characteristics and the average channel attenuation, d_0 is a reference distance for the antenna far-field, γ is the path loss exponent (The values for K, d_0, and γ can be obtained to approximate either an analytical or empirical model.), and X_σ represents the shadow fading exponent which is a Gauss-distributed random variable with mean zero and variance σ^2. This rule of signal propagation was used in both jamming signal and communication signals among sensor nodes. The parameters adopted in our simulation are listed in Table 1. Especially, the threshold of the Signal-to-Noise Ratio (SNR) is an empirical data which indicates the lowest received SNR for ensuring general communication among sensor nodes [9]. (Lower SNR represents the node is under jamming.)

$$\begin{cases} \frac{P_r}{P_t}(\text{dB}) = 10 \log_{10} K - 10\gamma \log_{10} \frac{d}{d_0} - X_\sigma \\ K = 20 \log_{10} \frac{\lambda}{4\pi d_0} \end{cases} \tag{7}$$

5.2   Evaluation Metrics

In our simulation, three important metrics are used to evaluate the performance of the proposed jammer tracking method. They can be described as follows:

- **Tracking errors:** The tracking errors are defined as the Euclidean distances between the estimated jammer location and the actual jammer location when the Meanshift based algorithm is triggered to work on the sensor nodes. In order to capture the statistical characteristics, we use the values of cumulative distribution function (CDF) to express the tracking errors obtained from the simulation experiments. The CDF indicates the probability of the tracking errors are less than a fixed value.

Table 1. Parameters of simulation

Parameter	Meaning	Value
n	The number of sensor nodes	200–1000
P_t	Transmitting power of sensor nodes	45 dBm
P_J	Transmitting power of mobile jammer	59–69 dBm
P_N	Power of environmental noise	−60 dBm
G	Gain of transmitter and receiver	1
γ	Path loss exponent	2
μ	Mean of shadow fading exponent	0
σ	Standard deviation of shadow fading exponent	1
f_c	Center frequency of wireless signal	900 MHz
v	Speed of mobile jammer	0 5 m/s
T_{SNR}	Threshold of the received signal to noise ratio	1.1 dB
$W_a \sim W_f$	Weight value of sensor nodes at state $S_a \sim S_f$	0, 1, 1.5, 2, 2.5, 3

- **Tracking times:** In the whole tracking process, the times of using our proposed Meanshift algorithm is an important parameter which illustrates the generated overhead to the network. More tracking times means more overhead is loaded onto the sensor nodes and network.
- **Occupancy rate of network:** In order to proof that our proposed method is a lightweight approach, we use the occupancy rate of network to evaluate the impact generated by the tracking method. This rate equals to the ratio of the packets produced by tracking method to the common packets transmitted among the sensor nodes.

5.3 Simulation Results and Analysis

The first simulation was implemented to validate the effectiveness of our proposed method. We used $n = 800$ sensor nodes and uniformly deployed them on the square map. The tracking results are shown in Fig. 2, where x-axis and y-axis indicates the horizontal coordinate and vertical coordinate of each node on the deployed map respectively. Actually, every point on the estimated trace is the average of the tracking results generated by all sensor nodes. We observe that the proposed method can correctly catch the moving trace of mobile jammer. It indicates that our method is effective in tracking.

Moreover, we studied the parameters which will affect the tracking performance of our method. We make a theoretical analysis at first. When the Meanshift based algorithm is used to track the jammer, it tries to search the window area which has the highest density. Thus, the density of sensor nodes must be an important factor which will make effects on the tracking errors. More sensor nodes indicate that more points with different "mass" will be involved to express the differences of density between the jammed region and no-jammed

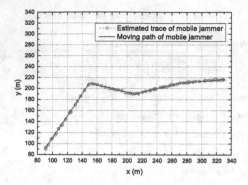

Fig. 2. Estimated moving trace of the mobile jammer

region. These differences will lead the algorithm to get a more accurate estimation. Similarly, the distribution of sensor nodes is also an important factor. The reason is that the uniformly distributed sensor nodes will average the density of jammed region, it can help the algorithm to converge to the barycenter of the jammed region. Otherwise, the nodes are located in a local area of jammed region. The density of this area will be too high to lead the algorithm to move toward this area. Also, the tracking errors will be increased in this condition. In order to validate our viewpoint, two simulations were performed. First, we uniformly distributed the sensor nodes and we adjusted the node density through varying the total number of sensor nodes. In particular, we used the number of sensor nodes $n = 300, 500, 800, 1200$ respectively. The CDF curves generated by tracking errors are presented in Fig. 3, where x-axis represents the tracking errors and y-axis represents the values of CDF. It is obvious that the tracking errors become more stable and more accurate with the increasing number of sensor nodes.

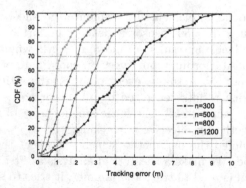

Fig. 3. CDF curves generated by tracking errors with different node number

The other simulation experiment was performed with random distribution and uniform distribution of sensor nodes respectively. And three different numbers of sensor nodes $n = 400, 600, 800$ were used in each distribution. The CDF curves of tracking errors generated by this simulation are shown in Fig. 4, where x-axis represents the tracking errors and y-axis represents the values of CDF. We can easily observe that the tracking errors are more accurate when using the uniform distribution. However, the errors generated by using random distribution is not big, we think they are still in an acceptable range. These two simulations powerfully proof that the performance of our proposed method is affected by the density and distribution of sensor nodes.

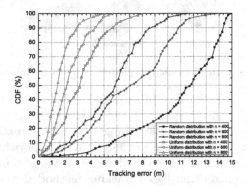

Fig. 4. CDF curves of tracking errors generated by using random and uniform distribution of sensor nodes

Furthermore, tracking times during the tracking process is another parameter which is affected by the node density and distribution. The reason is that our method is triggered by the changed state of any sensor node. The higher density of nodes will make the node states changing with a higher probability. Similarly, the distribution of sensor nodes affects the tracking times through the local node density. The tracking times reduces when the jammer is moving on the local area with a low density, and it increases when the jammer is moving on the local area with a high density. Therefore, this simulation focuses on the parameters which affect the tracking times. Because the main reason of the distribution can affect the tracking times is also due to the node density, we only used various node number $n = 300, 500, 800$ in this simulation. Also, two schemes which can reduce the tracking times were performed in this simulation. Both of them are changing the entry condition of our algorithm. One of them is that the algorithm is triggered when any jamming degree of node has been changed among jammed, unaffected jammed and no jammed. The other is that the algorithm is triggered when the states of any ten nodes have been changed. Each scheme ran ten times to get the average result of tracking times. The simulation results are shown in Fig. 5, where the y-axis represents the running times during the tracking. We can observe that the tracking times is affected by the node density, and it is proportional to the node density. The simulation results also validate that our optimization methods are effective in reducing the tracking times.

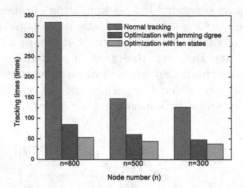

Fig. 5. Tracking times with different entry condition when the node number is fixed at 300, 500 and 800

Finally, in order to illustrate the advantages of our proposed tracking method, we compared our method with the range-free WCL algorithm and the range-based trilateration algorithm in the tracking errors. We also made a comparison with the trilateration algorithm based tracking method through the occupancy rate of network [16]. In these two scenarios, we simulated the WCL algorithm as same as our method which is triggered by the changed state of any node. In particular, we simulated the trilateration algorithm to localize the mobile jammer in a fixed timeslot. The reason is that this method needs to dynamically select and transfer the monitoring nodes at each time. We kept the node number $n = 500$ and uniformly distributed the sensor nodes. The CDF curves of tracking errors generated by this simulation are presented in Fig. 6, where x-axis represents the tracking errors and y-axis represents the values of CDF. We can observe that the WCL always get the worst tracking results, and the results generated by our method and trilateration algorithm are almost the same, but the results of trilateration algorithm seem more stable. In addition, the trilateration algorithm also relies on the uniform distribution and highest possible node density, to ensure that there are at least three nodes in unaffected jammed region at each tracking time when the jammer is moving and its transmit power is changing all the time.

Then, we evaluated the occupancy rate of network by using our method and trilateration algorithm respectively. The reason why we did not simulate the WCL is that the occupancy rate of network generated by WCL is as same as the occupancy rate of network generated by our method. Figure 7 presents the relational curves with $n = 300, 400, 500, 600$ and 800, where x-axis represents the node number and the y-axis represents the occupancy rate of network. We can see that our method maintains a stable lower occupancy rate of network than the trilateration based method. It is predictable that the occupancy rate of network generated by the trilateration based method will increase with the

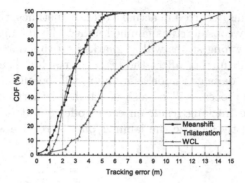

Fig. 6. CDF curves of tracking errors generated by Meanshift, Trilateration and WCL with node number n = 500

node number. And the over 50% occupancy rate must seriously affect the normal communications among sensor nodes, it will delay some exchanged information which are important for remaining the realtime function of WSN. In addition, we even not consider the waste of time when the nodes keep quiet to ensure the monitoring nodes can measure the accurate no-load RSS values.

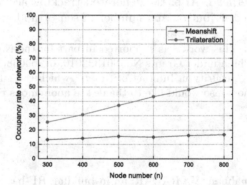

Fig. 7. Occupancy rate of network generated by Meanshift based tracking method and trilateration based tracking method with different node number

In summary, our proposed method does well in tracking the mobile jammer. And the tracking accuracy is sensitive to the node density and node distribution. Moreover, the triggered entry condition of our algorithm makes the method track the jammer in time when the jammed region is changing. Further, once the entry condition is determined, the occupancy rate of network generated by our method maintains at a stable level with lower percentage. Moreover, the larger node number leads to get better tracking results, but also heavier additional overhead. It is a trade-off choice when applying our method to be used in actual wireless sensor network. In addition, the simulation experiments cannot overally present some problems occurred in actual world. Sometimes, the damaged sensor nodes are mistakenly considered as jammed nodes, this condition will cause two effects: One is that wrong states will be marked on this damaged node and its neighbors, and it will further affect the tracking results. The other is that the nodes which use the damaged node as a "hop" will be out of touch with other nodes, the tracking process will be also affected. Furthermore, the end to end delay will affect the tracking result on each node, but it is unimportant that the nodes can correctly localize the jammer once it receive all changing states of sensor nodes.

6   Conclusion

In this paper, we introduce a novel mobile jammer tracking method which uses simple Meanshift algorithm as basis. We define six states of sensor nodes when the mobile jammer is active. We further use these states to weight the degree of "mass" associated with each sensor node. Then, the algorithm converges to the adaptive circle area which has the highest density, and the circle center is used as the estimated location of mobile jammer. The design of triggered entry condition makes our method can track the jammer in time. We simulate our method in Matlab. The experimental results indicate that our method is effective with lower additional overhead. Also, the generated tracking accuracy is acceptable and sensitive to the distribution and number of sensor nodes.

Acknowledgments. This work was supported in part by the National Natural Science Foundation of China under Grants No. 601332010, 61864068. This work was also supported in part by "Security in Internet of things" which is a subproject of Project Xuguangqi. The authors also would like to thank the anonymous reviewers for helpful comments.

References

1. Bahl, P., Padmanabhan, V.: RADAR: an in-building RF-based user location and tracking system. In: Proceedings IEEE INFOCOM 2000, vol. 2, pp. 775–784 (2000)
2. Blumenthal, J., Grossmann, R., Golatowski, F., Timmermann, D.: Weighted centroid localization in Zigbee-based sensor networks. In: 2007 IEEE International Symposium on Intelligent Signal Processing, WISP, pp. 1–6 (2007)
3. Broustis, I., Faloutsos, M., Krishnamurthy, S.: Overcoming the challenge of security in a mobile environment. In: Proceedings of the IEEE International Performance, Computing, and Communications Conference, vol. 2006, pp. 617–622 (2006)
4. Bulusu, N., Heidermann, J., Estrin, D.: GPS-less low-cost outdoor localization for very small devices. IEEE Pers. Commun. **7**(5), 28–34 (2000). Special Issue on Smart Spaces and Environments
5. Cheng, T., Li, P., Zhu, S.: An algorithm for jammer localization in wireless sensor networks. In: 2012 IEEE 26th International Conference on Advanced Information Networking and Applications, pp. 724–731 (2012)

6. Comaniciu, D., Ramesh, V., Meer, P.: Real-time tracking of non-rigid objects using mean shift. In: Proceedings of the IEEE Conference on Computer Vision and Pattern Recognition, 2000, p. 2142 (2002)
7. Elnahrawy, E., Martin, R.P.: The limits of localization using signal strength: a comparative study. In: 2004 First Annual IEEE Communications Society Conference on Sensor and Ad Hoc Communications and Networks, pp. 406–414 (2004)
8. Goldsmith, A.: Wireless communications (2006)
9. Liu, H., Liu, Z., Chen, Y., Xu, W.: Determining the position of a jammer using a virtual-force iterative approach. Wireless Netw. 17(2), 531–547 (2011)
10. Liu, H., Xu, W., Chen, Y., Liu, Z.: Localizing jammers in wireless networks. In: 7th Annual IEEE International Conference on Pervasive Computing and Communications, PerCom 2009, vol. 25, pp. 1–6. IEEE, March 2009
11. Misra, P., Enge, P.: Global Positioning System: Signal, Measurements, and Performance. Ganga-Jamuna Press, Massachusetts (2006)
12. Pelechrinis, K., Koutsopoulos, I., Broustis, I., Krishnamurthy, S.V.: Jammer localization in wireless networks: an experimentation-driven approach. Comput. Commun. 86, 75–85 (2016)
13. Pickholtz, R.L., Schilling, D.L., Milstein, L.B.: Theory of spread-spectrum communications: a tutorial. IEEE Trans. Commun. 32(2), 211–212 (1984)
14. Sun, Y., Wang, X., Zhou, X.: Jammer localization for wireless sensor networks. Chin. J. Electron. 4, 735–738 (2011)
15. Tuzel, O., Meer, P.: Mean shift clustering. In: 2013 IEEE 24th International Conference on Application-Specific Systems, Architectures and Processors (ASAP), pp. 370–374 (2005)
16. Wei, X., Wang, T., Tang, C., Fan, J.: Collaborative mobile jammer tracking in Multi-Hop Wireless Network. Future Generation Computer Systems (2016)
17. Wood, A.D., Stankovic, J., Son, S.: JAM: a jammed-area mapping service for sensor networks. In: 24th IEEE Real-Time Systems Symposium, RTSS 2003, pp. 286–297 (2003)
18. Xu, W., Ma, K., Trappe, W., Zhang, Y.: Jamming sensor networks: attack and defense strategies. IEEE Network Mag. Glob. Internetworking 20(3), 41–47 (2006)
19. Xu, W., Trappe, W., Zhang, Y., Wood, T.: The feasibility of launching and detecting jamming attacks in wireless networks. In: Proceedings of the 6th ACM International Symposium on Mobile ad hoc Networking and Computing - MobiHoc 2005, p. 46 (2005)
20. Xu, W.: Channel surfing: defending wireless sensor networks from interference. In: 2007 6th International Symposium on Information Processing in Sensor Networks, pp. 499–508 (2007)
21. Yang, Z., Ekici, E., Xuan, D.: A localization-based anti-sensor network system. In: Proceedings - IEEE INFOCOM, pp. 2396–2400 (2007)

New Upper Bounds on Degrees of Freedom for G-MIMO Relay Channel

Xiao Chen[1]($\boxtimes$), Liang Pang[1], Pengze Guo[1], Xingping Sun[2], and Zhi Xue[1]

[1] Shanghai Key Laboratory of Integrated Administration Technologies
for Information Security, Shanghai Jiao Tong University, Shanghai, China
{chenxiao,cyclone0000,guopengze,zxue}@sjtu.edu.cn
[2] Department of Mathematics, Missouri State University,
Springfield, MO 65897, USA
xingpingsun@missouristate.edu

Abstract. We study a general type of multiple-input multiple-output (G-MIMO) relay channels, which consist of two groups (A and B) of source nodes and one relay node. Both groups have arbitrarily many source nodes each of which is in turn equipped with an arbitrary number of antennas. A G-MIMO relay channel engages in two-way transmission of independent information via the relay node. We obtain a tight upper bound on the total degrees of freedom (DoF) for such G-MIMO relay channels. Under the reasonable assumption that the number of antennas at the relay node is no more than the total number of antennas of either Group A or Group B, we design an efficient transmission scheme to achieve the upper bound by using techniques of signal alignment and joint transceiver design for interference cancellation. At the end of the paper, we propose a future research topic to quantify the relationship between graded levels of network security and the corresponding DoF of the G-MIMO relay channels.

Keywords: Wireless channel · G-MIMO relay channel · Degrees of freedom · Network coding · Signal alignment

1 Introduction

Wireless communication is nowadays an indispensable part of modern life, and is omnipresent in such diverse fields as wireless sensor networks (WSN), satellite communication, and mobile networks, to name just a few. The exponential growth in demand for multimedia services and mobile communication is propelling scientists to develop innovative signal processing techniques with high spectral efficiency and capacity. As a result, more and more sophisticated mathematical tools are being introduced to the field of wireless communication. In a typical wireless communication system, the Degrees of Freedom (DoF) [1] is an important index for the capacity $C(\text{SNR})$ approximation of the system as expressed in the following equation:

$$C(\text{SNR}) = d \log(\text{SNR}) + o(\log(\text{SNR})), \tag{1}$$

© Springer Nature Singapore Pte Ltd. 2017
M. Xu et al. (Eds.): CTCIS 2017, CCIS 704, pp. 198–212, 2017.
https://doi.org/10.1007/978-981-10-7080-8_15

where d is DoF, and SNR is the signal-to-noise ratio. If SNR grows sufficiently large, then the accuracy of the approximation approaches 1 since the term $o(\log(\text{SNR})$ becomes negligible in comparison to $\log(\text{SNR})$. However, interference is a key bottleneck to limit the DoF of a wireless network. To alleviate the impact of interference, Jafar [2] and Maddah-Ali et al. [3] introduced the technique "interference alignment" to achieve the maximum DoF for the MIMO X channel. The key idea of the interference alignment is that interference signal spaces are aligned and corralled on the receiving side, allowing more space for free flow of useful signals in the system. By utilizing this technique, Cadambe and Jafar [4] showed that the capacity of the K-user time varying interference channel is characterized as in Eq. (1) with $d = \frac{2}{K}$. [5] reviewed the state of the art in the antenna selection (AS) schemes in energy efficient MIMO systems, the goal of which is to optimize the energy efficiency of the whole system. Based on this technique, blind interference alignment [6], ergodic alignment [7] and distributed interference alignment [8] were proposed.

Lee [9] introduced a new technique, dubbed "signal alignment", to solve the network information flow problem for an MIMO Y channel consisting of one relay node and three source nodes, each sending information to the other two via the relay node. One key feature of the technique is its capability of aligning signal streams for different source node pairs at the relay. When combined with the network coding technique, signal alignment can significantly increase the network throughput [10,11]. The two powerful techniques (interference alignment and signal alignment) have joined force in a few recent studies of an MIMO two-way relay X channel. This particular channel has two groups of source nodes, each of which includes two source nodes, and one relay node. Each source node is equipped with M antennas, and the relay node is equipped with N antennas. Via the relay node, every source node in one group exchanges two independent messages with two nodes in the other group. For the special case in which $M = 3$, and $N = 4$, Lee and Park [12] achieved the DoF of 8 by employing network coding. Xiang and Tao [13] considered a more general case with arbitrary M and N. They derived an upper bound on the total DoF as $\min\{2M, N\}$. Incorporating signal alignment and interference cancelation techniques, they proposed a transmission scheme to achieve the upper bound for the case where $M = 5$, $N = 8$. Similar schemes for achieving the upper bound with arbitrary M and N were also discussed in the same paper.

Network coding is an important approach to enhance spectrum efficiency. This technique was first introduced by Ahlswede and Cai [14] in the multi-hop wired network setting. Then [15] summarized the state-of-the-art research on network coding. A unique feature of network coding is that the intermediate node, i.e. the relay node, receives messages, mixes them, and forwards the mixed signals to several destinations simultaneously. Zhang [16] and Kitti et al. [17] first applied the technique to two-way relay channels, which has evidently increased the overall network throughput.

Scientists frequently use wireless MIMO relay channels to model varieties of communication systems. For instance, WSN is a typical wireless MIMO relay channel, where the relay node is the base station and the source nodes are the sensor nodes. In most practical applications, such as WSN, both the number of the source nodes and the number of each node's antennas are constantly subject to change. This motivates us to propose and study a general type of multiple-input multiple-output relay channels, for which we use the abbreviation G-MIMO. In a typical G-MIMO relay channel, there are two groups of source nodes (Group A and Group B). Each group has arbitrarily many source nodes. Via the relay node, each source node in Group A with an arbitrary number of antennas exchanges independent messages with each source node in Group B that is also equipped with an arbitrary number of antennas. The same process can be reversed in the sense that source nodes in Group B initiate the exchange of information. Thus, two-way information flow ensues. This broader setting includes the traditional MIMO two-way relay X channel as a special case. The purpose of the present paper is two-fold: (i) to derive an upper bound on the total DoF for G-MIMO relay channels; (ii) to design an efficient transmission scheme that allows the system to achieve the upper bound. The latter requires full utilization of the above mentioned techniques. We also briefly touch upon a future research topic to quantify the relationship between graded levels of network security and the corresponding DoF of the G-MIMO relay channels.

The remainder of this paper is organized as follows. In Sect. 2, we introduce and describe the G-MIMO relay channel model and give a tight upper bound on a corresponding DoF. These are the results in Theorem 1. In Sect. 3, we prove Theorem 1 and give three corollaries that are of independent interest. In Sect. 4, we show that the upper bound is tight by designing an efficient transmission scheme to achieve the upper bound. We also discuss various situations under which the upper bound is achieved. In Sect. 5, we give concluding remarks and propose future work.

2   Channel Model and Main Result

We divide the discussion of this section into two subsections. In Subsect. 2.1, we define and describe the G-MIMO relay channel model. In Subsect. 2.2, we state our main result on the DoF of G-MIMO relay channels.

2.1   Channel Model

A G-MIMO relay channel is shown in Fig. 1. For clarity, we make use of the superscript * to differentiate quantities associated with Group B from those associated with Group A. Source Node i in Group A has a_i antennas ($i = 1, 2, \ldots, L$), and Source Node j in Group B has a_j^* antennas ($j = 1, 2, \ldots, M$). Source Node i in Group A sends an independent message $W_{i,j}$ to Source Node j in Group B via the relay node. When the sending-receiving order is reversed, we use $W_{i,j}^*$ to denote the message sent to Source Node j from Group A by Source Node i from Group B. For example, a_1^*, a_1 represents, respectively, the numbers of the first source node's antennas in Group B and Group A. Likewise, $d_{1,1}^*, (d_{1,1}$

represents the DoF from the first source node in Group B (A) to the first source node in Group A (B). We emphasize that the channel consists of two groups of source nodes and one relay node. The entire transmission process is executed in two phases. In Phase I (the multiple-access phase), all source nodes transmit signals to the relay node. The received signals at the relay node is given by:

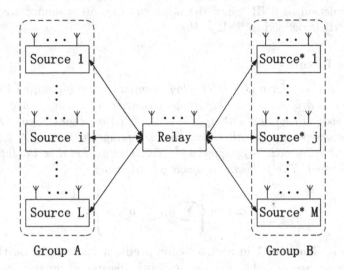

Source 1   Source* 1

Source i   Relay   Source* j

Source L   Source* M

Group A   Group B

Fig. 1. G-MIMO relay channel

$$\mathbf{y}_r = \sum_{i=1}^{L} \mathbf{H}_{i,r}\mathbf{x}_i + \sum_{j=1}^{M} \mathbf{H}_{j,r}^{*}\mathbf{x}_j + \mathbf{n}_r$$

where $\mathbf{y}_r$ denotes the $N \times 1$ received signal vector; $\mathbf{n}_r$ denotes the additive white Gaussian noise (AWGN) vector at the relay; $\mathbf{H}_{i,r}$ ($\mathbf{H}_{j,r}^{*}$) is the $N \times a_i$ ($N \times a_j^{*}$) channel matrix from source node $i(j)$ to the relay; $\mathbf{x}_i(\mathbf{x}_j^{*})$ is the $a_i \times 1$ ($a_j^{*} \times 1$) transmitted signal vector by source node i (j) with the power constraint $\mathbb{E}(\mathrm{Tr}\{\mathbf{x}_i\mathbf{x}_i^{H}\}) \leq P(\mathbb{E}(\mathrm{Tr}\{\mathbf{x}_j^{*}(\mathbf{x}_j^{*})^{H}\}) \leq P)$. Here we assume that all entries of the channel matrices $\mathbf{H}_{i,r}(\mathbf{H}_{j,r}^{*})$ and $\mathbf{n}_r$ are independent and identically distributed (i.i.d) zero-mean complex Gaussian random variables with unit variance, so all the channel matrices are of full rank with probability 1.

In Phase II (the broadcast phase), a new signal $\mathbf{x}_r$ is generated at the relay node and is broadcasted to all the source nodes. The received signals at the ith source node of Group A and the jth source node of Group B are, respectively, written as

$$\mathbf{y}_i = \mathbf{H}_{r,i}\mathbf{x}_r + \mathbf{n}_i, \quad i = 1, 2, \ldots, L$$
$$\mathbf{y}_j^{*} = \mathbf{H}_{r,j}^{*}\mathbf{x}_r + \mathbf{n}_j^{*}, \quad j = 1, 2, \ldots, M.$$

The total DoF of the G-MIMO relay channel is defined as follows:

$$d \triangleq \sum_{i=1}^{L} \sum_{j=1}^{M} (d_{i,j} + d_{j,i}^*) = \lim_{\text{SNR} \to \infty} \frac{R(\text{SNR})}{\log(\text{SNR})} \qquad (2)$$

where $d_{i,j}(d_{j,i}^*)$ is the DoF from source node i to j (j to i), $R(\text{SNR})$ is the sum rate as a function of SNR. Since the noise samples are assumed to have unit variance, SNR is defined as $\text{SNR} \triangleq P$.

2.2 Main Result

Theorem 1. *Consider a G-MIMO relay channel with two groups (A and B) of source nodes and one relay node. Group A consists of L source nodes, and the ith source node is equipped with a_i ($i = 1, 2, \ldots, L$) antennas; Group B consists of M source nodes, and the jth source node is equipped with a_j^* ($j = 1, 2, \ldots, M$) antennas; the relay node is equipped with N antennas. Let d be the total DoF of the relay channel. The following inequality holds true:*

$$d \leq 2 \min \left\{ \sum_{i=1}^{L} a_i, \sum_{j=1}^{M} a_j^*, N \right\}. \qquad (3)$$

We will prove Theorem 1 in Sect. 3. Some preliminary remarks on the results of the theorem are in order. Further in-depth discussion on the result of the theorem will be given in Sect. 3.

- Generally speaking, we have a full-duplex mode in this transmission scheme. Therefore, the presence of the factor 2 is necessary in the estimate. If the mode turns into half-duplex, then the factor 2 is not needed.
- From the results of Theorem 1, we observe the following interesting phenomenon. When $N \leq \min \left\{ \sum_{i=1}^{L} a_i, \sum_{j=1}^{M} a_j^* \right\}$, the DoF of the relay channel is bounded from above by twice of the number of the relay node's antennas, which is precisely the bottleneck for the spectrum efficiency of the network.
- In the present study, we work exclusively on the cases for which

$$N < \min \left\{ \sum_{i=1}^{L} a_i, \sum_{j=1}^{M} a_j^* \right\}.$$

Even within the same transmission scheme, the mathematical analysis for other cases seems to be quite different, to which future effort is warranted.

3 Proof of the Main Result and Further Discussion

In this section, we first prove Theorem 1. We then apply the result of the theorem to other kinds of MIMO relay channels, such as MIMO two-way relay channel, MIMO Y relay channel, and MIMO X relay channel.

3.1 Proof of Theorem 1

We first consider the situation in which the network information flows from Group A to Group B, as indicated in Fig. 2. In the first phase (see Cut 1 in Fig. 1), all the source nodes a_i ($i = 1, 2, \ldots, L$) in group A simultaneously transmit information to the relay node. As is customarily assumed, all antennas a_i ($i = 1, 2, \ldots, L$) fully cooperate. Thus, the channel essentially functions like an $N \cdot \left(\sum_{i=1}^{L} a_i \right) - $ MIMO channel. From the main result of [18], we conclude that the DoF for the channel under discussion is $\min \left\{ \sum_{i=1}^{L} a_i, N \right\}$. Similarly, in the second phase (see Cut 2 in Fig. 1), we obtain the DoF to be $\min \left\{ N, \sum_{j=1}^{M} a_j^* \right\}$. Combining the two DoF's from the two phases and resorting to the cut-set theorem [19], we obtain the following upper bound for the total DoF for one direction:

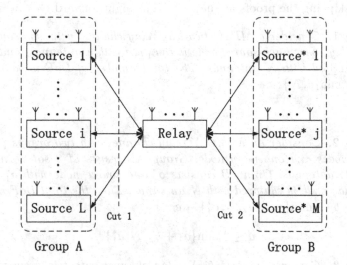

Fig. 2. G-MIMO relay channel

$$\sum_{i=1}^{L} \sum_{j=1}^{M} d_{i,j} \leq \min \left\{ \min \left(N, \sum_{i=1}^{L} a_i \right), \min \left[N, \sum_{j=1}^{M} a_j^* \right] \right\}$$

$$= \min \left\{ N, \sum_{i=1}^{L} a_i, \sum_{j=1}^{M} a_j^* \right\}.$$

In a similar way, we derive the total DoF for the other direction:

$$\sum_{i=1}^{L}\sum_{j=1}^{M} d_{j,i}^* \le \min\left\{N, \sum_{i=1}^{L} a_i, \sum_{j=1}^{M} a_j^*\right\}.$$

It follows that the DoF (denoted by d) for the entire channel is:

$$d = \sum_{i=1}^{L}\sum_{j=1}^{M} d_{i.j} + \sum_{i=1}^{L}\sum_{j=1}^{M} d_{j,i}^* \le 2\min\left\{\sum_{i=1}^{L} a_i, \sum_{j=1}^{M} a_j^*, N\right\}.$$

The proof is completed.

3.2 Discussion

In this subsection, we state three useful corollaries of Theorem 1. We take the liberty of skipping the proofs as they are all straight forward.

Corollary 1. *Consider a MIMO two-way relay channel with two source nodes and one relay node. Each source node is equipped with a antennas, and the relay node is equipped with N antennas. The total number of DoF is bounded from above by* 2 min$\{a, N\}$, *i.e.,*

$$d \le 2\min\{a, N\}.$$

Corollary 2. *Consider an MIMO Y relay channel with two groups (A and B) of source nodes and one relay node. Group A consists of 2 source nodes with $a_i(i = 1, 2)$ antennas; Group B consists of one source node with a_1^* antennas and the relay node is equipped with N antennas. Then the total DoF is bounded from above by* 2 min$\{a_1 + a_2, N, a_1^*\}$, *i.e.,*

$$d \le 2\min\{a_1 + a_2, N, a_1^*\}.$$

Corollary 3. *Consider an MIMO X relay channel with two groups of source nodes and one relay node. Each group consists of 2 source nodes with a antennas; and the relay node is equipped with N antennas. Then the total number of DoF is bounded from above by* 2 min$\{2a, N\}$, *i.e.,*

$$d \le 2\min\{2a, N\}.$$

Although the modalities of the MIMO relay channels covered by the three corollaries above are simple and naive, they exist in abundance among the hosts of the real world wireless communication apparatus. We use them as examples to show that the result of Theorem 1 is widely applicable in many different kinds of MIMO relay channels.

4   Achievability of the Upper Bound

In this section, we propose an efficient transmission scheme for the G-MIMO relay channel that achieves the DoF upper bound in Theorem 1. To facilitate the process, we will be making use of a variety of techniques, such as physical network coding, signal alignment, and joint transceiver design for interference cancelation,

For the direction $i \rightarrow j$, we make the reasonable assumption that the proposed scheme achieves

$$d_{i,j} = 2N\alpha_{i,j}, \quad i = 1, 2, \ldots, L, \quad j = 1, 2, \ldots, M,$$

where $\alpha_{i,j} = \frac{a_i + a_j^*}{2 \sum\limits_{i=1}^{L} \sum\limits_{j=1}^{M} (a_i + a_j^*)}$.

Similarly, for the direction $j \rightarrow i$, we have

$$d_{j,i}^* = 2N\alpha_{j,i}^*, \quad i = 1, 2, \ldots, L; \quad j = 1, 2, \ldots, M.$$

where $\alpha_{i,j} = \alpha_{j,i}^*$. Note that $d_{i,j}(d_{j,i}^*)$ are integers. It then follows that

$$d = \sum_{i=1}^{L} \sum_{j=1}^{M} d_{i.j} + \sum_{i=1}^{L} \sum_{j=1}^{M} d_{j.i}^* = 2N.$$

In the remainder of this section, we take source node 1 as an example for our analysis. All the other $(L + M - 1)$ source nodes can be dealt with in a similar fashion. Source node 1 transmits codewords $s_{1,j}^1, s_{1,j}^2, \ldots, s_{1,j}^{2N\alpha_{1,j}}$, $j = 1, 2, \ldots, M$ for message $W_{1,j}$, respectively, by using beamforming vector $\mathbf{V}_{1,j} = [\mathbf{v}_{1,j}^1, \mathbf{v}_{1,j}^2, \ldots, \mathbf{v}_{1,j}^{2N\alpha_{1,j}}]$, to source node j via the relay node. The other source nodes transmit their codewords accordingly. For clarity, we analyze the entire process in two phases.

4.1   Multiple-Access Phase

In the multiple-access phase, the transmitted signal of source node 1 is

$$\mathbf{x}_1 = \sum_{j=1}^{M} \mathbf{V}_{1,j}\mathbf{s}_{1,j} = \sum_{j=1}^{M} \left(\sum_{k=1}^{2N\alpha_{1,j}} \mathbf{v}_{1,j}^k s_{1,j}^k \right).$$

Based on the physical network coding [16], the relay node only needs to decode some mixture of the symbols, $W_{i,j} \oplus W_{j,i}^*$. By using the signal alignment for network coding [9], we choose beamforming vectors that satisfy the following conditions

$$\mathbf{H}_{1,r} \cdot \mathbf{v}_{1,1}^{k_1} = \mathbf{H}_{1,r} \cdot (\mathbf{v}_{1,1}^*)^{k_1} \triangleq \mathbf{g}_r^{k_1}; (k_1 = 1, 2, \cdots, 2N\alpha_{1,1})$$

$$\mathbf{H}_{1,r} \cdot \mathbf{v}_{1,2}^{k_2} = \mathbf{H}_{1,r} \cdot (\mathbf{v}_{2,1}^*)^{k_2} \triangleq \mathbf{g}_r^{2N\alpha_{1,1}+k_2}; (k_2 = 1, 2, \cdots, 2N\alpha_{1,2})$$

$$\vdots$$

$$\mathbf{H}_{1,r} \cdot \mathbf{v}_{1,h}^{k_h} = \mathbf{H}_{1,r} \cdot (\mathbf{v}_{h,1}^*)^{k_h} \triangleq \mathbf{g}_r^{2N\sum\limits_{j=1}^{h-1}\alpha_{1,j}+k_h} \quad ; (k_h = 1, 2, \cdots, 2N\alpha_{1,h})$$

$$\vdots$$

$$\mathbf{H}_{1,r} \cdot \mathbf{v}_{1,M}^{k_M} = \mathbf{H}_{1,r} \cdot (\mathbf{v}_{M,1}^*)^{k_M} \triangleq \mathbf{g}_r^{2N\sum\limits_{j=1}^{M-1}\alpha_{1,j}+k_M} \quad , (k_M = 1, 2, \cdots, 2N\alpha_{1,M})$$

where $\mathbf{g}_r^k, k = 1, 2, \ldots, 2N\sum\limits_{j=1}^{M}\alpha_{1,j}$, is the transmitting vector seen by the relay. These conditions imply that

$$\mathrm{span}([\mathbf{g}_r^1, \ldots, \mathbf{g}_r^{2N\alpha_{1,1}}]) \subseteq \mathrm{span}(\mathbf{H}_{1,r}) \cap \mathrm{span}(\mathbf{H}_{1,r}^*);$$

$$\mathrm{span}([\mathbf{g}_r^{2N\alpha_{1,1}+1}, \ldots, \mathbf{g}_r^{2N\alpha_{1,1}+2N\alpha_{1,2}}]) \subseteq \mathrm{span}(\mathbf{H}_{1,r}) \cap \mathrm{span}(\mathbf{H}_{2,r}^*);$$

$$\vdots$$

$$\mathrm{span}\left(\left[\mathbf{g}_r^{2N\sum\limits_{j=1}^{h-1}\alpha_{1,j}+1}, \ldots, \mathbf{g}_r^{2N\sum\limits_{j=1}^{h}\alpha_{1,j}}\right]\right) \subseteq \mathrm{span}(\mathbf{H}_{1,r}) \cap \mathrm{span}(\mathbf{H}_{h,r}^*);$$

$$\vdots$$

$$\mathrm{span}\left(\left[\mathbf{g}_r^{2N\sum\limits_{j=1}^{M-1}\alpha_{1,j}+1}, \ldots, \mathbf{g}_r^{2N\sum\limits_{j=1}^{M}\alpha_{1,j}}\right]\right) \subseteq \mathrm{span}(\mathbf{H}_{1,r}) \cap \mathrm{span}(\mathbf{H}_{M,r}^*).$$

Here $\mathrm{span}(\mathbf{H})$ stands for the column space. This allows us to rewrite the received signal at the relay as follows.

$$\mathbf{y}_r = \mathbf{G}_r\mathbf{s}_r + \mathbf{n}_r \tag{4}$$

where $\mathbf{G}_r \triangleq [\mathbf{g}_r^1, \mathbf{g}_r^2, \ldots, \mathbf{g}_r^N]$ which is an $N \times N$ matrix, and

$$\mathbf{s}_r \triangleq [s_{1,1}^1 + (s_{1,1}^*)^1, \ldots, s_{1,1}^{2N\alpha_{1,1}} + (s_{1,1}^*)^{2N\alpha_{1,1}}, \ldots,$$

$$s_{1,2}^1 + (s_{2,1}^*)^1, \ldots, s_{1,2}^{2N\alpha_{1,2}} + (s_{2,1}^*)^{2N\alpha_{1,2}}, \ldots,$$

$$s_{i,j}^1 + (s_{j,i}^*)^1, \ldots, s_{i,j}^{2N\alpha_{i,j}} + (s_{j,i}^*)^{2N\alpha_{i,j}}, \ldots,$$

$$s_{L,M}^1 + (s_{M,L}^*)^1, \ldots, s_{L,M}^{2N\alpha_{L,M}} + (s_{M,L}^*)^{2N\alpha_{L,M}}]^T,$$

which is a vector of N-components. As the entries of all the channel matrices are independently Gaussian, $\mathbf{G}_r$ is full-rank with probability 1. Thus, the relay node is able to decode $\mathbf{s}_r$ with probability 1. By applying the mapping principe of physical layer network coding, the mixture network coded messages

$$\hat{W}_{1,1} = W_{1,1} \oplus W_{1,1}^*, \hat{W}_{1,2} = W_{1,2} \oplus W_{2,1}^*, \cdots,$$
$$\hat{W}_{i,j} = W_{i,j} \oplus W_{j,i}^*, \cdots, \hat{W}_{L,M} = W_{L,M} \oplus W_{M,L}^*$$

can be obtained.

4.2 Broadcast Phase

In the broadcast phase, the relay node broadcasts the network messages shown below to all source nodes

$$\hat{W}_{1,1}, \hat{W}_{1,2}, \hat{W}_{1,3}, \cdots, \hat{W}_{1,M}$$
$$\hat{W}_{2,1}, \hat{W}_{2,2}, \hat{W}_{2,3}, \cdots, \hat{W}_{2,M}$$
$$\hat{W}_{3,1}, \hat{W}_{3,2}, \hat{W}_{3,3}, \cdots, \hat{W}_{3,M}$$
$$\cdots \quad \cdots$$
$$\hat{W}_{i,1}, \hat{W}_{i,2}, \hat{W}_{i,3}, \cdots, \hat{W}_{i,M}$$
$$\cdots \quad \cdots$$
$$\hat{W}_{L,1}, \hat{W}_{L,2}, \hat{W}_{L,3}, \cdots, \hat{W}_{L,M}.$$

The corresponding encoded symbol vectors are given by

$$[q_r^1, \cdots, q_r^{2N\alpha_{1,1}}], [q_r^{2N\alpha_{1,1}+1}, \cdots, q_r^{2N\alpha_{1,1}+2N\alpha_{1,2}}], \cdots,$$

$$\left[q_r^{(2N\sum\limits_{j=1}^{M-1}\alpha_{1,j})+1}, q_r^{(2N\sum\limits_{j=1}^{M-1}\alpha_{1,j})+2}, \cdots, q_r^{2N\sum\limits_{j=1}^{M}\alpha_{1,j}} \right];$$

$$\left[q_r^{(2N\sum\limits_{j=1}^{M}\alpha_{1,j})+1}, \cdots, q_r^{(2N\sum\limits_{j=1}^{M}\alpha_{1,j})+2N\alpha_{2,1}} \right], \cdots,$$

$$\left[q_r^{(2N\sum\limits_{j=1}^{M}\alpha_{1,j})+(2N\sum\limits_{j=1}^{M-1}\alpha_{2,j})+1}, \cdots, q_r^{(2N\sum\limits_{j=1}^{M}\alpha_{1,j})+(2N\sum\limits_{j=1}^{M}\alpha_{2,j})} \right];$$

$$\vdots$$

$$
\left[
\begin{array}{ccc}
q_r^{(2N\sum\limits_{i=1}^{l-1}\sum\limits_{j=1}^{M}\alpha_{i,j})+1} & ,\cdots, q_r^{(2N\sum\limits_{i=1}^{l-1}\sum\limits_{j=1}^{M}\alpha_{i,j})+2N\alpha_{l,1}}
\end{array}
\right], \cdots,
$$

$$
\left[
\begin{array}{cc}
q_r^{(2N\sum\limits_{i=1}^{l-1}\sum\limits_{j=1}^{M}\alpha_{i,j})+(2N\sum\limits_{j=1}^{M-1}\alpha_{l,j})+1} & ,\cdots, q_r^{(2N\sum\limits_{i=1}^{l}\sum\limits_{j=1}^{M}\alpha_{i,j})}
\end{array}
\right];
$$

$$\vdots$$

$$
\left[
\begin{array}{cc}
q_r^{(2N\sum\limits_{i=1}^{L-1}\sum\limits_{j=1}^{M}\alpha_{i,j})+1} & ,\cdots, q_r^{(2N\sum\limits_{i=1}^{L-1}\sum\limits_{j=1}^{M}\alpha_{i,j})+2N\alpha_{L,1}}
\end{array}
\right], \cdots,
$$

$$
\left[
\begin{array}{cc}
q_r^{(2N\sum\limits_{i=1}^{L-1}\sum\limits_{j=1}^{M}\alpha_{i,j})+(2N\sum\limits_{j=1}^{M-1}\alpha_{L,j})+1} & ,\cdots, q_r^{(2N\sum\limits_{i=1}^{L}\sum\limits_{j=1}^{M}\alpha_{i,j})}
\end{array}
\right];
$$

Then the transmitted signal at the relay node is rewritten as

$$
\mathbf{x}_r = \sum_{k=1}^{N} \mathbf{u}_r^k q_r^k
$$

where $\mathbf{U}_r = [\mathbf{u}_r^1, \ldots, \mathbf{u}_r^N]$ are beamforming vectors, which are designed at the relay node to make each component of the transmitted signal to lie in the null space of the effective channel matrices of the unintended source nodes. At source node 1, the received signal is

$$
\hat{\mathbf{y}}_1 = \tilde{\mathbf{H}}_{r,1}\mathbf{x}_r + \tilde{\mathbf{n}}_1 \tag{5}
$$

where $\hat{\mathbf{H}}_{r,1} \triangleq \mathbf{F}_1\mathbf{H}_{r,1}$ is the effective channel matrix from the relay node to the source node 1; $\mathbf{F}_1$ is the $2N\sum\limits_{j=1}^{M}\alpha_{j,1}^* \times a_1$ receiving filter matrix. So the received signal at source node 1 can be rewritten as

$$
\hat{\mathbf{y}}_1 = \mathbf{F}_1\mathbf{H}_{r,1}\left(\sum_{k=1}^{2N\sum\limits_{j=1}^{M}\alpha_{1,j}} \mathbf{u}_r^k q_r^k + \sum_{k=2N\sum\limits_{j=1}^{M}\alpha_{1,j}+1}^{N} \mathbf{u}_r^k q_r^k \right) + \hat{\mathbf{n}}_1.
$$

The first term in the bracket represents the useful network-coded messages $\hat{W}_{1,1}, \hat{W}_{1,2}, \hat{W}_{1,3}, \cdots, \hat{W}_{1,M}$, and the other term represents the combination of all unwanted interference messages

$$
\hat{W}_{i,j}, \quad i = 2, 3, ..., L; \quad j = 1, 2, ..., M.
$$

In order to cancel the interference, we need to design the transceivers for the source nodes and the relay node. For this purpose, We define

$$\mathbf{F}_i := [(\mathbf{f}_{1,i}^*)^1, \ldots, (\mathbf{f}_{1,i}^*)^{2N\alpha_{1,i}}, \ldots, (\mathbf{f}_{M,i}^*)^1, \ldots, (\mathbf{f}_{M,i}^*)^{2N\alpha_{M,i}}]^T, \quad i = 1, 2, \ldots, L;$$

$$\mathbf{F}_j^* := [\mathbf{f}_{1,j}^1, \ldots, \mathbf{f}_{1,j}^{2N\alpha_{1,j}}, \ldots, \mathbf{f}_{L,j}^1, \ldots, \mathbf{f}_{L,j}^{2N\alpha_{L,j}}]^T, \quad j = 1, 2, \ldots, M.$$

We then design the receiving matrices to align the effective receiving channel of each source node pair:

$$(\mathbf{f}_{1,1}^*)^k \mathbf{H}_{r,1} = \mathbf{f}_{1,1}^k \mathbf{H}_{r,1}^* \triangleq (\mathbf{w}_{1,1}^*)^{k_1}; \quad (k_1 = 1, 2, \cdots, 2N\alpha_{1,1}^*)$$

$$(\mathbf{f}_{2,1}^*)^k \mathbf{H}_{r,1} = \mathbf{f}_{1,2}^k \mathbf{H}_{r,2}^* \triangleq (\mathbf{w}_{2,1}^*)^{k_2}; \quad (k_2 = 1, 2, \cdots, 2N\alpha_{2,1}^*)$$

$$\cdots \qquad\qquad \cdots$$

$$(\mathbf{f}_{M,1}^*)^k \mathbf{H}_{r,1} = \mathbf{f}_{1,M}^k \mathbf{H}_{r,M}^* \triangleq (\mathbf{w}_{M,1}^*)^{k_M}. \quad (k_M = 1, 2, \cdots, 2N\alpha_{M,1}^*)$$

Here $\mathbf{f}_{i,j}^k$ ($(\mathbf{f}_{j,i}^*)^k$) is a $1 \times a_i^*$ ($1 \times a_i$) matrix; $\mathbf{w}_{i,j}^k$ is a $1 \times N$ effectively channel matrix between node i and j on the k-th data stream. The signal alignment of the broadcast phase is similar to that of the multiple-access phase. This allows us to choose the beamforming vectors $\mathbf{u}_r^k$ at the relay to lie in the null space of the intersection subspace of the corresponding effective channel as follows

$$\text{span}([\mathbf{u}_r^1, \ldots, \mathbf{u}_r^{2N\alpha_{1,1}}]) \subseteq \text{Null}([\hat{\mathbf{H}}_{r,2}, \hat{\mathbf{H}}_{r,3}, \ldots, \hat{\mathbf{H}}_{r,L}, \hat{\mathbf{H}}_{r,2}^*, \hat{\mathbf{H}}_{r,3}^*, \ldots, \hat{\mathbf{H}}_{r,M}^*]^T);$$

$$\text{span}([\mathbf{u}_r^{2N\alpha_{1,1}+1}, \ldots, \mathbf{u}_r^{2N\alpha_{1,1}+2N\alpha_{1,2}}])$$

$$\subseteq \text{Null}([\hat{\mathbf{H}}_{r,2}, \hat{\mathbf{H}}_{r,3}, \ldots, \hat{\mathbf{H}}_{r,L}, \hat{\mathbf{H}}_{r,1}^*, \hat{\mathbf{H}}_{r,3}^*, \ldots, \hat{\mathbf{H}}_{r,M}^*]^T);$$

$$\cdots\cdots\cdots\cdots$$

$$\text{span}\left(\left[\mathbf{u}_r^{2N\sum_{j=1}^{M-1}\alpha_{1,j}+1}, \ldots, \mathbf{u}_r^{2N\sum_{j=1}^{M}\alpha_{1,j}}\right]\right)$$

$$\subseteq \text{Null}([\hat{\mathbf{H}}_{r,2}, \hat{\mathbf{H}}_{r,3}, \ldots, \hat{\mathbf{H}}_{r,L}, \hat{\mathbf{H}}_{r,1}^*, \hat{\mathbf{H}}_{r,2}^*, \ldots, \hat{\mathbf{H}}_{r,(M-1)}^*]^T).$$

Here $\text{Null}(\mathbf{H})$ stands for the null space of the matrix $\mathbf{H}$. Next, we prove that the above condition can be satisfied with probability 1. We will give a complete proof to the first formula. The others can be taken care of in an almost identical way. It is straight forward to see that $\hat{\mathbf{H}}_{r,i}$ and $\hat{\mathbf{H}}_{r,j}^*$ are, respectively, $\left(2N\sum_{j=1}^{M}\alpha_{j,i}^*\right) \times N$ and $\left(2N\sum_{i=1}^{L}\alpha_{i,j}\right) \times N$ matrices. Hence, we have

$$\dim\left([\hat{\mathbf{H}}_{r,2}, \hat{\mathbf{H}}_{r,3}, \ldots, \hat{\mathbf{H}}_{r,L}, \hat{\mathbf{H}}_{r,2}^*, \hat{\mathbf{H}}_{r,3}^*, \ldots, \hat{\mathbf{H}}_{r,M}^*]^T\right)$$

$$= N \cdot \left(2N - 2N\sum_{j=1}^{M}\alpha_{j,1}^* - 2N\sum_{i=1}^{L}\alpha_{i,1}\right).$$

Denote $A_{L,M}$ the matrix on the left hand side of the above equation. Upon aligning the receiving-effective channels and canceling the repeated rows, we see that the row rank of the matrix $A_{L,M}$ is

$$\left(2N - 2N\sum_{j=1}^{M}\alpha_{j,1}^{*} - 2N\sum_{i=1}^{L}\alpha_{i,1}\right)/2+$$

$$\left(2N\sum_{j=2}^{M}\alpha_{j,1}^{*} + 2N\sum_{i=2}^{L}\alpha_{i,1}\right)/2 = N - 2N\alpha_{1,1}. \tag{6}$$

The overall rank of the matrix $A_{L,M}$ is $\min\{N - 2N\alpha_{1,1}, N\} = N - 2N\alpha_{1,1}$, so the dimension of its null space is $N - (N - 2N\alpha_{1,1}) = 2N\alpha_{1,1}$. Note that the intersection of the null spaces of the first two matrices is

$$\text{Null}([\hat{\mathbf{H}}_{r,2}, \hat{\mathbf{H}}_{r,3}, \ldots, \hat{\mathbf{H}}_{r,L}, \hat{\mathbf{H}}_{r,2}^{*}, \hat{\mathbf{H}}_{r,3}^{*}, \ldots, \hat{\mathbf{H}}_{r,M}^{*}]^{T})$$

$$\cap \text{Null}([\hat{\mathbf{H}}_{r,2}, \hat{\mathbf{H}}_{r,3}, \ldots, \hat{\mathbf{H}}_{r,L}, \hat{\mathbf{H}}_{r,1}^{*}, \hat{\mathbf{H}}_{r,3}^{*}, \ldots, \hat{\mathbf{H}}_{r,M}^{*}]^{T})$$

$$= \text{Null}([\hat{\mathbf{H}}_{r,2}, \hat{\mathbf{H}}_{r,3}, \ldots, \hat{\mathbf{H}}_{r,L}, \hat{\mathbf{H}}_{r,1}^{*}, \hat{\mathbf{H}}_{r,2}^{*}, \ldots, \hat{\mathbf{H}}_{r,M}^{*}]^{T}).$$

It follows that the row rank of the above matrix is

$$\left(2N - 2N\sum_{j=1}^{M}\alpha_{j,1}^{*}\right)/2 + \left(2N\sum_{j=1}^{M}\alpha_{j,1}^{*}\right)/2 = N. \tag{7}$$

It can be seen that the dimension of its null space is $N - N = 0$. For the other source node terms, we can get similar results. We conclude that the null space of the concatenated effective channel matrix for each source node team has no intersection with that of the other source node terms, so all the beamforming vectors $\mathbf{u}_{r}^{k}$ are linearly independent with probability 1. Thus the source node 1 can get the useful signals with no interference.

$$\tilde{\mathbf{y}}_{1} = \hat{\mathbf{H}}_{r,1}\left(\underbrace{\sum_{k=1}^{2N\alpha_{1,1}}\mathbf{u}_{r}^{k}q_{r}^{k}}_{\text{for } \hat{W}_{1,1}} + \underbrace{\sum_{k=2N\alpha_{1,1}}^{2N\alpha_{1,1}+2N\alpha_{1,2}}\mathbf{u}_{r}^{k}q_{r}^{k}}_{\text{for } \hat{W}_{1,2}} + \cdots + \underbrace{\sum_{k=2N\sum_{j=1}^{M-1}\alpha_{1,j}+1}^{2N\sum_{j=1}^{M}\alpha_{1,j}}\mathbf{u}_{r}^{k}q_{r}^{k}}_{\text{for } \hat{W}_{1,M}}\right).$$

From formulas (6) and (7), source node 1 can obtain the messages from all the source nodes $j(j = 1, 2, \ldots, M)$ at the other side. The corresponding messages are given by

$$W_{1,1}^{*} = W_{1,1} \oplus \hat{W}_{1,1};$$
$$W_{2,1}^{*} = W_{1,2} \oplus \hat{W}_{1,2};$$
$$\cdots$$
$$W_{M,1}^{*} = W_{1,M} \oplus \hat{W}_{1,M}.$$

In a similar fashion, the other source nodes obtain and handle the messages intended for themselves. Therefore, the transmission scheme as elucidated above reaches the desired upper bound $2N$.

5   Conclusion and Future Work

In the present paper, we study a general type of MIMO (G-MIMO) relay channels. We derived a tight upper bound on the DoF of these relay channel. In addition, by fully utilizing the techniques mentioned in the introduction of the paper, we design an efficient transmission scheme to achieve the upper bound under the assumption that $N \leq \min \left\{ \sum_{i=1}^{L} a_i, \sum_{j=1}^{M} a_j^* \right\}$. To conclude the present paper, we propose some research topics that are closely related to the main results here and are worthy of devoting future effort.

- In practical applications, the number of the relay node's antennas N may be more than the number of one side of the source nodes' antennas. That is

$$N > \min\{\sum_{i=1}^{L} a_i, \sum_{j=1}^{M} a_j^*\}.$$

  This is beyond the scope of what we have studied in the present paper. We are currently, investigating the important case and preparing a future publication.
- There are only one relay node and two groups of source nodes in the G-MIMO relay channel. However, relay channels boasting of having more relay nodes and more groups of source nodes widely exist in wireless communication. We anticipate that proper modifications of the current methods will be able to tackle the more general situations.
- Network security is becoming an utmost important issue in wireless communication. Understandably, the information transmission rates may be constrained by safety requirements, as shown by the following inequality:

$$\frac{1}{a_1^*}\mathrm{H}(\mathbf{W}_{\{1,2,...,L\}\rightarrow 2} \mid Y_1^*) \geq \sum_{i\in\{1,2,...,L\}} R_{i2},$$

where Y_1^* is the information accepted by source node 1 from Group B, and H represents entropy of the system. We are keenly interested in studying graded levels of network security and establishing quantitative relationships between levels of network security and the corresponding DoF of the relay channels.

Acknowledgments. Xiao Chen and Liang Pang contributed equally to this work and share first authorship. This work was supported in part by the National Natural Science Foundation of China under Grant No. 61332010.

References

1. Zheng, L., Tse, D.N.: Packing spheres in the grassmann manifold: a geometric approach to the non-coherent multiantenna channel. IEEE Trans. Inform. Theory **48**, February 2002

2. Jafar, S., Shamai, S.: Degrees of freedom region of the mimo x channel. IEEE Trans. Inform. Theory **54**(1), 151–170 (2008)
3. Maddah-Ali, M., Motahari, A., Khandani, A.: Communication over mimo x channels: interference alignment, decomposition, and performance analysis. IEEE Trans. Inform. Theory **54**(8), 3457–3470 (2008)
4. Cadambe, V., Jafar, S.: Interference alignment and degrees of freedom of the K-user interference channel. IEEE Trans. Inform. Theory **54**(8), 3425–3441 (2008)
5. Zhou, X., Bai, B., Chen, W.: Invited paper: antenna selection in energy efficient MIMO systems: a survey. China Communications **12**(9), 162–173 (2015)
6. Gou, T., Wang, C., Jafar, S.: Aiming perfectly in the dark-blind interference alignment through staggered antenna switching. IEEE Trans. Sig. Process. **59**(6), 2734–2744 (2011)
7. Jafar, S.: The ergodic capacity of phase-fading interference networks. IEEE Trans. Inform. Theory **57**(12), 7685–7694 (2011)
8. Gomadam, K., Cadambe, V., Jafar, S.: A distributed numerical approach to interference alignment and applications to wireless interference networks. IEEE Trans. Inform. Theory **57**(6), 3309–3322 (2011)
9. Lee, N., Lim, J., Chun, J.: Degrees of freedom of the MIMO Y channel: signal space alignment for network coding. IEEE Trans. Inform. Theory **56**(7), 3332–3342 (2010)
10. Lee, K., Lee, N., Lee, I.: Achievable degrees of freedom on k-user Y channels. IEEE Trans. Wireless Commun. **11**(3), 1210–1219 (2012)
11. Wang, N., Ding, Z., Dai, X., Vasilakos, A.: On generalized MIMO Y channels: precoding design, mapping, and diversity gain. IEEE Trans. Veh. Technol. **60**(7), 3525–3532 (2011)
12. Lee, K., Park, S., Kim, J., Lee, I.: Degrees of freedom on mimo multi-link two-way relay channels. In: Proceedings of the IEEE Globecom (2010)
13. Xiang, Z.Z., Tao, M.X., Mo, J.H., Wang, X.D.: Degrees of freedom for MIMO two-way X relay channel. IEEE Trans. Sig. Process. **61**(7), 1711–1720 (2013)
14. Ahlswede, R., Cai, N., Li, S., Yeung, R.: Network information flow. IEEE Trans. Inform. Theory **46**(4), 1204–1216 (2000)
15. Matsuda, T., Noguchi, T., Takine, T.: Survey of network coding and its applications. IEICE Trans. Commun. **E94-B**(3), 698–717 (2011)
16. Zhang, S., Liew, S., Lam, P.: Hot topic: physical-layer network coding. In: Proceedings of the ACM MobiCom, pp. 358–365, September 2006
17. Katti, S., Gollakota, S., Katabi, D.: Embracing wireless interference: analog network coding. In: Proceedings of the ACM SIGCOMM, September 2007
18. Zheng, L., Tse, D.: Diversity and multiplexing: a fundamental tradeoff in multiple-antenna channels. IEEE Trans. Inform. Theory **49**(5), 1073–1096 (2003)
19. Cover, T., Gamal, A.: Capacity theorems for the relay channel. IEEE Trans. Inform. Theory **25**(5), 572–584 (1979)

Formalizing and Verifying GP TEE TA Interface Specification Using Coq

Xia Yang[✉], Zheng Yang, Haiyong Sun, and Jingyu Liu

School of Information and Software Engineering, University of Electronic Science
and Technology of China, Sichuan, China
{26763018,510644493,1037792257,928153822}@qq.com

Abstract. The ARM TrustZone platform has provided a trusted execution environment (TEE) for mobile device to improve system security.
The Global Platform presents a TEE Internal Core API Specification
to define the TEE, the TEE system architecture, and the Internal and
Client API specifications. However, hackers can still attack the TEE by
means of the tampering the message stored in the communication buffer
that is used to exchange information between the TEE and REE world.
In order to solve this problem, this paper presents a formal security model
of the GP_TEE_TA_Interface and verifies the correctness of this model
using Coq based on the GP specification. The formalization identifies
the TA Interface specification as well as modelling the valid trace of TA
Interface based on a one-session application, which can effectively detect
and filter the invalid TA service request that from REE. These results
are useful for the standard institutions and TEE developers to develop
security TA software and prevent from hackers attack.

Keywords: GP TEE APIs specification · TA interface · Formal and
verification · Coq

1 Introduction

Smart connected devices, such as smartphones and others, are intrinsic to daily
life: they are used for business, social interactions, making purchases and enjoy-
ing media content. All of this data is susceptible to attacks from hackers. Also
millions of downloadable applications represent an even larger opportunity for
fraudsters. The Global Platform Trusted Execution Environment (TEE) System Architecture effectively addresses these concerns, which has been launched
in 2011 [1]. It includes the definition of the TEE, the TEE system architecture,
and the Internal and Client API specifications. The TEE is a secure area of the
main processor in a smart phone (or any connected device). It ensures that sensitive data is stored, processed and protected in an isolated, trusted environment.
The TEE's ability to offer isolated safe execution of an authorized security software, known as 'trusted application', enables it to provide end-to-end security
by enforcing protected execution of authenticated code, confidentiality, authenticity, privacy, system integrity and data access rights. The TEE offers a level of

© Springer Nature Singapore Pte Ltd. 2017
M. Xu et al. (Eds.): CTCIS 2017, CCIS 704, pp. 213–226, 2017.
https://doi.org/10.1007/978-981-10-7080-8_16

protection against attacks that has been generated in the Rich OS environment. It assists in the control of access rights and houses sensitive applications, which need to be isolated from the Rich OS. The APIs can reduce the coupling and protect the important sources and functions away from the illegal accessing caused by Rich Execution Environment (REE) [2]. However, even there is the Internal and Client API specifications, the function security, integrity and robustness still depend on developer's experience and proficiency, during the design and implementation of a TEE software system. Because Global Platform Specifications are expressed in natural language by informal or semi-formal notations, their ambiguity may confuse some developers and encounter potential risk of developing projects. For example: "Note that these annotations cannot be expressed in the C language. However, the [in], [in-buf], [instring], [instringopt], and [ctx] annotations can make use of the const C keyword.... However, the C header file of a compliant Implementation SHOULD use the const keyword when these annotations appear. Therefore, potential bugs that could be used by hackers still exist.

In 2014, Dan Rosenberg, the security expert, announced that there were some security vulnerabilities about integer overflow in the QSEE TrustZone Kernel [3]. In 2016, during the GeekPwn, the research group Shellphish, from America, showed the process of modifying the security module in the TrustZone Kernel of HUAWEI P9 Lite and disabled the function of fingerprint verification. These are vulnerabilities caused by the communication process between REE and TEE. In REE world, hacker can always find a method to attack the communication process and to tamper the message in the communication buffer that is used to exchange information between the TEE and REE world. For example, hackers may change the operation request stored in the buffer to make it become invalid, which will lead to TA service unable to correctly process it and to cause the critical information leaking. In order to avoid this risk, we build a security model for TA based on the TA interface specification of GP TEE, which can detect and filter the invalid or risky operation request that from REE. In this way, TEE world can be protected against from the potential attack caused by the communication vulnerability or malicious operation.

We have done following three contributions in this paper. Formalize the Global Platform TEE TA Interface in Coq and present a state transition model for TA Interface in the one-session TA case. Extract security properties of this model based on the GP TEE Specification. Verify the correctness of this model and check if it meets the security properties using Coq. This approach can guide user to develop a correct trusted application, and it also can protect TEE world from communication vulnerability. For example, the data (calling sequence, input value and function address) from the REE world will be checked, if it is not satisfied with valid preconditions and results of TA interface defined in the state transition model, the framework will reject this request and terminate the operation.

The paper is arranged as following: Sect. 2 gives a general overview of the proof assistant Coq and express why we choose it. Section 3 introduces the GP TEE API specification such as the TEE system architecture and the TA interface. Section 4 formalizes and models the TA interface based on the GP specification. Section 5 formalizes the model of system state transition, and verifies the model if it is correct and meet the GP TEE specification, using Coq prover. Conclusions and future works are discussed at the end of this paper.

2 Coq Proof Assistant

Coq is a Proof Assistant [4] for a Logical Framework known as the Calculus of Inductive Constructions. It is designed to develop mathematical proofs, and especially to write formal specifications, programs and to verify that programs are correct with respect to their specification. It provides a specification language named GALLINA. It allows the interactive construction of formal proofs, and also the manipulation of functional programs consistently with their specifications.

Nowadays, Coq still plays as a very important and essential role in the formalization field. A number of related tools and research are based on Coq, and it even can represent one of the highest achievements in this field. For instance, Krakatoa used to verify micro-programs implement by Java [5]. Verified Software Toolchain (VST) [6] designed by Princeton University used to verify C program. CompCert [7], which is a typical representation in verified trusted compiler field, and the breakthrough of Deep Specifications and Certified Abstraction Layers put forward by Yale University [8] using Proof Assistant Coq. Besides, Coq has been successfully applied in Trusted Logic industry project as the proof assistant for verifying the smart card system and the whole runtime environment of JavaCard Programming Language [5], DDF [19], a deep learning framework programming language, also is verified by Coq. From the above content, it is obvious that Coq has important theoretical value and practical significance in formalization field. It can help researcher create the specification and verification with high feasibility and high reliability. Therefore, we choose Coq as assistant prover for formalizing and verifying the GP TEE API specifications.

3 GP TEE API Specification

3.1 GP TEE System Architecture

In modern devices, such as smartphones, there is an extensive and versatile operating environment, the Rich Execution Environment (REE). It brings flexibility and capability, but at the same time leaves devices vulnerable to a wide range of security threats. The TEE is designed to reside alongside the REE and provide a safe area in the device to protect sensitive information and execute security related code (Fig. 1).

Global Platform defines the TEE as: At the highest level, a Trusted Execution Environment (TEE) is an environment where the following are true:

- Any code executing inside the TEE is trusted in authenticity and integrity.
- The other assets are also protected in confidentiality. The TEE shall resist all known remote and software attacks, and a set of external hardware attacks.

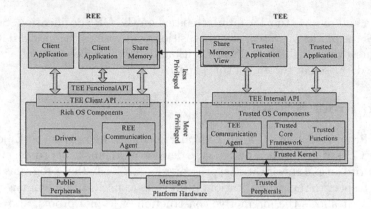

Fig. 1. TEE system architecture of GP

- Both assets and code are protected from unauthorized tracing and control through debug and test features.

The TEE described by Global Platform is an isolated execution environment. It can provide security features such as isolated execution, integrity of Trusted Applications along with confidentiality of their assets.

The TEE is a separate execution environment that runs alongside the Rich OS and provides security services to REE running inside the environment. The goal of the TEE Software Architecture is to make Trusted Applications (TA) that provides isolated and trustworthy capabilities for service providers, which can then be used through intermediary Client Applications (CA).

The TEE Functional API offers Client Applications a set of Rich OS-friendly APIs. These will allow access to some TEE services, such as cryptography or trusted storage, with a programming model familiar to Rich OS application developers. There are many components for supporting the secure services in the TEE software architecture, such as the Communication Agent and Trust OS component. The Communication Agent is an important module that is responsible for information exchange between TEE and REE through message. The client application of REE call this Communication Agent to exchange data with trusted application of TEE by means of the TEE Client API.

3.2 GP TA Interface (Entry Point)

There are a number of TEE APIs in the Global Platform Specification such as Trusted Core Framework API, Trusted Storage API and Cryptographic Operations API. Each TA must provide the Implementation with a number of functions, collectively called the "TA interface". These functions are the entry points called by the Trusted Core Framework to create the instance, notify the instance that a new client is connecting, notify the instance when the client invokes a command, etc. These entry points cannot be registered dynamically by the TA code:

They must be bounded to the framework before the TA code is started. There are five main APIs of trusted applications in the trusted framework, which is defined in the GP_TEE_TA_Interface Specification.

- **TA_CreateEntryPoint:** This is the TA constructor. It is called once and only once in the life-time of the TA instance. If this function fails, the instance is not created.
- **TA_DestroyEntryPoint:** This is the TA destructor. The Trusted Core Framework calls this function just before the TA instance is terminated. The Framework MUST guarantee that no sessions are open when this function is called. When TA_DestroyEntryPoint returns, the Framework MUST collect all resources claimed by the Trusted Application instance.
- **TA_OpenSessionEntryPoint:** This function is called whenever a client attempts to connect to the TA instance to open a new session. If this function returns an error, the connection is rejected and no new session is opened. In this function, the TA can attach an opaque void* context to the session. This context is recalled in all subsequent TA calls within the session.
- **TA_CloseSessionEntryPoint:** This function is called when the client closes a session and disconnects from the TA instance. The Implementation guarantees that there are no active commands in the session being closed. The session context reference is given back to the TA by the Framework. It is the responsibility of the TA to deallocate the session context if memory has been allocated for it.
- **TA_InvokeCommandEntryPoint:** This function is called whenever a client invokes a TA command. The Framework gives back the session context reference to the Trusted Application in this function call.

In the rest of this paper, we will call above five APIs as TA_CEP, TA_DEP, TA_OSEP, TA_CSEP, and TA_ICEP respectively.

When the user needs to start a TA for a critical application, for example the payment online, the communication agent will deliver this instruction to TEE and one of above five interface will be started. So if the instruction is tampered by hacker, the TA will become an untrusted server. In order to deal with this problem, in this paper, we formalize and verify the TA Interface using theorem proving and provide a guideline on how to correctly use TA Interface. In this way, the invalid and risk message produced by communication agent will be filtered and dropped, and the trusted applications in the TEE world will always execute valid instruction and return the correct result.

4   Formalization and Model of GPTEETA Interface

4.1   Formalizing the TA Interface Specification

Here we formalize the above 5 GP_TEE_TA_Interface using Coq prover and define the session state between TA Interfaces.

Definition 1 (Session State). There are three Session State, SS_None, SS_Open and SS_Close, which represents the current state of TA session. If the session does not exist, the initial state is SS_None. When the TEE world gets the instruction about session operation from REE, the session state change to SS_Open or SS_Close state according to the GP_TEE_TA_Interface function that shows in the Fig. 2:

Inductive GP_TEE_TA_Interface : Session_State $\rightarrow$ Set :=

| Start : SS_None $\rightarrow$ GP_TEE_TA_Interface

| TA_CreateEntryPoint : SS_Close $\rightarrow$ GP_TEE_TA_Interface

| TA_DestroyEntryPoint : SS_Close $\rightarrow$ GP_TEE_TA_Interface

| TA_OpenSessionEntryPoint : SS_Close $\rightarrow$ GP_TEE_TA_Interface

| TA_CloseSessionEntryPoint :SS_Open $\rightarrow$ GP_TEE_TA_Interface

| TA_InvokeCommandEntryPoint :SS_Open $\rightarrow$ GP_TEE_TA_Interface.

Fig. 2. Session state of TA

4.2 Modelling TA Interface Based on the One-Session Application

The current session state may change to another one based on the relation between TA Interfaces, for example, if the initial state is SS_None and the next state just only is SS_Open. So the state transition can check whether the TA in the correct way or not. We build a formal model for state transition based on the one-session TA service, which defines the relation and logic between TA Interfaces that used to ensure the correctness of session state. The invalid and malicious instruction from REE can be found and filtered out by this session state model.

The input and output states of each API defined in the model are extracted from the GP TEE Interface Specification one by one. The primitive elements and the respective explanations are given in the Definition 2. The basic state formal is defined in Definition 3.

Definition 2 (Primitive element). The **sl** is used to represent the list of session and the **t** is used to represent the current request. The **ident** stands for the identifier of every session including the uuid and login type. The ss records the session current state, SS_None, SS_Open and SS_Close. The **re** is used to record the return value from a TA interface. We also use the predicate Di_σ to check whether the data X is modified or not. If the X is changed, Di_σ will return an error message and throw out. Otherwise, it will return X directly.

Definition 3 (System State). In order to check the correctness of logic for the TA implementation and ensure the system is always valid state, we also formalize the system state as a tuple $\Gamma : \sigma <sl, t, i, ident, ss, re>$ for one session trusted application system. It is also used to trace the parameter passing between TA interfaces.

Definition 4 (Step state transition). The system state will change by single TA Interface operation, which is indicated as follows. Define the initial system state is $\Gamma : \sigma <None, None, None, None, None>$.

- **TA_CEP:** If the operation requested is TA_CEP, the state transition pre-condition must be the $\emptyset$ state. When the pre-condition satisfies, the session list will be created, the type of operation will be updated as the TA_CEP, the state of session will be set as SS_close and return value will be set as TEE_SUCCESS. The new system state $\Gamma : \sigma <sl, TA_{CEP}, None, close, TA_{SUCCESS}>$ will generate.

- **TA_OSEP:** If the operation requested is TA_OSEP and the pre-condition tuple $(ss, ops, re)\sigma_{last}$ is equivalent to $(close, TA\_CEP, TEE\_SUCCESS)$, the session list and the session identifier will be inherited from the last state directly. Then the state of session will be set as SS_open, the type of operation change to the TA_OSEP and the return value will be set as TEE_SUCCESS. The new system state $\Gamma : \sigma <Di_{\sigma last}(sl), TA_{OSEP}, ident, close, open, TEE_{SUCCESS}>$ will generate.

- **TA_CSEP:** If the operation requested is TA_CSEP and the pre-condition tuple $(sl, re)\sigma_{last}$ is equivalent to $(l_{\neq nil}, TEE\_SUCCESS)$, the session list will be set as nil and the session identifier will be inherited from the last state directly. Then the state of session will be set as SS_close, the type of operation updates to the TA_CSEP and return value will be set as TEE_SUCCESS. The new system state $\Gamma : \sigma <None, TA_{CSEP}, Di_{\sigma last}(ident), close, TEE_{SUCCESS}>$ will generate.

- **TA_DEP:** If the operation requested is TA_DEP and the pre-condition tuple $(ss, re)\sigma_{last}$ is equivalent to $(close, TEE\_SUCCESS)$, the session list, the type of operation, the session identifier and the session state will all be set none. The return value will be set as TEE_SUCCESS and will get the new system state $\Gamma : \sigma <None, None, None, None, TEE_{SUCCESS}>$. Actually, this new systems state equal the initial system state $\Gamma : \sigma <None, None, None, None, None>$.

- **TA_ICEP:** If the operation requested is TA_ICEP and the pre-condition tuple $(sl, t, ss, re)\sigma_{last}$ is equivalent to $(l_{\neq nil}, TA\_OSEP, open, TEE\_SUCCESS)$, the session list, the session identifier and session state will be inherited from the last state directly, the type of operation will change to TA_CSEP and the return value will be set as TEE_SUCCESS. The new system state $\Gamma : \sigma <Di_{\sigma last}(sl), TA_{ICEP}, Di_{\sigma last}(ident), \sigma_{last}ss, TEE_{SUCCESS}>$ will generate.

The model of the step state transition can be formalized from the above described system state transition which is caused by one TA Interface operation. The model is shown in the Fig. 3.

The paper is arranged as following: Sect. 2 gives a general overview of the proof assistant Coq and express why we choose it. Section 3 introduces the GP TEE API specification such as the TEE system architecture and the TA inter-face. Section 4 formalizes and model the TA inter-face based on the GP specification. Section 5 formalize the model of system state transition, and verify if the

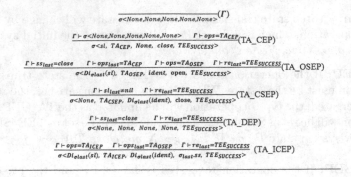

Fig. 3. Schematic of an HCE

model is correct and meet the GP TEE specification, using Coq. Conclusions and future works are discussed at the end of this paper.

Definition 5 (Trace state transition in one session case). If assume that only one session may be created during the communication TEE and REE, the model of state transition is defined as follows:

- The initial system state and the final system state must be $\emptyset$.
- The output state of the former operation is the input state of the latter operation.
- The valid trace of all TA operations in one session case is : $TA\_CEP \twoheadrightarrow TA\_OSEP \twoheadrightarrow TA\_ICEP \twoheadrightarrow TA\_CSEP \twoheadrightarrow TA\_DEP$.

This above model defines a strict rule for TA operation, if developer follows this model to implement trusted software system, the malicious attack from REE can be checked and filtered. In the next chapter, we will formalize and verify the abstract functions of five TA Interfaces using Coq, in order to certify whether the model is correct or not.

5   Formalizing and Verifying GP_TEE_TA Interface in Coq

We define five high-order abstract functions to express the functional requirements of TA Interface using Coq, and verify the consistency between the functions and the standard state transition have also been verified in Coq.

5.1   Formalization

In this section, the formalization of abstract functions is given out in Coq to express the definitions and transition relationships. First of all, the basic state which is transported among the functions should be defined.

Definition 6 (State in Coq). The session states are defined as dependent value within the inductive type explicitly, it can be checked by the inference mechanism of Coq. So the state S processed in the functions is a tuple $S = Record(sl, t, ident, re)$. The definition in Coq is shown as follow.

```
Record State : Set := {
  session : list TEE_Session;
  trace : option GP_TEE_TA_Interface;
  ident : option TEE_Identifier;
  re : option APIReType
}.
```

Definition 7 (State transition model). The high-order abstract requirement functions, which are needed to define, are similar to each other. So they can be abstracted as two main parts called **check** and **state_trace** where:

- **check** is defined for checking whether the input state is satisfied with model shown in the Fig. 3. If there are something wrong, the program will be terminated and return error code, else the **state_trace** will be called.
- **state_trace** is implemented for the data function. It is used to generate a new state for the requested trace of operations.
- **Set** is used to reset the state of TA_DEP back to the ∅ state.

Then we present a model of state transition in the Fig. 4, consisting of two components, **check** and **state_trace**. Besides, fun_{OPSE}, fun_{OPSE} and fun_{OPSE} need **Di** which we defined before to guarantee the consistency of session list and session identifier between two operations. The part of the **state_trace** defined in Coq is shown in the Fig. 5.

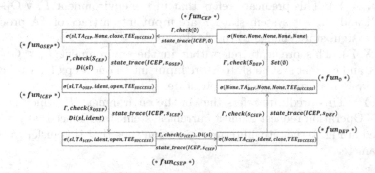

Fig. 4. Model of state transition

```
Function State_trace t (ops : GP_TEE_TA_Interface t) (s : State) : State
  match trace s with
    | None if   eqb (Value_GP2nat ops) (Value_GP2nat TA_CreateEntryPoint)
            then Build_State (cons State_session nil)
                                    (Some TA_CreateEntryPoint) None
                                    (Some TEE_SUCCESS)
            else Build_State (cons State_session nil)   None None
                                    (Some TEE_ERROR_BAD_PARAMETERS)
    | Some TA_CreateEntryPoint
            if   eqb (Value_GP2nat ops) (Value_GP2nat TA_CreateEntryPoint)
            then Build_State (cons State_session nil)   None None
                                    (Some TEE_ERROR_BAD_PARAMETERS)
            else Build_State (cons State_session nil)

    | Some TA_DestroyEntryPointBuild_State nil
      None None
      (Some TEE_SUCCESS)
    | Some TA_OpenSessionEntryPoint
            if   eqb (Value_GP2nat ops) (Value_GP2nat TA_CreateEntryPoint)
            then Build_State (cons State_session nil)...
```

Fig. 5. Formalization of state transition in Coq

5.2 Verification

In order to verify if the model mentioned above is correct and meet the GP TEE specification, we abstract high-order according to the requirement of GP TEE and proved them in Coq.

Definition 8 (Related predicates). The predicates used in the theorem and lemmas are defined as follows:

$S_{OPS}(X)$: This predicate refers that in the system environment Γ, which is used to check if $\forall$ system state satisfy the model formalized in Fig. 4.

$F_{multi}(X, Y)$: This predicate refers that in the environment Γ, $\forall$ Operation request X and current system state Y are input into a trace of TA processing, then the system state change to the final state.

$f_{ops}(X, Y)$: This predicate refers that in the environment Γ, $\forall$ Operation request X and current system state Y are input into a one step of TA processing, then the system state change to a new state.

$C(X, Y)$: This predicate refers that in the environment Γ, which is used to check if $\forall$ Operation request X meet current system state Y according to model formalized in Fig. 3, then it will return operation type that is transfer to the f_{ops} as a parameter.

Lemma 1 (TA_CEP). $\forall (s : State)(ops : GP\_TEE\_TA\_Interface), S_{preCEP}$ $(S) \rightarrow S_{CEP}(f_{TA\_CEP}(ops, s))$.

Proof. If the input pre-state **s** meets the one step operation request TA_CEP that is checked by the predicates S_{preCEP} based on the model defined in the Fig. 3, and the f is unfolded and simplified, the Lemma 1 can be verified. The Lemma 2 to Lemma 5 can be verified by the same way.

Lemma 2 (TA_OSEP). $\forall(s : State)(ops : GP\_TEE\_TA\_Interface)$, $S_{preOSEP}(S) \rightarrow \overline{S}_{OSEP}(f_{TA\_OSET}(ops, s))$.

Lemma 3 (TA_CSEP). $\forall(s : State)(ops : GP\_TEE\_TA\_Interface)$, $S_{preCSEP}(S) \rightarrow \overline{S}_{CSEP}(f_{TA\_CSEP}(ops, s))$.

Lemma 4 (TA_DEP). $\forall(s : State)(ops : GP\_TEE\_TA\_Interface)$, $S_{preDEP}(S) \rightarrow \overline{S}_{DEP}(f_{TA\_DEP}(ops, s))$.

Lemma 5 (TA_ICEP). $\forall(s : State)(ops : GP\_TEE\_TA\_Interface)$, $S_{preICEP}(S) \rightarrow \overline{S}_{ICEP}(f_{TA\_ICEP}(ops, s))$.

Theorem 1 (On step operation is always TEE_SUCCESS). $\forall(s : State)(ops : GP\_TEE\_TA\_Interface), (C(ops, s) \dashrightarrow id) \rightarrow f_{id}(ops, s) = TEE_{SUCCESS}$.

Proof. The system state **s** and the one step operation **ops** are checked by predicates **C**, if they match each other, it make sure that the **ops**, **s** and **f** are deterministic and it satisfy the model shown in the Fig. 3. Hence, **f** will always return.

Theorem 2 (System state is always security). $\forall(s : State)(ops : GP\_TEE\_TA\_Interface), S_{\emptyset}(S) \rightarrow S_{DEP}(F_{\emptyset \Rightarrow DEP}(ops, s))$.

Proof. This paper assumes the initial system state $\emptyset$ is security. The predicate is $F_{\emptyset \Rightarrow DEP}(ops, s)$ processes the all operations of the request trace based on the model shown in the Fig. 4, and it will get a final system state. Then the predicates $S_{DEP}(F_{\emptyset \Rightarrow DEP}(ops, s))$ verify if the final system state is $\emptyset$, which by means of the results proved by the Lemmas 1 to 5. If the final state is $\emptyset$, it means the system state did not change and still security, after the trace of TA operations.

According to the verification of Theorems 1 and 2 in Coq, we can verify that the model presented in this paper is correct and meet the GP_TEE_TA interface specification. So, if the implementation of a trusted application is in strict accordance with this model, the system state will keep in the safe state and the hacker cannot attack the TEE system from REE.

6 Related Work

The GP TEE specification is a pretty new software specification, which is used to implement a trusted software based on the ARM TrustZone in recent years. No formal analysis and verification has been done on it. However, formal technique has been used by researchers to formalize and verify the security of GP related fields, such as Santiago Zanella B'eguelin, formalized and verified the GP card specification using the B method in paper [9]. They gave an overview of an application of the B method to the formalization and verification of the Global Platform Card Specification. Pierre Neron and Quang-Huy Nguyen have presented a formal model of the smart card Web server specification and proofed its security properties. The formalization enables a thoughtful analysis of the specification that has revealed several ambiguities and potentially dangerous behaviors. Their formal model is built using a modular approach upon a model of Java Card and Global Platform.

However, the research of method of formalization and verification concentrates on the verifying of operating systems in the resent years. There are two outstanding achievements in verification of operating system. In November 2016, a team of Yale researchers, led by Professor Zhong Shao, had un-veiled CertiKOS [21], the worlds first operating system that ran on multi-core processors and shields against cyber-attacks. They presented a novel language-based account of abstraction layers and showed that they corresponded to a strong form of abstraction over a particularly rich class of specifications, which they called deep specifications [8]. Using these new languages and tools, Shao has successfully developed multiple certified OS kernels in the Coq proof assistant. Before that, there is another well-known certified OS called sel4 which was the most advanced member of the L4 microkernel family, notable for its comprehensive formal verification [20].

7   Conclusion and Future Work

7.1   Conclusions

The ARM TrustZone platform has provided a trusted execution environment for mobile device to improve system security. But hackers can still attack the TEE due to its vulnerability. Lack of commonly trusted standards for application management and their security concerns have slowed GP specification deployment. We strongly believe that this work will help improve the confidence in GP specifications and accelerate their acceptance as trusted standards. The objective of providing a formal and verification of the GP TA Interface specifications was successfully achieved in 2 man-months, a neglectable cost that considering the payback. As the work was in progress, vulnerability was detected in the TA software, including one that could lead to the execution of invalid or malicious TA service request from REE.

In this paper, we presented a formal security model of the GP_TEE_ TA_Interface and verified the correctness of this model using Coq. The formalization identified the TA Interface specification as well as modelling the valid trace of TA Interface based on a one-session application (see Sects. 4.1 and 4.2). In order to prove that if this model is correct and satisfy GP specification, we formalize and verify the model using Coq. This feedback is useful for the standard institutions such as Global Platform consortium, in order to improve their specifications. Besides, some of these issues were used to develop security TA software prevent from hacker's attack. Because the approaches presented in this paper can detect and filter the invalid or risk TA service request that from REE effectively. In this way, TEE world can be protected against from the potential attack caused by the communication vulnerability or malicious operation.

7.2   Future Work

Verification of the Implementation of the TA Interface. In order to furtherly certify the functional correctness of TA Interface implementation, we will formalize and verify the coding of TA interface for checking if it meets the GP TEE specification and our model presented in this paper, using Coq.

Verification of Security of Communication Buffer Between REE and TEE. Our design motivation is to ensure that software components belonging to TEE are adequately isolated from REE, such that only authorized communication can take place between them. In other words, confidentiality guaranteed by a TEE looks like a black box to the REE, only inputs and outputs to be observable. In the future, we need to model a security communication and verify that there is no information flow between TEE and REE, except the specific communication buffer.

Acknowledgments. The authors thank the anonymous reviewers for their very helpful comments. This work has been supported in part by the "Fundamental Research Funds for the Central Universities" grant (ZYGX2016J094), which is a large plan of the Chinese government.

References

1. GlobalPlatform Device Technology TEE Internal Core API Specification Version 1.1.1 (2016). http://www.globalplatform.org/specificationsdevice.asp
2. ARM TrustZone Technology. http://www.arm.com/products/processors/technologies/trustzone.php
3. Marche, C., Paulin-Mohring, C., Urbain, X.: The Krakatoa tool for certification of Java/JavaCard programs annotated in JML. J. Log. Algebraic Program. **59**, 89–106 (2004)
4. Appel, A.W.: Verified software toolchain. In: European Symposium on Programming, Heidelberg (2011)
5. Leroy, X.: The CompCert verified compiler (2005–2016). http://compcert.inria.fr/
6. Gu, R., et al.: Deep specifications and certified abstraction layers. ACM SIGPLAN Not. **50**(1) (2015). ACM
7. Béguelin, S.Z.: Formalisation and verification of the GlobalPlatform card specification using the B method. In: Barthe, G., Grégoire, B., Huisman, M., Lanet, J.-L. (eds.) CASSIS 2005. LNCS, vol. 3956, pp. 155–173. Springer, Heidelberg (2006). https://doi.org/10.1007/11741060_9
8. Yang, X., et al.: Trust-E: a trusted embedded operating system based on the ARM trustzone. In: 2014 IEEE 11th International Conference on Ubiquitous Intelligence and Computing and IEEE 11th International Conference on and Autonomic and Trusted Computing, and IEEE 14th International Conference on Scalable Computing and Communications and Its Associated Workshops (UTC-ATC-ScalCom). IEEE (2014)
9. GlobalPlatform Device Technology TEE Client API Specification, version 1.0 (2011). http://www.globalplatform.org/specificationsdevice.asp

10. GlobalPlatform Device Technology TEE Internal API Specification, version 1.0 (2011). http://www.globalplatform.org/specificationsdevice.asp
11. GlobalPlatform Device Technology TEE System Architecture, version 1.0 (2011). http://www.globalplatform.org/specificationsdevice.asp
12. Lehman, M.M.: Technical correspondence: uncertainty in computer application. Commun. ACM **33**(5), 584–587 (1990)
13. Sewell, T.A.L., Myreen, M.O., Klein, G.: Translation validation for a verified os kernel. In: PLDI, pp. 471–482 (2013)
14. Focardi, R., Gorrieri, R.: Classification of security properties. In: Focardi, R., Gorrieri, R. (eds.) FOSAD 2000. LNCS, vol. 2171, pp. 331–396. Springer, Heidelberg (2001). https://doi.org/10.1007/3-540-45608-2_6
15. Focardi, R., Gorrieri, R.: A classification of security properties for process algebras1. J. Comput. Secur. **3**(1), 5–33 (1995)
16. McCullough, D.: Noninterference and the composability of security properties. In: Proceedings of 1988 IEEE Symposium on Security and Privacy, 1988. IEEE (1988)
17. Barendregt, H., Geuvers, H.: Proof assistants using dependent type systems. In: Robinson, A., Voronkov, A. (eds.) Handbook of Automated Reasoning, chap. 18, vol. 2, pp. 1149–1238. Elsevier (2001)
18. MarisaKirisame. https://github.com/ThoughtWorksInc/DeepDarkFantasy
19. Klein, G., Elphinstone, K., Heiser, G., et al.: seL4: formal verification of an OS kernel. In: ACM Symposium on Operating Systems Principles, pp. 207–220 (2009)
20. Gu, R., Shao, Z., Chen, H., Wu, X.(N.), Kim, J., Sjoberg, V., Costanzo, D.: CertiKOS: an extenisble architecture for building certified concurrent OS Kernels. In: Proceedings of 2016 USENIX Symposium on Operating Systems Design and Implementation (OSDI 2016), Savannah, GA, pp. 653–669, November 2016

Research on Malicious Code Analysis Method Based on Semi-supervised Learning

Tingting He, Jingfeng Xue, Jianwen Fu, Yong Wang[✉], and Chun Shan

School of Software, Beijing Institute of Technology, Beijing, China
jianwenfu@126.com, wangyong@bit.edu.cn

Abstract. The research on classification method of malicious code is helpful for researchers to understand attack characteristics quickly, and help to reduce the loss of users and even the states. Currently, most of the malware classification methods are based on supervised learning algorithms, but it is powerless for the small number of labeled samples. Therefore, in this paper, we propose a new malware classification method, which is based on semi-supervised learning algorithm. First, we extract the impactful static features and dynamic features to serialize and obtain features of high dimension. Then, we select them with Ensemble Feature Grader consistent with Information Gain, Random Forest and Logistic Regression with L_1 and L_2, and reduce dimension again with PCA. Finally, we use Learning with local and global consistency algorithm with K-means to classify malwares. The experimental results of comparison among SVM, LLGC and K-means + LLGC show that using of the feature extraction, feature reduction and classification method, K-means + LLGC algorithm is superior to LLGC in both classification accuracy and efficiency, the accuracy is increased by 2% to 3%, and the accuracy is more than SVM when the number of labeled samples is small.

Keywords: Malicious code · Feature processing · K-means LLGC

1 Introduction

Malicious code refers to any computer software that has potential hazards to computers and networks. At present, the number and type of malwares increase gradually, and with the rapid development of malware generation technology, the global network environment is facing a huge threat. Signature based method is widely used in the commercial field of malware detection, but it is hard to detect malware variants [1]. The supervised learning method has been adopted to solve the problem of detection of malware variants, but the disadvantage is that it requires a large number of labeled benign software and malware samples [2]. So it is necessary and important to have a classification method that can classify a small number of labeled samples. Semi-supervised learning is a solution to a small number of labeled samples in practice, because the cost of marking label on data set is extremely high, which requires more time and labor costs.

© Springer Nature Singapore Pte Ltd. 2017
M. Xu et al. (Eds.): CTCIS 2017, CCIS 704, pp. 227–241, 2017.
https://doi.org/10.1007/978-981-10-7080-8_17

The classification of malicious code depends on the feature extraction, feature processing and the selection of classification models. The extraction and processing of features plays a crucial role in the classification. Currently, existing research related to the features for malware classification mainly concentrate in the single feature or multiple features [3–5]. In the malware classification contest (Kaggle) Microsoft launched [6], a group of winners extracted static features of disassembly documents and bytecode files, including file attributes, PE Section, Opcode sequence, bytecode sequence code, and used Random Forest algorithm for feature selection. Then they used NMF algorithm to do dimension reduction, and complete sample classification with supervised learning classification algorithm. Yi et al. [7] conducted the research of the feature selection in malware analysis, they extracted three kinds features: Opcode sequence, function calls graph and system calls, then finished multi-feature vector clustering based on DBSCAN. They proved that the system call sequence has the best effects for the single feature, and multi-feature clustering is better than the single feature.

There are few researches about malware classification methods based on semi-supervised learning. Shakya et al. [8] classified malwares using graph-based semi-supervised algorithm. Their approach used spectral embedding to re-encoding malware into a feature space based on the graph, and then performed classification in the derived feature space using a standard classifier (SVM). In addition, Santos et al. [9] proposed the LLGC (Learning with local and global consistency) algorithm can be used to detect unknown malware based on the sequence of opcodes. For the extracted features, they use malware execution trace (dynamic feature) or the sequence of Opcodes (static feature), but in our approach, we combine static features and dynamic features and get a higher classification accuracy. Moreover, these studies have proved that when the amount of labeled samples is small, semi-supervised classification algorithm can still maintain high accuracy. However, the LLGC algorithm is complex and require high computational overhead. Therefore, in this paper, we propose K-means + LLGC to classify malwares, which can reduce the complexity, enhance the scalability of LLGC for the new sample classification and obtain a higher classification accuracy.

2   Feature Extraction

There are two keys to feature extraction of malicious code classification: one is to define which feature in response to similarity and difference among malwares; the other is how to serialize these features. We extract 8 kinds of features totally, 4 of them are static features (disassembly files from IDA Pro) and 4 are dynamic features (dynamic behavioral analysis report from the sandbox). The methods and results of feature extraction and serialization are as shown in Table 1.

Table 1 shows we extract 8 kinds of features in total, they are packer feature, PE Section, Opcode, FUNCTION, API, registry path, released file and IP address. After obtaining the feature files, the features need to be preprocessed to transform them into the data type that can be used directly for feature selection. There are 5 kinds of features using the simple mathematical statistical

Table 1. Feature extraction and serialization

Feature	Extraction	Serialization	Result
Packer	If packed	Mark if packed with 0, 1. Calculate the number of packer types as N. Mark 0, 1 if packed with some type	0, 1 M * (N + 1) matrix
PE Section	Section between '.' and ':' of each line	Calculate the number of section types of all samples as N. Calculate the number of N sections in each sample	M * N matrix
Opcode	—	N-gram	M * 3000 matrix
FUNCTION	Function name between FUNCTION and PRESS	TF-IDF	M * 76 matrix
API	API sequence about file/service/process/network	N-gram	M * 3000 matrix
Registry	The registry path for APIs which modify 'reg_key'	Calculate the number of path types of all samples as N. Mark with 0, 1, whether modify 'reg_key' or not	M * N matrix
Released file	The number of type, the number of released file and the number of each type	The amount of released type of all samples is N. Then calculate the amount of each type for each sample	M * (N + 2) matrix
IP address	Region for IP address	Region kinds as N. Mark each sample with 0, 1	M * N matrix

method. The Opcode and system call sequence are divided by N-gram, while FUNCTION feature is processed by TF-IDF. Finally, we can get the feature matrix, the dimension of which is 6386. The details of packer feature, registry path, released file and IP address features are described:

(1) Packer feature

Packed malwares from the same family use same packers, as Table 2 shows. Distinguish the packer of each malware from 3 families with PEiD.

Table 2. Results of PEiD

Name	Packer
Mydoom.a.exe	UPX
Mydoom.d.exe	UPX
Mydoom.e.exe	UPX
Mydoom.g.exe	UPX
Mydoom.i.exe	UPX
NetSky.c.exe	PEtitle
NetSky.d.exe	PEtitle
NetSky.e.exe	PEtitle
NetSky.f.exe	PE Pack
NetSky.k.exe	tElock
Fujack.k.exe	ASPack
Fujack.r.exe	nSpack

As shown in Table 2, all the samples from family Mydoomare packed with UPX, while most samples from family NetSky are packed with PEtitle. Therefore, whether packed and packer name can effectively distinguish between types of malwares, as one of the static features.

(2) Registry path

Registry operational traces of different software are usually different. However, for malwares of the same family, they usually modify registry configuration as the former generation of malware do. As a result, registry changes can be used to classify malwares as one of the features that distinguishes malware families. When we extract registry features from JSON Report, first get API calls with 'category' = 'registry'. If API call names are among 'RegCreaKey', 'RegDeleteKey', 'RegSetValue', 'RegDeleteValue', 'RegReplaceKey' and 'RegUnloadKey', we extract registry path (the value of 'regkey'), which is corresponding to the API calls.

(3) Released file

Usually, malwares in the boot will release a part of the necessary setup files, these file names may be changed based on the original, but the type and amount of them maintain similar with the former generation of malware. As shown in Table 3, we select three types of malwares to compare the type and number of files they release. Among them, the sample A is a Ransomware, while the sample B and the sample C are the same family of Worm.

Table 3 shows there are distinct differences between the sample A and the sample B in the type and number of the released files, and the sample B is consistent with sample C in the type and number. By analyzing a large number of malware samples, it can be determined that the type of released files can perform the similarities and differences between malwares.

Table 3. Comparison among released files from three types of malwares

Sample	Data	PE32	JPG	HTML
A:pseudoDarkleech-Rig.tmp.exe	486	1	1	1
B:Worm.Win32.Agent.eq	0	1	0	0
C:Worm.Win32.Agent.kv	0	1	0	0

We extract the value of the keyword 'type' in the 'dropped' field from JSON Report as the type of released file.

(4) IP address

While the malwares of the same family start up, they usually communicates with the same network device or the network device in the same area. So, to distinguish the malwares based on different communication regions, we extract IP addresses from JSON Report with which malware establish a connection and the connection status is 'success', by identifying IP address regions via IP recognition interface. At last, the IP regions need de-duplication as a dynamic feature.

3   Feature Dimensionality Reduction

We can obtain high dimension features after feature extraction. However, in this paper, we focus on classification with few labeled samples. Using high dimension features may result in overfitting and decreasing the efficiency of classification. Therefore, it is necessary to reduce the dimensionality of features. Figure 1 shows the specific process of feature reduction.

3.1   Ensemble Feature Grader

The Ensemble Feature Grader (EFG) has 4 functions: feature grader, normalization, computing mean and selection. Feature grader consists of IG, RF and LR with L_1 and L_2.

IG, Information Gain [10], can evaluate the information amount for the classification system that when the amount of information is larger, the feature is more important. In malware analysis system, whether a feature F exists will influence the amount of information of the feature set. The variation of value is the IG size of feature F for feature set. As the calculation method of IG, for sample C and feature F, we compute document frequency in the case of F existence and non-existence to measure the IG of F of the sample C. When select features with IG only, we delete the features whose size is less than a threshold. Formula 1 is the formula for calculating IG of F.

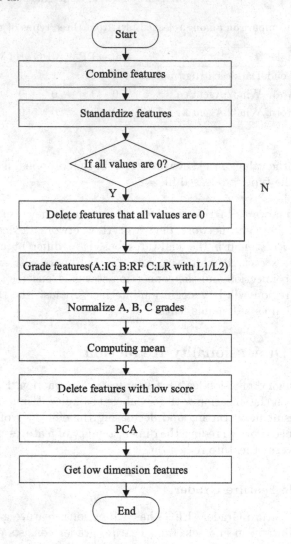

Fig. 1. Flowchart of feature dimensionality reduction

$$IG(F) = -\sum_{i=1}^{m} p(c_i) \log_2 p(c_i) + p(f) \sum_{i=1}^{m} p(c_i|f) \log_2 p(c_i|f)$$
$$+ p(\bar{f}) \sum_{i=1}^{m} p(c_i|\bar{f}) \log_2 p(c_i|\bar{f}) \tag{1}$$

or

$$IG(F) = H(C) - H(C|F) \tag{2}$$

Among them, C is category of sample, its value is $C_1, C_2, C_3, \ldots, C_n$, n is the total number of categories. $H(C)$ is the entropy of classification system, which represents the information amount of feature. When the feature set doesn't contain feature F, the entropy is conditional entropy as $H(C|F)$. The formula is unfolded as follows:

$$i \leq n, i \leq m \tag{3}$$

$$H(C) = -\sum_{i=1}^{n} P(C_i) \log_2 P(C_i) \tag{4}$$

$$H(C|F) = P(f)H(C|f) + P(\bar{f})H(C|\bar{f}) \tag{5}$$

Further:

$$H(C|\bar{f}) = -\sum_{i=1}^{n} p(C_i|\bar{f}) \log_2 p(C_i|\bar{f}) \tag{6}$$

$$H(C|f) = -\sum_{i=1}^{n} p(C_i|f) \log_2 p(C_i|f) \tag{7}$$

Among them, $p(C_i|f)$ is the probability that category of sample is C_i with feature F exists. $p(C_i|\bar{f})$ is the probability that category of sample is C_i with feature F doesn't exist. So, the IG of F to the feature set can be calculated as the variation between entropy and conditional entropy. The greater the IG is, the greater the effect on classification will be. Therefore, IG is used as a component of EFG.

Random forest [11] is composed of multiple CART (Classification And Regression Tree). In the training of each tree node, we get a feature set extracted from all features randomly without duplication. Then, we obtain the best feature for classification from the feature set by IG or Gini impurity.

In the process of establishing the classifier, the feature selection is carried out. When each decision tree is trained, we calculate Gini impurity reduction for each feature. For a decision tree forest, we can calculate the average reduction of Gini impurity for each feature. The Gini impurity average is a criteria for feature selection. In this paper, we calculate the score (Gini impurity average) by scikit-learn. When using Random Forest to calculate importances of features, the importance of the selected first feature is high, but the importance of other related features is usually low. So, the evaluation of the Random forest may be misleading. In this paper, we can use it to select the most important features.

Logistic Regression (LR) [12] is to perform the classification task. The algorithm needs to use the eigenvector and the corresponding label to estimate the parameters of the objective function to achieve better classification. In Logistic Regression, there is a logic function, and for a two-class classification problem, the function is transformed by the Formula 8.

$$\begin{aligned} logit(x) &= \ln(\frac{p(y=1|x)}{p(y=0|x)}) \\ &= \ln(\frac{p(y=1|x)}{(1-p(y=0|x))}) \\ &= \theta_0 + \theta_1 x_1 + \theta_2 x_2 + \cdots + \theta_m x_m \end{aligned} \tag{8}$$

From the Formula 8, we can see that the variable y is related to the multiple variables $x_1, x_2, \ldots, x_m$, but the influence of each argument on y is different. The regression coefficients $\theta_1, \theta_2, \ldots, \theta_m$ corresponding to the independent variables represent the weight of an independent variable. If the regression coefficient θ is determined, we can get the logic regression model.

In this paper, a logistic regression model with L_1 and L_2 regularization is used as a part of EFG. The regularization can be prevented from overfitting. The Eqs. 9 and 10 are as follows.

$$J = J_0 + \alpha \sum_w |w| \tag{9}$$

$$J = J_0 + \alpha \sum_w w^2 \tag{10}$$

L_1 regularization term is the sum of the absolute values of the elements in the weight vector w, while L_2 regularization term is the square sum of each element and then calculate the square root. α is the regularization coefficient.

The logistic regression with L_1 regularization can produce sparse matrix. So, it is used for feature selection. But when L_1 logistic regression selection is used only, it can merely retain one of the features that have the same correlation with respect to the target value, that is, the feature with coefficient 0 isn't unimportant. Therefore, in this paper, we optimize it with L_2 regularization. When using L_1 and L_2, if the weight of a feature A in L_1 is nonzero, then we choose the feature B whose weight is similar with A and weight in L_1 is 0. Feature A and B make up a feature set U. Finally, the features from U divide the weight equally. The equalized weights are the scores of the logistic regression with L_1 and L_2.

IG, RF and LR are 3 components of EFG. EFG integrates the three kinds of scores, which calculate the average of them as the score of EFG.

3.2   Principal Component Analysis (PCA)

The feature set processed by EFG proposed in Sect. 2 is lower dimension and sparse feature space. When reducing dimension in this feature space, we should ensure that the features after treatment can accurately represent the sample information. Therefore, we use Principal Component Analysis (PCA) algorithm for dimensionality reduction.

The Principal Component Analysis (PCA) [13] is an effective method to denoise and reduce the dimension by using the variable covariance matrix. The idea is to transform the high-dimensional feature matrix N into a low-dimensional matrix $K(K < N)$ by using a projection matrix composed of a multidimensional eigenvector, which achieves the purpose of dimensionality reduction of the high-dimensional feature matrix N.

4 Classification

In this paper, we propose a Learning with Local and Global Consistency (LLGC) algorithm based on the K-means for the malware classification, which utilizes the label information of the marked samples and obtains more label information by using the K-means method to reduce the iteration in the LLGC algorithm. The time complexity of the LLGC algorithm can be reduced by using the K-means algorithm. Moreover, the stable center point can be determined during the execution of the K-means algorithm. So it can solve the problem of LLGC whose low generalization ability for new data and improve scalability.

4.1 Learning with Local and Global Consistency (LLGC)

Learning with Local and Global Consistency (LLGC) [14] is a semi-supervised algorithm that provides smooth classification with respect to the intrinsic structure revealed by known labelled and unlabeled points. The method is a simple iteration algorithm that constructs a smooth function coherent to the next assumptions: (i) nearby points are likely to have the same label and (ii) points on the same structure are likely to have the same label [14].

Formally, the algorithm is started as follows. Let $X = \{x_1, \cdots, x_l, x_{l+1}, \cdots, x_n\} \subset R^m$ be data set. It contains the data instances x_1 to x_n, the set of labels $L = \{1, 2, \cdots, c\}$ and the unlabeled instances $x_u(l + 1 \leq u \leq n)$. Predicting labels of the unlabeled instances x_u is the LLGC algorithm need to do. $\mathcal{F}$ is the set of $n \times c$ matrices with condition of all values in matrix are non-negative. The matrices $F = [F_1^T, \ldots, F_n^T]^T$ is the classification result of each instance x_i in X. For the unlabeled instance, the label is assigned by $y_i = \arg\max_{j \leq c} F_{i,j}$, so F can be defined as a vectorial function like $F : X \to R^c$ to assign a vector F_i to the instances x_i. Define $Y(Y \in F)$ is an $n \times c$ matrix. The value $Y_{i,j} = 1$ if the label of x_i is set by $y_i = j$, otherwise $Y_{i,j} = 0$. The details of LLGC algorithm are as follows:

(1) Construct the adjacency graph using KNN.
(2) Construct the similarity matrix W; When $i \neq j, W_{i,j} = \exp(-||x_i - x_j||^2/2\sigma^2)$, otherwise $W_{i,j} = 0$.
(3) Calculate the regularized similarity matrix: $S = D^{-1/2}WD^{-1/2}$; Where D is a diagonal matrix $D_{ii} = \sum_{i=1}^{n} W_{i,j}$.
(4) Calculate iteratively $F(t + 1) = \alpha SF(t) + (1 - \alpha)Y$ until convergence, t is the number of iterations, $\alpha \in (0, 1)$ is a given parameter, $F(0) = Y$ is the initial state.
(5) We can prove that Step 4 is to obtain the convergence solution, let F^* be the limit of the sequence $\{F(t)\}$, $F^* = (1 - \alpha)(1 - \alpha S)^{-1}Y$, and mark each point $y^i = \arg\max_{j < c} F_{ij}^*$.

4.2 LLGC Based on K-means

LLGC algorithm need multiple iterations, the complexity of it is high. It is constrained by the graph-based semi-supervised classification algorithm, which has poor generalization ability for new sample data. Therefore, K-means [15] algorithm is used to optimize LLGC to improve the classification performance of LLGC, reduce the number of iterations and reduce the complexity. The implementation process of K-means + LLGC is shown as Fig. 2.

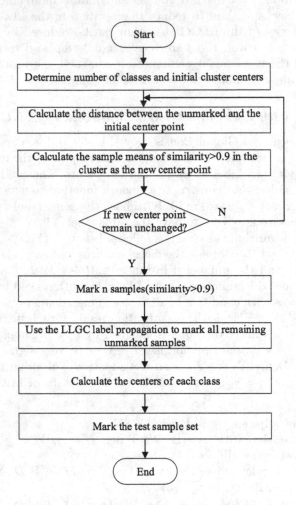

Fig. 2. Flowchart of K-means + LLGC

In Fig. 2, the algorithm is divided into eight steps:

(1) Calculate the means of the labeled samples from each class, and set them as initial clustering centers respectively.
(2) Measure the similarity of each unmarked sample to the initial clusters by using the Euclidean distance, then select the class with the largest similarity between the unmarked sample and the initial center points, and put this unlabeled node in this class.

(3) Select the samples with the similarity of more than or equal to 0.9 in each cluster, and then calculate the mean of these samples to obtain new clustering center points.

(4) Repeat Step 2 and Step 3 until the cluster center points are the same with the former center points.

(5) Mark sample nodes from all clusters with the similarity of more than or equal to 0.9.

(6) Based on label propagation of LLGC, mark the remaining unlabeled samples as described in Sect. 4.1.

(7) At this time, both the labeled samples and unlabeled samples from train set are marked, and then in accordance with each label class, calculate the centers of each class.

(8) When the test set is validated for this classifier, the test sample is marked with the highest similarity by calculating the similarity between each test sample and the center points.

By analyzing the flow of the algorithm, the K-means + LLGC algorithm obtain more label information with Step 5 to pre-mark the partial samples, which can reduce the complexity of the LLGC algorithm by reducing the number of iterations of the LLGC algorithm in Step 6. After the whole labels of the train set are obtained in Step 7, the sample center point of each class is calculated. If there are new samples, we can classify them by calculating similarity, enhancing the scalability of LLGC for the new sample classification.

5   Empirical Validation

In this paper, malware samples from 6 families are collected, a total of 600 samples as shown in Table 4.

Table 4. Malicious code samples

Family	Quantity
Virus.dos.Trivial.appaple	118
Virus.Win32.Virut	71
Trojan.Zbot	105
Virus.MSWord.Marker	89
Backdoor.Win32.Angent	96
Trojan.gangsir	121

The feature dimension obtained from feature extraction is 6386. In this paper, we use the Information Gain (IG), Random Forest (RF), Logical Regression with L_1 and L_2 (LR with L_1 and L_2) and EFG to reduce the dimension of

Table 5. Comparison of accuracy for 4 feature selection methods

Method	Top n(%)	Accuracy (%)
IG	n = 10	69.54
	n = 15	73.82
	n = 20	74.61
RF	n = 10	60.47
	n = 15	62.05
	n = 20	78.36
LR with L_1 and L_2	n = 10	74.02
	n = 15	81.34
	n = 20	78.97
EFG	n = 10	82.58
	n = 15	86.10
	n = 20	85.26

malicious code. The top 10%, 15% and 20% of the scores are extracted for classification respectively. The results are shown in Table 5.

As shown in Table 5, the classification accuracy using EFG is better than the single feature selection method; and when using EFG, we select the top 15% of the feature scores for classification to get a higher accuracy. So after dimensionality reduction, the dimension is 957. In this paper, the PCA algorithm is used to reduce the feature dimension again, and it can optimize the classification accuracy.

In feature extraction, using the Principal Component Analysis (PCA) algorithm can transform high-dimensional features into low-dimensional features. Since the feature data is mostly associated with each other, some valid information is taken away when some features are removed. Therefore, the feature space is transformed into features that are not related to each other before deleting the feature, and more effective feature information can be preserved. PCA is a de-related feature extraction method.

When using the PCA method to reduce the dimension, we can specify the dimension K of the low-dimensional feature space. In order to obtain the data dimension suitable for the training model of semi-supervised classification algorithm, the K values of [300, 400, 500] are selected in the experiment, and the accuracy of the classifier in the four dimensions are as shown in Table 6.

In the comparison of the dimension K and the classification accuracy in Table 6, it can be found that when the feature set is dimensioned, a relatively high accuracy can be achieved with $K = 400$. The following is the classification experiments using the dimension method above.

Among 600 samples, a total of 450 samples are selected as the training set and 150 samples as test set. Among them, 30% is the labeled samples (i.e., the number of labeled samples is 135). Using three kinds of malware classification algorithm,

Table 6. Accuracy for dimension K value

K	Accuracy
300	89.95
400	93.37
500	90.91

SVM, LLGC and K-means + LLGC to test sample classification accuracy. SVM is the supervised classification algorithm, and its number of samples of train set is 135. The classification results are shown in Table 7.

Table 7. Comparison of three classification algorithms

Algorithm	Num (classes)	Num (samples)	Num (train set)	Num (test set)	Accuracy
SVM	6	600	135 labeled samples	150	78.69
LLGC	6	600	135 labeled + 315 unlabeled samples	150	90.58
K-means + LLGC	6	600	135 labeled + 315 unlabeled samples	150	93.37

By comparing the results of classification, we can find that using K-means + LLGC algorithm for malware classification also improves the LLGC by using the unmarked sample auxiliary training model and obtains a higher classification accuracy when the number of labeled samples is small.

The number of labeled samples used in the experiment is 30%, which obtained by the following experiments. The experiment shows that which number of labeled samples is the most suitable for the train set when the semi-supervised classification method, K-means + LLGC, is used. Among them, there are a total of 450 labeled and unlabeled samples. To ensure that each category has a labeled sample, expand according to different proportions. Results of classification are as shown in Table 8.

In the experiment, it can be found that when the proportion of the labeled samples is not more than 20%, the accuracy of classification increases with the proportion of the increases. When the proportion of the labeled samples is more than 20%, the accuracy of classification tends to stable. Therefore, when using K-means + LLGC for semi-supervised classification, the number of labeled samples is selected to be around 20% or more.

Table 8. Results of classification

Proportions of the labeled samples	Accuracy for K-means + LLGC (%)
10%	82.37
15%	87.95
20%	89.76
25%	92.29
30%	93.37
35%	93.39

In this paper, K-means + LLGC is used for malware classification, compared with LLGC algorithm to reduce the number of iterations, improve the classification efficiency. By comparing the iteration time of LLGC and K-means + LLGC, it is proved that K-means + LLGC has optimized the classification efficiency of LLGC. The experimental results are shown in Table 9.

Table 9. Comparison for iteration runtime

Algorithm	Iteration runtime
LLGC	2.013 s
K-means + LLGC	1.697 s

It can be seen from the classification result of malware, classification performance of K-means + LLGC algorithm is better than LLGC algorithm, and the iteration time is also greatly reduced. Therefore, it is proved that the malware classification method used in this paper including feature extraction, preprocessing, dimension reduction and semi-supervised classification is effective.

6 Conclusion

Based on the research of the working principle and analysis method of malicious code, we have achieved the effective classification of malware families with the machine learning technology. By analyzing the dynamic behavior analysis report and disassembly file, four kinds of static features and four kinds of dynamic features are extracted. The original feature set is preprocessed, which involves n-gram and TF-IDF, to obtain a thousand dimension features. Feature scores used for selecting features are calculated by EFG, which consists of Information Gain, Random Forest and Logistic Regression with L_1 and L_2. PCA is also used to reduce the dimension. The features from extraction and dimensionality reduction can distinguish malware family effectively, to improve the accuracy of classification. In the classification of malware, we use the LLGC algorithm combined with K-mean to enhance the accuracy and efficiency of LLGC. The semi-supervised method can effectively deal with the classification of malicious code, and our method can optimize the classification performance of LLGC.

Acknowledgments. This work was supported by the National Key R&D Program of China (Grant No. 2016YFB0801304).

References

1. Cepeda, C., Dan, L.C.T., Ordonez, P.: Feature selection and improving classification performance for malware detection. In: IEEE International Conferences on Big Data and Cloud Computing, pp. 560–566. IEEE Computer Society (2016)
2. Comar, P.M., Liu, L., Saha, S., et al.: Combining supervised and unsupervised learning for zero-day malware detection. In: INFOCOM, 2013 Proceedings IEEE, pp. 2022–2030. IEEE (2013)
3. Xiao, X., Fu, P., Xiao, X., et al.: Two effective methods to detect mobile malware. In: International Conference on Computer Science and Network Technology, pp. 1041–1045. IEEE (2016)
4. Choi, Y.H., Han, B.J., Bae, B.C., et al.: Toward extracting malware features for classification using static and dynamic analysis. In: International Conference on Computing and NETWORKING Technology, pp. 126–129. IEEE (2013)
5. Shijo, P.V., Salim, A.: Integrated static and dynamic analysis for malware detection. Proc. Comput. Sci. **46**, 804–811 (2015)
6. Microsoft Malware Classification Challenge (BIG 2015). https://www.kaggle.com/c/malware-classification
7. Yi, W., Yong, T., Lu, Z., et al.: Research on feature selection in malicious code clustering. Inf. Netw. Secur. (9), 64–68 (2016)
8. Shakya, S., Zhang, J.: Towards better semi-supervised classification of malicious software. In: ACM International Workshop, pp. 27–33. ACM (2015)
9. Santos, I., Sanz, B., Laorden, C., Brezo, F., Bringas, P.G.: Opcode-sequence-based semi-supervised unknown malware detection. In: Herrero, Á., Corchado, E. (eds.) CISIS 2011. LNCS, vol. 6694, pp. 50–57. Springer, Heidelberg (2011). https://doi.org/10.1007/978-3-642-21323-6_7
10. Xueming, L., Hairui, L., Liang, X., et al.: TF-IDF algorithm based on information gain and information entropy. Comput. Eng. **38**(8), 37–40 (2012)
11. Rogers, J., Gunn, S.: Identifying feature relevance using a random forest. In: Subspace, Latent Structure and Feature Selection, Statistical and Optimization, Perspectives Workshop, SLSFS 2005, Bohinj, Slovenia, 23–25 February 2005, Revised Selected Papers, pp. 173–184. DBLP (2006)
12. Padmavathi, J.: Logistic regression in feature selection in data mining. Int. J. Sci. Eng. Res. **3**(8) (2012)
13. Guo, W., Dai, L., Wang, R., et al.: Feature mapping based on PCA. Acta Automatica Sinica **34**(8), 876–879 (2008)
14. Zhou, D., Bousquet, O., Lal, T.N., et al.: Learning with local and global consistency. Adv. Neural Inf. Process. Syst. **16**(4), 321–328 (2004)
15. Sahu, K., Shrivastava, S.K.: Kernel K-means clustering for phishing website, malware categorization. Int. J. Comput. Appl. **111**(9), 20–25 (2015)

Reliable Topology Control Algorithm in Cognitive Radio Networks

Yali Zeng[1], Li Xu[1(✉)], Xiaoding Wang[1], and Xu Yang[2]

[1] Fujian Provincial Key Laboratory of Network Security and Cryptology,
School of Mathematics and Computer Science, Fujian Normal University,
Fuzhou, China
xuli@fjnu.edu.cn
[2] School of Science, RMIT University, Melbourne, Australia

Abstract. In cognitive radio networks, the communication probability and available time of links among secondary uses are two important factors which are affected by the mobility of secondary users and the dynamism of primary user activities. Data packets are expected to be transmitted on stable links with high communication probability and long available time to avoid packet loss and retransmissions. However, existing topology control algorithms in cognitive radio networks only consider either the communication probability or the available time. To solve this problem, we propose a reliable topology control algorithm (RTCA) that employs such two factors to achieve reliable data transmission. RTCA first allows each pair of secondary users to communicate with each other by establishing a stable network, the topology of which is then optimized through reducing the edges while maintaining a high communication probability and a long available time. The simulation results and theoretical analysis demonstrate the effectiveness of the proposed algorithm.

Keywords: Cognitive Radio Networks · Topology control · Communication probability · Available time

1 Introduction

Topology control is one of the important approaches used in wireless networks to improve network reliability and reduce the packet loss rate meanwhile maintaining the network connectivity and high throughput [1–4]. Therefore, there are growing interests in this field.

Cognitive radio is emerging as a promising technique for alleviating spectrum scarcity and improving spectrum utilization [5–8]. The biggest difference between cognitive radio networks (CRNs) and the classical wireless networks is that users in CRNs have cognitive capacities. In CRNs, primary users (PUs) are the owners of the licensed spectrum, while mobile secondary users (SUs) are only allowed to operate on the vacant parts of the spectrum allocated to PUs. If the spectrum is reclaimed by PUs, SUs must vacate the spectrum to avoid

© Springer Nature Singapore Pte Ltd. 2017
M. Xu et al. (Eds.): CTCIS 2017, CCIS 704, pp. 242–254, 2017.
https://doi.org/10.1007/978-981-10-7080-8_18

interference with PUs [9]. The occupation of spectrums by PUs and the mobility of SUs make the topology of CRNs dynamic. Due to such characteristics, designing topology control algorithms for CRNs posed more challenges than classical wireless networks.

Many topology control algorithms have been proposed for classical wireless networks [10–16]. However, it is difficult to apply these algorithms directly to CRNs since users in classical wireless networks do not have cognitive abilities and the proposed algorithms do not consider the PUs activities.

On the other hand, existing topology control algorithms designed for CRNs usually consider either communication probability or available time. Huang et al. [13] propose a mobility-assisted routing algorithm based on communication probability in CRNs, which ignores the available time of the communication links. Guan et al. [14] present a prediction-based topology control and routing scheme named PCTC to construct a reliable topology to mitigate rerouting frequency and improve network performance, which overlooks the communication probability.

The other object of topology control is to construct a sparse network. As we all know, the more edges of a topology are, the more route request packets will be sent to find a path between two nodes during route discovery. Moreover, it will cost more resources for route maintenance. To avoid such problems, a proper topology control algorithm should be employed to eliminate the unnecessary links in CRNs while maintaining high performance. However, the topology control problem under restricted objectives is proved to be NP-hard [15]. Therefore, Li et al. [16] propose five heuristic algorithms to reduce the edges of a topology, but these algorithms are of high time complexity, except the UMCRP algorithm. Nonetheless, the connectivity of UMCRP cannot be guaranteed, especially setting a high threshold value or in the sparse topology.

To deal with these problems, we propose a reliable topology control algorithm (RTCA) to generate a double weights topology, which takes both communication probability and available time into consideration. After generating the original double weights topology, RTCA tries to cut the edges to construct a simplified topology while maintaining the high communication probability and long available time. With the help of the proposed topology control algorithm, classical routing protocols running on this topology can reduce the packet loss rate and re-transmissions in CRNs.

The rest of this paper is organized as follows. Section 2 introduces the system model. Section 3 presents the reliable topology control algorithm. Section 4 analyses the simulation results. Finally, Sect. 5 concludes the paper.

2   System Model

In cognitive radio networks (CRNs), two factors affect the direct communication between two secondary users (SUs). One is the mobility of the SUs. Two SUs can communicate with each other directly only when they meet so that they are in the communication range of each other. The other one is the activities of the

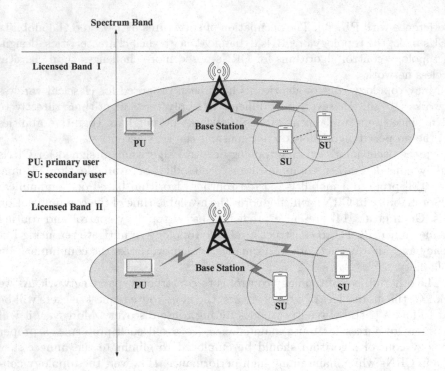

Fig. 1. Network architecture

primary users (PUs). PUs do not use the spectrum resources such that there are available channels for communication between two SUs. The latter factor also affects the available time of the communication links between two SUs. The less frequent of the PUs activities is, the longer time two SUs can stay connected. Thus, the communication probability and available time of links between two SUs depend on the mobility of SUs and the dynamism of PU activities. The network architecture is shown in Fig. 1.

2.1   Communication Probability of Links Calculation

Assume that there are N SUs in the networks, let $l_{i,j}$ be the link between two SUs n_i and $n_j, i,j \in [1,N], i \neq j$. We establish two probabilistic metrics for a pair of nodes (n_i, n_j), meet probability $p_{m_{i,j}} \in [0,1]$ and channel availability probability $p_{c_{i,j}} \in [0,1]$. When two SUs meet each other and there are available channels, they are able to communicate directly. The communication probability of a link $l_{i,j}$ is $p_{l_{i,j}}$.

Definition 1. The communication probability $p_{l_{i,j}}$ of a link $l_{i,j}$ between a pair of nodes (n_i, n_j) refers to the production of meet probability $p_{m_{i,j}}$ and channel availability probability $p_{c_{i,j}}$, i.e.,

$$p_{l_{i,j}} = p_{m_{i,j}} * p_{c_{i,j}} \tag{1}$$

Actually, the mobility of PUs and SUs is usually highly motivated [17,18]. They are not likely to move around randomly, but rather move in a predictable may based on repeating behavioral patterns such that if a node has visited a location several times before, it will probably visit that location again [19]. Therefore, the meet probability $p_{m_{i,j}}$ of two SUs is not constant. When two SUs encounter frequently, they have a higher $p_{m_{i,j}}$. If they do not meet for a period of time, they have a lower $p_{m_{i,j}}$.

The other requirement for two SUs to communicate is the available channels. The channel availability probability $p_{c_{i,j}}$ is affected by PUs. Since the PUs mobility is regular in reality, the channel availability probability can be deduced by analyzing the history data. Assume that the base station periodically broadcasts the available channel information for SUs. The method of deploying a centrally maintained base station to get available channel information is widely used in CRNs such as [20]. Thus, each SU can be aware of $p_{c_{i,j}}$ when they meet each other. Each SU saves $p_{l_{i,j}}$ in their route table. If $p_{c_{i,j}}$ or $p_{m_{i,j}}$ is updated, $p_{l_{i,j}}$ is updated too.

2.2 Available Time of Links Calculation

When two SUs communicate with each other, they can exchange their positions, velocities and directions. Assume that the communication range of each SU is R. For SU n_i and n_j, let (x_i, y_i) and (x_j, y_j) be the coordinate of n_i and n_j, respectively. Let v_i and v_j be the velocities, and α_i and α_j be the moving direction, respectively. If those motion parameters are known, the amount of time that two SUs will stay connected can be calculated as follow [19]

$$t_{l_{i,j}} = \frac{-(ab+cd) + \sqrt{(b^2+d^2)*R^2 - (ad-bc)^2}}{b^2+d^2} \tag{2}$$

where

$$a = x_i - x_j$$
$$b = v_i cos\alpha_i - v_j cos\alpha_j$$
$$c = y_i - y_j$$
$$d = v_i sin\alpha_i - v_j sin\alpha_j$$

In CRNs, the available time between two SUs is also affected by the PUs. If PUs do not use channels during time period t, two SUs can stay connected for t. Therefore, the available time of two SUs n_i and n_j is

$$T_{l_{i,j}} = t_{l_{i,j}} * p_{c_{i,j}} \tag{3}$$

Each SU also saves $T_{l_{i,j}}$ in their own route table. They periodically broadcast their route tables.

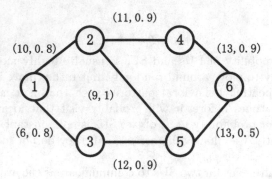

Fig. 2. Double weights network topology

2.3 Communication Probability and Available Time of the Topology Calculations

Using the route table information, we can obtain a double weights network topology. Take Fig. 2 as example, the weight values in each link (edge) are available time and communication probability, respectively.

Definition 2. A topology G is connected if and only if there exits at least one path for each pair of node $(n_i, n_j), i, j \in [1, N], i \neq j$.

Definition 3. The communication probability of a path $path_{n_i, n_{i+1}, , n_{k-1}, n_k}$ $(i, i + 1, k, k + 1 \in [1, N])$ is production of communication probability of all links, i.e.,

$$P_{path_{n_i, n_{i+1}, \ldots, n_{k-1}, n_k}} = Pl_{i,i+1} * \ldots * Pl_{k-1,k} \tag{4}$$

For example, in Fig. 2, the communication probability of the path $path_{1,2,4}$ from node 1 to node 4 is 0.8*0.9 = 0.72. Actually, there may be more than one path from one node to another in a connected topology.

Definition 4. The most reliable path $path_{n_i, n_j}^M$ from node n_i to n_j in topology G is the maximum communication probability among all paths from node n_i to n_j.

For instance, there are 3 paths from node 1 to node 2 in Fig. 2, $path_{1,2}$, $path_{1,3,5,2}, path_{1,3,5,6,4,2}$. The most reliable path is $path_{1,2}$ as the communication probability of this path is maximum. The most reliable path and the corresponding communication probability for each two nodes in Fig. 2 are shown in Table 1.

Definition 5. The communication probability of a topology G is the minimum communication probability among all most reliable paths among each pair of nodes (n_i, n_j), i.e.,

$$P^G = min\{path_{n_i,n_j}^M\} \tag{5}$$

As shown in Table 1, the communication probability of the topology in Fig. 2 is 0.648.

Table 1. Most reliable path and the corresponding communication probability for each two nodes in Fig. 2.

Source	Destination	Most reliable path	Communication probability
1	2	(1,2)	0.8
1	3	(1,3)	0.9
1	4	(1,2,4)	0.72
1	5	(1,3,5)	0.81
1	6	(1,2,4,6)	0.648
2	3	(2,5,3)	0.9
2	4	(2,4)	0.9
2	5	(2,5)	1
2	6	(2,4,6)	0.81
3	4	(3,5,2,4)	0.81
3	5	(3,5)	0.9
3	6	(3,5,2,4,6)	0.729
4	5	(4,2,5)	0.9
4	6	(4,6)	0.9
5	6	(5,2,4,6)	0.81

Definition 6. The available time of a topology G is the minimum available time among all links, i.e.,

$$T^G = min\{T_{l_{i,j}}\} \tag{6}$$

The available time of the topology in Fig. 2 is 6, which is the minimum available time among all links.

3   Reliable Topology Control Algorithm

As we can see, some links in Fig. 2 are of low communication probability or low available time. If data are transmitted on these links, it will cause a larger packet loss rate and frequent retransmissions. Thus, it is necessary to simplify the original topology so as to achieve the reliable data transmission and avoid frequent rerouting. In this paper, we propose a reliable topology control algorithm (RTCA) to construct a reliable sub-graph over the original topology.

The aim of RTCA is to construct a sparser subgraph from the obtained double weights topology such that for any pair of nodes, there exists a path connecting them with the available time higher than a required threshold and the communication probability is maximum. RTCA first keeps all most reliable paths between any two nodes such that the available time of each link of these paths is larger or equal to the threshold, and the communication probability of each path for each pair of nodes is maximum. The second step of RTCA is to delete some edges from the subgraph generated in the first step in an ascending order based on available time. A link is removed if without this link the subgraph is still connected. Detail of RTCA is shown below. It is assumed that the original double weights topology is connected.

Algorithm 1. RTCA

Input: original double weights topology G, subgraph $G' \longleftarrow \emptyset$, threshold of available time T_{th}, threshold of communication probability P_{th}

Output: G'

1: **for** each pair (n_i, n_j) **do**
2:     find the most reliable path $path^M_{n_i,n_j}$ in G such that the communication probability of $path^M_{n_i,n_j}$ is maximum and the available time of all links in $path^M_{n_i,n_j}$ is larger or equal to T_{th}
3:     **if** $l \in path^M_{n_i,n_j}$ and $l \notin G'$ **then**
4:         $G' = G' \cup \{l\}$
5:     **end if**
6: **end for**
7: **while** G' is not connected **do**
8:     $T_{th} = T_{th} - \zeta$ and repeat step 1 to step 6, $0 < \zeta \leq T_{th}$
9: **end while**
10: sort all links in G' in an ascending order based on available time
11: **while** $P^G(G' - \{l\}) \geq P_{th}$ **do**
12:     $G' = G' - \{l\}$
13: **end while**
14: **return** G'

An instance of RCTA is shown in Fig. 3. After combining all the most reliable path of the topology in Fig. 2, we can obtain the topology shown in Fig. 3a. The number of hops among some nodes may increase, but the communication probability is higher, such as the path between node 5 and node 6 of which the number of hops increases from 1 to 3 while the communication probability increases from 0.5 to 0.81.

As we can see from Fig. 3a, there exists a ring in this topology. Thus, we can continue to reduce some links if the communication probability of the generated subgraph is higher than P_{th}. Assume that P_{th} is equal to 0.6. According to RTCA, the link with the shortest available time, namely $l_{1,3}$, will be removed since without $l_{1,3}$ the subgraph is still connected and the communication probability of the subgraph is 0.648 which is larger than P_{th}. Hence, we can obtain a more simplified subgraph as shown in Fig. 3b.

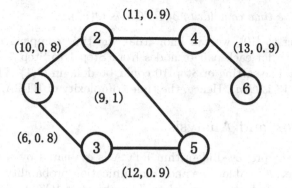

(a) Combining all the most reliable path

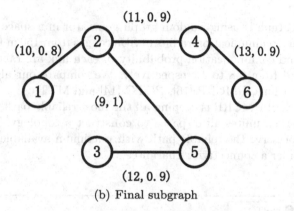

(b) Final subgraph

Fig. 3. Schematic diagram of RTCA

Note that the subgraph G' returned in Step 14 is named FSG short for final subgraph. FSG has the following properties.

Property 1. FSG is connected.

Proof. When the threshold of available time T_{th} is too large, the connectivity of generated subgraph from Step 1 to Step 6 cannot be guaranteed. Hence, from Step 7 to Step 9, RTCA checks the connectivity of subgraph. If subgraph is unconnected, T_{th} is reduced by ζ and the algorithm repeats Step 1 to Step 6, until the subgraph is connected. Therefore, FSG is connected.

Property 2. The minimum edge number of FSG is $n-1$.

Proof. RTCA reduces the edges from Step 11 to Step 13, and the subgraph FSG after reducing will be a tree if P_{th} is small enough. The edge number of a tree is $n-1$ with n nodes. Thus, the minimum edge number of FSG is $n-1$.

Theorem 1. *The time complexity of RTCA is* $O(n^3)$.

Proof. According to [10], we can know that the time complexity of finding a most reliable path for each pair of nodes from Step 1 to Step 6 and Step 7 to Step 9 is $O(n^3)$. The sorting of Step 10 could be done in $O(1)$. The deleting of Step 11 to Step 13 is $O(n)$. Hence, the time complexity of RTCA is $O(n^3)$.

4   Simulation and Analysis

In this section, the proposed algorithm RTCA is evaluated by simulations. We take edge number, available time and communication probability as the performance measurements for any algorithm. The object of RTCA is to construct a subgraph with small edge number, longer available time and larger communication probability.

The original graph is using random graph generator in a space $800 * 800$ m^2 with 10 SUs. The communication radius of SUs ranges from 150 m to 300 m. The available time and communication probability of each link are randomly chosen from 1 to 50 and from 0.8 to 1, respectively. We compare our algorithm with three other algorithms, UMCRP [16], PCTC [14] and MTT.

The basic idea of UMCRP is keeping all the most reliable paths between any two nodes, and then unites all of paths to construct a topology. The principle of PCTC is to preserve the reliable path with maximum available time for any pair of nodes under a connectivity guarantee.

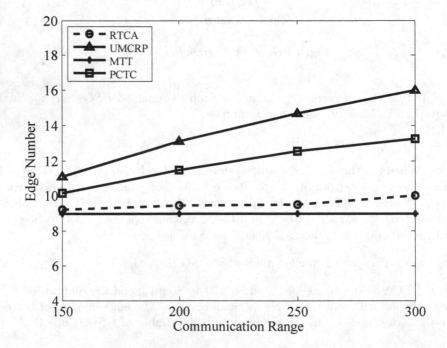

Fig. 4. Edge number of different algorithms

MTT uses the minimum spanning tree algorithm to generate a tree with maximum available time. In other word, MTT only considers the available time. It is obvious that the available time of MTT is longest and the edge number is smallest among four algorithms. The edge number of MTT is $n - 1$. Hence, in the terms of available time and edge number, MTT is optimal.

Figure 4 shows that the edge number of RTCA is approximate to that of MTT and is smaller than UMCRP and PCTC. It is because after union of all most reliable paths, UMCRP does not continue to reduce the edge of the generated subgraph, the edge number of UMCRP is thus larger than that of RTCA. RTCA tries to delete more edges to reduce the existence of ring topology, so the subgraph generated by RTCA is approximate to a tree and the edge number is approximate to MTT. As the subgraph generated by PCTC may exist some rings, the edge number of PCTC is larger than RTCA. The less the edges of a node are, the smaller the node degree is. The small node degree may mitigate contention in the shared wireless medium and the number of route request packets during the route discovery process.

As we can see from Fig. 5, the available time of MTT is longest as we have analyzed. Comparing with UMCRP, RTCA has a longer available time. This is because after finding all most reliable paths, RTCA reduces edges in an ascending order based on available time. The edge with shortest available time may be removed first and the edges with longer available time are leaved behind.

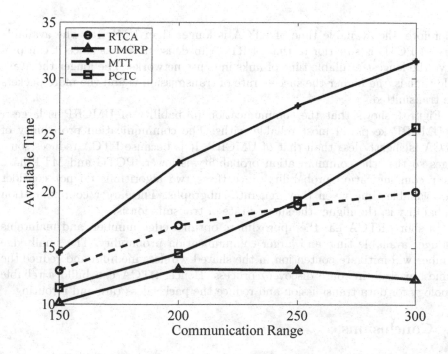

Fig. 5. Available time of different algorithms

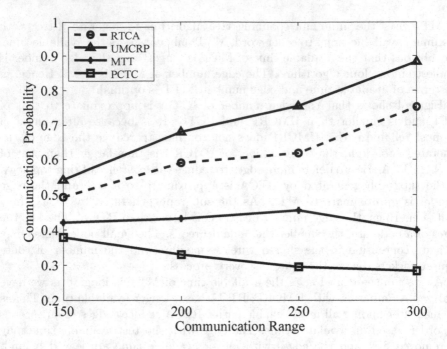

Fig. 6. Communication probability of different algorithms

Therefore, the available time of RTCA is longer than UMCRP. The available time of PCTC is superior to that of RTCA in dense networks since it can preserve the longest available time of links in dense networks. The longer the available time is, the higher the success rate of transmission is and the more packets are transmitted.

Figure 6 shows that the communication probability of UMCRP is largest, as UMCRP keeps all most reliable paths. The communication probability of RTCA is slightly less than that of UMCRP. It is because RTCA reduces some edges so that the communication probability is lower. PCTC and MTT have lower communication probability since these two algorithms do not consider the available time when they generate subgraphs. The larger communication probability is, the higher the success rate of transmission is.

In short, RTCA has the approximate optimal edge number, and maintains a longer available time and larger communication probability. The small edge number will mitigate contention in the shared wireless medium and reduce the request packets in route discovery process. Hence, RTCA can build a reliable topology for data transmission and reduce the packet loss rate and rerouting.

5   Conclusions

In this paper, we propose a reliable topology control algorithm (RTCA) in cognitive radio networks that takes both communication probability and available time into consideration. We employ simulation to validate our algorithm. By comparing with others algorithms, we observe that the topology generated by RTCA maintains smaller edge number, longer available time and larger communication probability. Routing algorithms conducted on such topology will reduce the packet loss rate and avoid the frequent rerouting.

Security is another important issue for the practical application of cognitive radio networks. In the future work, we will construct a topology with secure aware to achieve the reliable and secure transmission of data in cognitive radio networks.

Acknowledgments. This work was supported by the National Natural Science Foundation of China (Grant No. 61572010 and No. U1405255), Natural Science Foundation of Fujian Province (Grant No. 2013J01222 and No. 2016J01287), Fujian Normal University Innovative Research Team (Grant No. IRTL1207), Fujian Province Department of Education Project (Grant No. JAT160123), Fuzhou Science and Technology Bureau Project (Grant No. 2015-G-59), Fujian Province University industry Cooperation of Major Science and Technology Project (Grant No. 2017H6005).

References

1. Aziz, A.A., Sekercioglu, Y.A., Fitzpatrick, P., Ivanovich, M.: A survey on distributed topology control techniques for extending the lifetime of battery powered wireless sensor networks. IEEE Commun. Surv. Tutorials **15**(1), 121–144 (2013)
2. Zhang, X., Zhang, Y., Yan, F., Vasilakos, A.V.: Interference-based topology control algorithm for delay-constrained mobile ad hoc networks. IEEE Trans. Mobile Comput. **14**(4), 742–754 (2015)
3. Lin, L., Xu, L., Zhou, S., Wang, D.: Interference-based topology control algorithm for delay-constrained mobile ad hoc networks. IEEE Trans. Reliab. **64**(2), 807–818 (2015)
4. Zhang, J., Zhou, S., Xu, L., Wu, W., Ye, X.: An efficient connected dominating set algorithm in WSNs based on the induced tree of the crossed cube. Int. J. Appl. Math. Comput. Sci. **25**(2), 295–309 (2015)
5. Zheng, L., Tan, C.W.: Cognitive radio network duality and algorithms for utility maximization. IEEE J. Sel. Areas Commun. **31**(3), 500–513 (2013)
6. Akyildiz, I.F., Lee, W.-Y., Vuran, M.C., Mohanty, S.: NeXt generation/dynamic spectrum access/cognitive radio wireless networks: a survey. Comput. Netw. **50**(13), 2127–2159 (2006)
7. Feng, J., Zhang, Y., Lu, G., Zheng, W.: Securing cooperative spectrum sensing against ISSDF attack using dynamic trust evaluation in cognitive radio networks. Secur. Commun. Netw. **8**(17), 3157–3166 (2015)
8. Pei, Z., Liu, Y., Zhang, J., Wang, L.: Power allocation design and optimization for secure transmission in cognitive relay networks. Secur. Commun. Netw. **9**(18), 5133–5142 (2016)
9. Wang, X., Sheng, M., Zhai, D., Li, J., Mao, G., Zhang, Y.: Achieving bi-channel-connectivity with topology control in cognitive radio networks. IEEE J. Sel. Areas Commun. **32**(11), 2163–2176 (2014)
10. Li, M., Li, Z., Vasilakos, A.V.: A survey on topology control in wireless sensor networks: taxonomy, comparative study, and open issues. Proc. IEEE **101**(12), 2538–2557 (2013)

11. Guo, J., Liu, X., Jiang, C., Cao, J., Ren, Y.: Distributed fault-tolerant topology control in cooperative wireless ad hoc networks. IEEE Trans. Parallel Distrib. Syst. **26**(10), 2699–2710 (2015)
12. Stein, M., Kulcsár, G., Schweizer, I., Varró, G., Schürr, A., Mühlhäuser, M.:. Topology control with application constraints. In: IEEE 40th Conference on Local Computer Networks (LCN), pp. 229–232 (2015)
13. Huang, J., Wang, S., Cheng, X., Liu, M., Li, Z., Chen, B.: Mobility-assisted routing in intermittently connected mobile cognitive radio networks. IEEE Trans. Parallel Distrib. Syst. **25**(11), 2956–2968 (2014)
14. Guan, Q., Yu, F.R., Jiang, S., Wei, G.: Prediction-based topology control and routing in cognitive radio mobile ad hoc networks. IEEE Trans. Veh. Technol. **59**(9), 4443–4452 (2010)
15. Huang, M., Chen, S., Zhu, Y., Wang, Y.: Topology control for time-evolving and predictable delay-tolerant networks. IEEE Trans. Comput. **62**(11), 2308–2321 (2013)
16. Li, F., Chen, S., Huang, M., Yin, Z., Zhang, C., Wang, Y.: Reliable topology design in time-evolving delay-tolerant networks with unreliable links. IEEE Trans. Mobile Comput. **14**(6), 1301–1314 (2015)
17. Song, C., Qu, Z., Blumm, N., Barabsi, A.-L.: Limits of predictability in human mobility. Science **327**(5968), 1018–1021 (2010)
18. Willkomm, D., Machiraju, S., Bolot, J., Woliszl, A.: Primary user behavior in cellular networks and implications for dynamic spectrum access. IEEE Commun. Mag. **47**(3), 88–95 (2009)
19. Su, W., Lee, S.-J., Gerla, M.: Mobility prediction in wireless networks. In: IEEE 21st Century Military Communications Conference Proceedings, pp. 491–495 (2000)
20. Fitch, M., Nekovee, M., Kawade, S., Briggs, K., MacKenzie, R.: Wireless service provision in TV white space with cognitive radio technology: a telecom operator's perspective and experience. IEEE Commun. Mag. **49**(3), 64–73 (2011)

Practical Privacy-Preserving Outsourcing of Large-Scale Matrix Determinant Computation in the Cloud

Guangzhi Zhang[1,2], Shaobin Cai[1(✉)], Chunhua Ma[2], and Dongqiu Zhang[3]

[1] Computer Science Department, Harbin Engineering University, Harbin, China
409951652@QQ.com
[2] Suihua University, Suihua, China
[3] Qiqihaer Engineering College, Qiqihar, China

Abstract. Jaggi-Sanders algorithm is generalized to its nonlinear form for multicast network. Precise details of the algorithm implementation and the proof on the algorithm existence are given. It may has meaningful significance in the two following aspects. First, it may offer a thinking for the urgent need to find a nonlinear coding scheme for non-multicast network some of which can not be coded by linear coding. Second, some interesting mathematical concepts such as shared agreements, composite functions and n-dimensional maximal independent set (nMIS) based on combinatorics are proposed. These new concepts may offer beneficial lessons for further research on nonlinear network coding.

Keywords: Nonlinear network coding · Generalized Jaggi-Sanders algorithm · Shared agreements · Composite functions · n-dimensional maximal independent set

1 Introduction

Nonlinear network coding is paid more and more attention recently. It is regarded as a promising method to solve the theoretical dilemma of network coding. Until now, there have found many instances that show nonlinear network coding outperforms linear coding. For example, [1] shows that some networks have nonlinear network coding scheme rather than linear. [2] showed that with some help of nonlinear classical coding, the quantum version of some k-pair problem is solvable. [3] shows a polynomial separation between linear and non-linear network coding rates by connecting matroids and index coding. [4]designed optimal nonlinear network codes via performing a random walk over certain truth tables, and this optimal codes can not be got if using linear codes. [3] shows nonlinear codes outperforms linear codes in combating General Byzantine attacks. Even in the wireless environment, nonlinear codes also has a remarkable performance [5,6]. Though some papers shows that nonlinear codes still can not reach the upper bound of network coding capacity [7,8], but its also believed that nonlinear codes will have a better prospect of application. It is guessed that in the

© Springer Nature Singapore Pte Ltd. 2017
M. Xu et al. (Eds.): CTCIS 2017, CCIS 704, pp. 255–274, 2017.
https://doi.org/10.1007/978-981-10-7080-8_19

non-multicast network, the superiority of nonlinear codes is obvious, but for the multicast network, there is no need to apply nonlinear codes. [9] said that even in the multicast case, a somewhat smaller alphabet can be used if one employs nonlinear coding rather than linear, and they suspected the gap can actually be very large and exploring nonlinear coding was suggested to be a fruitful direction for future works.

Though nonlinear codes has great theoretical value, there has not systematic theory about nonlinear network coding both for multicast and non-multicast networks. The systematical theory is expected to be a algebraic representation just like the pre-existence exponential-time algorithm [10] and Jaggi-Sanders algorithm [11] in the linear codes. To perform network coding in non-multicast is a urgent because the benefits are enormous, and linear codes is insufficient for some non-multicast network [1]. To solve this problem, many ideas are introduced to handle nonlinear codes such as, motroids, the graph theory, information inequality, and so on, the general non-multicast can not be coded until now. For example, [4] performs nonlinear coding through random method, [3,5] use lexicographic or index way, [1] even use special property of finite field to construct special nonlinear instance. [9,12] make a progressive step to a algebraic representation systematically. But they just consider nonlinear codes in 2-dimensional messages space, meanwhile, how to do nonlinear in the higher dimensions is open.

The above methods may have limits to get the essence of nonlinear codes. May it is helpful to develop a algebraic representation of nonlinear codes just like the pre-existence exponential-time algorithm and Jaggi-Sanders algorithm in the linear codes. The two algorithm contributes a great deal to understand the essence of linear codes. Can we give a analogous algorithm to Jaggi-Sanders algorithm for multicast even for non-multicast network? That will be awarded to further our understanding of nonlinear network coding. Because it is too complicated to handle non-multicast, we confine this problem just for multicast network, i.e., generalize Jaggi-Sanders algorithm to its nonlinear form for multicast network. This typical problem may help us see the essence of nonlinear codes more clearly. The proposed generalized algorithm mainly based on some mathematical concepts from combinatorics perspective. Among them, the most important concept is n-dimensional maximal independent set, i.e., nMIS. These concepts have certain novelty, and it may offer some helpful mathematical tools to handle nonlinear network coding. The core idea of Jaggi-Sanders algorithm is to construct the global coding vector for any outgoing edge e which is in a edge-disjoint path using the independency of vectors. Our algorithm is also based on this idea. The changes are that global coding vector is generalized to nonlinear functions, and the independency of vectors is generalized to independency of nonlinear functions in finite field. There are also other matching concepts. The work of this paper is a direct revolution of the papers [9,12]. Though this method is not for non-multicast network, we have thoroughly solved the problem that constructing nonlinear codes for multicast networks. This contributes largely to understand the potential of nonlinear network coding. It also offers a beneficial lessons for the attempting to perform nonlinear coding on non-multicast network.

2   Basic Model and Definitions

The necessary concepts and notations are introduced here. For additional details
and definitions, see the references, in particular [12]. A multicast problem is a
quintuple (G, C, M, s, D).

- A directed acyclic graph $G := (V, E)$
- Capacities of edges, $C := \{c(e) | e \in E, c(e) \in Z\}$
- A message of dimension n, $M := (m_1, \ldots, m_n)$
- A single source, $s \in V$
- A set of destinations, $D \subseteq V$

In model of network coding, each edge is associated with an encoding function.
It determines the content to be transmitted on the edge when the input message
is M. Formally, for edge e from node v to node v', the encoding function ϕ_e can
be specified as:

$$\phi_e = \begin{cases} \sum^{|M|} \to F & if\ v = s \\ \sum^{|E_{I(v)}|} \to F & if\ v \neq s \end{cases}$$

where $E_{I(v)}$ is the set of input edges of node v. A network code is defined
as the set of encoding function associated with each edge. It characterizes the
transmission in the network. A network code is linear, if all the encoding functions are linear functions. Otherwise, it is a nonlinear. A code is feasible if
all destination nodes can recover the message M using the information they
received. Or else, it is infeasible. Original messages are $x_1, \ldots, x_n$ and the n
messages received by a sink are $f_1(x_1, \ldots, x_n), \ldots, f_n(x_1, \ldots, x_n)$. If $x_1, \ldots, x_n$
can be recovered, $\{f_1(x_1, \ldots, x_n), \ldots, f_n(x_1, \ldots, x_n)\}$ are one-to-one mapping to
$\{x_1, \ldots, x_n\}$. This implies the cardinality of $\{f_1(x_1, \ldots, x_n), \ldots, f_n(x_1, \ldots, x_n)\}$
and $\{x_1, \ldots, x_n\}$ are both $|F|^n$.

3   Related Concepts

3.1   Definition of Coding Dependent and n-Dimensional Maximal Independent Set

Definition 1. Let $F[x_1, \ldots, x_n]$ be the polynomial ring over F. A sequence of
polynomials $f_1, \ldots, f_n \in F[x_1, \ldots, x_n] \setminus 0$ is called nonlinear independent, if and
only if for any two distinct points $(x_1, \ldots, x_n), (x'_1, \ldots, x'_n) \in F^n$, satisfying

$$(f_1(x_1, \ldots, x_n), \ldots, f_n(x_1, \ldots, x_n)) \neq (f_1(x'_1, \ldots, x'_n), \ldots, f_n(x'_1, \ldots, x'_n))$$

Original messages can be recovered from the received messages sequence
$f_1, \ldots, f_n$ if they are nonlinear independent. Note that [12] define such concept as
nonlinear independent to be the concept of so-called algebraically independent.
But the definition of "algebraically independent" in [13] is not the same with the
implied meaning in this paper. The two kinds of definition can not be proven

to be equivalent for the lack ability of us in mathematics. So such concept as nonlinear independent is proposed in this paper to avoid ambiguity.

F is a finite field, then any function $f : F^n \to F$ can be uniquely represented by a polynomial with coefficients in the field F and with degree in each variable at most $|F| - 1$ [14]. Obviously, the number of such polynomials is $|F|^{|F|^n}$. These polynomials can be expressed as followings:

$$g(x_1, x_2, \ldots, x_n) = \sum_{a_1, a_2, \ldots, a_n \in \{0, 1, \ldots, |F|-1\}} c(a_1, a_2, \ldots, a_n) x_1^{a_1} x_2^{a_2} \ldots x_n^{a_n}$$

Let V^n denote all the polynomials as $g(x_1, x_2, \ldots, x_n)$ with n variables. For example, $|F| = 2$, then such functions as $f : F^2 \to F$ have 16 kinds of different expressions like {0, x, y, x+y, xy, x+xy, y+xy, x+y+xy, 1, x+1, y+1, x+y+1, xy+1, x+xy+1, y+xy+1, x+y+xy+1} [12].

In [9], $|F| + 1$ functions independent of each other are constructed, meanwhile in [12], maximal independent set is defined. The concepts above are both limited to 2-dimensional vector space. To get the minimal coding field needed by multicast network coding with nonlinear coding scheme, we introduce a new concept of so-called n-dimensional maximal independent set.

Definition 2. A set of functions $f_1, \ldots, f_m$ is called a n-dimensional independent set, if every n $(n < m)$ functions are nonlinear independent. A set is called a n-dimensional maximal independent set (nMIS), if m is maximal. Denote m, which is the cardinality of nMIS of all the functions over a finite field, with C_{noline}. C_{noline} is a generalized concept and it bases on the nMIS which includes both linear and nonlinear functions.

3.2 $|F|^{(n-1)}$-to-1 Mapping

In this section, we will point out what kind of functions can be the candidates of nMIS.

Theorem 1. For the input message of dimension n and a finite field F, all the functions of a nMIS are $|F|^{(n-1)}$-to-1 mapping.

Proof. In [9], it has been proven that the function must be a $|F|$-to-1 mapping when $n = 2$ by pigeonhole principle. Combinatorics is used here to prove the theorem when $n > 2$. With $f_1, \ldots, f_n$ denote the functions sequence which are nonlinear independent of each other.

Suppose at least one function among $f_1, \ldots, f_n$ is not $|F|^{(n-1)}$-to-1 mapping. Denote this function with $f_{i,1}$, and a new permutation of $f_1, \ldots, f_n$ is denoted as $f_{i,1}, \ldots, f_{i,n}$. Because $f_{i,1}$ is not $|F|^{(n-1)}$-to-1 mapping, then $\exists r_1 \in F$ makes the cardinality of X_1 more than $|F|^{(n-1)}$ where X_1 is the collection of elements satisfying $f_{i,1}(x_1, \ldots, x_n) = r_1$. Consider X_1 in the function $f_{i,2}$, then $\exists r_2 \in F$ makes the cardinality of $X_{1,2}$ more than $|F|^{(n-2)}$ where $X_{1,2}$ is the collection of elements satisfying $f_{i,2}(x_1, \ldots, x_n) = r_2$ and $X_{1,2} \sqsubset X_1$. The reason is that, the elements in X_1 are more than $|F|^{(n-1)}$, so, $\frac{|F|^{(n-1)}}{|F|} + 1$ points in X_1 are injected into a same value in domain.

By that analogy, a sequence of $X_1, X_{1,2}, ..., X_{1,2,...,n-1}$ is got where $X_1 \sqsupseteq X_{1,2} \sqsupseteq \cdots \sqsupseteq X_{1,2,...,n-1}$. Collections of points $X_{1,2,...,n-1}$ is referred to function $f_{i,n-1}$ and $X_{1,2,...,n-1}$ has more than $|F|$ elements. Consider $X_{1,2,...,n-1}$ in the function $f_{i,n-1}$, all the elements more than $|F|$ are mapped into a domain with size $|F|$. This indicates that there exists a set $X_{1,2,...,n}$, and the cardinality of $X_{1,2,...,n}$ is at least 2 where $X_{1,2,...,n-1}$ is the collection of elements satisfying $f_{i,n}(x_1, \ldots, x_n) = r_n$ and $X_{1,2,...,n-1} \sqsupseteq X_{1,2,...,n}$. Denote the two points $a = (a_1, a_2, \ldots, a_n), b = (b_1, b_2, \ldots, b_n)$. Obviously,

$$\begin{cases} f_{i,1}(a_1, \ldots, a_n) = f_{i,1}(a_1, \ldots, a_n) \\ \qquad \cdots\cdots\cdots \\ f_{i,n}(b_1, \ldots, b_n) = f_{i,n}(b_1 \ldots, b_n) \end{cases}$$

then

$$(f_{i,1}(a_1, \ldots, a_n), \ldots, f_{i,n}(a_1, \ldots, a_n)) = (f_{i,1}(b_1, \ldots, b_n), \ldots, f_{i,n}(b_1, \ldots, b_n))$$

This contradicts the assumption that $f_{i,1}, \ldots, f_{i,n}$ are nonlinear independent of each other. So it is impossible that at least one function among $f_1, \ldots, f_n$ is not $|F|^{(n-1)}$-to-1 mapping. The theorem has been proven until now.

3.3 Cardinality of Maximal Independent Set of Nonlinear Coding Functions

Theorem 2. For the input message of dimension n and a finite field F, $C_{noline} = \left\lfloor (n-1)\frac{q^n-1}{q^{n-1}-1} \right\rfloor$.

Proof. n functions algebraically independent means that if and only if for distinct points $(x_1, \ldots, x_n), (x'_1, \ldots, x'_n) \in F^n$, satisfying

$$(f_1(x_1, \ldots, x_n), \ldots, f_n(x_1, \ldots, x_n)) \neq (f_1(x'_1, \ldots, x'_n), \ldots, f_n(x'_1, \ldots, x'_n))$$

Among n functions, there are no more than $n-1$ functions (arbitrary one of them is represented by function f_i) meeting $f_i(x_1, \ldots, x_n) = f_i(x'_1, \ldots, x'_n)$. Or else, there will be n functions $f_1, \ldots, f_n (1 \leq i \leq n)$, and any of them f_i meeting $f_i(x_1, \ldots, x_n) = f_i(x'_1, \ldots, x'_n)$. That is to say, the n functions become not algebraically independent, contradicting the assumption that every n functions of nMIS are algebraically dependent. Inspired by [9], now define an agreement of the function f_i to be a pair of distinct points $(x_1, \ldots, x_n), (x'_1, \ldots, x'_n) \in F^n$ such that $f_i(x_1, \ldots, x_n) = f_i(x'_1, \ldots, x'_n)$. It has been proven in Theorem 1 that all the candidate functions of nMIS are $|F|^{(n-1)}$-to-1 mapping. Each function f_i has $|F| * \frac{|F|^{n-1}(|F|^{n-1}-1)}{2}$ agreements; because for each of the $|F|$ elements $\gamma \in F$, we can choose $\frac{|F|^{n-1}(|F|^{n-1}-1)}{2}$ pairs of distinct points from among the $|F|$ points in $(y_1, \ldots, y_n) \in F$ such that $f_i(y_1, \ldots, y_n) = \gamma$.

Now, let $[f_1, \ldots, f_m]$ be a nMIS in F. Because among n functions, there are no more than $n-1$ functions (arbitrary one of them is represented by function f_i)

meeting $f_i(x_1, \ldots, x_n) = f_i(x'_1, \ldots, x'_n)$, or else there will be n functions $f_1, \ldots, f_n (1 \leq i \leq n)$ meeting $f_i(x_1, \ldots, x_n) = f_i(x'_1, \ldots, x'_n)$. So, all the agreements of functions of nMIS are $(n-1)\frac{|F|^n(|F|^n-1)}{2}$ at most. If not, again by the pigeonhole principle, there must exist n functions $f_i, f_{i+1}, \ldots, f_{i+n-1}$ that share an agreement if

$$m * |F| \frac{|F|^{n-1}(|F|^{n-1}-1)}{2} > (n-1) * \frac{|F|^n(|F|^n-1)}{2}$$

But, if $f_i, f_{i+1}, \ldots, f_{i+n-1}$ share an agreement $(x_1, \ldots, x_n)$ and $(x'_1, \ldots, x'_n)$, we will have

$$\begin{cases} f_i(x_1, \ldots, x_n) = f_i(x'_1, \ldots, x'_n) \\ \quad \cdots \\ f_{i+n-1}(x_1, \ldots, x_n) = f_{i+n-1}(x'_1, \ldots, x'_n) \end{cases}$$

This contradicts the assumption that arbitrary n functions are algebraically independent. Therefore, it must

$$m < (n-1)\frac{|F|^n - 1}{|F|^{n-1} - 1}$$

m must be the biggest possible value for the cardinality of nMIS (n-dimensional maximal independent set should be bigger as much as possible). Because m is the counting number of the cardinality of nMIS, m must be an integer, then

$$m = \left\lfloor (n-1)\frac{|F|^n - 1}{|F|^{n-1} - 1} \right\rfloor$$

From other perspective, because no more than n−1 functions satisfying $f_i(x_1, \ldots, x_n) = f_i(x'_1, \ldots, x'_n)$ where $(x_1, \ldots, x_n), (x'_1, \ldots, x'_n)$ are different points in domain, the number of all the agreements of nMIS is limited to $(n-1) * [n * (n-1)/2]$. Meanwhile, the number of agreements of every function is $(n-1) * ((n-1) - 1)/2$, then, dividing one by the other gives C_{noline}. For $n = 2, |F| = 3$, based on this theorem, we can construct a nMIS that

$$\begin{cases} [x + 2y^2] \\ [x^2 + xy^2 + 2x + 2y^2 + y] \\ [x^2 + xy^2 + x + y] \\ [2x^2 + 2xy^2 + 2y^2 + 2y] \end{cases}$$

3.4 Composite Function

Assume a graphical representation of the concept of functions and composite functions. Consider the case where $n = 2, |F| = 3$, for the function f(x, y), there are n combinations of (x, y) in the domain, i,e, (0 0), (0 1), (0 2), (1 0), (1 1), (1 2), (2 0), (2 1), (2 2). For brevity, designate the above tuple sequence with the numbers in order, i.e., 1, 2, 3, 4, 5, 6, 7, 8, 9. To represent a function of two variables, divide a circle into $|F|$ sectors when each sector corresponds to one value of the range, and assign the above 9 tuples to the $|F|$ sectors, each sector can include 9 tuples at most and 0 tuple at least. The rest situations as $n \neq 2, |F| \neq 3$ can be deduced by analogy. Then, the way, how these $|F|^n$ tuples are distributed in the circle represents a certain function. We call such circle as function mapping distribution graph.

Now, we come to the concept of composite functions, and there is a composite function: $K[f_1(x,y), f_2(x,y)]$ where $n = 2, |F| = 3$. Composite function model can be expressed with the Fig. 1. Given three determined functions f_1, f_2, $K(X, Y)$, we will show how to get the ultimate composite function $K_{f_1,f_2}(x,y)$.

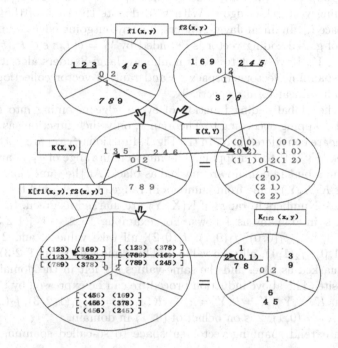

Fig. 1. Interpretation of the concept of composite function from the perspective of graphics

Because the global coding function of every edge incoming into a node is $|F|^{(n-1)}$-to-1 mapping according to Theorem 1, only such functions as $|F|^{(n-1)}$-to-1 mapping are considered here. In the Fig. 1, functions f_1, f_2 are both uniform mapping, i.e., $|F|^{(n-1)}$-to-1 mapping. The numbers in range of f_1, f_2 are marked as red when numbers in domain are marked as black. At the same time, numbers in domain of $K(X, Y)$ come from numbers in range of f_1, f_2, and they are both marked as red. Numbers in range of K(X,Y) are marked as green. In $K(X, Y)$, replace tuples in domain as follows. For example, $(0, 2) \rightarrow [(1\ 2\ 3)\ (2\ 4\ 5)]$ because 1 2 3, i.e., $f_1(0,0)$, $f_1(0,1)$, $f_1(0,2)$, all take value 0, and 2 4 5, i.e., $f_2(0,1)$, $f_2(1,0)$, $f_2(1,1)$, all take value 2. The same values in (1 2 3) between

(2 4 5) are marked as blue, and the same values are left in the domain of ulti-mate composite. The above induction procedure can be expressed by the follow-ing equation. $K(X,Y)(X = 0, Y = 2) = K(0,2) = K(f_1(1,2,3), f_2(2,4,5)) = K_{f_1,f_2}(2) = K_{f_1,f_2}(0,1)$. 2 is on behalf of $(0, 1)$ in domain.

At last, we get the intended composite function $K_{f_1,f_2}(x,y)$. The rest situa-tions as $n \neq 2, |F| \neq 3$ can be deduced easily by analogy.

3.5   Spanning Function Space

In vector space theory, the notation $\langle . \rangle$ will designate the spanning vector sub-space by a group of vectors. For a node t, let $V_t = \langle \{f_e : e \in In(t)\} \rangle$ where f_e is global coding vector for edge e. With v to denote the rank of the spanning vector subspace $\langle . \rangle$. In linear Jaggi-Sanders, for any outgoing edge e of node t, its value range of global coding vector is bounded by $V_t = \langle \{f_e : e \in In(t)\} \rangle$. That is to say, $f_e \in V_t$. If we want to study nonlinear Jaggi-Sanders algorithm, such concepts as spanning vector subspace $\langle . \rangle$ and rank of vector collections should be extend to nonlinear form respectively.

Because the global coding function of every edge incoming into a node is $|F|^{(n-1)}$-to-1 mapping according to Theorem 1, only such functions as $|F|^{(n-1)}$-to-1 mapping are considered here. In the Fig. 1, functions f_1, f_2 are both uniform mapping, i.e., $|F|^{(n-1)}$-to-1 mapping. The numbers in range of f_1, f_2 are marked as red when numbers in domain are marked as black. At the same time, numbers in domain of $K(X, Y)$ come from numbers in range of f_1, f_2, and they are both marked as red. Numbers in range of K(X, Y) are marked as green. In $K(X, Y)$, replace tuples in domain as follows. For example, $(0, 2) \rightarrow [(1\ 2\ 3)(2\ 4\ 5)]$ because 1 2 3, i.e., $f_1(0,0)$, $f_1(0,1)$, $f_1(0,2)$, all take value 0, and 2 4 5, i.e., $f_2(0,1)$, $f_2(1,0)$, $f_2(1,1)$, all take value 2. The same values in (1 2 3) between (2 4 5) are marked as blue, and the same values are left in the domain of ulti-mate composite. The above induction procedure can be expressed by the follow-ing equation. $K(X,Y)(X = 0, Y = 2) = K(0,2) = K(f_1(1,2,3), f_2(2,4,5)) = K_{f_1,f_2}(2) = K_{f_1,f_2}(0,1)$. 2 is on behalf of $(0, 1)$ in domain.

First, we extend spanning vector subspace to so-called spanning function subspace.

Definition 3. Given n polynomial functions $f_1(x_1, \ldots, x_n), \ldots, f_m(x_1, \ldots, x_n)$, and $K(Y_1, \ldots, Y_n)$ over finite field F, such that, $K_{f_1,\ldots,f_m}(x_1, \ldots, x_n) = K(f_1, \ldots, f_m)$. Keeping coefficients of $f_1, \ldots, f_m$ invariant and exhaust all the possible coefficients of $K(Y_1, \ldots, Y_n)$, the collection of all the possible $K_{f_1,\ldots,f_m}(x_1, \ldots, x_n)$ is called the spanning function subspace of $f_1, \ldots, f_m$.

Following the familiar notation in vector space, with

$$\langle \{f_1(x_1, \ldots, x_n), \ldots, f_m(x_1, \ldots, x_n)\} \rangle$$

to denote the spanning function subspace. Note that it has nothing to do with $K(f_1, \ldots, f_m)$ for $\langle \{f_1, \ldots, f_m\} \rangle$ because the spanning function space is the intrin-sic attribute of collection of $f_1, \ldots, f_m$.

If background is concerned here, $f_i(x_1, \ldots, x_n)$ refers to the global coding function of ith leading edge into node t, and $K(Y_1, \ldots, Y_n)$ refers to local coding function for edge leaving node t. All the functions are generalized nonlinear functions. If the function is restricted to linear functions, the global coding function will degenerated to global coding vector, and spanning function subspace will degenerated to spanning vector subspace.

In practice, it is more convenient to grasp the concept of spanning function space from different direction by so-called shared agreements.

Definition 4. For m functions with n variables, the notation

$$share\{f_1, \ldots, f_m\} = \begin{cases} \bigcap_{i=1}^{n} A(f_i), f_i \in \{f_1, \ldots, f_m, f_{m+1}, \ldots, f_n, \}, if \ m < n \\ \bigcap_{i=1}^{m} A(f_i), f_i \in \{f_1, \ldots, f_n\}, if \ m \geq n \end{cases}$$

is called shared agreements of collections of $f_1, \ldots, f_m$. It is equivalent to

$$share\{f_1, \ldots, f_m\} = \bigcap_{i=1}^{m} A(f_i)$$

For example, in Fig. 1, $share\{f_1, f_2\} = \{(4, 5), (7, 8)\}$.

Theorem 3. The number of elements in spanning function space is inversely proportional to the cardinality of $share\{f_1, \ldots, f_m\}$. Specially, when $share\{f_1, \ldots, f_m\}$ is $\emptyset$, the spanning function space is identical with the collection of all the polynomials with degree n on the finite field F.

Proof. There is a shared agreements $[(x_1', \ldots, x_n'), (x_1'', \ldots, x_n'')]$, denoted as $[X'X'']$ for convenience, such that $[X'X''] \in share\{f_1, \ldots, f_m\}$. That is to say, in any function f_i, such that $f_i(X') = f_i(X'')$. Based on the forgoing composite function model of Fig. 1, we have $K(f_1, \ldots, f_m) = K_{f_1, \ldots, f_m}(x_1, \ldots, x_n)$. For the values $a_1, \ldots, a_m$ in field F, we assume $a = K(f_1(), \ldots, f_m()) = K(a_1(), \ldots, a_m())$ such that

$$\left.\begin{matrix} f_1(X_{1,1}) \\ \cdots \\ f_1(X') \\ f_1(X'') \\ \cdots \\ f_1(X_{1,r}) \end{matrix}\right\} = a_1 \ \cdots \ \left.\begin{matrix} f_i(X_{i,1}) \\ \cdots \\ f_i(X') \\ f_i(X'') \\ \cdots \\ f_i(X_{i,r}) \end{matrix}\right\} = a_i \ \cdots \ \left.\begin{matrix} f_m(X_{m,1}) \\ \cdots \\ f_m(X') \\ f_m(X'') \\ \cdots \\ f_m(X_{m,r}) \end{matrix}\right\} = a_m$$

then

$$(\{X_{1,1}, \ldots, X', X'', \ldots, X_{1,r}\} \bigcap, \ldots, \bigcap \{X_{m,1}, \ldots, X', X'', \ldots, X_{m,r}\})$$

$$= \bigcap_{i=1}^{m} \{X_{i,1}, \ldots, X', X'', \ldots, X_{i,r}\} \sqsupseteq \{X', X''\}$$

Based on Fig. 1, we know that $K_{f_1,...,f_m}(X') = K_{f_1,...,f_m}(X'') = a$. That is to say, for certain function $f'()$, such that $f'(X') = f'(X'')$, we have $f'() \notin \langle\{f_1,...,f_m\}\rangle$. It means, $\langle\{f_1,...,f_m\}\rangle$ is just a proper subset of collections of all the polynomials with degree n on the F. The cardinality of is inversely proportional to the cardinality of $\langle\{f_1,...,f_m\}\rangle$. Specially, when $share\{f_1,...,f_m\}$ is Ø, the spanning function space $\langle\{f_1,...,f_m\}\rangle$ is identical with the collection of all the polynomials with degree n on the finite field F.

We also introduce a concept relative with spanning function space, and it is the rank of collections of functions which will be used in a subsequent proof.

Definition 5. The notation

$$dim\{f_1,...,f_m\} = \begin{cases} m, if(1 \leq m < n \ \& \ \bigcap_{i=1}^{m} A(f_i) = \varnothing) \\ non-integer \ in(1,m) \ \& \ \propto \frac{1}{|share\{f_1,...,f_m\}|}, if(1 \leq m < n \ \& \ \bigcap_{i=1}^{m} A(f_i) \neq \varnothing) \\ n, if(n \leq m \ \& \ share\{f_1,...,f_m = 0\}) \\ non-integer \ in(1,n) \ \& \ \propto \frac{1}{|share\{f_1,...,f_m\}|}, if(n \leq m \ \& \ share\{f_1,...,f_m\} \neq 0\}) \end{cases}$$

will designate the rank of collections of functions of $f_1,...,f_m$. It is observed easily that $dim\{f_1,...,f_m\}$ is generalized from the rank of vector space. Compared with the "rank" of vector space which can only take integer values, the rank of collections of generalized nonlinear functions can take non-integer values. It is continuous change rather than continuous jump like the rank of vector space.

For example, in Fig. 1, (4, 5), (7, 8) showed as italics are shared agreements respectively, i.e., $f_1(4) = f_1(5) \ \& \ f_2(4) = f_2(5), f_1(7) = f_1(8) \ \& \ f_2(7) = f_2(8)$. If $f'(4) = f'(5)$ or $f'(7) = f'(8)$, then $f'() \notin \langle\{f_1,...,f_m\}\rangle$. That means, $\langle\{f_1,...,f_m\}\rangle$ excludes such mapping form as $f'()$ such that $f'(4) = f'(5)$ or $f'(7) = f'(8)$.

3.6   To Get the Local Coding Function with Algebraic Method

For a node t, if we know all the global coding functions for its leading edges, and the global coding function for a leaving edge e is also known, how can we get the local coding function $\phi(Y_1,...,Y_m)$ for edge e in node t. Without lose of generality, consider the case $n = 2, |F| = 3$. Two leading edge global coding functions are

$$f_1(x,y) = a_1x^2 + a_2x^2y + a_3x^2y^2 + a_4x + a_5xy + a_6xy^2 + a_7y + a_8y^2 + a_9$$

$$f_2(x,y) = b_1x^2 + b_2x^2y + b_3x^2y^2 + b_4x + b_5xy + b_6xy^2 + b_7y + b_8y^2 + b_9$$

the global coding function of outgoing edge e is

$$f_c(x,y) = c_1x^2 + c_2x^2y + c_3x^2y^2 + c_4x + c_5xy + c_6xy^2 + c_7y + c_8y^2 + c_9$$

Algorithm 1:

1, Assume $K(Y_1, Y_2) = d_1Y_1^2 + d_2Y_1^2Y_2 + d_3Y_1^2Y_2^2 + d_4Y_1 + d_5Y_1Y_2 + d_6Y_1Y_2^2 + d_7Y_2 + d_8Y_2^2 + d_9$

2, It turns out $\phi(f_1(x,y), f_2(x,y)) = f_3(x,y)$. Choose g points in domain arbitrary, such that $g \geq 9$, then, obtain g equations with 9 unknowns of $d_1, d_2, ..., d_9$. If the rank of these g equations is not enough to 9, we add the value of g until the rank of these g equations is equal to 9.

3, To get the values of $d_1, d_2, ..., d_9$. Through solving equations set, then, $\phi(Y_1, Y_2)$ is determined.

Note that, if $f_3(x,y) \notin \langle\{f_1, f_2\}\rangle$, the equations set has no solution.

The rest situations as $n \neq 2, |F| \neq 3$ can be deduced easily by analogy.

4 Nonlinear Generalization of Jaggi-Sanders Algorithm to Its Nonlinear Form

With the previous preparation work, we will make a formal statement of the nonlinear generalized form of Jaggi-Sanders algorithm. The two are nearly the same, except that global coding vector and local coding vector are replaced by global coding function and local coding function respectively. As shown in Fig. 1, we intend to construct a nonlinear multicast scheme. The number of sinks which are consistent with maxflow $(T_q) \geq n\,(1 \leq q \leq \eta)$ is η. Denote these sink nodes with $T_1, T_2, ..., T_\eta$ such that $|F| > n$. For the arbitrary sink node T_q, it will exist n edge-disjoint paths $P_{q,1}, P_{q,2}, ..., P_{q,n}\ (1 \leq q \leq \eta)$. The number of all these edge-disjoint paths are n at most. The most important point is that, coding field is $|F| = \eta + 1$ [15].

Notation description:

1, "(q, i) pair": to denote every edge along a edge-disjoint path $P_{q,i}$. Because a edge may appear in different edge-disjoint path, some edge may have more than one "(q, i) pair".

2, $e_{q,i}$: predecessor edge of e in edge-disjoint $P_{q,i}$, to denote the just finished processing edge in edge-disjoint $P_{q,i}$. $P_{q,i}$ looks very much like "points" in programming language.

Algorithm 2:

1, Initialize global coding function f_e of n imaginary leading edge, and they are established as $x_1, x_2, ..., x_n$. The global coding function of the rest no-imaginary edges are established as 0.

2, Initialize "(q, i) pair": Every edge of every edge-disjoint path $P_{q,i}$ is labeled by (q, i); Initialize preprocessor $e_{q,i}$: for every (q, i) path, $e_{q,i}$ is initialized to imaginary edge respectively, that is, $e_{q,i}$ points to the first edge of every path $P_{q,i}$.

3, In any upstream-to-down stream orderconsider every node t and every channel $e \in out(t)$. With respect to every "(q, i) pair", other global coding functions $f_{e_{q,j}} : j \neq i$ which are nonlinear independent of $f_{e_{q,j}}$ have been already assigned in the previous time where $1 \leq q \leq \eta$. Establish the corresponding agreements $A_{f_{q,j}}$ referred to $f_{e_{q,j}}$. Based on the dependency theorem of global coding functions, $f_e \notin (\bigcup_{(q,i):a\ pair} \langle\{f_{e_{q,j}} : j \neq i\}\rangle)$, it is equivalent to that, $A_{f_e} \notin (\bigcup_{(q,i):a\ pair} \langle\{A_{f_{q,j}} : j \neq i\}\rangle)$, i.e., $A_{f_e} \sqsubseteq A_{C_{|F|n}^2} \setminus (\bigcup_{(q,i):a\ pair} \langle\{A_{f_{q,j}} : j \neq i\}\rangle)$

From Theorem 2, we know $|A_{C^2_{|F|^n}} \setminus (\bigcup_{(q,i):a\ pair} \langle\{A_{f_{q,j}} : j \neq i\}\rangle)| \geq |F| *$ $A_{C^2_{|F|^n}}$.

4, Establish the shared agreements $share\{f_1, ..., f_m\}$ of all the global coding functions for m leading edges at node based on Theorem 2. It is also need to confirm that $f_e \in V_t$, i.e., $share\{f_1, ..., f_m\} \sqsubseteq A_{f_e}$. It is induced from Theorem 3 that if $share\{f_1, ..., f_m\} \sqsubseteq A_{f_e}$, f_e will exist in the spanning function space of global coding functions for leading edges $\langle\{f_1, ..., f_m\}\rangle$.

5, Construct f_e. It should $f_e \in V_t \setminus (\bigcup_{(q,i):a\ pair} \langle\{f_{e_{q,j}} : j \neq i\}\rangle)$, equivalently, $A_{f_e} \sqsubseteq A_{C^2_{|F|^n}} \setminus (\bigcup_{(q,i):a\ pair} \langle\{A_{f_{q,j}} : j \neq i\}\rangle)$ & $share\{f_1, ..., f_m\} \sqsubseteq A_{f_e}$. Subsequently, we will give a compound proof to see the existence of A_{f_e}, i.e., f_e. It maybe unintelligibility to grasp this step, so, we give a practical construction example to illustrate this step in appendix. What calls for special attention is that in this example in the butterfly network, $share\{f_1, ..., f_m\}$ in all the node t is $\emptyset$because the n leading global coding functions of all the node t are independent of each other. So, the example is just the simple case of this algorithm.

6, According to sub-algorithm 2, establish the local coding function K_e for edge e in the node t where $e \in out(t)$.

7, With respective to every "(q, i) pair", update preprocessor edge, that is $e_{q,i} = e$.

8, For every sink node, assign $x_1, ..., x_n$ as the global coding functions of imaginary leaving edges respectively, from left to right. With respect to every imaginary edge e_i with global coding function x_i which is also a part of original messages, establish the local coding function ϕ_{e_i}. Such local coding functions are also decoding functions for original functions.

5   Proof on the Existence of Global Coding Function for Edge e

To see the existence of f_e in the step 5 in Algorithm 2 is given in this section.

Theorem 4. If the multicast scheme is constructed in field F where $|F| > \eta$, the global coding function f_e in Algorithm 3 always exists.

Proof. In Algorithm 2, for every "(q, i) pair", f_e needs to not only independent of $f_{e_{q,j}}$ already assigned, but also be in the spanning function space of leading edges global coding functions in node t. That is, equivalently, $f_e \in V_T \setminus (\bigcup_{(q,i):a\ pair} \langle\{f_{e_{q,j}} : j \neq i\}\rangle)$, it's, $A_{f_e} \sqsubseteq A_{C^2_{|F|^n}} \setminus (\bigcup_{(q,i):a\ pair} \langle\{A_{f_{q,j}} : j \neq i\}\rangle)$ & $share\{f_1, ..., f_m\} \sqsubseteq A_{f_e}$. m is to denote the number of leading edges in node t. We mainly utilize shared agreements in Theorem 3 to confirm it is in the spanning function space of leading $edges'$ global coding functions in node t. Meanwhile, utilize concept of agreements in Theorem 3 to confirm f_e is independent of $f_{e_{q,j}}$ already assigned. By default, all the global coding functions of leading edges in node t are $f_1(x_1, ..., x_n), ..., f_m(x_1, ..., x_n)$ respectively where the number of leading edges in node t is m. There are several following conditions.

1, m = 1, and the global coding function of leading edge is f.

In this case, $f_e = \lambda * f$ such that $\lambda \in F$ & $\lambda \neq 0$. By the property of induction of Algorithm 2, f has satisfied the condition of needing to independent of global coding function for other edge-disjoint edge. Further more, $\lambda * f$ is certainly in the spanning function space of function f. So, f_e exists.

2, m = n, and $dim\{f_1(x_1, \ldots, x_n), \ldots, f_m(x_1, \ldots, x_n)\} = n$.

In this case, the spanning function space is identical with V^n. Its equivalent to that $share\{f_1, \ldots, f_m\}$ is $\emptyset$. From Theorem 2, we know $c_{noline} \geq (n-1) * (|F| - 1) + 1$. This inequality can be proved easily, and for space the proving process is omitted. In extreme cases, the maximum of each $dim(\langle\{f_{e_{q,j}} : j \neq i\}\rangle)$ is n−1, and f_e should exist beyond the function space spanned by $\bigcup_{(q,i):a\ pair}\{f_{e_{q,j}} : j \neq i\}$. So, except $\bigcup_{(q,i):a\ pair}\langle\{f_{e_{q,j}} : j \neq i\}\rangle$, there must be at least 1 function left to be assigned for the processor edge e. It implies $(n-1) * (|F| - 1) + 1 >= (n-1) * \eta + 1$, i.e., $|F| >= \eta + 1$. In the other words, if $|F| >= \eta + 1$, f_e exists. From another perspective, the collection of functions $\bigcup_{(q,i):a\ pair}\{f_{e_{q,j}} : j \neq i\}$ occupies $\eta * |F| * \frac{|F|^{n-1}(|F|^{n-1}-1)}{2}$ different agreements at most. If f_e exists, at least another $|F| * \frac{|F|^{n-1}(|F|^{n-1}-1)}{2}$ agreements which used for construct f_e must be offered by the field F. All the agreements offered by field F is $(n-1) * \frac{|F|^n(|F|^n-1)}{2}$, so, if another $|F| * \frac{|F|^{n-1}(|F|^{n-1}-1)}{2}$ needs to be offered, it implies that

$$(n-1)*\frac{|F|^n(|F|^n - 1)}{2} - \eta*|F|*\frac{|F|^{n-1}(|F|^{n-1} - 1)}{2} \geq |F|*\frac{|F|^{n-1}(|F|^{n-1} - 1)}{2}$$

This inequality implies $|F| >= \eta + 1$. In all, if $|F| >= \eta + 1$, f_e exists. For example, in the butterfly graph of appendix, node t is the case of this situation.

3, $2 \leq m < n$, unknowns of $x_1, x_2, \ldots, x_n$ are degraded into $x_1, x_2, \ldots, x_m$ and $dim\{f_1(x_1, \ldots, x_n), \ldots, f_m(x_1, \ldots, x_n)\} = m$.

With respect to the m unknowns $x_1, x_2, \ldots, x_m$ except $x_{m+1}, \ldots, x_n$, we can choose a function with variables $x_1, x_2, \ldots, x_m$ to be assigned for processor edge e. Specially with regard to $x_1, x_2, \ldots, x_m$ rather than $x_1, x_2, \ldots, x_n$, we can apply Theorem 3 to conclude that there exists $|F| * \frac{|F|^{n-1}(|F|^{n-1}-1)}{2}$ to construct f_e. The proving process analogy of proof in situation 2. So, f_e exists.

For example, if $|F| = 3, n = 3, \eta = 3$, there is a intermediate node t which has 2 leading edges. The global functions for the 2 edges are independent of each other, and they only depend on the variables x_1, x_2 rather than x_1, x_2, x_3.

4, $2 \leq m < n$, the global coding functions of leading edges are, in order, $f_1(x_1, \ldots, x_n), \ldots, f_m(x_1, \ldots, x_n)$, and $dim\{f_1(x_1, \ldots, x_n), \ldots, f_m(x_1, \ldots, x_n)\} = m$.

This condition implies that all the variables depended on by the global coding functions are $x_1, x_2, \ldots, x_n$. Random variables $x_1, x_2, \ldots, x_m$ are selected from these variables of $x_1, x_2, \ldots, x_n$. With $f_i(x_1, \ldots, x_n)_{(x_1,\ldots,x_m)}$ to denote the function degraded from f_i with variables $x_1, x_2, \ldots, x_n$ and $f_i(x_1, \ldots, x_n)_{(x_1,\ldots,x_m)}$ just depend on the variables of $x_1, x_2, \ldots, x_m$. From Theorem 3, If

$$dim\{f_1(x_1, \ldots, x_n), \ldots, f_m(x_1, \ldots, x_n)\} = m$$

from Theorem 3,

$$f_1(x_1,\ldots,x_n)_{(x_1,\ldots,x_m)},\ldots,f_m(x_1,\ldots,x_n)_{(x_1,\ldots,x_m)}$$

are independent of each other. Just for the variables $x_1, x_2, ..., x_m$, the situation is the same with the situation 2. So, at least exist 1 function $f_j(x_1, ..., x_n)_{(x_1,...,x_m)}$ just depend on $x_1, x_2, ..., x_m$ can be selected, and its corresponding upgrade function $f_i(x_1, ..., x_n)$ can be as the global coding function for the processor edge e. This implies $|\{f_j(x_1, ..., x_n)_{(x_1,...,x_m)}\}| = |\{f_j(x_1, ..., x_n)\}|$. So, f_e exists.

For example, if $|F| = 3, n = 3, \eta = 3$, the global coding functions of leading edges in node t are $f_1(x_1, x_2, x_3) = (x_1 + 2 * x_2^2 + x_1 * x_3) + x_2^2 * x_3$, $f_2(x_1, x_2, x_3) = (x_1^2 + x_1 * x_2^2 + x_1 + x_2) + x_1 * x_3 + x_2 * x_3^2$. The corresponding degrade functions which are independent of each other are $f_1(x_1, x_2, x_3)_{(x_1,x_2)} = x_1 + 2 * x_2^2$, $f_2(x_1, x_2, x_3)_{(x_1,x_2)} = x_1^2 + x_1 * x_2^2 + x_1 + x_2$. The selected function is $f_3(x_1, x_2, x_3)_{(x_1,x_2)} = 2 * x_1^2 + 2 * x_1 * x_2^2 + 2 * x_2^2 + 2 * x_2$. Because $f_3(x_1, x_2, x_3)_{(x_1,x_2)}$ are coding dependent of $f_1(x_1, x_2, x_3)_{(x_1,x_2)}$ and $f_2(x_1, x_2, x_3)_{(x_1,x_2)}$. Based on Theorem 3, the corresponding upgrade function of $f_3(x_1, x_2, x_3)_{(x_1,x_2)}$ must exist certainly. With the help of MATLAB, and after lots of calculation are played, we reach that $f_3(x_1, x_2, x_3) = (2 * x_1^2 + 2 * x_1 * x_2^2 + 2 * x_2^2 + 2 * x_2) + 2 * x_2^2 * x_3 + 2 * x_1 * x_3 + x_1^2 * x_3$.

5, Other situations: $share\{f_1, ..., f_m\} \neq \varnothing$

This is equivalent to that $dim\{f_1, ..., f_m\} = n$ is not integer value, i.e., $k_1 \leq dim\{f_1(x_1, ..., x_n), ..., f_m(x_1, ..., x_n)\} \leq k_2$, where $1 < k_1 \leq k_2 < n$ and k_1, k_2 are both non-integer. This implies at least $\lfloor k_1 \rfloor$ variables can be selected. Just for the $\lfloor k_1 \rfloor$ variables, there will exist $\lfloor k_1 \rfloor$ polynomials in these $\lfloor k_1 \rfloor$ variables which are coding dependent. a analogy of induction procedure in situation 4 can be done. Just for the $\lfloor k_1 \rfloor$ variables, the spanning function space is denoted by $V^{\lfloor k_1 \rfloor}$, then, $V^{\lfloor k_1 \rfloor} \neq \varnothing$. Because $dim\{f_1(x_1, ..., x_n), ..., f_m(x_1, ..., x_n)\} \geq k_1$, $|\langle\{f_1, ..., f_m\}\rangle| \geq |V^{\lfloor k_1 \rfloor}|$. So, f_e exists.

In all, f_e exists.

6   Conclusion

This work generates the Jaggi-Sanders algorithm the its non-linear style, and it offers a new approach and a new frame for network coding study. It is completely new idea. This idea help decrease the coding filed. It can code for non-multicast network. This work has the model significance for network coding study. It has special advantages in error recovery and energy saving.

7   Open Problems

Intuitively, if the network coding construction algorithm is a accurate algorithm, rather than a heuristic algorithm, it looks rather unlikely that its time complexity can be reduced to polynomial complexity. After private communications with several exporters at network coding, their advices also back this guess. Can we give a proof of this guess? May it can be solved by proving that this problem is logically equivalent to a known NP-complete problem. If this guess is true, we need to develop heuristic nonlinear network coding algorithm for purpose of engineering applications.

Acknowledgment. This work is supported by Suihua technology office program (SHKJ2015-015, SHKJ2015-014), National Science foundation of China (61571150), Education Office of Heilongjiang province science and technology program (Study on integrated network application in smart factory), Suihua university program (K1502003).

Appendix

A Case of Nonlinear Jaggi-Sanders Algorithm in Butterfly Network

Based on the proposed nonlinear Jaggi-sanders algorithm, a nonlinear multicast scheme was constructed as the graph 2 illustrates.

When field $|F| = 3$, and messages dimension is $n = 2$, all the points in domain of function with 2 variables can be denoted by a numbers sequence. Thats, $(0, 0) \rightarrow 1, ..., (2, 2) \rightarrow 9$. There are 36 agreements, i.e., $A_{C^2_{|F|^n}} = 36$, illustrated

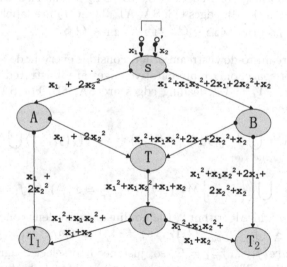

Fig. 2. A case of constructing nonlinear network coding scheme with nonlinear Jaggi-Sanders algorithm

in the list 1. 9 agreements points are selected to construct a function and how to select is based on Algorithm 2.

$a1 = [1\ 2]\ (0,0)(0,1);$ $a10 = [2\ 4]\ (0,1)(1,0);$ $a19 = [3\ 7]\ (0,2)(2,0);$ $a28 = [5\ 7]\ (1,1)(2,0)$

$a2 = [1\ 3]\ (0,0)(0,2);$ $a11 = [2\ 5]\ (0,1)(1,1);$ $a20 = [3\ 8]\ (0,2)(2,1);$ $a29 = [5\ 8]\ (1,1)(2,1)$

$a3 = [1\ 4]\ (0,0)(1,0);$ $a12 = [2\ 6]\ (0,1)(1,2);$ $a21 = [3\ 9]\ (0,2)(2,2);$ $a30 = [5\ 9]\ (1,1)(2,2)$

$a4 = [1\ 5]\ (0,0)(1,1);$ $a13 = [2\ 7]\ (0,1)(2,0);$ $a22 = [4\ 5]\ (1,0)(1,1);$ $a31 = [6\ 7]\ (1,2)(2,0)$

$a5 = [1\ 6]\ (0,0)(1,2);$ $a14 = [2\ 8]\ (0,1)(2,1);$ $a23 = [4\ 6]\ (1,0)(1,2);$ $a32 = [6\ 8]\ (1,2)(2,1)$

$a6 = [1\ 7]\ (0,0)(2,0);$ $a15 = [2\ 9]\ (0,1)(2,2);$ $a24 = [4\ 7]\ (1,0)(2,0);$ $a33 = [6\ 9]\ (1,2)(2,2)$

$a7 = [1\ 8]\ (0,0)(2,1);$ $a16 = [3\ 4]\ (0,2)(1,0);$ $a25 = [4\ 8]\ (1,0)(2,1);$ $a34 = [7\ 8]\ (2,0)(2,1)$

$a8 = [1\ 9]\ (0,0)(2,2);$ $a17 = [3\ 5]\ (0,2)(1,1);$ $a26 = [4\ 9]\ (1,0)(2,2);$ $a35 = [7\ 9]\ (2,0)(2,2)$

$a9 = [2\ 3]\ (0,1)(0,2);$ $a18 = [3\ 6]\ (0,2)(1,2);$ $a27 = [5\ 6]\ (1,1)(1,2);$ $a36 = [8\ 9]\ (2,1)(2,2)$

1, Initializing f_e imaginary edges are set as $f_{OS} = x_1, f_{OS'} = x_2$, while the rest $f_e = 0$. The spanning function space of node S is V^n, i.e., all the 2-dimensional mappings in field F (because $f_{OS} = x_1$ is nonlinear independent of $f_{OS'} = x_2$ in variables x_1, x_2) [15].

2, Label "(q, i) pair" for every edge, consider sinks T_1, T_2.

(1) for $T_1(q = 1)$ there are 2 edge-disjoint paths O-S-A-T1 and O'-S-B-T-C-T_1. For the first path (i=1), edges OS, SA, AT_1 are labeled with (1, 1). For the second path (i=2), edges OS, SB, BT, TC, CT_1 are labeled with (1, 2).

(2) for T_2 (q = 2) there are 2 edge-disjoint paths O'-S-B-T2 and O-S-A-T-C-T2. For the first path (i=1), edges O'S, SB, BT_2 are labeled with (2, 1). For the second path (i=2), edges OS, SA, AT, TC, CT_2 are labeled with (2, 2).

(3) Initializing $e_{q,i}$. $e_{1,1} = e_{2,2} = OS, e_{1,2} = e_{2,1} = O'S$.

3, In an upstream-to-downstream order, consider every node and its leading edges. For lack of space, only representative edges are illustrated here.

(1) For node S, $V_t = V^n$, leading edges are SA, SB. For SA, its (q, i) are (1, 1), (2, 2). Then

$$f_{SA} \in V_S \setminus \left(\bigcup_{(q,i):a\ pair} \langle\{f_{e_{q,j}} : j \neq i\}\rangle \right) = V_S \setminus \left(\langle\{f_{e_{1,2}}\}\rangle \bigcup \langle\{f_{e_{2,1}}\}\rangle \right)$$

$$= V_S \setminus \left(\langle\{f_{e_{OS'}}\}\rangle \bigcup \langle\{f_{e_{OS'}}\}\rangle \right) = \left(\langle\{f_1 = x_1, f_2 = x_2\}\rangle \right) \setminus \left(\langle\{f_1 = x_1, f_2 = x_2\}\rangle \right)$$

Based on step 5 in Algorithm 2, the nonlinear equivalent condition is

$A_{f_e} \sqsubseteq A_{C^2_{|F|^n}} \setminus (\bigcup_{(q,i):a\ pair} \langle\{A_{f_{q,j}} : j \neq i\}\rangle)$ & $share\{f_1, ..., f_m\} \sqsubseteq A_{f_e}$

Of them, $share\{f_1, ..., f_m\} = \emptyset$, so, just need to select 9 agreements in to construct a function. The 9 corresponding agreements of the function $f = x_2$ are as the followings.

$$a[3] = [1\ 4]; 1(0,0)\ 4(1,0)\ 7(2,0) \to 0$$
$$a[6] = [1\ 7];$$
$$a[24] = [4\ 7];$$

$$a[11] = [2\ 5]; 2(0,1)\ 5(1,1)\ 8(2,1) \rightarrow 1$$
$$a[14] = [2\ 8];$$
$$a[29] = [5\ 8];$$

$$a[18] = [3\ 6]; 3(0,2)\ 6(1,2)\ 9(2,2) \rightarrow 2$$
$$a[21] = [3\ 9];$$
$$a[33] = [6\ 9];$$

Select 9 agreements to form a function from the rest 27 agreements after removing the 9 agreements of function $f - x_2$ in list 1. Note that not any 9 agreements can form a function, for example, if [1 5], [1 6] are selected, [5 6] has to be included. Then the 3 points 1, 5, 6 are mapped into a same value in the range, for example, 0. The rest 2 groups of points are mapped into 2 different values respectively where each group includes 3 points. For $share\{f_1, ..., f_m\} = \emptyset$, in the procedure of selecting 9 agreements, there is no need to mapping certain 2 points (2 leading edges) into a same value in range. For example, in the Fig. 1 in text, we need to map 2 points 4, 5 into a same value in range, and treat 7, 8 in the same manner. The reason is $[4,5] \in share\{f_1, ..., f_m\}\&[7,8] \in share\{f_1, ..., f_m\}$. But there is no need to do so in this case. The function corresponding to the selected agreements can be got through solving linear equations in 9 coefficients of this being solved function. That is, to assume

$$f(x_1, x_2) = c_1 x_1^2 + c_2 x_1^2 x_2 + c_3 x_1^2 x_2^2 + c_4 x_1 + c_5 x_1 x_2 + c_6 x_1 x_2^2 + c_7 x_2 + c_8 x_2^2 + c_9$$

The ultimate solved function is $f = x_1 + 2x_2^2$, then, $f_e = x_1 + 2x_2^2$ The 9 corresponding agreements of the function are as the followings.

$$a[4] = [1\ 5]; 1(0,0)\ 5(1,1)\ 6(1,2) \rightarrow 0$$
$$a[5] = [1\ 6];$$
$$a[27] = [5\ 6];$$

$$a[25] = [4\ 8]; 4(1,0)\ 8(2,1)\ 9(2,2) \rightarrow 1$$
$$a[26] = [4\ 9];$$
$$a[36] = [8\ 9];$$

$$a[9] = [2\ 3]; 2(0,1)\ 3(0,2)\ 7(2,0) \rightarrow 2$$
$$a[13] = [2\ 7];$$
$$a[19] = [3\ 7];$$

In node S, the local coding function for outgoing edge e is $F(X,Y) = X + 2Y^2$. (2) For the outgoing edge TC of node T, its (q,i) are (1, 2), (2, 2). From Subsect. 3.3, we know global coding functions $f_{e_{AT_1}}, f_{e_{BT_2}}$ both belongs to a nMIS, so they are independent of each other. Then the spanning functions of node T are all the mappings in field F with degree 2, i.e., $V_t = V^n$.

$$f_{TC} \in V_T \setminus (\bigcup_{(q,i):a \ pair} \langle\{f_{e_{q,j}} : j \neq i\}\rangle) = V_T \setminus (\langle\{f_{e_{1,1}}\}\rangle \bigcup \langle\{f_{e_{2,1}}\}\rangle)$$

$$= V_T \setminus (\langle\{f_{e_{AT_1}}\}\rangle \bigcup \langle\{f_{e_{BT_2}}\}\rangle)$$

$$= (\langle\{f_1 = x_1 + 2x_2^2, f_2 = x_1^2 + x_1x_2^2 + 2x_1 + 2x_2^2 + x_2\}\rangle)$$

$$\setminus \{(\langle\langle\{f_1 = x_1 + 2x_2^2\}\rangle) \bigcup (\langle\{f_2 = x_1^2 + x_1x_2^2 + 2x_1 + 2x_2^2 + x_2\}\rangle))\}$$

$$= V^n \setminus (\langle\langle\{f_1 = x_1 + 2x_2^2\}\rangle) \bigcup (\langle\{f_2 = x_1^2 + x_1x_2^2 + 2x_1 + 2x_2^2 + x_2\}\rangle)$$

Based on step 5 in Algorithm 2, the nonlinear equivalent condition is $A_{f_e} \sqsubseteq A_{C^2_{|F|^n}} \setminus (\bigcup_{(q,i):a \ pair} \langle\{A_{f_{q,j}} : j \neq i\}\rangle)$ & $share\{f_1, ..., f_m\} \sqsubseteq A_{f_e}$
Of them, $share\{f_1, ..., f_m\} = \varnothing$, so, just need to select 9 agreements in $= A_{C^2_{|F|^n}} \setminus (A_{f_1 = x_1 + 2x_2^2} \bigcup A_{f_2 = x_1^2 + x_1x_2^2 + 2x_1 + 2x_2^2 + x_2})$ to construct a function. The corresponding functions of $f_1 = x_1 + 2x_2^2$ and $f_2 = x_1^2 + x_1x_2^2 + 2x_1 + 2x_2^2 + x_2$ are marked as red and green respectively in list 1. Among the rest 18 agreements, 9 agreements are selected and marked as blue. As doing for edge SA, the 9 agreements construct a function $f_{TC} = x_1^2 + x_1x_2^2 + x_1 + x_2$ as $f_{e_{TC}}$ which is certainly independent of $f_1 = x_1 + 2x_2^2$ and $f_2 = x_1^2 + x_1x_2^2 + 2x_1 + 2x_2^2 + x_2$ based on Theorem 2. At last, we will use Algorithm 2 to get the local coding function for TC in node T, and it is $F = 2X + Y$.

(3) For node T_1 using the step 6 of Algorithm 2, assume the two imaginary outgoing edges are $f_1 = x_1, f_2 = x_2$. Establish the two local coding functions for the two imaginary outgoing edges. Actually, they are the decoding functions in sink node. For example, the local coding function for right imaginary edge in node T_1 is $K_{T_1x_2}(X, Y) = 2X^2 + 2X + Y$, and it is also the decoding function for original message x_2 in node T_1. $\phi_{T_1x_2}(x_1 + 2x_2^2, x_1^2 + x_1x_2^2 + 2x_1 + 2x_2^2 + x_2) = 2x_2^4 + x_2^2 + x_2$, for the operation of mod 3 in field $F = \{0, 1, 2\}$, $2x_2^4 + x_2^2 + x_2 = x_2$ and this can be verified easily by MATLAB. x_1 can be decoded in the same manner. The ultimate global coding functions are illustrated in the Fig. 2. The local coding functions for every outgoing edge in a node are listed in the chart 1. If there are 2 leading edges in a node, the variables X, Y of $\phi(X, Y)$ delegate the left and right messages respectively received by a node. Meanwhile, if there is only one leading edge, the local coding function is $\phi(X)$ (Table 1).

Notation

F: the finite field used.

n: the block length of the original codes, i.e., the dimension of original messages.

m: the number of leading edges of a intermediate node and $m \geq 1$.

C_{noline}: Cardinality of maximal independent set of nonlinear coding functions.

Table 1. Local coding functions for every outgoing edges including imaginary outgoing edges in sinks

S	$\phi(X,Y) = X + 2Y^2$	$\phi(X,Y) = X + XY^2 + 2X + 2Y^2 + 2Y$
A	$\phi(X) = X$	$\phi(X) = X$
B	$\phi(X) = X$	$\phi(X) = X$
T	$\phi(X,Y) = 2X + Y$	
C	$\phi(X) = X$	$\phi(X) = X$
T_1	$\phi(X,Y) = XY^2 + 2X^2 + XY + Y^2$	$\phi(X,Y) = 2X^2 + 2X + Y$
T_2	$\phi(X,Y) = X + X^2Y + 2X^2 + XY^2 + 2Y^2$	$\phi(X,Y) = 2X^2 + 2XY + 2X + 2Y^2 + 2Y$

nMIS: a n-dimensional maximal independent set.

ϕ_e: the local coding function for edge e which is a outgoing edge of intermediate t. This function is in the variables which are the messages of leading edges of intermediate node t.

$\phi_e(X,Y)$: a special case of ϕ_e which is in the variables X, Y, i.e., there are two edges in node t.

$K_{T_1 x_2}$: a special case of ϕ_e where edge e is specialized as the second imaginary outgoing edge.

x_2 of the sink T_1. It is also the decoding function for messages x_2 in sink node T_1.

$K_{f_1 f_2}(x,y)$: the arithmetic result of composite the function $K[f_1(x,y), f_2(x,y)]$.

f_e: global coding function for edge e in the variables of original messages $x_1, ..., x_n$.

(q, i): two-tuple to represent the $i'th$ edge-disjoint path of the $q'th$ sink.

$e_{(q,i)}$: the predecessor edge e of on a path.

$P_{q,i}$: denote the path that the $i'th$ edge-disjoint path of the $q'th$ sink.

V^n: all the mappings in n variables in field F where one of these mappings can be uniquely represented by a polynomial with coefficients in the field F and with degree in each variable at most $n-1$. It is the generalization of the vector space concept.

$\langle \{f_1, ..., f_m\} \rangle$: the spanning function space which is a subspace of V^n.

t: a intermediate node.

V_t: the spanning function space of node t, and it is a alternative representation of $\langle \{f_1, ..., f_m\} \rangle$.

$dim\{f_1, ..., f_m\}$: the rank of collection of functions $f_1, ..., f_m$, and it is the generalization of the rank of vectors set concept.

$share\{f_1, ..., f_m\}$: the shared agreements of collection of functions $f_1, ..., f_m$.

A_{f_e}: all the agreements of function f_e.

$A_{C^2_{|F|^n}}$: all the agreements of all the functions where there are n variables in the finite field F.

ϕ: the number of sinks.

q: the sequence number to denote the $q'th$ sink of ϕ sinks.

E: the set of edges.

$f_i(x_1, ..., x_n)_{(x_1,...,x_m)}$: to denote the function degraded from functions f_i with variables $x_1, x_2, ..., x_n$ and $f_i(x_1, ..., x_n)_{(x_1,...,x_m)}$ just depend on the variables of $x_1, x_2, ..., x_m$.

References

1. Dougherty, R., Freiling, C., Zeger, K.: Insufficiency of linear coding in network information flow. IEEE Trans. Inf. Theor. **51**(8), 2745–2759 (2005)
2. Kobayashi, H., Le Gall, F., Nishimura, H., Rotteler, M.: Constructing quantum network coding schemes from classical nonlinear protocols. In: 2011 IEEE International Symposium on Information Theory Proceedings (ISIT), pp. 109–113. IEEE (2011)
3. Blasiak, A., Kleinberg, R., Lubetzky, E.: Lexicographic products and the power of non-linear network coding. In: 2011 IEEE 52nd Annual Symposium on Foundations of Computer Science (FOCS), pp. 609–618. IEEE (2011)
4. Shadbakht, S., Hassibi, B.: MCMC methods for entropy optimization and nonlinear network coding. In: 2010 IEEE International Symposium on Information Theory Proceedings (ISIT), pp. 2383–2387. IEEE (2010)
5. Li, Q., Ting, S.H., Ho, C.K.: Nonlinear network code for high throughput broadcasting with retransmissions. In: IEEE International Symposium on Information Theory, ISIT 2009, pp. 2853–2857. IEEE (2009)
6. Wernersson, N., Skoglund, M.: Nonlinear coding and estimation for correlated data in wireless sensor networks. IEEE Trans. Commun. **57**(10), 2932–2939 (2009)
7. Dougherty, R., Freiling, C., Zeger, K.: Unachievability of network coding capacity. Inf. Theor. IEEE Trans. **52**(6), 2365–2372 (2006)
8. Langberg, M., Sprintson, A.: On the hardness of approximating the network coding capacity. In: IEEE International Symposium on Information Theory, ISIT 2008, pp. 1008–1014 (2008)
9. Lehman, A.R., Lehman, E.: Complexity classification of network information flow problems. In: Proceedings of the Fifteenth Annual ACM-SIAM Symposium on Discrete Algorithms, Society for Industrial and Applied Mathematics, pp. 142–150 (2004)
10. Medard, M., Koetter, R.: Beyond routing: an algebraic approach to network coding. Proc. IEEE INFOCOM **1**(5), 122–130 (2002)
11. Sanders, P., Egner, S., Tolhuizen, L.: Polynomial time algorithms for network information flow. In: ACM Symposium on Parallel Algorithms and Architectures, pp. 286–294 (2003)
12. Li, L., Fan, K., Long, D.: Nonlinear network coding: a case study. Comput. Sci. **7**, 020 (2008)
13. Bachmann, O., Greuel, G.-M., Lossen, C., Pfister, G., Schönemann, H.: A Singular Introduction to Commutative Algebra. Springer, Berlin (2007)
14. Liaoqunying, F.: The Finite Field and its Application. Dalian University of Technology Press, Dalian (2011)
15. JiaqingHuang, Z.: Network Coding Principles. National Defence Industry Press, Beijing (2012)

Universal Secure Error-Correcting (SEC) Schemes for Network Coding via McEliece Cryptosystem Based on QC-LDPC Codes

Guangzhi Zhang[1,2], Shaobin Cai[1(✉)], Chunhua Ma[2], and Dongqiu Zhang[3]

[1] Computer Science Department, Harbin Engineering University, Harbin, China
4099516520QQ.com
[2] Suihua University, Suihua, China
[3] Qiqihaer Engineering College, Qiqihar, China

Abstract. The McEliece cryptosystem based on quasi-cyclic low-density parity check (QC-LDPC) codes is presented to offer both security and error-correction simultaneously in network coding system. The characteristics of the cryptosystem make it does not need to reduce information rate additionally to offer security. The messages μ is coded into x with QC-LDPC. x is transmitted through a network where a MDS network coding error-correcting scheme is performed. ρ links are observed by adversary and t errors occurs in the network. The characteristic of MDS codes make the errors can't be spread, therefore, the corrupted packets which occur in t links will cause at most t errors in the received messages in the sink. As long as the number of errors occurs in the intermediate links is not beyond the minimum distance of QC-LDPC codes, the hybrid scheme can perform error-correcting and security simultaneously. The information rate reaches $(n - 2t)/n$ instead of $(n - \rho - 2t)/n$ where n is the max-flow min-cut.

Keywords: McEliece cryptosystem · QC-LDPC codes · Security · Error-correction · Network coding

1 Introduction

1.1 The Existing Works About Error-Correcting and Security Schemes in Network Coding

Network coding is a effective technique to achieve the increment of information transport throughput in multicast. It also can increase the robustness of the network transport. However, network coding poses new challenges for secure and reliable communication. We identify the challenges in addressing the security vulnerabilities and the difficulties of error-correcting. The network may be subject to two major kinds of performance degradations: the eavesdrop and the pollution. In network coding, its very nature of combining information in the intermediate nodes makes it is very sensitive to transmission errors. A single error will be propagated by every node further downstream. This will thus

© Springer Nature Singapore Pte Ltd. 2017
M. Xu et al. (Eds.): CTCIS 2017, CCIS 704, pp. 275–289, 2017.
https://doi.org/10.1007/978-981-10-7080-8_20

prevent reconstruction of even a small portion of the file in the sink. Also, the information and coding vector of the packets in the intermediate nodes are exposed to eavesdroppers if they are unprotected. Then, the eavesdropper can reconstruct the original information by the coding vectors of the network coding.

To well understand our original intention of the upcoming proposal, we should address the ins and outs of pre-existing works about error-correction scheme and security scheme. For limited space, we will just outline the most relevant and typical works. Looking for more detailed references, readers are invited to the latest survey [1]. There are some specifications to judge the quality of a scheme:

(a) low complexity
(b) high rate
(c) universality
(d) high security of offering resilience against an arbitrary fraction of malicious nodes
(e) desirable fusion of error-correction and security.

Solutions can be categorized into cryptographic approaches and information theoretic approaches. Generally speaking, cryptographic approaches have high rate and high security, but have high complexity. Meanwhile, information theoretic approaches have low complexity, but it can't cope with the adversary who can eavesdrop on the entire network.

Cryptographic approaches includes such methods as keys, signatures, null space, and authentication [2–4]. And also it is really worthwhile to mention that homomorphic signatures. In this scheme, the intermediate nodes can combine and encode the incoming hash packets and forward them without knowing the content of native packets or private key of the source node. But almost all the existing homomorphic signature schemes have high complexity [5–10]. Many researches are aimed at reducing the complexity. For example, using symmetric keys [11,12] and batch verification to alleviate computational complexity. Some works even apply powerful CPUs [13,14]. But these researches are far from practical application. They lead to traffic overhead or they need frequently pre-distributing verification codes between nodes in a communication or require a large bandwidth [1,15].

In the existing works about information theoretic approaches, in the sense of methodology, there are mainly three kinds of approaches in my opinion. The representative works of the first category are as in [16–18]. They generalizes the concepts of traditional blocks codes, and the typical methods in blocks codes are adopted naturally. They treat the network based on network coding as a known quantity. For example, in [17], $y_u = (xA + z)FB$, the transfer matrix is known (details of these symbols therein [17]). In [18], the transfer matrix is also determinate. However, this kind of approach is just suited for coherent network. The second approach is as in [19]. In equation $Y = TX + T_{Z \rightarrow Y}Z$, the transfer matrix T is unknown. After both parity symbols and hash values are sent over secret channels, the original messages can be recovered through solving equations. However, parity symbols and hash values are used to counteract the uncertainty of the transfer matrix in the network coding. The third kind of skills are as in [20–23]. The original messages are coded with a MDS codes in the source. The network is abstracted as a point-to-point transparent channel where the topology and transfer matrix is unknown. The routine errors and eavesdrops, even the network coding performing in intermediate nodes are all treated as a disturbance to the source coding with MDS codes. As long as the disturbance is within an appropriate range, the decoding in the sink can be performed. The only profound difference among this kinds of approaches are different MDS codes with different mathematic metrics. The mathematic metrics include rank-metric [20], subspace distance metric. [20] is a part of the grand sweep of security schemes in network coding. It composes an inner error-correcting code with the outer network coding scheme. We just need to design a MDS codes in the source regardless of the network topology and underline network coding coefficients. Subsequent other rank-metric codes and subspace codes come down in one continuous line with this seminal intention [21–23]. It is worth to mention that, in [24], information is encoded in a choice of vector space rather than a vector where the distance between subspaces is introduced. MDS, MRD subspaces distance are just different metrics. As long as the interference strength in network is weaker than the minimum distance of the inner error-correcting code in the source, we can recover the original messages. For convenience, we will call the third kind of schemes as source MDS scheme. Because the third scheme has no need of a additional secret channel and the knowing of the transfer matrix, it is very suit for non-coherent network coding, and seems a promising approach.

1.2 The Secure Error-Correcting (SEC) Schemes for Network Coding

As is shown above, in the existing works about information theoretic approaches, most of schemes consider error-correction scheme and security scheme separately. A simple concatenation of the two schemes is mediocre, however, it is not necessarily work. There are still a few works to consider the combination of the two problems simultaneously in network coding. [19] is a such scheme, but both the field size and the packet length are needed to be sufficiently large. A secret channel is also needed. So, it would not be a promising practical scheme. [25] and [26, 27] process the issues of combining error-correction scheme and security scheme in coherent and non-coherent networks respectively. [26] based on [20] is an important work. It can be performed in a decentralized manner for non-coherent network. It just needs to afford a maximum-distance-separable (MDS) codes as an inner codes in the source and sends the coded messages with network coding to the sink. It is regardless of the fusion of MDS codes in the source and the network coding performing in the intermediate nodes. Because it is based on information theoretic approaches, it also has polynomial-time complexity. But this scheme has two drawbacks. One is that it can just resist Byzantine wiretap, i.e., just the eavesdropper having limited power can be coped with rather than the eavesdropper having omniscient power. Another one is that the rate will decline as the strength of the eavesdropper becomes stronger. Meanwhile, the rate may be a constant if we adopt so-called Cryptographic codes as an inner codes instead of traditional MDS codes in the source. It will be a perfect scheme to deal with the combination of error-correction scheme and security scheme. It will offer resilience against an adversary who eavesdrops on the entire network and controls an arbitrary fraction of malicious nodes. Meanwhile, some errors occurred in the network can also be corrected.

The McEliece cryptosystem in the point-to-point communication just has above characteristics [28]. We introduce this scheme from point-to-point communications to multicast with network coding. The right characteristic of the McEliece cryptosystem is very suitable for the problem of combining error-correction scheme and security scheme simultaneously. McEliece proposed a cryptosystem based on the usage of the generator matrix of a linear block code as the private key and its linear matrix operation transformation as the public key. The spirit of the McEliece scheme is in the inherent complexity of decoding a large linear block code with no visible structure that, in fact, is known to be an NP complete problem. In his original proposal, McEliece used Goppa codes having large public key size and low transmission rate. Replacing Goppa codes with Quasi-cyclic low density parity-check (QC-LDPC) codes, in the framework of the McEliece system will reduce the key length, resulting from the sparse character of their parity-check matrices [29].

With cryptosystem based on QC-LDPC Codes replacing the inner codes in the so-called source MDS scheme, the whole system can deal with both error-correcting and secure communications simultaneously. From the perspective of information theoretic, if the disturbance raised by the errors is small than the half of the minimum distance of source codes, i.e., McEliece cryptosystem based on QC-LDPC Codes, the errors can be corrected. In sense of cryptosystem, McEliece cryptosystem based on QC-LDPC Codes provided security resisting on eavesdroppers with arbitrary strength.

In all, with the McEliece cryptosystem replacing of the inner codes of [20], we make [20] based on McEliece cryptosystem has the capacity against omniscient eavesdropper instead of a limited adversary like Byzantine eavesdropper.

1.3   The Construction of MDS Codes for Coherent Network Coding

But there is an important issue to deal with: the error spread in network coding. In network coding, its very nature of combining information in the intermediate nodes makes it is very susceptible to transmission errors. A single error will be propagated by every node further downstream. This will thus prevent reconstruction of even a small portion of the file in the sink. When QC-LDPC is adopted in the source for a SEC scheme, and t errors occur in the network, the SEC scheme will fails if the t errors are spread. We have to delicately construct the network coding scheme to avoid errors spread.

If rank metric or subspace metric are adopted, the error spread problem is solved both for coherent or non-coherent network coding. The network coding can be constructed without considering the errors. For space distance metric, Theorem 1 shows in [21] that

$d_s(\langle TX \rangle, \langle Y \rangle) \leq 2 rank T_{Z \to Y} Z \leq 2 rank Z \leq 2t$ where $rank Z$ is the rank of the error vector Z. That means, based on space metric, t corrupted errors can make $2t$ dimension change at most even though the network is not known at all. For rank distance metric, it is obvious that t corrupted errors can make t rank changes in the received messages at most. It is for that, the rank of $T_{Z \to Y} \cdot Z$ is no more than what of Z even though the $T_{Z \to Y}$ is not known at all. So, from the perspective of rank metric, the errors Z won't spread, not as it does when hamming metric is adopted. So, the spread of original corrupted errors in non-coherent work is avoided by adopting the subspace metric or the rank metric. Naturally, for coherent network, the spread of original corrupted errors is also avoided.

However, there are also some reasons for us not to completely give up hamming metric in the network coding for coherent network. First, the basic prerequisite for subspace and rank metric both is that, $|Q| \geq |q|^n$. Q is the coding field in all the nodes, q is the finite field from which the coefficients of local coding kernel is selected, and n is the max flow min cut. Second, the hamming metric is the first metric which are broadly researched. Many efficient coding and decoding algorithms based on hamming metric haven been presented.

If hamming metric is considered, we have to constructed network coding scheme delicately to avoid the error spread. [30–33] each gives a construction algorithm of a MDS codes in NEC. [32,33] all modifies the Jaggi-Sanders algorithm [34] to get a efficient construction algorithm. In finding the global coding kernel for the processing link, they select a vector from the candidate vectors. Through the exhaustive search, the candidate vectors are promised as legal by avoiding all the error patters. Except [30–33], there are no other important construction schemes for coherent network with hamming metric as far as we know. Especially what deserves to be mentioned is that only the Algorithm 2 in [30] suit for our proposed SEC scheme in this paper. Except Algorithm 2 in [30], all other constructing schemes directly transmits the original messages μ into the network. The received messages in the sink is $G^{\#} \cdot \mu$ where $G^{\#}$ is the transfer matrix of network coding. In Algorithm 2 in [30], μ is coded with a classical error-correcting code as the codebook. $G \cdot \mu$ is sent from the source where G is the generate matrix of a classical error-correcting code. The received messages in the sink is $T \cdot G \cdot \mu$ where T is the transfer matrix of network coding. The main task of the network coding algorithm is to design a set of local encoding kernels such that the minimum distances of the network code, roughly speaking, are the same as the classical error-correcting code.

So, in the source coding, QC-LDPC is adopted. For the network coding, a MDS network coding error correcting scheme based on Algorithm 2 in [30] is constructed.

The remainder of this paper is organized as follows. Section 2 presents a brief review of McEliece cryptosystem based on QC-LDPC Codes. In Sect. 3, we will formally give our scheme. Section 4 gives the simulation result. Finally, Sect. 5 presents our conclusions.

2   McEliece Cryptosystem with QC-LDPC Codes

The below description about McEliece cryptosystem with QC-LDPC codes is mainly derived from [29].

The low-density parity-check (LDPC) code has the parity-check matrices which are sparse. The quasi-cyclic (QC) LDPC codes to reduce the secret key length is a slightly modified version of LDPC.

Quasi-cyclic (QC) codes form an important class of linear block codes, characterized by the use of very simple encoder and decoder circuits. It defines a systematic quasi-cyclic code as a linear block code with dimension $k = p.k_0$ and length $n = p.n_0$. It possesses the following properties:

 (i) each no symbol section (sub-block) of a codeword is composed of k_0, information symbols followed by $r_0 = n_0 - k_0$ parity checks;
(ii) each cyclic shift of a codeword by no symbols yields another codeword.

Property (i) can be obviously generalized for the non-systematic case.

McEliece cryptosystem is proposed firstly in [28]. It is based on Goppa codes which shows two major drawbacks: (i) large public key size and (ii) low transmission rate. Replacing Goppa codes with low-density parity-check (LDPC) codes, in the framework of the McEliece system, is proposed in [29]. The parameters of QC-LDPC selected in this paper are set as follows. $n_0 = 4$, $k_0 = 3$, $p = 4032$, rate is 0.75($R = k_0/n_0$). The decoding radius d_{min} of QC-LDPC is determined as 212 by evaluation rather than theoretical derivation. So, cautiously, we can assume $d_{min} = 190$ as an estimate of the correction capability of the considered code. It has parity-check matrix H, and produces a generator matrix G.

Matrix H will be part of Bob's private key. The remaining part of the private key is formed by two other matrices: a random sparse $k * k$ on-singular "scrambling" matrix S and a random sparse n x n non-singular "transformation" matrix Q. S and Q are regular matrices, formed by $k_0 * k_0$ and $n_0 * n_0$ blocks of $p * p$ circulants, respectively. Bob, in order to receive encrypted messages from Alice, computes the public key as follows:

$$G' = S^{-1}.G.Q^{-1} \tag{1}$$

It should be noted that G' preserves the quasi-cyclic structure of G, due to the block circulant form of S and Q. The public key G' is made available in a public directory. Alice, who wants to send an encrypted message to Bob, extracts the public key from the public directory and divides her message into k-bit blocks. If u is one of these blocks, Alice obtains its encrypted version as follows:

$$x = \mu G' + e = c + e \tag{2}$$

where e is a locally generated random vector of length n and weight t'. When Bob receives the encrypted message x, he first computes:

$$x' = x.Q = \mu.S^{-1}.G + e.Q \tag{3}$$

Vector x' is a codeword of the QC-LDPC code chosen by Bob (corresponding to the information vector $u' = u.S^{-1}$), affected by the error vector $e.Q$ whose maximum weight is d_{min}. Using belief propagation, Bob should be able to correct all the errors, thus recovering u', and then u through a post multiplication by S.

3   Proposed Scheme

In this section we will formally propose our scheme: universal secure error-Correcting schemes for network coding via McEliece cryptosystem based on QC-LDPC Codes. This scheme is to cope with the non-coherent network.

3.1   Source Coding

The general process is as follows. In a multicast network, there are one source Alice and η sinks: Bob1, Bob2,..., Bobη. Hereinafter we will denote any of the sink by Bobi. One of the sinks, for example, Bob1, produces a generator matrix G of the QC-LDPC Codes described in Sect. 2. The parameters of QC-LDPC is also same with Sect. 2.2, i.e., a (16128,12096) linear block codes. The coding field is F_2. Then, the corresponding "scrambling" matrix S and "transformation" matrix Q are generated respectively. So, the public key G' can be determined where $G' = S^{-1}.G.Q^{-1}$. Bob1 will share the secret keys G, S and Q with the rest sinks through a secret channel. Among all the transmissions, there is just one time for sharing the secret key. So, it is a constant overhead that can be ignored. The source Alice gets her public key from the public directory and divides her message into k-bit blocks. If u is one of these blocks, Alice obtains its encrypted version as follows:

$$x = uG' + e = c + e \tag{4}$$

where e is a locally generated random error vector of length n and weight t'.

3.2   Encoding and Decoding About Network Coding

One time encoding with QC-LDPC in the source produces a x with 16128 bits. x can be seen as a vector and transmitted through the network where the network coding approach is adopted. The network coding field is F_q (usually F_{256}) rather than F_2 which is the QC-LDPC coding field. In our scheme, x is not transmitted through the network as a vector. The vector x is reformulated into a matrix form which is denoted by X. X is a $n \times m$ matrix where n is the max-flow min-cut in the multicast network. Then, based on the batch (or generation) scheme of network coding, matrix X is transmitted through the network. Specifically, when 16128 bits is sent through network, the reformulation procedure is as follows. In F_{256}, one symbol is 8bits. If $n = 8$, for example, m will be set as 252. The transport procedure can be expressed by the formulation

$$Y = TX + T_{Z \to Y} Z \tag{5}$$

X is the batch of packets sent by Alice, Z refers to the packets errors injected into Alices batch, and Y is the received batch by sinks. The variable T refers to the linear transform from Alice to Bobi, while $T_{Z \to Y}$ refers to the linear transform from error edges to Bobi. T is $n \times n$, $T_{Z \to Y}$ is $n \times z_o$ and Z is $z_o \times m$. A classical random network codes X includes the identity matrix as part of each batch. The identity matrix sent by Alice incurs the same transform as the rest of the batch. Thus,

$$T_{Z \to Y} L \tag{6}$$

where $\widehat{T}$ and L are the columns corresponding to I's location in Y and Z respectively. $\widehat{T}$ is $n \times n$, and L is $z_o \times n$. By substituting T from (6), (5) can be simplified to get

$$Y = \widehat{T}X + T_{Z \to Y}(Z - LX) \tag{7}$$
$$= \widehat{T}X + E \tag{8}$$

where E is a $n \times m$ matrix that characterizes errors. Note that the matrix $\widehat{T}$, which Bobi knows, acts as a proxy transfer matrix for T, which he doesn't know. Note that the above is mainly in reference to [19]. If there is no other information, X can't be decoded. Certainly, if a hash of original messages is sent through a secret channel like [19], X will be decoded. This skill will cost optional resources, and we will adopt another method. In a sink Bobi, the packets are collected until the proxy transfer matrix $\widehat{T}$ is invertible. Matrix $\widehat{T}^{-1}$ is left multiplied in equation (9), we get

$$\widehat{T}^{-1}Y = X + \widehat{T}E \tag{9}$$

That means

$$X = \widehat{T}^{-1}Y - \widehat{T}^{-1}E \tag{10}$$

where $\widehat{T}^{-1}Y$ can be got, and $\widehat{T}^{-1}E$ is unknown. Denote $X^d = \widehat{T}^{-1}Y$. Based on the traditional linear block codes theory, X^d can be regarded as a deviation value of X. Denote $\widehat{X}$ as the probability estimate of X. In principle, in the decoding about network coding, $\widehat{T}$ is seen as a proxy transfer matrix of the true transfer matrix T to perform decoding.

3.3   Decoding About McEliece Cryptosystem with QC-LDPC Codes

In Sect. 3.2, X^d, the deviation value of X, is got through decoding of network coding scheme. Matrix X^d is reformulated into a vector x^d. Obviously, x^d is the deviation value of x. Respectively, denote $\widehat{x}$ the probability estimate of x. Based on the McEliece cryptosystem with QC-LDPC codes in Sect. 2, there is a block codes C' whose generation matrix is G' where $x=\mu G'+e$, and $x=\mu G'+e$, and $x \in C'$. Because there is a difference between x^d and x. This difference is responding to $\widehat{T}^{-1}T_{Z\rightarrow Y}(Z-LX)$ which is the error matrix injected into X^d. $\widehat{T}^{-1}T_{Z\rightarrow Y}(Z-LX)$ is reformulated into its vector form, and this vector form is denoted by $\psi(Z)$ which is the vector injected into x^d. Then,

$$x^d = \mu G' + e + \psi(Z) \tag{11}$$

Equation (11) shows that Based on maximum likelihood decoding principle, μ can be decoded. That's

$$\widehat{\mu} = \underset{\mu G' \in C'}{\text{argmin}} \ d_{G'}(\mu.G', x^d) \tag{12}$$

where $\widehat{\mu}$ is the probability estimate of μ, and $d_{G'}$ is the common hamming distance in sense of generation matrix $G'.\mu.G'$ is a legal-codes in codes C' where x^d is usually a illegal in codes C'. The above procedure is the typical maximum likelihood decoding principle in the traditional linear block codes.

In McEliece cryptosystem, the specific effective decoding algorithm referring to codes C' (defined by generation matrix G') does not exist. Specifically, in McEliece cryptosystem with QC-LDPC codes, the effective decoding algorithm is specific to the codes C which is determined by the generation matrix G rather than G'. In spirit of McEliece cryptosystem, we will compute $x^d.Q$, and let

$$x^{d'} = x^d.Q = \mu.S^{-1}.G + e.Q + \psi(Z).Q \tag{13}$$

Instead of using Eq. (11) to decode, the equation below is adopted.

$$\widehat{\mu.S^{-1}} = \underset{\mu S^{-1}.G \in C}{\text{argmin}} \ d_G(\mu S^{-1}.G, x^{d'}) \tag{14}$$

Because S is determined, $\widehat{\mu.S^{-1}} = \widehat{\mu}.S^{-1}$. So,

$$\widehat{\mu}.S^{-1} = \underset{\mu S^{-1}.G \in C}{\text{argmin}} \ d_G(\mu S^{-1}.G, x^{d'}) \tag{15}$$

From Eq. (12), we know that as long as the hamming weight of vector $e.Q + \psi(Z).Q$ is less than half d_{min}, the minimum distance of codes C, the decoding can be successful. The codes C is QC-LDPC. With t denote the number of the non-zero components in the error vector z. Form the analysis in the introduction, the Algorithm 2 in [30] can provide $e.Q + \psi(Z).Q \leq t$ because the error z won't be spread. We know as long as $t \leq d_{min}/2$, the decoding can success. The specific decoding algorithm responding to Eq. (14) is the belief propagation decoding algorithm of QC-LDPC. The decoding algorithm is effective. After decoding, $\widehat{\mu}.S^{-1}$ is got, and then $\widehat{\mu}$ through a post-multiplication by S. $\widehat{\mu}$ is the probability estimate of μ. We have got the original messages μ up to now. The whole decoding procedure is completed finally.

The basic idea is as follows. The coded information vector x in original McEliece cryptosystem is sent by point-to-point communication channel, and

x is lossless. In contrast, in our scheme, the packets X, reformulated from vector x, is sent through network by network coding scheme. Vector x represented by matrix X, is disturbed because there are errors occurred in the network. After decoding with network coding scheme, x^d is got where x^d is the deviation value of x. Because the proxy transfer matrix, rather than the true transfer matrix, is used to decode X in network coding, the corresponding vector x^d includes the errors from the network. The errors are denoted by vector $\psi(Z)$. Considering the original message u and the generation matrix G rather than G′, all the errors are $e.Q + \psi(Z).Q$. This scheme is to correct not only the locally generated random error vector, but also the errors incurred in the network. It certainly possesses the ability of security and error-correcting simultaneously. The network coding also increases the throughput.

3.4　Remarks

There are some important points which may be difficult to understand. It is necessary to clarify them to avoid confusion.

First point is what kinds of mathematics metric is adopted in the source codes. Not like the metrics such as rank metric, subspace metric in [20,24], the metric here is the traditional hamming distance of linear block codes. Denote the propagated errors hamming weight $W(e.Q + \psi(Z).Q)$. As long as $t \leq d_{\min}/2$, it will appear $2.W(e.Q + \psi(Z).Q) \leq d_{\min} - 1$, then u can be recovered correctly. The weight of e is t', and the weight of $\psi(Z)$ is t. Algorithm 2 in [30], starts with a classical error-correcting code as the codebook. The main task of the algorithm is to design a set of local encoding kernels such that the minimum distances of the network code, roughly speaking, are the same as the classical error-correcting code. It prevents the t original corrupted errors to be spread through exhaustedly searching all the error pattern. That's to say, $W(e.Q + \psi(Z).Q) \leq t$.

Second point is that, the source code QC-LDPC is not a MDS code. Existing work for error-correcting in non-coherent network generally produce a MDS codes in the source. The basic idea of this intension is to increase the distance of the codes. It will make the damage of error is decline. From the information theory view, the rate of MDS reaches the upper-bound. In order to offer the security of McEliece cryptosystem and sparse characteristic for effective decoding algorithm, the source codes would not adopt the MDS codes. Because the information rate will not decline as the strength of eavesdroppers becomes stronger, the ultimate comprehensive rate is considerable.

Third point is that the errors from the network will enhance the security of McEliece cryptosystem. In the original McEliece cryptosystem,e is locally generated random vector to enhance the security. In our scheme, the weight of e will smaller than its own weight in the original proposal. $\psi(Z)$ and e offer the security function together. So, the errors produced by the network no longer are negative factors, but positive factors.

Fourth point is that effectiveness of decoding about McEliece cryptosystem. When we want to multicast the information u with network coding, it's not hard to dope out an idea that u is going to be encrypted into x, and x is sent through the network with some error-correcting mechanism. Such ideas as above are not going to work because most cryptosystems have high computational complexity, and then they are not suit for the large scale digital transmission. McEliece cryptosystem has effective decoding algorithm. Another drawback of the idea is that it needs two codes schemes: one for encryption in the source, the other for error correction in the transmission. This will lead to much overhead. However, McEliece cryptosystem just offers himself to do the works of security and error-correcting both at the same time. With our ingenious design as described above, McEliece cryptosystem is perfectly fused with the network coding.

4   Evaluation

4.1   Experiment environment

We compare Silva's scheme [26], Yu's scheme [11] and our schemes in experiments. Silva's scheme and Yu's scheme are typical works of information theoretic approaches and cryptographic approaches respectively. Because cryptographic approaches involve a large number of mathematical operations, MATLAB is adopted instead of usual network simulation platform such as OMNET. This will give a unified platform for different type of demands. This experiment is operated in Windows machine with 3.4 GHZ Intel Core i5. Generally speaking, in this experiment, The latency of the three schemes will be compared. We also want to know how the ratio of delivery is influenced by the errors occurred in the network.

4.2   Latency

This section, we will compare the latency of three schemes. In the existing schemes, the latency is a main bottleneck. Typically, the maximum flow minimum cut of the network will be set about 8 though the number of nodes is variable. The network coding field is F_{256} for all three schemes. For Silva's scheme, Gabidulin codes is adopted in the source coding. [35] will be as a reference. Parameter Settings are as follows: $n = m = 8$, $q = 256$, $k = 5$. The minimum information for a transfer is $k * log_2(q^m)$, i.e., 320 bits. 5 messages will be coded into 8 messages with Gabidulin codes. 12096 bits will sent 38 times. For Yu's scheme, $n = 8$, $m = 6$. The other parameters are set as [35] except that p is 1023-bit (in [11] p is 1024 bits long). The minimum information for a transfer in Yu's scheme here is $m * n * log_2 p$, i.e., 49104 bits that is about 4 times 12096 bits. For our scheme, the elements of source messages are selected from F_{256}. The network coding field is also F_{256}. 12096 bits messages will be coded into 16128 bits, and then 16128 bits will be sent through network with network coding. 16128 bits will be organized into $n * m$ matrix where $n = 8$, $m = 252$. These messages will be decoded by the method described in Sect. 3. The decoding method for QC-LDPC codes is same as that described in [29]. Note that the meaning of m in Silva's scheme [26] is different from that in Yu's scheme [11] and our scheme. m in Silva's scheme is used to the extension field wherein m in Yu's scheme and our scheme is used to represent the packets number included in every block.

The minimum information for a transfer in Silva's scheme, our scheme and Yu's scheme are 320 bits, 12096 bits and 49104 bits respectively. Assume 12096 bits are sent with every scheme, and then we computer the normalized latency respectively which is illustrated in Fig. 1. The value of latency in Yu's scheme is divided by 5, and then illustrated in the figure.

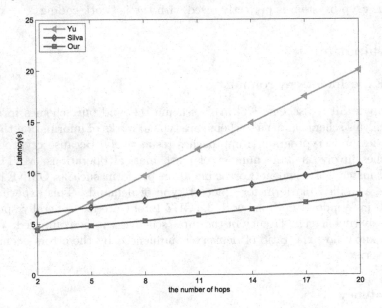

Fig. 1. A secure system model for outsourcing LMDC

From Fig. 1, we know Silva's scheme and our scheme based on information theoretic approaches are faster than Yu's scheme. For Silva's scheme and our scheme, the most time consuming operations are the decoding for Gabidulin codes and QC-LDPC codes in the sinks. The intermediate nodes just need to do network coding operations without operations like hash signatures. The consuming time for network coding in the settings here is microsecond level, so the consuming time can be ignored. For Yu's scheme based on cryptosystem approaches, every intermediate nodes involve hash signature and verification which are time consuming. Total time is increased while the number of hops increased.

The time for network coding solely is about 4.032 s. It is mainly about the decoding operation for 16128 bits.

4.3   The Information Rate

We will focus on the information rate in this section. The rate is illustrated in Table 1. The experiment results accord with it.

Table 1. The rate of three schemes

Silva	Yu	Our
$(n - \rho - 2t)/n$	$(m-1)/m$	$(n-2t)/n$

n in Silva's scheme is the maximum flow minimum cut of the network. ρ is arbitrarily chosen links which are eavesdropped. t is the number of errors. m in Yu's scheme is the packets number included in every block. According to the parameters in Subsect. 4.2, the information of our scheme is 0.75.

5 Conclusions

In this paper, McEliece cryptosystem based on QC-LDPC codes in the point-to-point environment is generalized to its another variant in the network coding environment. Based on a QC-LDPC codes, a MDS network coding scheme based on hamming metric is constructed to avoid the error spread. It doesnt need to reduce information rate to offer security. The information rate reaches $(n-2t)/n$ instead of $(n - \rho - 2t)/n$. It offers security and error-correcting simultaneously. Especially, it first offers cryptosystem level security when security and error-correcting scheme are combined in the information theoretic fashion. It has both high security of the cryptosystem and low computing complexity of information theoretic approaches.

Acknowledgments. This work is supported by Suihua technology office program (SHKJ2015-015, SHKJ2015-014), National Science foundation of China (61571150), Education Office of Heilongjiang province science and technology program (Study on integrated network application in smart factory), Suihua university program (K1502003).

References

1. Bahramgiri, H., Lahouti, F.: Robust network coding against path failures. IET Commun. **4**(3), 272–284 (2010)
2. Baldi, M., Chiaraluce, F.: Cryptanalysis of a new instance of McEliece cryptosystem based on QC-LDPC codes. In: IEEE International Symposium on Information Theory, pp. 2591–2595 (2007)
3. Charles, D., Jain, K., Lauter, K.: Signatures for network coding. In: 2006 Conference on Information Sciences and Systems, pp. 857–863 (2006)
4. Chi, K.N., Yang, S.: Deterministic secure error-correcting (SEC) network codes. In: Information Theory, Workshop, pp. 96–101 (2007)
5. Boneh, D., Freeman, D., Katz, J., Waters, B.: Signing a linear subspace: Signature schemes for network coding. In: Jarecki, S., Tsudik, G. (eds.) PKC 2009. LNCS, vol. 5443, pp. 68–87. Springer, Heidelberg (2008). https://doi.org/10.1007/978-3-642-00468-1_5

6. Gkantsidis, C., Rodriguez, P.R.: Cooperative security for network coding file distribution. In: IEEE International Conference on Computer Communications, Proceedings, INFOCOM 2006, pp. 1–13 (2005)
7. Jaggi, S., Langberg, M., Katti, S., Ho, T.: Resilient network coding in the presence of byzantine adversaries. In: IEEE International Conference on Computer Communications, INFOCOM 2007, pp. 616–624. IEEE (2008)
8. Katz, J., Waters, B.: Compact signatures for network coding (2009)
9. Kehdi, E., Li, B.: Null keys: limiting malicious attacks via null space properties of network coding. In: INFOCOM, pp. 1224–1232 (2009)
10. Kim, M.J., Zhao, F., Koetter, R., Han, K.J., Han, K.J.: On counteracting byzantine attacks in network coded peer-to-peer networks. IEEE J. Sel. Areas Commun. **28**(5), 692–702 (2010)
11. Koetter, R., Kschischang, F.R.: Coding for errors and erasures in random network coding. IEEE Trans. Inf. Theor. **54**(8), 3579–3591 (2007)
12. Krohn, M.N., Freedman, M.J., Mazires, D.: On-the-fly verification of rateless erasure codes for efficient content distribution. In: Proceedings, 2004 IEEE Symposium on Security and Privacy, pp. 226–240 (2004)
13. Matsumoto, R.: Construction algorithm for network error-correcting codes attaining the singleton bound. IEICE Trans. Fundam. Electron. Commun. Comput. Sci. **E90–A**(9), 1729–1735 (2007)
14. Mceliece, R.J.: A public-key cryptosystem based on algebraic coding theory. Deep space network progress report, pp. 114–116 (1978)
15. Oliveira, P.F., Barros, J.: A network coding approach to secret key distribution. IEEE Trans. Inf. Forensics Secur. **3**(3), 414–423 (2008)
16. Sanders, P., Egner, S., Tolhuizen, L.: Polynomial time algorithms for network information flow. In: Fifteenth ACM Symposium on Parallel Algorithms and Architectures, pp. 286–294 (2003)
17. Shang, T., Pei, H., Liu, J.: Secure network coding based on lattice signature. Chin. Commun. **11**(1), 138–151 (2014)
18. Siavoshani, M.J., Fragouli, C., Diggavi, S.N.: Subspace properties of network coding and their applications. IEEE Trans. Inf. Theor. **58**(5), 2599–2619 (2012)
19. Silva, D., Kschischang, F.R.: Security for wiretap networks via rank-metric codes. In: IEEE International Symposium on Information Theory, pp. 176–180 (2008)
20. Silva, D., Kschischang, F.R.: Universal secure error-correcting schemes for network coding. **41**(3), 2428–2432 (2010)
21. Silva, D., Kschischang, F.R.: Using rank-metric codes for error correction in random network coding. In: IEEE International Symposium on Information Theory, pp. 796–800 (2007)
22. Silva, D., Kschischang, F.R.: Universal secure network coding via rank-metric codes. IEEE Trans. Inf. Theor. **57**(2), 1124–1135 (2011)
23. Silva, D., Kschischang, F.R., Koetter, R.: A rank-metric approach to error control in random network coding. IEEE Trans. Inf. Theor. **54**(9), 3951–3967 (2008)
24. Talooki, V.N., Bassoli, R., Lucani, D.E., Rodriguez, J., Fitzek, F.H.P., Marques, H., Tafazolli, R.: Security concerns and countermeasures in network coding based communication systems: a survey. Comput. Netw. **83**, 422–445 (2015)
25. Venturelli, R.B., Silva, D.: An evaluation of erasure decoding algorithms for Gabidulin codes. In: Telecommunications Symposium, pp. 1–5 (2014)
26. Wang, O., Long, V., Nahrstedt, K., Khurana, H.: MIS: Malicious nodes identification scheme in network-coding-based peer-to-peer streaming. In: IEEE INFOCOM, pp. 296–300 (2010)

27. Xuan, G., Fu, F.W., Zhang, Z.: Construction of network error correction codes in packet networks. In: International Symposium on Networking Coding, pp. 1–6 (2011)
28. Yang, S., Chi, K.N., Yeung, R.W.: Construction of linear network codes that achieve a refined singleton bound. In: IEEE International Symposium on Information Theory, pp. 1576–1580 (2008)
29. Yangm, S., Yeung, R.W.: Characterizations of network error correction/detection and erasure correction. In: Proceedings Netcod (2007)
30. Yang, S., Yeung, R.W., Chi, K.N.: Refined coding bounds and code constructions for coherent network error correction. IEEE Trans. Inf. Theor. **57**(3), 1409–1424 (2011)
31. Yu, Z., Wei, Y., Ramkumar, B., Guan, Y.: An efficient signature-based scheme for securing network coding against pollution attacks. In: The Conference on Computer Communications, INFOCOM 2008, pp. 1409–1417. IEEE (2008)
32. Yu, Z., Wei, Y., Ramkumar, B., Guan, Y.: An efficient scheme for securing XOR network coding against pollution attacks. In: INFOCOM, pp. 406–414 (2009)
33. Zhang, Z.: Linear network error correction codes in packet networks. IEEE Trans. Inf. Theor. **54**(1), 209–218 (2008)
34. Zhao, F., Kalker, T., Medard, M., Han, K.J.: Signatures for content distribution with network coding. In IEEE International Symposium on Information Theory, pp. 556–560 (2007)
35. Zhao, K., Chu, X., Wang, M., Jiang, Y.: Speeding up homomorpic hashing using GPUs. In: IEEE International Conference on Communications, pp. 856–860 (2009)

A Research of Power Analysis Based on Multiple Classification Models

Biao Liu[1](✉), Yang Pan[1], Jiali Li[2], and Huamin Feng[1,2]

[1] Beijing Electronic Science and Technology Institution, Beijing, China
liubiao521@aliyun.com
[2] Xidian University, Xi'an, China

Abstract. Aiming at the problem that the single model classification algorithm has a low success rate when the number of training samples is low, We present a power analysis method that combines multiple classification models. We use DPA_Contest_V4 dataset to complete our experiment. First we use the traditional method to break the mask, and then we use SVM, RF and kNN classification algorithm to train and predict as base learners. Finally, we combine these models with ensemble learning or semi-supervised learning. The experimental results show that these two methods are both superior to the single model. Especially when the number of traces in the training set is small, the accuracy can be increased by more than 10%.

Keywords: Semi-supervised learning · Ensemble learning · Power analysis

1 Introduction

Power analysis is a technique that enables attacks by analyzing the power consumed during the operation of a cryptographic device. When the cryptographic algorithm used by the device is known, it will be possible for us to analyze the intermediate values in the encryption process. Different intermediate values tend to reflect different characteristics at specific locations of the energy trace. Therefore, the process of power analysis can be transformed to a classification problem [1].

Template attack use the idea of classification problem, but this method requires a relatively high number of energy trace, [2] and actual attacks are often difficult to obtain enough traces. To solve this problem, Lerman et al. [3] applied the SVM algorithm to the template attack, and the result shows that the addition of the machine learning algorithm can reduce the request of the number and quality of the traces.

However, the accuracy of the single-model classification algorithm will be low when the training set is small. Therefore, this paper will combine multiple classification models for the first time in the field of power analysis. Our method starts from two perspectives. One is improving the performance of classification

© Springer Nature Singapore Pte Ltd. 2017
M. Xu et al. (Eds.): CTCIS 2017, CCIS 704, pp. 290–302, 2017.
https://doi.org/10.1007/978-981-10-7080-8_21

algorithms with ensemble learning, see Sect. 2.1. The other is making full use of unlabeled samples with semi-supervised learning, see Sect. 2.2. For this, when the number of traces is small, the accuracy of the classifier can be significantly improved.

2   The Combination of Multiple Classification Models

2.1   Ensemble Learning

Ensemble learning is done by combining multiple learners to complete learning tasks. Usually train a group of learners, called individual learners, and then combine these individual learners through a certain strategy.

Usually, the ensemble of multiple learners with comparable performance will result in a better learning performance than an individual learner. As shown in Fig. 1, although the accuracy rate of the three individual learners is only 66%, it improves to 100% after the voting method.

There are some common ensemble strategies, such as bagging, boosting, and some other simple strategies like Averaging, Voting and Learning. Averaging: averaging or weighted averaging the output of multiple individual learners to compute the final result. Voting: vote the results of several individual learners, and then use the classification result which appeared most among those individual learners. Learning: combine individual learners through another learner which called secondary learner, while the individual learner called primary learner. Use the primary learner's output to train the secondary learner. To solve the problem of over-fitting, the output of the primary learner should be obtained by cross-validation. In other words, we should use the unused sample when computing the primary learner's output [5].

This paper adopts two ensemble strategies, one is linear weighted ensemble, and the other is voting ensemble. Since the Hamming weight of intermediate value has a linear relationship with the voltage at the corresponding point in the traces, regression prediction is used in Support Vector Machine, Random Forest and k-Nearest Neighbor, but not classification prediction. Then we turn the regression prediction to classification prediction when output the result.

	Sample1	Sample2	Sample3
Model1	√	√	✗
Model2	✗	√	√
Model3	√	✗	√
Ensemble	√	√	√

Fig. 1. Accuracy rate improves after voting

During the process of Weighted Averaging Ensemble Learning (WAEL), we first train some individual learners and then use these individual learners to compute results through weighted average. In order to ensure reasonableness of the weight of each learner, we use the least squares method to calculate the weight of each individual learner. See Sect. 3.3 for details.

During the process of Voting Ensemble Learning (VEL), we first train some individual learners, and then vote the results of these learners. The specific steps are shown in Sect. 3.4.

Generally, in order to have a better result of ensemble learning, the individual learners should have roughly equal and not too bad performance, and there should be a greater difference among these individual learners. Therefore, considering the above factors, this paper chooses three algorithms, including SVM, RF and kNN, as the individual learner to form the ensemble model, see Sect. 2.3.

2.2 Semi-supervised Learning [6]

Semi-supervised learning is a learning strategy that allows learners to rely on external interactions and automatically use unlabeled samples to improve learning performance. It is an inexpensive way to use unlabeled samples.

In a semi-supervised study that combines multiple algorithms, we usually use labeled samples to train and predict with a base learner. Next we put the higher confidence samples in the prediction results into the training set of other classifiers. Then we make it iterate over and over again.

In this paper, we use Tri-training as our semi-supervisory strategy. We choose SVM, RF and kNN as our base learners which is same as ensemble learning, see Sect. 2.3 for details. Tri-training was presented by Zhou and Li in 2005. The core idea of Tri-training is to deal with the confidence with implicitly handle way to select unmarked samples. The Tri-training algorithm uses three classifiers for training. During the iteration process, we choose a classifier as a main classifier while the remaining as auxiliary classifiers in turn. If the two auxiliary classifiers predict the same result for a sample, we will add this sample into the marked sample set of the main classifier. See Sect. 3.5 for details.

2.3 Base Learner

2.3.1 Support Vector Machines (SVM) [7]

SVM is a machine learning algorithm based on the principle of statistical learning theory and structural risk minimization, which can be used to deal with classification and regression problems.

The basic idea of SVM is to divide a hyperplane in the sample space to separate the different samples. The hyperplane can be represented by the linear equation $\omega^T x + b = 0$, ω denotes the normal vector, b denotes the displacement term. As shown in Fig. 2.

The goal of optimization is to find the hyperplane when the interval γ reaches the maximum. Usually the sample is not linearly separable in the low-dimensional space. Therefore, it is necessary to map the sample from the original

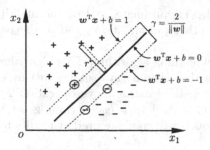

Fig. 2. Support vector machines

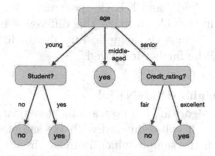

Fig. 3. Decision tree

space to the higher dimension space by means of using the kernel function, which makes the sample show linearly separable characteristics in the high dimension space. Solve α in following formula to find the final model.

$$\max_{\alpha} \sum_{i=1}^{m} \alpha_i - \frac{1}{2} \sum_{i=1}^{m} \sum_{j=1}^{m} \alpha_i \alpha_j y_i y_j \kappa \left(x_i, \ x_j \right)$$

$$\text{s.t.} \ \sum_{i=1}^{m} \alpha_i y_i = 0, \alpha_i \geq 0, \ i = 1, 2, \ldots, m.$$

Where α is the Lagrangian multiplier and $\kappa \, ()$ is the kernel function.

2.3.2 Random Forest (RF) [8]

Random Forest is an ensemble learning algorithm with method of Bagging based on Decision Tree.

Decision tree is a tree-based decision-making classification algorithm, when classifying, usually conduct a series of judgments based on a number of features.

As shown in Fig. 3, the root node is the entire data set, each child node represents a part of the data set, and the leaf node represents a part of the final classification result. The ultimate goal of the algorithm is to generate a generalized decision tree that can maintain good predictive power for unknown data.

Bagging is a parallel learning algorithm. This algorithm uses the Bootstrap method to sample from the original data set for m times, the m samples will be obtained as a data set. Repeat the above operation T times to get T data sets containing m samples. And then each training set train a model alone, and ultimately these models will combine predict results by voting or averaging method.

Random forest also uses random attribute selection in the decision tree training on the basis of Bagging. For each decision tree node, a subset with k attributes is randomly selected from the attributes set of the node, and then an optimal attribute is selected to divide, and k is the parameter for controlling the randomness. This makes it possible to make the difference between the different decision trees not only include the sample, but also include the attributes, so that the final result will be further improved.

2.3.3 k-Nearest Neighbor (kNN) [9]

The k-nearest neighbor algorithm is a no-training classification algorithm. When predicting a new sample, it will compared with the samples in the training set, and then the label from the sample which is most similar to the sample to be predicted will be the prediction result. Usually we will select top k most similar samples in the training set, the highest number of classifications (classification) or the average of the labels (regression) will be the prediction of the new sample. In this paper, the Euclidean distance formula is used to calculate the similarity between samples: $d = \sqrt{\sum_{i=0}^{n} (xA_i - xB_i)^2}$, where d is the distance between samples and n is the number of features in one sample.

3 Power Analysis Based on Multiple Classification Models

In this paper, we attack the AES-256 encryption algorithm with rotating mask from DPA_Contest V4 datasets [10]. During the process, first we crack the mask with SVM; then we do training and prediction on the value of the S-box output's Hamming weight with SVM, RF and kNN; finally, we combine the results of these three single models by ensemble model or semi-supervised model to reach the final result.

3.1 Feature Extraction

Research has shown that the mask offset or the Hamming weight of intermediate value is only highly correlated with the small portion of the trace. Therefore, in order to improve the accuracy and reduce the cost of calculation, we need to extract the feature of traces. The methods of extracting features are principal component analysis [11], correlation coefficient [12] and so on. In this paper, we use the correlation coefficient to extract the feature, the concrete steps are as follows.

Select the value of all the traces on a certain time as $v_{i,j}$ ($i = [1, N]$, $j \in [1, T]$) and the offset of all traces as $offset_i$ ($i = [1, N]$) or the hamming weight of the intermediate value as hw_i ($i = [1, N]$), where N is the total number of traces used to extract the feature, and T is the total number of points on the data set. According to the Pearson formula

$$\rho = \frac{Cov(X, Y)}{\sqrt{D(X)}\sqrt{D(Y)}} = \frac{E((X - E(X))(Y - E(Y)))}{\sqrt{D(X)}\sqrt{D(Y)}}$$

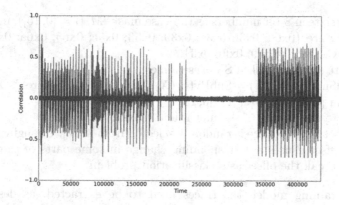

Fig. 4. Correlation coefficient between the offset and the point on the trace, x-axis is the time point and y-axis is the correlation coefficient

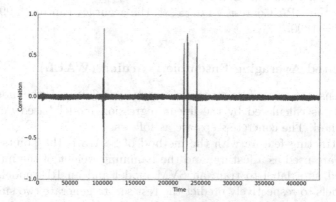

Fig. 5. Correlation coefficient between the first S-box and the point on the trace, x-axis is the time point and y-axis is the correlation coefficient

Calculate the correlation coefficients of the two variables. And then sort the absolute values of the correlation coefficients at all times. Finally, select m points with the largest correlation coefficient to build the training set.

As shown in Figs. 4 and 5, the correlation coefficient appears some peaks at some time, indicating that at these moments an operation with a large correlation with the mask offset or intermediate value occurs, such as plaintext blind or S-box operation, our goal is to extract features at these moments.

3.2   Crack the Offset with SVM [13]

Since the trace in the data set only includes the first round of AES-256 encryption, the masked S-box in the first round of encryption is considered.

Mask operation step:

(1) Choose sixteen 8-bit numbers as the base mask M_i $(i = [0, 15])$, in this data set, they are {0x00; 0x0f; 0x36; 0x39; 0x53; 0x5c; 0x65; 0x6a; 0x95; 0x9a; 0xa3; 0xac; 0xc6; 0xc9; 0xf0; 0xff}.

(2) Generate sixteen masked S boxes to meet
MaskedSubBytes$_i$ (X_i) = SubBytes $(X_i \oplus M_i) \oplus M_{i+1}$, where X_i represents a certain plaintext byte, $i \in [0, 15]$.

(3) Calculate the output of the first round mask S box:
The offset of each trace is randomly selected from [0,15]. Changing the value of the offset causes a corresponding change in some parts of the trace. So we can break the offset as a classification problem.

Before training model, the traces need to be extracted, as described in Sect. 3.1.

We train SVM model with extracted $dataset_{i,j}$ $(i = [1, N]$, $j = [1, m])$ and offset values, then use this model to predict the offset value. We make experiments under the DPA_Contest_V4 data set, the accuracy can reach 99.4% when $m = 100$, $N = 1000$.

3.3   Weighted Averaging Ensemble Learning (WAEL)

In order to ensure reasonableness of each single-model weight, the model weight in this paper is calculated by the linear regression model based on the least squares method. The concrete steps are as follows.

After extracting feature with the method of Sect. 3.1, the points extracted from traces are used as a feature, and the hamming weight of the intermediate value is used as a label to train an SVM model and an RF model. And use the two models to respectively predict the test set, to generate two single-model prediction results $result_{svm}$ and the $result_{rf}$. To prevent over-fitting, there is a need for cross-prediction of the training set, resulting in two sets of long-term results with the training set $cross_r esult_{svm}$ and the $cross_r esult_{rf}$. Next, the $cross_r esult_{svm}$ and the $cross_r esult_{rf}$ are used as the feature, the hamming weight of the intermediate value as the label to train the linear regression model;

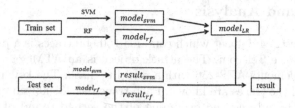

Fig. 6. Weighted averaging ensemble learning

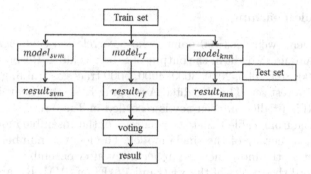

Fig. 7. Voting ensemble learning

finally, using the $result_{svm}$ and the $result_{rf}$ as the test set, we use the trained linear regression model to predict the result. The result is the ensemble of SVM and RF. The basic steps are shown in Fig. 6. This paper also carries out a three-model WAEL experiment, the steps similar to the two models.

3.4 Voting Ensemble Learning (VEL)

This section uses the same features and labels in Sect. 3.3 to train an SVM model, a RF model, and a kNN model respectively. We use these three models to predict the test set respectively, to generate three single-model prediction results $result_{svm}$, $result_{rf}$ and $result_{knn}$. Then the three predictions are voted on, and the voting results are output as an ensemble result. The basic steps are shown in Fig. 7.

3.5 Tri-training [14]

This section uses the same features and labels as in Sect. 2.3. During the first round of the iteration the learners of the training set are all labeled samples. Due to the performance of each learner is weak at the beginning of Tri-training, we only select a part of unlabeled samples which meet the conditions to join the training set. Also, during the first round of iteration, we only select the sample which was predicted as the same result from all the three models to join the training set.

4   Results and Analysis

The DPA_Contest_V4 dataset which contains 100,000 traces is a public data set provided by France Telecom. The attack object is an ATMega 163 microcontroller that implements AES-256 with a rotating mask. The key, plaintext, and offset used in all the traces are known. Each trace has 435002 sample points and covers the first round and the beginning of the second round of the AES-256 encryption algorithm [5].

4.1   Ensemble Learning

In this experiment, we select 100 points whose correlation coefficient is max as feature, the Hamming weight of the output of S-box as label. Respectively, select 50, 100, 200, 500, 800, 1000, 2000, 3000, 4000, 5000 traces as training set, another 10000 traces as a test set. The Weighted Averaging Ensemble Learning (WAEL) of SVM and RF's prediction accuracy is recorded in Table 1.

It can be seen from Table 1 that the accuracy of the ensemble model is always higher than the accuracy of the single model. The less the number of traces of the training set is, the more increase in accuracy after ensemble.

Table 2 record the results of the VEL and WAEL of SVM, RF and kNN. The training set and the test set are selected as described above. Since the samples are randomly selected, the results are slightly different from those in Table 1.

As can be seen from Table 2, with the increase in the number of training traces, the accuracy of all three models is gradually increased. The accuracy of SVM, RF and kNN is basically the same, while the ensemble model of the accuracy is significantly higher than a single model.

In contrast to the two methods of ensemble in Table 2, we found that the accuracy of WAEL was consistently higher than that of VEL.

Table 1. Accuracy of SVM, RF and WAEL

	SVM	RF	WAEL
50	0.675	0.669	0.755
100	0.736	0.747	0.826
200	0.815	0.832	0.873
500	0.847	0.853	0.882
800	0.862	0.874	0.907
1000	0.871	0.882	0.913
2000	0.879	0.893	0.918
3000	0.887	0.902	0.927
4000	0.892	0.910	0.933
5000	0.904	0.923	0.941

Table 2. Accuracy of SVM, RF, kNN and ensemble model

	SVM	RF	kNN	VEL	WAEL
50	0.698	0.680	0.654	0.754	0.804
100	0.739	0.753	0.748	0.821	0.855
200	0.802	0.824	0.792	0.866	0.883
500	0.842	0.858	0.824	0.887	0.908
800	0.851	0.867	0.829	0.904	0.916
1000	0.878	0.875	0.851	0.910	0.924
2000	0.882	0.893	0.871	0.918	0.930
3000	0.891	0.908	0.879	0.922	0.937
4000	0.901	0.914	0.893	0.931	0.943
5000	0.903	0.923	0.898	0.936	0.952

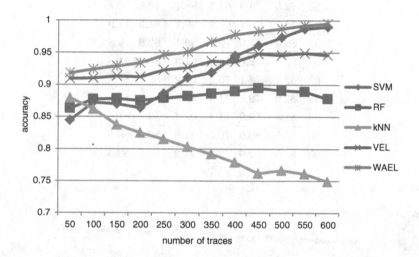

Fig. 8. Comparison of SVM, RF, kNN and ensemble model when the number of features is different

In contrast to the results of WAEL in Tables 1 and 2, we found that the results of WAEL have been further improved after the kNN model has been added.

We also do some experiment when the number of features is different. The training set has 1000 traces. We respectively select 50, 100, 150, 200, 250, 300, 350, 400, 450, 500, 550, 600 points whose correlation coefficient is max as feature to train models. The accuracy of each model is shown in Fig. 8. As can be seen from the figure, the less the number of features is, the more WAEL improve.

4.2   Semi-supervised Learning

In this experiment, we select 100 points whose correlation coefficient is max as feature, the Hamming weight of the output of S-box as label. Respectively, select 10, 15, 20, 30, 40, 50, 60, 70, 80, 90, 100 traces as labeled datasets, another 5000 traces as unlabeled datasets, 10000 traces as test set. The results after 10 iterations are shown in Table 3.

Table 3. The results of Tri-training

	First round			Last round		
	SVM	RF	kNN	SVM	RF	kNN
10	70.7	60.8	59.2	60.4	62.4	61.6
15	68.9	64.9	65.2	78.6	73.6	72.1
20	72.5	68.9	67.7	88.1	80.6	78.7
30	74.1	70.1	69.9	89.1	81.6	77.9
40	80.4	71.6	70.3	90.1	82.8	79.8
50	81.9	72.6	71.6	91.3	85.2	81.3
60	82.1	78.1	70.4	92.2	85.1	81.3
70	82.9	79.8	71.4	92.4	83.8	81.5
80	81.3	79.9	71.4	92.7	83.7	81.6
90	84.6	80.6	70.3	92.9	83.3	80.9
100	82.5	82.9	72.4	93.2	84.8	82.5

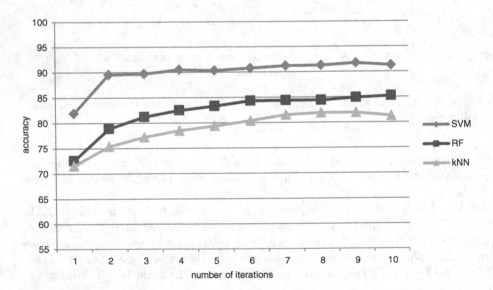

Fig. 9. The accuracy of three base learners in each iteration

As we can see in Table 3, as the number of energy traces of the marked samples has increased, the accuracy of the result is gradually increased. Through Tri-training, the accuracy of the three base classifiers have been greatly improved, especially SVM, more than 10%.

When the number of labeled samples is only 10, the accuracy rate has decreased because of the low accuracy of each base learner. When the number of labeled samples is above 15, the situation has improved.

Figure 9 records the accuracy of each learner after tri-training with 50 labeled samples. It can be seen from the figure that when the iterations to the fifth round, the accuracy of the base learners gradually tend to be stable.

5   Conclusions and Prospects

This article combine multiple classification models in the field of power analysis for the first time. It can be seen from the experiment that, in terms of ensemble learning, both VEL and WAEL can achieve higher accuracy than single models. In addition, the WAEL can also increase the accuracy of the model by more than 10% when the number of traces is low. In terms of semi-supervised learning, under the tri-training strategy, we can achieve the same effect with much less labeled traces.

The experiment show that whether it is ensemble learning or semi-supervised learning can increase the accuracy significantly when the number of labeled traces is low (<500). In ensemble learning strategy, WAEL is better than VEL, three models is better than two models. The experiment also shows that semi-supervised learning is a more effective method. Because semi-supervised learning not only combines several classification algorithms, but also uses a large number of unlabeled data compared to ensemble learning.

References

1. Lerman, L., Poussier, R., Bontempi, G., Markowitch, O., Standaert, F.-X.: Template attacks vs. machine learning revisited (and the curse of dimensionality in side-channel analysis). In: Mangard, S., Poschmann, A.Y. (eds.) COSADE 2014. LNCS, vol. 9064, pp. 20–33. Springer, Cham (2015). https://doi.org/10.1007/978-3-319-21476-4_2
2. Hospodar, G., Gierlichs, B., Mulder, E.D., et al.: Machine learning in side-channel analysis: a first study. J. Cryptographic Eng. 1(4), 293–302 (2011)
3. Markowitch, O., Lerman, L., Bontempi, G.: Side channel attack: an approach based on machine learning. In: International Workshop on Constructive Side-Channel Analysis and Security Design (2011)
4. Liu, Y., Yao, X.: Ensemble learning via negative correlation. Neural Netw. Official J. Int. Neural Netw. Soc. 12(10), 1399 (1999)
5. Zhou, Z.-H.: Machine Learning. Tsinghua University Press (2016). (in Chinese)
6. Blum, A., Mitchell, T.: Combining labeled and unlabeled data with co-training. In: Eleventh Conference on Computational Learning Theory, pp. 92–100. ACM (1998)

7. Vapnik, V.N.: The nature of statistical learning theory. IEEE Trans. Neural Netw. **8**(6), 1564 (1997)
8. Liaw, A., Wiener, M.: Classification and regression by randomForest. R News **23**(23), 18–22 (2002)
9. Altman, N.S.: An introduction to kernel and nearest-neighbor nonparametric regression. Am. Stat. **46**(3), 175–185 (1992)
10. TELECOM ParisTech SEN research group. DPA Contest (4th edn.), 2013-2014[EB/OL]. [2014-5-12]. http://www.dpacontest.org/V4/
11. Gilmore, R., Hanley, N., O'Neill, M.: Neural network based attack on a masked implementation of AES. In: IEEE International Symposium on Hardware Oriented Security and Trust, pp. 106–111. IEEE (2015)
12. Lerman, L., Medeiros, S.F., Bontempi, G., Markowitch, O.: A machine learning approach against a masked AES. In: Francillon, A., Rohatgi, P. (eds.) CARDIS 2013. LNCS, vol. 8419, pp. 61–75. Springer, Cham (2014). https://doi.org/10.1007/978-3-319-08302-5_5
13. Zeng, Z., Gu, D., Liu, J., et al.: An improved side-channel attack based on support vector machine. In: Tenth International Conference on Computational Intelligence and Security, pp. 676–680. IEEE (2014)
14. Zhou, Z.H., Li, M.: Tri-Training: Exploiting Unlabeled Data Using Three Classifiers. IEEE Educational Activities Department (2005)
15. Rechberger, C., Oswald, E.: Practical template attacks. In: Lim, C.H., Yung, M. (eds.) WISA 2004. LNCS, vol. 3325, pp. 440–456. Springer, Heidelberg (2005). https://doi.org/10.1007/978-3-540-31815-6_35
16. Bartkewitz, T., Lemke-Rust, K.: Efficient template attacks based on probabilistic multi-class support vector machines. In: Mangard, S. (ed.) CARDIS 2012. LNCS, vol. 7771, pp. 263–276. Springer, Heidelberg (2013). https://doi.org/10.1007/978-3-642-37288-9_18

Classification of Video-Based Public Opinion via Projection Metric Learning with Riemannian Triplet Constraint

Junfeng Tian[1,3] and Yan Ha[2,3(✉)]

[1] School of Computer Science and Technology, Hebei University,
Baoding 071002, China
[2] School of Management, Hebei University, Baoding 071002, China
hayanhbu@163.com
[3] Key Laboratory on High Trusted Information System in Hebei Province,
Baoding 071002, China

Abstract. Network public opinion acts an important role in the field of information security. With the rapid development of internet technology applications, network public opinion has achieved great changes in the aspects of data size, category, and complexity. Furthermore, the video content information plays a more and more important role in the data of network public opinion. How to efficiently manage and utilize the video content information within network public opinion becomes a research hot spot in the field of the analysis of network public opinion. The main task of tackling video information is classifying the video contents in social networks which could strengthen the ability of public opinion classification. All the traditional video contents based classification methods consider the image sequence among the videos in the Euclidean space and extract the temporal and spatial features of the image sequence for utilizing. However, these approaches have not considered the implicit geometric construct among the frame images in the given video. Fortunately, every video can be considered as an element in the Riemannian manifold. Moreover, the Riemannian triplet constraint can be utilized to exploit more discriminative information from negative samples. In this paper, projection metric learning and Riemannian triplet constraint are integrated together to carry on the analysis of network public opinion upon the videos chosen from Youtube. Furthermore, two datasets selected from Youtube are utilized to validate the proposed method. In comparison with the existing related methods, the proposed method demonstrates better performance on matching rate and impostor removal efficiency.

Keywords: Network public opinion · Video content classification · Riemannian triplet constraint · Metric learning

1 Introduction

In recent years, network content security in the field of network security has been increasingly important. Moreover, network public opinion analysis in the

M. Xu et al. (Eds.): CTCIS 2017, CCIS 704, pp. 303–317, 2017.
https://doi.org/10.1007/978-981-10-7080-8_22

field of information content security plays a very important role. Now, with the development of mobile Internet, a variety of types of information is generated on the network. Video-based public opinion information in the network is more and more common and becomes an important form of information in the network public opinion management. The question of how to effectively explore and manage network public opinion in the video public opinion information becomes an important issue of network public opinion analysis. The video public opinion content classification is the main task of network public opinion analysis. The goal of the video-based public opinion content classification is to determine the specific classification of videos and the series of images in the network. In order to solve this problem, some methods are specifically proposed. In the actual situations, the classification of video-based public opinion content often encounters serious challenges due to the differences in view-direction, lighting, background clutter, location and its resolution. In addition, the sequence of images in the same video has a strong inherent geometry relationship, and this structure introduces a more important question: how to make full use of these geometries correlations.

So far, many methods have focused on video-based identifying [1–3]. According to these methods, we can divide them into two categories: considering temporal or spatial feature information and considering subspace information. The goal of the former is to extract the temporal and spatial features from the sequence of images to be identified [4–6]. The subspace-based method computes a series of images through a low-dimensional linear subspace [7–9]. The linear subspace feature extraction method is often used to learn an effective distance metric (which minimizes the matching error rate of two identical images and maximizes the difference in different classes of images). However, these methods do not adequately exploit the discriminative ability of the negative samples has not been exploited with the method. At the same time, the subspace-based video or image sets are non-linear in the real world and there is a great challenge to exploit more discriminatory information from negative samples using their inherently unique geometric features.

At present, most of the research for nonlinear subspace is focused on the discriminant analysis of video-based object classification in the Grassmann manifold. They are mainly classified into two categories: one is to get a number of kernel functions which are used to take Grassmann elements embedded in a Hilbert space which is with high-dimensional (this is consistent with non-linear subspace but inconsistent with Euclidean space in practice) [7,8,10]. The other class does not consider the embedded Hilbert space, while learns a mapping metric that uses SPD matrices on Grassmann manifold [11–13].

However, most of the metric learning (ML) based methods on Grassmann manifold work in a distance metric that does not make full use of the intrinsic geometry and information of positive and negative samples. In the actual cases, the impostor sample is more discriminative than the simple negative sample. Assuming samples x_i and x_j in one class, while the class of x_k is not the same class as that of x_i. If $\|x_i - x_k\|^2 < \|x_i - x_j\|^2$, x_k is an impostor of x_i w.r.t. x_j. So, x_i, x_j and x_k constitute a triplet, and it is denoted by $< i,j,k >$ [14].

[15,16] proposed to utilize the impostor sample. However, the geometric structure in manifold has not been considered.

Related studies [15–17] have shown that multiple types of negative samples are rich in discriminant information on Grassmann manifold and that the impostor samples often have more identical information than well separable negative samples (WSN-samples) in object recognition and classification. However, we discover some drawbacks in existing methods, as stated as follows:

(1) The existing ML-based methods on Grassmann manifold [11,18] treat all negative samples equally, resulting that more identical information carried by others like impostors is regardless.
(2) The existing metric learning methods with considering impostor [15,16] with the following disadvantages:

- Those methods eliminate the samples which is impostor on Grassmann manifold when these samples are in the same triplet on Grassmann manifold rather than in Euclidean space.
- They ignore the geometry structure features of the WSN-samples, which include some significant discriminative information for recognition task on Grassmann manifold in practice.

To deal with these drawbacks, we consider these factors to design an effective approach to solve the video contents classification problem. We first proposed a new metric learning method for video content classification on Grassmann manifold, which learns the distance metric computed by adjust impostors with Riemannian triplet constraint and excavates the Grassmann geometry information of well separable negative samples together. Then, A novel Remannian triplet constraint is designed, which demands the distance between impostor in Riemannian space and the relative two positive samples in a Riemannian triplet with the Grassmann distance criterion is maximized, and in such a way the impostors can be removed more suitable for Riemannian geometry practically. Finally, several related experiments are conducted in this paper to show the consequence of our method in classification accuracy rate comparisons and influence of the designed symmetric Riemannian triplet constraint and WSN-samples.

In the paper, there exist a brief demonstration of Riemannian triplet constraint in Sect. 2, and our proposed PMRTCL Method is illustrated in Sect. 3. Finally, we conduct several experiments as shown in Sect. 4 and draw a conclusion in Sect. 5.

2 Riemannian Triplet on Grassmann Manifold

Before we introduce our method, as background of our paper, we will briefly introduce the geometric characteristics of Riemannnian space, and the detailed introduction and related topics referred to [18–20].

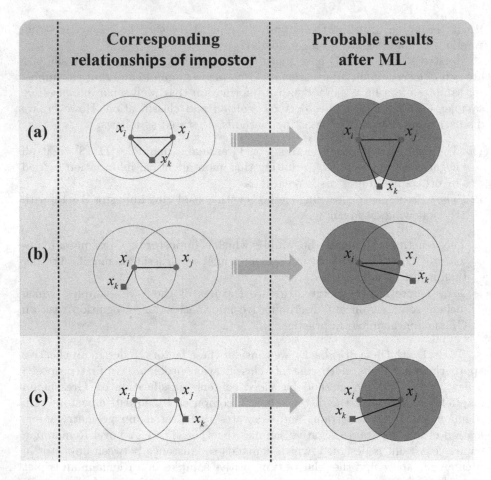

Fig. 1. Demonstration of relationship between the impostor and WSN-samples in before and after metric learning. (a) is to SCR, (b) and (c) is to ACR.

2.1   Riemannian Distance on Grassmann Manifold

Grassmann manifold $\mathcal{G}(q, D)$ are constituted of collection of linear subspaces which is of the $\mathbb{R}^D$ and its dimensional is q. The $\mathbb{R}^D$ is in $q(D - q)$ dimensional Riemannian space. Thus, each element on $\mathcal{G}(q, D)$ is span(Y) which constituted of a linear subspace which is segmented by its orthonormal basis metric X of size $D \times q$ such as to make $Y^T Y = I_q$ and I_q is the identity metric of size $q \times q$.

On a Grassmann $\mathcal{G}(q, D)$, it use smooth curves to connect points in the manifold. The manifold distance in two elements is calculated as the distance of the minimal curve linking them on the Grassmann manifold. The minimal curve and its distance are named geodesic and geodesic distance, respectively. On the Riemannian space, the geodesic distance in two elements X_1 and X_2 is defined by

$$d_g(X_1, X_2^T) = \|\Theta\|_2, \tag{1}$$

where Θ is the vector of principal angles between X_1 and X_2. For its computation, readers can acknowledge it in [18].

One of the most traditional methods to compute the true Grassmann geodesic distance is the projection mapping computation $\Phi(X) = XX^T$ proposed by [18]. As the projection $\Phi(X)$ is a $D \times D$ symmetric metric, a desirable method of computing intrinsic relationship is $< X_1, X_2 >_\Phi = tr(\Phi(X_1)^T \Phi(X_2))$. The intrinsic relationship induces a distance named projection metric:

$$d_p(X_1, X_2) = 2^{-1/2} \|X_1 X_1^T - X_2 X_2^T\|_F, \qquad (2)$$

where $\|\cdot\|_F$ indicates the metric Frobenius-norm. Referred to [20], the projection metric can evaluate the real geodesic distance Eq. 1 with $\sqrt{2}$ scale.

2.2   Riemannian Triplet Constraint

The corresponding relationships of impostor in Euclidean space is illustrated in Fig. 1. The correlative positive element pair can be divided into two categories: symmetric corresponding relationship (SCR) and asymmetric corresponding relationship (ACR) [14]. In this paper, we introduce the triplet in to Riemannian space. Assuming X_i and X_j denote the two videos which share the same class label, X_k denotes another video with different class label with X_i. If $d_p(X_i, X_k) < d_p(X_i, X_j)$, X_k denotes the impostor with X_i w.r.t. X_j. From this case, X_i, X_j and X_k constitute a Riemannian triplet, and designed by $<i,j,k>_{\in \mathcal{G}}$.

For each goal video sample X_i, all the negative videos of it are divided into two parts: impostors and other relative negative samples which named WSN-sample, based on the following rules.

(1) Assuming X_i and X_j share the same class label and X_k with another different class label, if X_k indeed impostor which is correlative with X_i w.r.t. X_j and correlative with X_j w.r.t. X_i, we build one Riemannian triplet $<i,j,k>_{\in \mathcal{G}}$ to avoid double formation which is represented in Grassmann manifold $\mathcal{G}$.

(2) If X_j has a different class label with X_i, but not an impostor of X_i, then X_j is called a well separable negative sample (WSN-sample) of X_i. X_i and X_j construct a well separable negative pair (WSN-pair) $<i,j>$. we make D represent the set of WSN-pairs in all samples.

3   Our Proposed PMRTCL Method

Firstly, we divide the Heterogeneous videos into impostor and WSN-samples on Riemannian space, then introduce the Projection Metric learning method that is based on Grassmann manifold, which is named the Projection Metric Learning with Riemannian Triplet Constraint method(PMRTCL) for video-based public opinion classification. Then we will describe it in detail of the PMRTCL and its optimization.

3.1 Formulation

Let $X_1, X_2, ..., X_m$ are the training sequences of video with different number frames in m videos, where $X_i \in \mathbb{R}^{D \times d}$ represent a video matrix of i-th image set or video which has n_i frames, every image in them being denoted as a vector containing a D-dimensional feature. In these matrices, every video or image set attributes to a classes indicated by C_i. The i-th image set or video sample X_i is indicated by a q-dimensional linear subspace spanned by an orthonormal basis metric $Y_i \in R^{D \times d}$, s.t. $X_i X_i^T \simeq Y_i \Lambda Y_i^T$, where Λ_i, Y_i is relate with the matrices which is of q largest eigenvalues and eigenvectors Individually.

Supposing a linear subspace on Riemannian space denoted as $\text{span}(Y_i)$, we consider $Y_i Y_i^T$ as an element on the manifold, and our goal is to find a suitable mapping function to satisfy the symmetric Riemannian triplet constraint, and the mapping $f : g(q, D)$ is defined as

$$f(Y_i Y_i^T) = W^T Y_i Y_i^T W = (W^T Y_i)(W^T Y_i)^T. \tag{3}$$

Where $W \in R^{D \times d}$ denotes a projection metric which rank is full in column. This projection can convert the elements on original Grassmann manifold $g(q, D)$ to another lower dimensional Grassmann manifold $g(q, d)$. However, in normal case, $W^T Y_i$ is not always orthonormal matrix. So in order to maintain the geometric properties of the Grassmann manifold, we have to find a way to ensure that the converted $W^T Y_i$ into orthonormal basic matrix. In order to solve this problem, we momentarily let the element $W^T Y_i'$ to represent the orthonormal matrix $W^T Y_i$ after mapping. This problem uses QR decomposition as an optimization method for iterative processing and the detailed iterative procedure will demonstrated later. First, we introduce the projection metric learning method and the symmetric Riemannian triplet constraint objective function, and then describe the optimization procedure.

Projection Metric Learning for Video-based Content classification on Grassmann Manifold. The Projection Metric of any pair video matrices which need to transformed $W^T Y_i' Y_i'^T W$, $W^T Y_j' Y_j'^T W$ is defined by:

$$
\begin{aligned}
d_p^2(&W^T Y_i' Y_i'^T W, W^T Y_j' Y_j'^T W) \\
&= 2^{-1/2} \| W^T Y_i' Y_i'^T W - W^T Y_j' Y_j'^T W \|_F^2 \\
&= 2^{-1/2} tr(P A_{ij} Aij^T P).
\end{aligned} \tag{4}
$$

where $A_{ij} = Y_i' Y_i'^T - Y_j' Y_j'^T$ and $P = WW^T$. Since W is demanded a matrice whose rank of column is full, P is a rank-d symmetric positive semidefinite (PSD) matrix of size $D \times D$, which is a Mahalanobis-like matrix for computing distance.

Riemannian Triplet Objective Function. For the pre-obtained symmetric Rimennian triplet set and the WSN-pair set, we focus on a Riemannian mapping metric, which aims to eliminate the distance between the impostor and WSN-pair in the triplets. In order to eliminate the impostor in ACR more efficiently, we designed a new constraint. This constraint is to minimize the Riemannian distance of the positive pair and maximize the Riemannian distance which is constituted from two negative pair in the same Riemannian triplet at the same time. We call the triplet constraint on Riemannian space as symmetric Riemannian triplet constraint. Specifically, for a given Riemannian triplet $< i, j, k >_{\in \mathcal{G}}$, we require $d_p(f(Y_i'Y_i'^T), f(Y_j'Y_j'^T)) < d_p(f(Y_i'Y_i'^T), f(Y_k'Y_k'^T))$ and $d_p(f(Y_i'Y_i'^T), f(Y_j'Y_j'^T)) < d_p(f(Y_j'Y_j'^T), f(Y_k'Y_k'^T))$. $d_p(\cdot)$ should be the function of Riemannian distance obtained when learn the distance metric on Riemannian manifold as Eq. 4.

To come to the goal, the discriminant function $\overset{*}{P}$ is designed as follows:

$$\overset{*}{P} = \arg\max_P J(P) = \arg\max_P J_1(P) + \lambda J_2(P) \qquad (5)$$

where

$$J_1(P) = \frac{1}{|G|} \sum_{<i,j,k> \in G} \left\{ \begin{array}{l} (\rho_1 2^{-1/2} tr(PA_{ik}A_{ik}^T P) - \\ 2^{-1/2} tr(PA_{ij}A_{ij}^T P) + \\ (\rho_2 2^{-1/2} tr(PA_{jk}A_{jk}^T P) - \\ 2^{-1/2} tr(PA_{ij}A_{ij}^T P)) \end{array} \right\}$$

$$J_2(P) = \frac{1}{|D|} \sum_{<i,j> \in D} 2^{-1/2} tr(PA_{ij}A_{ij}^T P)$$

λ represent a parameter which is used to balance terms in objective function. ρ_1 and ρ_2 is the penalty parameters of the negative pairs solely.

$$\rho_1 = \exp(-\frac{\left\| Y_i'Y_i'^T - Y_k'Y_k'^T \right\|}{\left\| Y_i'Y_i'^T - Y_j'Y_j'^T \right\|})$$

$$\rho_2 = \exp(-\frac{\left\| Y_j'Y_j'^T - Y_k'Y_k'^T \right\|}{\left\| Y_i'Y_i'^T - Y_j'Y_j'^T \right\|})$$

The first term $J_1(P)$ is used to guarantee that the Riemannian distance between the positive pair samples in the same triplet is smaller than the distance between the other two negative pairs and only in this case, in every Riemanian triplet the impostor can be efficiently eliminate. The term $J_2(P)$ is used to guarantee that the Riemannian distance of WSN-sample pairs is maximized after mapping. The demonstration of our method can be seen in Fig. 2.

Our PMRTCL method can more effectively remove the impostor in the Riemannian triplet, and it combine the discriminative information and that in WSN-samples. Therefore, our projection Riemannian metric carry better identical ability.

3.2   Optimization for Our PMRTCL Method

A novel optimization method for PMRTCL will be described, including two key steps, one for optimizing P and the other for optimizing Y'. Although Y' can not be accurately represented by P, it's not easy to look an effective method for optimization of P. We design an iterative optimization method for P and Y',

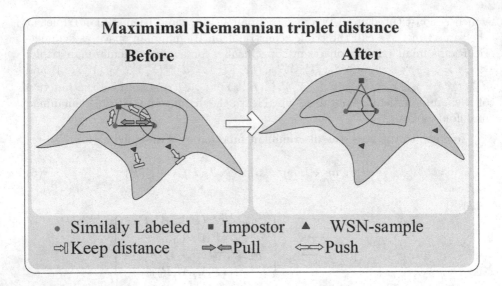

Fig. 2. The basic idea of our proposed method

by fixing one of the iterations to optimize another and repeat it in several times and get the final optimization result.

We aim to make $W^T Y$ be orthonormal with Y normalized. In case of P denote a PSD matrix with rank-d and size $D \times D$ as demonstrated, we also use a nonlinear Riemannian Conjugate Gradient (RCG) method [18,19] on the Grassmann manifold for look the suitable P with the Y' fixed.

Normalization of Y. With fixed $P = WW^T$, we normalized all matrix Y_i into Y_i' for all i so as to make the $W^T Y_i$ is orthonormal matrix. Therefore, we perform QR-decomposition to $W^T Y_i$ s.t. $W^T Y_i = Q_i R_i$, where $Q_i \in R^{D \times q}$ is the orthonormal matrix adjusted by the first q columns and $R_i \in R^{q \times q}$ denotes the invertible upper-triangular matrix. Because R_i is invertible and Q_i is orthonormal, we let $W^T Y_i'$ to be an orthonormal basis matrix with Y_i normalized as

$$Q_i = W^T(Y_i R_i^{-1}) \to Y' = Y_i R^{-1} \tag{6}$$

Computation of P. With fixed Y_i, we compute the optimal PSD matrix P by using RCG optimization algorithm on Grassmann manifold of PSD matrices with rank-d and size $D \times D$. For P alway on the larger than the normal trace in Eq. (5), the discriminative objective function $J(P)$ in Eq. (5) is innovate into:

$$\overset{*}{P} = \arg\max_P tr(PS_G P) - \lambda tr(PS_D P). \tag{7}$$

where S_G and S_D are defined as:

$$S_G = \frac{1}{N_G} \sum_{<i,j,k> \in G} 2^{-1/2}(\rho_1 tr(A_{ik}A_{ik}^T) - tr(A_{ij}A_{ij}^T))$$
$$+ 2^{-1/2}(\rho_2 tr(A_{jk}A_{jk}^T) - tr(A_{ij}A_{ij}^T)). \tag{8}$$

$$S_D = \frac{1}{N_D} \sum_{<i,j> \in D} 2^{-1/2} tr(A_{ij}A_{ij}^T). \tag{9}$$

For the Conjugate Gradient(CG) optimization algorithm develops in Euclidean, the RCG optimization algorithm on the Riemannian space executes with an iterative steps. As is demonstrated of the iterative procedure as listed below: at the $k-$th iterative step, finding P_k by finding the minimum of J together with the geodesic γ in the orientation $H_k - 1$ from $P_k - 1 = \gamma(k - 1)$, computing the gradient of Riemannian manifold $\nabla_P J(P_k)$ at this location, choosing new probe orientation to be a association of the old probe orientation and the new gradient on Riemannian space, i.e., $H_k \longleftarrow -\nabla_p J(P_k) + \eta\tau(H_{k-1}, P_{k-1}, P_k)$, iterate it and stop when it is convergence. In this step, the Riemannian gradient $\nabla_P J(P_k)$ will be evaluated from its correlative Euclidean gradient $D_P J(P_k)$ by $\nabla_P J(P_k) = D_P J(P_k) - P_k P_k^T D_P J(P_k)$, and $\tau(H_{k-1}, P_{k-1}, P_k)$ denotes the parallel transformation of tangent vector $H_k - 1$ from P_{k-1} to P_k. We refer the reader to [18,19] if you want to know more detailed procedure. At this moment, we only need to compute the Euclidean gradient $D_P J(P_k)$ of Eq. (7) as:

$$D_P J(P_k) = 2(S_G - \lambda S_D)P_k \tag{10}$$

When the optimal P is determined, the Riemannian distance of two linear subspaces is calculated using Eq. (4). Although it is difficult to prove the convergence of the proposed optimization algorithm, it is shown by experiment that our method is usually able to let the objective function Eq. (7) get a stable and ideal result with some iterations.

4   Experiments

In this section, extensive video-based content classification experiments are performed on two publicly available datasets to show the performance of the proposed PMRTCL approach.

4.1   Datasets and Experimental Settings

We conduct experiments for our proposed method on two widely used available video datasets for video-based content classification:YouTube Celebrities (YTC) [21] and YouTube Face (YTF) [22]. The YouTube Celebrities (YTC) is a very challenging and widely applied video face dataset. It has 1910 video clips of 47 subjects collected from YouTube. Most clips contain hundreds of frames, which

Table 1. Top ranked matching rates (%) on the YTC dataset

Method	YTC	YTF
MSM	60.25 ± 3.05	65.20 ± 1.97
PM	62.17 ± 3.65	65.12 ± 2.00
AHISD	63.70 ± 2.89	64.80 ± 1.54
CHISD	66.62 ± 2.79	66.30 ± 1.21
CMSM	63.81 ± 3.70	66.46 ± 1.54
SSDML	68.85 ± 2.32	65.38 ± 1.86
DCC	65.48 ± 3.51	68.28 ± 2.21
GDA	65.02 ± 2.91	67.00 ± 1.62
GGDA	66.37 ± 3.52	66.56 ± 2.07
PML	66.69 ± 3.54	67.30 ± 1.76
PMRTCL	**68.36 ± 2.34**	**67.89 ± 1.63**
PMRTCL-GDA	**70.52 ± 2.58**	**70.98 ± 2.01**
PMRTCL-GGDA	**72.39 ± 2.37**	**70.53 ± 1.89**

are often low resolution and highly compressed with noise and low quality. The YTF contains 3425 videos of 1595 different persons collected from the YouTube website. In this dataset, there exist large variations in pose, illumination, and expression in each video sequence.

In all experiments, we regarded every video as an image set with data matrix $X_i = [x_1, x_2, x_3, \cdots, x_{n_i}]$, where $x_j \in \mathbb{R}^D$ is the feature vector which computed from j-th frame in videos. The video or image sequence can be described using a linear subspace from the singular value decomposition (SVD) of X_i. In detail, we apply the q left singular-vectors to the orthonormal basis matrix Y_i to represent a q-dimensional linear subspace for X_i, which is considered as an element on Grassmann manifold $\mathcal{G}(q, D)$. The parameters setting will illustrated along with the experiments conducted using cross-validation.

To evaluate the performance of our PMRTCL approach, we conduct four comparable experiments by several unsupervised subspace-based methods including Mutual Subspace Method (MSM) [23], Metric learning [18], Affine Hull based Image Set Distance (AHISD) [24] and Convex Hull based Image Set Distance (CHISD) [24]. In addition, we also test several state-of-the-art supervised subspace-based learning method including Constrained Mutual Subspace Method (CMSM) [25], Set-to-set distance metric learning(SSDML) [26], Discriminative Canonical Correlations (DCC) [27], Grassmann Discriminative Analysis (GDA) [7] and Grassmann Graph-Embedding Discriminant Analysis (GGDA) [10]. As for fair comparison, the key parameters of each method are empirically tuned based on the recommendations in the original works. As for MSM/AHISD, the first canonical correlation or leading component is exploited when comparing two subspaces. As for CMSM/DCC, the dimensionality of the resulting discriminant subspace is tuned from 1 to 10. For SSDML, its key parameters are tuned and empirically set as: $\lambda_1 = 0.001$, $\lambda_2 = 0.5$, the number of positive and negative pairs per sample are 10 and 20 respectively. As for GDA/GGDA, the final dimensionality is set $c - 1$ (c is the number of face classes in training). In GGDA, the other parameter β is tuned at the range of $\{1e^2, 1e^3, 1e^4, 1e^5, 1e^6\}$. For our PMRTCL, the parameter λ is set to 0.2.

To make the comparable results persuasive, we use the same features as the four comparable experiments. For appraisal, the average classification accuracy rate is reported after 10 random trials. Then, we report the different result of PMRTCL method in rank-1 with the comparable four methods. The enforcement of PMTRCL approach is superior to the existing methods with pretty performance. On account of the PSD metrics which computed from the optimization can be resolved into a low-dimensional space for transformations, this Riemannian manifold can be embedded into the approach GDA and GGDA which search the equal Riemannain metric. As reports in results, both the PMRTCL-GDA and the PMRTCL-GGDA promote the preliminary approaches (i.e., GDA and GGDA) and exceed the other comparable methods, which is shown in Table 1.

4.2 Evaluation on YTC and YTF Dataset

For YTC dataset, each object is resized to a 20×20 image as [28,29], every frame of video is preprocessed by the histogram equalization to eliminate lighting effects. Then we extract gray features for each image. Following the prior works [28–30], we go on random ten trials cross evaluate experiments, i.e., 10 randomly constitute the train and test data from gallery and probe. In every trial, we choose half of the person to train and the other half is to test. With carried out our experiment on PMRTCL, each video is represented by a linear subspace of order 20. And then, the average classification accuracy rates of our methods and every comparable methods are shown in Table 1.

For YTF dataset, we straightly gather the face images through the YTF data and then resize them into 20×40 pixels as [31] and extract the raw intensity features of resized video frames, and then follow the standard evaluation protocol [22] to evaluate standard, ten-trials, cross validation, matching tests. Explicitly, we take advantage of the officially provided 5000 video pairs, which are equally divided into 10 trials. Each trials contains 250 intra-personal pairs and 250 inter-personal pair. In the end, the average classification matching rates of these methods are shown in Table 1.

The Table 1 report the top ranked classification accuracy rates of our approach and comparable methods on two datasets. It can be demonstrated that our PMRTCL method is coincidentally superior to all compared approaches on the classification accuracy rate.

4.3 Evaluation of Riemannian Triplet Constraint

The symmetric Riemannian triplet constraint is proposed for eliminate impostors more efficiently. To make a judgment about the constraint, we contrast the impostor removal capability (IRC) [14] of our method and other impostor-based approaches. The IRC measure is computed as follows:

$$IRC = \frac{N_{before} - N_{after}}{N_{before}} \tag{11}$$

where N_{after} and N_{before} denote the count of impostors in dataset with or without using the PMRTCL approach, separately. Figure 3 reveals the IRCs of PMRTCL and two typical impostor-based ML methods (LMNN and EIML) on two datasets. We discover that our PMRTCL method come true better IRCs than the two methods, which reveals the effectiveness of the proposed symmetric Riemannian triplet constraint for impostor eliminated.

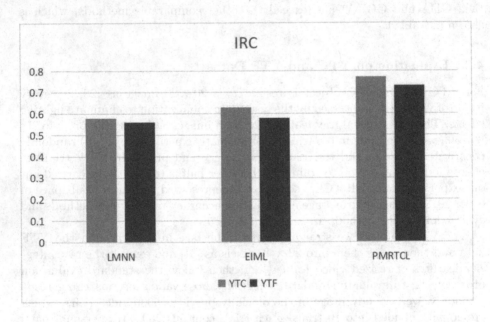

Fig. 3. IRC comparison between PMRTCL and impostor-based methods LMNN and EIML

Table 2. Top ranked matching rates (%) of PMRTCL and PMR

Method	YTC	YTF
PMR	67.04	66.87
PMRTCL	**68.36**	**67.89**

4.4 Evaluation of WSN-Samples on Riemannian Manifold

We conduct experiments on YTC and YTF dataset with or without using WSN-samples which aim to measure the effects of using WSN-samples. We denote the regard PMRTCL without using WSN-samples as PMR. Table 2 reveals the rank 1 classification accuracy rates of PMRTCL and PMR on two datasets. We discover that utilizing the WSN-samples promotes the rank 1 classification accuracy rate by 1.02%, which reveals that the WSN-samples involve certain identical information which is helpful for Video content classification.

5 Conclusion

In this paper, PMRTCL approach for video-based content classification in public opinion analysis is proposed, which eliminates impostors more efficiently and makes the distance of WSN-samples be enlarged in video content classification at the same time. It can be observed from the experimental results: (1) PMRTCL can exploit the intrinsic geometry structure to strengthen the discriminative capability and is superior to several metric learning based methods by considering classification accuracy rate. (2) With the proposed symmetric Riemannian triplet constraint, PMRTCL can eliminate impostors on Grassmann manifold more efficiently. (3) There presents several available information in WSN-pairs, moreover, making use of these discriminative information appropriately can promote the performance. In comparison with its related methods, the proposed PMRTCL achieves better performance in video-based public opinion classification. Therefore, it can be widely used in the network public opinion analysis in the field of network security.

Acknowledgments. This project is supported by National Natural Science Foundation of China (61170254, 61379116), the Natural Science Foundation of Hebei province (Grant No. F2016201244) and the Natural Science Foundation of Hebei institution (Grant No. ZD2015088).

References

1. Wu, B., Hu, B.G., Ji, Q.: A coupled hidden markov random field model for simultaneous face clustering and tracking in videos. Pattern Recognition (2016)
2. Dewan, M.A.A., Granger, E., Marcialis, G.L., Sabourin, R., Roli, F.: Adaptive appearance model tracking for still-to-video face recognition. Pattern Recogn. 49(C), 129–151 (2015)
3. Lee, S.H., Baddar, W.J., Ro, Y.M.: Collaborative expression representation using peak expression and intra class variation face images for practical subject-independent emotion recognition in videos. Pattern Recogn. 54(C), 52–67 (2016)
4. Fathy, M.E., Alavi, A., Chellappa, R.: Discriminative log-Euclidean feature learning for sparse representation-based recognition of faces from videos. In: Proceedings of the Twenty-Fifth International Joint Conference on Artificial Intelligence, IJCAI 2016, New York, NY, USA, 9–15 July 2016, pp. 3359–3367 (2016)

5. Shen, J., Zuo, X., Li, J., Yang, W., Ling, H.: A novel pixel neighborhood differential statistic feature for pedestrian and face detection. Pattern Recogn. **63**, 127–138 (2016)
6. Wu, X., Li, Q., Xu, L., Chen, K., Yao, L.: Multi-feature kernel discriminant dictionary learning for face recognition. Pattern Recogn. **66**(C), 404–411 (2017)
7. Hamm, J., Lee, D.D.: Grassmann discriminant analysis: a unifying view on subspace-based learning. In: International Conference, pp. 376–383 (2008)
8. Ham, J., Lee, D.D.: Extended grassmann kernels for subspace-based learning. In: Conference on Neural Information Processing Systems, Vancouver, British Columbia, Canada, December, pp. 601–608 (2008)
9. Chen, S., Sanderson, C., Harandi, M.T., Lovell, B.C.: Improved image set classification via joint sparse approximated nearest subspaces. In: IEEE Conference on Computer Vision and Pattern Recognition, pp. 452–459 (2013)
10. Harandi, M.T., Sanderson, C., Shirazi, S., Lovell, B.C.: Graph embedding discriminant analysis on grassmannian manifolds for improved image set matching. In: IEEE Conference on Computer Vision and Pattern Recognition, pp. 2705–2712 (2011)
11. Harandi, M.T., Salzmann, M., Hartley, R.: From manifold to manifold: geometry-aware dimensionality reduction for SPD matrices. In: Fleet, D., Pajdla, T., Schiele, B., Tuytelaars, T. (eds.) ECCV 2014. LNCS, vol. 8690, pp. 17–32. Springer, Cham (2014). https://doi.org/10.1007/978-3-319-10605-2_2
12. Jung, S., Dryden, I.L., Marron, J.S.: Analysis of principal nested spheres. Biometrika **99**(3), 551 (2012)
13. Huang, Z., Wang, R., Shan, S., Chen, X.: Projection metric learning on grassmann manifold with application to video based face recognition. In: IEEE Conference on Computer Vision and Pattern Recognition, pp. 140–149 (2015)
14. Zhu, X., Jing, X.Y., Wu, F., Zheng, W., Hu, R., Xiao, C., Liang, C.: Distance learning by treating negative samples differently and exploiting impostors with symmetric triplet constraint for person re-identification. In: IEEE International Conference on Multimedia and Expo, pp. 1–6 (2016)
15. Weinberger, K.Q., Saul, L.K.: Distance Metric Learning for Large Margin Nearest Neighbor Classification. JMLR.org (2009)
16. Hirzer, M., Roth, P.M., Bischof, H.: Person re-identification by efficient impostor-based metric learning. In: IEEE Ninth International Conference on Advanced Video and Signal-Based Surveillance, pp. 203–208 (2012)
17. Dikmen, M., Akbas, E., Huang, T.S., Ahuja, N.: Pedestrian recognition with a learned metric. In: Kimmel, R., Klette, R., Sugimoto, A. (eds.) ACCV 2010. LNCS, vol. 6495, pp. 501–512. Springer, Heidelberg (2011). https://doi.org/10.1007/978-3-642-19282-1_40
18. Edelman, A., Arias, T.A., Smith, S.T.: The geometry of algorithms with orthogonality constraints. Siam J. Matrix Anal. Appl. **20**(2), 303–353 (1998)
19. Absil, P.A., Mahony, R., Sepulchre, R.: Optimization Algorithms on Matrix Manifolds. Princeton University Press, Princeton (2009)
20. Harandi, M., Sanderson, C., Shen, C., Lovell, B.: Dictionary learning and sparse coding on grassmann manifolds: an extrinsic solution. In: IEEE International Conference on Computer Vision, pp. 3120–3127 (2013)
21. Kim, M., Kumar, S., Pavlovic, V., Rowely, H.: Face tracking and recognition with visual constraints in real-world videos. In: IEEE International Conference on Computer Vision, pp. 1–8 (2008)

22. Wolf, L., Hassner, T., Maoz, I.: Face recognition in unconstrained videos with matched background similarity. In: Computer Vision and Pattern Recognition, pp. 529–534 (2011)

23. Yamaguchi, O., Fukui, K., Maeda, K.: Face recognition using temporal image sequence. In: International Conference on Face Gesture Recognition, p. 318 (1998)

24. Cevikalp, H., Triggs, B.: Face recognition based on image sets. In: Computer Vision and Pattern Recognition, pp. 2567–2573 (2010)

25. Fukui K., Yamaguchi O.: Face recognition using multi-viewpoint patterns for robot vision. In: The Eleventh International Symposium on Robotics Research, ISRR, 19–22 October 2003, Siena, Italy, pp. 192–201 (2005)

26. Zhu, P., Zhang, L., Zuo, W., Zhang, D.: From point to set: extend the learning of distance metrics. In: IEEE International Conference on Computer Vision, pp. 2664–2671 (2013)

27. Kim, T.K., Kittler, J., Cipolla, R.: Discriminative learning and recognition of image set classes using canonical correlations. IEEE Trans. Pattern Anal. Mach. Intell. **29**(6), 1005 (2007)

28. Davis, L.S.: Covariance discriminative learning: a natural and efficient approach to image set classification. In: Computer Vision and Pattern Recognition, pp. 2496–2503 (2012)

29. Lu, J., Wang, G., Moulin, P.: Image set classification using holistic multiple order statistics features and localized multi-kernel metric learning. In: IEEE International Conference on Computer Vision, pp. 329–336 (2013)

30. Wang, R., Chen, X.: Manifold discriminant analysis. In: IEEE Conference on Computer Vision and Pattern Recognition. CVPR 2009, pp. 429–436 (2009)

31. Cui, Z., Li, W., Xu, D., Shan, S., Chen, X.: Fusing robust face region descriptors via multiple metric learning for face recognition in the wild. In: Computer Vision and Pattern Recognition, pp. 3554–3561 (2013)

A Trusted Routing Mechanism Suitable for the Sensing Nodes in Internet of Things

Yubo Wang, Bei Gong$^{(\boxtimes)}$, and Yichen Wang

Faculty of Information Technology, Beijing University of Technology,
Beijing, China
tekkman_blade@126.com

Abstract. The sensing layer of Internet of Things is composed of heterogeneous sensing networks, sensing layer data is fast and reliable transmission is the basis of trusted operation of the Internet of things, the choice of routing in the data transmission process is critical to the life cycle of the sensing node, the success rate of data transmission, and the feedback control of the network layer and application layer. But the current sensing layer routing mechanism lacks credible considerations for data transmission paths and its environmental adaptability is poor. In order to ensure that the Internet of things perceived layer of data quickly and reliably transmitted, this chapter presents a trusted routing mechanism for sensing nodes, based on the node trust measure, this model calculates the bandwidth and energy available between nodes, taking into account the influence of available bandwidth and energy on data transmission between nodes. It uses the dynamic programming method to calculate the trusted path of data transmission between nodes, to ensure that the data transmission between trusted nodes trusted. The routing mechanism proposed in this chapter has the characteristics of low overhead, high scalability and easy project realization. Simulation experiments show that the routing mechanism is good to against attack, extensive environmental adaptability, can effectively resist selective forwarding attacks, node hijacking attacks. Compared with the existing scheme, this mechanism effectively reduces the communication overhead in the routing establishment process, and significantly improves the network performance and has a good application prospect.

Keywords: Internet of Things · Link bandwidth · Dynamic planning · Trusted route · Trusted measure

1 Introduction

The Internet of Things connects a large number of end entities in the physical world through the Internet to the sensing environment, the rise of the Internet of Things makes the terminal and the Internet between the long gully to fill, and after the rise of the Internet, once again opened a new information technology revolution [1]. Internet communication is no longer controlled by people and the end of each other, but the material and things, people and things, things and each other's interaction and communication also included, this change also makes the object more intelligent and the process of the completion of people and things, things and things and people interact

© Springer Nature Singapore Pte Ltd. 2017
M. Xu et al. (Eds.): CTCIS 2017, CCIS 704, pp. 318–347, 2017.
https://doi.org/10.1007/978-981-10-7080-8_23

with each other, resulting in a number of new implementation techniques and application scenarios [2], and further promote the integration of man and nature, social environment. From the inner demand and the external presentation form, the Internet of Things is a reality in the information world, through information technology as a bridge between the real world and the virtual world, the real world of people and things mapped to cyberspace [3, 4].

There are a variety of heterogeneous sensing networks in the sensing layer of the Internet of things. The channel characteristics, the dynamic and the distribution of the nodes of the different structures are different. The existing data transmission protocols are susceptible to various attacks [5, 6]. Researchers at home and abroad have done a lot of research on the security routing of sensing nodes, but the current research is still based on the traditional data encryption and identity authentication mechanism, the lack of active confidence from the node and the source of data from the perspective of trusted data safe transmission mechanism. Due to the presence of multiple heterogeneous sensing networks in the sensing layer, the existing secure routing mechanism does not apply to such environments. As we all know, in the study of security routing of Internet of Things, the trusted measure and remote proof mechanism of nodes can effectively identify malicious nodes, which can effectively guarantee the trustworthy operation of sensor nodes. The node trusted metric is currently considered as an effective solution to ensure reliable transmission of node data. More specifically, the credible metric mechanism can be applied to a trusted routing mechanism to ensure that the relay nodes that are passing through the data are credible.

At present, domestic and foreign scholars have a lot of research on the security route based on the trusted value [7, 8]. However, there are still some problems to be solved in the current routing mechanism of the perceived network based on the trusted metric. First, the existing routing scheme based on the trusted metric only considers a certain type of sensing layer network, its environment adaptability is poor, and it can only resist some of the currently known attacks against the route. Although the route management scheme after fusing node trusted value can effectively improve the security of the network, it may also bring a series of potential security risks, such as node key information exposure, energy consumption increase and data theft. In order to solve this problem, this chapter is based on the defects of the trustworthiness metric routing mechanism, and puts forward the related solutions for these defects. Secondly, the routing mechanism based on the trusted metric is fundamentally different from the traditional routing protocol using Qos metrics, such as the selection of the next hop of the node, the choice of the load algorithm and the bandwidth, and so on. For example, compared with the Qos-based routing mechanism, the calculation of the routing mechanism based on the trusted metric is more complex and requires consideration of the constraints of the physical link and the node's trusted metric in the data transmission process. In addition, because the node trustworthiness does not have transitivity, symmetry and full real-time, there is also a significant difference between the routing mechanism based on the Qos metric [9, 10]. However, the current research on sensing layer routing is usually the difference between ignoring the credible metric and the Qos-based selection mechanism, which results in the unclear logic of the routing mechanism, the low adaptation of the environment.

In view of the above problems, this chapter proposes a new trusted routing mechanism for the sensing layer of Internet of Things on the basis of the trusted node measurement model. The bandwidth of the link between the nodes is calculated first, and then the trusted metric of the candidate relay node is calculated. A data transmission route is selected with the dynamic planning integrated bandwidth and the trusted metric value. The mechanism can be applied to different types of sensing networks, with good environmental adaptability, and can effectively use the limited bandwidth resources in the knowledge network to improve the utilization of resources and effectively extend the working life of nodes. Simulation results show that the routing mechanism has good anti-aggression and extensive environmental adaptability, which can effectively resist various attacks against nodes, and reduce the communication cost in the route establishment process, which greatly improves the network performance and has good application prospect. Subsequent sections of this article are organized as follows: In Sect. 2, we introduce the trusted route selection process; Sect. 3 discusses the node credibility measurement model; Sect. 4 discusses the trusted routing mechanism; Sect. 5 is the simulation experiment; the first Sect. 6 is the conclusion.

2 Related Work and Routing Establishment Process Description

2.1 Research on Trusted Routing

Unlike the Internet, the object-sensing layer nodes are composed of heterogeneous nodes, the computing power of the sensing nodes and the difference in the quality of service requirements, making the real-time transmission of data between the sensing nodes become a difficult problem. The literature [11] thinks, due to the unique openness of the Internet of Things, the traffic of the data transmission, the control of the routing and the quality of service will be the core problem that the data transmission layer of the Internet of Things urgently needs to be solved. The study of the trusted routing mechanism suitable for the sensing layer can effectively improve the success rate of data packets, and can make more effective use of the existing bandwidth in the sensing network, guarantee the rationality of resource utilization, reduce the data transmission time, The credibility of the operation has a very important role.

Internet of things is currently widely used in intelligent transportation, medical monitoring, industrial control of the emerging information physical system (CPS) [12], So the Internet and the real object directly connected between the composition of the overall security logic is the key to secure the Internet of things, but the two are connected to the safety of communication channels are less concerned about. Especially in the open Internet of Things sensing computing environment, the data transmission link between the sensing nodes of the Internet of Things is common, so it is difficult to comprehensively manage and control the data transmission path. In order to ensure the security of the data transmission in the control process, we must fully consider the heterogeneous sensing network problem in the data transmission process: the node computing ability and the communication ability in the different sensing networks will not be much different, but the node communication Protocol and data forwarding strategy may be different, which needs to solve the perception layer heterogeneous sense of the network routing problem.

The problem of heterogeneous network routing in the sensing layer of Internet of Things is currently very popular among domestic and foreign scholars. It is usually forwarded by the same protocol in the process of selecting traditional network data transmission routes. However, because of the diversity of data acquisition types and applications in the Internet, it is necessary to design a route suitable for heterogeneous sensing layer networks. Today, most of the work focuses on the following two parts:

(1) Isomorphism based on the network type

This type of heterogeneous network routing research focuses on the interconnection of different types of subnet (WIFI; 3G...), and finally from the logic to form a whole virtual network. The logic of the nodes in each subnet is the same, but the boundaries of the different subnets are clear. In the document [13] the network layer protocol of the subnet is abstracted as a unified protocol, and different types of subnet connections are realized through a unified logical link. This mechanism is based on the same physical attributes and inherits the subnet nodes of the existing routing mechanism. According to the document [14] through the structure of the hierarchical network structure, through the dynamic address of different sub-network link, in the process to maintain the original routing protocol. The above-mentioned heterogeneous network routing and routing mechanism has little change to the routing protocol itself, so the cost is low, but it cannot be applied to the physical layer and the variable layer.

(2) Sensing layer node physical attributes and routing protocol variable environment

In this environment, the different sensing layers of the computing power, the remaining energy and energy consumption may be different. In order to improve the node's life cycle, the node is bound to use a different routing strategy. The physical attribute index of the node in this type of sensing network is different. The node may choose different routing strategies, usually choose the lowest energy routing strategy, but this strategy often cannot guarantee that the selected path is trusted. Therefore, the literature [15] combined with the node trustworthiness measure and the probability of data transmission to select the optimal data transmission path, the advantage is to effectively protect the data transmission credible, but it cannot achieve the stable use of energy, may cause energy consumption Unstable, thus reducing the node's life cycle. In literature [16], the data transmission route is selected from the angle of time delay and data transmission success rate, and the most routing path is searched by data flow. However, this method will cause the path driver to be uncontrollable and cannot guarantee the next hop the node is trusted. However, the prerequisite of the above research is that the routing protocol of the sensing layer node is unified. Only when selecting the predecessor node will consider its own condition, lack consideration of the sum of energy, confidence measure, delay and bandwidth, cannot be effective satisfying the choice of trusted routes in heterogeneous awareness networks.

The above research is the main research content of heterogeneous sensing network data transmission routing at home and abroad, but still does not cover the problem of heterogeneous node data transmission routing. Although in the traditional Internet, there have been some on the physical properties of different transmission strategies are also different network abstract integration of the routing problem research, For example, the literature [17] proposed a mechanism for identity mapping and data routing identifier mapping in the process of identity identification based on node access. Literature [18] proposed multi-routing identification and access scheme, through the network layer unified abstraction to achieve different Network routing convergence, and thus data transmission efficiency and network quality of service. However, the similar scheme mainly deals with the logical integration of heterogeneous networks, mainly for networks such as 3G and 4G. The scheme does not necessarily apply to the network of sensing networks, and the energy consumption and data transmission rate of the above scheme are lacking. The overall test, while the current network logic integration research is mainly based on theoretical research, the lack of practical application of the case.

The Internet of Things sensing layer is composed of a variety of multi-source heterogeneous cognitive networks, and the security of data transmission between sensing nodes is extremely important. To ensure the safety of data transmission, and now there are two main research ideas: one is a security for data transmission, mainly through symmetric encryption and asymmetric encryption to ensure the confidentiality of data, such a wide range of applications and effective, but the energy consumption High; the second is for the data transmission routing, by calculating the trusted next routing node to protect the data transmission security. In literature [19], a data protection mechanism based on bilinear encryption is proposed. The scheme has good security, but the time cost and energy consumption are high. The perceived node is limited by the energy and the computing ability. The environmental adaptability is not good. Compared with the data encryption, the trusted routing mechanism can better adapt to the sensing layer and the perceived network. Due to the computational power and the energy limit of the node, the trusted routing mechanism can better control the data flow, and the environment adaptability is not good. In the literature [20], we design a trusted route construction method based on the n-dimensional spatial sensing network, construct a trusted route based on the node trustworthiness measure and route picking probability. However, in the heterogeneous sensing network, the two nodes communicate with each other the relay node data forwarding strategy in the transit route, so the program cannot be used directly, need to fully consider the forwarding strategy before use. In the literature [21], a cluster-based data transmission route is proposed. The scheme can calculate each hop on the route through the abstract heterogeneous sensing layer node, which can guarantee the trustworthiness of the transmission path, but lack the coping strategy of route failure.

2.2 Description of Establishing Trusted Route

2.2.1 Description for Sensing Node

In a sensor node network, according to the node computing power and energy nodes, the nodes can be divided into ordinary nodes, cluster head nodes and data aggregation nodes. Different nodes have different tasks: ordinary nodes only need collect and transmit data, cluster head nodes need certificate the ordinary nodes and collect data from ordinary nodes and send data to data aggregation nodes, while data aggregation nodes monitor all other nodes in a region and send data to the application layer of

Internet of Things. According to tasks of different nodes, different nodes can be formally described. The ordinary nodes should include the identity information, the computing environment and the data transmission status, and the formal description is as follows:

(1) Node identifier

The ordinary node consists of two elements: the node identity information id (identity information contains the network identification number ni, identity authentication key k and the attached access information pm) and the actual physical address pa in the wireless sensor network, so the ordinary node can be described with two tuple $ID = (id, pa)$;

(2) Node computing environment

The node computing environment includes the basic information of hardware and software, the programs and the communication protocols of node. Node computing environment can be described by the four tuples: $NE = (hw, ho, ap, cp)$: the node hardware information hw (the main hardware abstract value), ho (the node operating system and key processes of the value), $ap = (p_1, p_2 \ldots p_n)$ (the current running the programs of node), $cp = \{cp_1, cp_2 \ldots cp_n\}$ (the current running the communication protocols of node);

(3) Data transfer status

Since the core task of sensing layer nodes is to collect and send data, data transmission should contain the requested transmission amount of data, the actual transmission of data and data transmission time. The following sequence description $Da = (dr, ds, t_b, ad)$ can describe the data transfer status, in $Da = (dr, ds, t_b, ad)$: dr is the requested data, ds is actually transmitted data, t_b is the time when data is sent, ad is the destination address of data. So the ordinary node description can be described by three tuple (ID, NE, Da).

To cluster head nodes and data aggregation nodes, these identity description and computation environment description are similar to ordinary nodes. But the cluster head nodes have an ordinary node list and the data aggregation nodes have a cluster head node list, which means that ordinary nodes are managed and measured by the cluster head nodes, the cluster head nodes are managed and measured by the data aggregation nodes. So the data transfer status and the list are the follows.

(4) Data transfer status of cluster head node/data aggregation node

The data transfer status of cluster head node and data aggregation are similar, in addition to receiving the data, cluster head node/data aggregation node needs to transmit data, which can be described by the following sequence:

$Ds = (D, T, dr, ds, t_b)/D = \{d_1, d_2 \ldots d_n\}$ represents a cluster head node/data aggregation node. It requests the data which each ordinary node/cluster head node sent, $T = \{t_1, t_2 \ldots t_n\}$ represents the time that each ordinary node/cluster head node send data to the cluster head node/data aggregation node, the definitions of dr, ds, t_b, ad are the same with the ordinary node.

(5) The list of nodes maintained by cluster head nodes/data aggregation nodes

Cluster head nodes/data aggregation nodes measure common nodes/cluster head nodes, and each node maintains a common node/cluster head node list, which can be described by the sequence $L = (N, T)$. In $L = (N, T)$, $N = (w_1, w_2 \ldots w_n)$ represents ordinary nodes/cluster nodes (the basic hardware, operating system information and critical processes are stored as w_i), $T = (t_1, t_2 \ldots t_n)$ represents the trust of each node, so the cluster head node/data aggregation node can be described by the sequence (ID, NE, Ds, L).

2.2.2   A Description of a Trusted Route Establishment Process

Suppose that a number of sensing nodes $\{Se_1, Se_2, \ldots, Se_n\}$ are deployed in a certain region, the distribution of the perceived layer nodes follows a random even distribution. The spatial location satisfies the minimum power transfer requirement for the sensing node to communicate. The perceived nodes are divided into data aggregation nodes, cluster head nodes and ordinary nodes according to energy. The data transmission of the sensing node includes the sending between the nodes and the two behaviors that the node sends the data to the cluster head node. In the process of data transmission, the predecessor node will announce the data forwarding strategy, and the successor node will announce its support data forwarding strategy, and combine the link bandwidth between nodes and the trusted value of the node to calculate the most reasonable data transmission route. Assume that all nodes can choose the next hop honestly according to the data forwarding strategy. If a malicious node exists, the malicious node can be isolated and removed from the perceived network according to the node trusted metric model.

For a period of time t, a data transmission node (usually the node is a common node) generates the data packet $\{D_1, D_2, \ldots, D_n\}$, according to the description of node data transmission status $Da = (dr, ds, t_b, ad)$ in Sect. 3. Each packet contains a feature description, The characteristic description of the packet is $\{cd_1, cd_2, \ldots, cd_n\}$, C_i contains the packet source address pa, destination address ad, transmission time t_b, link bandwidth l_b, residual energy e_b, belonging to the sensing network ni, etc. Part of the above information is extracted from the node identity description attribute and the data transmission state, and the part is based on the routing policy of the node.

The given packet D_i and the characteristic description cd_i of the packet, the current node of the packet needs to calculate the matching degree of the data forwarding policy of the successor node and the description of the current packet characteristic, and determines whether to select the node as the next relay node based on the trusted value and energy of the node. Given the logical description of the sensing network cluster as shown in Fig. 1, the logical calculation process of the trusted route can be described as follows:

1. When the packet currently holds the node to select the next relay node, the node preferred to find its neighbors, the information requested by the neighboring nodes includes the link bandwidth l_b, the adjacent nodes and the remaining energy of the node e_b;
2. Neighboring nodes and packets holding nodes Perform Sect. 4 based on the node dynamic trust of the remote protocol, if credible to each other, the node is used as an alternative. If the neighboring nodes are not trusted, the node with the highest value

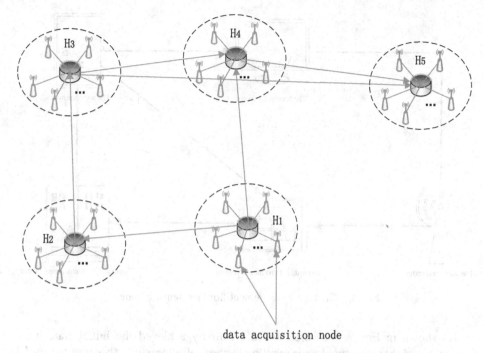

data acquisition node

Fig. 1. Logical description of the perceived network cluster

of r trusted metric is selected according to the routing security policy. The adjacent node then returns its bandwidth value.

3. The next relay node is calculated based on the link bandwidth l_b, the residual energy e_b, and the trusted measure of the node.

4. If you have reached the destination node, stop the calculation, otherwise turn to the second step.

3 The Dynamic Trusted Measure Model of Sensing Node

3.1 The Trust Measurement Model for Sensing Nodes

If a new sensing node begins to work, its parent node (parent node may be the cluster node or the data aggregation node) needs to confirm whether its initial state is trusted. Its initial state is trusted, it can collect and transmit data, and at this time the parent node needs to confirm whether the node is trusted during operation by the dynamic measurement.

In the sensing layer, the measurement of the data aggregation node is achieved by the upper layer nodes. Therefore, this section discusses the trusted measurement process that the ordinary node and the cluster head node are regarded as measured nodes. Figure 2 describes the trusted metric flow of the nodes logically:

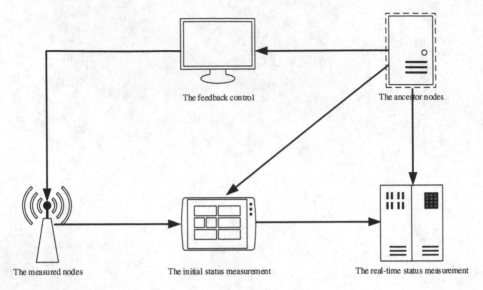

The feedback control

The ancestor nodes

The measured nodes

The initial status measurement

The real-time status measurement

Fig. 2. The trust measurement flow for sensing nodes

As shown in Fig. 2, measured nodes are firstly achieved the initial state measurement, and then measured nodes will be dynamically measured (because the initial trusted state of nodes is not represent for trusted behavior of nodes, which needs comprehensive node dynamic state to judge whether the node is trusted). Then the superior nodes feedback control according to the measurement results of measured nodes.

3.2 The Initial State Trust Measurement for the Sensing Node

The cluster head node has more energy than each ordinary node, so the ordinary node is measured by the cluster head node. The cluster head node is measured by the data aggregation node, and the data aggregation node is measured by the higher layer. Through the measurement from layer to layer, the initially security of internet of things can be ensured. $MTC = \{hw, ol, ck, \eta[1], \ldots, \eta[n]\}$ is the value of the basic trusted configure measure elements of the node, and the hash of hardware configuration is hw, the hash of osloader is ol, the hash of operating system kernel is ck, the expansion measurement hash of the applications in the node is $\eta[1], \ldots, \eta[n]$. Given the expected measurement value for the measured nodes in high level node is $P = \{hw', ol', ck', \eta[1]', \ldots, \eta[n]'\}$ and the higher level node will compute $V = (hw \& hw') \& (ol \& ol') \& (ck \& ck')$. If the value of V is 0, the status of node is not trusted, and the node will be not allowed to start, otherwise IST is defined as the initial state measurement function IST described as follows:

$$IST = \sum_{i=1}^{n} \eta[i] \& \eta[i]'$$

Given a threshold value I_t, if $IST > I_t$, the measurement for the basic configuration is in line with the security policy, the node can join.

3.3 The Dynamic Trust Measurement Model for Sensing Nodes

In a given sensing network area, the sensing node of the region is $N = \{\eta_1, \eta_2, \ldots, \eta_n\}$ η_π is cluster head node, η_i is ordinary node in the communication range η_π, η_π do the trusted measurement from the dimensions of the l on η_i, the trusted measurement of l dimensions are respectively $M_1(\eta_\pi, \eta_i), M_2(\eta_\pi, \eta_i), \ldots, M_k(\eta_\pi, \eta_i)$. Among $0 \leq M_i(\eta_\pi, \eta_i) \leq 1$, α_i is the weight of each $M_i(\eta_\pi, \eta_i)$, α_i satisfies:

$$0 \leq \alpha_i \leq 1, \ \sum_{i=1}^{l} \alpha_i = 1 \tag{1}$$

Definition 3-1. Suppose that $TM(\eta_\pi, \eta_i, t)$ is the trusted measure function of cluster head node η_π for ordinary node η_i, and $TM(\eta_\pi, \eta_i, t)$ is calculated as follows:

$$TM(\eta_\pi, \eta_i, t) = \sum_{i=1}^{l} \alpha_i M_i(\eta_\pi, \eta_i) \tag{2}$$

According to Eq. (2) represents the trusted measure of η_i, the trusted level of η_i can be confirmed by the calculation result of Eq. (2), the closer the trusted measure of η_i is close to 1, the higher the trusted level of η_π is, the higher the service priority within the communication radius of η_π, which means the priority of η_π receives and processes the data sent by η_i is higher. The trusted measure of η_i is time-dependent, so it is necessary to mark the trusted measure of η_i with the time stamp t.

Definition 3-2. According the calculation result of $TM(\eta_\pi, \eta_i, t)$, k trusted levels can be determined, $(\beta_1, \beta_2, \ldots, \beta_k), 0 \leq \beta_i \leq 1, (i = 1, 2, \ldots, k)$, β_i meets $\beta_1 < \beta_2 < \ldots < \beta_k$ (There are three types of trustworthiness in this chapter: untrustworthy, pending and trusted), suppose $\{sf_1, sf_2, \ldots, sf_k\}$ is a set of service levels of η_i within the communication radius of η_π, then the service level function calculation process is described as follows:

$$\Phi(TM(\eta_\pi, \eta_i, t)) = \begin{cases} sf_m, & \beta_m \leq T(TM(\eta_\pi, \eta_i, t)) \leq 1 \\ sf_m, & \beta_{m-1} \leq T(TM(\eta_\pi, \eta_i, t)) \leq \beta_m \\ \ldots \\ sf_2, & \beta_1 \leq T(TM(\eta_\pi, \eta_i, t)) \leq \beta_2 \\ sf_1, & 0 \leq T(TM(\eta_\pi, \eta_i, t)) \leq \beta_1 \end{cases} \tag{3}$$

$\{sf_1, sf_2, \ldots, sf_k\}$ is determined by the actual need of perceived network, according to Eqs. (2) and (3), η_π can confirm the service level of η_i and then η_π classifies the node service sequence within the communication radius according to node trusted, to make sure the data is trusted.

3.4   The Trust Measurement Function

In order to achieve real-time feedback control of perceived nodes, the upper node of the sensing node needs to monitor the trusted state of its lower node in real time, So it is necessary to make real-time trusted metrics for perceived nodes.

Definition 3-3. Sensing node data transmission state metric function $M_1(\eta_\pi, \eta_i)$.

The main task of a sensing node is to perceive and send data, so its data transmission status is an important indicator of whether its state is trusted, suppose η_π requires η_i to send dr data packets in time ε, η_i sent ds data packets actually (ds $\leq$ N), Then η_π's calculated value for η_i's trusted in the data sending state at time ε is calculated as follows:

$$D_t = ds/dr + 1 \tag{4}$$

The repetition rate of the packet sent by the sensing node is an important basis for judging whether the sensing network is trusted, assume that R is the repetition rate sent by the sensing node data packet, and θ is the malicious node threshold, The closer the R is to θ, the more entrusted the node data transmission status is. The trusted rate of the perceived node data transmission status based on the data packet repetition rate can be described as follows:

$$D_t = \begin{cases} 2 - \lambda^R & R < \theta \\ 0 & other \end{cases} \tag{5}$$

Where $\lambda > 1, \lambda^\theta = 2$, θ is determined by the security policy of the perceived network.

The data transmission delay is also an important indicator of whether the node data transmission status is trusted, Suppose t is the delay when η_i sends data to η_π. If t is less than the delay threshold γ specified in the sensing network, the data transmission state of η_i is trusted. On the contrary, if t is more than the delay threshold γ, the possibility that η_i is a malicious node increases. So the trusted interval of the sensing node data transmission state based on the data transmission delay can be described as follows:

$$D_d = \begin{cases} \rho^{\frac{t-\gamma}{\gamma}}, & t \geq \gamma \\ 1, & other \end{cases} \tag{6}$$

Where ρ and γ θ is determined by the security policy of the perceived network.

Equations 4 to 6 is a trusted measure of the state of data transmission for a time at η_i time, in order to calculate the trusted state of η_i's data transmission status more comprehensive and accurately, need to take a comprehensive look, at a period of time, η_i's data transmission status. Assume in T_w time, η_π requests n times to send data to node η_i, Assume that the measure of the state of the n times data transmissions of η_π to η_i is $\{D_{t1}, D_{t2} \ldots D_{tm}\}$, suppose D_{t1} is the oldest measure of the past, D_{tm} is the measure of the current data transmission status, then $M_1(\eta_\pi, \eta_i)$ can be described as follow:

$$M_1(\eta_\pi, \eta_i) = \begin{cases} \sum_{i=1}^{m} D_{ti}f(i)/i & i \neq 0 \\ 0 & i = 0 \end{cases} \tag{7}$$

$f(i)$ is the time decay function, $f(i) \in [0, 1]$, $f(i)$ can smooth data which at different time by sending State trusted measure. As trust falls over time, the closer the metric to the current moment is, the higher the weight. The time decay function reflects the characteristics of the trust age lag. The time decay function can be described as follows:

$$f(i) = \begin{cases} 1 & i = n \\ f(i-1) = f(i) - \frac{1}{n}, & 1 \leq i \leq n \end{cases} \tag{8}$$

The data transmission behavior trusted computing function proposed in this section based on the time attenuation function has the following advantages:

Risk and trust are interdependent, and trusting an entity is necessarily associated with the risk of failure of trust. Therefore, for the risk behind the perceived node's trusted value, this chapter solves the risk benefit theory in economic theory. According to the value of the function $\Phi(TM(\eta_\pi, \eta_i, t))$, the risk function of the node's trusted measurement value is described as follows:

$$R(\eta_\pi, \eta_i) = \beta_i(1 - \Phi(TM(\eta_\pi, \eta_i, t))) = \Gamma(TM(\eta_\pi, \eta_i, t))(1 - TM(\eta_\pi, \eta_i, t-1)) \tag{9}$$

In the Eq. (9), $\beta_i(1 - \Phi(TM(\eta_\pi, \eta_i, t)))$ is the expected service level of η_i. Similar to the risk benefit theory in economics, the higher the expected service level, the higher the risk of trust η_i, so $R(\eta_\pi, \eta_i)$ is inversely proportional to $\beta_i(1 - \Phi(TM(\eta_\pi, \eta_i, t)))$. $TM(\eta_\pi, \eta_i, t-1)$ is the trusted measure of the last data transmission status by η_π to η_i. The closer the $TM(\eta_\pi, \eta_i, t-1)$ is to the one, the lower the risk is, so $R(\eta_\pi, \eta_i)$ is inversely proportional to $\beta_i(1 - \Phi(TM(\eta_\pi, \eta_i, t)))$.

Definition 3-4. Formula (9) is used to describe the influence of the uncertainty of the data transmission state on the trusted of nodes. Due to the uncertainty of data transmission status, the effect of risk on the transmission state of data of nodes is shown below:

$$M_2(\eta_\pi, \eta_i) = 1 - R(\eta_\pi, \eta_i) \tag{10}$$

According to (9) and (10), $M_2(\eta_\pi, \eta_i)$ considers the impact of risk on the trusted of nodes from two aspects. The first consideration is that η_i is the probability of a malicious node within the radius η_π of the communication. The higher the value of confidence level of η_i, the lower the probability of it being a malicious node; The second consideration is the relationship between service level and risk, the higher the level of service η_i enjoys, the higher the risk of trust η_i. According to (9) and Definition 3-2, $M_2(\eta_\pi, \eta_i)$ is inversely proportional to $R(\eta_\pi, \eta_i)$.

Definition 3-5. If the set of nodes that have interacted with η_i is $\{\eta_{r1}, \eta_{r2}, \ldots, \eta_{rL}\}$, $\eta_\pi \in \{\eta_{r1}, \eta_{r2}, \ldots, \eta_{rL}\}$. Referring to the trust model in human relations, to assess whether a person is trusted, it not only needs to assess whether his own behavior is trusted, but also needs to refer to the trust of their interpersonal counterparts. The confidence level of people whose communicative object is highly trusted and whose communication object is obviously different. Similarly, the trusted measurement value η_i is also affected by its surrounding interaction nodes, so the interactive confidence measure of η_i can be described as follow:

$$M_3(\eta_\pi, \eta_i) = \sum_{j=1}^{L} \upsilon(\eta_{rj}) \cdot M_1(\eta_\pi, \eta_i) / \sum_{j=1}^{L} \upsilon(\eta_{rj}) \tag{11}$$

$\upsilon(\alpha_{rj})$ is the interactive trusted factor function of η_i, and the analytic expression of $\upsilon(\alpha_{rj})$ is as follows:

$$\upsilon(\alpha_{rj}) = \begin{cases} M_1(\eta_\pi, \eta_{rj}) & Hop = 1 \\ \prod_{\chi=1}^{k} M_1(\eta_{\pi i}, \eta_{rj}) & Hop > 1 \end{cases} \tag{12}$$

From (12), if η_{rj} and η_i belong to the same cluster, then the number of hops is 1, so $\upsilon(\alpha_{rj}) = M_1(\eta_\pi, \eta_{rj})$; Otherwise, the number of hops is larger than 1, then $\upsilon(\eta_{rj}) = \prod_{\chi=1}^{k} M_1(\eta_{\pi i}, \eta_{rj})$. At this time, $\upsilon(\eta_{rj})$ is obtained by multiplying the data transmission state confidence metric of each relay node in the calculation communication path. Similar to the trust in human relations, as for direct interaction and after a number of relay interactions, the trust value is obviously different. Equation (11) describes the influence of the communication distance and the number of relay objects on the trusted value of the node interaction, $\upsilon(\eta_{rj})$ clearly reflects the effect of the distance and the number of interacting objects on the reciprocal confidence measurement of η_i.

Definition 3-6. With the increasing application of Internet of Things, the attack on nodes in the perceived layer is endless, and the trusted operation of the sensing nodes is closely related to the trust of the nodes. Therefore, this chapter acts the perceived nodes trusted measure as an important component of node confidence measurement, the evaluation function of the trust of nodes is described as follows:

$$M_4(\eta_\pi, \eta_i) = 1 - \frac{\sum_{Log} L(\eta_\pi, \eta_i)}{Log} \tag{13}$$

In the Eq. (13), $\sum_{Log} L(\eta_\pi, \eta_i)$ represents Log the number of data transmission or interaction failures of η_i in the η_π record, η_π energize the nodes according to the trusted evaluation of η_i. The higher the trust of η_i is, the more trusted η_i is respectively.

Definition 3-7. Node activity degree is used to characterize the stability of running state of nodes in the perceived network. The more interactive objects η_i has, the more the number of successful interactions is and the more trusted the nodes are. The node activity can be described by the following formula:

$$M_5(\eta_\pi, \eta_i) = \frac{\mu(J) + \mu(P)}{2} \tag{14}$$

Among them, $\theta(x) = 1 - \frac{1}{x+\varepsilon}$, J represents the number of objects that interact with η_i, and P represents the total sum of the clusters which interaction nodes belongs that interact with η_i. ε is the adjustment constant of function $\theta(x)$ and satisfies $\varepsilon > 0$. When $\varepsilon \to \infty$, $\theta(x) \to 1$.

Definition 3-8. According to D $M_i(\eta_\pi, \eta_i)$ in the Definitions 3-3–3-7, the information entropy calculation process for the i dimension of η_i is described as follows:

$$H(M_i(\eta_\pi, \eta_i)) = -M_i(\eta_\pi, \eta_i) \log M_i(\eta_\pi, \eta_i) - (1 - X_i(\eta_\pi, \eta_i)) \log(1 - M_i(\eta_\pi, \eta_i)) \tag{15}$$

In the formula (15), $M_i(\eta_\pi, \eta_i)$ represents the confidence level of nodes η_i in a certain metric dimension, $1 - M_i(\eta_\pi, \eta_i)$ represents the entrusted degree of η_i in the ith metric dimension, so formula (15) has two information sources $1 - M_i(\eta_\pi, \eta_i)$ and $M_i(\eta_\pi, \eta_i)$ from the perspective of information entropy. Given trusted measurement function $M_i(\eta_\pi, \eta_i)$, $M_j(\eta_\pi, \eta_i)$ in the two dimensions, $H(M_i(\eta_\pi, \eta_i))$ and $H(M_j(\eta_\pi, \eta_i))$ can be obtained by calculating the information entropy. If $H(M_i(\eta_\pi, \eta_i)) > H(M_j(\eta_\pi, \eta_i))$, it stands that the average uncertainty in this metric dimension is large in this $M_i(\eta_\pi, \eta_i)$ metric dimension. Before the node η_i is measured, the weights of the two metric dimensions are the same.

Definition 3-9. Given different $M_i(\eta_\pi, \eta_i)$, Assuming β_i is the confidence distinction of $M_i(\eta_\pi, \eta_i)$, then the calculation of α_i can be described as follows:

$$\beta_i = \begin{cases} 1 - \frac{1}{\log M} H(X_i(\alpha_\pi, \alpha_i)), & H(X_i(\alpha_\pi, \alpha_i)) > \rho \\ 0, & H(X_i(\alpha_\pi, \alpha_i)) < \rho \end{cases} \tag{16}$$

Given a differentiated degree of confidence, a different metric dimension weight can be obtained:

$$\alpha_i = \beta_i / \sum_{i=1}^{k} \beta_i, i = 1, 2, \ldots, k \tag{17}$$

In Eq. (16), M is the number of stages of rating given in Definition 3-1. According to the formula above, obviously: $0 \le \beta_i \le 1$ and $\sum_{i=1}^{k} \beta_i = 1$ at the same time, the weight of $M_i(\eta_\pi, \eta_i)$ can be obtained according to the Eqs. (16) and (17). If the value of $M_i(\eta_\pi, \eta_i)$ information entropy is less than ρ, it will determined that β_i is 0. And the according to the Eq. (17), its classification weight is 0. This can effectively reduce the risk of perceived networks and improve the perceived network operation of its trust.

So the overall trustworthy measure of the node can be calculated according to Definitions 3-1–3-9:

$$TM(\eta_\pi, \eta_i, t) = \sum_{i=1}^{5} \alpha_i M_i(\eta_\pi, \eta_i) \tag{18}$$

4 Trusted Routing Mechanism of Sensing Layer

4.1 The Calculation of the Available Bandwidth of Any Link Between Nodes

The link measurements in this section place more focus on the microscopic measurement of the network, the emphasis of the measurement is to determine the no-load rate of the link. In order to be able to carry out micro-and accurate measurement of the data transmission link between nodes, this section proposes a method of sending random small packets to detect the status of the link between nodes. The available status for data and link between nodes lies on judgment to time delay of small data packets. The ideal state is that the transmission delay is 0. The measurement process of the data link bandwidth between nodes is described as follows:

1. Node N_i randomly selects a small packet of length l and transports it to node N_{i+1}.
2. And then, the delay of each detection message in the transmission queue $Link_{ii+1}$ is determined according to the feedback time of the small packet.
3. Statistics the number η of data message with a delay of 0 on the link $Link_{ii+1}$ transmission. Let σ be the total number of data packets sent. The idle rate of the link can be calculated as $fr = \eta/\sigma$.
4. Therefore, in the premise of the link bandwidth of a given node N_i and N_j is C_i. The bandwidth that can be used on the link is $available\_C_i = fr \cdot C_i$.

The network bandwidth measurement of the above link is for a direct link connection between the nodes, if N_i to N_j has a data path, but need to go through x segment of data link can be reached, then the available bandwidth of the entire data link at this time depends on the link with the least bandwidth. Assuming that the link can use the minimum bandwidth of the data link is $Link_\varepsilon$. The same message is placed in the two links are next to each other. At this time, the forward link and the queuing delay of the link are related to each other, the front link is $Link_{\varepsilon-1}$, so the focus of the bandwidth can be used in that path is to calculate the link idle rate of $Link_\varepsilon$, End-to-end multi-short available bandwidth can be calculated by the following methods:

1. Node N_i randomly selects a small packet of length l and send it to node N_j.
2. And then, the delay of each detection message in the transmission queue $Link_\varepsilon$ and $Link_{\varepsilon-1}$ is determined according to the feedback time of the small packet.
3. Statistics the number η of data message with a delay of 0 on the link $Link_{ii+1}$ and $Link_{\varepsilon-1}$ transmission. Let σ be the total number of data packets sent. The idle rate of the link can be calculated as $fr = \eta/\sigma$.

4. Therefore, under the premise that the minimum bandwidth of the link in the data path of a given node N_i and N_j is C_m, the bandwidth that can be used in the link is $available\_C_i = fr \cdot C_m$.

The above calculation process is concerned with the message transmission delay and the remaining bandwidth of the link. If there is a data path between any two nodes, then the delay between the two nodes can be calculated. If you need to calculate the specific packet transmission delay, you need to know in advance the queue delay between the two nodes when you want to get the message, and it is necessary to accurately measure the minimum delay of data transmission in the network, that is, the time required to detect the packet sent to the destination in the case where the queuing delay of all packets is 0. When the transmission delay data of the probe packet is obtained, the minimum value is taken as the minimum network transmission delay. It should be noted that in the simulation test environment, due to accurate time synchronization, so the measurement results are accurate. However, in the actual data transmission network, due to the complexity of the network environment, the underlying switch performance differences will cause relatively large error, so it is necessary to have multiple measurements to calculate the corresponding mathematical expectations for correction.

4.2 Adjacent Node Selection Based on the Trusted Measure of Node

In view of the limited computing power and energy of perceived nodes, storage capacity and communication bandwidth are also severely limited, therefore, the choice of relay nodes in the data transmission route according to the existing security mechanism is a significant challenge. The confidence measure of the perceived node is the basis of trusted routing, in this section, we consider a neighbor node selection mechanism based on the node trustworthiness measure in Sect. 3. Since the node trustworthiness value has been described in detail in Sect. 3. In this section we will discusses how to select the next node from the current packet holding node in combination with the rationality of routing.

Assume that the current packet holding a node Se_μ. Assuming that it has passed the bandwidth and data link query, Get a set $\{Se_{r1}, Se_{r2}, \ldots, Se_{rk}\}$ that can reach the destination node sent by the packet and that is adjacent to Se_μ, according to Sect. 3 - node trusted metric model, the calculated value of the calculated node A is calculated by its parent node. In order to ensure the trustworthiness of the data transmission routing relay node, the node can be three types according to its trusted measure value, namely the trusted node, the relay trusted node and the untrusted node, which is defined as follows:

1. Untrusted, under such conditions $0 \leq T(Se_{\mu\pi}, Se_\mu, t) \leq T_0$
2. Relay trusted, meet the conditions of $T_0 \leq T(Se_{\mu\pi}, Se_\mu, t) < T_1$
3. Trusted, at this time $T_1 \leq T(Se_{\mu\pi}, Se_\mu, t) < 1$

A is the cluster head node of the cluster where B is located, $0 \leq T_0 \leq T_1 \leq 1$, The value of T_0, T_1 depends on the degree of rigor of the perceived computing environment requirements for trusted metric, and the most stringent degree is $T_0 = T_1 = 1$.

The choice of the next-hop node in this case is the most restrictive, but usually A does not take such a harsh value.

In order to ensure the trusted of the relay node, a packet holding node Se_μ should try to select a trusted node. Because its neighbor node $\{Se_{r1}, Se_{r2}, \ldots, Se_{rk}\}$ is not all nodes belong to a cluster head node, may be in a different cluster, so the node in the selection process will encounter the following circumstances:

1. Se_{ri} and Node Se_μ are in the same cluster, and Se_{ri} is not a cluster head node
2. Se_{ri} and Node Se_μ are in the same cluster, and Se_{ri} is a cluster head node
3. Se_{ri} and Node Se_μ are not in the same cluster, and Se_{ri} is not a cluster head node
4. Se_{ri} and Node Se_μ are not in the same cluster, and Se_{ri} is a cluster head node

For situation 1, Node Se_μ may query the cluster head node Se_μ of its cluster for the trusted metric of node Se_{ri}. For situation 2, since node Se_{ri} is the cluster head node, then Se_μ can be considered to be unconditionally trusted. For situation 3, Se_{ri} and Node Se_μ do not belong to the same cluster, and Se_{ri} is not a cluster head node, for such a situation, it is necessary to confirm whether Se_{ri} is credible according to the remote certification based on the trusted value in Sect. 4. If it is trusted, put it in the list of trusted nodes, and inquire the cluster where the node Se_{ri} is located and records its credible metrics. If it is not trusted, its measure is recorded. For situation 4, Se_μ and Node Se_{ri} also need to complete the remote certification. The difference is that Se_{ri} is the cluster head node, if Se_μ is not a cluster head node, it cannot be inquired, at this point Se_μ to its cluster head node Se_π query Se_{ri} trusted measure, now the cluster head node Se_π will query its parent-data sink node, if Se_μ is already a cluster head node, it can query the trusted value of A from the higher level data sink node.

4.3   The Energy Calculation Model of Link Between Sensory Nodes

In Sects. 4.1 to 4.2, the calculation of the bandwidth in the routing process of the sensing node and the calculation of the next trusted node of the routing node are discussed, but the remaining node energy also has a significant impact on the selection of trusted routes, therefore, it is necessary to calculate the route from the data source node to the trusted node of the data target node, and then build the trusted route by combining the link bandwidth, the node route and the remaining energy of the sensing node.

The perceived node routing model can be summarized as a undirected graph of the weight $G = (V, A)$. In this formula V represents the collection of all the sensing nodes in the sensor network $V = (V_i, \cdots, V_{k-1}, V_k)$; each sensing node V_i has energy E_i; A represents the set of edges, and each side has its own weight, it is mainly expressed as the energy connecting two nodes. The energy of link (V_i, V_j) can be calculated as follows:

The value of the energy of link (V_i, V_j) is related to the number of V_i and V_j node links and the energy consumed for each bit (The energy consumed by sending a bit is closely related to the distance between V_i and V_j). For link $V_i V_j$, Node V_i may have more than one link, the amount of data that node V_i sends and receives per second is α bit, in link $V_i V_j$, the data that V_i sent per second is μ bit, so the energy that node V_i can use for link V_iV_j is $E_i \times \frac{\mu}{\alpha}$. Likewise, node V_j may have more than one link, the amount of data that node V_j sends and receives per second is β bit, in link V_iV_j, the data that node V_j received per second is η bit, so the energy that node V_j can use for link V_iV_j is $E_j \times \frac{\eta}{\beta}$. Therefore, the energy $E(V_i, V_j)$ of link (V_i, V_j) is described as:

$$E(V_i, V_j) = \begin{cases} E_i \times \frac{\mu}{\alpha}, E_i \times \frac{\mu}{\alpha} < E_j \times \frac{\eta}{\beta} \\ E_j \times \frac{\eta}{\beta}, E_i \times \frac{\mu}{\alpha} \ge E_j \times \frac{\eta}{\beta} \end{cases}.$$

4.4 The Description of the Construction of a Trusted Route

According the calculation of bandwidth, selection of trusted measurable based adjacent node and energy calculation of data transmission route in Sects. 4.2 to 4.3, this section would combine taking bandwidth, trusted and energy to calculate optimal data trusted transmission route. Combining with data diagrams of sensing network, this section will describe the construction process of trusted route. Figure 3 is a schematic diagram of the data of sensing network:

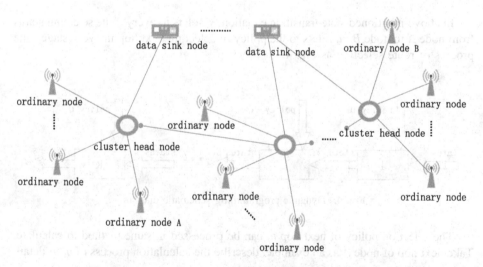

Fig. 3. The schematic diagram of the data of sensing network

As the figure above, the set of data packets generated by sensing node A is $\{D_1, D_2, \ldots, D_n\}$. At time t_i, node A is scheduled to send D_i to node B. After the search for bandwidth and data link, the set of nodes that node B-reachable and node A adjacency is $\{Se_{r1}, Se_{r2}, \ldots, Se_{rk}\}$. Take sensing node A as an example, dynamic planning in operations research can be regarded as a method to address the problem that the analysis for trusted route. The model as following:

$$s_2 = T_1(s_1, u_1)$$
$$s_3 = T_2(s_2, u_2)$$
$$\ldots$$
$$s_{k+1} = T_k(s_k, u_k)$$

There are multiple stages in the process of selecting trusted route, the aim of every stage is to find out the optimal next hop of data-packet-holding node. Every stage has to make decision to control the process of selecting trusted route. The development of decision making in multiple stages depends on state transition equation, after ascertaining the status of trusted route in certain stage, the selection of route in next stage would not be influenced by the status before this stage. In other words, in the process of selection of next hop, previous stage can only influence further stage by current status, this selection therefore have the characteristics of no-after effect. When structuring dynamic planning model to decision making of trusted route, the characteristics of no-aftereffect can be utilized. The state transition equation as following (general format):

$$s_2 = T_1(s_1, u_1)$$
$$s_3 = T_2(s_2, u_2)$$
$$\ldots$$
$$s_{k+1} = T_k(s_k, u_k)$$

In above-mentioned state transition equation, s_i refers to every route selecting status from node A to node B. u_i refers to the policy of selecting next hop in every stage. The process of route selecting as Fig. 4:

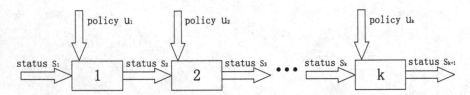

Fig. 4. Dynamic programming schematic diagram

The selection policy of next hop u_i can be processed in same method to calculate. Take next hop of node A as an example, describe the calculation process of u_i in detail.

1. Then calculate the set of trusted compute nodes $\{Se'_1, Se'_2, \ldots, Se'_1\} \subseteq \{Se_{r1}, Se_{r2}, \ldots, Se_{rk}\}$ according to the selection algorithm of the neighboring nodes based on the node confidence measure as discussed in Sect. 4.3, if there is no trusted node, the critical set $\{Se'_1, Se'_2, \ldots, Se'_1\} \subseteq \{Se_{r1}, Se_{r2}, \ldots, Se_{rk}\}$ of the trusted node is output, if there is no credible critical set, calculate $\bar{T} = \frac{1}{k} \sum_{i=1}^{k} T(Se_{ri}, Se_{ri\pi}, t)$, export all nodes that $T(Se_{ri}, Se_{ri\pi}, t) > \bar{T}$ of the set $\{Se'_1, Se'_2, \ldots, Se'_1\} \subseteq \{Se_{r1}, Se_{r2}, \ldots, Se_{rk}\}$.

2. Assume that the bandwidth of the link from node A to any node Se'_{ri} in set $\{Se'_1, Se'_2, \ldots, Se'_1\} \subseteq \{Se_{r1}, Se_{r2}, \ldots, Se_{rk}\}$ is set to $\{C_1, C_2, \ldots, C_l\}$, it is possible to obtain the available bandwidth set $\{available\_C_1, available\_C_2, \ldots, available\_C_l\}$ of node A and node Se'_{ri} according to the link trusted bandwidth formula of 4.1

3. According to the link energy calculation model between sensed nodes in 4.2, and the set of links between node A and node Se'_{ri}, we can calculate the link energy set $\{C_1, C_2, \ldots, C_l\}$, among them $C_i = (A, Se'_{ri})$.

4. According to the set $\{Se'_1, Se'_2, \ldots, Se'_1\} \subseteq \{Se_{r1}, Se_{r2}, \ldots, Se_{rk}\}$, at this moment, assume that the set of trusted measures at node $\{Se'_1, Se'_2, \ldots, Se'_1\}$ is $\{T_1, T_2, \ldots, T_l\}$, the available bandwidth set for A and Node Se_{ri} is $\{available\_C_1, available\_C_2, \ldots, available\_C_l\}$, and the link energy set is $\{E(C_1), E(C_2), \ldots, E(C_l)\}$, The node that the next hop of the sensing node A in the data transmission can calculate $Selelt\_Node_i = \max\{T_i \times E(C_i)/available\_C_i\}$ on the basis of the trusted measure value, $Selelt\_Node_i$ is the optimal index function in the next hop of the strategy trusted route selection process. According to the calculated value of $Selelt\_Node_i$ can be obtained next hop $Se'_i \in \{Se'_1, Se'_2, \ldots, Se'_1\}$ of data transmission routing of node A, so the next hop of the routing in state $s_2 = T_1(s_1, u_1)$ is Se'_i.

5. Because there is more than one link from node $Se'_i \in \{Se'_1, Se'_2, \ldots, Se'_1\}$ to target node B, assume that the set of links is $\{l_1, l_2, \ldots l_m\}$, calculate $Selelt\_Link_i = best\{l_i\}$. $Selelt\_Link_i$ represents the optimal link between node Se'_i and node B. So from node A to the optimal link of node B is $l_{AB} = Selelt\_Node_i + Selelt\_Link_i$. The choice of each hop of the routing node in link $Selelt\_Link$ follows the selection strategy of the next hop node in the trusted route.

Therefore, based on each hop routing strategy u_i, the optimal index function $Selelt\_Node_i$ and the state transition function $s_{k+1} = T_k(s_k, u_k)$ can calculate the optimal trusted route from node A to node B.

Table 1. Experiment parameters

Experimental parameters	Parameter value
Simulation time	1000 s
Spreading area of perceived nodes	200 m * 200 m
Number of perceived nodes	50
Communication range of nodes	50 m
Packet generation interval of node	2 s
Packet length	50 bytes
Supported routing protocol	LEACH, PEGASIS, TEEN
Physical layer supported protocol	IEEE 802.15.4
Untrusted threshold	0.4
Trusted threshold	0.8
Accurate rate of trusted metric value	0.95
Radio of malicious nodes	20%

(*continued*)

Table 1. (*continued*)

Experimental parameters	Parameter value
Energy consumption in circuit	30 nJ/bit
Amplification factor (short distance)	0.0004 pJ/bit/m
Amplification factor (long distance)	5.0 nJ/bit/m
Data fusion overhead	2 nJ/bit/signal Data
Initial energy of data convergence node	256 J
Initial energy of cluster head	64 J
Initial energy of normal node	16 J
Number of cluster head nodes	3 s
Number of cluster head nodes	5
Number of data sinks	2

5 Experimental Simulation

This section uses the NS2 simulation environment on the Ubuntu platform to verify the performance, correctness, and environmental adaptability of the trusted routing mechanism presented in this section. First, 50 perceived nodes are deployed in the 200 m * 200 m area. In this 50 sensor nodes, there are two categories of nodes. One is a normal node, the other is a malicious node. Malicious nodes can launch node hijacking attacks, flood attacks, gray hole attacks and intermittent attacks. Table 1 shows the experimental parameters of this chapter.

According to the description of the above experimental parameters, the distribution of nodes is shown in Fig. 5 below:

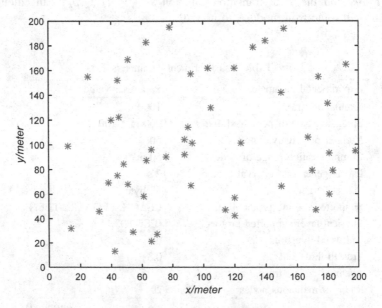

Fig. 5. The distribution of nodes

The experimental content of this section analyses the influence of these attacks on the trusted route proposed in this section by introducing several attacks against the nodes. In the face of various attacks, the efficiency and the safety of the trusted routing model and other sensing nodes model are compared in this chapter.

5.1   Attack Analysis of Malicious Attacks

In order to verify the validity of the proposed route defense attack, the experiment first assumes that the malicious node initiates selective forwarding attacks on the network (when the node as a routing node will intentionally discard at least 30% of the packets or forward all packets to the unrelated node), and then analyze the influence on the success rate of sending packets to the perceived node when using the trusted routing mechanism or not using the mechanism in the face of selective forwarding attacks. The experimental results are shown in Fig. 6. When there is no selective forwarding attack in the sensing network, the average success rate of the data transmission in the sensing network is close to 100%. However, it is assumed that starting from 100 s, some malicious nodes began to selectively forward attacks without using a trusted routing mechanism. Through Fig. 6, it can be found that the average success rate of node data transmission began to quickly reduce. If the trusted routing mechanism proposed in this section is used, it can be seen from Fig. 6 that the average success rate of the data transmitted by the sensing node is gradually higher compared with not using the trusted

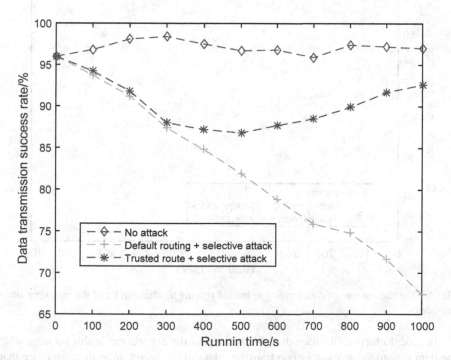

Fig. 6. The success rate of data sending in trusted routing mechanism faced the selective transmit attack

routing mechanism. This is because the use of trusted routing mechanism can ensure that each node could select trusted. The trusted confirmation of the node can effectively reduce the impact of selective forwarding attacks.

In addition, the real-time operation and the threshold of node's trusted measure value is also an important factor in ensuring that the path is trusted. Comparing the selection of two different trusted value (for example, 0.8 and 0.7), the trusted value threshold of higher nodes could use a more stringent standard to select a trusted next hop and better discover malicious nodes. Theoretically, the setting of higher trusted value thresholds can lead to higher success rates for packet forwarding. However, in the actual knowledge network, according to Sect. 3, the assessment of trustworthy measurement model for the trust of the node cannot ensure that the node is 100% trusted. The trusted value threshold is too high, which makes the node trusted neighbor choice difficult and is not conducive to the next hop choice of trusted routing. The threshold of the trusted value of the node needs to be determined according to the deployment environment of the sensing network. As shown in Figs. 7 and 8, the malicious nodes launch node hijacking attacks and witch attacks, the simulation results is similar. The specific experimental results are as follows:

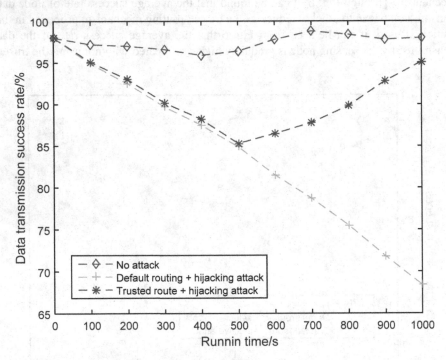

Fig. 7. The success rate of data sending in trusted routing mechanism faced the hijacking attack of nodes

In order to further illustrate the effectiveness of the experiment in this section, when the data transmission source node transmits data to the target node through more than one relay node, it needs to calculate the trusted measurement value of each relay node,

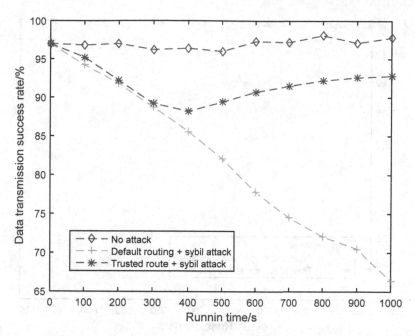

Fig. 8. The success rate of data sending in trusted routing mechanism faced the sybil attack

so it is possible to calculate the trusted measurement value of the entire data transmission path based on the trusted measure of the nodes on the entire data transmission path. In general, the trusted value of the node does not have a transfer relationship. In other words, the trusted measurement value cannot increase with the data transmission path. That is to say, the trusted measurement value of the data transmission path should not be greater than that of the relay node. The data destination node should be treated as an entity with a trusted measurement value of 1 because the destination node is not trusted and the trusted route calculation is meaningless. Since the trusted measurement value between nodes are independent of each other, the trusted measurement value of the data transmission path can be defined as follows:

$$Trust(r) = \sqrt{\prod_{i=1}^{m} T_{sei}} \qquad (20)$$

Among them, r represents the data transmission path from the source node to the target node and T_{sei} represents the trusted degree of the relay node between the source node and the target node. Figures 8, 9 and 10 show that the network does not have any malicious attacks and the trusted value of data transmission path will not change, but when node initiates a forward attack, a node hijacking attack, and a witch attack in a sensing network environment, the trusted metric value drops significantly in the transmission path without using a trusted routing mechanism. After using of trusted routing mechanism presented in this section, the trusted measurement value of the path changes less, which can effectively protect that the data transmission is trusted.

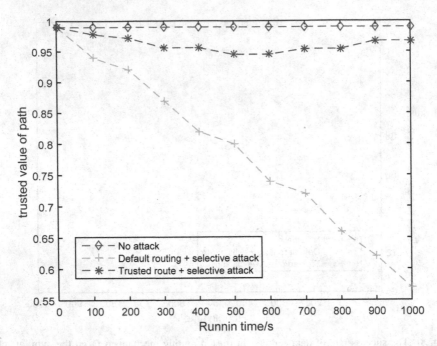

Fig. 9. The change of trusted measurement value in trusted transmission route faced the selective transmit attack

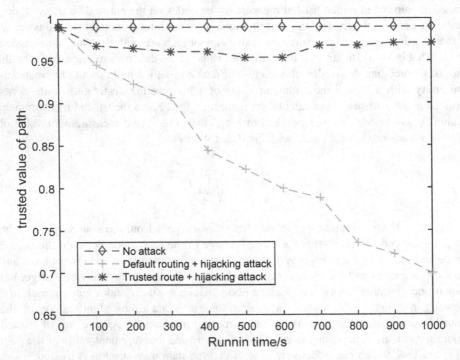

Fig. 10. The change of trusted measurement value in trusted transmission route faced the hijack attack of nodes

From the Figs. 9, 10 and 11 which demonstrates the changes of trusted metric value of data transmission path, the trusted routing mechanism designed in this section is better against malicious node, which can effectively protect the data transmission.

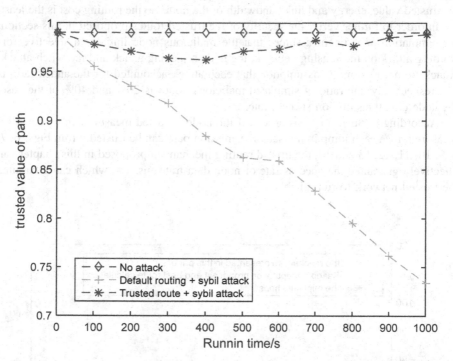

Fig. 11. The change of trusted metric value when data transmission path are in face of the witch attacks

5.2 Security Comparison

In addition to the traditional routing mechanism of the sensing layer node, the routing protocol adopting the additional security mechanism will increase the energy consumption in the data transmission process. The route cost becomes the key factor that needs to be considered when designing the sensing layer routing protocol. The trusted routing mechanism proposed in this section takes full account of the trusted value of the node, the available bandwidth of the link, and the energy of the communication link. The simulation experiment will first compare the trusted routing scheme in this section with the path calculation scheme based on the least route in the literature [22] based on the best route and reputation broadcasting scheme and the literature [23]. By analyzing their respective performance, comparing the energy consumption and safety characteristics between the schemes. As can be seen from Figs. 6, 7, 8, 9, 10, 11 and 12, the literature [22] based on the best routing and reputation broadcast program due to the need to frequently confirm the best path, so the data packet repeat transmission rate is high, with the number of adjacent nodes increased, the routing establishment time is far higher than other programs. Literature [23] program routing overhead is not the introduction of credit broadcast, so the lower cost, but the reliability of its route cannot guarantee. The scheme proposed in this chapter uses dynamic programming method to calculate each hop of the route, so theoretically every hop is the best node to balance the trusted value, energy and link bandwidth of the node, so the routing cost is the least.

In order to further verify the security of the trusted routes proposed in this section, the simulation experiment assumes that the malicious node initiates a selective forwarding attack on the sensing network, the node hijacking attack and the witch attack. Attack from 100 s on the assumption that each attack accounted for the attack ratio is 1/3, respectively, the ratio of simulated malicious nodes is 20% and 40% of the case, the node data transmission success rate.

According to Sect. 3 of this article, if the node's trusted measure can be correctly measured, then each jump in the data transmission path can be trusted. From Figs. 6, 7, 8, 9, 10, 11, 12, 13 and 14, the trusted routing mechanism proposed in this chapter can effectively guarantee the success rate of node data transmission, which can guarantee the trusted network to run reliably.

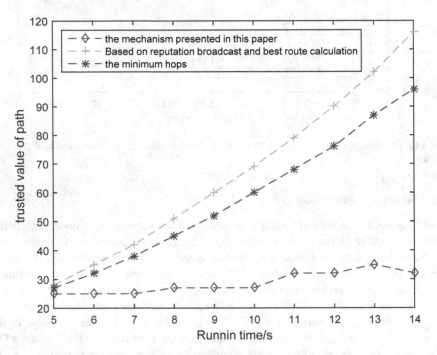

Fig. 12. Time comparison chart of route establishment

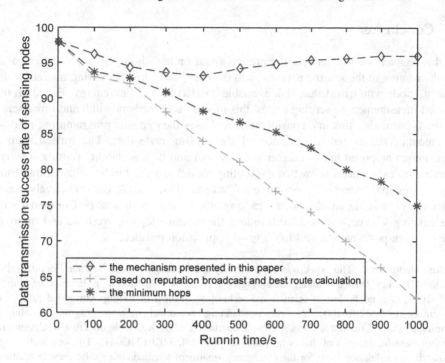

Fig. 13. When the malicious node accounts for 20%, the node data transmission success rate

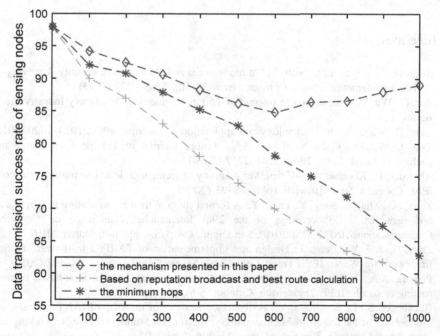

Fig. 14. When the malicious node accounts for 40%, the node sends the data success rate

6 Conclusion

In this chapter, we first analyze the present situation and shortcomings of the research on the routing of the sensing network, and then propose a trusted routing model for the sensing node with trust value, link available bandwidth and link energy. Based on the trusted measurement of sensing nodes, this model takes the bandwidth and link energy of the transmission link into consideration and uses the dynamic programming method to calculate the trusted transmission of the sensing node data. The trusted routing mechanism proposed in this chapter is a low cost and high scalability routing scheme. Simulation experiments show that the routing model proposed in this chapter has good anti-aggression, extensive environmental adaptability, and it can effectively resist selective forwarding attacks, node hijacking attacks and witch attacks. Compared with the existing scheme, the model can reduce the communication overhead and improve the network performance, and has a good application prospect.

Acknowledgments. This work was supported by the National Natural Science Foundation of China (The key trusted running technologies for the sensing nodes in Internet of things: 61501007, General Project of science and technology project of Beijing Municipal Education Commission: KM201610005023, the outstanding personnel training program of Beijing municipal Party Committee Organization Department (The Research of Trusted Computing environment for Internet of things in Smart City: 2014000020124G041). The key technology research and validation issue for the emergency treatment telemedicine public service platform which integrates the military and civilian and bases on the broadband wireless networks (No. 2013ZX03006001-005), the issue belongs to Major national science and technology projects.

References

1. Romana, R., Zhoua, J., Lopezb, J.: On the features and challenges of security & privacy in distributed Internet of Things. Comput. Netw. **57**(10), 2266–2279 (2013)
2. Wu, G., Wu, Y.: Introduction to Internet of Things Engineering. Machinery Industry Press, Beijing (2012)
3. Qian, Z., Wang, Y.: IoT technology and application. J. Electron. **40**(5), 1023–1029 (2012)
4. Tsai, C.-W., Lai, C.-F., Vasilakos, A.V.: Future Internet of Things: open issues and challenges. Wirel. Netw. **20**(8), 2201–2217 (2014)
5. Abusalah, L., Khokhar, A., Guizani, M.: A survey of secure mobile ad hoc routing protocols. IEEE Commun. Surv. Tutorials **10**(4), 78–93 (2008)
6. Zhang, C., Zhu, X., Song, Y., Fang, Y.: A formal study of trust-based routing in wireless ad hoc networks. In: Proceedings of the 29th International Conference on Computer Communications (INFOCOM 2010), San Diego, CA, USA, pp. 1–9, March 2010
7. Zhan, G., Shi, W., Deng, J.: Design and implementation of TARF: a trust-aware routing framework for WSNs. IEEE Trans. Dependable Secure Comput. **9**(2), 184–197 (2012)
8. Pirzada, A.A., McDonald, C., Datta, A.: Performance comparison of trust-based reactive routing protocols. IEEE Trans. Mob. Comput. **5**(6), 695–710 (2006)
9. Buchegger, S., Le Boudec, J.-Y.: Performance analysis of the CONFIDANT protocol. In: Proceedings of the 3rd ACM International Symposium on Mobile Ad Hoc Networking and Computing, Lausanne, Switzerland, pp. 226–236, June 2002

10. Garcia-Luna-Aceves, J.J., Spohn, M.: Source-tree routing in wireless networks. In: Proceedings of the 7th International Conference on Network Protocols, Toronto, Canada, pp. 273–282, October 1999
11. Paris, S., Nita-Rotaru, C., Martignon, F., Capone, A.: EFW: a cross-layer metric for reliable routing in wireless mesh networks with selfish participants. In: Proceedings of the 2011 IEEE INFOCOM, Shanghai, China, pp. 576–580, April 2011
12. Wolf, W.: Cyber-physical systems. Embedded Comput. **42**(3), 88–89 (2009)
13. Bhargava, B., Wu, X., Lu, Y., Wang, W.: Integrating heterogeneous wireless technologies: a Cellular Aided Mobile Ad Hoc Network (CAMA). Mob. Netw. Appl. **9**(4), 393–408 (2004)
14. Ge, Y., Lamont, L., Villasenor, L.: Hierarchical OLSR - a scalable proactive routing protocol for heterogeneous ad hoc networks. In: IEEE International Conference on Wireless and Mobile Computing, Networking and Communications (WiMob 2005), pp. 17–23 (2005)
15. Dong, P., Qin, Y., Zhang, H.: Research on universal network supporting pervasive services. J. Electron. **35**(4), 599–606 (2007)
16. Yang, D., Li, S., Wang, B., Zhang, H.: New transport layer architecture for pervasive service. J. Comput. Sci. **32**(3), 359–370 (2009)
17. Liu, F., Zhang, K., Zhang, H.: Low computational load anonymous routing protocol for ad-hoc networks. Comput. Sci. **38**(11), 48–53 (2012)
18. Helmy, A.: Small worlds in wireless networks. IEEE Commun. Lett. **7**(10), 490–492 (2003)
19. Latvakoski, J.: Towards hierarchical routing in small world wireless networks. In 2009 Fifth International Conference on Wireless and Mobile Communications, pp. 322–327 (2009)
20. Cavalcanti, D., Agrawal, D., Kelner, J., Sadok, D.: Exploiting the small-world effect to increase connectivity in wireless ad hoc networks. In: Telecommunications and Networking-ICT 2004, pp. 1–6 (2004)
21. Helmy, A., Garg, S., Nahata, N., Pamu, P.: CARD: a Contact-based Architecture for Resource Discovery in wireless ad hoc networks. Mob. Netw. Appl. **10**(1), 99–113 (2005)
22. Almasri, M., Elleithy, K., Bushang, A., Alshinina, R.: TERP: a Trusted and Energy Efficient Routing Protocol for wireless sensor networks. In: Proceedings of the 2013 IEEE/ACM 17th International Symposium on Distributed Simulation and Real Time Applications, Delft, Netherlands, pp. 207–214, October 2013
23. Zahariadis, T., Trakadas, P., Leligou, H.C.: A novel trust-aware geographical routing scheme for wireless sensor networks. Wireless Pers. Commun. **69**(2), 805–826 (2013)

An Efficient ID-Based Mutual Authentication and Key Agreement Protocol for Mobile Multi-server Environment Without a Trusted Registration Center and ESL Attack

Wei Li[1(✉)], Xue-lian Li[1], Jun-tao Gao[2], and Hai-yu Wang[1]

[1] School of Mathematics and Statistics,
Xidian University, Xi'an, Shaanxi Province, China
liwei3013@126.com, xuelian202@163.com, slimshady225@163.com
[2] School of Telecommunications engineering,
Xidian University, Xi'an, Shaanxi Province, China
jtgao@mail.xidian.edu.cn

Abstract. As the rapid development of Internet technology, more and more ID-based mutual authentication and key agreement (ID-MAKA) protocols for mobile multi-server environment have been proposed. However, almost all ID-MAKA schemes for multi-server architecture are based on a trusted registration center (RC). In the real world, RC may record and leak the user or server registration information. Through careful analysis, we found that a large number of related protocols are insecure under RC disclosure registration information (RCDRI) attack. At the same time, these protocols are likely to be attacked by ephemeral secret leakage (ESL) in view of the computing power of mobile clients. To solve the above problems, we propose a new ID-MAKA protocol for mobile multi-server that uses self-certified public key (SCPK) cryptography to achieve resistance to RCDRI attack and ESL attack. Because our scheme is based on an untrusted RC, the adversary has the ability to obtain the registration information from RC. In view of the above feature, we demonstrate the security of our scheme in a more robust security model, where the adversary has more ability. Finally, compared with previously proposed schemes, we show that our protocol has a high efficiency. Taking into account the security and efficiency, our protocol is more suitable for mobile clients.

Keywords: ESL attack · ID-based · RCDRI attack · No trusted center · Mobile device · Self-certified public key

1 Introduction

In recent years, handheld and wearable mobile devices are widely used in many cases, such as online shopping, online banking transaction and file sharing. Because a large number of clients have access to remote servers through public

© Springer Nature Singapore Pte Ltd. 2017
M. Xu et al. (Eds.): CTCIS 2017, CCIS 704, pp. 348–369, 2017.
https://doi.org/10.1007/978-981-10-7080-8_24

channels, identity authentication technique is required to ensure the legitimacy of clients for protecting resources from unauthorized usages. On the other hand, servers must prove themselves to users in order to protect users from being spoofed by fake servers. After mutual authentication, the client and the remote server compute to produce a mutual session key, which will be used for secure information exchange between them in subsequent communication.

To achieve this goal, in 1981, Lamport first proposed an authentication protocol based on one-hash function [1]. Later, various single-server authentication systems [2–12] and multi-server authentication systems [14–16, 18–20, 22–30] have been proposed. As the Internet user exponential growth, the single-server structure is not suitable for practical applications. In order to meet the actual demands, mutual authentication and key agreement (MAKA) protocols for multi-server environment are studied widely. In general, there are three types of MAKA for multi-server situation, namely: password-based protocols, public-key based protocols and ID-based protocols. In the password-based schemes, servers need to maintain the password table. If an attacker finds the servers vulnerability, he can get the private key information. For the public-key based schemes, there must be a public key infrastructure to maintain and manage each user's public key certificate. In 1984, Shamir pointed out the shortcomings of using the traditional public key encryption system [13]. Therefore, in this paper we only concern with designing ID-based MAKA schemes for multi-server environment.

1.1 Related Works

In 2004, Juang [14] proposed a MAKA protocol for multi-server architecture by using hash function and symmetric key cryptosystem. In the same year, Chang et al. [15] pointed out that Juang's protocol lacks efficiency. In order to solve the problem of efficiency, they proposed a more efficient MAKA scheme for multi-server environment, but in their scheme RC and servers share the same system private key. This feature will undoubtedly cause many security vulnerabilities. Based on this issue, in 2008, Tsai [16] proposed a MAKA protocol for multi-server environment by using hash functions, but Lee pointed out that the protocol is vulnerable to impersonation attack by users [17].

Since many previous protocols did not provide anonymity, in order to solve this problem, Geng et al. [18] and Liao et al. [19] proposed dynamic ID-MAKA schemes for multi-server environment, respectively. Later on, Hsiang and Shih [20] found that the protocol in [19] is vulnerable to insider attack, masquerade attack, server spoofing attack and is not reparable. To remedy these flaws, they proposed an improvement on the scheme in [19]. However, in 2009, Chuang et al. [21] analyzed that Geng et al. [18] suffers from a user-spoofing attack and Hsiang et al. [20] is vulnerable to insider attack and a server-spoofing server attack. After that, in 2011, Lee et al. [22] pointed out that Hsiang et al.'s protocol [20] does not provide mutual authentication and suffers from masquerade attack and server spoofing attack. To overcome these weaknesses, Lee et al. proposed an improvement on Hsiang and Shih's protocol. Later, Li et al. [23] pointed out that the scheme of Lee et al. is still insecure under the forgery attack and server spoofing attack and cannot provide proper authentication. In order to overcome these weaknesses, they also proposed an ID-MAKA for multi-server environment. In the subsequent study, Zhao et al. [24] found that the scheme in [23] is vulnerable to the stolen smart card and offline dictionary attack, replay attack, impersonation attack and server spoofing attack.

In 2012, Chuang and Tseng [25] proposed a provably secure ID-based MAKA protocol based on the elliptic curve cryptography (ECC), bilinear pairing and ID-based encryption. Because of the low efficiency of Chuang et al.'s protocol, in 2014, Han and Zhu [26] proposed an improved ID-based scheme for multi-server environment by using ECC to achieve better performance. However, in the same year, Islam [27] pointed out that most of the above protocols are vulnerable to the ephemeral secret leakage (ESL) attack and designed a new ID-MAKA protocol for multi-server architecture which can resist the ESL attack. Since Islam's scheme needs quartic bilinear pairing leading to inefficiency, Tseng et al. [11], as well as Tsai et al. [12] respectively proposed more efficient ID-MAKA protocols in 2015, but their schemes do not apply to multi-server environment. In 2016, Tseng, Huang and Tsai et al. [28] proposed a more efficient ID-MAKA protocol for multi-server environment to solve the problem of user/server revocation. Unfortunately, as they described in the paper, the protocol did not reach the ESL security. In the same year, Wang et al. [29] also proposed a MAKA protocol for multi-server environment and claimed that their scheme can achieve higher efficiency and withstand various security attacks. Recently, Reddy et al. [30] pointed out that Wang et al. protocol's users are sharing personal identifiable information with the servers during the registration and authentication process, which will cause a series of security issues. However, after careful study, we found that most of the ID-MAKA schemes discussed above are insecure under RCDRI attack or ESL attack. In Tables 1 and 2 below, we summarize the resistance of the above schemes to ESL and RCDRI attacks.

Table 1. About resistance to RCDRI attack

Schemes	[14]	[15]	[16]	[18]	[19]	[20]	[22]	[25]	[26]	[27]	[28]	[30]
C-RCDRI	No	No	No	Yes	No	Yes	Yes	No	No	No	No	Yes
S-RCDRI	No	No	No	No	No	No	No	No	No	No	No	No
Env	Multi	Multi	Multi	Multi	Multi	Multi	Multi	Multi	Multi	Multi	Multi	Multi

Table 2. About resistance to ESL attack

Schemes	[5]	[10]	[18]	[24]	[25]	[26]	[28]	[29]
ESL	No	No	No	No	No	No	No	No
Env	Single	Single	Multi	Multi	Multi	Multi	Multi	Multi

1.2 Contributions

From Tables 1 and 2, we found that most of the schemes are unable to resist the joint attack of RCDRI and ESL, and even some of them could not resist any of the RCDRI or ESL attacks. In order to address the above mentioned weaknesses and achieve complete security feature, it is very necessary for designing an ID-MAKA for multi-server without a trusted center. In this paper, we propose an RCDRI attack-free and ESL attack-free ID-MAKA scheme by using ECC, bilinear pairing [31], SCPK [32] for mobile multi-server architecture. In short, our protocol based on SCPK not only needs to provide an ID when the user/server registers, but also submits their secret values of the packaging. During mutual authentication and key agreement phase, only the user/server holding the secret value and private key distributed by the RC can complete the phase. Based on the above characteristics, our protocol can resist RCDRI attack. On the other hand, in order to achieve better security and more practical, our scheme also achieve security under the ESL attack. After rigorous security analysis and performance comparison, it is confirmed that our scheme achieves complete security requirements and has a high efficiency than the existing related schemes. These properties make it more suitable for mobile devices.

The rest of the paper is organized as follows. The basic knowledge will be introduced in Sect. 2. Section 3, proposes our protocol. The security model and proof are presented in Sect. 4. Section 5 compares the security and efficiency with the same type schemes. Section 6 gives the conclusions.

2 Preliminaries

Let G_1 be a cyclic additive group of prime order q, which is a subgroup of the group of points on elliptic curve over a finite field F_q, and G_2 be a cyclic multiplicative group of the same order q. A bilinear pairing is a map $e : G_1 \times G_1 \to G_2$ if the following properties hold.

- Bilinear: we have $e(aP, bQ) = e(P, Q)^{ab}$, for all $a, b \in Z_q^*$ and $P, Q \in G_1$.
- Non-degeneracy: $e(P, P) \neq 1_{G_2}$, for some $P \in G_1$.
- Computability: There must be an efficient algorithm to compute $e(P, Q)$ for all $P, Q \in G_1$.

The map e can be obtained either from the modified Weil pairing or from Tate pairing over a finite field [31]. In the following, we define two hard mathematical problems and assumptions.

Definition 1 (Computational Diffie-Hellman (CDH) Problem). *Given* (P, aP, bP), *where* $P \in G_1$ *and* $a, b \in Z_q^*$, *it is difficult to compute* abP *within polynomial time.*

Definition 2 (Collision Attack Assumption (k-CCA) Problem). *Given* $P \in G_1, sP$, $\{h_1, h_2, ..., h_k \in Z_q^*\}$ *and* $\{\frac{1}{s+h_1}P, \frac{1}{s+h_2}P, ..., \frac{1}{s+h_k}P\}$, *it is difficult to compute* $\frac{1}{s+h}P$ *for some* $h \notin \{h_1, h_2, ..., h_k\}$ *within polynomial time [33].*

3   The Proposed Protocol

In this section, we propose a new ID-MAKA scheme for multi-server environment by using elliptic curve, SCPK and bilinear paring. The proposed protocol can be divided into three phases: setup, extract, and mutual authentication and key agreement. The detailed description of the proposed scheme is follows:

3.1   Setup

After entering the security parameter l, we take the following actions:

1. RC chooses an l-bits prime q and the tuple $(F_q, E/F_q, G_q, P)$, where G_q is a q-order additive subgroup of the group of points on an elliptic curve over a finite field F_q and P is a generator of G_q.
2. RC picks the master private key $x \in Z_q^*$ and computes the public key

$$P_{pub} = xP.$$

3. RC selects a bilinear pairing $e : G_q \times G_q \to G_m$, where G_m is cyclic multiplicative group of the same order q and seven secure one-way hash functions

$$H_0 : \{0,1\}^* \to Z_q^*, H_1 : \{0,1\}^* \to Z_q^*, H_2 : \{0,1\}^* \to Z_q^*,$$
$$H_3 : \{0,1\}^* \to Z_q^*, H_4 : \{0,1\}^* \to Z_q^*, H_5 : \{0,1\}^* \to Z_q^*,$$
$$H_6 : \{0,1\}^* \to Z_q^*.$$

4. RC computes $e(P, P) = g \in G_m$.
5. RC publishes

$$\Omega = (F_q, E/F_q, G_q, G_m, P, P_{pub}, H_0, H_1, H_2, H_3, H_4, H_5, H_6, e)$$

as system parameters.

3.2   Extract

At this phase, user registration and server registration are based on self-certified public key (SCPK) [31]. Extraction can be divided into the server registration and user registration.

Extraction Phase for the Server. RC inputs system parameters, the master key, a server's $ID_{sj}(1 \leq j \leq m)$ and the server's secret packaging value $V_{sj} = s_{sj}P$, then computes the private key for the corresponding server.

1. In this phase, the server S_j chooses a desired secret value s_{sj}, then computes $V_{sj} = s_{sj}P$ and submits (V_{sj}, ID_{sj}) to RC.
2. RC selects a random $y_{sj} \in Z_q^*$, then computes

$$Y_{sj} = y_{sj}P, h_{(sj,0)} = H_0(ID_{sj}, (Y_{sj} + V_{sj})),$$

$$d_{sj} = (y_{sj} + h_{(sj,0)}x) mod q.$$

3. RC delivers (d_{sj}, Y_{sj}) to S_j through an out of band (secure) channel.

Upon receiving d_{sj} and Y_{sj}, the S_j server can validate the private key by checking whether the equation

$$d_{sj}P = Y_{sj} + H_0(ID_{sj}, (Y_{sj} + V_{sj}))P_{pub}$$

holds. If the equation holds, the private key is valid and vice versa.

Extraction Phase for the User. Client registration is different from server-side registration. According to the different requirements and validity periods [25–27], there are two different scenarios.

1. Long validity period: in this situation, a user $U_i(1 \leq i \leq n)$ has a long validity period. In order to manage member revocation, RC maintains an ID revocation list (IDRL).
2. Anonymity and short validity period: In this case, a user $U_i(1 \leq i \leq n)$ can be anonymous login server and then access to resources.

For scenario 1

1. A U_i selects a desired secret value $s_{ui} \in Z_q^*$ and computes $V_{ui} = s_{ui}P$, then submits (V_{ui}, ID_{ui}) to RC.
2. RC picks a random $y_{ui} \in Z_q^*$ and computes

$$Y_{ui} = y_{ui}P, h_{(ui,1)} = H_1(ID_{ui}, (Y_{ui} + V_{ui}), validity\ period),$$

$$d_{ui} = (y_{ui} + h_{(ui,1)}x)mod q.$$

3. RC delivers $(d_{ui}, Y_{ui}, validity\ period)$ to U_i through an out of band (secure) channel.

Upon receiving d_{ui}, Y_{ui} and $validity\ period$, the U_i can validate the private key by checking whether the equation

$$d_{ui}P = Y_{ui} + H_1(ID_{ui}, (Y_{ui} + V_{ui}), validity\ period)P_{pub}$$

holds. If the equation holds, the private key is valid and vice versa.

For scenario 2

Because the temporary registration situation faces the following problem, if RC does not check the user ID information, the attacker may have the opportunity to initiate the denial of service (DoS) attack. In order to prevent the DoS attack on RC while ensuring anonymous characteristics, we improved the anonymous user registration based on the literature [12], so that only a legitimate ID user can complete the registration.

1. A user U_i selects a random $a \in Z_q^*$ and a secret value $s_{ui} \in Z_q^*$, then U_i computes

$$F_{ui} = H_5(ID_{ui})P + P_{pub}, A_{ui} = (a + s_{ui})P, CID_{ui} = ID_{ui} \oplus H_6(A_{ui}),$$

$$V_{ui} = s_{ui}P, B_{ui} = (a + s_{ui})F_{ui}.$$

Finally U_i submits anonymous request $(CID_{ui}, B_{ui}, H_5(ID_{ui}), V_{ui})$ to RC through an open channel.

2. On receiving $(CID_{ui}, B_{ui}, H_5(ID_{ui}), V_{ui})$, RC computes

$$A_{ui} = (x + H_5(ID_{ui}))^{-1}B_{ui}, ID_{ui} = CID_{ui} \oplus H_6(A_{ui}).$$

Then RC checks the legitimacy of ID, if the ID is an arbitrarily string, RC refuses to register, otherwise; turn to the next step.
3. RC picks a random $y_{ui} \in Z_q^*$ and computes

$$Y_{ui} = y_{ui}P, h_{(ui,1)} = H_1(CID_{ui}, (Y_{ui} + V_{ui}), validity\ period),$$

$$d_{ui} = (y_{ui} + h_{(ui,1)}x)modq.$$

4. RC delivers $(d_{ui}, Y_{ui}, validity\ period)$ to U_i through an out of band (secure) channel.

Upon receiving d_{ui}, Y_{ui} and $validity\ period$, the U_i can validate the private key by checking whether the equation

$$d_{ui}P = Y_{ui} + H_1(CID_{ui}, (Y_{ui} + V_{ui}), validity\ period)P_{pub}$$

holds. If the equation holds, the private key is valid and vice versa. At this point, the user can use the anonymous CID_{ui} login server.

3.3 Mutual Authentication and Key Agreement Phase

At this phase scenario 1 and scenario 2 are identical except the transmitted identity. For simplicity, in this section, we use the client U_i with the identity ID_{ui} throughout this phase. Without loss of generality, we assume that the client U_i wants to log in the remote server S_j with the identity ID_{sj}. This phase is described as follows (Refer to Fig. 1):

1. User U_i randomly selects $r_{ui} \in Z_q^*$ and a current timestamp T_{ui}. Then, U_i computes $M_{ui} = (s_{ui} + r_{ui})P$,

$$h_{(ui,2)} = H_2(P_{pub}, ID_{ui}, ID_{sj}, V_{ui}, Y_{ui}, M_{ui}, T_{ui}),$$

$$V = \frac{1}{s_{ui} + d_{ui} + h_{(ui,2)}}P.$$

Finally, user U_i sends $(V, V_{ui}, Y_{ui}, ID_{ui}, M_{ui}, T_{ui}, validity\ period)$ to server S_j.
2. Upon receiving $(V, V_{ui}, Y_{ui}, ID_{ui}, M_{ui}, T_{ui}, validity\ period)$ at time T'_{ui}. S_j checks whether $validity\ period$ is overdue or not, whether $T'_{ui} - T_{ui} \leq \Delta T_{ui}$ holds, whether $ID_{ui} \in IDRL$ and then whether

$$e(V, h_{(sj,2)}P + V_{ui} + P_{ui}) = e(P, P) = g$$

where $h_{(sj,2)}$ and P_{ui} are

$$h_{(sj,2)} = H_2(P_{pub}, ID_{ui}, ID_{sj}, V_{ui}, Y_{ui}, M_{ui}, T_{ui}),$$

$$P_{ui} = Y_{ui} + h_{(sj,1)}P_{pub}, h_{(sj,1)} = H_1(ID_{ui}, (Y_{ui} + V_{ui}), validity\ period).$$

If any condition is not satisfied, S_j stops the session; otherwise, continue to the next step.

User		Server

$r_{ui} \leftarrow Z_q^*$ and T_{ui}
$M_{ui} = (s_{ui} + r_{ui})P$
$h_{(ui,2)} = H_2(P_{pub}, ID_{ui}, ID_{sj}, V_{ui}, Y_{ui}, M_{ui}, T_{ui})$
$V = \dfrac{1}{s_{ui} + d_{ui} + h_{(ui,2)}}P$

$$(V, V_{ui}, Y_{ui}, ID_{ui}, M_{ui}, T_{ui}, \textbf{\textit{validity period}})$$
$$\longrightarrow$$

Check T_{ui}, ***validity period***, ID_{ui}
$h_{(sj,1)} = H_1(ID_{ui}, (Y_{ui} + V_{ui}), \textbf{\textit{validity period}})$.
$P_{ui} = Y_{ui} + h_{(sj,1)}P_{pub}$
$h_{(sj,2)} = H_2(P_{pub}, ID_{ui}, ID_{sj}, V_{ui}, Y_{ui}, M_{ui}, T_{ui})$
$e(V, h_{(sj,2)}P + V_{ui} + P_{ui})? = g$
$r_{sj} \leftarrow Z_q^*$ and T_{sj}
$M_{sj} = (s_{sj} + r_{sj})P$
$R_{sj} = (d_{sj} + s_{sj})M_{ui}$
$\textbf{\textit{Auth}} = H_3(P_{pub}, ID_{ui}, ID_{sj}, M_{sj}, M_{ui}, R_{sj})$
$K_{ji} = (s_{sj} + r_{sj})M_{ui}$
$SK_{ji} = H_4(ID_{ui}, ID_{sj}, M_{ui}, M_{sj}, K_{ji}, P_{pub}, R_{sj})$.

$$(Y_{sj}, ID_{sj}, \textbf{\textit{Auth}}, M_{sj}, V_{sj}, T_{sj})$$
$$\longleftarrow$$

Check T_{sj}, ID_{sj}
$P_{sj} = Y_{sj} + H_0(ID_{sj}, (Y_{sj} + V_{sj}))P_{pub}$
$R_{ui} = (s_{ui} + r_{ui})(V_{sj} + P_{sj})$
$H_3(P_{pub}, ID_{ui}, ID_{sj}, M_{sj}, M_{ui}, R_{ui})? = \textbf{\textit{Auth}}$
$K_{ij} = (s_{ui} + r_{ui})M_{sj}$
$SK_{ij} = H_4(ID_{ui}, ID_{sj}, M_{ui}, M_{sj}, K_{ij}, P_{pub}, R_{ui})$

Fig. 1. Mutual authentication and key agreement phase

3. Server S_j chooses an integer $r_{sj} \in Z_q^*$ and a current timestamp T_{sj}. Then, S_j computes the response values $M_{sj} = (s_{sj} + r_{sj})P$, $R_{sj} = (d_{sj} + s_{sj})M_{ui}$ and $Auth = H_3(P_{pub}, ID_{ui}, ID_{sj}, M_{sj}, M_{ui}, R_{sj})$. And S_j computes

$$K_{ji} = (s_{sj} + r_{sj})M_{ui}$$

and session key

$$SK_{ji} = H_4(ID_{ui}, ID_{sj}, M_{ui}, M_{sj}, K_{ji}, P_{pub}, R_{sj}).$$

Finally the server sends $(Y_{sj}, ID_{sj}, Auth, M_{sj}, V_{sj}, T_{sj})$ to U_i.

4. Upon receiving the messages $(Y_{sj}, ID_{sj}, Auth, M_{sj}, V_{sj}, T_{sj})$ at time T'_{sj}, U_i checks whether $T'_{sj} - T_{sj} \leq \Delta T_{sj}$ holds and whether ID_{sj} is the ID of the requesting server. If any condition does not hold, U_i terminates the session; otherwise , U_i computes

$$P_{sj} = Y_{sj} + H_0(ID_{sj}, (Y_{sj} + V_{sj}))P_{pub}, R_{ui} = (s_{ui} + r_{ui})(V_{sj} + P_{sj})$$

and verifies whether $Auth$ is equal to $H_3(P_{pub}, ID_{ui}, ID_{sj}, M_{sj}, M_{ui}, R_{ui})$ or not. If holds, U_i computes $K_{ij} = (s_{ui} + r_{ui})M_{sj}$ and the session key

$$SK_{ij} = H_4(ID_{ui}, ID_{sj}, M_{ui}, M_{sj}, K_{ij}, P_{pub}, R_{ui}).$$

Otherwise U_i terminates the session.

4   Analysis of Our Scheme

4.1   Correctness

The correctness of the protocol is as follows:

$$
\begin{aligned}
R_{sj} &= (d_{sj} + s_{sj})M_{ui} \\
&= (d_{sj} + s_{sj})(s_{ui} + r_{ui})P \\
&= (s_{ui} + r_{ui})(d_{sj} + s_{sj})P \\
&= (s_{ui} + r_{ui})(d_{sj}P + s_{sj}P) \\
&= (s_{ui} + r_{ui})(Y_{sj} + H_0(ID_{sj}, (Y_{sj} + V_{sj}))P_{pub} + V_{sj}) \\
&= R_{ui} \\
K_{ji} &= (s_{sj} + r_{sj})M_{ui} \\
&= (s_{sj} + r_{sj})(s_{ui} + r_{ui})P \\
&= (s_{ui} + r_{ui})(s_{sj} + r_{sj})P \\
&= (s_{ui} + r_{ui})M_{sj} \\
&= K_{ij}
\end{aligned}
$$

4.2   Security Analysis

In this section, we discuss the security of the proposed protocol in the random oracle model. In the model, each party involved in a session is treated as an oracle, and an adversary can access the oracle by issuing some specified queries.

Security Model

In this subsection, we define the capabilities of an adversary and list security requirements of an ID-MAKA protocol for multi-server environment. The security model for ID-MAKA protocol is described in the literatures [25–28], but these schemes are insecure under RCDRI attack, so their models are not allowed to query some specific users of the private key. So on the basis of the schemes [25–28], we propose a more robust security model in which each participants private key distributed by the RC can be queried. Suppose A is a probabilistic polynomial time adversary. We allow A to potentially control all communications in the proposed protocol via accessing to a set of oracles as described below. Let $\alpha \in \{U, S\}$ and $\prod_\alpha^m$ be the mth instance of α.

- Extract(ID_α): With this query, the corresponding participant's private key can be obtained.
- Send($\prod_\alpha^m, M$): In this query, the adversary A can send a message M to the oracle $\prod_\alpha^m$. On receiving M, the oracle $\prod_\alpha^m$ performs some computation and replies to the adversary A according to the proposed scheme.
- $H_i(m_i)$: When an adversary A makes H_i query with the message m_i, the oracle returns a random number r and records (m_i, r) into a list L_i, where L_i is initially empty and $i = 0, 1, 2, 3, 4, 5, 6$.
- Reveal($\prod_\alpha^m$): This query is executed by A to obtain a session key SK from the oracle $\prod_\alpha^m$. If SK negotiation is completed, $\prod_\alpha^m$ returns the corresponding session key SK, otherwise outputs a null value.
- Corrupt(ID_α): An adversary A can issue this query to the oracle and get back the user/server private key from RC.
- Secret($\prod_\alpha^m$): With this query, the adversary can get the secret value of the corresponding user/server.
- Test($\prod_\alpha^m$): The adversary A is allowed to send a Test query to the oracle $\prod_\alpha^m$. On receiving a Test query, $\prod_\alpha^m$ chooses a bit $b \in \{0, 1\}$ and returns the session key if $b = 1$, otherwise outputs a random string $SK \in Z_q^*$ as the session key.

Definition 3 (Partnership). *Two oracles $\prod_{U_i}^m$ and $\prod_{S_j}^m$ is said Partnership, if they mutually authenticates each other and computes a mutual session key between them.*

Definition 4 (Freshness). *An oracle $\prod_{U_i}^m$ with its partner $\prod_{S_j}^m$ is said freshness i.e., the participants hold a fresh key SK if the following two conditions hold:*

1. *Both the oracles $\prod_{U_i}^m$ and $\prod_{S_j}^m$ accept SK as session key, but the Reveal query has not been invoked by U_i and S_j.*
2. *It is allowed to ask the Send ($\prod_{U_i}^m$) query or Send ($\prod_{S_j}^m$) query after the Corrupt query is executed.*

In a specific protocol P, we define the adversary A wins if a single Freshness Test oracle queried by A and correctly guesses the bit b that is picked by the Freshness Test oracle.

Definition 5 (AKA-secure). *The authenticated key agreement (AKA) advantage is defined as*

$$Adv_p^{aka}(A) = |2Pr[Asucceeds] - 1|$$

where $Pr[Asucceeds]$ is the probability of A wins the game. We say the protocol P is AKA-secure if $Adv_p^{aka}(A)$ is negligible.

In a specific protocol P, we say the adversary A breaks client to server authentication if A can fake the 'V'. We denote this event and its probability by $C2S$ and $Pr[C2S]$ separately. Similarly, we say adversary A breaks server to client authentication if A can fake the '$Auth$'. We denote this event and its probability by $S2C$ and $Pr[S2C]$ respectively.

Definition 6. *We say protocol P is mutual authentication-secure (MA-secure) if both $Pr[C2S]$ and $Pr[S2C]$ are negligible.*

Security Proof
Here, we show that the proposed protocol can achieve the expected security features under the random oracle model. Due to the proof process of specific identity situation and anonymous situation is similar. For simplicity, we only prove the specific identity of the situation.

Theorem 1. *In the random oracle model, our scheme is MA-secure i.e., it achieves client-to-server ($C2S$) authentication and server-to-client ($S2C$) authentication under the k-CCA assumption and CDH assumption respectively.*

Proof. **Case1 (C2S).** Assume that the adversary A breaks $C2S$ authentication of the proposed scheme with a non-negligible ε, then we can construct a probabilistic time adversary F that will solve an instance of k-CCA problem by interacting with A.

For an instance of the k-CCA problem $\{P, Q_1 = xP, e_1, e_2, ..., e_k \in Z_q^*\}$ and $\{\frac{1}{x+d_{uI}+e_1}P, ..., \frac{1}{x+d_{uI}+e_k}P\}$, F simulates the system initializing algorithm to generate the system parameters

$$(F_q, E/F_q, G_q, P, P_{pub} = zP, H_0, H_1, H_2, H_3, H_4, e, G_m),$$

where $z \in Z_q^*$ is a random integer and d_{uI} can be obtained by Corrupt (ID_{uI}) query. H_0, H_1, H_2, H_3 and H_4 are five random oracles controlled by F. Let q_i, q_n, q_m and q_s be the number of hash queries, clients, servers and send queries, where $i = 0, 1, 2, 3, 4$. F picks $I \in \{1, 2, ..., q_n\}$, $J \in \{1, 2, ..., q_m\}$, assuming that A can violate the client-to-server authentication against the oracles $\prod_{S_J}^m$ and $\prod_{U_I}^m$, i.e. A can generate legal message $(V, V_{uI}, Y_{uI}, ID_{uI}, M_{uI}, T_{uI}, validity\, period)$. F interacts with A as follows.

- H_1-query: F maintains a list L_1 of tuples $(ID_{ui}, V_{ui}, Y_{ui}, h_{ui}, validity\, period)$. When A queries the oracle H_1 on $(ID_{ui}, V_{ui}, Y_{ui}, validity\, period)$. F responds as follows: If $(ID_{ui}, V_{ui}, Y_{ui}, h_{ui}, validity\, period)$ is recorded on L_1, then F responds with h_{ui}; otherwise, F randomly chooses $h_{ui} \in Z_q^*$ that has not been chosen by F, and inserts $(ID_{ui}, V_{ui}, Y_{ui}, h_{ui}, validity\, period)$ into L_1 and responds with h_{ui}.
- $H_i(m_i)$-query: F maintains a list L_i of the form (m_i, h_i), where $i = 2, 3, 4$. On receiving the queries, F checks L_i. If (m_i, h_i) is on the list L_i, F responds with h_i; otherwise, F randomly chooses $h_i \in Z_q^*$ that has not been chosen by F, and inserts (m_i, h_i) into L_i and responds with h_i.

- Extract-query: F maintains a list L_E of tuples $(d_{ui}, ID_{ui}, V_{ui}, Y_{ui}, h_{ui}, validity$ $period)$. When A queries the oracle Extract on (ID_{ui}, V_{ui}), F responds as follows: If $(d_{ui}, ID_{ui}, V_{ui}, Y_{ui}, h_{ui}, validity\, period)$ is on L_E, then F responds with $(d_{ui}, Y_{ui}, validity\, period)$; otherwise, F randomly chooses $a, b \in Z_q^*$, then computes $Y_{ui} = aP + bP_{pub}$, sets the registered private key

$$d_{ui} \leftarrow a, h_{ui} = H_1(ID_{ui}, V_{ui} + Y_{ui}, validity\, period) \leftarrow -b\,mod\,q,$$

finally F inserts

$$(d_{ui}, ID_{ui}, V_{ui}, Y_{ui}, h_{ui}, validity\, period), (ID_{ui}, V_{ui}, Y_{ui}, h_{ui}, validity\, period)$$

into L_E and L_1 respectively and responds with $(d_{ui}, Y_{ui}, validity\, period)$.
- Corrupt-query: When A queries (ID_{ui}, V_{ui}), F responds with $(d_{ui}, Y_{ui}, validity$ $period)$.
- Secret-query: if $ID_{ui} \neq ID_{uI}$, F responds with the secret value s_{ui}; otherwise, F cancels the game.
- Send-query:
  - When adversary A makes a Send $(\prod_U^m, 'Start')$ query, F responds as follows: If $U \neq ID_{uI}$, F responds with $(V, V_{ui}, Y_{ui}, ID_{ui}, M_{ui}, T_{ui}, validity$ $period, r_{ui})$ according to the description of protocol, since F knows r_{ui}, d_{ui} and s_{ui} of the client U_i; otherwise, F selects $V = \frac{1}{x + d_{uI} + e_m} P, a \in Z_q^*$, then computes $M_{uI} = Q_1 + aP, V_{uI} = Q_1$ and inserts a new tuple $(P_{pub}, ID_{uI}, ID_{sj}, V_{uI}, Y_{uI}, M_{uI}, T_{uI}, h_2 = e_m)$ into L_2, finally responds with $(V, V_{uI}, Y_{uI}, ID_{uI}, M_{uI}, T_{uI}, validity\, period, a)$.
  - F answers other A's Send queries according to the description of the protocol, because F knows the private key and secret value of other users and servers.
- Reveal-query: When the adversary A makes a Reveal $(\prod_\alpha^m)$ query, F responds as follows. If $\prod_{U_i}^m$ is not accepted, F responds with $\perp$. Otherwise F checks L_4 and responds with the corresponding h_4.

The event $U = ID_{uI}$ and $\prod_\alpha^m = \prod_{S_j}^m$ occurs with the probability $\frac{1}{q_n q_m}$. In this case, adversary A would not have made Secret (ID_{uI}) query, so F would not have aborted. If F wins such a game, then F must output

$$V = \frac{1}{x + d_{uI} + e} P$$

for some $e \notin \{e_1, e_2 ..., e_k\}$. Thus, according to the assumption, F can find e, d_{uI} from L_2 and Corrupt-query with the probability $\frac{1}{q_2}$ and output $(e + d_{uI}, V)$ as a solution to the k-CCA problem. So if the adversary A can compute the fake V with a non-negligible probability ε, then F is able to solve an instance of k-CCA problem with the probability $\frac{\varepsilon}{q_m q_n q_2}$, which is non-negligible. Therefore, $Pr[C2S]$ is negligible and the proposed protocol can provide the client-to-server authentication.

Case 2 (S2C). Assume that the adversary A breaks $S2C$ authentication of the proposed scheme with a non-negligible probability ε, then we can construct a probabilistic time adversary F that will solve an instance of CDH problem by interacting with A.

For an instance of the CDH problem $\{P, Q_1 = xP, Q_2 = yP\}$, F simulates the system initializing algorithm to generate the system parameters

$$(F_q, E/F_q, G_q, P, P_{pub} = zP, H_0, H_1, H_2, H_3, H_4, e, G_m),$$

where $z \in Z_q^*$ is random integer. H_0, H_1, H_2, H_3 and H_4 are five random oracles controlled by F. Let q_i, q_n, q_m and q_s be the number of hash queries, clients, servers and send queries, where $i = 0, 1, 2, 3, 4$. F picks $I \in \{1, 2, ..., q_n\}$, $J \in \{1, 2, ..., q_m\}$, assuming that A can violate the server-to-client authentication against the oracle $\prod_{S_J}^m$ and $\prod_{U_I}^m$. F interacts with A as follows.

- H_0-query: F maintains a list L_0 of tuples $(ID_{sj}, V_{sj}, Y_{sj}, h_{sj})$. When A queries the oracle H_0 on $(ID_{sj}, Y_{sj}, V_{sj})$. F responds as follows: If

$$(ID_{sj}, V_{sj}, Y_{sj}, h_{sj})$$

is on L_0, then F responds with h_{sj}; otherwise, F randomly chooses $h_{sj} \in Z_q^*$ that has not been chosen by F, then inserts $(ID_{sj}, V_{sj}, Y_{sj}, h_{sj})$ into L_0 and responds with h_{sj}.

- $H_i(m_i)$-query: F maintains a list the L_i of form (m_i, h_i), where $i = 2, 3, 4$. On receiving the queries, F checks L_i. If (m_i, h_i) is on the list L_i, F responds with h_i; otherwise, F randomly chooses $h_i \in Z_q^*$ that has not been chosen by F, then inserts (m_i, h_i) into L_i and responds with h_i.

- Extract-query: F maintains a list L_E of tuples $(d_{sj}, ID_{sj}, V_{sj}, Y_{sj}, h_{sj})$. When A queries the oracle Extract on (ID_{sj}, V_{sj}) F responds as follows: If

$$(d_{sj}, ID_{sj}, V_{sj}, Y_{sj}, h_{sj})$$

is on L_E, then F responds with (d_{sj}, Y_{sj}). Otherwise, F randomly chooses $a, b \in Z_q^*$, computes $Y_{sj} = aP + bP_{pub}$, sets

$$d_{sj} \leftarrow a, h_{sj} = H_0(ID_{sj}, V_{sj} + Y_{sj}) \leftarrow -b \bmod q,$$

inserts $(d_{sj}, ID_{sj}, V_{sj}, Y_{sj}, h_{sj})$ and $(ID_{sj}, V_{sj}, Y_{sj}, h_{sj})$ into L_E and L_0 respectively and responds with (d_{sj}, Y_{sj}).

- Corrupt-query: When A queries (ID_{sj}, V_{ui}) or (ID_{ui}, V_{ui}), F responds with (d_{sj}, Y_{sj}) or (d_{ui}, Y_{ui}).

- Secret-query: if $ID_{sj} \neq ID_{sJ}$ and $ID_{ui} \neq ID_{uI}$, F responds with secret value s_{sj} or s_{ui}. Otherwise, F cancels the game.

- Send-query:
  - When the adversary A makes a Send $(\prod_U^m, 'Start')$ query, F answers this query as in Case 1.
  - When the adversary A makes a Send $(\prod_S^m, (V, V_{ui}, Y_{ui}, ID_{ui}, M_{ui}, T_{ui},$ *validity period*$))$ query, F responds as follows: If $\prod_\alpha^m \neq \prod_{U_I}^m$ and $S \neq ID_{sJ}$, F responds with $(Y_{sj}, ID_{sj}, Auth, M_{sj}, V_{sj}, T_{sj}, r_{sj})$ according to description of protocol, since F knows r_{sj}, d_{sj} and s_{sj} of the

server S_j. Else, if $\prod_{\alpha}^{m} = \prod_{U_I}^{m}$ and $S \neq ID_{sJ}$, F first checks whether *validity period* is overdue or not, whether $T'_{uI} - T_{uI} \leq \Delta T_{uI}$ holds, whether $ID_{uI} \in IDRL$ and whether

$$e(V, h_{(sj,2)}P + V_{uI} + P_{uI}) = e(P, P) = g.$$

If any condition is not true, $\prod_{S}^{m}$ terminates the session. Otherwise, $\prod_{S}^{m}$ continues to compute the response values

$$M_{sj} = (s_{sj} + r_{sj})P, R_{sj} = (d_{sj} + s_{sj})M_{uI}$$

and $Auth = H_3(P_{pub}, ID_{uI}, ID_{sj}, M_{sj}, M_{uI}, R_{sj})$. And $\prod_{S}^{m}$ computes $K_{jI} = (s_{sj} + r_{sj})M_{uI}$ and

$$SK_{jI} = H_4(ID_{uI}, ID_{sj}, M_{uI}, M_{sj}, K_{jI}, P_{pub}, R_{sj}).$$

Finally the oracle sends $(Y_{sj}, ID_{sj}, Auth, M_{sj}, V_{sj}, T_{sj}, r_{sj})$ to A. Else, if $\prod_{\alpha}^{m} \neq \prod_{U_I}^{m}$ and $S = ID_{sJ}$, F first checks whether *validity period* is overdue or not, whether $T'_{ui} - T_{ui} \leq \Delta T_{ui}$ holds, whether $ID_{ui} \in IDRL$ and whether $e(V, h_{(sj,2)}P + V_{ui} + P_{ui}) = g$. If any condition is not true, $\prod_{S}^{m}$ terminates the session. Otherwise, $\prod_{S}^{m}$ randomly picks $c \in Z_q^*$, then the oracle $\prod_{S}^{m}$ computes the response values $M_{sJ} = (Q_2 + cP)$, $V_{sJ} = Q_2$,

$$R_{sJ} = (s_{ui} + r_{ui})(Q_2 + Y_{sJ} + H_0(ID_{sJ}, (Y_{sJ} + Q_2))P_{pub})$$

and $Auth = H_3(P_{pub}, ID_{ui}, ID_{sJ}, M_{sJ}, M_{ui}, R_{sJ})$. And $\prod_{S}^{m}$ computes $K_{Ji} = (s_{ui} + r_{ui})M_{sJ}$ and session key

$$SK_{Ji} = H_4(ID_{ui}, ID_{sJ}, M_{ui}, M_{sJ}, K_{Ji}, P_{pub}, R_{sJ}).$$

Finally the server sends $(Y_{sJ}, ID_{sJ}, Auth, M_{sJ}, V_{sJ}, T_{sJ}, c)$ to A. Else, if $\prod_{\alpha}^{m} = \prod_{U_I}^{m}$ and $S = ID_{sJ}$, $\prod_{S}^{m}$ randomly chooses $c, d \in Z_q^*$, then computes the response values $M_{sJ} = (Q_2 + cP)$, $V_{sJ} = Q_2$, $R_{sJ} = dP$ and $Auth = H_3(P_{pub}, ID_{uI}, ID_{sJ}, M_{sJ}, M_{uI}, R_{sJ})$, then F responds with $(Y_{sJ}, ID_{sJ}, Auth, M_{sJ}, V_{sJ}, T_{sJ}, c)$ to A.

- Reveal-query: When the adversary A makes a Reveal($\prod_{\alpha}^{m}$) query, F responds as follows. If $\prod_{U_i}^{m}$ is not accepted or $\prod_{U_I}^{m}$ and $\prod_{S_J}^{m}$, the session key is queried, F responds with $\perp$; otherwise F checks L_4 and responds with the corresponding h_4.

The events $S = ID_{sJ}$ and $\prod_{\alpha}^{m} = \prod_{U_I}^{m}$ occur with the probability $\frac{1}{q_n q_m}$. In this case, adversary A would not have made Secret (ID_{uI}) or Reveal $(\prod_{U_I}^{m} and \prod_{S_J}^{m})$ queries , so F would not have aborted. If F wins such a game, F only outputs xyP with a non-negligible probability. As H_3 is a random oracle, thus, according to the assumption, F can find the corresponding item in table L_3 with the probability $\frac{1}{q_3}$ and output R_{sJ} as a solution to CDH problem, i.e.

$$xyP = R_{sJ} - d_{sJ}xP - ayP - ad_{sJ}P = R_{sJ} - d_{sJ}Q_1 - aQ_2 - ad_{sJ}P,$$

where d_{sJ} can be queried by Corrupt-query oracle. Therefore, if the adversary A can successfully impersonate the server with a non-negligible probability ε, then F is able to solve an instance of CDH problem with probability $\frac{\varepsilon}{q_n q_m q_3}$, which is non-negligible. Therefore, $Pr[S2C]$ is negligible and the proposed protocol can provide the server-to-client authentication.

Theorem 2. *In the random oracle model, our scheme is AKA-secure i.e., the inequality $Adv_p^{aka}(A) < \varepsilon$ holds under CDH assumption, where ε is negligible.*

Proof. Assume an adversary A correctly output the bit b which is chosen by F in the Test query with a non-negligible probability ε, then there must be a polynomial time bounded adversary F that can address the CDH problem with a non-negligible probability.

Similar to the Theorem 1, for an instance of the CDH problem

$$\{P, Q_1 = xP, Q_2 = yP\},$$

F simulates the system initializing algorithm to generate the system parameters

$$(F_q, E/F_q, G_q, P, P_{pub} = zP, H_0, H_1, H_2, H_3, H_4, e, G_m),$$

where $z \in Z_q^*$ is random integer. H_0, H_1, H_2, H_3 and H_4 are five random oracles controlled by F. Let q_i , q_n, q_m and q_s be the number of hash queries, clients, servers and send queries, where $i = 0, 1, 2, 3, 4$. F picks $I \in \{1, 2, ..., q_n\}$, $J \in \{1, 2, ..., q_m\}$ and $l_1, l_2 \in \{1, 2, ..., q_s\}$, assuming that A can violate key agreement against the oracle $\prod_{U_I}^{l_1}$ and $\prod_{S_J}^{l_2}$. F interacts with A as follows.

- H_0-query: F maintains a list L_0 of tuples $(ID_{sj}, V_{sj}, Y_{sj}, h_{sj})$. When A queries the oracle H_0 on $(ID_{sj}, Y_{sj}, V_{sj})$. F responds as follows: If

$$(ID_{sj}, V_{sj}, Y_{sj}, h_{sj})$$

  is on L_0, then F responds with h_{sj}; otherwise, F randomly chooses $h_{sj} \in Z_q^*$ that has not been chosen by F, then inserts $(ID_{sj}, V_{sj}, Y_{sj}, h_{sj})$ into L_0 and responds with h_{sj}.
- H_1-query: F maintains a list L_1 of tuples $(ID_{ui}, V_{ui}, Y_{ui}, h_{ui}, validity\ period)$. When A queries the oracle H_1 on $(ID_{ui}, Y_{ui}, V_{ui}, validity\ period)$. F responds as follows: If $(ID_{ui}, Y_{ui}, V_{ui}, h_{ui}, validity\ period)$ is on L_1, then F responds with h_{ui}; otherwise, F randomly chooses $h_{ui} \in Z_q^*$ that has not been chosen by F, then inserts $(ID_{ui}, Y_{ui}, V_{ui}, h_{ui}, validity\ period)$ into L_1 and responds with h_{ui}.
- $H_i(m_i)$-query: F maintains a list L_i of the form (m_i, h_i), where $i = 2, 3, 4$. On receiving the queries, F looks up L_i. If (m_i, h_i) is on the list L_i. F responds with h_i; otherwise, F randomly chooses $h_i \in Z_q^*$ that has not been chosen by F, then inserts (m_i, h_i) into L_i and responds with h_i.
- Extract-query: Oracle responses similar to Theorem 1.

- Corrupt-query: When A queries ID, F responds to the corresponding registration information.
- Secret-query: If $ID_{sj} \neq ID_{sJ}$ or $ID_{ui} \neq ID_{uI}$, F responds with the secret value s_{sj} or s_{ui}; otherwise, F cancels the game.
- Send-query: F's answer is similar to Case1 and Case2 in Theorem 1.
- Reveal-query: When the adversary A makes a Reveal ($\prod_{U_i}^m$) query, F responds as follows. If $\prod_{U_i}^m$ is not accepted or $\prod_{U_i}^m$ and $\prod_{S_j}^m$ the session key is queried, F responds with $\perp$; otherwise F checks L_4 and responds with the corresponding h_4.
- Test-query: If the query is not between $\prod_{U_I}^{l_1}$ and $\prod_{S_J}^{l_2}$, then F cancels the game; otherwise F flips an unbiased coin b and returns the session key if $b = 1$, otherwise outputs a random string $SK \in Z_q^*$ as the session key.

Let B be the event that A chooses the oracle $\prod_{S_J}^{l_2}$ to ask its Test query and the partnership of $\prod_{S_J}^{l_2}$ is $\prod_{U_I}^{l_1}$. According to the assumption and Definition 5, it is clear that the equation

$$\frac{1}{2} + \varepsilon = Pr[A succeeds]$$
$$= Pr[A succeeds | B \vee S2C] Pr[B \vee S2C]$$
$$+ Pr[A succeeds | \overline{B \vee S2C}] Pr[\overline{B \vee S2C}]$$

holds. Since H_4 is a random oracle, and $\prod_{U_I}^{l_1}$ and $\prod_{S_J}^{l_2}$ remain freshness,

$$Pr[A succeeds | \overline{B \vee S2C}] = \frac{1}{2}.$$

So we have

$$1/2 + \varepsilon = Pr[A succeeds | B \vee S2C] Pr[B \vee S2C]$$
$$+ Pr[A succeeds | \overline{B \vee S2C}] Pr[\overline{B \vee S2C}]$$
$$\leq Pr[A succeeds | B \vee S2C] Pr[B \vee S2C] + \frac{1}{2}.$$

After simplification, we get

$$Pr[B] + Pr[S2C] \geq Pr[B \vee S2C] \geq \varepsilon, Pr[B] \geq \varepsilon - Pr[S2C].$$

However, we have proved in Theorem 1 that $Pr[S2C]$ is negligible. Therefore, in this case, the probability that H_4 has previously been queried on by A is non-negligible.

The events $\prod_{U_I}^m$ and $\prod_{S_J}^m$ occur with the probability $\frac{1}{q_n q_m}$ and the adversary A chooses Test $\prod_{U_I}^{l_1}$ as Test oracle with the probability $\frac{1}{q_s}$. In this situation, adversary A would not have made Secret (ID_{uI}, ID_{sJ}) queries or Reveal Reveal($\prod_{U_I}^m$ and $\prod_{S_J}^m$) query, so F would not have aborted. If A can win such a game, after the above analysis, we know that A will execute the corresponding H_4 hash query of the tuples

$$(ID_{uI}, ID_{sJ}, M_{uI}, M_{sJ}, K_{JI}, P_{pub}, R_{sJ})$$

with a non-negligible probability $Pr[B]$. As H_4 is a random oracle, thus F can find corresponding item in table L_4 with the probability $\frac{1}{q_4}$ and output K_{JI} or R_{sJ} as a solution to CDH problem, i.e.

$$xyP = K_{JI} - cxP - ayP - acP = K_{JI} - cQ_1 - aQ_2 - acP,$$

$$xyP = R_{sJ} - d_{sJ}xP - ayP - ad_{sJ}P = R_{sJ} - d_{sJ}Q_1 - aQ_2 - ad_{sJ}P.$$

So if the adversary A can win the game with a non-negligible probability ε, then F can solve an instance of CDH problem with the probability at least

$$\frac{2Pr[B]}{q_n q_m q_s q_4} \geq \frac{2(\varepsilon - Pr[S2C])}{q_n q_m q_s q_4}$$

which is non-negligible. Therefore, $Adv_p^{aka}(A)$ is negligible and the proposed protocol can provide the AKA-security.

Theorem 3. *Under the CDH assumption, our protocol can offer prefect forward security.*

Proof. According to Theorem 2, the session key in our protocol depends not only on the registered private key but also on the secret value of the user or server. On the other hand, we prove in Theorem 2 that our protocol is still secure even if the registered private key is leaked. Therefore, our protocol can offer perfect forward security.

5   Efficiency and Security Discussion

In this section, we will give an efficiency analysis and security analysis of our scheme and compare it with other similar schemes. In Table 3, we compare the security of our scheme and related schemes under ESL attack and RCDRI attack.

Table 3. Security comparison

Schemes	[10]	[18]	[25]	[26]	[27]	[28]	[29]	Our scheme
ESL	No	No	No	No	Yes	No	No	Yes
Clint-RCDRI	–	Yes	No	No	No	No	Yes	Yes
Server-RCDRI	–	No	No	No	No	No	No	Yes
Environment	Single	Multi	Multi	Multi	Multi	Multi	Multi	Multi

As can be seen from Table 3, whether it is based on smart card or ID, many of the previous schemes are based on a trust RC. In these protocols, the user submits the password directly to the RC or the user's private key is generated by the RC unilaterally in the user registration phase. Similarly, the server side is also built on the RC trusted basis. However, this is very dangerous because RC in the real world may record and divulge the user's or server's registration information. And because mobile devices have limited computing power, they tend to store the required random numbers in advance. So if the security of the protocol depends on these random numbers, it is prone to ESL attack. Combined with the above analysis, a secure ID-MAKA for multi-server environment scheme must resist RCDRI attack and ESL attack.

In mutual authentication and key agreement phase, our protocol not only requires the user/server to have a private key generated by RC, but also requires the user/server to have a secret value, and both must satisfy the relationship established during the registration phase. In this way, our protocol can achieve the resistance to RCDRI attack. We then take into account the limited computing power of mobile devices. In order to make our protocol more secure and more practical, we use the user/server secret value to achieve security under ESL attack. In this way, because our protocol is not affected by the ESL attack, we can use the pre-calculation to improve efficiency. Combined with the above analysis, our scheme can resist ESL attack and RCDRI attack and give the proof under the random oracle model. Therefore, it has a stronger security than similar schemes.

In the following, we compare our protocol with the related MAKA protocols for multi-server environment from the point view of computational cost. For simplicity, we define the following symbols.

- TG_e : The time of performing a bilinear map.
- TG_{mul}: The time of executing paring-based scalar multiplication operation of point.
- TG_{mtph}: The time of executing a map-to-point hash operation of point.
- TG_{inv}: The time of performing a modular inversion operation.
- TG_{exp}: The time of performing a modular exponentiation operation.
- T_h: The time of performing a one-way hash function.

In [34], Scott, Costigan and Abdulwahab implemented some cryptographic paring operations on the Philips HiPersmart (client-side) card and a Pentium IV computer (server-side) with maximum clock speeds of 36 MHz and 3 GHz, respectively. On the other hand, for the protocols based on bilinear pairing can meet the standard security requirement, a popular and valid choice would be an elliptic curve over a finite field $E(F_p)$ with $p = 512$ bits and a large prime $q = 160$ bits. Based on the above parameters, we give their test results in Table 4. The data in Table 4 depends on the specific operating system and the development environment. Details can be found in Ref. [34]. Note that TG_e, TG_{mul}, TG_{exp} and TG_{mtph} are more time consuming than T_h.

Table 4. Corresponds to the time of the operation

	TG_e	TG_{mul}	TG_{mtph}	TG_{inv}	TG_{exp}	T_h
Server	3.16 ms	1.17 ms	<1 ms	<0.3 ms	0.62 ms	<0.01 ms
Client	0.38 s	0.13 s	<0.01 s	<0.03 s	0.07 s	<0.001 s

As our protocol is secure under the ESL attack, we can compute M_{ui} in advance. Likewise, if a user needs to interact with a server frequently, the user can store P_{sj} after the first successful authentication. Combined with the above analysis, we compare the efficiency of our protocol and other similar protocols in Table 5.

In Table 5, we show the comparisons among our scheme and some previously proposed schemes [11, 25, 27] in terms of the computational cost, number of rounds and environment. The execution time spent is measured by using the data in Table 4. Because of the unequal computing power of the server and the client, our proposed scheme also uses this asymmetry to reduce the client's stress based on different security assumptions. As shown in Table 5, since $e(P, P)$ can be pre-calculated, our protocol is more advantageous on server-side computational cost. It is important to ease the server's operating pressure and improve the user experience.

On the other hand, since our scheme can withstand the ESL attack and the RCDRI attack, our protocol can compute or cache some the parameters of the mutual authentication phase in advance to improve efficiency. So, as shown in Table 5, our scheme also has a great advantage in terms of client computing costs.

Table 5. Efficiency comparison

	Scheme [25]	Scheme [27]	Scheme [11]	Our scheme
Computational cost (client)	$4TG_{mul}+5T_h$ $+TG_{exp}$	$4TG_{mul}+2T_h+$ $2TG_e+2TG_{mtph}$	$4TG_{mul}+3T_h+$ TG_{mtph}	$3TG_{mul}+4T_h+$ $TG_{inv}+(2TG_{mul})$
Computational cost (server)	$2TG_e+3TG_{mul}$ $+TG_{exp}+3T_h$	$4TG_{mul}+2TG_e$ $+2T_h+2TG_{mtph}$	$2TG_{mul}+4T_h$ $+2TG_{mtph}+3TG_e$	$TG_e+5TG_{mul}+4T_h$
Execution time (client)	About 0.6 s	About 1.3 s	About 0.6 s	About 0.42 s
Execution time (server)	About 10.6 ms	About 13.2 ms	About 9.8 ms	About 9.4 ms
Number of rounds	2	2	3	2
Environment	Multi-server	Multi-server	Single-server	Multi-server

Note that "()" indicates that it can be pre-calculated or can be cached after the first successful authentication. Therefore, according to Table 3 and above analysis, our protocol provides more security features, that is, it can achieve security under the ESL attack and RCDRI attack. Even in the latest protocol of the same type [28], it can't resist ESL attack nor resist RCDRI attack. According to Table 5, our scheme also has a higher efficiency. Therefore, it is more suitable for practical applications.

6 Conclusion

In this paper, according to the review of relevant works, we found that many ID-MAKA schemes are insecure under RCDRI attack and ESL attack. We proposed a more secure ID-MAKA scheme for mobile multi-server architecture that can resist RCDRI attack and ESL attack. According to the CDH and k-CCA assumptions, we have shown that the proposed protocol can securely implement mutual authentication and key agreement in the random oracle model. According to the comparison in Sect. 5, the proposed protocol has a good efficiency and strong security.

Since our scheme is still based on the [25–27] user revocation mechanism, this revocation mechanism is not efficient enough. Achieving more efficient revocation mechanism and stronger security will be at the heart of our future research.

Acknowledgments. This work was supported in part by the National Key Research and Development Program of China (No. 2016YFB0800601), the Natural Science Foundation of China (No. 61303217, 61502372), the Natural Science Foundation of Shaanxi province (No. 2013JQ8002, 2014JQ8313).

References

1. Lamport, L.: Password authentication with insecure communication. Commun. ACM **24**(24), 770–772 (1981)
2. Das, M.L., Saxena, A., Gulati, V.P., et al.: A novel remote user authentication scheme using bi-linear pairings. Comput. Secur. **25**(3), 184–189 (2006)
3. Khan, M.K., Zhang, J.: Improving the security of a flexible biometrics remote user authenti-cation scheme. Comput. Stand. Interfaces **29**(1), 82–85 (2007)
4. Tseng, Y.M., Wu, T.Y., Wu, J.D.: A pairing-based user authentication scheme for wireless clients with smart cards. Informatica **19**(2), 285–302 (2008)
5. Wu, T.Y., Tseng, Y.M.: An efficient user authentication and key exchange protocol for mobile client-server environment. Comput. Netw. **54**(9), 1520–1530 (2010)
6. He, D., Chen, J., Hu, J.: Further improvement of Juang et al.'s password-authenticated key agreement scheme using smart cards. Kuwait J. Sci. Eng. **38**(2A), 55–68 (2011)
7. Debiao, H., Jianhua, C., Rui, Z.: A more secure authentication scheme for telecare medicine information systems. J. Med. Syst. **36**(3), 1989–1995 (2012)
8. He, D.: Cryptanalysis of an authenticated key agreement protocol for wireless mobile communications. ETRI J. **34**(3), 482–484 (2012)
9. He, D., Chen, J., Chen, Y.: A secure mutual authentication scheme for session initiation protocol using elliptic curve cryptography. Secur. Commun. Netw. **5**(12), 1423–1429 (2012)

10. He, D.: An efficient remote user authentication and key agreement protocol for mobile client server environment from pairings. Ad Hoc Netw. **10**(6), 1009–1016 (2012)
11. Tseng, Y.M., Huang, S.S., Tsai, T.T., et al.: A novel ID-based authentication and key exchange protocol resistant to ephemeral-secret-leakage attacks for mobile devices. Int. J. Distrib. Sens. Netw. **2015**, 1–12 (2015)
12. Tsai, J.L., Lo, N.W.: Provably secure and efficient anonymous ID-based authentication protocol for mobile devices using bilinear pairings. Wirel. Pers. Commun. **83**(2), 1–14 (2015)
13. Shamir, A.: Identity-based cryptosystems and signature schemes. In: Blakley, G.R., Chaum, D.E. (eds.) CRYPTO 1984. LNCS, vol. 196, pp. 47–53. Springer, Heidelberg (1984). https://doi.org/10.1007/3-540-39568-7_5
14. Juang, W.S.: Efficient multi-server password authenticated key agreement using smart cards. IEEE Trans. Consum. Electron. **50**, 251–255 (2004)
15. Chang, C.C., Lee, J.S.: An efficient and secure multi-server password authentication scheme using smart cards. In: International Conference on Cyberworlds, pp. 417–422. IEEE Computer Society (2004)
16. Tsai, J.L.: Efficient multi-server authentication scheme based on one-way hash function without verification table. Comput. Secur. **27**(3–4), 115–121 (2008)
17. Lee, S.G.: Cryptanalysis of multiple-server password-authenticated key agreement schemes using smart cards. J. Inf. Commun. Convergence Eng. **9**(4), 431–434 (2011)
18. Geng, J., Zhang, L.: A dynamic ID-based user authentication and key agreement scheme for multi-server environment using bilinear pairings. In: The Workshop on Power Electronics and Intelligent Transportation System, pp. 33–37. IEEE Computer Society (2008)
19. Liao, Y.P., Wang, S.S.: A secure dynamic ID based remote user authentication scheme for multi-server environment. Comput. Stand. Interfaces **31**(1), 24–29 (2009)
20. Hsiang, H.C., Shih, W.K.: Improvement of the secure dynamic ID based remote user authen-tication scheme for multi-server environment. Comput. Stand. Interfaces **31**(6), 1118–1123 (2009)
21. Chuang Jr., Y.H.: Security weaknesses of two dynamic ID-based user authentication and key agreement schemes for multi-server environment (2009)
22. Lee, C.C., Lin, T.H., Chang, R.X.: A secure dynamic ID based remote user authentication scheme for multi-server environment using smart cards. Expert Syst. Appl. **38**(11), 13863–13870 (2011)
23. Li, X., Ma, J., Wang, W., et al.: A novel smart card and dynamic ID based remote user authentication scheme for multi-server environments. Math. Comput. Modell. **58**(s 1–2), 85–95 (2013)
24. Zhao, D., Peng, H., Li, S., et al.: An efficient dynamic ID based remote user authentication scheme using self-certified public keys for multi-server environment. Comput. Sci. (2013)
25. Chuang, Y.H., Tseng, Y.M.: Towards generalized ID-based user authentication for mobile multi-server environment. Int. J. Commun Syst **25**(4), 447–460 (2012)
26. Han, W., Zhu, Z.: An ID-based mutual authentication with key agreement protocol for multi-server environment on elliptic curve cryptosystem. Int. J. Commun Syst **27**(8), 1173–1185 (2015)
27. Islam, S.H.: A Provably Secure ID-Based Mutual Authentication and Key Agreement Scheme for Mobile Multi-server Environment Without ESL Attack. Kluwer Academic Publishers, Hingham (2014)

28. Tseng, Y.M., Huang, S.S., Tsai, T.T., et al.: List-free ID-based mutual authentication and key agreement protocol for multiserver architectures. IEEE Trans. Emerg. Top. Comput. **4**(1), 102–112 (2016)
29. Wang, C., Zhang, X., Zheng, Z.: Cryptanalysis and improvement of a biometric-based multi-server authentication and key agreement scheme. PLoS ONE **11**(2), e0149173 (2016)
30. Reddy, A.G., Yoon, E.J., Das, A.K., et al.: Design of mutually authenticated key agreement protocol resistant to impersonation attacks for multi-server environment. IEEE Access **5**(99), 3622–3639 (2017)
31. Boneh, D., Franklin, M.: Identity-based encryption from the weil pairing. In: Kilian, J. (ed.) CRYPTO 2001. LNCS. Springer, Heidelberg (2001). https://doi.org/10.1007/3-540-44647-8_13
32. Liao, Y.P., Hsiao, C.M.: A novel multi-server remote user authentication scheme using self-certified public keys for mobile clients. Elsevier Science Publishers B.V. (2013)
33. Mitsunari, S., Sakai, R., Kasahara, M.: A new traitor tracing. IEICE Trans. Fund. Electron. Commun. Comput. Sci. **E85-A**(2), 481–484 (2002)
34. Scott, M., Costigan, N., Abdulwahab, W.: Implementing cryptographic pairings on smart-cards. In: Cryptographic Hardware and Embedded Systems - CHES 2006, International Workshop, Yokohama, Japan, 10-13 October 2006, Proceedings, D-BLP, pp. 134–147 (2006)

Research on Cryptographic Algorithm Recognition Based on Behavior Analysis

Fei Yan[1,2(✉)], Yunlong Xing[1,2], Shiwei Zhang[2], Zhihan Yue[2], and Yamin Zheng[2]

[1] Key Laboratory of Aerospace Information Security and Trusted Computing of Ministry of Education, Wuhan 430072, China
[2] School of Computer, Wuhan University, Wuhan 430072, China
{yanfei,yunlong.xing}@whu.edu.cn

Abstract. Due to the abuse of cryptography technology and the difficulty to break encryption algorithm, ransomware has a huge threat to cyberspace. So how to detect the cryptographic algorithm in the recognition program plays an important role in the protection of information security. However, existing cryptographic algorithm identification and analysis technology has the disadvantages of low recognition efficiency, single analysis strategy, and they cannot identify program variants effectively. In view of these problems, this paper presents a cryptographic algorithm based on behavior analysis. Based on the behavior analysis, combined with the static structure and dynamic statistical characteristics of the key data, the subroutine of the target program is gradually screened, and the execution logic of the subroutine is analyzed. Finally, the cryptographic algorithm in the binary code of the program is obtained. Compared with the traditional signature-based technology, our technology has a better recognition rate with less resource occupation. What's more, this technology can identify the program variants accurately, so it has a good application prospects.

Keywords: Cryptographic algorithm identification · Behavior analysis · Signature recognition

1 Introduction

With the popularity of the Internet, computer application technology and network communication technology develop rapidly, especially in the process of information exchange, cryptography plays an important role in ensuring information security. However, if a high-security cryptographic algorithm is exploited by malicious programs, it poses a huge threat to the critical data and file systems of the average user. So, it is important in the identification and analysis of binary code in the password algorithm for malicious code detection and password security analysis.

This work is sponsored by National Science Foundation of China (No. 61272452), National High-tech R&D Program of China (863 Program) 2015AA016002, and National Basic Research Program of China (973 Program) 2014CB340601.

© Springer Nature Singapore Pte Ltd. 2017
M. Xu et al. (Eds.): CTCIS 2017, CCIS 704, pp. 370–382, 2017.
https://doi.org/10.1007/978-981-10-7080-8_25

The traditional cryptographic algorithm identification is mainly based on the idea of signature matching [1], by analyzing the existing cryptographic algorithm and extracting the corresponding eigenvalue, the feature library is constructed. When the target program is detected, the characteristic value of the program is matched with the library feature. If matching succeeds, the program contains built-in cryptographic algorithm. Many anti-virus software is based on the construction of the signature library. But there are several obvious flaws in the method of signature matching: (1) the identification is not in time, only after obtaining a program sample characteristics, we can detect the program; (2) rely on the upgrading of the signature database and consume system resources seriously; (3) cannot detect new malware. Although the development of technology, the detection has more rich characteristics, and classification technology is more accurate, but if the statistical code is too rigid, the malicious program is easy to avoid the detection of signatures [2–6].

In addition to signature matching, there are some new cryptographic algorithm recognition techniques, for example, the detection of cryptographic algorithm based on the cipher text randomness [7] and the cipher text statistics detection [8]. We can predict the cryptographic algorithms of the program to be tested by statistical correlation of cipher text, but this detection technique is complicated and cannot recognize the public key cryptography algorithm effectively.

In view of these problems, this paper presents a new technology for cryptographic algorithm recognition based on behavior analysis. Based on the behavior analysis and the static structure and dynamic statistical characteristics of the key data, the subroutine of the target program is gradually screened and positioned after the encryption subroutine to analyze the execution logic. Then, according to the different characteristics of each type of cryptographic algorithm, we can identify the code in the binary code of the program accurately.

The main contributions of this paper are as follows:

(1) Based on behavior analysis, and focusing on program execution results and algorithmic logic, this technology has a high efficiency for the program using traditional cryptographic algorithmic;
(2) Combined with the binary code of the program static feature matching and compilation level instruction dynamic piling comprehensive analysis, false negative rate and false positive rate are low and the accuracy is very high;
(3) Provide new ideas for new cryptographic algorithms and provide technical support for malware protection.

2 Related Technology

In the process of realizing the system, the DynamoRIO dynamic binary jacking platform is used to extract the index of metric of training data set and the naive Bayesian classifier is used to train data for coming into been probability model. The following two techniques will be introduced briefly and respectively:

2.1 DynamoRIO Dynamic Binary Jacking Platform

DynamoRIO is the simulation software at the process level working between the application layer and the operating system, whose working principle is been showing below:

As shown in Fig. 1, when DynamoRIO platform is debugging the program plug, the program will call the core components of the platform first. Then the code will be divided into basic blocks by built-in basic block builder and stored in the basic block cache. At the same time, non-control flow instruction in the cache will be running in sequential way until it encounters a control flow instruction. The tracking selection module then counts the call relationship between the basic blocks based on the control flow instruction and determines whether continuing the trace according to the context or not.

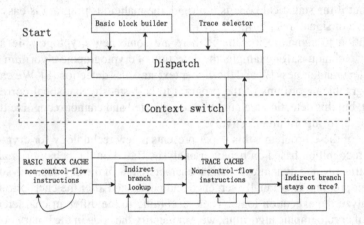

Fig. 1. The working principle of each component

To realize the efficient of instrumentation and debugging, DynamoRIO uses many kinds of optimization strategy such as code caching, linking, tracking builds and transparent use of resources. The code cache uses the local principle to use the basic block as a unit for the local use of the code cache processing to improve the efficiency of instruction read. The code cache uses the local principle to use the basic block as a unit for the local use of the code cache processing to improve the efficiency of instruction read. If target instructions already exist in code cache, and pointed by the direct jump instruction, DynamoRIO can jump directly to the code cache target instructions, to avoid context switching overhead. And in the process of debugging, DynamoRIO tries to be transparent and does not affect the use of the program itself.

2.2 Naive Bayesian Classifier

Naive Bayesian classifier is a very simple classification algorithm, whose ideological basis is as follows. As for the items to be sorted, naive Bayesian classifier can calculate the probability of occurrence of each category under the condition of this occurrence of the items and match with maximum probability value [10]. Its formal definition is as follows:

Step 1: Set x = {a1, a2, a3, …, am} as one item to be sorted, every a as one feature attribute of x;

Step 2: Set category collection C = {y1, y2, y3, …, yn};

Step 3: Calculate P(y1|x), P(y2|x), …, P(yn|x);

Step 4: If P(yk|x) = max{P(y1|x), P(y2|x), …, P(yn|x)}, x∈yk.

The key of the definition is the calculation of every conditional probability in step 3. First, find a collection of known categories to be classified, then add up conditional probability of every feature attribute to this category. That is to say P(a1|y1), P(a2|y1), …, P(am| y1); P(a1|y2), P(a2|y2), …, P(am|y2); …; P(a1|yn), P(a2|yn), …, P(am|yn). If every feature attribute condition is independent, we can get conclusion according to Bayesian formula which is:

$$P(yi|x) = (P(x|yi)P(yi))/(P(x)) \tag{1}$$

3   System Design and Analysis

This paper is based on the behavior analysis of the program to identify the cryptographic algorithm. The technology is based on the behavior analysis, through the subroutine screening in the target program, and gradually positioning to the encryption subroutine, and then analyze its execution logic. With the helping of static structure matching and dynamic statistical features, you can accurately identify the program binary code in the cryptographic algorithm and the algorithm accurate positioning. The general idea of cryptographic algorithm recognition is as follows (Fig. 2):

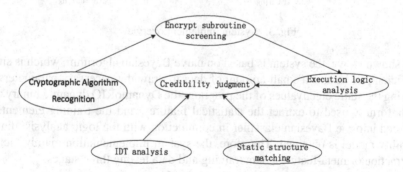

Fig. 2. Design method of system design

In order to realize the automatic identification of the system, we define the filtering rule of the encryption subroutine: (1) encryption subroutine is usually located in the subroutine call tree leaf node; (2) the number of basic block in encryption subroutine will not exceed 20; (3) the relative proportion of instruction mov in encryption subroutine is usual 40%–60% [9]. The execution logic analysis is mainly for the hash function, packet encryption algorithm, public key encryption algorithm and stream cipher. By extracting chain value initialization, cyclic shift and S box initialization, modular exponentiation and stream key generation logic, we can match with the general encryption algorithm. IDT (import directory table) analysis is mainly for the process of implementation of reference to the dynamic link library and analyses whether to call suspicious library functions, such as registry operations and reference encryption function library. Finally, the static structure matching is applied to the initialization chain value in hash function and the matching of the static structure such as the S-box and the P-box in packet encryption function. Through the execution logic analysis and help with the IDT analysis and static structure matching, we can make an accurate decision in the credibility of the program. What's more, the system introduces DynamoRIO dynamic binary analysis platform and naive Bayesian algorithm, the system frame is as follows (Fig. 3):

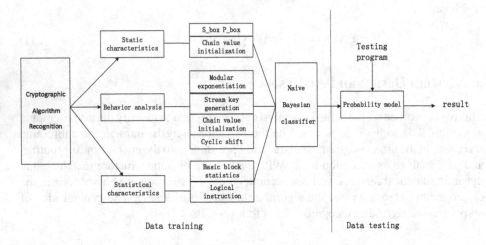

Fig. 3. System implement overview

As shown above, the system is based on naive Bayesian algorithm, which is simple and efficient, and trains a small amount of data to draw the necessary parameters. By extracting the static eigenvalues of the program, the DynamoRIO dynamic binary analysis platform is used to extract the statistical features, and the training elements are introduced into the Bayesian classifier in conjunction with the logic analysis, thus the probability model is obtained. Therefore, the system implementation mainly includes the extraction of meta-features, data training and data testing three stages.

3.1 Extract Metric Features

In the extraction meta-feature stage, many programs are mainly divided into two sets according to whether or not they contain the cryptographic function: the cryptographic assembly and the ordinary assembly. Then, DynamoRIO dynamic binary jacking platform is used to simulate the operation of each program, and calculates the probability relation between the program and the correlation quantity.

3.1.1   Extract Static Features

The static characteristics of this part in the extraction program mainly include S box and some static matrix structure. S box is widely used in block cipher, completing the confusion of cryptographic algorithms, and maintaining the relative stability in the process of implementation. For example, in AES encryption algorithm, S and S^{-1} are both 16 * 16 matrix, completing one mapping 8 bit input to 8 bit output; the DES function uses eight S-boxes, and each S-box is converted into the 6 bit input to 4 bit output. S box construction is generally in front of the implementation of the process and exists with static structure in the program for the internal table operation [11].

The static matrix is another static structure in the implementation of the encryption algorithm, which mainly completes the diffusion of the cryptographic algorithm. Diffusion is used to make the relationship between plaintext and cipher text acting as complex as possible. Any small changes in the plaintext will make the cipher text very different, and the realization of the diffusion is mainly based on the matrix multiplication. For example, in the AES encryption algorithm, the row shift is a 4 * 4 matrix for byte-to-byte permutations that provide the diffusivity of the algorithm. Column confusion is also used to adjust the relative position of the elements of the matrix transformation to improve the security of the algorithm. During the implementation, several key constants of the column confusion matrix are: 0x02, 0x01, 0x01, 0x03.

The static feature extraction flow chart is as follows:

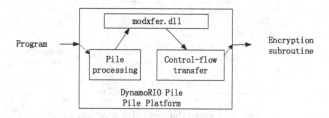

Fig. 4. Extract static features

As shown in Fig. 4, in order to identify whether the program contains S-box and static matrix and other key static structure, we first use the DynamoRIO dynamic stakes platform to run the test program, and then use the platform to compile the dynamic link library modxfer.dll on the target program Pile processing, reporting the flow of control flow between the modules, through the control flow call relationship to the encryption subroutine and its program entry, use the hexadecimal editor to open the program, jump to the encryption subroutine to static structure Of the keyword search, according to the search results and a small amount of experience we can determine whether the program contains S boxes and static matrix and other static structure.

3.1.2   Extract Dynamic Characteristics

The dynamic characteristic, a kind of statistical characteristic, is the obvious difference shown in the cryptographic program and the ordinary program in the process of executing the program. The dynamic extraction of this part mainly includes the relative proportion of the mov instruction of the subroutine during the execution of the program and the multiple cyclic encryption mode.

The mov instruction carries out the transfer function in the assembly level code, transfers the data between the CPU internal registers, transfers the immediate data to the general register inside the CPU, the data transfer between the register and the external memory, and the immediate value to the storage unit. The In the cryptographic algorithm subroutine, the mov instruction is usually used to complete the lookup operation of static structure such as S box, and the mov instruction is used to complete the temporary transmission of plaintext and cipher text data. Therefore, the relative instruction ratio of the mov instruction in the subroutine General subroutine is much higher.

The loop feature mainly completes the generation of block key in the block cipher algorithm, the iterative encryption, and optimizing the encryption efficiency of modal square residual algorithm in the public key cryptography. In the high-security encryption algorithm, the round robin plays a key role in the RC5 algorithm, the round robin is set to 18–20 to resist the differential analysis. In the DES algorithm, the subkey generates 16 cycles of iteration, and the key pair data is encrypted 16 times.

The dynamic feature extraction flow chart is as follows:

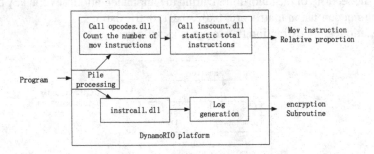

Fig. 5. Extract dynamic characteristics

As shown in Fig. 5, in order to extract the mov instruction relative proportion in the process of executing the program, in the implementation of DynamoRIO pile under the premise of the use of inscount.dll dynamic technology all the number of instructions and op codes.dll dynamic implementation of the decomposition of different instructions Code, and report the number, and then the number of instructions to move the number of instruction instructions, the mov instruction in the subroutine in the relative proportion. Through a large number of statistical data analysis, cryptographic algorithm subroutine mov instruction relative proportion should be more than 40%. The extraction of the loop pattern is based on the instrcalls.dll statistics direct call, indirect call and return the log file generated by the instruction to determine the number of iterations of the key function of the encrypted subroutine. According to the statistical results, the number of cycles of the subroutine must be more than 16 times to satisfy the metric measurement requirement.

3.1.3   Behavioral Analysis

The behavior analysis of the cryptographic program mainly focuses on the four main encryption algorithms: hash function, packet encryption algorithm, public key encryption algorithm and stream cipher. The hash algorithm is used to initialize the corresponding chain value. The packet encryption algorithm corresponds to the operation of the S-box and the P-box and the cyclic shift. The public key algorithm corresponds to the call of the large tree and the modular exponent operation. The stream cipher algorithm mainly analyzes the generation of the stream key.

Hash functions typically include an initialization module and a summary value generation module when the code is implemented. The initial memory unit requested in the initialization module plays the role of saving the initialized chain value, the intermediate block hash result, and the last hash value. In the disassembly result, the initial chain value is stored in the continuous memory unit (imm is the initial chain value) using successive mov imm, imm instructions, and the continuous memory unit uses add reg1, reg2; mov mem, reg1 or xor Mem, reg instruction form, the last packet processing is completed, the continuous memory unit to store the input data hash value.

In order to implement the "confusion" and "diffusion" of the plaintext data, the block cipher is usually used in static data such as S-boxes and P-boxes in feistel, SP and other network structures and stored in a binary executable file in a binary executable file in the data segment. In the disassembly results, the block password is usually used mov reg1, dword_addr [reg2] instruction on the P box, S box and other static array access.

The public key cryptography usually uses large primes in the implementation process. These large primes are usually generated by the random number generator. In the disassembly result, the RSA algorithm will show more obvious exponentiation operation. To optimize the modular exponentiation efficiency, the algorithm usually uses modulo residual implementation.

RC4 is the most widely used stream cipher, the algorithm generates a byte pseudo-random key stream, which is mixed with the plaintext operation to achieve the purpose of encryption, decryption, the generated pseudo-random flow and cipher text XOR operation to restore the plaintext.

3.2   Data Training

In the stage of data training, the probability statistic model is obtained based on the correspondence between each program and the five metric elements, the relative proportion of the cryptographic program and the common program.

The structure of the stage is as follows:

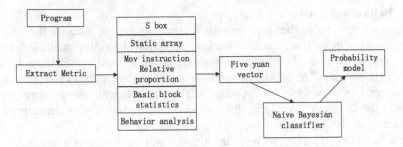

Fig. 6. Data training structure

As shown in Fig. 6, five metrics referred to as 5 yuan S_N -S boxes, static matrix- N_{ST}, mov instruction accounting for Nmov, cyclic mode Ncyc, behavior analysis- Nsh, for each of the programs there are (N_S, N_{ST}, Nmov, Ncyc, Nsh) five yuan vectors, each vector element value is 0 or 1.

As can be seen from the Eq. (1) Bayes' theorem, first we divide all the programs in the training data set into two categories according to whether the program is a cryptographic program, wherein the assembly referred to as a code C1, referred to as a common assembly C2. when the training data, all five of first element vector is introduced into all the program code Bayesian classifier, then count the number of each vector element value and class values that satisfy this condition, for example, the S-box train, first Count the number of cryptographic procedures, and then calculate the number of S boxes to meet the characteristics of the two can be compared to the S box can be obtained in the password program probability, the other meta-like solution.

Respectively, in the cryptographic program in the probability of the emergence of P1, P2, P3, P4 and P5, then in the password program, the proportion of each metric is the proportion of:

$$Qi = Pi/(P1 + P2 + P3 + P4 + P5) \tag{2}$$

The "i" above is in the range of 1 to 5, and the proportion of the probability of each meta-element in the common program can be solved by the same token, and the proportion of each metric element in the cipher program and the common program is recorded. The probability matching model of the cryptographic program can be obtained.

3.3 Data Testing

In the data testing phase, the probability model of data training is used to match the metric of the test program, to judge whether the program contains the cryptographic algorithm.

As can be seen from (2), the cryptographic program and the common proportion of each program in the proportion of the data in the test phase, for each test program, first in accordance with the provisions of Sect. 2.1 to extract the characteristics of the five elements of the program (0, 1, 1, 1, 1), and multiply the vector by multiplying the vector by the inverse of the vector. The probability of matching the program to the category is as follows:

$$X = (0, 1, 1, 1, 1) * (Q1, Q2, Q3, Q4, Q5)^{-1} \tag{3}$$

To recognize a cryptographic algorithm, we only need to compare X with Y, the expected value. If $X \geq Y$, the program is more likely to be a cryptographic program, and vice versa. Besides, because the password program and the ordinary procedure are opposite events, so we only need to judge one of these two cases.

4 Experiments and Assessment

In this essay, experimental environment is equipped with Intel i5-5200U CPU, 8 GB RAM, 128 GB SSD + 512 GB HDD, Windows 7 SP1 and DynamoRIO dynamic Pile Platform. Experiments and Assessment in this chapter contain three main stages: data collection, function assessment and effect assessment.

4.1 Data Collection

Collected data in this essay contains 563 programs which include 506 password programs and 57 normal programs and password programs accounted for 90% of whole programs. Password programs are mainly collected from famous on-line virus analysis websit-virustotal and academic support provided by AnTian company. All of code programs are assessed by virustotal and every program has only one category. Data categories are showed in a form below (Table 1):

Table 1. Collect data classification

	Cryptography	Normal	Total
Training	461	52	513
Testing	45	5	50

As No.1 form demonstrates, all of programs are divided into two parts: training set and testing set. Training set contains 513 programs, including 461 password programs and 52 normal programs. Two kinds of programs belong to different categories. Testing set contains 50 programs, including 45 password programs and 5 normal programs. This two kinds of programs are not distinguished.

4.2 Function Assessment

The aim of function assessment is to test that whether cryptographic algorithm recognition technology can distinguish the password programs from programs or not. The main body of the validation here is whether the naive Bayesian algorithm can generate the probability matching model according to the input training data set and whether the test data set can be detected and identified according to the probability model.

4.2.1   Production of Probabilistic Models

Production of probabilistic models needs to extract 5 metrics of static characteristics dynamic characteristics and behavioral characteristics and every 5 metric of each programs will produce 0/1 five yuan vector.

First, testing set's static characteristics which is the steady data structure when programs are processing should be extracted. Therefore, once encryption subroutine inside can be located, we can find whether the search subroutine contains the static structure through the string. In Sect. 3.1.1, we know that DynamoRIO binary digit analysis platform can identify programs control flow transfer through the transfer of program dynamic pile and modxfer.dll. and that help us find the entrance of the subroutine. The statistics for this section are as follows:

Table 2.   Static feature information collection

	Sbox	Static array	Total
Cryptography	273	150	423
Normal	3	9	12

It can be seen from Table 2 that the probability that the two static features of the S-box and the static matrix exist in the cryptographic program is much larger than that of the ordinary program.

The dynamic characteristics include the relative proportion of the mov instruction and the loop pattern. As can be seen from Sect. 3.1.2, the relative proportion of the mov instruction is to call the opcodes.dll and inscount.dll statistics subroutines in the program via the DynamoRIO platform. The number of instructions and the total number of instructions are compared with 40%–60%. For comparison, you can determine whether the indicator is met. Similar to the static structure, the search of the loop pattern is also done by locating it into the subroutine. From analysis, the part of the statistical results shown in the following table:

Table 3.   Dynamic feature information collection

	Mov	Cyclic shift	Total
Cryptography	403	125	528
Normal	10	23	33

As can be seen from Table 3, the general program may also contain more mov instructions and multiple loop structure, but compared to the password program is still less.

The extraction of behavioral characteristics is relatively simple, only need to locate the encryption subroutine, and then analyze its execution logic to determine whether it is modular exponentiation, stream key generation, cyclic shift or chain value initialization of one of them. The results are as follows:

Table 4. Behavioral feature information collection

	Behavioral characteristics	Total
Cryptography	453	453
Normal	5	5

As can be seen from the table, almost all of the password procedures are inline with the metrics.

4.2.2 Data Testing

According to the three tables in Sect. 4.2.1, we can get the frequency of the training data and the frequency of the common program. The frequency is approximately equal to the probability, and the following formula can be obtained by combining the formula (2):

Table 5. Cryptographic algorithm probabilistic mode

i=	1	2	3	4	5
Pi	59.2	32.5	87.4	27.1	98.2
Qi	29.3	10.7	28.7	9.0	32.3

From Table 5, we can get the probability model of the cryptographic function, which has the statistical probability and the relative proportion of each metric.

For the test data set, extract the meta-generated 0/1 five-dimensional vector, according to Table 4 data and calculation formula (3), take Y is 65%, that can determine whether the program is a password program.

4.3 Performance Evaluation

In order to compare the effectiveness of the technology, all the programs in the test set were tested and analyzed separately using the technique and the signature detection technique, respectively, the false alarm rate, the false negative rate and the accuracy rate. The results are as follows:

Table 6. Experimental comparison

	False positives	True negatives	Accuracy
Signature	10%	18%	86%
Behavior	4%	2%	97%

It can be seen from Table 6 that the algorithm is superior to the algorithm based on the signature matching algorithm in terms of false positive rate, false negative rate and accuracy rate, and the technology can identify unknown cryptographic procedures. Therefore, Naive Bayesian classifier cryptographic algorithm identification research technology has obvious practical value.

5   Conclusion

Based on the behavior analysis, combined with the key static structure and dynamic statistical characteristics, the subroutine of the target program is gradually screened, and the execution logic of the subroutine is analyzed. Finally, the cryptographic algorithm in the binary code of the program is obtained. In this process, DynamoRIO dynamic insertion technique is introduced to simulate the running, synchronous tracking and naive Bayesian classifier probability model. Whenever the cryptographic algorithm in the test program is used, the relative ratio of the S-box, the static data, the mov instruction in the subroutine, the cyclic shift operation and the behavioral characteristics are extracted, and then matched with the probability model whether the program contains a cryptographic algorithm inside. Compared with the traditional signature-based recognition technology, the technology occupies less resources, higher recognition rate, but also accurately identify the program variants.

References

1. Traynor, P., Chien, M., Weaver, S., et al.: Noninvasive methods for host certification. ACM Trans. Inf. Syst. Secur. (TISSEC) **11**(3), 16 (2008)
2. Chen, X., Andersen, J., Mao, Z.M., et al.: Towards an understanding of anti-virtualization and anti-debugging behavior in modern malware. In: 2008 IEEE International Conference on Dependable Systems and Networks With FTCS and DCC, DSN 2008, pp. 177–186. IEEE (2008)
3. Maiorca, D., Corona, I., Giacinto, G.: Looking at the bag is not enough to find the bomb: an evasion of structural methods for malicious pdf files detection. In: Proceedings of the 8th ACM SIGSAC Symposium on Information, Computer and Communications Security, pp. 119–130. ACM (2013)
4. Jana, S., Shmatikov, V.: Abusing file processing in malware detectors for fun and profit. In: 2012 IEEE Symposium on Security and Privacy (SP), pp. 80–94. IEEE (2012)
5. Marpaung, J.A.P., Sain, M., Lee, H.J.: Survey on malware evasion techniques: state of the art and challenges. In: 2012 14th International Conference on Advanced Communication Technology (ICACT), pp. 744–749. IEEE (2012)
6. Ugarte-Pedrero, X., Balzarotti, D., Santos, I., et al.: SoK: deep packer inspection: a longitudinal study of the complexity of run-time packers. In: 2015 IEEE Symposium on Security and Privacy (SP), pp. 659–673. IEEE (2015)
7. Yang, W., Tao, W., Meng, X., et al.: Recognition scheme of block cipher algorithm based on categorical randomness metrics distribution. J. Commun. **36**(4), 147–155 (2015)
8. Yang, W., Tao, W., Jindong, L.: A new method of statistical detection for cryptography of block cipher algorithm. J. Ordnance Eng. Coll. **27**(3), 58–64 (2015)
9. Jizhong, L.: Research on key technology of cryptographic algorithm identification and analysis. The PLA Information Engineering University (2014)
10. Jizhong, L., Liehui, J., Qing, Y., et al.: Recognition algorithm of cryptographic algorithms based on Bayes decision. Comput. Eng. **34**(20), 159–160 (2008)
11. Liu, T.M., Jiang, L., He, H., et al.: Researching on cryptographic algorithm recognition based on static characteristic-code. In: Security Technology, pp. 140–147 (2009)

A Struts2 Unknown Vulnerability Attack Detection and Backtracking Scheme Based on Multilayer Monitoring

Anqi Hu[1,2], Guojun Peng[1,2(✉)], Zhenhang Chen[1,2], and Zejin Zhu[1,2]

[1] Key Laboratory of Aerospace Information Security and Trusted Computing,
Ministry of Education, Wuhan University, Wuhan 430072, China
huanqiwhu@163.com, guojpeng@whu.edu.cn
[2] School of Computer Science, Wuhan University, Wuhan 430072, China

Abstract. For Struts2, attacks using unknown vulnerabilities are difficult to be detected and the details of the exploit are hard to be figured out. In this paper, we analyze the internal structure of Struts2 framework and the details of recent remote code execution vulnerabilities. Then we implement the monitoring mechanism on Struts2 application source layer, OGNL language layer and Java virtual machine system layer, and build a common detection framework and vulnerability detail backtracking scheme of Struts2 unknown vulnerability attack. Finally, through the experiments based on almost all (including nine "unknown" and three known) of the Struts2 remote code execution vulnerabilities since 2013, the result shows that the scheme can detect all the vulnerabilities and quickly locate the exploiting details, while the average performance loss is only 2.4%.

Keywords: Unknown vulnerability detection · Struts2 framework · Detail backtracking · Remote code execution

1 Introduction

The rapid development of information industry has brought unprecedented prosperity of information technology [1–3]. At the same time, web applications spring up. In order to develop applications quickly, developers often use many mature components and frameworks to build them. Struts2 framework is widely used in software development [4], which is a free, open-source, MVC framework for creating elegant, modern Java web applications. Moreover, it is widely used by banks, governments, and e-business.

The number of network security vulnerabilities presents a steady growth phase [5]. In addition, there are many vulnerabilities in the history of Struts2 framework, which caused great losses to enterprise and related agencies. Table 1 lists the remote code execution vulnerability (hereinafter referred to as RCE) published in 2016–2017. So far, Struts2 official announced 46 vulnerabilities, including 22 RCE vulnerabilities, which accounted for a large proportion. Moreover, the historical events indicate that Struts2 RCE vulnerability has a huge impact on the enterprise.

© Springer Nature Singapore Pte Ltd. 2017
M. Xu et al. (Eds.): CTCIS 2017, CCIS 704, pp. 383–396, 2017.
https://doi.org/10.1007/978-981-10-7080-8_26

Table 1. 2016–2017 Struts2 RCE vulnerability list [13]

Label	Type	Hierarchy of affects	Affects version	Year
S2-046	RCE	Critical	2.3.5 – 2.3.31, 2.5 – 2.5.10	2017
S2-045	RCE	Critical	2.3.5 – 2.3.31, 2.5 – 2.5.10	2017
S2-042	RCE	High	2.3.20 – 2.3.31	2016
S2-037	RCE	High	2.3.20 – 2.3.28.1	2016
S2-036	RCE	Medium	2.0.0 – 2.3.28.1	2016
S2-033	RCE	High	2.3.20 – 2.3.28 (except 2.3.20.3 and 2.3.24.3)	2016
S2-032	RCE	High	2.3.20 – 2.3.28 (except 2.3.20.3 and 2.3.24.3)	2016
S2-031	RCE	Medium	2.3.20 – 2.3.28 (except 2.3.20.3 and 2.3.24.3)	2016
S2-029	RCE	Important	2.0.0 – 2.3.24.1 (except 2.3.20.3)	2016

At present, the official and security researchers have proposed different detection and protection schemes. When Struts2 RCE vulnerabilities appear, the official will quickly analyze and release patches. The remediation strategy for known vulnerabilities is: (1) Maintain blacklist and whitelist at the entrance of the vulnerability and filter the user input data; (2) Modify the source code in the code execution place, so that it is no longer used OGNL language for processing. Nevertheless, we found that there are problems in such a patch program. Such as S2-037, which was found after the S2-033 appeared, is discovered by the attacker in the same class file and different point.

In the case of unknown vulnerability protection, Struts2 official also limited the execution ability of the OGNL language at the bottom. The main strategy is to maintain a blacklist of sensitive classes and methods. When OGNL statement executes, it will firstly perform a series of grammar analysis, and finally call the specified class and method. Therefore, before calls the class and method functions, the official will add blacklists to filter dangerous classes and methods. However, due to the power of the OGNL language, it can control the blacklist through the "#_memberAccess" global object. Therefore, the attacker repeatedly bypassed the unknown vulnerability protection scheme in the subsequent exploits of vulnerability.

OWASP security team proposed a mitigation strategy for Struts2 vulnerability attacks: Using the JDK's security manager, which imposes restrictions on the implementation of the underlying code interface [6]. This scheme can actually alleviate the unknown RCE vulnerability attacks. When the Web application tries to execute command, JDK will report an error and block it. Nevertheless, this scheme cannot get the entire process information about the vulnerability from the entrance to the final implementation, cannot define strategy flexibly, and can only make protection according to the functionality provided by the official API.

In the industry, OWASP security team has made comprehensive analysis about Struts2 framework [7]. IBM's analysis of Struts2 historical vulnerabilities shows that the blacklist and whitelist strategy of the Struts2 framework cannot guarantee safety. Furthermore, Struts2 create vulnerabilities in the same location more than once [8]. The academia has also done a lot of research on Struts2 framework and Java Web application vulnerability detection. The paper published by Olgierd Pieczul described how to use Runtime Detection technology to discover the 0-day vulnerability on the modern software system, and used Struts2 framework as a component representative to validate 19 known vulnerabilities successfully [9]. The detection methodology needs to define the range of monitoring and the level of abstraction, which will produce huge data. Therefore, it cannot be applied to enterprise-level software. Matthias Rohr has developed a visualization tool called Kieker [10] which can constantly monitor the behavior of Java software. For discovering Java Web application system vulnerability, the researchers often perform static analysis on the source code [11, 12].

In short, Struts2 framework is widely used and the impacts of the vulnerability of the framework are huge. Nevertheless, for Struts2 unknown vulnerability detection, the schemes of the official and the security experts have some flaws.

This paper proposed a scheme that can detect unknown vulnerabilities and restore the exploiting details, which effectively compensate for the above shortcomings. The scheme summarized common exploit model of vulnerability through systematically analyzing the source architecture of the Struts2 and its history RCE vulnerabilities. Based on this, we designed an unknown vulnerability attack detection scheme, which can quickly backtrack details of the exploit.

Experiments confirmed the protection scheme proposed in the paper can successfully intercept all payloads used by attackers, make up the lack of the Struts2 official protection strategy in defending the unknown vulnerability attack. At the same time, the scheme perform interception at all levels including the JDK layer, and output function calls and parameter information. Based on the scheme, we can intercept unknown vulnerabilities, get more details about the code execution process and define protection policies flexibly. Experiments proved that this scheme is simple and effective, which can be used in the real Web application environment with lower performance loss.

The main contributions of this paper are listed as follows:

1. Make a comprehensive analysis on the Struts2 overall architecture and historical vulnerabilities; summarize the common exploit model of framework RCE vulnerabilities.
2. Propose an accurate and efficient scheme to detect unknown vulnerabilities and trace back vulnerability details.

2 Design of Unknown Vulnerability Attack Detection Scheme

In Struts2 RCE vulnerabilities, there are typical representatives such as S2-016, S2-029, S2-045 and so on. This section analyzes the overall architecture of Struts2, and perform an execution path analysis at the source level on the typical vulnerabilities. Combined with the historical RCE vulnerabilities, we summed up a RCE common exploit model. Based on this, we intercept the key part of the common exploit model and give the details of the scheme.

2.1 Architectural Analysis of Struts2

The process from the request to the response of Struts2 is shown in Fig. 1. In the Struts2 architecture, user requests (HttpServletRequest) should go through the filters first, and then query ActionMapper to determine whether need to call the developer's customized Action program to process business logic. If we need to call Action, we can find the invoked class, method and view pages through the configuration file Struts.xml. Then we can generate an ActionInvocation by ActionProxy to complete a call execution on developer's customized Action class. During this time, the framework will use multiple interceptors to process the data in a recursive manner. Finally, according to different processing results, we can jump to the specified front-page (JSP, FreeMarker, Velocity, etc.), and return results to client side.

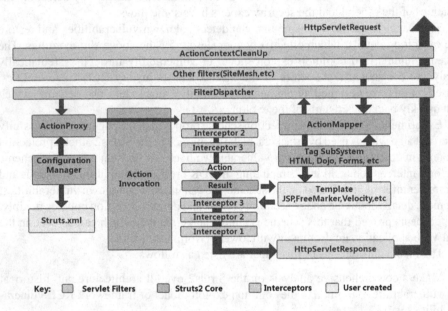

Fig. 1. Struts2 architecture

According to the process analysis, we can find that Struts2 will do some default internal processing in the whole procedure from the user input to the final output, such as filters, interceptors, and URL handling. An ordinary programmer always focuses on the logic of the business level, but does not pay attention to the logic of the component's internal processing. Therefore, once security problems occurred in the internal processing of Struts2, it will be difficult to locate and repair it timely. In addition, the analysis of the previous vulnerabilities shows that these internal processes will often lead to new security issues.

2.2　Common Struts2 Vulnerability Exploit Model

After combing the user request processed by Struts2, we analyze the historical RCE vulnerability at the source level and find that there are common characteristics of attacks against the framework. As a result, we can extract a common exploit model for Struts2 vulnerability attacks.

In 2013, a typical vulnerability raised in Struts2, whose principle and process are shown in Fig. 2. The vulnerability takes advantage of the redirection function, it can transfer the user input URL and data to the ActionMapper for parsing. If it includes redirect command (redirect: specify the URL), then jump to the specified page. However, if the user enters a redirection URL address that contains malicious code, the framework will use the OGNL language API to parse. Finally, it makes a remote code execution vulnerability. OGNL language is a very powerful language, which can create any Java object and modify the Struts2 internal object properties. As a result, you can finally achieve the purpose of executing system commands and reading or writing files.

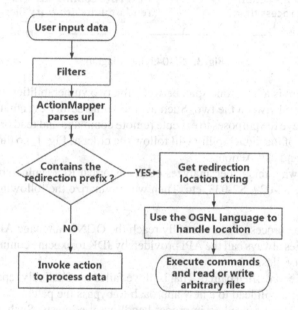

Fig. 2.　S2-016 flow diagram

In 2017, there was a new RCE vulnerability S2-045 in Struts2, whose principle and process are shown in Fig. 3. It uses the upload function of Struts2. When user uploads a file whose Content-Type attribute is embedded in the malicious code, the framework will resolve the internal error. The error message will be handled by the OGNL language, which contains the injected malicious OGNL code. Ultimately, the attack can achieve to execute the command, read and write arbitrary files.

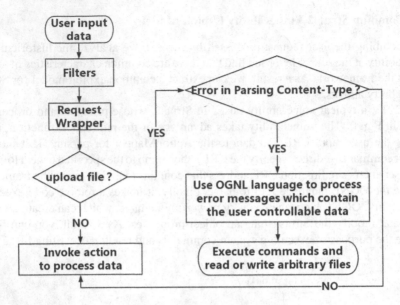

Fig. 3. S2-045 flow diagram

Although there is a long time span between the two vulnerabilities, but there is still some resemblance between the two. Such as: the vulnerability eventually uses OGNL language to achieve the purposes to execute remote command and read or write arbitrary file. The process of the vulnerability will follow the order as Fig. 1: go through the filter, parse the URL, and call Action.

In the same way, this paper analyzes other historical RCE vulnerabilities process, such as: S2-020, S2-029, S2-033, etc. Then we summarize the following similar characteristics:

1. The execution process will eventually reach the OGNL language API.
2. Vulnerabilities always call the API provided by JDK to execute commands, read and write arbitrary files.
3. Vulnerabilities are often paired. That is, if we failed to effectively repair the previous vulnerability, it will lead to a new approach to bypass the patch.
4. Vulnerabilities are caused by improper handling of requests. Such as: the problem focused on the process of parsing the URL by filters, uploading data, handling parameters by parameter interceptor and parsing URL request by the official plugin's special rules.

Based on the above characteristics, this paper summarizes the common exploit model of Struts2 historical vulnerabilities, as shown in Fig. 4.

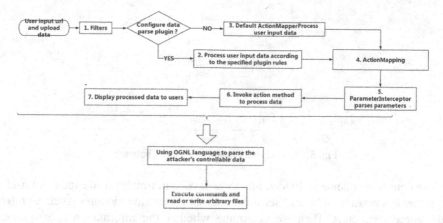

Fig. 4. Common Struts2 vulnerability exploit model

Figure 4 marked 1–7, which is the data processing section of the framework, but also the key points that the RCE vulnerabilities trigger, and the only way to process user's requests. User's input will firstly go through the filter and package processing (S2-045 and S2-046 trigger point). Then, if configured by a plugin, the ActionMapper (S2-033 and S2-037 trigger points) passed to the REST plugin, and then generates an Action-Mapping object. Otherwise, it is handled by the default ActionMapper class (S2-016 trigger point). The ActionMapping object includes called Action, method name, and the final display of the Result, parameter values and other important information. Then, the parameters are processed by the ParameterInterceptor (S2-003, S2-005, S2-009 trigger points). Finally, the ActionProxy calls the Action's method to handler business logic (S2-032 trigger point). After the business process is completed, the program will find the corresponding result class (Result) to display the results to the user. If Struts2 cannot find the corresponding JSP and other view files and is configured with the Convention plugin, it will find view pages (S2-042 trigger point) in accordance with the default rules. In addition, these trigger points and processes will eventually converge to the underlying OGNL language API, and then call the underlying Java API to achieve executing commands, and reading or writing arbitrary files.

2.3 Detection Scheme Design

According to the summary in Sect. 2.2, this paper presents a scheme for Struts2 unknown RCE vulnerability detection and backtracking details, as shown in Fig. 5.

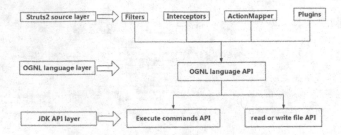

Fig. 5. Struts2 vulnerability detection scheme

The detection scheme is divided into three levels: in first level, we intercept useful parameter information in Struts2 sensitive internal processing modules (such as: filters and interceptors, etc.). Then we determine whether the information is suspicious according to the historical vulnerabilities. In level two, we inject hook code in the OGNL syntax parsing API, to get the incoming parameter value and use the blacklist to determine whether it is a suspicious Payload. In level three, we intercept sensitive operations' API in the underlying Java virtual machine. The scheme mainly intercepts two relatively important sensitive operations: execute commands, read or write files. The details of this interception scheme will be discussed in Sect. 3.

Through the above interception scheme, we can get the detail about the process from the input to the bottom of the implementation of OGNL language. If the system performs sensitive operation, the bottom JDK API will capture the information. Therefore, by analyzing the sensitive information generated at each level, we can determine the type of attack, such as unknown vulnerabilities, known vulnerabilities, and whether do harm to the system. In addition, we can combine information from all levels to review the details of the vulnerabilities quickly.

Vulnerability detection rules are shown in Table 2. In the first four lines of the table, we can find that JDK has intercepted the sensitive API call and it proves that the vulnerability has been exploited successfully and done some harm. According to the intercepted information of historical vulnerability entries in the application layer and OGNL

Table 2. Vulnerability detection rules

Source	OGNL	JDK	Result
✓	✓	✓	Known vulnerability, Successful attack
✗	✓	✓	Unknown vulnerability, Successful attack
✓	✗	✓	Unknown vulnerability, Successful attack
✗	✗	✓	Unknown vulnerability, Successful attack
✓	✓	✗	Known vulnerability, Unsuccessful attack
✗	✓	✗	Unknown vulnerability, Unsuccessful attack
✓	✗	✗	Known vulnerability, Unsuccessful attack
✗	✗	✗	Normal request

Note: "✓" represents it can intercept the suspicious information,
"✗" represents it cannot intercept the suspicious information.

layer, we can determine whether it is an unknown vulnerability attack. Moreover, the fifth and sixth lines indicate that the attack has not occur at the system level, but the OGNL layer intercepted the suspicious Payload, which means that there have been suspicious vulnerability attacks. In addition, we can confirm whether they are unknown vulnerability attack through follow-up backtracking analysis.

According to the process of Fig. 4, we can restore the vulnerability from the input to the end of the entire process by combining the parameters value intercepted by the seven modules and the return information of functions with the OGNL language layer and JDK underlying information. If it is an unknown vulnerability, according to the above interception information and the underlying JDK functional call stack, we can backtrack the entire attack exploit details.

3   Implementation of the Detection and Backtracking of Unknown Vulnerabilities

3.1   Overall Implementation

1. Struts2 source code layer. We add our interception code in the seven modules marked in Fig. 4, output the parameters of sensitive function calls and their return values. We audit the parameters of the sensitive functions which had been used as vulnerabilities before, determine whether the call is dangerous according to the instance of former exploits.
2. OGNL Language layer. We need to filter out the suspicious payload because there is a lot of OGNL language execution inside the framework. Therefore, we maintain a blacklist of regular expression. When an OGNL language statement is detected, we match this statement with each regex in the blacklist. If the statement is matched, for instance, the statement has some sensitive strings as Class, Runtime, Process-Builder and so on, the statement will be considered as suspicious and its relevant information will be output to the log.
3. JDK API layer. We add our interception code in the sensitive underlying API of JAVA, which is the API of execution instructions and IO system. When these API are called, we output the information of instructions to be executed, or the file name and time of the call. We also output the information of the call stack at this moment for backtracking.

Based on the results of the interception in each layer and the rules presented in Table 2, we determine whether there is an unknown vulnerability attack. When there is one, we backtrack the start point of this attack based on the call stack information in the JDK API layer. Furthermore, we can analyze the information retrieved in Struts2 source code layer and the payload obtained in OGNL language layer, backtracking and positioning the exploit detail quickly.

3.2 Important Interception Point in Struts2 Source Code Layer

With the purpose of implementing the interception of the important information inside Struts2 framework, we analyze the source code of the seven sensitive modules presented in the exploit pattern showed in Fig. 4. Combing it with our former experience of debugging vulnerabilities, we list a part of key functions handling user information inside the framework, which is presented in Table 3.

Table 3. Interception points in Struts2 functions.

Class name	Method name	Function
DefaultActionMapper	getMapping()	Handle user requests
StrutsPrepareAndExecuteFilter	doFilter()	Entry point of the filter
Dispatcher	serviceAction()	Call action
DebuggingInterceptor	intercept()	Debug mode interceptor
StrutsResultSupport	execute()	Result support class
ParametersInterceptor	doIntercept(), setParameters()	Parameter interceptor
OgnlUtil	setValue(), getValue()	OGNL language interface

The last line of Table 3 is our interception for OGNL language. All the payloads aiming to OGNL language will finally get to this interface. Therefore, we use regular expressions right before this interface to audit the calls, determining whether there will be a suspicious attack. Struts2 framework is an open-source software build by Maven. In order to intercept each important function in each layer, we need to re-compile the source code of Struts2. By reading the source code of Struts2 we have found that Struts2 have official logging interface, which provides us with the convenience to intercept the important functions. Therefore, by configuring the logging interface, we use Logback, which is an open-source logging component, to add our interception code with the purpose of logging the important information. By doing this we finally get the custom version of Struts2 which has interception ability. Then we can use the information provided by this version of Struts2 to help us restore the detail of exploits.

3.3 JDK API Interception and Backtracking on Call Stack

Different from Oracle JDK, OpenJDK is an open-source version of JAVA development kit. Although it differs from Oracle JDK, OpenJDK can be considered as the same as Oracle JDK in the aspects of performance, functionality and running logic. Therefore, we edit the source code of OpenJDK and re-compile it to make it can intercept the calls on sensitive APIs. More specifically, we intercept these sensitive operations: executing directives, reading, and writing files, and the relevant classes to these operations are ProcessImpl, FileInputStream and FileOutputStream.

By the effort we have made, we can now obtain the command line, PID, the call stack, the name of the file and the time when a process calls the sensitive functions mentioned above. We then write the information we obtained into the log. The pseudo code is showed in Table 4. In Table 4, we list some simple ways to obtain the PID and Java call stack of the process which tends to operate some sensitive operations. Java call stack is created the same time when a process is being created. It belongs to the private part of the process and stores key information of the stack. By making use of the Java call stack, we can backtrack the procedure of the call, from the underlying API to the entry of the program.

Table 4. Pseudo code of interception function

1.	Obtain command line of name of the file to be read/written
2.	String pid = ManagementFactory.getRuntimeMXBean().getName();//obtain PID
3.	Throwable ex = new Throwable();
4.	StackTraceElement[] stackElements = ex.getStackTrace();//obtain call stack
5.	Use FileWriter to log the information.

3.4   The Method of Backtracking Exploits Details

We start our backtracking from the JDK API where it calls from OGNL layer. By combing the information of the attacking code of OGNL language layer and application layer interception, we can restore the whole exploit detail. Taking S2-032 for an example, the information we write into the log is presented in Table 5.

Table 5. The backtracking log of S2-032

[1]	[http-bio-8080-exec-3]: Try to exec command:touch s2-032 //the directive attacker tried to execute
[2]	com.opensymphony.xwork2.ognl.OgnlUtil.getValue(OgnlUtil.java:333)
[3]	com.opensymphony.xwork2.DefaultActionInvocation.invokeAction (DefaultActionInvocation.java:423) //Key point of OGNL execution.
[4]	[http-bio-8080-exec-3] try to exec Ognl expression:'Payload' //The payload is intercepted in OGNL language layer.
[5]	[http-bio-8080-exec-3] StrutsPrepareAndExecuteFilter – ActionMapping{name='HelloWorld',namespace='/example', method='Payload',......}// ActionMapping

In Java call stack, we find that in line 423 of the file DefaultActionInvocation.java, directives that will call OGNL is executed. The key of the exploit is in this line of code is shown in Table 6.

Table 6. Key code of S2-032

[1] methodResult = ognlUtil.getValue(methodName + "()", getStack().getContext(), action);

Then, the interceptor in OGNL language layer obtain the complete payload of the attack. In addition, the same payload string is found in the parameter interceptor in application layer and the output of the ActionMapper.

Taking all the information we obtained into consideration, the detail of the exploit is that: by setting the "method:" prefix attacker set the Action call method name to OGNL language. When Struts2 finally call that method by calling DefaultActionInvocation, OGNL language will resolve the method, resulting in the vulnerability.

4 Experimental Design and Data Analysis

4.1 Experiment Platform and Test Scenario

In order to verify the scheme's effectiveness to the unknown vulnerabilities attack detection and details backtracking. This paper uses the platform environment as Table 7.

Table 7. Experiment platform

Operating system	Strut2 version	JDK	Attack vector
Ubuntu 14.04.1 LTS	2.3.20	OpenJDK 7u40	Previous RCE vulnerability

Test scenario selected the Linux platform and used the OpenJDK 7u40 as underlying Java virtual machine environment. Experiment collect almost all (including nine "unknown" and three known) Struts2 remote code execution vulnerabilities since 2013 to attack Struts2 web application.

Experiment uses Struts 2.3.20 to test. Based on 2.3.20 release time, the RCE vulnerabilities that occurred after this time are defined as "unknown vulnerability". The code injected for 2.3.20 version will not specifically do intercept for "unknown vulnerabilities". According to the detection rule of Table 2 and experiment data, we obtain the result as Table 8.

Table 8. Vulnerability attack experimental results

Label	Source layer	OGNL	JDK	Detection results	Actual results	Details backtracking
S2-016	✓	✗	✗	Known vulnerability	Known vulnerability	✓
S2-020	✓	✗	✗	Known vulnerability	Known vulnerability	✓
S2-021	✓	✗	✗	Known vulnerability	Known vulnerability	✓
Debug mode	✓	✓	✓	Known vulnerability	Unknown vulnerability	✓
S2-029	✗	✓	✓	Unknown vulnerability	Unknown vulnerability	✓
S2-031	✗	✗	✓	Unknown vulnerability	Unknown vulnerability	✓
S2-032	✗	✓	✓	Unknown vulnerability	Unknown vulnerability	✓
S2-033	✗	✓	✓	Unknown vulnerability	Unknown vulnerability	✓
S2-037	✗	✓	✓	Unknown vulnerability	Unknown vulnerability	✓
S2-042	✗	✓	✓	Unknown vulnerability	Unknown vulnerability	✓
S2-045	✗	✓	✓	Unknown vulnerability	Unknown vulnerability	✓
S2-046	✗	✓	✓	Unknown vulnerability	Unknown vulnerability	✓

4.2 Analysis of Results

This paper collects nine "unknown vulnerabilities" and three "known RCE vulnerabilities" in the Struts2 application to perform attack tests. As shown in Table 8, this scheme can successfully discover 12 vulnerabilities attack. Detection rate is 100%. Eight "unknown vulnerabilities" were detected as "unknown vulnerabilities", and one "unknown vulnerabilities" was detected as "known vulnerability". All three "known vulnerabilities" were detected as "known vulnerabilities".

.The first three lines of Table 8 vulnerabilities are the known vulnerabilities, which can be all discovered by our scheme. Their exploits didn't apply to Struts 2.3.20 version, so they were unable to reach OGNL layer and JDK layer, and the actual attack is invalid. The vulnerability of line 4 is in the struts2's debug mode. Official security bulletin in the S2-008 has described this vulnerability, but has not patched it. Scheme intercepted the vulnerability attack vector, and the attack was successful, so the scheme detected it as a "known vulnerability". Nevertheless, it uses the OGNL language features, bypassing the underlying OGNL protection mechanism, so it should belong to an "unknown vulnerability".

Of the eight "unknown vulnerabilities" discovered, only S2-031 did not intercept suspicious attacks on the OGNL language layer. The vulnerability exploits the XSLT template injection method, directly call the underlying Java API execution system command. Therefore, the scheme only intercepted the attack vector in the JDK layer.

No false positives were found during the experiments. However, in the actual Web application, users also call the OGNL language API while sending a normal request. Therefore, you should adjust the API blacklist regular expression when deploying the actual Web application to avoid excessive false positives.

Table 8 shows that the scheme can trace all exploit details. Through the integration of the various levels of interception information and function call stack information, according to the method described in Sect. 3.4, can quickly locate the vulnerability details in the source code.

In order to test the performance loss of the application, this paper respectively examines the original framework and the modified framework that was injected with hook code. The experiment uses vulnerability packet to send 1200 requests. As shown in Table 9, by comparing the time consuming before and after the interception, the performance loss is about 2.4% (three mean) of the interception scheme.

Table 9. Results of performance

System	The number of requests	Time-consuming 1	Time-consuming 2	Time-consuming 3
Before interception	100 * 12	35.517 s	28.632 s	27.994 s
After interception	100 * 12	36.466 s	29.421 s	28.524 s

In summary, the proposed scheme has no significant loss of system performance. It can effectively discover unknown Struts2 RCE vulnerability attacks. Furthermore, it can use the various levels of interception information to help quickly trace the vulnerability details.

5 Conclusion

In this paper, we propose a comprehensive system level detection scheme to discover unknown vulnerability attack and quick locate the exploit details. Through the analysis of historical vulnerability and system architecture, we summarize the common exploit model of vulnerability. We inject hook code in the Struts2 source layer, OGNL language layer and the Java virtual machine system layer. In this way, we can get the internal processing details of the vulnerability from the entry to the attack endpoint. Based on this, we can determine whether the request is an unknown vulnerability attack. Furthermore, by analyzing intercept information, we can restore the vulnerability details. Finally, we design an experiment scenario based on the historical RCE vulnerability of the Struts2 framework, and the experimental results show that the scheme is effective. The next step is to achieve a fully automated inspection system.

References

1. Wang, J., Shi, Y., Peng, G., et al.: Survey on key technology development and application in trusted computing. China Commun. **13**(11), 70–90 (2016)
2. Shen, C., Zhang, H., Feng D., et al.: Information security overview. Scientia Sinica (Technologica) **37**(1), 129–150 (2007)
3. Huanguo, Z., Jie, L., Gang, J., et al.: Development of trusted computing research. Wuhan Univ. J. Nat. Sci. **11**(6), 1407–1413 (2006)
4. Brown, D., Davis, C.M., Stanlick, S.: Struts 2 in Action. Dreamtech Press, New Delhi (2008)
5. He, P., Fang, Y.: A Risk assessment model of intrusion detection for web applications based on web server logs and website parameters. Netinfo Secur. **1**, 61–65 (2015)
6. OWASP: Attacking and Defending Struts2, 06 September 2013. https://prezi.com/yydldqt0dep-/attacking-and-defending-struts2/
7. Dabirsiaghi, A.: A Gap Analysis of Application Security in Struts2, 04 May 2009. https://www.owasp.org/images/b/be/A_Gap_Analysis_of_Application_Security_in_Struts2.pdf
8. Ashraf, Z.: Analysis of recent struts vulnerabilities in parameters and cookie interceptors, their impact and exploitation. IBM Security Intelligence portal (2014)
9. Pieczul, O., Foley, Simon N.: Runtime detection of zero-day vulnerability exploits in contemporary software systems. In: Ranise, S., Swarup, V. (eds.) DBSec 2016. LNCS, vol. 9766, pp. 347–363. Springer, Cham (2016). https://doi.org/10.1007/978-3-319-41483-6_24
10. Rohr, M., van Hoorn, A., Matevska, J., et al.: Kieker: continuous monitoring and on demand visualization of Java software behavior (2008)
11. Livshits, V.B., Lam, M.S.: Finding security vulnerabilities in java applications with static analysis. In: Usenix Security (2005)
12. Kong, Y., Zhang, Y., Fang, Z., et al.: Static detection of logic vulnerabilities in java web applications. In: 2012 IEEE 11th International Conference on Trust, Security and Privacy in Computing and Communications (TrustCom), pp. 1083–1088. IEEE (2012)
13. Apache Struts 2. Security bulletins (2017). https://struts.apache.org/docs/security-bulletins.html

An Approach of Implementing Core Role Based Access Control Model Using Attribute Based Encryption

Yong Wang[1]([envelope]), Xuemin Tong[1], Ming Li[2], Jingfeng Xue[1], Ji Zhang[1], Zhenyan Liu[1], Dan Hao[1], and Ning Wang[1]

[1] School of Software, Beijing Institute of Technology, Beijing, China
wangyong@bit.edu.cn
[2] The Third Research Institute Ministry of Public Security, Shanghai, China

Abstract. Cloud Storage, which provides cost-efficient and scalable storage services, has emerged as a hot paradigm today. However, in the resource outsourcing environment such as cloud storage, the resource owner is separated from the resource superintendent, and the authorization decision is made by the untrusted outsourcing server, as a result of which the correct enforcement of the access control policies cannot be ensured. To keep the data confidential against unauthorized parties, cryptographic access control must be applied. In this paper, we present a new cryptographic approach of implementing Core Role based Access Control Model named ABE-RBAC. We use Attribute Based Encryption (ABE) to manage users, roles, permissions, as well as user role assignments (URA) and role permission assignments (RPA), which enables the resource owner to fully control the authorization management, and ensures the proper enforcement of access control polices. This is the first cryptographic core RBAC enforcement that completely conform to the standard GB/T 25062-2010.

Keywords: Cryptographic access control · ABE · RBAC · GB/T 25062-2010 · Cloud Storage

1 Introduction

Storing data in Cloud Storage has become the most popular choice for personal and enterprise users during recent years. There are many Cloud Service Providers available, such as Amazon AWS, Microsoft Azure and Alibaba Aliyun. Cloud Storage provides effective and cost-efficient storage service, security concern has risen upon the fact that the data no longer reside within user's physical possession.

Cryptographic access control has been widely researched to protect the user's data in the Cloud Storage [1,8,9,11]. Because the revocations of user roles will cause large numbers of related users' secret keys updates, key distribution base schemes cannot apply to the environment with a huge number of strange users

M. Xu et al. (Eds.): CTCIS 2017, CCIS 704, pp. 397–408, 2017.
https://doi.org/10.1007/978-981-10-7080-8_27

and data owners. For improving these disadvantages, Sahai and Waters proposed an attribute-based encryption (ABE) scheme, where attributes have been exploited to generate a public key for encrypting data and have been used as an access policy to control users' access [12]. The access policy can be categorized as either key-policy (KP-ABE) or ciphertext-policy (CP-ABE). The key-policy is the access structure on the user's private key, and the ciphertext-policy is the access structure on the ciphertext.

Zhu et al. proposed an Attribute-based Encryption with Attribute Lattice, which makes use of RBAC concepts, while they didn't discuss how to use ABE to implement the whole (core) RBAC model [2]. Zhou et al. use ID-based Broadcast Encryption (IBBE) to send encrypted data to a group of users with specific roles by public broadcasting channel [8]. However, this proposal assumes that the user role assignments (URA) have already been assigned through traditional methods (Non-cryptographic methods), and it merely uses IBBE to implement role permission assignment (RPA), hence URA is easy to become a failure point. In addition, their approach cannot support the revocation of RPA. Hong et al. proposed a practical ABE based RBAC [3]. Their system applied CP-ABE to URA, where the user assigned a role can decrypt the key of the role, and the role key is used to encrypt the encryption key for all files that the role can access. Hence the RPA essentially encrypts the set of encryption keys corresponding to all the files that the role has access to with the role key. However, this scheme cannot achieve a fine-grained RPA policy and is less efficient when the user is revoked because it needs to update the encryption key for all files that the user can access. The data owner has to not only update the key of the role that is being revoked by the user and re-encrypt the file key set, but also to gather the re-encrypted file key corresponding to other users who have access to these files, and the user involved need to re-obtain and decrypt the file key collection.

In order to keep all the role based access control phases being protected by ABE, we propose a cryptographic core RBAC scheme to implement the core RBAC model specified by GB/T 25062-2010, which consists of management of users, roles, permissions, as well as user role assignments (URA) and role permission assignments (RPA). The scheme is named ABE-RBAC. It needs to be emphasized that we also provide flexible authorization and efficient user revocation, role revocation, URA revocation, RPA revocation. Our approach can provide technical basis and implementation reference for secure access control of enterprise application in untrusted outsourcing environment.

2   Preliminaries

2.1   Core Role Based Access Control

GB/T 25062-2010 defines three RBAC models: core RBAC, hierarchical RBAC and constrained RBAC, the core RBAC defines the essential elements and the minimal set of relations to implement a RBAC system. The management of the core RBAC features include user (USERS) and the character sets (ROLES) of creation and revocation, the assignment and revocation of the user-role assignment (URA) and role-permission assignment (RPA).

2.2 Ciphertext Policy-Attribute Based on Encryption (CP-ABE)

In 2007, Bethencourt et al. proposed a ciphertext policy attribute-based scheme, and the access policy in the encrypted data (ciphertext) [5]. A set of descriptive attributes are associated with the user's private key, and the access policy is built in the encrypted data. The access structure of the encrypted data is corresponding to the user's private key with a set of descriptive attributes. If a set of attributes in the user's private key satisfy the access structure of the encrypted data, the data user can decrypt the encrypted data; if not, the data user cannot obtain the message. For example, the access structure in the encrypted data is {MIS ∧ (Teacher ∨ Student)}. If a set of attributes in the user's private key is {MIS ∧ Teacher}, the user can recover the data.

2.3 Decisional q-MEBDH Assumption

Let $\mathbb{G}$ be a bilinear group of prime order p. the decisional q-MEBDH problem in $\mathbb{G}$ is stated as follows: first the challenger picks a generator g and the random exponents, $s, \alpha, \alpha_1, \cdots, \alpha_q$, The attacker is given a vector X =

$$g, g^s, e(g,g)^\alpha$$

$$\forall_{1 \leqslant i,j \leqslant q}, g^{\alpha_i}, g^{\alpha_i s}, g^{\alpha_i \alpha_j}, g^{\alpha/(\alpha_j^2)}$$

$$\forall_{1 \leqslant i,j,k \leqslant q, i \neq j}, g^{\alpha_i \alpha_j s}, g^{(\alpha \alpha_j)/(\alpha_i^2)}, g^{(\alpha \alpha_i \alpha_j)/(\alpha_k^2)}, g^{\alpha \alpha_i^2 / \alpha_j^2}$$

and an element $Z \in \mathbb{G}$ as input, determine if $Z = e(g,g)^\alpha s$. An algorithm A that outputs $b \in \{0,1\}$ has advantage ϵ in solving Decision q-MEBDH in $\mathbb{G}$ if:

$$|Pr[A(X, T = e(g,g)^{\alpha s} = 1)] - P[A(X, T = Z) = 1]| \geq \epsilon$$

We say that the Decisional q-MEBDH assumption holds in $\mathbb{G}$ if no polynomial-time algorithm has a non-negligible advantage in solving the problem.

3 Construction

The ABE-RBAC scheme includes a data owner (DO), a resource user and Cloud Service Provider (CSP), and the resource owner performs an access control scheme construction method, saves the generated public password information to the outsourcing server. The resource user from the outsourcing server can download the relevant ciphertext, and obtain the key information from the resource owner, and finally decrypt the resource. The scheme architecture is shown in Fig. 1.

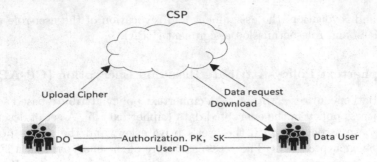

Fig. 1. ABE-RBAC scheme architecture

3.1 Access Control Model

In the Role-Based Access Control model, access permissions are assigned to roles rather than users, and users must activate a role to gain permissions. In our scheme, we completely use the basic concepts of users, roles and permissions in the core RBAC model. The structure of the whole model is consistent with the basic structure of the RBAC model. As shown in Fig. 2, for each user, his roles and the related permissions owned by the roles are identified by a unique ID, which is the only attribute of the user, role, and permission.

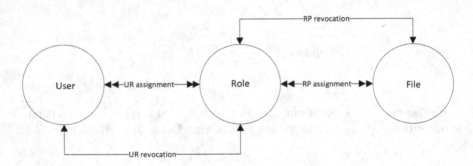

Fig. 2. ABE-RBAC Access control model

3.2 Scheme Construction

ABE-RBAC scheme contains 12 access control management functions specified by GB/T 25062-2010. These functions are listed in Table 1, the relationship among them and the enforcement architecture is shown in Fig. 3.

A. System Initialization–Setup(), used for creating system public key PK and system main encryption key MK. It includes following steps:

Step A1: Select biliner group $\mathbb{G}_0$ and $\mathbb{G}_1$ which with prime order p, randomly select two generators g and h of $\mathbb{G}_0$, then define bilinear mapping $e : \mathbb{G}_0 \times \mathbb{G}_0$

Table 1. Access control management function list

Function name	Function detail
Setup	System initialization generate PK and SK
Encrypt	Encrypt Privilege key
AddUser	Create a new user
AddRole	Create a new role
AssignUser	Assign user to a role
AddPermission	Create a new file
GrantPermission	Assign File to a role
CheckAccess	judge whether user IDU have access to resource IDF or not
DeassignUser	revoke the assigned relationship between user IDU and role IDR
RevokePermission	revoke the assigned relationship between role IDR and file IDF
DeleteUser	delete user IDU and update related key information
DeleteRole	delete user IDR and update related key information

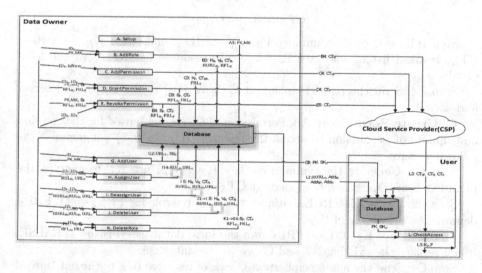

Fig. 3. Relationships among access control functions and the scheme's enforcement architecture

$\rightarrow \mathbb{G}_1$, select two stochastics $\alpha, \beta \in \mathbb{Z}_p$, select two hash function H1: $\{0,1\}^* \rightarrow \mathbb{G}_0$ and H2: $\mathbb{G}_0 \rightarrow \mathbb{Z}_p$.

Step A2: Generate system public key PK and system main encrypted key MK:

$$PK = (g, g^\beta, g^{\beta^2}, e(g,g)^\alpha, H1, H2)$$

$$MK = (\alpha, \beta, g^\alpha)$$

B. Create Role–AddRole (ID_R), used for new role $ID_R \in \{0,1\}^*$ to generate related key information, it includes following steps:

Step B1: Select randomly $ID_{U_0} \in \mathbb{Z}_p$, initialize revocation list of role user $RURL_R = \{ID_{U_0}\}$. It is the set of identities of user's revoked role ID_R. Initialize role resource list $RFL_R = \{\}$, RFL_R denotes the set of accessible resources ID_R.

Step B2: Select randomly V_R, $K_R \in \mathbb{Z}_p$, which are respectively regarded as the random number and key of role ID_R, assume $V_R{}^0 = V_R$, the computing process related to CT_R is as follows:

$$C_1 = g^{1/H2(K_R)}, C_2 = H(ID_R)^{1/H2(K_R)},$$

$$C = K_R \cdot e(g,g)^{\alpha V_R}, C_0 = g^{V_R},$$

$$C_{0,1} = g^{\beta V_R{}^0}, C_{0,2} = g^{\beta^2 V_R ID_{U_0}} h^{\beta V_R{}^0}$$

$$CT_{R,1} = (C_1, C_2, C, C_0)$$

$$CT_{R,2} = (C_{0,1}, C_{0,2})$$

$$CT_R = (C_{R,1}, C_{R,2})$$

Step B3: Save random number V_R, $V_R{}^0$ of ID_R, encrypted K_R, ciphertext CT_R, revoked list of role user $RURL_R$, role resource list RFL_R to the local database.

Step B4: Send the related ciphertext CT_R of ID_R to the outsourced server and save it.

C. Create Permission–AddPermission (ID_F, isNew): used for the creation and update of permission to access the resource $ID_F \in \{0,1\}^*$, it includes the following steps:

Step C1: Generate the symmetrical key $K_F \in \mathbb{Z}_F$: use K_F to encrypt the plaintext F of ID_F, generate ciphertext CT_{SF}.

Step C2: If isNew is TRUE, initialize the resource role list $FRL_F = \{\}$, FRL_F denotes the set of role of ID_F.

Step C3: Save K_F, CT_{SF}, FRL_F into the local database. If isNew is FALSE, it can replace the existing K_F and CT_{SF} in the database.

Step C4: Send the related ciphertext CT_{SF} of resource ID_F to the outsourced server and save it.

D. Role Permission Assignment–GrantPermission (ID_R,ID_F): used for the permission assignment of role $ID_R \in \{0,1\}^*$ for accessing resource $ID_F \in \{0,1\}^*$, it includes following steps:

Step D1: If ID_F is the resources newly created, that is FRL_F is empty, select randomly $S_F \in \mathbb{Z}_F$, executive $CT_F = $ Encrypt (ID_R, S_F,K_F,TRUE) to encrypt K_F. If FRL_F is not empty, resource owner gets random number related to ID_F and ciphertext CT_F from local database. Then $CT_F' = $ Encrypt $(ID_R, S_F, K_F, FALSE)$, and combine the result with CT_F, that is $CT_F \cup = CT_F'$.

Step D2: Update role resources list $RFL_R \cup = \{IDF\}$. Update resource role list as $RFL_F \cup = \{IDR\}$.

Step D3: Save S_F, CT_F, role resource list RFL_R, resource role list FRL_F into the local database.

Step D4: Send CT_F to the outsourced server and save it.

E. Role Permission Revocation–RevokePermission (ID_R, ID_F); used for renovation of role ID_R's access of ID_F, it includes the following steps:

Step E1: Update resource role list $FRL_{F^-} = \{ID_R\}$; Update role resource list $RFL_R -= \{IDF\}$.

Step E2: Execute AddPermission $(ID_F, FALSE)$. Encrypt K_F' after getting the update of resource ID_F.

Step E3: If FRL_F is not empty, then select randomly $S_F' \in \mathbb{Z}_p$. FRL_F consists of $|FRLF|$ factors (role). Denote the ith element of $FRL_F (i = 1,...,|FRLF|)$ as ID_{Ri}.

Compute $CT_{F1} = $ Encrypt $(PK, ID_{R1}, S_F', K_F', TRUE)$, then define variable j, j is successively set to be 2 to $|FRL_F|$, and compute $CT_{Fj} = $ Encrypt $(PK, ID_{Rj}, S_F', K_F', FALSE)$.

Step E4: Save S_F' and ciphertext $CT_F' = (CT_{F1}, CT_{F2}, CT_{F3}...CTF_{|FRLF|})$ into the local database. Respectively replace the original random number S_F and ciphertext CT_F related to access rights. Save resource role list FRL_F and role resource list RFL_R into the database.

Step E5: Send $CT_F' = (CT_{F1}, CT_{F2}, CT_{F3}...CTF_{|FRLF|})$ to the outsourced server and save it. Replace the existed ciphertext CT_F.

F. Encrypt–Encrypt $(ID_R, S_F, K_F, isNewOrReencrypt)$, used for encryption based on the characteristic of role when doing the role permission assignment and role permission revocation. Input parameter ID_R is the identification of accessible role, S_F is a random number related to resource ID_F. K_F is the symmetric encryption key of resource ID_F. isNewOrReencrypt is Boolean variable. When the value is TRUE, it means encryption is caused by the authorization when creating new resource or revocation of permission. Encryption includes the following steps:

Step F1: Compute $CT_{FR} = H(ID_R)^{S_F}$.

Step F2: If isNewOrReencrypt is TRUE, compute $C_3 = g^{S_F}$, $C_4 = K_F \cdot e(g,g)^{\alpha S_F}$, $C_5 = g^{\beta S_F}$, output encrypted text $CT_F = (C_3, C_4, C_5, CT_F{}^R)$, otherwise output CT_F^R.

G. Create User–AddUser (ID_U), used for new user ID_U to create key information, it includes following steps:

Step G1: Select randomly $t \in \mathbb{Z}_F$, as follows, compute the private key related to user ID_U:

$$D_0 = g^\alpha g^{\beta^2 t}, D_1 = (g^{\beta ID_U} h)^t, D_2 = g^{-t}$$

$$SK_U = (D_0, D_1, D_2)$$

Step G2: Initialize user role list $URL_F = \{\}$, URL_U denotes the set of roles owned by ID_U. Save URL_U and SK_U into the local database.

Step G3: Send the private key SK_U related to user's identity and system public key PK to user ID_U.

H. User Role Assignment–AssignUser (ID_U, ID_R), used for assigning role ID_R to user ID_U, it includes following steps:

Step H1: Update the role user list $RUL_R \cup = \{ID_U\}$and user role list URL_U $\cup = \{ID_R\}$. In which, RUL_R denotes the set of users with role ID_R, while URL_U denotes the set of users with role ID_U.

Step H2: Obtain ciphertext $CT_{R,1} = (C_1, C_2, C, C_0)$ related to role ID_R from the database.

Step H3: Select randomly r,w $\in \mathbb{Z}_p$, compute the private key related to role ID_R and user ID_U as follows:

$$D_3 = g^{(\alpha+w)}/\beta$$

$$D_R = g^{w/H2(K_R)} \cdot H(ID_R)^{r/H2(K_R)} = (C_1)^w \cdot (C_1)^r$$

$$D'_R = g^{r/H2(K_R)} = (C_2)^r$$

$$SK_U{}^R = (D_3, D_R, D'_R)$$

Step H4: Save role user list RUL_R, user role list URL_U, user role related private key SK_U^R and version number $Ver_U^R = 0$ into the local database.

I. User Role Revocation–DeassignUser (ID_U, ID_R), used for the revocation of the assigned relationship between user ID_U and role ID_R. It includes following steps:

Step I1: Name the sequence number of the revoked user ID_U in the role user revocation list as n, that is $n = |RURL_R|$. Identify user ID_U as ID_{U_n}. Update role user revocation list $RURL_R \cup = \{ID_{U_n}\}$. Update role user list $RUL_R - = \{ID_U\}$. Update the user role list: $URL_U - = \{ID_R\}$.

Step I2: Select randomly $V_R{}^n \in \mathbb{Z}_p$, $K'_R \in \mathbb{Z}_p$. Update the related random number $V_R = V_R + V_R{}^n$ of role ID_R. Update role of ID_R encryption key K_R to K'_R.

Step I3: compute C'_1, C'_2, C', C'_0, $C_{n,1}$, $C_{n,2}$ as follows:

$$C'_1 = g^{1/H2(K'_R)}, C'_2 = H1(ID_R)^{1/H2(K'_R)}$$

$$C' = K'_R \cdot e(g,g)^{\alpha V_R}, C'_0 = g^{V_R}, C_{n,1} = g^{\beta V_R^n}$$

$$C_{n,2} = (g^{\beta^2 ID_{U_0}} h^\beta)^{V_R^n}$$

$$CT'_{R,1} = (C'_1, C'_2, C', C'_0)$$

$$CT'_{R,2} = CT_{R,2} \| (C_{n,1}, C_{n,2})$$

Step I4: Update the encryption key of every user ID_U in RUL_R, select randomly r,w $\in \mathbb{Z}_p$, the following is to compute the private key related to role ID_R of user ID_U:

$$D_3 = g^{(\alpha+w)/\beta}, D_R = (C')^w \cdot (C'_2)^r, D'_R = (C'_1)^r$$

$$SK_U^R = (D_3, D_R, D_R')$$
$$Ver_U^R + = 1$$

Step I5: Save random number V_R, private key K_R' and ciphertext $CT_{R,1}'$, $CT_{R,2}'$ into the local database. Replace the existing random number V_R, private key K_R and ciphertext $CT_{R,1}$, $CT_{R,2}$ related to role ID_R.

Save role user list RUL_R, role user revocation list $RURL_R$ and user role list URL_U into the local database. Save the related private key and version number Ver_U^R in the role user list RUL_R into the local database.

J. Delete User–DeleteUser (ID_U), used for deleting user ID_U and updating related key information. It includes the following steps:

Step J1: Respectively execute the user role revocation DeassignUser (ID_U, ID_R) for all the roles ID_R in the user role list.

K. Delete Role–DeleteRole (ID_R), used for deleting role ID_R, and update the related key information. It includes the following steps:

Step K1: Respectively execute role permission revocation RevokePermission (ID_R, ID_F) in the role resource list RFL_R. Respectively execute role permission revocation.

L. Authorization–CheckAccess (ID_U, ID_F) for all the resources ID_F in the role resource list of ID_R, to decide whether user ID_U have access to resource ID_F or not. If it has access, then decrypt the ciphertext CT_F of ID_F. It includes the following steps:

Step L1: Resource owner compute the set RU_F. If $URL_U \cap FRL_F = RU_F$ is not empty, select any role ID_R from RU_F, and then gather $RURL_R$, the download address Add_R in the encryption CT_R, the download address Add_{SF} and Add_F in the outsourced server in CT_F and the related ciphertext CT_{SF} in ID_F, private key SK_U^R related to role ID_R and version number Ver_U^R, send it to user ID_U.

Step L2: If RU_F is empty, user ID_U have no access to resource ID_F, cancelled.

Step L3: User ID_u downloads ciphertext $CT_R = (C_1, C_2, C, C_0, C_{0,1}, C_{0,2}, C_{1,1}, C_{1,2},..., C_{|RURL_R|,1}, C_{|RURL_R|,2})$ related to role ID_R and CT_{SF}, $CT_F = (C_3, C_4, C_5, CT_F^R)$ related to role ID_R from the outsourced server. Continue to execute Step L4.

Step L4: User ID_U use private key $SK_U = (D_0, D_1, D_2)$ related to identity and private key $SK_U^R = (D_3, D_R, D_R')$ related to role and ciphertext CT_R and to decrypt the ciphertext CT_{SF} related to resource ID_F.

The computing process is as follows:

$$\frac{e(C_0, D_0)}{e\left(D_1, \prod_{i=0}^{|RURL_R|-1}(C_{i,1})^{\frac{1}{ID_U-ID_{U_i}}}\right) \cdot e\left(D_2, \prod_{i=0}^{|RURL_R|-1}(C_{i,2})^{\frac{1}{ID_U-ID_{U_i}}}\right)}$$

$$= e(C_0, D_0) / \left(\prod_{i=0}^{|RURL_R|-1} (e(D_1, C_{i,1}) \cdot e(D_2, C_{i,2}))^{1/(ID_U, ID_{U_i})} \right)$$

$$= e(g,g)^{\alpha V_R} \cdot e(g,g)^{V_R \beta^2 t} / \left(\prod_{i=0}^{|RURL_R|-1} (e(g,g)^{V_R^i \beta^2 t}) \right)$$

$$= e(g,g)^{\alpha V_R} \cdot e(g,g)^{V_R \beta^2 t} / e(g,g)^{V_R \beta^2 t}$$

$$= e(g,g)^{\alpha V_R} \tag{1}$$

Then compute:

$$C/D' = K_R \cdot e(g,g)^{\alpha V_R}/e(g,g)^{\alpha V_R} = K_R$$

Then Compute:

$$A = e((D_R)^{H2(K_R)}, C_3)/e((D'_R)^{H2(K_R)}, CT_F^R)$$

$$= e((g^{w/K_R} \cdot H(ID_R)^{r/H2(K_R)})^{H2(K_R)}, g^{S_F})/e((g^{r/H2(K_R)})^{H2(K_R)}, H(ID_R)^{S_F})$$

$$= e(g^w \cdot H(ID_R)^r, g^{S_F})/e(g^r, H(ID_R)^{S_F})$$

$$= e(g,g)^{w S_F}$$

Finally compute:

$$C_4/e(C_5, D_3)/A = K_F \cdot e(g,g)^{\alpha S_F}/e(g^{\beta S_F}, g^{(\alpha+w)/\beta})/e(g,g)^{w S_F} = K_F$$

Step L5: The resource user decrypts the ciphertext CT_{SF} of the resource ID_F using the key K_F obtained by the step L4 decryption, and the plaintext F, K_F and F will be stored into the local database.

4   Performance

This section evaluates the performance of our ABE-RBAC scheme. The role creation and permission assignment operations correspond to cryptographic operations in our scheme, where user creation and role assignment correspond to key generation operations, and authorization decisions correspond to decryption operations in the encryption scheme. The number of users, roles and files, the number of users assigned by each role, the number of roles authorized by each file, and so on, can affect the actual operation efficiency. So, we analyze the performance of the ABE-RBAC scheme under three different scenarios (A, B, C) with different parameters. The scenarios we designed are listed in Table 2.

Table 2. Scenarios for performance analysis

	A	B	C
Number of users	100	1000	10000
Number of roles	10	50	100
Average number of roles assigned to each user	2	5	10
Number of files	10000	100000	1000000
Average number of files assigned to each role	1000	10000	100000

We set the size of each file to 1 KB, and all the data stored in memory, does not involve network transmission and database access operations. The test environment used is Intel i5 2.7 Ghz, the memory is 4G, and the operating system is Ubuntu 16.04LTS. The part of cryptography implementation uses the JPBC (Java Pairing-Based Cryptography Library). After running the three scenarios ten times, the average running time of each key algorithm is obtained, as shown in Table 3. And compared with the running time of role access control scheme implemented by Hong [3].

As we can see from Table 3, the URA, RPA, and file access operations are computationally expensive and stable, regardless of the number of users in the scenario, the number of roles, and the number of files, and the cost is lower than the Cheng Hong's scheme. While the cost of UR revocation and the RP revocation of higher, because we use costly paring operations to assure the security, which is different from Cheng Hong. In fact, the cost is no higher than hundreds of microseconds, which is acceptable by most use cases. That is a balance between security and performance.

Table 3. Comparison of average time cost between our scheme and Cheng Hong's scheme

	ABE-RBAC (ms)			Cheng Hong (ms)		
Operations	A	B	C	A	B	C
UR assignment	62	65	88	170	190	194
UR revocation	269	590	1134	160	189	189
RP assignment	115	154	175	143	189	26
RP revocation	143	932	1830	160	197	293
File Access	94	172	152	140	185	260

Our scheme uses the CP-ABE [5] and its revocation schemes [6] as basic building blocks in a straightforward way, so it can be easily proved to be secure in the generic group model under the qDecisional Multi-Exponent Bilinear Diffie-Hellman assumption.

5   Conclusions

In this paper, we use ABE to implement a cryptographic role-based access control scheme (ABE-RBAC). To the best of our knowledge, this is the first cryptographic core RBAC enforcement that completely conform to the standard GB/T 25062-2010. The whole process of role access control are based on attribute based encryption can securely support user-role and role-permissions grant and direct revocation. At the same time, the application of attribute based encryption also avoids the illegal rights escalation and unauthorized access of authorized users in traditional system. Our scheme not only keeps the flexible and efficiency of RBAC model and the strong security provided by ABE. In the future, we should consider how to improve the computational efficiency of ABE-RBAC, reduce computation overhead, and provide more fine-grained access control.

References

1. Qin, B., Deng, H., Wu, Q., et al.: Flexible attribute-based encryption applicable to secure e-healthcare records. Int. J. Inf. Secur. 14(6), 499–511 (2015)
2. Zhu, Y., Ma, D., Hu, C.J., et al.: How to use attribute-based encryption to implement role-based access control in the cloud. In: International Workshop on Security in Cloud Computing, pp. 33–40. ACM (2013)
3. Hong, C., Lv, Z., Zhang, M., Feng, D.: A secure and efficient role-based access policy towards cryptographic cloud storage. In: Wang, H., Li, S., Oyama, S., Hu, X., Qian, T. (eds.) WAIM 2011. LNCS, vol. 6897, pp. 264–276. Springer, Heidelberg (2011). https://doi.org/10.1007/978-3-642-23535-1_24
4. Goyal, V., Pandey, O., Sahai, A., et al.: Attribute-based encryption for finegrained access control of encrypted data. In: ACM Conference on Computer and Communications Security, pp. 89–98. ACM (2006)
5. Bethencourt, J., Sahai, A., Waters, B.: Ciphertext-policy attribute-based encryption. IEEE Symposium on Security & Privacy, pp. 321–334. IEEE (2007)
6. Lewko, A., Sahai, A., Waters, B.: Revocation systems with very small private keys. In: IEEE Symposium on Security and Privacy, pp. 273–285. IEEE Computer Society (2008)
7. Ostrovsky, R., Sahai, A., Waters, B.: Attribute-based encryption with non-monotonic access structures. In: CCS 2007 ACM Conference on Computer & Communications Security, pp. 195–203 (2007)
8. Zhou, L., Varadharajan, V., Hitchens, M.: Enforcing role-based access control for secure data storage in the cloud. Comput. J. 54(10), 1675–1687 (2011)
9. Liu, W., Liu, X., Liu, J., et al.: Auditing and revocation enabled role based access control over outsourced private EHRs. In: IEEE, International Conference on High PERFORMANCE Computing and Communications, pp. 336–341. IEEE (2015)
10. Chow, S.S.M.: A framework of multi-authority attribute-based encryption with outsourcing and revocation. In: ACM on Symposium on Access Control MODELS and Technologies, pp. 215–226. ACM (2016)
11. Chase, M., Chow, S.S.M.: Improving privacy and security in multi-authority attribute-based encryption. In: ACM Conference on Computer and Communications Security, pp. 121–130. ACM (2009)
12. Sahai, A., Waters, B.: Fuzzy identity-based encryption. In: Cramer, R. (ed.) EUROCRYPT 2005. LNCS, vol. 3494, pp. 457–473. Springer, Heidelberg (2005). https://doi.org/10.1007/11426639_27

Author Index

Printed in the United States
By Bookmasters